INVESTMENT AND PORTFOLIO ANALYSIS

Wiley Series In Finance

Alexander A. Robichek, Editor

▮▮

Financial Research And Management Decisions
    Alexander A. Robichek
Investment And Portfolio Analysis
    Haim Levy and Marshall Sarnat

INVESTMENT AND PORTFOLIO ANALYSIS

IIIIIIIIIIIIIIIIIIIIIIIIIIIIIIIIIIIIIIIIIIIIIIIIIIII

Haim Levy
and
Marshall Sarnat

JOHN WILEY & SONS, INC.
New York · London · Sydney · Toronto

Copyright © 1972 by John Wiley & Sons, Inc.

All rights reserved. Published simultaneously in Canada.

No part of this book may be reproduced by any means, nor transmitted, nor translated into a machine language without the written permission of the publisher.

Library of Congress Catalog Card Number: 74-175793

ISBN 0-471-53152-9

Printed in the United States of America.

10 9 8 7 6 5 4

To Our Families

17819

HG
4521
.L67

Preface

This book was born of our conviction that the proper place to study risk is within the confines of the security market which specializes in that "commodity." It represents an attempt to integrate traditional security analysis (the analysis of a single investment opportunity, considered in isolation) with the more recently developed theories of risk diversification and portfolio balance. The resulting analytical framework is then applied to the analysis of perfect and imperfect securities markets, conglomerate mergers, and international investment.

The book incorporates recent advances in efficiency analysis (by no means all our own) which permit the derivation of decision rules from easily understood assumptions regarding investors underlying attitudes toward risk. A great deal of effort has been expended (with some success, we hope) to make the innovations in efficiency analysis which have shaped the "New Finance" accessible to the nonmathematical reader. The text is almost exclusively based on a diagrammatic presentation which can readily be followed without formal mathematical training. Technical appendices have been added for those readers who desire more rigorous proofs of the verbal and geometric arguments of the text. It should be emphasized, however, that although the text can be read independently of the appendices, some familiarity with the text is necessary if the appendices are to be placed in their proper perspective. More specifically, we have had in mind the requirements of that by now proverbial student of business and economics "who knows only high school algebra," but since we are "risk averters," two brief elementary Mathematical and Statistical Supplements have been included just in case. Thus, students of investment analysis who have common sense enough to wish to learn more than common sense alone can teach them about a fascinating, albeit complex, subject are well prepared to follow the arguments of the book.[1]

---

[1] Cf. Hans Reichenbach, *The Rise of Scientific Philosophy*, University of California Press, Berkeley, 1951.

The book provides a flexible teaching instrument and has been used as the basis for both one and two semester courses in investment analysis and portfolio selection at the University of California at Berkeley and the Hebrew University. Both the students and their teachers survived, and with no apparent ill effects. Chapters 1–5, 9, and 10 provide material for a one semester introduction to investment and security analysis. Parts II and III provide material for a one semester course for advanced students. Alternatively, Part II, taken alone, provides the core, or supplemental reading, for courses in decision-making for students of economics.

We also hope that the book will prove of more than passing interest to professional investment analysts and portfolio managers, thereby helping to bridge part of the gap which has emerged between these more experienced practitioners of the art of decision-making under risk and uncertainty and some of their academic colleagues.

In essence, a book such as this, which represents a synthesis of the work of a generation of scholars, makes even the listing of acknowledgments practically impossible and certainly infeasible. The rather extensive bibliographies will have to serve as an indicator, however inadequate, of the extent of the debts incurred, but we would indeed be remiss not to mention, at least, our very obvious indebtedness to the pioneering work of Harry Markowitz, James Tobin, William F. Sharpe, John Lintner, and Jack L. Treynor. Similarly, we also should like to thank our students at the University of California and Hebrew University for their criticisms and often penetrating comments, as well as our colleagues, Giora Hanoch, Fred Arditti, and Jehuda Kahane for correcting errors and suggesting improvements of both style and substance. Our thanks are also due to Professors M. J. Arlington and Nancy L. Jacob who read the entire book in manuscript and offered numerous suggestions. Special mention should also be made of the advice and valuable comments received from Professor Alexander Robichek; Part I and Chapter XIV, in particular, were considerably expanded and improved at his suggestion. Finally, it is a very pleasant duty to thank Moshe Ben Horim who, for two years, provided research assistance far beyond the call of duty (or of salary).

Jerusalem, Israel HAIM LEVY
MARSHALL SARNAT

Contents

Introduction   3

  1. Positive and Normative Aspects of the Theory of Finance   3
  2. Realism vs Abstraction in the Theory of Finance   4
  3. Plan of Book   5

PART I: SECURITY ANALYSIS AND THE VALUATION OF THE FIRM   3

Chapter I: The Capital Market   7

  1. Introduction   7
  2. The Primary Securities Market   7
  3. The Secondary Securities Market   8
  4. The New York Stock Exchange   11
    4.1 The Exchange Community   12
    4.2 Listing Requirements   13
    4.3 Placing an Order   14
    4.4 The Specialist   16
  5. Margin Trading   17
  6. Short Selling   18
  7. Stock Price Indexes   19

Chapter II: Measuring Corporate Profits   27

  1. Introduction   27
  2. Sources of Accounting Data   27
  3. Economic Profits vs. Accounting Profits   28
  4. Earnings Per Share   32
  5. Adjusted Earnings Per Share   35
  6. Adjusting EPS for Stock Splits and Stock Dividends   37

7. Adjusting EPS for Rights Issues	39
8. The Adjustment for New Public Issues	44
9. Adjusting EPS in Practice	45
10. Summary	50

Chapter III: Alternative Measures of Profitability — 59

1. Introduction	59
2. The Time Value of Money	59
3. Net Present Value (NPV)	62
4. The Internal Rate of Return (IRR)	67
5. The Relationship Between the IRR and NPV Methods: Independent Projects	69
5.1 Ranking Investment Proposals	71
6. The Relationship Between IRR and NPV: Dependent Projects	73
6.1 Differences in the Scale of Investment	73
6.2 Reinvestment Rates	76
7. Measuring the Profitability of Financial Investments	79
7.1 The Rate of Return on Common Stocks	80
7.2 Adjusting the Rate of Return	83
8. Calculating the Adjusted Rate of Return: Some Examples	85
9. Summary	88

Chapter IV: Valuation of Securities: Bonds and Preferred Stock — 99

1. Introduction	99
2. Alternative Formulations of the Yield on Bonds and Preferred Stock	99
2.1 The Rate of Return	99
2.2 Bond Yields	100
3. The Risks of Bonds	104
3.1 Credit Risk	104
3.2 Purchasing Power Risk	109
3.3 Interest Rate Risk	111
4. The Time Pattern of Yields: The Yield Curve	114
5. Other Features of Fixed-Income Securities	121
5.1 Retirement Provisions	121
5.2 Call Provision	122
5.3 Convertibility	123
6. Summary	125

Chapter V: Valuation of Securities: Common Stocks — 131

1. Introduction	131
2. The Net Asset Value Approach	131

CONTENTS

3. Present Value of Earnings	133
4. Pragmatic Valuation: Using Price–Earnings Ratios	136
4.1 Adjusting the Price–Earnings Ratio	137
5. The Present Value of Dividends	139
6. Dividend Policy and Valuation	143
7. Growth Stocks	147
7.1 The IBM Paradox	150
8. Financial Leverage	153
9. Leverage and Valuation	157
10. The Modigliani and Miller Analysis of Leverage and Valuation	162
10.1 Proposition I: Capital Structure and Valuation	163
10.2 M & M's Proposition II	167
11. Price–Earnings Ratios and Financial Risk	170
12. Summary	175
Appendix V-1: The Present Value of Earnings with Continuous Discounting	179
Appendix V-2: The Dividend Growth Model with Continuous Discounting	181

PART II: PORTFOLIO SELECTION   187

Chapter VI: The Investment Decision Under Conditions of Uncertainty   189

1. Introduction	189
2. The Maximum Return Criterion	192
3. The Maximum Expected Return Criterion	193
3.1 The St. Petersburg Paradox	194
3.2 Daniel Bernoulli's Solution	196
3.3 Cramer's Solution	200
4. The Modern Theory of Utility	201
4.1 The Axiomatic Basis for Expected Utility	202
4.2 The Meaning of Utility	204
5. Alternative Attitudes Toward Risk	207
6. The Special Case of a Linear Utility Function	212
7. State-Preference Theory	215
8. Summary	217
Appendix VI-1: Proof that the Expected Utility Principle Follows from the von Neumann-Morgenstern Axioms	226

Appendix VI–2: A Graphical Representation of Expected
Utility 228

Chapter VII: Alternative Shapes of the Utility Function 231

1. Introduction 231
2. The Friedman-Savage Hypothesis 235
3. The Subjective Utility Approach 240
4. Risk Attitudes in the Stock Market: Some Empirical Evidence 244
    4.1 Implications for Utility Functions 249
5. Summary 251

Appendix VII–1: Empirical Estimates of Risk Attitudes in the
Stock Market, Selected Periods, 1943–67 256
Appendix VII–2: The Shape of a Cubic Utility Function 258

Chapter VIII: The Efficiency Analysis of Investment
Under Uncertainty 261

1. Introduction 261
2. The Concept of an Efficiency Criterion 261
3. A General Efficiency Criterion (GC) 264
    3.1 An Intuitive Interpretation of the General Criterion 267
    3.2 The Concept of an Optimal Efficiency Criterion 268
    3.3 The Relationship of the General Criterion to the First Two
         Distribution Moments 276
4. A Risk Aversion Criterion 278
    4.1 Some Basic Properties of the Risk Aversion Criterion 283
5. Efficiency Criteria and Diversification 285
6. Summary 291

Appendix VIII–1: Proof of the General Criterion 296
Appendix VIII–2: Proof of the Risk Aversion Criterion 299
Appendix VIII–3: Proof of the Risk Aversion Criterion when the
Cumulative Distributions Intersect Only Once 302

Chapter IX: The Mean–Variance Criterion 303

1. Introduction 303
2. The Nature of Investment Risk 304
3. The Mean Variance Criterion (MVC) 307
4. The Utility Foundations of the MVC 310
5. The Two-Stage Criterion (TSC) 315
6. A Graphical Representation of the Mean–Variance Criterion 318

CONTENTS   xiii

   7. A Graphical Representation of the Two-Stage Criterion   323
   8. Some Empirical Evidence on Two-Parameter Distributions   325
   9. Summary   330

Appendix IX-1: Proof of the Optimality of the Mean-Variance Criterion for the Case of Concave Utility   339

Chapter X: The Mean–Variance Criterion and Portfolio Selection   341

   1. Introduction   341
   2. The Investment in Liquid Assets   341
   3. Portfolios of Two Securities   349
   4. A Three-Security Portfolio   359
   5. The Gains from Diversification   363
   6. The Impact of Interdependence on the Gains from Diversification   365
   7. The Number of Securities and the Gain from Diversification   368
   8. The Efficiency Frontier—The General Case   370
   9. Summary   373

Chapter XI: The Mean–Variance Criterion and Quadratic Utility   379

   1. Introduction   379
   2. The Meaning of Quadratic Utility   379
      2.1 β Less than Zero   380
      2.2 β Greater than Zero   382
   3. The Mean–Variance Criterion for the Case of Quadratic Utility   383
   4. The Quadratic Utility Criterion (QUC)   385
   5. The Expected Gain–Confidence Limit Criterion (EGC)   388
      5.1   The Relationship of the EGC to Other Efficiency Criteria   390
      5.2   The EGC and the Efficiency Frontier   391
   6. A Comparison of Alternative Efficiency Criteria: An Example   393
   7. Summary   395

Chapter XII: Investors' Wealth, the Discount Rate, and the Relative Effectiveness of Efficiency Criteria   401

   1. Introduction   401
   2. Investors' Wealth   402
      2.1   Wealth as a Nonstochastic Variable   403
      2.2   Wealth as a Stochastic Variable   404
   3. Discounting Investment Returns   406
   4. Relative Effectiveness of Alternative Efficiency Criteria   410
   5. Summary   414

Appendix XII–1:	Proof that the General and Risk Aversion Criteria Are Independent of Initial Wealth	418
Appendix XII–2:	Proof that the MVC and QUC Are Independent of Initial Wealth	420
Appendix XII–3:	Proof that the Efficiency Criteria Are Independent of the Discount Rate	422
Appendix XII–4:	Proof that the Efficiency Criteria Are Transitive	425
Appendix XII–5:	Composition of the Efficient Sets of Mutual Funds, Based on 1958–67 Data	427

Chapter XIII: Price Determination in the Stock Market 429

1. Introduction 429
2. Some Simplifying Assumptions 429
3. Single-Stock Portfolios with Lending or Borrowing 431
   3.1   Choosing Among Alternative Single-Stock Portfolios 436
   3.2   Equilibrium in the Stock Market: Single-Stock Portfolios and a Unique Interest Rate 439
   3.3   The Case of Multiple Interest Rates 441
4. Multiple-Stock Portfolios 443
   4.1   A Graphical Analysis 444
   4.2   The Optimal Investment Proportions 446
   4.3   Optimal Investment Proportions: An Alternative Approach 448
5. The Relationship of Expected Return to Risk 451
6. Equilibrium in the Stock Market 452
7. Summary 455

Appendix XIII–1:	Proof that Optimal Investment Proportions Are Independent of the Scale of Investment	462
Appendix XIII–2:	The Shape of Investors' Indifference Curves	463
Appendix XIII–3:	Equilibrium Prices in a Perfect Securities Market	466
Appendix XIII–4:	The Effects of Investors' Expectations on Equilibrium Prices in the Securities Market	468
Appendix XIII–5:	Derivation of the Equilibrium Risk–Return Trade-off in a Perfect Market	470

PART III: APPLICATIONS OF PORTFOLIO THEORY 473

Chapter XIV: The Assessment of Portfolio Performance 475

1. Introduction 475

CONTENTS xv

   2. Measuring the Investment Performance of Mutual Funds 476
      2.1 The Benchmarks of Mutual Fund Performance 477
   3. Alternative Measures of Investment Performance 479
      3.1 Reward-to-Variability Ratio 480
      3.2 Volatility and the Characteristic Line 482
      3.3 Systematic and Unsystematic Risk 483
      3.4 Treynor's Performance Indicator 486
   4. Some Empirical Results of Mutual Fund Performance 487
   5. Mutual Fund Performance in an Imperfect Securities Market 489
   6. Predictions of Performance from Past Data 491
      6.1 The Random Walk Hypothesis 492
      6.2 Implications for Investment Analysis 494
      6.3 Implications for Portfolio Theory 495
   7. Predicting Portfolio Performance 496

Chapter XV: Two Studies in Corporate Diversification: Conglomerate Mergers and Multiperiod Capital Investments 505

   1. Introduction 505
   2. Conglomerate Mergers 505
      2.1 The Portfolio Analysis of Conglomerate Diversification 507
      2.2 Capital Costs 511
   3. Capital Investments 512
      3.1 The Variance as a Measure of Risk in Capital Budgeting 512
      3.2 The Portfolio Analysis of Capital Investments 518
   4. Summary 522

   Appendix XV-1: Proof of the Neutrality of Conglomerate Mergers in a Perfect Securities Market 526

Chapter XVI: International Diversification of Investments 529

   1. Introduction 529
   2. Co-Movements of Security Prices 529
   3. The Gains from International Diversification 531
   4. The Efficiency Frontier 534
   5. The Composition of the Optimal Portfolios 535
   6. Some Further Implications of the Analysis 543

   Appendix XVI-1: Classification of 28 Countries by Groups 548

PART IV: TECHNICAL SUPPLEMENT — 549

A. Mathematical Supplement — 551
The Derivative — 551
   Definition, Geometrical Interpretation — 551
The Derived Function — 552
Increasing and Decreasing Functions — 553
Rules of Differentiation — 554
   Some Remarks, Examples — 555
Higher-Order Derivatives — 556
Partial Derivatives — 556
Local Maxima and Minima — 557
Constrained Maxima and Minima — 560
   The Elimination Method — 560
   Lagrange Multiplier Method — 561
   Graphical Interpretation of the Constrained Maximum — 563
Integrals — 563
   The Indefinite Integral as an Area Under a Curve — 565
   Changing the Integration Variable — 567
   The Double Integral — 568
The Sum of Geometric Series — 569
Taylor Series: Power Expansion of Functions — 570

B. Statistical Supplement — 573
The Distribution Function — 574
Moments — 577
   Examples and Further Developments, The Uniform (Rectangular) Distribution — 582
The Expected Value and the Variance of the Uniform Distribution — 582
The Normal Distribution — 583
   The Normal Distribution Parameters — 584
Linear Transformation of Random Variables — 587
Covariance and the Correlation Coefficient — 588
Expected Value and Variance of the Sum of Random Variables — 591
Chebychev Inequality — 592

Author Index — 595

Subject Index — 599

INVESTMENT AND PORTFOLIO ANALYSIS

PART I
SECURITY ANALYSIS AND THE VALUATION OF THE FIRM

Introduction

> Man should always divide his wealth into three parts: one-third in land, one-third in commerce and one-third retained in his own hands.
>
> Babylonian Talmud

The sages of the Talmud suggested what is perhaps the world's first diversified investment portfolio, and despite the vicissitudes of fifteen hundred years their device is not without merit even today. A formal statement of the theory of risk diversification and portfolio selection, however, did not become available until the 1950s when Harry Markowitz and James Tobin published their pioneering studies.[1] This book is nothing more than an attempt to explain, in a systematic manner, why for almost two millennia most investors (but not necessarily economists) have been following the advice implied in the Talmudic dictum.

1. POSITIVE AND NORMATIVE ASPECTS OF THE THEORY OF FINANCE

Such attempts, following Markowitz, are usually classified as belonging to the theory of portfolio selection. Portfolio theory, like most economic theories, has two distinct aspects: viewed as a *positive* theory, it attempts to explain and predict phenomena in capital markets; viewed as a *normative* theory, or as an art, it sets out criteria concerning the way in which investment decisions *should* be made and stipulates the rules for attaining desired ends.

---

[1] H. M. Markowitz, "Portfolio Selection," *Journal of Finance* VII (March 1952), and *Portfolio Selection*, New York: Wiley, 1959. J. Tobin, "Liquidity Preference As Behavior Towards Risk," *Review of Economic Studies* XXVI (February 1958).

We owe this distinction to John Neville Keynes, the distinguished Victorian logician and political economist, and the father of a very famous son who made his mark not only in economics but in the art of finance as well.[2]

Considerable confusion results when normative and positive theory are not distinguished. Positive theory can be, and often is, divorced from any normative considerations—attempts to explain the operation of securities markets do not necessarily imply normative judgments as to the manner in which these markets *ought* to operate. But normative theory and the art of finance cannot be independent of positive theory, since normative prescriptions usually imply predictions of the outcomes of alternative choices or courses of action, and such predictions are the province of positive theory. Thus one can construct a model of price determination in the securities market (see Chapter XIII) without taking a normative stand on the desirability of the existence of such a market. But this relationship is not symmetrical: normative attempts to outline an "ideal" framework for achieving optimal security prices invariably require the use of some model for explaining (and predicting) how security prices respond to various stimulae.

2. REALISM VS. ABSTRACTION IN THE THEORY OF FINANCE

The distinction of positive from normative theory can also provide a long overdue funeral for that old chestnut, "Well, that may be all right in theory but it is no good in practice." From the positive standpoint, a theory whose explanations and predictions do not hold true for the class of phenomena to which it applies is simply a "bad" theory and should be replaced. This also follows from more general considerations of the philosophy of science which suggest that an infinity of theories exists to explain the necessarily finite number of observed facts.[3] Thus to be acceptable a theory must provide the best available explanation (prediction) of the phenomena being studied.

In the above sense we seek a realistic explanation of investment behavior and of security markets. But it should be noted that to be useful, a theory

---

[2] The significance of the elder Keynes' distinction was rediscovered and analyzed in detail by Milton Friedman in a brilliant and very readable essay, "The Methodology of Positive Economics," in *Essays in Positive Economics*, Chicago and London: University of Chicago Press, 1953. The remainder of this, and the following, sections are drawn from Friedman's essay.

[3] *Ibid.*, p. 9. It also follows that although a theory can be rejected, we cannot establish the "truth" of a particular theory since there always exists the possibility of finding an alternative hypothesis which can account for the same phenomena.

must be abstract; we seek a map which can guide us through the complex maze of decision making under uncertainty rather than a detailed photograph which only reproduces the complexities of the maze itself. The need for abstraction is almost self-evident once you think of it, but it has some interesting implications:

(a) The "realism" of a theory's assumptions can be judged only by the degree to which the theory provides valid and meaningful explanations and predictions, and this requires an examination of the logical consequences of the theory against observed matter.

(b) To be meaningful a theory's assumptions will have to be almost invariably "unrealistic" in the sense that they must be abstract, and therefore cannot provide an exhaustive description (photograph) of the phenomena to be explained.[4] Again this is really self-evident; few would argue that the hair color of the president of the New York Stock Exchange is germane to the problem of explaining price determination in that market. Far from being desirable, descriptive realism must be avoided if meaningful explanations are to be provided. How far can the degree of abstraction go? This again can be answered only by checking on whether the theory yields explanations and predictions which are sufficient for our purposes.

3. PLAN OF BOOK

Like Gaul, this book is divided into three parts. Part I, in essence, is an analysis of the single security, treated in isolation. In the five chapters which comprise this section of the book we present our version of the traditional corpus of security analysis. Chapter I summarizes the institutional background required to place the problem of investment selection in proper perspective. Chapter II discusses some basic problems relating to the measurement of corporate profitability. Chapter III sets out the fundamentals underlying the measurement of profitability to the investor in securities. Chapters IV and V present a framework for the valuation of a firm's fixed-income securities (bonds and preferred stock) and common stock, respectively. These chapters deal with two aspects of risk: the interest rate risk which influences the term structure of interest rates on bonds, and the financial risk associated with the use of leverage in a firm's capital structure, which influences the required rate of return on a firm's common stock.

---

[4] Of course, they *cannot* be "unrealistic" in the sense of not providing an explanation (prediction) of observed phenomena.

In Part II the analysis of risk is expanded to reflect the interaction among the returns of alternative investments. Chapter VI sets out the utility foundations which underly portfolio analysis, and in Chapter VII two alternative hypotheses regarding the shape of investors' utility functions, and their implications for investment analysis, are examined. Chapter VIII derives decision rules for investors directly from the underlying utility considerations. In Chapters IX, X, and XI Markowitz's normative mean–variance theory of portfolio selection is expounded and critically examined; Chapter XII is devoted to an analysis of the influence of initial wealth and time discounting on the efficiency analysis as well as to a comparative analysis of the relative effectiveness of the alternative efficiency criteria developed in the previous chapters of the book. Chapter XIII presents a positive model of price determination in the stock market.

Part III of the book is devoted to applications of the normative and positive portfolio theory of Part II. Chapter XIV discusses several measures of investment performance and tests the ability of alternative efficiency criteria to *predict* portfolio performance on the basis of ex-post returns. Chapter XV is devoted to corporate, rather than individual investors', diversification. The efficacy of conglomerate mergers is critically examined and the implications of portfolio balance for problems of capital budgeting are analyzed. Chapter XVI concludes the book with an application of the portfolio model to problems of international finance by examining empirically the possibilities for risk reduction by means of internationally diversified investment portfolios.

The technical appendices should be consulted by the reader who desires more rigorous proofs of the verbal and graphical analysis presented in the text.

Chapter I
The Capital Market

1. INTRODUCTION

Investment and portfolio decisions are taken within the framework provided by a complex of financial institutions and intermediaries which together comprise the capital market. It is this market which provides the mechanism for channeling current savings into investment in productive facilities, that is, for allocating the country's capital resources among alternative uses. In effect, the capital market provides an economy's link with the future, since current decisions regarding the allocation of capital resources are a major determining factor of tomorrow's output. The crucial role played by the capital market in shaping the pattern and growth of real output imparts a social significance to individual investment and portfolio decisions.

The capital market can be defined in any number of ways, but for the purposes of this chapter we shall give the term a rather narrow meaning, confining it to those institutions which deal with relatively long-term financial instruments, for example, stocks, government and corporate bonds. We exclude commercial banking and short-term loans[1] not because they cannot legitimately be considered part of the capital market, but simply on the grounds of the "division of labor." This enables us to focus attention on the allocation of long-term funds and for this purpose we shall first consider the new issue market for equity capital and bonds.

2. THE PRIMARY SECURITIES MARKET

To place the capital market in proper perspective it is useful to distinguish between the "primary" and "secondary" securities markets. The primary

---

[1] This corresponds to the familiar distinction between the "capital market" and the "money market."

market for securities is the *new issues* market which brings together the "supply and demand" or "sources and uses" for new capital funds. In this market the principal source of funds is the domestic savings of consumers and nonfinancial businesses; other suppliers include foreign investors and State and local governments. The principal uses of funds are: the long-term financing of the investment in housing (mortgages), the long-term investment of corporations and other businesses, and the long-term borrowing of federal, state, and local government. The ultimate suppliers of funds are those sectors with a surplus of current income over expenditure (savings); and these funds flow to their ultimate users, namely, economic units which issue securities to finance a surplus of expenditures over their current incomes.

In a highly developed capital market by far the largest proportion of individuals' savings reaches the new issues market *indirectly* via a financial intermediary. For example, the savings of most individuals are channeled to an ultimate user, say a corporation desiring to finance an expansion of its productive facilities, via a pension fund, insurance company, investment company, or similar institution. Moreover, most individual investors are unfamiliar with the new issues market and its institutions, such as underwriters and selling syndicates which serve as middlemen between the corporate demanders of funds and the individual investors and financial institutions which supply the funds. To most investors the term *securities market* is synonymous with the "stock exchange."

3. THE SECONDARY SECURITIES MARKET

The purpose of a stock exchange or *secondary* securities market, like any other organized market, is to enable buyers and sellers to effect their transactions more quickly and cheaply than they could otherwise. However, since a stock exchange typically deals in *existing* securities rather than in new issues, its economic significance may be misunderstood.

As we noted above, the primary function of the capital market relates to the channeling of savings into capital formation; hence the capital market's economic significance stems from its impact on the allocation of capital resources among alternative uses. But an increase in the volume of securities trading in the stock market does *not* represent an increase in the economy's aggregate savings, every purchase of an *existing* security being exactly offset by the sale of the same security. For the economy as a whole, an increase in savings in the form of securities ownership is measured by the volume of net new issues of securities, transactions in existing securities representing shifts among owners, which always cancel out in the aggregate. Similarly, transactions in existing securities do not provide additional funds to finance

3. THE SECONDARY SECURITIES MARKET

capital formation; here again it is the volume of net new issues which provides additional financing to business enterprise. An analogy can readily be drawn from the automobile market. The sales of new Ford cars (new issues) by the Ford Motor Company (issuing firms) provide revenue (investment funds) to the company; transactions in older models of Ford cars (existing securities) in the used car market (stock exchange) do not. But just as the existence of a resale market for cars affects the willingness of consumers to purchase new Fords, the availability of an efficient secondary market for securities is one of the more important factors inducing investors to acquire new issues of securities. And the connection between the primary and secondary markets is even stronger in the case of the securities market, since new issues are often close, or even perfect, substitutes for outstanding securities.

The basic economic function of a stock exchange is to provide marketability for long-term investments, thereby reducing the personal risk incurred by investors and broadening the supply of equity and long-term debt capital for the financing of business enterprise. For example, even though the investment in a common stock is fixed for the life of the firm, the ability to shift ownership to others during the course of this period permits more individuals to participate in the long-term financing of companies. In a modern economy possessing a well developed secondary securities market the fixed investment of firms is provided by a changing group of individuals, none of whom may have been willing to commit his personal resources for the entire or even a substantial part of the life of the enterprise. Thus in an efficient stock exchange the supply of credit, which from the private investor's viewpoint is often inherently short-term, is transformed into a supply of long-term investment funds for the financing of capital formation. The ability to transfer the risks of investment forges a link between the stock exchange and the new issues market, and this greatly enhances the ability of business enterprises to mobilize additional long-term capital to finance the creation of new, or the expansion of existing, production facilities.

To effectively fulfill its functions as an allocator of capital, the securities market should be influenced solely by economic considerations; the prices of the various securities should reflect their expected returns and risk characteristics. In an efficient market current prices for a company's securities will reflect the investors best estimates of firms' anticipated profitability and of the risks attaching to these profits.[2] And since—other things being equal—rising stock prices attract investors, the allocation of capital will be *biased* in favor of firms with relatively high levels of risk-adjusted profits. On the other hand,

---

[2] The implications of a market in which all available information is fully reflected in prices are discussed in Chapter XIV.

firms with low profitability or excessive riskiness will find it difficult, expensive, or on occasion even impossible to raise additional capital for expansion.

The prerequisites for such an efficient securities market are roughly the same as those of any "perfect" or purely competitive market:

(a) the products traded in the market must be homogeneous;

(b) the market must be comprised of many relatively small buyers and sellers;

(c) there must be free entry and exit into and out of the market.

Although a securities market is made up of many types of securities (common stocks, preferred stocks, and bonds) of a large number of companies, each class of securities is homogeneous in the sense that the risk-adjusted rates of return of the various classes of securities comprise homogeneous commodities. One share of a given risk class is as good as any other and therefore they must sell at the same price. In addition, a modern securities market is made of a large number of relatively small buyers and sellers so that it is difficult for any individual to influence prices. In 1969, for example, there were over 3 million shareholders of record of American Tel. & Tel. stock, no one of whom owned as much as 1% of the outstanding shares. The day of the "corner" appears to be over. On the other hand, although anyone who owns a security can always sell it to anyone willing to buy it, entry into the market proper, for example acquiring a seat on the stock exchange, is not free. But even when such deviations are taken into account, it is to the stock exchange that we often point when in need of a real life model which approximates the "perfect" market of economic theory.[3]

This rather sanguine view of the stock market and its impact on the allocation of capital is not universally held. To some the New York Stock Exchange is a den of iniquity; to other, more sophisticated, observers stock market prices reflect mass psychology with little if any connection to underlying economic values. The case against the stock exchange was most forcibly expressed during the 1930s by the most famous economist of the time, John Maynard Keynes. In a characteristically brilliant passage which goes a long way toward explaining his own success as an investor, Keynes described the stock exchange as a place where most investors attempt to guess what average opinion thinks average opinion will be like one month hence, while others practice the "fourth, fifth and higher degrees" of this art.[4]

---

[3] See William J. Baumol, *The Stock Market and Economic Efficiency*, New York: Fordham University Press, 1965.

[4] John Maynard Keynes, *The General Theory of Employment Interest and Money*, New York: Harcourt Brace, 1936, p. 156.

It should be recalled that Keynes was writing at a time when a worldwide financial crisis had so undermined public confidence that stock prices did often appear to be unconnected with any underlying economic values. Taking a somewhat longer view, however, there is really no inherent contradiction between the kind of speculative behavior which Keynes described and the thesis that stock prices, in the long run, reflect economic values. For this purpose it is sufficient that some investors become conditioned to the fact that stock prices rise when profits and dividends increase, so that it "pays" to exploit all available information in an attempt to anticipate such possibilities. The available statistical evidence suggests that Keynes notwithstanding, the pure speculator does *not* rule the roost, and therefore the quest for quick capital gains has not divorced the trend in the price of a company's stock from the expectation of future profits.[5]

4. THE NEW YORK STOCK EXCHANGE

Although regional stock exchanges exist in a dozen cities throughout the country, the two largest markets are located a stone's throw from one another in the heart of the New York financial district. These are the so-called "Big and Little Big Boards," the New York and American Stock Exchanges. Taken together these two national exchanges dominate the capital market: over 90% of all listed stocks and 99% of all listed bonds are registered on the two New York exchanges. We shall confine ourselves to the larger of the two, the New York Stock Exchange.

The New York Stock Exchange, founded in 1792, is the nation's oldest organized securities market. Today the Exchange dominates the U.S. securities market; measured in terms of market value, almost 75% of all listed stocks and 79% of all listed bonds were registered on the Big Board at the end of 1969.[6] Some indication of the growth of the market can be gleaned from the fact that on March 16, 1830, the dullest day in the history of the Exchange, only 31 shares were traded; 138 years later, on April 10, 1968, the Exchange recorded its first 20-million-share trading day!

---

[5] For an early example of the use of stock market prices to approximate management's expectations of future profits, see the late Yehuda Grunfeld's, "The Determinants of Corporate Investment" in A. Harberger (ed.), *The Demand for Durable Goods*, Chicago: University of Chicago Press, 1960. Grunfeld's evidence is particularly impressive since he was not concerned with the stock market per se and hit upon the "market value of the firm" as a surrogate for "expected profits" in an attempt to explain the fluctuations of corporate investment.

[6] Securities and Exchange Commission, *Statistical Bulletin* (March 1970).

The New York Stock Exchange is an unincorporated association and is registered as a "national securities exchange" under the Securities Exchange Act. Administrative Authority is vested in a 33-man Board of Governors, 29 of whom are elected by the members of the Exchange. The President of the Exchange and three other governors representing the public are elected by the Board.

4.1 THE EXCHANGE COMMUNITY

The Exchange provides a meeting place of the "demand and supply" for securities rather than of the buyers and sellers themselves, trading in securities being limited to members, most of whom act as agents for the ultimate buyers and sellers. Since 1953 the Exchange membership has been 1,366. A member may choose to trade on his own behalf (the so-called floor or registered traders), but if he does, he cannot carry customer accounts. Subject to the Board's approval members may also combine with other individuals to form a partnership or corporation for the purpose of doing business with the public. The Board must approve all members or stockholders of such *member organizations.* Today all of the principal securities brokers are members of the New York Stock Exchange.

The privilege of trading on the Exchange is not a free good and can be acquired (subject to the Board's approval) only by purchasing the "seat" of one of the members.[7] The price of a seat is a good indicator of the volume of trading, and incidentally of the "risks" of investment in general. At the crest of the stock market boom of the 1920s (October 31, 1925) a seat on the exchange fetched a price of $495,000; by 1942 the price of such membership had fallen to $17,000. In the early 1960s seats were selling for $200,000, but not until 1968 did the price of a seat on the Exchange surpass the previous 1929 high, the last membership transfer of 1968 being effected for a price of $515,000.

Under the pressure of the rise in trading volume, the number of NYSE employees increased from 1,223 in 1956 to 2,714 in 1968. However, if we focus attention on the entire Exchange community—members, registered representatives, and other employees of member firms, and the employees of the Exchange—the total labor force involved in the buying and selling of securities was 152,000 in 1968 as compared with only 60,000 in 1956. This 150% increase in the labor force reflects the 350% increase in the volume of shares traded during the same period. Of course, all the above figures relate to the New York Stock Exchange, so that the actual labor force involved in

---

[7] Partners and stockholders of member organizations may apply for "allied membership" in the Exchange, but such members are not permitted to go on the floor of the Exchange.

4. THE NEW YORK STOCK EXCHANGE

securities trading could be expanded to include employees of the other exchanges and perhaps of the financial press (*Wall Street Journal*, *Barron's*, *Forbes Magazine*, *Commercial and Financial Chronicle*, and so on); investment advisory services (Moody's, Standard & Poor's, Value Line); and trust departments of banks. Moreover, if we ignore the convention by which the labor of housewives is not reflected in gross national product, we might also include those wives of individual investors who diligently prepare charts and diagrams of stock price movements in that never ending search for an undervalued stock.

4.2 LISTING REQUIREMENTS

Just as individual investors are precluded from actively buying and selling on the floor of the Exchange unless they are members, only the securities of a "listed" company are eligible for trading.[8] To be listed, a company is expected to meet certain qualifications and to be willing to keep the investing public informed of the progress of its affairs. Although each case is determined on its own merits, the following minimum requirements have been laid down:

> (1) Demonstrated earning power under competitive conditions of $2.5 million before federal income taxes for the most recent year prior to listing and $2 million for each of the two preceding years
>
> (2) Net tangible assets of $14 million
>
> (3) A total of $14 million in market value of publicly held common stock
>
> (4) One million shares outstanding, of which 800 thousand must be publicly held
>
> (5) Two thousand shareholders, 1,800 of which must be round-lot shareholders, that is, owners of 100 or more shares

In addition, it has been the policy of the Exchange for many years not to list nonvoting common stocks, and as a result all of the common stocks listed on the Big Board have the right to vote.

The New York Stock Exchange is an international, as well as a national, securities market in the sense that the stocks and bonds of many foreign governments and corporations have been accepted for listing. At the end of 1968 26 stocks of foreign corporations, comprising about 2% of all listed

---

[8] The listing requirements are taken from New York Stock Exchange, *Fact Book 1969*.

corporations, and 247 foreign bond issues, out of a total of 1,455, were listed on the Exchange. There has also been an increasing tendency to list "Eurodollar" bonds, that is, the bonds of foreign subsidiaries of U.S. corporations. These bonds are issued abroad and the New York listing is usually sought to improve the securities' marketability.

The advantages of listing to the corporation and its shareholders are often considerable.[9] Listing on the Exchange enhances a security's marketability and collateral value. It also facilitates, and often lowers the cost of, additional equity financing. Similarly, the availability of a continuous "objective" valuation of the firm's shares is often very advantageous to the shareholders, as well as to the corporation when a merger or other acquisition requiring an exchange of stock is contemplated. Finally, listing on the Big Board often increases the number of shareholders and provides a great deal of "free" advertising for the company; the activities, announcements, and periodic earning reports of listed corporations are all newsworthy items on the financial pages of the nation's leading newspapers.[10]

4.3 PLACING AN ORDER

The New York Stock Exchange provides a continuous auction market in listed securities, but as active trading on the floor of the Exchange is limited to members, the typical investor desiring to buy or sell a listed security must first contact a brokerage firm which handles such orders. The broker acts as the customer's agent, and for simplicity we shall assume that the investor has selected a member firm of the New York Stock Exchange. The initial step is to open an account which typically can be of two types:

a. Cash Account

A cash account is limited to purchases and sales for cash; that is, the securities must be paid for in cash upon delivery.

b. General Account

A general account is opened for an investor who in addition to cash transactions may also wish to purchase securities on credit or to sell them short.

---

[9] Listing, however, does not appear to have had a significant effect on stock prices in recent years. See James C. Van Horne, "New Listings and Their Price Behavior," *Journal of Finance* (September 1970).

[10] However, to the corporation experiencing serious financial or other difficulties the disclosure required by the Exchange can prove an embarrassment.

4. THE NEW YORK STOCK EXCHANGE   15

For the moment let us assume that a cash account is opened, and that our hypothetical investor wants to buy the stock of the Ford Motor Company. However, simply stipulating the stock one wants to buy does not provide the broker with sufficient information. The customer must also indicate the number of shares to be purchased and the type of order. The number of shares to be acquired has special significance in the securities business since lower commissions are payable on shares purchased in *round lots*, that is, in multiples of 100 shares.[11] Any fractional purchases or sales are considered *odd lots* and an additional commission is charged on such transactions. Similarly the customer must indicate the type of order, usually a "market" or "limit" order, which he desires to place. The market order instructs the broker to buy (sell) the securities in question at the best obtainable price. The limit order, as its name implies, instructs the broker to buy (sell) the security at the stipulated limit price or better. In the case of a purchase, this means to buy at the limit price or below; in the case of a sale, to sell at the limit price or above. The customer must also indicate the length of time he wishes the limit order to remain in effect, should the broker be unable immediately to obtain the stipulated price in the market.

A special type of limit order, the so-called *stop-loss* order, has gained considerable notoriety. For example, an investor who is holding a particular stock in the hope that its price may rise might give his broker a limit order to sell the stock should the price fall ten points below the current market price of, say, 92.[12] Thus, if the price should fall to 82, the limit order becomes a market order to sell. Note, however, that the placing of such a stop-loss order does *not* guarantee that the stock will be sold at the limit price. If the market drops sharply, the broker may be unable to sell the customer's shares until they have fallen considerably below the stop-loss price. Since a backlog of stop-loss orders could conceivably set off a chain reaction of automatic selling, should the price of the stock fall, the Exchange on occasion has suspended the placing of such orders for certain stocks.

Now let us return to our hypothetical investor at the broker's office. At most local offices a remote terminal hooked to a computer-fed information system provides up-to-date information on the last recorded sale and current bid and asked prices for listed stocks. After checking on the prices, our investor puts in a market order to buy a round lot of 100 shares of Ford common. This order is relayed to the broker's partner on the floor of the Exchange, who takes it to the area or "post" at which Ford stock is traded.

---

[11] For stocks whose unit prices are relatively high, 10 rather than 100 shares constitutes a round lot.

[12] If a customer is short in the stock, he might try to limit his losses should the price rise. In such cases the procedure is reversed and he orders the broker to buy the shares, in order to cover his short position, should the price rise above a given limit.

4.4 THE SPECIALIST

The actual transaction is effected by approaching a member of the Exchange who specializes in the trading of Ford stock and who, by his readiness to buy and sell Ford stock, creates a continuous market for the stock. The *specialist*, as he is called, keeps a "book" in which he records limit orders from all over the country to buy and sell Ford stock. In our example, when the broker's representative approaches the specialist he will ask for the current quotation. The specialist consults his book and answers, say, 62 to $62\frac{1}{2}$, which means that the highest bid price in his book is $62 and the lowest price at which he has an offer to sell is $62.50. Our broker's floor partner might bid $62\frac{1}{4}$ in the hope that one of traders standing around the specialist might have received a sale order at that price. If not, he raises his bid to $62\frac{1}{2}$ and the transaction is effected when the specialist calls out "sold." The broker and specialist record this transaction, and a report of the transaction is transmitted by an Exchange employee to the Exchange's computer center. Within seconds the report is flashed by ticker to subscribers all over the country. If our investor waits at his broker's office, he can watch the ticker report of his transaction which the broker usually projects electronically on a wall display panel.

The role of the specialist is crucial to the functioning of the market. He is in possession of very valuable information. In effect the specialist is the only person on the floor of the Exchange with up-to-date, albeit partial, knowledge of the supply and demand for the security in question.[13] His book, at any moment of time, summarizes investors' offers to buy and sell the stock at varying prices. The specialist does not share this information with other traders; that is, he is a "monopolist" with respect to this information. That fact is very important since the specialist not only serves as an intermediary, but can also trade on his own account and could conceivably exploit his knowledge by buying and selling selectively to maximize his own profits.

It should be noted that the specialist is not free to act solely on his own behalf. His primary function is to help maintain a "fair and orderly" market by buying and selling on his own account.[14] Thus he is constrained in his own trading to transactions which narrow the price changes between sales, thereby achieving greater price continuity than would otherwise be the case. The Exchange regularly checks the activities of the specialists; in 1968 over

---

[13] The information is only partial, since the specialist's book includes only limit orders which have been placed in advance of anticipated changes in market price. Should the price change, other investors may also be induced to buy or sell at that price, and will do so by means of market orders.

[14] NYSE *Fact Book 1969*, p. 52.

95% of specialists' transactions on own account were "stabilizing," in the sense that they represented purchases at prices below, or sales at prices above, the previous different price. Thus by buying and selling *against* the market the specialist dampens price fluctuations. Some measure of the effectiveness of the specialist system can be gleaned from the results of an examination carried out by the Exchange of 6 million transactions in 1968. The examination showed that 94% of the transactions took place at the same price as the preceding transaction, or within a spread of not more than $\frac{1}{4}$ point.[15]

5. MARGIN TRADING

The extension of credit to finance the purchase of securities, or "trading on margin" as such transactions are usually called, has been subject to federal regulation since 1934. The Securities Act of 1934 empowers the Board of Governors of the Federal Reserve System to regulate the extension of credit by banks and brokers to customers for the purchase of stocks or bonds. The regulation stipulates the *margin*, that is, the cash amount a credit customer must pay when purchasing a security, the balance being advanced by the broker. Thus an 80% margin requirement essentially means that the customer's initial equity in the purchase of, say, $10,000 of common stocks must be at least $8,000. Credit can be extended by the broker only up to $2,000.[16]

In addition to the Fed's *initial* margin requirement, the Exchange also sets requirements for *maintenance* margins, that is, the minimum equity requirements which apply to the account after the day of the transaction. In general, a customer's equity must be at least 25% of the market value of the securities carried in the margin account, and therefore serving as collateral for the broker's loan. This is the *minimum* requirement; individual brokers may, and often do, set maintenance margins at higher levels. In addition, the Exchange imposes higher margins on especially volatile issues. Continuing margin control is necessary if the broker's loan is to be safeguarded. When falling stock prices reduce the collateral value of the stock held in the margin account, the maintenance margin requirement ensures that the value of the collateral will always exceed the customer's debit balance with the broker.

---

[15] For a less favorable evaluation of the specialist's functions, see Baumol, *op cit.*, Chapter 2.

[16] Should the margin of equity fall below the initial requirement subsequent to the purchase, the customer's account is considered "restricted," and federal regulations stipulate the percentage of the proceeds from any sale of securities of such accounts which must be retained in the account in order to reduce the investor's debit balance. However it should be emphasized that "the Fed" does *not* object to restricted accounts per se, and does not force the sale of securities so held.

Should the value of the stock fall below the continuing margin requirement, a call goes out to the customer "for more margin," that is, to deposit additional cash in the account. If the customer fails to do this, the broker can restore the minimum margin by selling off a sufficient quantity of the stock held in the margin account.

Since the maintenance margin (25%) is considerably below the Fed's initial margin (70–80% in recent years), the price of a stock must decline drastically before any distress selling will occur owing to lack of margin. Thus the two regulations interact to permit federal regulation of the volume of stock market credit and the protection of brokers' loans without inducing distress selling, which even minor fluctuations in price would induce if the Fed's initial margin requirements applied subsequent to the purchase.

6. SHORT SELLING

When an investor feels confident about a stock's chances he can purchase that stock. If he is particularly "bullish" about the stock, he will borrow money to finance further purchases; that is, he will acquire the stock on margin. But what about the proverbial "bear" who thinks that the price of a particular stock is going to fall significantly in the near future? If he owns the stock he can sell it, but what can the bearish investor do if he doesn't own the stock in question, or after he has sold off his holdings? The answer to this dilemma is to sell the stock short, a short sale being defined as the sale of stock which an investor does not own. Thus the investor can borrow the stock and sell it on the market at the current price in anticipation of buying it back at reduced prices, thereby profiting from the decline.[17]

Although the very term *short sale* smacks of speculation, short sales are made for a variety of reasons, not all of them speculative. For example, an investor may "sell short against the box"; that is, borrow a stock and sell it even though he owns the stock himself. The "box" in this case refers to the safe deposit box of the short seller. The motives for such a short sale are usually not speculative. For example, having made a profit in a particular stock in December, the owner may sell the stock short and then deliver his own stock to the lender to cover the short sale in January, thereby carrying his profit over to the next tax year. Similarly short sales are used for a variety of hedging purposes, but the specialists and professional traders on

---

[17] The lender of the stock is compensated for the loan of the stock since the proceeds of the short sale can be invested by the lender; the lender is also entitled to any dividends declared during the time the stock is out on loan.

the floor of the Exchange account for the majority of short sales, most of which are technical in nature. Thus a heavy wave of buying orders may be met by the specialist partially out of his own inventory and partially by short selling the stock.

7. STOCK PRICE INDEXES

Almost all investors are concerned with general market conditions as well as with the particular securities comprising their portfolios. In 1965 the New York Stock Exchange introduced a comprehensive measure of the market trend. The composite index covers all listed stock; changes in the index are printed every half hour on the ticker tape. Four subgroup indexes— Industrial, Transportation, Utility, and Finance—and their net changes also appear on the tape every hour. The indexes are adjusted to eliminate the effects of changes in capitalization (splits and stock dividends) and of new listings and delistings.[18] The prices of each stock are weighted by the number of shares listed, and the aggregate market value is expressed relative to the base period (December 1955 equals 50). But despite the fact that the New York Stock Exchange is the nation's paramount securities market, this index is a relative newcomer to the financial scene; most investors, and the general public as well, turn to a much better known indicator of market trends, which is not strictly speaking an index: the Dow-Jones Averages.

If the NYSE Index is the newest of the major market indicators, the Dow-Jones Average is the oldest. In 1884, Dow, Jones and Company began publishing stock price averages in a daily newsletter which was the precursor of the *Wall Street Journal*. Today the company publishes four averages of prices for selected stocks listed on the New York Stock Exchange: 30 industrials, 20 railroad stocks, 15 utilities, and the composite average for the 65 stocks. The averages are reported regularly during days of trading on the Exchange, and are sent out at half hour intervals over the Dow-Jones news ticker service. The Dow-Jones averages appear in the *Wall Street Journal* and in the financial pages of leading newspapers all over the world.

The 30 industrials constitute the best known of the four averages, and when the financial press reports new highs or lows for the D-J average, the reference is invariably to the industrials. As the name implies, the D-J indicators are actual *averages* of stock prices; the divisor, however, is adjusted for stock splits in order not to disturb the average.[19] Figure I.1 charts the Dow-Jones industrial average for the period 1929–70.

---

[18] These alterations are handled by adjusting the base period to eliminate their impact on the index.
[19] The type of adjustment needed is illustrated in the next chapter.

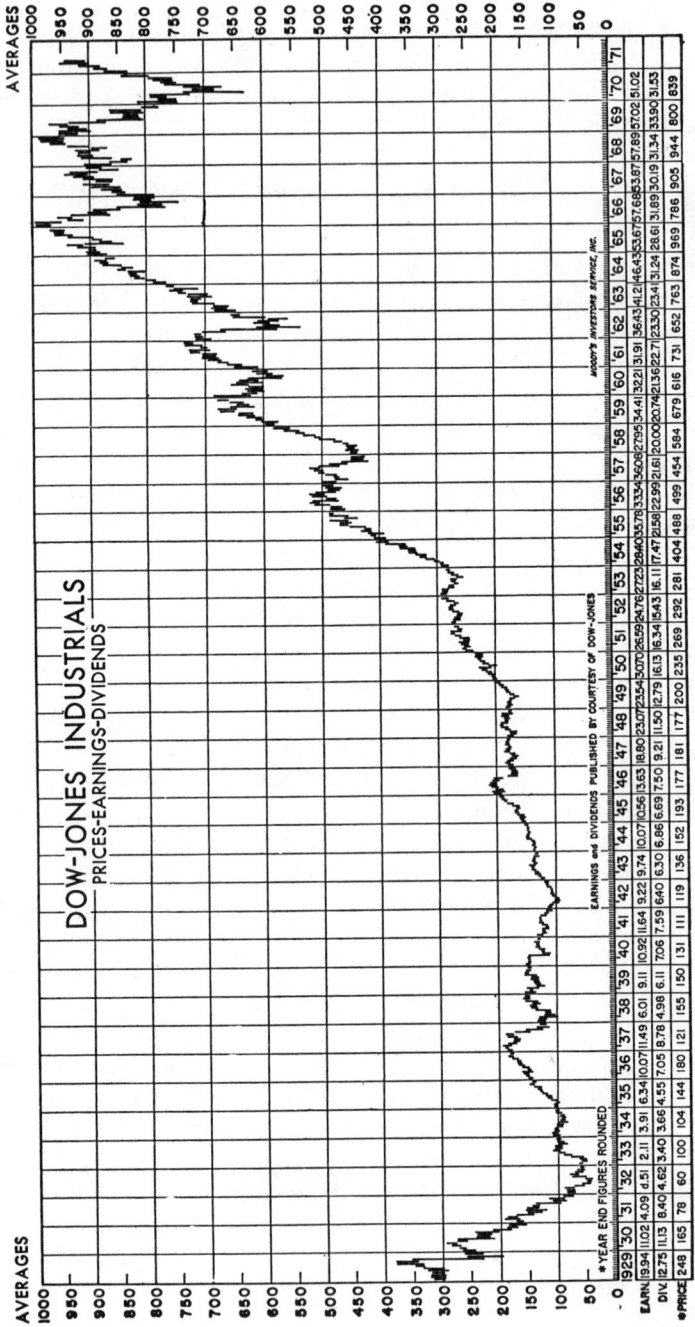

FIGURE I.1. Dow-Jones industrial average 1929–1970. Source: Moody's Industrial Manual, 1971, p. 32a.

7. STOCK PRICE INDEXES

The industrial average is a "blue chip" average, since the 30 stocks included represent a cross section of the best known and largest companies listed on the Exchange. These include American Tel. & Tel., American Tobacco, Dupont, General Electric, General Motors, Sears Roebuck, and U.S. Steel. From time to time substitutions have taken place in the list; perhaps the best known substitution was the removal of IBM from the list in 1939. Had this not occurred, the D-J industrials would have "broken 1,000" at the beginning of the 1960s, which suggests that some care should be exercised when interpreting the averages. In particular, no significance attaches to the absolute *level* of the average and attention should be directed to the change (preferably the *percentage* change) in the average over time. Thus when the average stands at, say, 800 points, a fall of 16 points to 784 does not necessarily indicate a national disaster, but rather that the prices of the 30 D-J industrial stocks have declined by 2% on the average.

Standard & Poor's Corporation publishes another well known series of stock price indexes:

>500 stocks, composite index
>425 industrials
>25 railroads
>50 utilities

All of these indexes are reported regularly during the day by the various news services.[20] Unlike the D-J averages, the S&P indexes are "indexes" in the full sense of the term, that is, current market value (price times number of shares) is expressed as a percentage *relative* to the market value of a common base period. In the case of the S&P indexes, a base of 10 is given to the average stock prices during the years 1941–1943. A base of 10 rather than the more common 100 was chosen so that the resulting index number would more closely approximate the actual average of prices on the NYSE. The new index was chained to the older S&P 90 stock composite index, so that the indexes are available for earlier years as well.

Figure I.2 sets out the Standard & Poor's Composite Index for the period 1925–1970 in nominal terms and in constant prices (deflated by the consumer price index). Inflation accounts for about one half of the rise in stock prices over the period. An examination of Figure I.2 also indicates the crucial importance of the timing of investments. For the unlucky individual who invested in a representative cross section of common stocks in 1929, on the eve of the Great Depression, stock prices did not regain their initial levels until 1954 in nominal terms, and not until 1956 in constant real terms. On the other hand, investments made at the trough of the depression in 1931

---

[20] Standard & Poor's publishes indexes for many industry subgroups, as does Moody's.

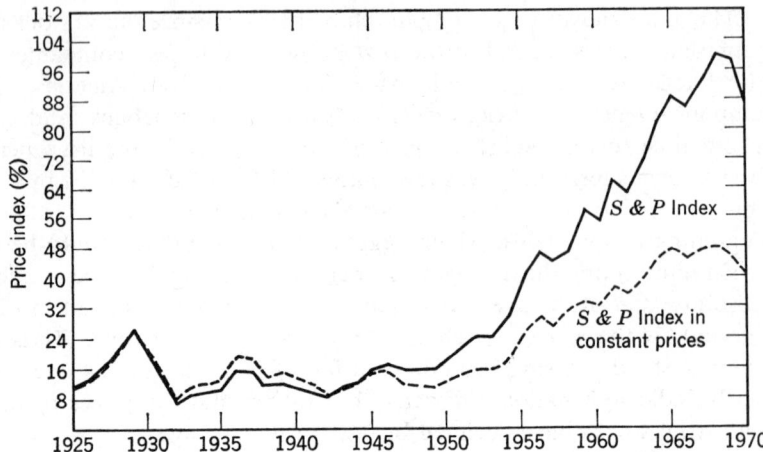

FIGURE I.2. S&P composite stock index in nominal and constant prices, 1925–1970. Source: Standard & Poor's Trade and Securities Statistics: Security Price Index Record.

fared much better; by 1936 the S&P index had doubled both in nominal and real terms, and by 1954 the nominal index was more than 4 times its 1931 level, while in real terms, stock prices more than doubled between 1931 and 1954.

An alternative way of using the indexes is to calculate the rate of return on the stocks included in the index.[21] This is done by computing the capital gain or loss for the year, that is, the change in the index during the year plus the average dividend paid on the same stocks during the year, and then expressing this sum as a percentage of the index at the beginning of the year:

$$\frac{I_1 - I_0 + D_1}{I_0} = \text{rate of return}$$

where: I_0 = level of index at beginning of year
I_1 = level of index at end of year
D_1 = average dividend paid during the year

Figure I.3 plots the annual rates of return, calculated as above, for the Dow-Jones Industrials for the 41 year period 1930–1970. The rate of return was positive in 29 of the 41 years, and for the period as a whole the average annual rate of return was 7.8%. Again the crucial importance of timing can

---

[21] For details of the procedure see Chapter III.

7. STOCK PRICE INDEXES

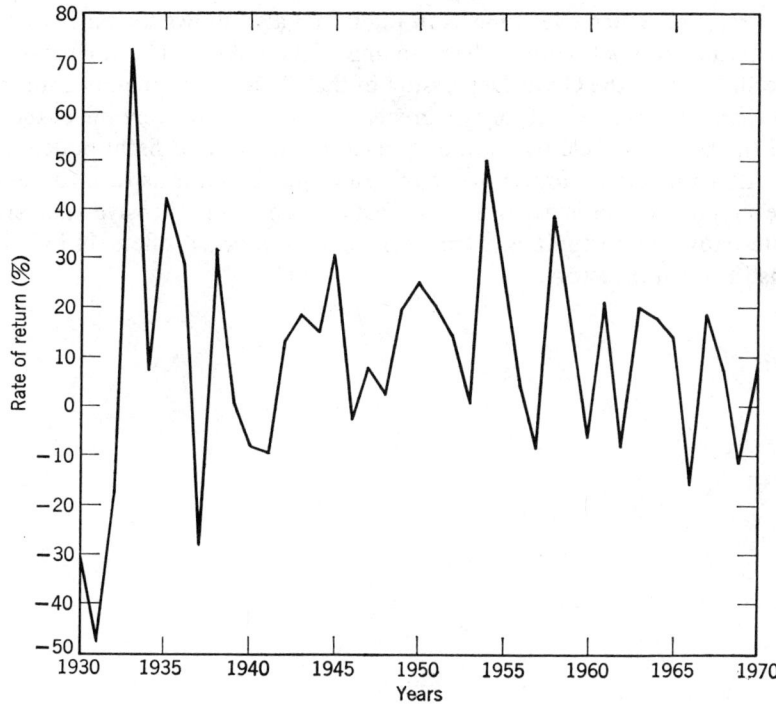

FIGURE I.3. Rates of Return of Dow-Jones Industrials, 1930–1970.

be seen by examining the following figures on the rate of return for selected sub-periods:

Period	Annual Geometric Average Rate of Return (%)
1930–1970	7.8
1930–1932	−32.5
1933–1941	11.9
1942–1970	10.2

The advantages of using the rate of return are obvious. This figure reflects the total benefits (dividends and capital gains) emanating from the investment in stocks and is perhaps easier to interpret than the rather cryptic announcements that the Dow-Jones Average is up (or down) by $7\frac{1}{8}$ points. Plotting the rates of return over time as in Figure I.3 also shows the narrowing of the amplitude of fluctuations (the lessening of the risks of investment) which has occurred since the Great Depression of the 1930s. This phenomenon reflects, perhaps, the public authority's greater ability to effectively offset the impact of the business cycle by counter-cyclical monetary and fiscal policies.

After this brief glimpse of the securities markets, let us turn to the task of developing the tools necessary to effect a more comprehensive analysis of the alternative opportunities a modern capital market offers individual and institutional investors.

QUESTIONS

1.1 Distinguish between the primary and secondary securities markets.

1.2 What are the principal economic functions of a stock exchange?

1.3 How do stock market prices affect the allocation of capital resources in the economy?

1.4 What is the logic behind the NYSE listing requirements?

1.5 What are the advantages of listing to the corporation? Can you think of any disadvantages?

1.6 What is the function of the specialist on the NYSE? Can you think of a feasible alternative for the "specialist system of trading"?

SELECTED REFERENCES

Baumol, W. J., *The Stock Market and Economic Efficiency*. New York: Fordham University Press, 1965.

Brown, J. M., "Post-Offering Experience of Companies Going Public," *Journal of Business* (January 1970).

Cohen, J. B., and Zinbarg, E. D., *Investment Analysis and Portfolio Management*. Homewood, Ill.: Irwin, 1967.

Eiteman, W. J.; Dice, C. A.; and Eiteman, D. K., *The Stock Market*, 4th ed. New York: McGraw-Hill, 1966.

Furst, R. W., "Does Listing Increase the Market Price of Common Stocks?" *Journal of Business* (April 1970).

Leffler, G. L., and Farwell, L. C., *The Stock Market*, 3rd ed. New York: Ronald Press, 1963.

Molodovsky, N., "Building A Stock Market Measure—A Case Story," *Financial Analysts Journal* (May–June 1967).

Renshaw, E. F., "Estimating the Return on S & P's Industrial Price Index," *Financial Analysts Journal* (January–February 1969).

Van Horne, J. C., "New Listings and Their Price Behavior," *Journal of Finance* (September 1970).

West, S., and Miller, N., "Why the New NYSE Common Stock Indexes?" *Financial Analysts Journal* (May–June 1967).

Chapter II
Measuring Corporate Profits

1. INTRODUCTION

Many readers will be familiar with the signs "garbage in" and "garbage out" which adorn the computation centers of some American universities. Cynicism aside, they may well serve as a sobering warning to the budding analyst that owing to rapid technological advances, our ability to manipulate figures far outstrips our ability to provide meaningful data in many disciplines. Nowhere is this more true than in security analysis.

One key variable in the evaluation of the current desirability of acquiring (or holding) a company's securities is its anticipated earnings performance. But even an intelligent guess as to future profitability depends on our estimate of what the company is currently earning, and perhaps even more important, on how its earnings have been growing in the recent past. The purpose of this chapter is to lay the groundwork for an evaluation of a firm's securities by first analyzing the conceptual problems inherent in the measurement of corporate income.

2. SOURCES OF ACCOUNTING DATA

One of the most important sources of information for evaluating corporate earnings and the desirability of investing in securities is the quarterly and annual reports published by companies listed on a major stock exchange (and by some which are not). By far the most important of these is the annual report, which typically includes the company's balance sheet and income statement as well as a review of company activities during the current year and its plans for the future. In addition to these periodic reports a company occasionally prepares special reports. The most important of these is the prospectus, which is prepared prior to a new issue of securities by companies desiring to raise additional capital from the public. The prospectus provides information on a company's development and past activities, the terms of the new issue, the investors to whom the securities are being offered, and the purpose of the issue. Properly used, these two types of reports can provide a great deal of information relevant to the investment decision process.

The way in which these reports should be used depends, of course, on the analyst's objectives. Generally he turns to a company's annual report or to its prospectus with a threefold purpose in mind:

(1) Analysis of the company's current and past profitability

(2) Estimation of its potential future profitability

(3) Evaluation of its expected profitability against the present price of its stock

An understanding of past trends in a company's earnings is a vital first step when trying to gauge future earnings. In addition, the analysis of past data may shed some light on the degree of earnings stability: How much (and why) did earnings fluctuate? Has the company been able to pay dividends regularly or was it compelled to forego dividend payments in years of low earnings? Thus, while it is true that an investor who weighs the purchase of a company's stock "buys future earnings," his decision often rests on an evaluation of past trends as well as on very partial information regarding possible future developments.

3. ECONOMIC PROFITS VS. ACCOUNTING PROFITS

As we have already noted, much of the relevant information regarding a company's activities often comes to us in the form of an accounting report, chiefly a balance sheet and income statement. These reports are prepared in accordance with *accounting* principles, which often leads to very significant differences between the accountant's "estimate"[1] of past and current earnings and that of the investment analyst or economist.

Important conceptual differences exist between "accounting profits" and "economic profits." Many of these differences reflect basic disagreement regarding the realization of income and the definition of costs, but they also

---

[1] Note that even the most objective accounting report of historical earnings is, of necessity, an estimate, based as it must be on the accountant's estimate of the length of life of equipment, salvage value, and so on.

3. ECONOMIC PROFITS VS. ACCOUNTING PROFITS

reflect the very different objectives of the accountant and of the economist.[2] The accountant's primary concern is to measure past periodic (usually annual) earnings; in a way the accountant is the firm's economic historian, albeit a very quantitative one. The economist, on the other hand, is solely concerned with the future stream of earnings over the expected life span of the firm; the periodic milestones so vital to the preparation of a balance sheet of assets and liabilities are of no particular concern to him.

The sympathies of the financial analyst tend to lie with the economist since it is the estimation of future trends which provides the *raison d'être* for his analysis of the past. And although a complete adjustment of company reports to reflect economic profits is usually not possible, it is often desirable to make at least some rough adjustment especially when comparing the performance of two firms.

Differences between accounting and economic profits arise from a number of sources; some of the more important, but certainly not all, of the differences arise for the following reasons:[3]

(a) Economic analysis is based on the concept of a *cash* flow, while a firm's accounts typically are kept on an accrual basis. This, of course, is a special case of the accountant's concern with the allocation of revenues and costs to specific years. The "matching" of costs and revenues, which occupies much of an accountant's time and even more of his ingenuity when transactions relate to more than one year, is not crucial to the economist. The latter can forego the one year income statement and replace it with a two or three year or for that matter with a "life of the asset" income statement.

A major advantage of the economist's approach for the investment analyst is that by focusing attention on the timing of receipts and expenditures, the cash flow concept leads directly to the need for discounting future earnings, which lies at the heart of the valuation problem.[4]

(b) The economist and the accountant are not only in disagreement with respect to the timing of revenues and costs, but often do not agree on what costs should be deducted from what revenues when calculating a net income or profit figure. Owing to his quest for objectivity the accountant tends to recognize recorded historical events only, with respect to both costs and

---

[2] Where the functions of managerial accounting and economics overlap—for example, in the capital budgeting analysis of new investments—the common objective leads to an almost complete narrowing of the differences in both concepts and methods.

[3] The reader who desires to pursue this question at greater depth is referred to S. S. Alexander, "Income Measurement in a Dynamic Economy," in *Five Monographs on Business Income*, American Institute of Accountants, 1948; a revised version by David Solomons appears in W. T. Baxter and S. Davidson, *Studies in Accounting Theory*, Homewood, Ill.: Irwin, 1962, pp. 126–200.

[4] The discounting of cash flows is discussed in detail in Chapter III.

revenues. Thus *opportunity costs*, which reflect what might have been had another course of action been chosen, are not deducted from revenues when accounting profits are calculated. For example, while the economist imputes an interest cost on the equity capital employed in the firm, the accountant recognizes an interest cost only to the extent that an actual outlay of money takes place. As a result, accounting profits tend to overstate economic profits, where opportunity costs are significant.

(c) Depreciation, on the other hand, is one nonoutlay cost which is recognized by both accountants and economists. However, the way in which the cost is estimated differs. The accountant is primarily concerned with *allocating* the historical cost of the asset to particular years during its expected lifetime, since such an allocation is necessary if periodic income statements (and balance sheets) are to be calculated. To the economist, the historical cost of a machine is irrelevant; for a century now economists, following Jevons, have intoned "Bygones are bygones"; this allows them to slide into current replacement costs without even shifting gears. For them capital wastage, or economic depreciation as it is often called, is measured by the difference in the *market* values of the asset at the beginning and end of the period.[5] The accountant's concern with historical costs and the economist's dictum that once incurred, a cost is irrelevant for all current evaluations and future decisions, are responsible for much of the divergence between the accounting and economic concepts of profits.[6]

(d) Another area where the approaches of accounting and economics diverge is in the treatment of capital gains or losses. This, of course, is of special interest to the investment analyst. The accountant treats realized capital gains or losses as income or as deductions from income. The unrealized appreciation on an asset is not recognized. However, it should be noted that the conservative accounting rule of valuing assets at "cost or market, whichever is lower" anticipates capital losses, which are recognized, while deferring unrealized capital gains, which are not considered as income. To the economist a rise in price of General Motors stock is no more or less a fact because its owner has decided to sell or not to sell the stock. The effects of differential taxation aside, the economist treats realized and unrealized capital gains on an equal par with other income items.

The accounting treatment of capital gains is particularly troublesome to the financial analyst since it often creates difficulties in evaluating the trend of past earnings. The reporting of capital gains only on realization may create artificial irregularities in the trend of earnings. Consider, for example,

---

[5] The length of the period usually reflects the life span of the asset or investment.
[6] The economist's concern for price level–adjusted values can be viewed as a special case of the rejection of historical prices as a measure of economic values.

3. ECONOMIC PROFITS VS. ACCOUNTING PROFITS

an investment company holding a diversified portfolio of common stocks, or for that matter any company holding marketable assets such as oil leases or real estate. The year to year appreciation (if any) of the portfolio is not reflected in the company's income statement unless the assets are actually sold in the market, thereby creating a recordable transaction. Unless a company sells off assets at a regular rate, large sales will create "jumps" in the accounting record of earnings which have no economic basis.

To illustrate this point let us take the concrete example given in Table II–1, which sets out the consolidated income statement of General Foods Corporation in 1968 and 1969. A "bottom line" comparison of the two years shows a 30% jump in General Foods' net after-tax earnings in 1969 as compared with 1968. But before picking up the hot line to the broker's office a more careful reading of the statement might be in order. Fortunately, General Foods is concerned with providing a readily understandable earnings statement, and therefore has clearly identified $29 million of net extraordinary items which, while part of accounting earnings, should be given special consideration. Moreover, in the notes to the accounting statements, the extraordinary item is identified as the net capital gain from the sale of a subsidiary company.

TABLE II–1. Consolidated statement of earnings of General Foods Corporation*

	March 29, 1969	March 30, 1968
Net sales	1,893,760	1,739,686
Other Income	9,130	8,819
	1,902,890	1,748,505
Cost and Expenses		
Cost of Sales	1,152,842	1,058,195
Marketing, General, and Administrative Expenses	522,983	485,058
Interest Expense	10,401	6,219
	1,686,226	1,549,472
Earnings Before Income Taxes and Extraordinary Items	216,664	199,033
Taxes on Income	113,274	97,690
Earnings Before Extraordinary Items	103,390	101,343
Extraordinary Items, Net of Tax	29,496	----------
NET EARNINGS	132,886	101,343

* All dollar amounts expressed in thousands.

How should the financial analyst handle this item when evaluating GF's profitability? Certainty no one will argue that the capital gain is not a gain, but it might be legitimate to question the propriety of assigning the entire gain to 1969. But having ignored any *unrealized* appreciation on the investment in the subsidiary company during past years, the entire capital gain is automatically attributed to the year in which it was realized, and the company's accounting staff is to be commended for having clearly identified the transaction in a way that permits the reader of the statement to make his own decision regarding the trend in the company's earnings. Thus we might be closer to the truth if we note that earnings (net of extraordinary items) remained stable in 1969. But before doing this it might be advisable to examine the company's statements during the past few years. Should we find, for example, large extraordinary income items in all or most years, it might pay to recast the earnings record to reflect these gains. An "extraordinary" item appearing regularly in a firm's income statement might usefully be considered as "ordinary" income. This is probably true for the "other income" entry in the GF statement. (This item is perhaps also too small in magnitude to warrant a great deal of research effort.)

Thus, in the absence of a revaluation of assets each year, great care should be taken to ensure that the trend in a company's earnings is not distorted by the differential treatment of various income components. Similarly, care must be exercised when comparing the earnings records of two different companies whose accounting practices may differ. For example, should we wish to compare General Foods with Brand X, the latter's extraordinary income must be identified and evaluated before a meaningful comparison of earnings records can be made.[7]

4. EARNINGS PER SHARE

Even if we succeed in adjusting all the income statements to reflect economic profits, a number of questions regarding the validity of profitability comparisons arise. These questions arise whether we are comparing the profitability of the same company over a period of years or making a cross-section comparison of the earnings of a number of different companies in a given year.

First, consider the question of using total net earnings as our profitability indicator. This raises the following problem: Consider the hypothetical

---

[7] This is not meant to imply that such an adjustment by itself is sufficient to ensure comparability. See Section 5.

4. EARNINGS PER SHARE

TABLE II–2. Income data for a hypothetical company

	1968	1970
Net Earnings after Tax	1,000,000	1,500,000
Number of Shares of Stock Outstanding	100,000	200,000
Earnings per Share (EPS)	10	7.5

company whose net earnings were $1,000,000 in 1968 and $1,500,000 in 1970 (Table II–2). We have also assumed that the company issued (on January 1, 1969) 100,000 additional shares of stock, thereby doubling the shares outstanding. However, since the new stock issue doubled the number of shares outstanding, while profits increased by only 50% over the two year period, earnings per share (EPS) declined from $10 per share in 1968 to $7.50 per share in 1970. Thus, owing to a new stock issue[8] an increase in total earnings may or may not reflect an increase in the profitability rate of new investments relative to existing investments. In fact, in our example the new investments have not generated a comparable level of profitability, and as a result, earnings per share declined. Similarly, there is no significance to total earnings when companies of different sizes are being compared. Since the investor is concerned with the profitability per unit of investment, a per share calculation can readily be made to eliminate the influence of size.

Many companies recognize the shortcomings of total profits for investment analysis and therefore provide per share calculations in their annual reports. Such a calculation is illustrated in Table II–3 for International Business Machines. On December 31, 1968 IBM had about 113 million shares outstanding and net earnings of about $871 million, so that earnings per share (net earnings divided by the number of shares) were $7.71. Alternatively, if we take earnings before taxes in the numerator, IBM's pre-tax earnings per

TABLE II–3. Selected data from the IBM Annual Report for the year 1968

Net Earnings, Before Income Taxes	$1,864,497,991
U.S. Federal and Foreign Income Taxes	993,000,000
Net Earnings, After Taxes	871,497,991
Number of Shares Outstanding	112,968,369
Net Earnings per Share	7.71

[8] We assume that sufficient time has elapsed for the investments which were financed by the issue to reach fruition. See p. 44.

share were:

$$\frac{\$1,864,497,991}{112,968,369} = \$16.50$$

Clearly after-tax profits are more meaningful to the investor than pre-tax profits; even if the investor is tax exempt, the company still must pay the corporate income tax. Thus the maximum dividend that can be paid out of earnings is measured by the after-tax earnings per share. Still the analyst may wish to examine the pre-tax figure, especially when attempting to derive the all important trend in a company's earnings over a particular period of time. Basic tax rates may change or an excess profits tax may be introduced in a particular year which may distort the trend in the firm's economic performance. But more important, owing to tax adjustments, loss carry-forwards, investment credits, and the like, a corporation may in some years incur a significantly different tax liability on the *same* magnitude of pre-tax income, even if the basic tax rate remains the same.

As a result, after-tax earnings per share may fluctuate even when pre-tax earnings (and tax rates) are stable. To avoid drawing incorrect inferences both figures should be examined and any major discrepancies between trends in pre-tax and post-tax per share earnings explained. For example, a break in the growth rate of per share earnings which results from the imposition of an excess corporate profits tax might well lead to far different conclusions than would a fall in profitability due to a break in sales or a rise in the cost of goods sold.

When comparing the profitability of two *different* companies it is very important to use the after-tax figures. Some corporations are required to pay less tax per dollar of income than others. Several examples leap to mind. An oil company which benefits from liberal depletion allowances will tend to have a higher after-tax income for a given level of pre-tax earnings. Similarly, many countries encourage investments by offering partial or full tax exemption to selected enterprises.

Take the simple example given in Table II–4, which assumes that Company A has been given the status of an approved enterprise, say in Northern Ireland or Israel, and therefore, pays only 25% tax. Company B, which does not enjoy a privileged position, pays the regular tax rate of 50%.

A comparison of the pre-tax earnings per share is very misleading in this case. Although both companies earn $10 per share on a pre-tax basis, Company A, which benefits from the preferential tax treatment, earns a considerably higher post-tax profit per share—$7.50 as against only $5 for company B.[9] Since the tax concessions are of direct benefit to the investor,

---

[9] The reader should note that a comparison of total profits is meaningless owing to the difference in the sizes of the two companies.

5. ADJUSTED EARNINGS PER SHARE

TABLE II–4

	Company A	Company B
Net Earnings Before Tax	$100,000	$500,000
Income Tax	25,000	250,000
Net Earnings After Tax	75,000	250,000
Number of Shares Outstanding	10,000	50,000
Pre-tax Earnings per Share	10	10
Post-tax Earnings per Share	7.5	5

he should be willing, other things being equal, to pay more for a share of A's common stock, and therefore such concessions should not be overlooked when estimating profitability.

5. ADJUSTED EARNINGS PER SHARE

Having calculated earnings per share, and having checked for irregularities in tax liabilities, it would appear plausible that studying the time series of EPS for a company should be helpful in determining the past trends in its profitability. To this end Table II–5 presents EPS data for IBM for the years 1960–1968. Contrary to what one might have expected, the earnings record

TABLE II–5. Unadjusted earnings per share* of IBM, 1960–68

Year	Net Earnings (thousands of $) (1)	Number of Shares Outstanding (thousands) (2)	Earnings per Share ($) (1) ÷ (2) = (3)
1960	204,915	18,392	11.14
1961	254,119	27,691	9.18
1962	304,726	27,808	10.96
1963	364,255	27,922	13.05
1964	431,160	35,048	12.30
1965	476,902	35,225	13.54
1966	526,130	54,448	9.66
1967	651,500	56,114	11.61
1968	871,498	112,968	7.71

* Net earnings after taxes.

TABLE II-6. Earnings per share for a hypothetical company

Year	Net Earnings	Number of Shares	Earnings per Share
1969	100,000	50,000	2
1970	100,000	100,000	1

is very uneven; EPS rose in four years and *fell* in four other years. Moreover, between 1960 and 1968 EPS *dropped* from $11.14 to $7.71, which is contrary to all our preconceptions of the profitability of this popular growth stock. The explanation is not hard to find; from time to time IBM split its stock. For example, in 1968 IBM declared a 2 for 1 split, so that at the end of 1968 a shareholder had two shares for every one share he had held at the end of 1967. Thus the drop in EPS from $11.61 in 1967 to 7.71 in 1968 is illusory. Since every 1967 shareholder had double the number of shares without additional investment, the *adjusted* EPS in 1968 is 2 7.71 = $15.42, which represents a steep rise in profitability relative to the previous year. The unadjusted fall in EPS is merely technical and, of course, can be very misleading. Under no circumstances should such a technical fall in EPS be identified as a decline in profitability.

The need to adjust the EPS figures in order to ensure comparability between years can be illustrated by the example given in Table II-6. Although net after-tax profits remained the same between 1969 and 1970, the number of shares doubled in 1970, thereby reducing EPS by 50%, that is, from $2 per share in 1969 to $1 per share in 1970. How should we interpret this drop in EPS?

To the degree that the company issued new shares to the public, and that sufficient time has elapsed for the new investments financed by the issue to reach fruition, the conclusion that profitability dropped drastically seems justified. If the company issued new shares and the funds were not properly used, this is tantamount, from the investor's point of view, to acquiring a new partner who adds nothing to the company's overall profitability but shares in the earnings. However, if the drop in EPS is due to a 2 for 1 stock split, no additional capital was raised, but neither have the former shareholders acquired new partners. For every share owned in 1969 a shareholder now has two shares, so EPS did not really drop but remained stable at $2 per *adjusted* share in 1970. Hence, if paradoxical results are to be avoided, EPS figures must be adjusted; in the next three sections we shall briefly discuss the major adjustments:

(a) for stock splits and stock dividends;
(b) for rights issues; and
(c) for public stock issues.

6. ADJUSTING EPS FOR STOCK SPLITS AND STOCK DIVIDENDS

In a stock dividend or split a company's stockholders are given additional shares to represent their ownership interest. No additional investment on the part of the shareholders is required, and of course, no additional capital is raised by the corporation. The difference between the stock dividend and the split is technical and need not concern us here: in a split, as the name suggests, the par or stated value of the stock is reduced, while in a stock dividend the par or stated value remains unchanged, and a transfer is effected from earned surplus to the capital account. In both instances no transaction takes place, and the split or stock dividend represents a bookkeeping entry.[10]

To clarify the procedure for adjusting EPS for splits or stock dividends, let us consider the example given in Table II–7 of a company which declared a 10% stock dividend in 1967 and a 2 for 1 split (equivalent for our purposes to a 100% stock dividend) in 1969. As a first step, a base year is chosen; in our example it is 1965. An "index" of the *number* of shares a 1965 shareholder owns in each of the following years, *without additional investment*, is constructed. Such an index is given in Table II–8. For simplicity, consider a shareholder with 100 shares in 1965. In 1967, following the 10% stock

TABLE II–7. Unadjusted earnings per share and stock dividends (splits) of a hypothetical company

Year	Net Earnings after Tax (1)	Number of Shares (2)	Unadjusted Earnings per Share (3)	Splits and Stock Dividends (4)
1965	1,000	1,000	1.00	—
1966	1,100	1,000	1.10	—
1967	1,200	1,100	1.09	10%
1968	1,500	1,100	1.36	—
1969	1,500	2,200	0.68	2:1
1970	1,600	2,200	0.73	—

[10] Large stock dividends and splits may broaden the market for a firm's stock by lowering the per unit price, thereby lowering the minimum investment required to secure the preferential commission on 100 share round lots. The case for a small stock dividend or split is far less clear, although where the cash dividend rate remains unchanged it affords management the opportunity of "announcing" a dividend rise in advance.

TABLE II–8.

Year	Number of Shares at Beginning of Each Year	Splits and Stock Dividends	Number of Shares at End of Each Year
1965	100	——	100
1966	100	——	100
1967	100	10%	110
1968	110	——	110
1969	110	2:1	220
1970	220	——	220

dividend, the *number* of shares which he owned increases to 110, without any additional investment, and the index is set at 110 from 1967 on. In 1969 following the 2 for 1 split the number of shares which he owned increased to 220 (not 200, since he held 110 shares when the split occurred). From that date the index becomes 220. When calculating the adjusted EPS, Table II–9, the observed EPS (Column 1) is multiplied by the index (Column 2), and the resulting product (Column 3) represents the EPS, adjusted for stock splits and stock dividends.[11]

The need for the adjustment becomes clear when we compare the record of unadjusted earnings per share for the company (Column 1 of Table II–9) with its adjusted EPS (Column 3 of Table II–9). Those fluctuations in

TABLE II–9.

Year	Unadjusted Earnings per Share (1)	Index (2)	Adjusted Earnings per Share $[(1) \cdot (2)]/100 = (3)$
1965	1.00	100	1.00
1966	1.10	100	1.10
1967	1.09	110	1.20
1968	1.36	110	1.50
1969	0.68	220	1.50
1970	0.73	220	1.61

[11] Alternatively 1970 could be chosen as the base year and the index constructed backwards by *dividing* the annual unadjusted earnings-per-share data by 1 plus the relevant percentage change in the number of shares. This is the procedure commonly employed by Moody's and other reporting services when adjusting for splits or stock dividends. See Section 9.

unadjusted EPS which were induced by the accounting manipulations clearly are of no significance to the investor and must be offset when the *rate of growth* in earnings is being calculated. The company did not experience a 27% drop in profitability between 1965 and 1970, as the unadjusted EPS figures suggest. On the contrary, a glance at Table II-9 suffices to show that the company's profits (for a given investment) *increased* by 61% (adjusted EPS were $1.61 in 1970 compared with $1.00 in 1961) during those years. Similarly the increase in profitability between 1967 and 1965 was 20% (adjusted) and not 9% as the unadjusted figures suggest. Since the analyst usually examines the past record of EPS in order to discern *trends* in the rate of growth, only the *adjusted* record is relevant for this purpose.

7. ADJUSTING EPS FOR RIGHTS ISSUES

A firm's shareholders are often given the prior privilege of purchasing their pro rata share of new issues of common stock at a fixed subscription price, or of selling the claims (that is, rights) to this privilege on the open market. The legal *raison d'etre* of this preemptive right is to afford stockholders an opportunity of preserving their share in the company, but from the standpoint of the investment analyst, raising additional equity capital by means of a rights offering is equivalent to a stock dividend paid to the existing shareholders accompanied by a new issue, at a fixed price, to which these same shareholders have a prior right (but no obligation) to subscribe. To clarify this, consider the example of a rights offering in which the company grants each shareholder the right to purchase a new share of stock at a subscription price (P_s) which is below the market price for the company's shares, P_c. Note that in this case the allocation ratio, N, is equal to 1, that is, the shareholder can acquire one additional share at the subscription price for every old one which he owns. Now let us identify the stock dividend component of the rights offering. In the extreme case where $P_s = 0$ and $N = 1$ the rights offering "vanishes," and is replaced by a 100% stock dividend; for every old share the stockholder receives one new share, without an additional investment. Alternatively if we set the subscription price equal to the market price, $P_s = P_c$, the rights issue becomes a public issue at the market price and the stock dividend component vanishes. The stock dividend component depends not only on the subscription price but also on the allocation ratio, N. If $N = 2$ in the first example, and *two* old shares are required to receive one new share, the stock dividend is only 50%, rather than 100%, even though the subscription price is zero.

To adjust a company's EPS data for *all* stock dividends and splits, the stock dividend component of any rights issues must be identified. This is very easy in the extreme cases where $P_s = 0$ or $P_s = P_c$, but as the subscription price is never set at these extremes in practice, we now turn to the problem of isolating the stock dividend component of a rights offering when $0 < P_s < P_c$.

Assuming a perfect market, the market price of a share will fall automatically on the day a stock dividend is allocated, in the same proportion as the stock dividend. The new market price is given by

$$P_{c_1} = \frac{P_c}{1 + \alpha}$$

where: P_{c_1} = the market price of a share after the stock dividend
P_c = the market price of a share before the stock dividend
α = the stock dividend as a percentage of the initial number of shares outstanding.

This formula reflects the assumption that in a perfect market the total value of the firm will not change when the ownership interest is split into a larger number of certificates. Assume that the number of shares outstanding before the stock dividend was A, and therefore the total market value of the firm was AP_c. Following the stock dividend the number of shares is increased in proportion to the stock dividend rate, and becomes $A(1 + \alpha)$, so that its total market value is given by $A(1 + \alpha)P_{c_1}$. Since, by assumption, the total market value of the firm does not change because of the stock dividend, the following equation holds:

$$AP_c = A(1 + \alpha)P_{c_1} \tag{2.1}$$

Dividing both sides of Equation (2.1) by $A(1 + \alpha)$ and cancelling terms yields the desired formula:

$$P_{c_1} = \frac{P_c}{1 + \alpha} \tag{2.2}$$

Thus if we assume a market price $P_c = \$2.00$ and a 100% stock dividend we have

$$P_{c_1} = \frac{2}{1 + 1} = 1$$

And since the number of shares has doubled and the market price has been halved, the total market value of the firm's shares remains unchanged.

When the subscription price of a rights issue is set below the market price (and this is invariably the case), the price of the firm's shares, following the rights issue, typically falls. The stock dividend component of a rights offering can be identified by showing that the fall in market value of the old shares, implied by a rights offering, is equivalent to the fall in price induced by a stock dividend.

7. ADJUSTING EPS FOR RIGHTS ISSUES

The theoretical price of a newly issued share following the execution of the rights issue is a weighted average of the pre-rights share price P_c and the subscription price P_s:

$$P_t = \frac{AP_c + BP_s}{A + B} \tag{2.3}$$

where: P_t = the theoretical[12] market price of a share following the rights issue
A = the number of shares outstanding before the rights offering
B = the number of new shares issued.

Dividing the numerator and denominator of (2.3) by B yields:

$$P_t = \frac{(A/B)P_c + P_s}{A/B + 1} \tag{2.4}$$

And since A/B equals the allocation ratio—the number of old shares required to purchase one new share, usually denoted by N—we rewrite (2.4) to obtain the familiar formula for the theoretical *ex-rights* price of a share:

$$P_t = \frac{NP_c + P_s}{N + 1} \tag{2.5}$$

We can now calculate the stock dividend component of the rights issue by finding the hypothetical stock dividend, α, which will induce the same price effect as the rights issue, that is, a fall from P_c to P_t. Recalling Equation (2.2), this can readily be done as follows:

$$\frac{P_c}{1 + \alpha} = P_t \tag{2.6}$$

Hence,

$$\alpha = \frac{P_c}{P_t} - 1 \tag{2.6'}$$

Thus the stock dividend component of the rights issue is measured by the ratio of the pre-rights market price to the ex-rights market price, reduced by unity. This formula obviously fits our extreme examples: if $P_s = P_c$ the *ex-rights* theoretical price is given by

$$P_t = \frac{NP_c + P_c}{N + 1} = P_c$$

---

[12] It must be emphasized that P_t is the theoretical price in the absence of other influences. Generally the market price following a rights issue will differ from P_t owing to changes in investors' expectations, general fluctuations on the stock exchange, and so on.

and therefore the stock dividend component is

$$\alpha = \frac{P_c}{P_t} - 1 = \frac{P_c}{P_c} - 1 = 0$$

If we let $P_s = 0$, the rights issue vanishes and becomes a pure stock dividend:

$$P_t = \frac{NP_c + P_s}{N + 1} = \frac{NP_c}{N + 1}$$

$$\alpha = \frac{P_c}{P_t} - 1 = \frac{P_c(N + 1)}{NP_c} - 1 = \frac{N + 1 - N}{N} = \frac{1}{N}$$

Thus if $N = 1$, we have a 100% stock dividend, if $N = 2$ we have a 50% stock dividend, and so on.

Having identified the stock dividend component of a rights offering, let us now illustrate the required adjustment of EPS by considering the hypothetical example, given in Table II–10, of a company which issued rights in 1968 and again in 1969, the terms of which were as follows:

1968: $P_s = 120$ and $N = 1$; the market price at the time was $P_c = 200$.
1969: $P_s = 150$ and $N = 4$; the market price at the time was again $P_c = 200$.

To adjust the EPS for the rights issue we must first identify the stock dividend component: For the 1968 issue this can be done as follows:

$$P_t = \frac{200 + 120}{1 + 1} = 160$$

Hence the dividend component is

$$\alpha = \frac{P_c}{P_t} - 1 = \frac{200}{160} - 1 = 0.25, \quad \text{or } 25\%.$$

TABLE II–10.

Year	Net Earnings after Tax	Number of Shares Outstanding	Unadjusted Earnings per Share
1967	1,000	100	10
1968	1,800	200	9
1969	2,250	250	9
1970	2,500	250	10

7. ADJUSTING EPS FOR RIGHTS ISSUES

TABLE II-11.

Year	Number of Shares at Beginning of Year	Dividend Component of Rights Offering	Number of Shares at End of Year
1967	100	—	100
1968	100	25%	125
1969	125	5%	131.25
1970	131.25	—	131.25

The relevant calculations for the 1969 rights issue are:

$$P_t = \frac{NP_c + P_s}{N + 1} = \frac{4 \cdot 200 + 150}{5} = \frac{950}{5} = 190$$

and the stock dividend component is

$$\alpha = \frac{P_c}{P_t} - 1 = \frac{200}{190} - 1 \simeq 0.05, \quad \text{or approximately } 5\%.$$

As can be seen, the 1969 rights issue has a lower spread between P_c and P_s and a higher allocation ratio N than the 1968 issue. Both of these factors serve to *lower* the stock dividend component of the rights offering, which is only 5% in 1969 as compared with 25% in 1968.

Having identified the equivalent stock dividend, we calculate the relevant index of the number of shares as for a regular stock dividend in Table II-11, and we apply it to the unadjusted EPS data in Table II-12. As was true in the case of a stock dividend, a comparison of the unadjusted and adjusted EPS figures in Table II-12 clearly shows the need for the adjustment. Failure to recognize the stock dividend component of the rights issue implies a reduction in profitability and a concomitant loss to the investor where no loss occurred.

TABLE II-12.

Year	Unadjusted Earnings per Share (1)	Index (2)	Adjusted Earnings per Share $\frac{(1) \cdot (2)}{100} = (3)$
1967	10	100	10
1968	9	125	11.25
1969	9	131.25	11.81
1970	10	131.25	13.12

As can readily be shown, the investor could have exercised his rights and sold off the new shares until his additional investment was repaid, and he would still have had the extra shares indicated by the stock dividend adjustment. Thus in 1968 an investor having 100 shares who exercised his rights would acquire 100 new shares at a subscription price of $120 per share, which amounts to an investment of $12,000. He could then immediately sell 75 of these shares at the *ex-rights* price of $160, that is, for $12,000. The remaining 25 shares represent the stock dividend component of the rights issue, namely a 25% increase in the number of his shares *without* additional investment.[13]

8. THE ADJUSTMENT FOR NEW PUBLIC ISSUES

On the surface no adjustment for a new public issue seems necessary. By definition, the stock dividend component of such a new issue is zero, and any dilution of EPS which takes place as a result of a new public stock issue should be retained in the EPS figure. Thus there is no need for an adjustment.

On reflection, however, one type of adjustment might prove helpful in some cases. Consider the data in Table II–13, which gives the EPS for a company before and after a new public issue. Note that the EPS fell from $10 in 1969 to $5 in 1970, the year of the new issue. If we assume that the issue took place on December 30, 1970, the company had only one day in which to use the proceeds of the issue, and the drop in profitability is only technical and should perhaps be smoothed out when estimating past trends. On the other hand, if the new issue took place on January 1, 1970, the com-

TABLE II–13.

Year	Earnings after Tax (in thousands of dollars)	Number of Shares (in thousands)	Earnings per Share (in dollars)
1969	1,000	100	10
1970	1,000	200	5

[13] Alternatively, the same result can be derived by assuming that the investor sells the rights and uses the proceeds to purchase additional shares. The theoretical price of the rights R is given by the formula:

$$R = \frac{P_c - P_s}{N + 1}$$

In this case the measure of the stock dividend component is $\alpha = \dfrac{R}{P_t}$.

pany had a full year in which to use the funds, so that the drop in EPS apparently reflects some difficulties connected with the use of the funds. A simple type of adjustment which can sometimes prove helpful in discerning profitability trends is to adjust the EPS figures for a year in which a new public issue took place as follows:[14] If the capital was available for, say, six months, that is, if the issue took place in the middle of the year, the number of new shares is divided by 2 when calculating the EPS for that year. If the issue was made at the end of the first quarter, $\frac{9}{12}$ of the shares are included; and so on.[15] Thus, taking the example given in Table II–13, and assuming the issue had been made at the end of the first quarter of 1970, adjusted EPS would be calculated as follows:

$$\frac{\text{Earnings for year}}{\text{Old shares} + \text{Annual equivalent of new shares}}$$

$$= \frac{1{,}000}{100 + (9/12) \cdot 100} = \frac{1{,}000}{175} = 5.7$$

Of course, this adjustment, unlike the adjustment for stock splits and stock dividends, is arbitrary. But fortunately most stock issues are small relative to the overall size of the corporation and the adjustment can safely be ignored. However, in cases where very large amounts of capital are raised, an adjustment of EPS in the year of issue may be helpful in eliminating a decrease in EPS which merely reflects the *timing* of the new issue rather than a change in profitability.

9. ADJUSTING EPS IN PRACTICE

To illustrate the EPS adjustments in practice, let us consider an actual case of a corporation which declared a stock dividend, split its stock, and raised new capital by means of a rights issue. Table II–14 sets out the necessary data for calculating a time series of adjusted earnings per share for IBM for the period 1960–1968. The index of the number of shares (1960 = 100) is

---

[14] Clearly, the adjustment is appropriate for rights issues as well. This adjustment is applied to the proceeds from the rights issue and is *not* a substitute for the adjustment for the stock dividend component discussed in the previous section.

[15] Of course, the appropriate adjustment may not always be limited to one year. For example, if the analyst feels that three years are required until the investments begin paying off, the increase in shares should be prorated over the three year period following the new issue.

TABLE II-14. Selected data for IBM, 1960–1968

	1960	1961	1962	1963	1964	1965	1966	1967	1968
Net Earnings after Tax (thousands of $)	204,915	254,119	304,726	364,255	431,160	476,902	526,130	651,500	871,498
Number of Shares* (thousands)	18,391	27,691	27,808	27,921	35,048	35,225	54,448	56,114	122,968
Unadjusted Earnings per Share ($)	11.14	9.18	10.96	13.05	12.30	13.54	9.66	11.61	7.71
Rights Issues	—	—	—	—	—	—	†	—	—
Stock Dividends and Splits	—	50%	—	—	25%	—	50%	2½%	100%

*The company offers small amounts of stock to its executives and employees at prices somewhat below the market. Theoretically this calls for the same type of adjustment made for any new issue, but owing to the relatively small size of those "issues," the adjustment has not been made.

† The allocation ratio was 1:40 at a subscription price (P_s) of $285 at a time when the market price (P_c) was $371.

9. ADJUSTING EPS IN PRACTICE   47

TABLE II–15. Index of number of shares for IBM (1960 = 100)

Year	Number of Shares at Beginning of Year (1)	Additional Shares Via Splits and Stock Dividends (2)	Additional Shares Via Rights (2)	Number of Shares at End of Year (4)
1960	100	—	—	100
1961	100	50	—	150
1962	150	—	—	150
1963	150	—	—	150
1964	150	37.5	—	187.50
1965	187.50	—	—	187.50
1966	187.50	93.75	1.60	282.85
1967	282.85	7.05	—	289.90
1968	289.90	289.90	—	579.80

given in Table II–15, and was calculated as follows:

(1) In 1961 the company split its stock, and one new share was given for each two shares held; as a result 50 shares are added to the index in that year, which becomes 150 at the end of 1961.

(2) In 1964 the company declared a 25% split. Since in 1964 our base-year investor already held 150 shares (100 original shares + 50 received in 1961), 37.5 shares (25% of 150) are added to the index.

(3) In 1966 the company declared a 50% split and also allocated rights. Here the chronological order is important if we are to determine the number of rights granted. A study of the annual report indicates that the split was made on March 5, 1966, while the rights were allocated on July 5, 1966. All outstanding shares including those received through the split were entitled to subscribe to the rights. Accordingly, in the first stage, the index rises by 93.75 shares as a result of the split (50% of 187.50), and in the second stage, 1.60 shares are added to reflect the stock divided component of the rights offering. The calculation, using the IBM data, is as follows:

$$N = 40$$
$$P_s = 258$$
$$P_c = 371$$
$$P_t = \frac{NP_c + P_s}{N + 1} = \frac{40 \cdot 371 + 285}{41} = \frac{15{,}125}{41} = 368.9$$
$$\alpha = \frac{371}{368.9} - 1 = 1.0057 - 1 = 0.0057, \quad \text{or} \quad 0.57\%.$$

Since the base-year investor held 281.25 (187.50 + 93.75) shares prior to the rights issue, the number of shares added to the index by the stock dividend component of the rights issue is: $0.0057 \cdot 281.25 = 1.60$ shares.

(4) A small $2\frac{1}{2}\%$ stock dividend increased the index to 289.90 at the end of 1967.

(5) Finally, a 2 for 1 stock split brought the index to 579.8 shares at the end of 1968.

Thus an investor who held 100 shares of IBM stock at the beginning of 1960 had 579.8 shares at the end of 1968, *without* making any additional investments. Table II–16 applies the appropriate index number to the calculation of IBM's adjusted earnings per share in each of the years 1960–1968. A comparison of the unadjusted EPS figures (Column 1) with their adjusted counterparts (Column 3) is eloquent testimony for the need to use adjusted data when analyzing trends. The adjustment converts a 40% *decline* in unadjusted EPS into a fourfold *increase* in IBM's profitability during these same years.

The index presented in Table II–16 takes the end of 1960 as its base so that adjusted EPS = unadjusted EPS, by definition, for that year. Many analysts prefer to have this identity in the last year for which data are available, in our example, 1968 would be taken as the base year. This can easily be done by dividing the index of Table II–16 by 579.80, which results in the index given in Table II–17. Note that dividing all the index numbers by a constant

TABLE II–16. Calculation of adjusted earnings per share for IBM, 1960–1968

Year	Unadjusted Earnings per Share (1)	Index (2)	Adjusted Earnings per Share $\frac{(1) \cdot (2)}{100} = (3)$
1960	11.14	100.00	11.14
1961	9.18	150.00	13.77
1962	10.96	150.00	16.44
1963	13.05	150.00	19.58
1964	12.30	187.50	23.05
1965	13.54	187.50	25.39
1966	9.66	282.85	27.32
1967	11.61	289.90	33.66
1968	7.71	579.80	44.70

9. ADJUSTING EPS IN PRACTICE

TABLE II–17. Alternative calculation of adjusted earnings per share for IBM, 1960–1968

Year	Unadjusted Earnings Per Share (1)	Index* (2)	Adjusted Earnings Per Share† $\frac{(1) \cdot (2)}{100} = (3)$
1960	11.14	17.25	1.92
1961	9.18	25.87	2.37
1962	10.96	25.87	2.84
1963	13.05	25.87	3.38
1964	12.30	32.34	3.98
1965	13.54	32.34	4.38
1966	9.66	48.78	4.71
1967	11.61	50.00	5.81
1968	7.71	100.00	7.71

* This is the index of Table II-16 divided by 579.80 and multiplied by 100.

† IBM published its *adjusted* earnings in its annual report for 1968 with 1968 as the base year. Adjustments were made for stock dividends and for splits, but *not* for rights. Thus, the numbers appearing in column (3) are slightly different from those published by IBM. The differences are negligible (1–2 cents per share) since the stock dividend component of the rights issue was very small.

(579.80) leaves the percentage relationship between the numbers unchanged. The data of Table II–17 are fully equivalent to the former calculations with the exception that the last year, 1968, is now the base year and the number of shares of previous years is reduced. The interpretation, however, is straightforward: An investor who owned 17.25 shares of IBM in 1960 had 100 shares of IBM in 1968, without additional investment. And the EPS of $7.71 in 1968 represents the same (percentage) fourfold increase over the *adjusted* EPS of 1960, $1.92.

Both calculations give the same results. The calculation using 1960 as the base year allows us to show clearly how the number of shares grows over time as a result of splits, stock dividends, and rights issues. The advantage of using the current year as the base is that adjusted EPS will then be equal to EPS as calculated directly from the current balance sheet, which may avoid misunderstandings.[16]

---

[16] However the downward adjustments of previous years' earnings or stock prices can also be misleading, as can be discerned in the implicit answer to the often repeated question, "Do you know what GM stock was selling for in 1931?"

10. SUMMARY

Expected profitability constitutes the key variable in the evaluation of a company's common stock. But an evaluation of the future must usually begin with an assessment of the firm's past and present performance. Data on corporate earnings and other pertinent information are available for many companies in their annual reports to shareholders as well as in the special reports, prospectuses, prepared on the eve of a flotation of new securities. The analysis of past trends in earnings and of their fluctuations can often provide investors with a benchmark from which a current evaluation of the company's future outlook can be made.

Owing to the different objectives of the accountant and the economist, important differences exist between the concept of accounting profits and the concept of economic profits. Since the financial analyst is concerned with estimating future earnings, rather than with measuring past earnings, some adjustment of company reports to reflect economic concepts is desirable, especially when making inter-company or inter-industry comparisons.

One major advantage of the economist's approach to the measurement of earnings is the emphasis given to the timing of actual receipts and outlays. This cash flow concept leads directly to the need for discounting the stream of future earnings, which lies at the heart of the valuation problem confronting the financial analyst. Similarly, the economist's concern with current market values rather than with historical costs is also more appropriate for financial analysis.

The handling of capital gains often presents a serious problem to someone attempting to evaluate trends in earnings. Large extraordinary income items may create fluctuations in earnings trends without economic justification. On the other hand, where extraordinary income items appear regularly in a company's income statement, they might more appropriately be considered as ordinary income. Thus in the absence of a revaluation of assets each year, great care has to be exercised to ensure that the earnings trend has not been distorted by the differential treatment afforded various income components.

Difficulties also arise when making earnings comparisons of the same company over time, or between two different companies. A large new public stock issue may make subsequent comparisons of total earnings meaningless; similarly there is no significance to the comparison of total earnings of two companies of different sizes. Many companies recognize the shortcomings of the total profits figure for investment analysis and provide per share calculations in their annual reports.

Because of changes in the tax treatment of income over time, the analyst

10. SUMMARY 51

may wish to examine both pre-tax and post-tax earnings, especially when attempting to discern trends. However, when comparing the profitability of different companies, post-tax figures should be used, since not all corporations pay the same rate of tax on a given level of pre-tax income.

Because of stock splits and/or stock dividends, EPS figures must be adjusted to ensure comparability between years. Similarly an adjustment must be made for the stock dividend component of a rights offering, and for new public issues in the year of issue. Since the analyst typically examines a firm's past EPS record to discern trends in the growth rate, only the adjusted record is relevant for this purpose.

Although the prospective investor in a company's shares is primarily concerned with estimating the expected return (and risk) of the share itself, the analysis of trends and fluctuations in earnings provides a more solid base for reaching an investment decision. In the long run, the rate of return to investors in a company's stock reflects the trend in underlying earnings; the adjustments of accounting data, discussed in this chapter, are designed to facilitate the analysis and interpretation of these trends.

QUESTIONS AND PROBLEMS

||||||||||||||||||||||||||||||||||||||||||||||||

2.1 For what purpose does an investment analyst examine a company's financial statements?

2.2 Distinguish between "accounting" depreciation and "economic" depreciation.

2.3 Compare the treatment afforded capital gains in economics with that of accounting. From the viewpoint of security analysis, which approach do you prefer?

2.4 What are the shortcomings of using *total pre-tax* figures in investment analysis?

2.5 Are comparisons of *pre-tax* earnings per share ever meaningful? Explain.

2.6 For what purpose does the analyst compute *adjusted* earnings per share?

2.7 Identify the stock dividend component of a rights offering.

2.8 What is the purpose of the adjustment for new public issues? How does this adjustment differ from the adjustment for stock dividends and splits?

2.9 Mr. Jordan, a shareholder in the Alpha Company, wrote the company a letter complaining that the cash dividend had remained fixed at $1.00 per share at a time when other companies in the industry had raised their dividend rates by as much as 50%. To answer the complaint the company's secretary gathered the following data relating to the past three years:

	Cash Dividends per Share	Stock Dividends	Stock Split
1968	1.00	5%	1 new share for every 2 old shares
1969	1.00		
1970	1.00	5%	

(1) Write a letter to Mr. Jordan. Assume that the cash dividends were paid on the last day of each year, and that the stock dividends and splits occurred in June of each year.

(2) How would your answer be affected had the company issued rights in 1968? What other information would you require in order to write a more comprehensive answer? Be specific.

2.10 *The Brosh Investment Company.* On January 15, 1963 the Investments Committee of the Brosh Investment Company met to consider the possibility of increasing the share of the fine chemical industry in its overall portfolio. The Brosh Company is a closely held corporation controlled by the Brosh family, and is perhaps one of the largest family-controlled diversified investment companies. After an extensive discussion, the committee decided to invest $100,000 in *one* of two companies: GADOL Chemicals or the KATAN Corporation.

The choice had previously been narrowed to these two alternatives by the president of Brosh, Mr. Jay Gold. Mr. Gold had decided that these two companies represented the most promising possibilities in the fine chemical industry and had obtained options from both firms to acquire 40,000 shares at the market price which prevailed on December 31, 1962. In both cases the

TABLE 1. KATAN Corporation: Selected Balance sheets (in thousands of dollars)

	December 31, 1958	December 31, 1960	December 31, 1962
ASSETS			
CURRENT ASSETS			
Cash	20	32	29
Receivables	40	45	60
Inventories	70	87	91
Total Current Assets	130	164	180
Fixed Assets	250	290	345
Total Assets	380	454	525
LIABILITIES AND NET WORTH			
Current Liabilities	50	70	80
Long-term Debt	200	200	215
NET WORTH			
Capital Stock (par value $1)	100	140	160
Undistributed Profits	30	44	70
TOTAL LIABILITIES AND NET WORTH	380	454	525

December price represented a 1% discount from the current price of the stock.

Since the options were good only to the end of January, the committee asked Mr. John Gordon, a recent business school graduate who had joined the Brosh staff as an investment analyst, to prepare a comparative analysis of the two firms based on the financial statements which they had presented to Brosh for the committee's meeting next week. To this end, Mr. Gordon assembled the data in Tables 1–6 and set about writing his evaluation.

2.11 At the beginning of 1971, ABC Investors Inc., an investment counseling firm, was making its annual recommendations regarding the investment in common stocks. As a first step, the various companies were grouped into equivalent economic risk classes (for example, domestic oil companies, computer manufacturers, and so on) and each firm's performance records during the past four years were studied. On the basis of this review and the current market prices of the shares, ABC Investors Inc. *ranked* the firms in each class by relative desirability to the investor.

Using the data in Tables A, B, C, and D, on seven companies belonging to a particular risk class, analyze the performance records and *rank* the seven firms. As a first step, divide the firms into two classes: (a) potentially profitable investments which can be recommended; (b) nonrecommended investments. Give your reasons for your decision. (For the purpose of this exercise, assume that the data are a representative sample of performance during the past decade.)

TABLE 2. KATAN Corporation: Selected income statements and allocation of profits accounts (in thousands of dollars)

	1958	1960	1962
SALES	600	800	1,005
Less:			
Cost of Goods Sold	420	572	700
Depreciation	10	18	25
General Expenses	80	90	130
Net Profit before Taxes	90	120	150
Taxes (50%)	45	60	75
Net Profit after Taxes	45	60	75
Undistributed Profit at Beginning of Year	9	10	23
Net Profit during Year	45	60	75
Cash Dividends	4	6	8
Stock Dividends	20	20	20
Undistributed Profit at End of Year	30	44	70

QUESTIONS AND PROBLEMS

TABLE 3. KATAN Corporation: Dividend record and share prices, 1957–1962

Year	Cash Dividends ($ per share)	Stock Dividends	End of Year Share Prices
1957	0.05	—	2.61
1958	0.05	25%	2.36
1959	0.05	20%	2.13
1960	0.05	17%	2.15
1961	—*	—*	1.83
1962	0.057	14%	2.20

* The "break" in dividend payment was explained in the following note, which was appended to the Financial Statement for 1961. "The loss of a major patent in 1961 necessitated the temporary discontinuation of dividends in order to develop an alternative production method for one of the firm's major products." In 1962 the company reported that the new process had proved a complete success, and resumed dividend payments in that year.

TABLE 4. GADOL Chemicals: Selected balance sheets (in thousands of dollars)

	December 31, 1958	December 31, 1960	December 31, 1962
ASSETS			
CURRENT ASSETS			
Cash	100	120	135
Receivables	70	80	100
Inventories	130	160	190
Total Current Assets	300	360	425
Fixed Assets	658	1,010	1,290
Total Assets	958	1,370	1,715
LIABILITIES AND NET WORTH			
Current Liabilities	138	150	190
Longterm Debt	350	350	350
NET WORTH			
Capital Stock* ($1 par value)	300	600	800
Undistributed Profit	170	270	375
TOTAL LIABILITIES AND NET WORTH	958	1,370	1,715

* The company floated public stock issues in 1960 and 1962.

TABLE 5. GADOL Chemicals: Selected income statements and allocation of profits accounts (in thousands of dollars)

	1958	1960	1962
SALES	1,700	2,022	2,350
Less:			
Cost of Goods Sold	1,139	1,255	1,500
Depreciation	35	52	70
General Expenses	150	155	180
Net Profit before Taxes	376	560	600
Taxes (50%)	188	280	300
Net Profit after Taxes	188	280	300
Undistributed Profits at Beginning of Year	—	32	139
Net Profit during Year	188	280	300
Cash Dividends	18	42	64
Undistributed Profit at End of Year	170	270	375

TABLE 6. GADOL Chemicals: Dividend record and share prices, 1957–1962

Year	Cash Dividends ($ per share)	Stock Dividends	End of Year Share Prices
1957	0.06	—	1.19
1958	0.06	—	1.37
1959	0.06	—	1.59
1960	0.07	—	1.84
1961	0.07	—	1.81
1962	0.08	—	2.00

TABLE A. Rate of growth of sales (%)

Company	1968	1969	1970
A	12	26	11
B	12	8	30
C	61	7	−2
D	37	1	16
E	39	38	−15
F	20	10	2
G	19	18	10

TABLE B. Unadjusted earnings per share,[1] 1967–1970
($ per share)

Company	1967	1968	1969	1970
A	0.14	0.19	0.30	0.37
B	0.15	0.03	*	0.05
C	0.51	0.12	0.11	0.06
D	*	0.16	0.21	0.31
E	0.20	0.20	0.21	*
F	0.11	0.27	0.01	*
G	0.07	0.05	0.17	0.13

[1] Net profit after taxes divided by average number of shares outstanding during the year.
* Loss.

TABLE C. Adjusted earnings per share, 1967–1970
($ per share)

Company	1967	1968	1969	1970
A	0.45	0.65	1.01	1.35
B	0.15	0.03	*	0.06
C	0.51	0.27	0.25	0.12
D	*	0.18	0.25	0.40
E	0.20	0.20	0.23	*
F	0.11	0.31	0.01	*
G	0.07	0.05	0.17	0.26

* Loss.

TABLE D. End of year market price quotation, 1967–1970
($ per share)

Company	1967	1968	1969	1970
A	1.18	1.14	1.18	1.12
B	1.42	1.33	1.26	0.97
C*	——	——	1.22	0.91
D	1.43	1.41	1.45	1.55
E	0.97	1.03	1.34	1.07
F	3.20	3.47	5.45	4.05
G	1.47	1.35	1.70	0.92

* The company was listed in 1969.

SELECTED REFERENCES

Alexander, S. S., "Income Measurement in a Dynamic Economy," *Five Monographs on Business Income*, American Institute of Accountants, 1948.

Baxter, W. T., and Davidson, S., *Studies in Accounting Theory*. Homewood, Ill.: Irwin, 1962.

Block, F. E., "Per Share Adjustments for Rights," *Financial Analysts Journal* (May–June 1965).

Dean, Joel, *Managerial Economics*. New York: Prentice-Hall, 1951.

Graham, B.; Dodd, D. C.; and Cottle, S., *Security Analysis*. New York: McGraw-Hill, 1961.

Hicks, J. R., *Value and Capital*, 2nd edition. Oxford: Oxford University Press, 1953.

Weston, F. T., "Increased Emphasis on Reporting Earnings Per Share," *Financial Analysts Journal* (July–August 1967).

Weston, F. T., and Davidson, S., "What Will Accounting Changes Do to Earnings?" *Financial Analysts Journal* (September–October 1968).

Williams, W. D., "A Look Behind Reported Earnings," *Financial Analysts Journal* (January–February 1966).

Chapter III
Alternative Measures of Profitability

1. INTRODUCTION

In a discussing the profitability of a business firm in the previous chapter, the *timing* of receipts and outlays was ignored. In practice, however, firms (or investors) have productive alternative uses for their money, and these alternatives must be taken into account when formulating measures of an investment's profitability. In this chapter we shall initially discuss decision rules by which the firm (or an individual) chooses among capital investment opportunities, a process that is usually referred to as the capital budgeting problem. Capital budgeting techniques will then be generalized and extended to the problem of measuring the return on financial assets such as common stocks.

2. THE TIME VALUE OF MONEY

In a typical investment decision the decision-maker makes a commitment of current resources to secure a stream of benefits (or a once-and-for-all benefit) in future years. Such decisions have the following characteristics:

(a) the magnitude and timing of the benefits and outlays are usually highly uncertain;
(b) a significant period of time (usually more than one year) elapses between the initial investment outlay and the receipt of the final benefits from the project.

The first characteristic leads to the perplexing problem of how to evaluate risk and uncertainty when reaching an investment decision. A satisfactory handling of this problem requires the use of concepts which are developed in Part II of the book; therefore the analysis of risky investments is deferred to Chapter VI. We shall confine ourselves here to the analysis of alternative investments where the costs and benefits are known with certainty. This assumption enables us to focus attention on the second characteristic of an investment—the time lag between the investment outlay and the receipt of the benefits.

In evaluating the desirability of an investment proposal, consideration must be given not only to the magnitude of the cash flows but to their timing as well. This will become clear if we consider the following example of a project which requires an immediate investment outlay of $1,000, and which returns $1,100 exactly one year later. Does it pay to make such an investment, that is, does it pay to give up $1,000 today in order to receive $1,100, one year hence? Clearly our answer depends on the alternative use which we have for the $1,000. If we assume that we can earn 12% interest by depositing the $1,000 in a bank, the value of the deposit at the end of the year will be $1,120; since $1,120 > $1,100, the previous investment is not desirable. On the other hand if the bank pays only 8% interest, the value of the account at the end of the year will be $1,080, and since $1,080 < $1,100, the original proposal is worthwhile and, other things being equal, is to be preferred over the bank account.

Clearly, an intelligent investment decision requires the weighing of alternatives. The fact that money always can earn a positive return (interest) lends importance to the time dimension of the typical investment proposal. A dollar given up today is not the equivalent of a dollar received in the future as long as there exists the alternative of earning a positive return on the dollar during the interim.[1]

Let us denote the relevant alternative rate of return which can always be earned in the market, independent of the decision under consideration, by the letter k. Now what is the value to the firm of a dollar which will be received one year from now? To answer this question we first check the *future* value of one dollar, that is, the initial amount plus interest at the end of the year. Given the alternative return of k, the future value of a dollar is

$$V_1 = 1 \cdot (1 + k)$$

If $k = 10\%$ we have

$$V_1 = 1 \cdot (1 + 0.1) = 1 + 0.10 = \$1.10$$

where V_1 denotes the future value at the end of year 1.

---

[1] To avoid confusion, it should be noted that this statement is independent of changes in the purchasing power of money, and depends *solely* on the existence of a positive interest rate.

2. THE TIME VALUE OF MONEY

What is the future value of one dollar at the end of two years? As we have already noted, its value at the end of the first year will be $1.10, so that in the second year an additional 10% will be earned on the $1.10:

$$V_2 = 1.10 + 0.11 = 1.21$$

where V_2 denotes the future value at end of 2 years, or in symbols:

$$V_2 = 1(1 + k)(1 + k) = 1(1 + k)^2$$

In general, the future value of one dollar at the end of n years will be

$$V_n = 1 \cdot (1 + k)^n$$

Of course, this equation is nothing more than the familiar formula for compound interest over time. It can be applied to any amount of money. Thus if we want to know the future value to which P dollars will accumulate in n years when it is compounded annually at k rate of interest, we have:

$$V_n = P(1 + k)^n$$

It requires only a minor extension of the familiar interest rate formula to derive the formula for *present value*, rather than future value. Dividing both sides of the formula by $(1 + k)^n$ we derive:

$$P = \frac{V_n}{(1 + k)^n}$$

which can be read as, the present value of V_n dollars received at the end of n years is equal to P. This is perhaps the less familiar formula for discounting future sums to their present values, and is, as we have seen, the obverse side of the compound interest formula. Applying the formula to our previous one year example we get

$$\frac{V_1}{1 + k} = \frac{1.10}{1 + 0.10} = 1$$

That is, the present value of $1.10 to be received at the end of one year is one dollar. Similarly the present value of $1.21 to be received at the end of two years is one dollar:

$$\frac{V_2}{(1 + k)^2} = \frac{1.21}{(1 + 0.10)^2} = 1$$

The line of reasoning behind the formula is very simple: given the alternative of earning 10% on its money, the firm (or individual) should never be willing to pay (invest) more than $1,000 to secure $1,100 with certainty at the end of the year. If it pays $1,010, for example, it could have reached a higher future value by investing the $1,010 at 10%, thereby achieving a future value of

$$1{,}010(1 + 0.10) = 1{,}101 > 1{,}100$$

Alternatively we can apply the present value formula directly by noting

$$P = \frac{1{,}100}{1 + 0.10} = 1{,}000 < 1{,}010$$

That is, the present value of $1,100 received one year hence is $1,000, which is less than the proposed investment outlay of $1,010; therefore the investment is not worthwhile. Modern time-discounted methods for evaluating investment projects are nothing more than straightforward generalizations of the future value–present value relationship.

3. NET PRESENT VALUE (NPV)

The Net Present Value (NPV) method of evaluating the desirability of investments can be defined as follows:

$$NPV = \frac{S_1}{1+k} + \frac{S_2}{(1+k)^2} + \frac{S_3}{(1+k)^3} + \cdots + \frac{S_n}{(1+k)^n} - I_0$$

$$NPV = \sum_{t=1}^{n} \frac{S_t}{(1+k)^t} - I_0$$

where: S_t = net cash receipt at the end of year t
I_0 = the initial investment outlay[2]
k = the discount rate = the required rate of return

An investment proposal's NPV is derived by discounting the cash receipts to their present values, summing them over the life of the proposal, and deducting the initial outlay. The actual calculation can be reduced to a very simple procedure by using Table A. Table III–1 illustrates the calculation for two hypothetical investments. The 10% discount factors used to reduce the receipts to their present values are defined as follows:[3]

$$\alpha_{1,10} = \frac{1}{1 + 0.10} = 0.909$$

$$\alpha_{2,10} = \frac{1}{(1 + 0.10)^2} = 0.826$$

$$\alpha_{3,10} = \frac{1}{(1 + 0.10)^3} = 0.751$$

---

[2] Since the investment outlay may stretch over an extended period, a more general formulation would be to define I_0 as the present value of the investment outlay.

[3] Since investment B is an annuity, the calculation can be even further simplified by choosing the appropriate discount factor from Table B, 2.487; in which case the NPV is given by:

$$400 \cdot 2.487 - 1,100 = 994.8 - 1,100 = -105.2$$

The slight discrepancy in the results is due to rounding of the discount factor to three decimal places in Tables A and B.

3. NET PRESENT VALUE (NPV)

TABLE III-1.

Year	Project A Net Cash Flow	Discount Factor (10%)	PV of Cash Flow	Project B Net Cash Flow	Discount Factor (10%)	PV of Cash Flow
1	400	0.909	363.6	400	0.909	363.6
2	600	0.826	495.6	400	0.826	330.4
3	500	0.751	375.5	400	0.751	300.4
	$\sum$ PV of Receipts		1,234.7	$\sum$ PV of Receipts		994.4
	Less Investment Outlay		−1,100	Less Investment Outlay		−1,100
	NPV		+134.7	NPV		−105.6

where the two subscripts of each α denote the year in which the dollar was received and the 10% discount rate, respectively.[4] Generalizing this for all years and discount rates, we obtain

$$\alpha_{tk} = \frac{1}{(1+k)^t}$$

the solution of which over the domains $t = 1, 2, \ldots, 50$ and $k = 1, 2, \ldots, 50$, generates Table A. To find the PV of a given sum S received in year t, we multiply S by the appropriate discount factor:

$$S\alpha_{tk} = S\frac{1}{(1+k)^t}$$

Table B, which is used for annuities, is merely a summation of the relevant annual discount factors of Table A; for example, to find the present value a 10-year one dollar annuity at 10% discount, we multiply one dollar by the factor appearing in line 10 of the 10% column of Table B, 6.145, which is a summation of the first 10 factors in the 10% column of Table A.

To apply the NPV method to problems of investment choice a decision rule must be defined, but to do this we must first assume a goal for the firm (or investor). Some of you may recall the South Sea Island tribe whose members, according to anthropologists, seek to give away all their wealth. Without taking a normative stand on the desirability of such behavior, we can indicate that an appropriate investment decision rule would be one which

---

[4] The subscripts also indicate the relevant line (year) and column (discount rate) of Table A. Thus, $\alpha_{6,20}$ is found by taking the factor appearing in line 6 and column 20 of Table A, 0.335.

TABLE A. Present value of 1 $

Periods until Payment	1%	2%	4%	6%	8%	10%	12%	14%	15%	16%	18%	20%	22%	24%	25%	26%	28%	30%	35%	40%	45%	50%
1	0.990	0.980	0.962	0.943	0.926	0.909	0.893	0.877	0.870	0.862	0.847	0.833	0.820	0.806	0.800	0.794	0.781	0.769	0.741	0.714	0.690	0.667
2	0.980	0.961	0.925	0.890	0.857	0.826	0.797	0.769	0.756	0.743	0.718	0.694	0.672	0.650	0.640	0.630	0.610	0.592	0.549	0.510	0.476	0.444
3	0.971	0.942	0.889	0.840	0.794	0.751	0.712	0.675	0.658	0.641	0.609	0.579	0.551	0.524	0.512	0.500	0.477	0.455	0.406	0.364	0.328	0.296
4	0.961	0.924	0.855	0.792	0.735	0.683	0.636	0.592	0.572	0.552	0.516	0.482	0.451	0.423	0.410	0.397	0.373	0.350	0.301	0.260	0.226	0.198
5	0.951	0.906	0.822	0.747	0.681	0.621	0.567	0.519	0.497	0.476	0.437	0.402	0.370	0.341	0.328	0.315	0.291	0.269	0.223	0.186	0.156	0.132
6	0.942	0.888	0.790	0.705	0.630	0.564	0.507	0.456	0.432	0.410	0.370	0.335	0.303	0.275	0.262	0.250	0.227	0.207	0.165	0.133	0.108	0.088
7	0.933	0.871	0.760	0.655	0.583	0.513	0.452	0.400	0.376	0.354	0.314	0.279	0.249	0.222	0.210	0.198	0.178	0.159	0.122	0.095	0.074	0.059
8	0.923	0.853	0.731	0.627	0.540	0.467	0.404	0.351	0.327	0.305	0.266	0.233	0.204	0.179	0.168	0.157	0.139	0.123	0.091	0.068	0.051	0.039
9	0.914	0.837	0.703	0.592	0.500	0.424	0.361	0.308	0.284	0.263	0.225	0.194	0.167	0.144	0.134	0.125	0.108	0.094	0.067	0.048	0.035	0.026
10	0.905	0.820	0.676	0.558	0.463	0.386	0.322	0.270	0.247	0.227	0.191	0.162	0.137	0.116	0.107	0.099	0.085	0.073	0.050	0.035	0.024	0.017
11	0.896	0.804	0.650	0.527	0.429	0.350	0.287	0.237	0.215	0.195	0.162	0.135	0.112	0.094	0.086	0.079	0.066	0.056	0.037	0.025	0.017	0.012
12	0.887	0.788	0.625	0.497	0.397	0.319	0.257	0.208	0.187	0.168	0.137	0.112	0.092	0.076	0.069	0.062	0.052	0.043	0.027	0.018	0.012	0.008
13	0.879	0.773	0.601	0.469	0.368	0.290	0.229	0.182	0.163	0.145	0.116	0.093	0.075	0.061	0.055	0.050	0.040	0.033	0.020	0.013	0.008	0.005
14	0.870	0.738	0.577	0.442	0.340	0.263	0.205	0.160	0.141	0.125	0.099	0.078	0.062	0.049	0.044	0.040	0.032	0.025	0.015	0.009	0.006	0.003
15	0.861	0.743	0.555	0.417	0.315	0.239	0.183	0.140	0.123	0.108	0.084	0.065	0.051	0.040	0.035	0.031	0.025	0.020	0.011	0.006	0.004	0.002
16	0.853	0.728	0.534	0.394	0.292	0.218	0.163	0.123	0.107	0.093	0.071	0.054	0.042	0.032	0.028	0.025	0.019	0.015	0.008	0.005	0.003	0.002
17	0.844	0.714	0.513	0.371	0.270	0.198	0.146	0.108	0.093	0.080	0.060	0.045	0.034	0.026	0.023	0.020	0.015	0.012	0.006	0.003	0.002	0.001
18	0.836	0.700	0.494	0.350	0.250	0.180	0.130	0.095	0.081	0.069	0.051	0.038	0.028	0.021	0.018	0.016	0.012	0.009	0.005	0.002	0.001	0.001
19	0.828	0.686	0.475	0.331	0.232	0.164	0.116	0.083	0.070	0.060	0.043	0.031	0.023	0.017	0.014	0.012	0.009	0.007	0.003	0.002	0.001	
20	0.820	0.673	0.456	0.312	0.215	0.149	0.104	0.073	0.061	0.051	0.037	0.026	0.019	0.014	0.012	0.010	0.007	0.005	0.002	0.001	0.001	
21	0.811	0.660	0.439	0.294	0.199	0.135	0.093	0.064	0.053	0.044	0.031	0.022	0.015	0.011	0.009	0.008	0.006	0.004	0.002	0.001		
22	0.803	0.647	0.422	0.278	0.184	0.123	0.083	0.056	0.046	0.038	0.026	0.018	0.013	0.009	0.007	0.006	0.004	0.003	0.001	0.001		
23	0.795	0.634	0.406	0.262	0.170	0.112	0.074	0.049	0.040	0.033	0.022	0.015	0.010	0.007	0.006	0.005	0.003	0.002	0.001			
24	0.788	0.622	0.390	0.247	0.158	0.102	0.066	0.043	0.035	0.028	0.019	0.013	0.008	0.006	0.005	0.004	0.003	0.002	0.001			
25	0.780	0.610	0.375	0.233	0.146	0.092	0.059	0.038	0.030	0.024	0.016	0.010	0.007	0.005	0.004	0.003	0.002	0.001	0.001			
26	0.772	0.598	0.361	0.220	0.135	0.084	0.053	0.033	0.026	0.021	0.014	0.009	0.006	0.004	0.003	0.002	0.002	0.001				
27	0.764	0.586	0.347	0.207	0.125	0.076	0.047	0.029	0.023	0.018	0.011	0.007	0.005	0.003	0.002	0.002	0.001	0.001				
28	0.757	0.574	0.333	0.196	0.116	0.069	0.042	0.026	0.020	0.016	0.010	0.006	0.004	0.002	0.002	0.002	0.001	0.001				
29	0.749	0.563	0.321	0.185	0.107	0.063	0.037	0.022	0.017	0.014	0.008	0.005	0.003	0.002	0.002	0.001	0.001	0.001				
30	0.742	0.552	0.308	0.174	0.099	0.057	0.033	0.020	0.015	0.012	0.007	0.004	0.003	0.002	0.001	0.001	0.001					
40	0.672	0.453	0.208	0.097	0.046	0.022	0.011	0.005	0.004	0.003	0.001	0.001										
50	0.608	0.372	0.141	0.054	0.021	0.009	0.003	0.001	0.001	0.001												

SOURCE: Robert N. Anthony, *Management Accounting: Text and Cases* (rev. ed.; Homewood, Ill.: Richard D. Irwin, Inc., 1960), p. 656.
AUTHORS' NOTE: These values are obtained by compounding at the end of each period. Other tables use different schemes of compounding, without changing the magnitudes greatly.

TABLE B. Present value of $1 received annually

Periods to Be Paid	1%	2%	4%	6%	8%	10%	12%	14%	15%	16%	18%	20%	22%	24%	25%	26%	28%	30%	35%	40%	45%	50%
1	0.990	0.980	0.962	0.943	0.926	0.909	0.893	0.877	0.877	0.862	0.847	0.833	0.820	0.806	0.800	0.794	0.781	0.769	0.741	0.714	0.690	0.667
2	1.970	1.942	1.886	1.833	1.783	1.736	1.690	1.647	1.626	1.605	1.566	1.528	1.492	1.457	1.440	1.424	1.392	1.361	1.289	1.224	1.165	1.117
3	2.941	2.884	2.775	2.673	2.577	2.487	2.402	2.322	2.283	2.246	2.174	2.106	2.042	1.981	1.952	1.923	1.868	1.816	1.696	1.589	1.493	1.405
4	3.902	3.808	3.630	3.465	3.312	3.170	3.037	2.914	2.855	2.798	2.690	2.589	2.494	2.404	2.362	2.320	2.241	2.166	1.997	1.849	1.720	1.602
5	4.853	4.713	4.452	4.212	3.993	3.791	3.605	3.433	3.352	3.274	3.127	2.991	2.864	2.745	2.689	2.635	2.532	2.436	2.220	2.035	1.876	1.731
6	5.795	5.601	5.242	4.917	4.623	4.355	4.111	3.889	3.784	3.685	3.498	3.326	3.167	3.020	2.951	2.885	2.759	2.643	2.385	2.168	1.983	1.824
7	6.728	6.472	6.002	5.582	5.206	4.868	4.564	4.288	4.160	4.039	3.812	3.605	3.416	3.242	3.161	3.083	2.937	2.802	2.508	2.263	2.057	1.883
8	7.652	7.325	6.733	6.210	5.747	5.335	4.968	4.639	4.487	4.344	4.078	3.837	3.619	3.421	3.329	3.241	3.076	2.925	2.598	2.331	2.108	1.922
9	8.566	8.262	7.435	6.802	6.247	5.759	5.328	4.946	4.772	4.607	4.303	4.031	3.786	3.566	3.463	3.366	3.184	3.019	2.665	2.379	2.144	1.948
10	9.471	8.983	8.111	7.360	6.710	6.145	5.650	5.216	5.019	4.833	4.494	4.192	3.923	3.682	3.571	3.465	3.269	3.092	2.715	2.414	2.168	1.965
11	10.368	9.787	8.760	7.887	7.139	6.495	5.937	5.453	5.234	5.029	4.656	4.327	4.035	3.776	3.656	3.544	3.335	3.147	2.752	2.438	2.185	1.977
12	11.255	10.575	9.385	8.384	7.536	6.814	6.194	5.660	5.421	5.197	4.793	4.439	4.127	3.851	3.725	3.606	3.387	3.190	2.779	2.456	2.196	1.985
13	12.134	11.343	9.986	8.853	7.904	7.103	6.424	5.842	5.583	5.342	4.910	4.533	4.203	3.912	3.780	3.656	3.427	3.223	2.799	2.468	2.204	1.990
14	13.004	12.106	10.563	9.295	8.244	7.367	6.628	6.002	5.724	5.468	5.008	4.611	4.265	3.962	3.824	3.695	3.459	3.249	2.814	2.477	2.210	1.993
15	13.865	12.849	11.118	9.712	8.559	7.606	6.811	6.142	5.847	5.575	5.092	4.675	4.315	4.001	3.859	3.726	3.483	3.268	2.825	2.484	2.214	1.995
16	14.718	13.578	11.652	10.106	8.851	7.824	6.974	6.265	5.954	5.669	5.162	4.730	4.357	4.033	3.887	3.751	3.503	3.283	2.834	2.489	2.216	1.997
17	15.562	14.292	12.166	10.477	9.122	8.022	7.120	6.373	6.047	5.749	5.222	4.775	4.391	4.059	3.910	3.771	3.518	3.295	2.840	2.492	2.218	1.998
18	16.398	14.992	12.659	10.828	9.372	8.201	7.250	6.467	6.128	5.818	5.273	4.812	4.419	4.080	3.928	3.786	3.529	3.304	2.844	2.494	2.219	1.999
19	17.226	15.678	13.134	11.158	9.604	8.365	7.366	6.550	6.198	5.877	5.316	4.814	4.442	4.097	3.942	3.799	3.539	3.311	2.848	2.496	2.220	1.999
20	18.046	16.351	13.590	11.470	9.818	8.514	7.469	6.623	6.259	5.929	5.353	4.870	4.460	4.110	3.954	3.808	3.546	3.316	2.850	2.497	2.221	1.999
21	18.857	17.011	14.029	11.764	10.017	8.649	7.562	6.687	6.312	5.973	5.384	4.891	4.476	4.121	3.963	3.816	3.551	3.320	2.852	2.498	2.221	2.000
22	19.660	17.658	14.451	12.042	10.201	8.772	7.645	6.743	6.359	6.011	5.410	4.909	4.488	4.130	3.970	3.822	3.556	3.323	2.853	2.498	2.222	2.000
23	20.456	18.292	14.857	12.303	10.371	8.883	7.718	6.792	6.399	6.044	5.432	4.925	4.499	4.137	3.976	3.827	3.559	3.325	2.854	2.499	2.222	2.000
24	21.243	18.914	15.247	12.550	10.529	8.985	7.784	6.835	6.434	6.073	5.451	4.937	4.507	4.143	3.981	3.831	3.562	3.327	2.855	2.499	2.222	2.000
25	22.023	19.523	15.622	12.783	10.675	9.077	7.843	6.873	6.464	6.097	5.467	4.948	4.514	4.147	3.985	3.834	3.564	3.329	2.856	2.499	2.222	2.000
26	22.795	20.121	15.983	13.003	10.810	9.161	7.896	6.906	6.491	6.118	5.480	4.956	4.520	4.151	3.988	3.837	3.566	3.330	2.856	2.500	2.222	2.000
27	23.560	20.707	16.330	13.211	10.935	9.237	7.943	6.935	6.514	6.136	5.492	4.964	4.524	4.154	3.990	3.839	3.567	3.331	2.856	2.500	2.222	2.000
28	24.316	21.281	16.663	13.406	11.051	9.307	7.984	6.961	6.534	6.152	5.502	4.970	4.528	4.157	3.992	3.840	3.568	3.331	2.857	2.500	2.222	2.000
29	25.066	21.844	16.984	13.591	11.158	9.370	8.022	6.983	6.551	6.166	5.510	4.975	4.531	4.159	3.994	3.841	3.569	3.332	2.857	2.500	2.222	2.000
30	25.808	22.396	17.292	13.765	11.258	9.427	8.055	7.003	6.566	6.177	5.517	4.979	4.534	4.160	3.995	3.842	3.569	3.332	2.857	2.500	2.222	2.000
40	32.835	27.355	19.793	15.046	11.925	9.779	8.244	7.105	6.642	6.234	5.548	4.997	4.544	4.166	3.999	3.846	3.571	3.333	2.857	2.500	2.222	2.000
50	39.196	31.424	21.482	15.762	12.234	9.915	8.304	7.133	6.661	6.246	5.554	4.999	4.545	4.167	4.000	3.846	3.571	3.333	2.857	2.500	2.222	2.000

SOURCE: Robert N. Anthony, *Management Accounting: Text and Cases* (rev. ed.: Homewood, Ill.: Richard D. Irwin, Inc., 1960), p. 657.
AUTHOR'S NOTE: These values are obtained by compounding at the end of each period. Other tables use different schemes of compounding, without changing the magnitudes greatly.

results in a minimum future value, or, what comes to the same thing, a minimum present value. And if the anthropologists are correct, such a decision rule should also have the property of providing a good explanation and prediction of the investment behavior of the tribe.

With regard to the business firm, one may well feel that a more appropriate approach might be to assume that the firm seeks to maximize (rather than minimize) the wealth of its shareholders. Note that this wealth-maximizing behavior is an *assumption* and not a conclusion of the analysis, and is not intended to imply a normative prescription for the behavior of the firm or of individual investors. But given this goal, we can devise a consistent set of optimal rules for reaching the goal, and if some economists are correct, these decision rules should provide a good explanation, and prediction, of the firm's investment decisions in practice.[5]

Given the assumptions of wealth maximization and perfect certainty, the following decision rules should be adopted:[6]

$$\text{when the NPV} > 0, \quad \text{accept the project}$$

$$\text{when the NPV} < 0, \quad \text{reject the project}$$

where the present values are calculated using a discount rate which reflects the alternative use of capital, that is, its opportunity cost.[7] Thus the firm will accept those proposals whose net present values are positive, and will reject those projects whose net present values are negative. These decision rules follow directly from the assumption that firms operate to maximize the wealth of their shareholders, since under the assumed conditions of certainty the prices of all assets, *including common stocks*, are determined by their discounted present values.[8] These decision rules result in an optimal choice of projects since, under the assumed conditions, no other set of projects can be found which will increase the value of the firm.

---

[5] If the decision rules derived from wealth maximization do not provide such an explanation, the wealth maximization assumption ought to be replaced with another one, and the decision rules implied by the new goal of the firm should be determined and tested empirically.

[6] We ignore projects with a zero NPV since by definition the firm is indifferent to such proposals.

[7] Given the assumption of certainty, the opportunity cost will be equal to the riskless rate of interest.

[8] A formal proof of this proposition is given in Paul A. Samuelson, "Some Aspects of the Pure Theory of Capital," *Quarterly Journal of Economics* 51 (May 1937), pp. 469–96.

4. THE INTERNAL RATE OF RETURN (IRR)

The internal rate of return (IRR) is another time-discounted measure of investment worth.[9] The internal rate of return is defined as that rate of discount which equates the present value of the stream of net receipts with the initial investment outlay:

$$I_0 = \frac{S_1}{1+r} + \frac{S_2}{(1+r)^2} + \frac{S_3}{(1+r)^3} + \cdots + \frac{S_n}{(1+r)^n}$$

$$= \sum_{t=1}^{n} \frac{S_t}{(1+r)^t}$$

where r denotes the internal rate of return. An alternative and equivalent definition of the IRR is that rate of discount which equates the NPV of the cash flow to zero:

$$\sum_{t=1}^{n} \frac{S_t}{(1+r)^t} - I_0 = 0$$

The latter formula is somewhat more helpful in calculating the IRR, which for investments whose cash flow is received over a period of years requires an iterative or "trial and error" solution. The computational procedure is as follows: Given the cash flow and investment outlay, choose a discount rate at random and calculate the project's NPV. If the NPV $>$ 0, choose a *higher* discount rate and repeat the procedure; if the NPV is negative, that is, NPV $<$ 0, choose a *lower* discount rate and repeat the procedure. That discount rate which makes the NPV $=$ 0 is the IRR, and the procedure is completed.[10] Table III–2 gives an example of such a calculation.

In cases of projects with equal annual receipts, Table B enables us to make a convenient short cut:

Consider the following project:

$$\sum_{t=1}^{n} \frac{S}{(1+r)^t} = I_0$$

where: $S =$ a constant, that is, $S_1 = S_2 = \cdots = S_n$

---

[9] Applied to the investment in real assets, this method is known under a variety of names including "marginal efficiency of capital," "discounted cash flow," "investor's method," and so on. This is also the method which has been used in financial circles for centuries to compute the yield to maturity on a bond. The term *internal rate of return* was introduced by K. Boulding, "The Theory of a Single Investment," *Quarterly Journal of Economics* (May 1935), pp. 475–94.

[10] For most projects the IRR can be calculated by hand in a few minutes, but where necessary, standard computer programs are available to calculate the IRR.

TABLE III–2.

Year	Net Cash Flow	Discount Factor	PV of Cash Flow
	First Iteration: 8% Discount Rate		
1	452	0.926	418.6
2	500	0.857	428.5
3	278	0.794	220.7
		PV of Receipts	1,067.8
	Less: Investment Outlay		−1,000
		NPV	+67.8
	Second Iteration: 15% Discount Rate		
1	452	0.870	393.2
2	500	0.756	378.0
3	278	0.658	182.9
		PV of Receipts	954.1
	Less: Investment Outlay		−1,000
		NPV	−45.9
	Final Iteration: 12% Discount Rate		
1	452	0.893	403.6
2	500	0.797	398.5
3	278	0.712	197.9
		PV of Receipts	1,000
	Less: Investment Outlay		−1,000
		NPV	0

If we let β_t denote the discount factor in line (t) of Table B, we can rewrite the IRR formula for an equal annual annuity as

$$\beta_t \cdot S = I_0$$

$$\beta_t = \frac{I_0}{S}$$

Now let us apply the simplified formula to a concrete example:

Let $S = \$20$ per year

$t = 40$ years

$I_0 = \$100$

First we find the discount factor

$$\beta_{40} = \frac{I_0}{S} = \frac{100}{20} = 5$$

5. RELATIONSHIP BETWEEN THE IRR AND NPV METHODS

A glance at line 40 of Table B shows that $\beta_{40} = 4.997 \simeq 5$ in the 20% column, and therefore the IRR of the annuity is approximately 20%.

The decision rules associated with the IRR are:[11]

> If the IRR exceeds k, accept the project;
> if the IRR is less than k, reject the project;

where: k denotes the firm's opportunity cost of capital.

5. THE RELATIONSHIP BETWEEN THE IRR AND NPV METHODS: INDEPENDENT PROJECTS

Clearly the IRR and NPV methods are closely related. To bring out this relationship let us consider the set of all "conventional" investment projects, where a conventional project is defined as one in which the initial outlay is followed by a stream of net receipts of the form: $-++ +$ (or if the outlay takes place over more than one year we have a cash flow of the form: $--+++$). The necessary and sufficient condition for a project's inclusion in the set of conventional investment projects is that there be only one *change* in sign in the cash flow. Thus a project with large terminal costs: $-+++-$ is precluded since there are *two* changes in sign: the first following the initial investment outlay and the second preceding the terminal year.

The IRR for any conventional project can be written as:

$$\sum_{t=1}^{n} \frac{S_t}{(1+r)^t} = I_0 \tag{3.1}$$

where r denotes the IRR.

The NPV for the *same* project can be written as

$$\sum_{t=1}^{n} \frac{S_t}{(1+k)^t} > I_0, \quad \text{if the NPV} > 0 \tag{3.2}$$

or

$$\sum_{t=1}^{n} \frac{S_t}{(1+k)^t} < I_0, \quad \text{if the NPV} < 0 \tag{3.3}$$

If we assume that the project has a positive NPV, Equation (3.1) and inequality (3.2) must hold simultaneously. This implies that the left-hand side of (3.1) is smaller than the left-hand side of (3.2). Since by definition their numerators are identical, this implies that $r > k$, and conversely for the

---

[11] We ignore the possibility of $r = k$ in which case the firm would be indifferent to the project.

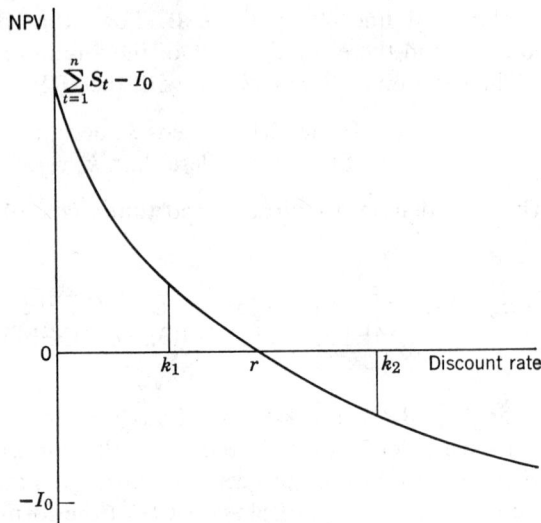

FIGURE III.1.

assumption of a negative NPV. Thus, the IRR and NPV methods imply the same investment decision: if a project is acceptable by the NPV rule—NPV > 0—it is also acceptable by the IRR rule since we have just shown that $r > k$; but if a project fails the NPV test, that is, its NPV is negative, it will also be rejected by the IRR rule since in such a case $r < k$.[12]

This relationship is also shown in Figure III.1, which graphs the NPV of a conventional investment project as a function of the discount rate. When the discount rate = 0 (at the intercept with the vertical axis) the NPV equals the algebraic sum of the stream of net receipts minus the initial outlay: $\sum_{t=1}^{n} S_t - I_0$; as the discount rate approaches infinity the NPV is reduced to $-I_0$. Since we have assumed the project to be conventional in form, the function slopes downward monotonically as the discount rate increases. (For every increase in the discount rate the positive cash flow is reduced while the initial investment outlay remains constant, and therefore the NPV declines).[13] The intercept with the horizontal axis denotes the internal rate of return r, since by definition r is that rate of discount which reduces the NPV of a project to zero.

---

[12] Note that if the NPV is assumed to be zero, this implies $r = k$, and by both methods the investor is indifferent to the project.

[13] In general this function is a n-degree polynomial, and therefore will *not* be linear even in the limiting case where $n = 1$, that is, in the case of a one period investment project.

5. RELATIONSHIP BETWEEN THE IRR AND NPV METHODS

From Figure III.1 we can again see that where the NPV is positive, for example at a discount rate of k_1, $r > k_1$. Conversely, where the NPV is negative, for example, using a discount rate equal to k_2, $r < k_2$. In sum, both methods give the same accept–reject decisions. If a project is profitable by the NPV criterion it will also be profitable by the IRR criterion, and vice versa. Thus, faced with the problem of differentiating acceptable from unacceptable investments, both decision criteria yield the same answers.

5.1 RANKING INVESTMENT PROPOSALS

Despite the fact that both the NPV and the IRR criteria result in the same accept and reject decisions, this equivalence does not necessarily hold for the *ranking* of investment proposals. Consider, for example, the cash flows of the following two investment projects.

Project/Year	0	1	2	3
A	−1,000	639	639	——
B	−1,000	——	——	1,520

The internal rates of return of the projects are

$$r_A = 18\%$$
$$r_B = 15\%$$

Their NPV's, using a 6% discount rate, are:

$$\text{NPV}_A = \$171$$
$$\text{NPV}_B = \$277$$

To clarify this differential ranking, we graph the NPV of each of the projects as a function of the discount rate in Figure III.2. The ranking of the projects by their internal rates of return is constant, and does *not* depend on the discount rate used—clearly 18% always exceeds 15%. But it is equally clear from Figure III.2 that the ranking of projects by the NPV need not be constant, and that it does depend on the discount rate used. If the two functions cross in the positive quadrant of the diagram, and such is the case in Figure III.2, the dominance of one project over another will not be absolute. In our example, if the discount rate is less than r_0, Project B is ranked first, but for higher discount rates project A is ranked ahead of B.

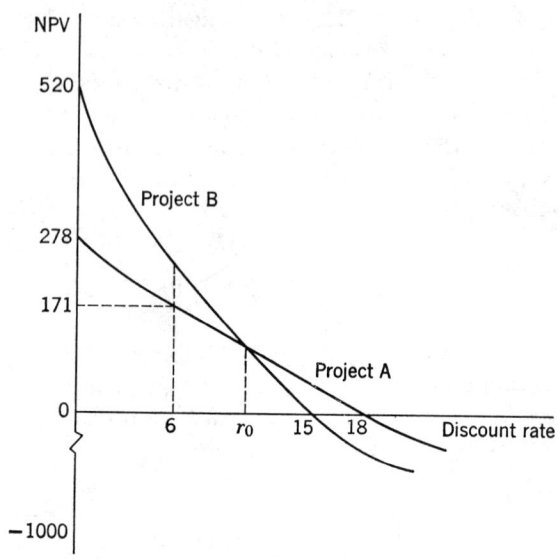

FIGURE III.2.

Which ranking is to be preferred? On the surface the difference in ranking might not seem too serious. After all, a maximizing firm will not accept the first five or ten projects, but will choose all those whose NPV's are positive. And as we have already shown, this set of projects, despite differences in the relative rankings, is identical to the set which results when we use the IRR. Unfortunately, the world is not always so simple as to permit a straightforward accept–reject decision. For a variety of reasons, the firm may be confronted with two or more mutually exclusive investment projects, projects which if accepted imply the rejection of other proposals. Where this is true, the firm must choose *between* the two alternatives, and the ranking becomes crucial. Clearly if A and B in our example are mutually exclusive, the NPV and IRR rankings indicate different orders of priority. At a 6% discount rate the firm would prefer B by the NPV rule; however, should it use the IRR rule, A would be preferred.

The problems raised by the possible existence of mutually exclusive projects cannot be brushed aside with the remark that they are theoretical curiosities. Numerous examples can be found:

> (a) Putting up a three storey or four storey apartment building on a given lot.
>
> (b) Which product gets the preferential spot near the entrance of a supermarket? If it is orange juice it can't be coffee, and vice versa.

6. THE RELATIONSHIP BETWEEN IRR AND NPV

(c) Locating a manufacturing plant. If it is to be near the sources of raw materials, this may mean that it will not be close to the customer.

(d) Shipping oil. If the firm decides to build a pipeline, it in effect excludes the alternative of using tankers, and vice versa.

Finally, it should be noted that even where the initial decision is not inherently mutually exclusive, the firm often must choose among a number of alternative means of carrying out the project, and these alternatives are mutually exclusive.

6. THE RELATIONSHIP BETWEEN IRR AND NPV: DEPENDENT PROJECTS

When the relationships among projects create mutually exclusive choice situations, the relative ranking of projects becomes important. In this context the fact that the IRR ranks projects once-and-for-all without regard to the discount rate, that is, without regard to the opportunity cost of the capital, is cause for concern. This will become clear if we consider a number of examples.

6.1 DIFFERENCES IN THE SCALE OF INVESTMENT

Differences in the ranking of projects by the two methods arise for a variety of reasons. Consider the cash flows of the following two projects:

	0	1	2	3
Project A	−1,000	505	505	505
Project B	−11,000	5,000	5,000	5,000

If we assume a 10% opportunity cost, that is, if we assume that the firm can acquire funds or find alternative uses for funds at 10%, both projects are acceptable by either the IRR or NPV methods since the IRR's of both projects are greater than the cost of capital, and therefore both projects also have positive net present values:

	IRR	NPV
Project A	24%	+256
Project B	17%	+1,435

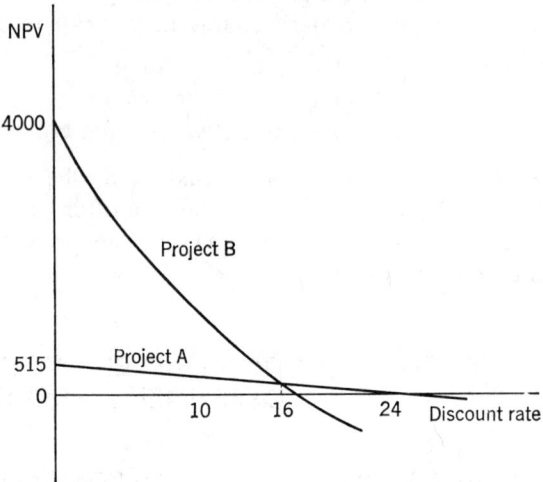

FIGURE III.3.

Now let us assume that these two projects are mutually exclusive. If we invoke the IRR rule, Project A with a 24% rate of return is preferable to project B with only a 17% rate of return. However, by the NPV rule, Project B should be preferred over project A since the former's NPV is larger. What is the reason for this disparity in the rankings of the projects? Figure III.3 graphs the NPV's of the two projects as functions of the discount rate.

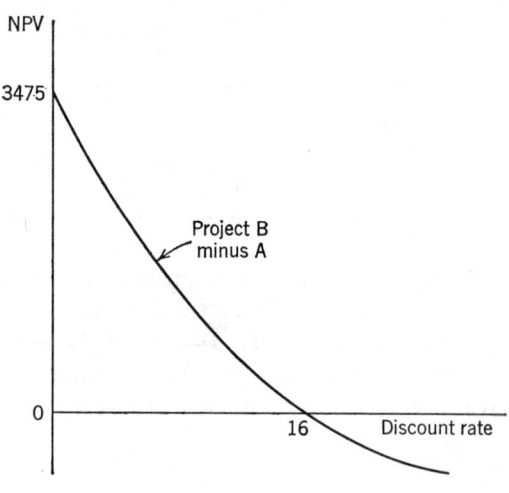

FIGURE III.4.

6. THE RELATIONSHIP BETWEEN IRR AND NPV

As we can see from the diagram, the functions intersect at a discount rate of 16%. The interpretation of the diagram is straightforward: given the necessity of choosing between the two projects, firms whose costs of capital are below 16% will prefer the larger project to the smaller project, while those with costs of capital above 16% (but below 17%) will prefer the smaller project. For costs of capital above 17% only the smaller project is feasible since the NPV of project B is negative after that point.

The arithmetic of capital budgeting aside, how can we account for the fact that for discount rates below 16%, which is probably the relevant domain for most business firms, the relatively low rate of return from project B would be chosen in a mutually exclusive situation by the optimal NPV method? The reason for this preference can be clarified by considering the incremental cash flow which such a choice represents. This is done in the following table and in Figure III.4:

	0	1	2	3
Project B	−11,000	5,000	5,000	5,000
Project A	−1,000	505	505	505
B minus A	−10,000	4,495	4,495	4,495

Choosing Project B rather than Project A is tantamount to choosing a hypothetical project "B minus A" which represents the *incremental* cash flow resulting from such a decision. Thus the choice of the larger project is equivalent to choosing the smaller project plus an additional investment of $10,000 on which $4,495 will be realized each year, for three years. The internal rate of return on this incremental cash flow is 16%, and to a firm with a 10% cost of capital this represents a profitable opportunity and should be accepted. To a firm whose cost of capital is greater than 16% it does not pay to make the additional commitment of resources, and the incremental cash flow should be rejected. This is precisely what the NPV method prescribes: looking at Figure III.3 we note that the intersection of the two functions takes place at a discount rate of 16%, which is the same as the internal rate of return on the incremental cash flow (see Figure III.4). This follows from the fact that the point of intersection represents a discount rate which equates the net present values of the two projects, which is equivalent to the discount rate which equates their difference to zero. And the latter, by definition, is the internal rate of return on the incremental cash flow.

By automatically examining and evaluating the incremental cash flows at the firm's cost of capital, the NPV method ensures that the firm will reach the optimal scale of investment. The IRR method—which is independent of the scale of investment, that is, it is set out in terms of percentage rather than in terms of absolute dollar returns—ignores this important facet of an investment decision. Put in the crudest form, the IRR will always prefer a 50% return on a dollar to a 20% return on 100 dollars. To most of us (assuming a cost of capital below 20%), the optimal solution is to take advantage of both opportunities, but where a choice between the two must be made, few indeed would argue in favor of the IRR solution. Most individuals, as is true of most firms, have goal functions which are set out in terms of absolute returns, not in percentage terms.[14] And since the NPV reflects absolute returns, this ensures its optimality in mutually exclusive choice situations.

6.2 REINVESTMENT RATES

A glance at the example given in Figure III.2 is sufficient to show that the differences in ranking cannot be explained solely in terms of different scales of investment. Even when initial investment outlays are the same, that is, when the projects have the same scale, the two methods can still give contradictory rankings; in other words, the functions may still intersect (see Figure III.2). In general, it is the failure of the IRR method to evaluate properly the alternative use of funds (it ranks projects *independent* of the opportunity cost of capital) which leads to differences in ranking. This can occur even if the projects have the same initial outlays and even the same durations, so long as they do not have identical annual cash flows.[15] Any difference in the magnitude or timing of the cash flow may cause a difference in the rankings of projects by the two methods. The reason for this lies in the implicit assumptions made by the two methods regarding the reinvestment of the cash flows of the projects: The IRR assumes that a project's annual cash flows can be reinvested at the project's internal rate of return; the NPV method assumes that the cash flows can be reinvested at the firm's opportunity cost of capital, that is, at the discount rate.

Since these assumptions are implicit, a more formal demonstration may help to clarify the meaning and significance of the reinvestment rates. Consider any project with a given initial outlay I_0, a given duration of n years, and a stream of cash receipts $S_1, S_2, \ldots, S_n$. The internal rate of

---

[14] As we shall show in Part II, such choices can also be explained in terms of utility, which also depends on the absolute dollar returns, and not on the percentage returns, from investments.

[15] If they did, of course, the projects would be identical.

6. THE RELATIONSHIP BETWEEN IRR AND NPV

return of this project is

$$I_0 = \frac{S_1}{1+r} + \frac{S_2}{(1+r)^2} + \cdots + \frac{S_{n-1}}{(1+r)^{n-1}} + \frac{S_n}{(1+r)^n}$$

$$= \sum_{t=1}^{n-1} \frac{S_t}{(1+r)^t} + \frac{S_n}{(1+r)^n} \quad (3.4)$$

For simplicity let us further assume that the project has a positive NPV at the firm's cost of capital, k. Therefore, the NPV formula for the same project can be written as

$$I_0 < \frac{S_1}{1+k} + \frac{S_2}{(1+k)^2} + \cdots + \frac{S_{n-1}}{(1+k)^{n-1}} + \frac{S_n}{(1+k)^n}$$

$$I_0 < \sum_{t=1}^{n-1} \frac{S_t}{(1+k)^t} + \frac{S_n}{(1+k)^n} \quad (3.5)$$

To make the reinvestment rates explicit, let us rewrite (3.4) and (3.5) in their future value forms. We do this by multiplying both sides of (3.4) by $(1+r)^n$:

$$I_0(1+r)^n = \sum_{t=1}^{n-1} S_t(1+r)^{n-t} + S_n \quad (3.6)$$

Similarly, we multiply both sides of (3.5) by $(1+k)^n$:

$$I_0(1+k)^n < \sum_{t=1}^{n-1} S_t(1+k)^{n-t} + S_n \quad (3.7)$$

Thus even if the initial investment outlays and the durations of the projects are the same, it is clear from Equations (3.6) and (3.7) that the interim receipts are compounded forward (the obverse side of discounting) at different rates—r in the IRR formula and k in the NPV formula. Nor can this problem be avoided, since it arises out of the very need to discount the cash flows of different time periods to some common denominator.

The economic counterpart of these compounding rates is a "reinvestment" rate; that is, the time-discounting process which underlies both methods implicitly makes an assumption regarding the value of the interim receipts to the firm. In the NPV method it is assumed, as it should be, that all receipts can be reinvested at the firm's opportunity cost of capital k.[16] This makes sense, since by definition k reflects the alternative use of funds, and in calculating the profitability of a project we want to evaluate it against that alternative use. This, of course, is the very essence of an NPV calculation.

---

[16] If this does not hold true, the opportunity cost of capital has been incorrectly estimated.

The IRR method, on the other hand, assumes reinvestment at the project's rate of return r. This assumption has no economic basis, since the alternative cost of capital to the firm cannot be r and k at one and the same time. If $r \neq k$, and this is the only case where differences in ranking are of interest, then assuming the future reinvestment of the interim proceeds at the rate r might be unrealistic to the extent that such high-return projects simply may not be available in the future. But even if we could be certain of their physical availability, the IRR's reinvestment assumption is still in error. Such high-return projects, if available, will always be executed by a firm whose cost of capital is equal to k, *independent* of the decision on the current project under consideration.[17] It is an error, therefore, to "credit" the current project with any future benefits accruing from the reinvestment of the interim proceeds at rates of return above k. The NPV method isolates and evaluates the profitability of the current project alone, since the net present value of the proceeds reinvested at a rate of return *equal* to the cost of capital is zero.

The crucial importance of the reinvestment rate assumption can be made even more explicit if we assume that for any one of a variety of reasons, the firm (or individual) expects the opportunity cost of capital to differ in future years. For simplicity, let us assume a case where the discount rate is expected to rise over time, so that $k_1 < k_2 < k_3 < \cdots < k_n$. Clearly, no change occurs in the internal rate of return calculation, and Equation (3.6) still holds, that is, the interim proceeds are still assumed to be reinvested at the average rate of return r. But it is no longer clear that the IRR decision rule which relates the rate of return to the cost of capital can be used. Comparison of a single-valued rate of return with a vector of discount rates $k_1, k_2, \ldots, k_n$ will not, in general, yield meaningful results. It is sufficient to consider an example of a three year project with a rate of return equal to 15%, and the following costs of capital: $k_1 = 10\%$, $k_2 = 15\%$, $k_3 = 20\%$.

A similar problem does not arise with respect to the net present value method. Given the vector of discount rates the NPV of a three year project can be written as follows:

$$I_0 \lessgtr \frac{S_1}{(1+k_1)} + \frac{S_2}{(1+k_1)(1+k_2)} + \frac{S_3}{(1+k_1)(1+k_2)(1+k_3)}$$

Multiplying both sides of this equation by the expression

$$(1+k_1)(1+k_2)(1+k_3)$$

we obtain

$$I_0(1+k_1)(1+k_2)(1+k_3) \lessgtr S_1(1+k_2)(1+k_3) + S_2(1+k_3) + S_3$$

---

[17] If they are not independent the present and future cash flows should be combined and the composite project evaluated by the NPV method.

7. MEASURING THE PROFITABILITY OF INVESTMENTS

Thus the net present value calculation remains meaningful even if we assume nonuniform short-term discount rates. The interim receipts are compounded forward (reinvested) in this case at the appropriate opportunity cost for each relevant period. Thus the first year receipts are reinvested during the second year at that year's cost of capital, k_2, during the third year at k_3, and so on.

To summarize, the NPV method provides an optimal solution to the capital budgeting problem given the assumption that future cash flows and the appropriate cost of capital (discount rate) are known. Both the NPV and IRR are weighted averages, the former using the appropriate short-term weights $k_1, k_2, \ldots, k_n$ while the latter uses the inappropriate long-term rate of return, r.

7. MEASURING THE PROFITABILITY OF FINANCIAL INVESTMENTS

The Net Present Value method was developed to solve the capital budgeting problem of the business firm. But the investment in financial securities, by its very nature, tends to differ from the investment in physical assets: financial assets tend to be highly divisible—you cannot build two-thirds of a bridge but you can buy one-millionth of a share in the ownership of AT&T. Thus for all practical purposes, scale problems can usually be ignored when analyzing securities.[18]

The investment in capital goods usually involves a long-term commitment of resources over a fixed number of years (that is, disinvestment is costly and often uneconomic); most securities, independent of their date of maturity (if any),[19] can be held for as short or as long a period as is desired; in other words, investments in securities are highly reversible. Finally, while the firm is often faced with mutually exclusive alternatives, the decision to purchase a share of AT&T does not generally preclude the purchase of GM stock.

Thus, when analyzing investments in securities, differences in scale and duration among alternative investments can safely be ignored. This property of financial investments is of considerable importance since we seek a measure of return which can rank the alternative investments for all investors without determining their individual discount rates.[20] What is required is a measure

---

[18] Except when transaction costs are introduced. See Chapter XV.
[19] Common stock or preferred stock as well as perpetual bonds have no formal redemption dates.
[20] The vast number of investors in a financial market precludes any attempt at making meaningful NPV calculations of stocks and bonds.

of return which provides a ranking of financial investments equivalent to the ranking that would have been obtained through the use of present values, at any positive discount rate.

7.1 THE RATE OF RETURN ON COMMON STOCKS[21]

Two alternative formulations of a time-adjusted rate of return[22] on common stocks have been advocated in the financial literature. Both of these measures are based on the total cash flow, dividends and capital gains (losses), emanating from the ownership of common stock. The first method simply applies the familiar formula for the internal rate of return to the problem of determining the rate of return on investments in common stock:

$$P_0 = \frac{D_1}{(1+r)} + \frac{D_2}{(1+r)^2} + \cdots + \frac{D_{n-1}}{(1+r)^{n-1}} + \frac{D_n + P_n}{(1+r)^n}$$

$$= \sum_{t=1}^{n} \frac{D_t}{(1+r)^t} + \frac{P_n}{(1+r)^n} \qquad (3.8)$$

where: r = the internal rate of return
D_t = the cash dividend received in period t; $(t = 1, 2, \ldots, n)$
P_n = the market price of a share at the close of period n
P_0 = the initial market price of a share of common stock

This formula is perfectly general and can be adapted to any holding period. It views the cash flow to the investor as the stream of dividends plus the share's terminal market value.

The alternative formulation views the return on a common stock as the geometric mean of a series of annual rates of return, and hence we shall refer it as the "geometric mean rate of return." This formulation defines the rate of return in any period t as

$$i_t = \frac{D_t + (P_t - P_{t-1})}{P_{t-1}}$$

$$= \frac{D_t + P_t}{P_{t-1}} - 1 \qquad (3.9)$$

---

[21] The analysis of this section follows that of H. Ben-Shahar and M. Sarnat, "Reinvestment and the Rate of Return on Common Stocks," *Journal of Finance*, Vol. XXI (December 1966).

[22] Since we require a measure for multi-period investment, undiscounted measures of return such as the dividend yield, D/P are unsatisfactory for our purposes. The dividend yield also includes only part of the benefits accruing to the shareholder since it ignores capital gains.

7. MEASURING THE PROFITABILITY OF INVESTMENTS

where: i_t = the rate of return in period t
P_t = the share's market price at the end of period t.

For multi-period investments the geometric mean is taken:[23]

$$1 + \bar{i} = \sqrt[n]{\prod_{t=1}^{n} \frac{D_t + P_t}{P_{t-1}}}$$

$$= \sqrt[n]{\prod_{t=1}^{n} (1 + i_t)} \qquad (3.10)$$

where: $\bar{i}$ = the geometric mean rate of return.

A comparison of the two formulas shows that they provide identical measures of return for single-period investments. Setting t equal to one in Equation (3.8) and multiplying both sides by $(1 + r)/P_0$ gives

$$1 + r = \frac{D_1 + P_1}{P_0}$$

$$r = \frac{D_1 + P_1}{P_0} - 1 \qquad (3.11)$$

which is the same as (3.9). In the general case where shares are held for more than one period, both formulations implicitly assume reinvestment of the interim cash dividends. It should be recalled in this context that as already noted in Section 6 above, "reinvestment" is the obverse side of "compounding," and therefore is an inherent property of any time-discounted formula. It is *not* a behavioral assumption regarding the investment habits of individuals. However it does raise the problem of the implicit rates at which the interim receipts are assumed to be reinvested (compounded).

To make these rates explicit we multiply both sides of the IRR formula (3.8) by $(1 + r)^n/P_0$:

$$(1 + r)^n = \frac{1}{P_0} \left[\sum_{t=1}^{n} D_t(1 + r)^{n-t} + P_n \right]$$

$$= \frac{1}{P_0} \left[\sum_{t=1}^{n-1} D_t(1 + r)^{n-t} + D_n + P_n \right] \qquad (3.12)$$

The geometric mean formula presents a somewhat more difficult problem. Let us start with a case where $t = 2$. Squaring both sides of (3.10) and

---

[23] The symbol $\prod$ indicates multiplication, just as the symbol Σ indicates summation. For example,

$$\prod_{t=1}^{3} (1 + i_t) = (1 + i_1)(1 + i_2)(1 + i_3)$$

setting $t = 2$, we have

$$(1 + \bar{i})^2 = \prod_{t=1}^{2} \frac{D_t + P_t}{P_{t-1}} = \frac{D_1 + P_1}{P_0} \cdot \frac{D_2 + P_2}{P_1}$$

$$= \frac{D_1}{P_0} \cdot \frac{D_2 + P_2}{P_1} + \frac{P_1}{P_0} \cdot \frac{D_2 + P_2}{P_1}$$

$$= \frac{1}{P_0}\left[D_1 \cdot \frac{D_2 + P_2}{P_1} + D_2 + P_2\right] \quad (3.13)$$

But since $(D_2 + P_2)/P_1 \equiv (1 + r_2)$, this can be written as

$$(1 + \bar{i})^2 = \frac{1}{P_0}[D_1(1 + r_2) + D_2 + P_2] \quad (3.14)$$

Generalizing this result for n investment periods, we get

$$(1 + \bar{i})^n = \frac{1}{P_0}\left[\sum_{t=1}^{n-1} D_t \prod_{j=t}^{n-1}(1 + i_{j+1}) + D_n + P_n\right] \quad (3.15)$$

A comparison of Equations (3.15) and (3.12) shows that the two alternative formulations do not provide identical measures of return in the multiperiod case if dividends are paid,[24] and that the only difference between them stems from differing assumptions regarding the reinvestment rate. Thus the IRR implicitly assumes reinvestment at the long-run average rate r, while the geometric mean rate, despite its name, implicitly assumes reinvestment at the short-term rates of return which actually obtained in the market during the periods subsequent to the receipt of the dividend. The use of short-term rates rather than an average rate has important theoretical advantages; as a result, the vector of short-term rates more accurately reflects the opportunity cost of the dividend in the market.[25] And since the initial investment outlay can be considered free of size constraints, and the cash flows are brought to common terminal dates, a ranking of common stocks using the geometric mean rate of return in consistent with an NPV ranking, independent of the discount rate. Thus this measure of return is appropriate for all investors.[26]

---

[24] If no dividends are paired both the internal and geometric mean rates of return are equal to

$$\sqrt[n]{\frac{P_n}{P_0}} - 1$$

[25] Optimum solutions to investment problems require the use of short-term rates. The use of a long-term average is not permissible, since an infinity of short-term combinations can be defined which are compatible with any given long-term average rate. See M. J. Bailey, "Formal Criteria for Investment Decisions," *The Journal of Political Economy* LXVII (October 1959).

[26] Since common stocks represent risky investments, an investment decision requires a measure of risk as well as a measure of return. Here we consider only the question of return; the problem of risk is taken up in Chapter VI.

7. MEASURING THE PROFITABILITY OF INVESTMENTS

7.2 ADJUSTING THE RATE OF RETURN

The empirical application of the geometric mean formula requires a number of adjustments. More specifically, procedures must be defined for handling the following problems:

    a. Current dividends plus the change in share prices do not always accurately represent the total return to shareholders, owing to a wide variety of splits, stock dividends, and rights offerings.

    b. Cash dividends are typically received at varying dates during the year and not necessarily on the last day of the year, as might seem to be implied by Equation (3.15).[27]

An operational solution to these problems can be found by redefining the geometric mean rate of return in a manner which consistently reinvests upon receipt all cash dividends, stock dividends, and the market value of rights.[28] With respect to stock dividends (splits) and rights the adjustments are identical to those made for EPS in the previous chapter.[29] An index of shares is set up to equal 100 in the base year; shares received via subsequent splits or stock dividends are added to the index at the time they are allocated. We assume that rights are sold in[30] the market on the first day of trading and the proceeds of the "sale" (that is, the market value of the rights) are used to "purchase" additional shares. These shares are then added to the index.[31]

Since a lag exists between the date a share is listed ex-dividend and the time the company's check becomes available, the reinvestment of the cash dividends should be lagged as well. For simplicity, we use the proceeds of cash dividends to purchase additional shares on the fifteenth of the month following the ex-dividend date, and the shares so acquired are also added to the index of shares on that date.

---

[27] Problems of intra-year timing arise owing to the convention of calculating *annual* rates of return. If investment periods are defined to coincide with the ex-dividend dates, this problem disappears.

[28] The reader who is interested in the detailed procedures, including programming instructions, is directed to Fisher and Lorie, "Rates of Return on Investments in Common Stocks," *Journal of Business* XXXVII (January 1964).

[29] See pp. 37 through 44.

[30] These reinvestment "transactions" are theoretical, and therefore, commissions and taxes should not be charged.

[31] An equivalent procedure would be to exercise the rights and immediately sell enough of the shares to cover the subscription price of all the shares previously acquired via the exercise of the rights.

The reinvestment of stock dividends (splits) and the value of rights is designed to keep the initial investment intact throughout the investment period. Failure to do this implies the sale of part of the shareholder's ownership interest in the firm. The reinvestment of cash dividends, as we have shown, is an inherent theoretical property of the geometric mean rate of return, or for that matter of any compounded rate of return. It should also be emphasized that the reinvestment of the interim cash dividends is necessary to ensure comparability among the shares of different companies. This procedure preserves the equivalence between current income and capital appreciation.[32] Investors can be assumed to remain indifferent to a 10% per annum increase in stock prices or to an annual 10% cash dividend (with no price appreciation) if and only if they are permitted to reinvest the cash dividends in the original shares.

The adjusted rate of return for any given year[33] is derived using the following formula:

$$i_t^* = \frac{V_t - V_{t-1}}{V_{t-1}} = \frac{V_t}{V_{t-1}} - 1 \qquad (3.16)$$

where: i_t^* = the adjusted rate of return in year t
V_t = the market value of the investment at the end of year t.

The market value of the investment is calculated by multiplying the index of shares (reflecting the reinvestment of stock dividends, splits, value of rights, and cash dividends) by the market price of a share at the end of the year. For multi-period investments the formula becomes

$$1 + i^* = \sqrt[n]{\prod_{t=1}^{n} \frac{V_t}{V_{t-1}}} = \sqrt[n]{\frac{V_n}{V_0}} \qquad (3.17)$$

To this point we have ignored taxes and transaction costs. Clearly we can have as many rates of return as we have income tax brackets, and no theoretical consideration is involved beyond "making the punishment fit the crime." Thus, a calculation of rates of return on common stock for a pension fund would presumably be made on a pre-tax basis if the fund is exempt from both income and capital gains taxes. The appropriate calculation for individuals would have to reflect their marginal tax rates, and, of course, these rates vary from individual to individual. In the examples which follow we shall confine ourselves to the calculation of pre-tax rates of return.

---

[32] Abstracting from differences which may properly exist owing to the differential taxation of current income and capital gains.
[33] The rate of return is calculated from January 15 to January 14 of the following year to avoid any possible bias due to the use of the calendar year.

8. CALCULATING THE ADJUSTED RATE OF RETURN: SOME EXAMPLES

To illustrate the calculation of the rate of return in practice, let us consider a number of actual examples. We start with AT&T common stock in 1968. Table III–3 sets out the necessary data for adjusting the number of shares. There were four quarterly dividends of $0.60 per share paid during the year. If we assume that an investor had 100 shares at the beginning of the year, he was entitled to dividends equal to $60 ($0.60 · 100 = $60) at the end of the first quarter. Since the price of AT&T common was $50 per share on the fifteenth of the following month (the date on which actual dividend payment is assumed to have been made), 1.20 additional shares can be acquired out of the proceeds of the dividend. The index of shares is now set at 101.20. At the end of the second quarter, the investor receives a $0.60 dividend on 101.20 shares, but as the price of a share on the fifteenth of the following month was $51, the increased dividend proceeds suffice to acquire only 1.19 shares, and the index of the number of shares rises to 102.39. Similar calculations are made at the end of the next two quarters. If the proceeds of all dividends are consistently reinvested on the fifteenth of the month following the ex-dividend date, the index of shares rises from 100 at the beginning of the year to 104.68 at the end of the year. It should be noted that failure to reinvest the interim dividends would be tantamount to ignoring the need for time discounting *within* the year, and since the dividend payment dates of various firms do not always coincide, the comparability of the rates of return would be impaired.

TABLE III–3. Calculation of index of shares for AT&T common, 1968*

Cash Dividends ($ per share)	Share Price on 15th of Following Month	Additional Shares Purchased	Index of Number of Shares
			100.00
0.60	50	1.20	101.20
0.60	51	1.19	102.39
0.60	$52\frac{6}{8}$	1.16	103.55
0.60	$54\frac{7}{8}$	1.13	104.68

* All transactions within the year are given in chronological order.

TABLE III–4. Calculation of index of shares for Goodrich Common, 1968*

Cash Dividends ($ per share)	Split	Share Price on 15th of Following Month	Additional Shares Acquired	Index of Number of Shares
				100.00
0.60		$58\frac{6}{8}$	1.02	101.02
0.60		$64\frac{5}{8}$	0.94	101.96
	3 for 2		50.98	152.94
0.60		$41\frac{7}{8}$	1.57	154.51
0.60		$46\frac{1}{8}$	1.44	155.95

* All transactions within the year are given in chronological order.

The actual calculation of the rate of return requires the following additional data:

Share price at beginning of year = $53.00

Share price at end of year = $54.00

Applying formula (3.17) we have

$$i^*_{1968} = \frac{104.68 \cdot 54}{100 \cdot 53} - 1 = 5.7\%$$

that is, the pre-tax rate of return to investors in AT&T common stock was 5.7% in 1968.

Table III–4 sets out the share index for Goodrich common stock in 1968. This is a slightly more complicated calculation since in addition to the quarterly dividends, the company split its stock 3 for 2 in the middle of the year. Note that in calculating the index care must be taken to consider each transaction in its proper chronological order. For example, an investor who started the year with 100 shares had a total of 101.96 shares (owing to the reinvestment of cash dividends) when the split was declared. These extra shares are eligible for the split, and therefore are taken into account in the calculation of the index. By the end of the year an investor who started with 100 shares, reinvested cash dividends, and held the split shares had 155.95 shares in his closing portfolio.

The calculation of the rate of return on Goodrich common stock for 1968 is as follows:

$$i^*_{1968} = \frac{155.95 \cdot 53\frac{2}{8}}{100 \cdot 68} - 1 = 22.1\%$$

8. CALCULATING THE ADJUSTED RATE OF RETURN

where: 155.95 = the index of number of shares at the end of year
$53\frac{2}{8}$ = price of the share at end of the year
68 = price of the share at the beginning of the year

Thus the rate of return on Goodrich Common stock was 22.1% in 1968. The importance of making the adjustments can readily be seen if we calculate the *meaningless* unadjusted rate of return by the formula

$$\frac{D + P_t}{P_{t-1}} - 1 = \frac{2.40 + 53\frac{2}{8}}{68} - 1 = -18\%$$

Thus failure to adjust the calculation results in a large negative rate of return. It should be clear from this example that care must be exercised when making rough rule of thumb calculations of rates of return from, for example, the financial pages of your newspaper.

The final example considered is that of IBM. Table III-5 sets out the index of the number of shares for IBM common stock in 1966. This particular year was chosen since IBM paid cash dividends, split its stock, and also floated a rights issue. Once again, it should be noted that all of the above benefits must be listed in exact chronological order. An investor who held

TABLE III-5. Calculation of index of shares for IBM, 1966

Cash Dividends ($ per share)	Split and Rights†	Share Price on 15th of Following Month	Additional Shares Acquired	Index of Number of Shares
				100.00
$1.50		$513\frac{4}{8}$	0.29	100.29
	3 for 2		50.14	150.43
$1.10		$342\frac{4}{8}$	0.48	150.92
	1 for 40 $P_s = 285$	355	0.74	151.66
$1.10		348	0.48	152.14
$1.10		$352\frac{4}{8}$	0.47	152.61

† For rights no time lag is necessary and the relevant calculation is:

$$\frac{150.92 \cdot \$1.75}{\$355} = 0.74 \text{ shares}$$

where 150.92 = number of shares eligible for rights offering
$1.75 = market value of the right attaching to one share
$355 = market price of shares on first day of trading after rights issue.

100 shares of IBM at the beginning of the year and reinvested the cash dividends, held the split stock, and used the proceeds from the sale of the rights to purchase additional shares had 152.61 shares at the end of the year. The rate of return on IBM common for 1966 was:

$$i^*_{1966} = \frac{152.61 \cdot 384\frac{4}{8}}{100 \cdot 492\frac{4}{8}} - 1 = 19.15\%$$

where: $384\frac{4}{8}$ = the price of a share at the end of the year
$492\frac{4}{8}$ = the price of a share at the beginning of the year.

Thus the rate of return on IBM Common stock was about 19% in 1966. Once again care has to be taken to adjust the calculation; a rough rule of thumb calculation, based on beginning- and end-of-year prices and the dividend, results in a very large and meaningless *negative* rate of return.

9. SUMMARY

This Chapter sets out the principles underlying the firm's analysis of capital budgeting decisions and the measurement of the return on financial investment under conditions of certainty, that is, on the assumption that the estimate of future cash flows is given. The latter assumption, which is relaxed in Part II of the book, permits us to focus attention on the implications of the time value of money for investment analysis.

In evaluating the desirability of an investment proposal, consideration must be given not only to the magnitude of the cash flows but to their timing as well. A dollar received tomorrow is not the equivalent of a dollar invested today, so long as there exists an alternative of earning a positive return on the dollar during the interim. Two time-discounted methods for evaluating capital investment expenditures are discussed in this chapter: Net Present Value (NPV), which is derived by discounting a project's cash receipts using the firm's opportunity cost of capital, summing them over the life of the proposal, and deducting the initial investment outlay; and the Internal Rate of Return (IRR), which is defined as that rate of discount which equates the present value of the stream of net receipts with the initial investment outlay. All of the necessary calculations are reduced to very simple procedures by using present value tables constructed for this purpose.

Assuming that a firm desires to maximize the wealth of its shareholders, the following decision rules can be derived for the NPV method:

(a) When NPV > 0, accept the project.
(b) When NPV < 0, reject the project.

9. SUMMARY

These rules, consistently applied, maximize the net present value of the firm; and since under the assumed condition of certainty the prices of all assets are determined by their discounted present values, these decision rules are optimal in the sense that no alternative set of projects can be chosen which will increase the value of the shareholders' equity.

The following decision rules are associated with the IRR method:

(a) If the IRR exceeds k, accept the project.
(b) If the IRR is less than k, reject the project, where k denotes the firm's opportunity cost of capital.

The IRR and NPV decision rules are closely related. For conventional investment projects (those projects characterized by initial outlays followed by a stream of net receipts) they result in identical accept or reject decisions. Thus with respect to the problem of differentiating acceptable proposals both decision criteria yield the same results.

Despite the fact that both the NPV and IRR criteria result in the same accept and reject decisions, this equivalence does not hold when mutually exclusive investments are considered. (Two alternatives are defined as mutually exclusive if the acceptance of one implies the rejection of the other.) Here the *ranking* of projects is of paramount importance, and it can readily be shown that the two methods generally do not assign the same relative priorities to a given set of projects. The reason for this stems from an important conceptual difference in the two methods: The IRR method ranks projects by their rates of return, *independent* of the discount rate; the NPV method ranks projects by the size of their net present values, and it does depend on the discount rate.

Differences in the ranking of projects by the two methods arise in a variety of circumstances:

(a) Since the IRR is given as a pure number, it is independent of the scale of investment, and therefore ignores this important facet of an investment decision. The IRR cannot distinguish between a 50% return on a dollar and a 50% return on a thousand dollars; the NPV, which is defined in terms of absolute returns, can. Faced with the necessity of choosing between two such options, few indeed would argue in favor of the IRR solution.

(b) Even if the initial outlays of the projects are the same, differences in the magnitude and timing of the cash flows may result in differences in the rankings of the projects by the two methods. This stems from the implicit assumptions regarding the rate at which interim receipts can be reinvested: The IRR formula assumes reinvestment at the project's internal rate of return; the NPV formula implicitly assumes reinvestment at the firm's cost of capital. The latter assumption is preferable, since high return projects may not be available in the future; and even more important, should they be available they will be accepted without regard to the decision on the current project under consideration. Therefore it would be an error to "credit" the current projects with any future benefits accruing from the possible reinvestment of interim proceeds at rates of return which exceed the opportunity cost of capital.

When analyzing the profitability of investments in common stocks, we seek a measure of return which provides an appropriate ranking of investments for all investors, independent of their individual discount rates. Two alternative formulations, based on the total cash flow, have been advocated. The first applies the IRR formula to the stream of dividends and the share's terminal market value; the second is defined as the geometric mean of the annual returns (taking dividends and capital gains or losses into account). The only difference between the two measures of return reflects differing implicit assumptions regarding the reinvestment rate. The geometric mean's assumption of reinvestment at the short-term rates which actually obtained in the market is conceptually more appropriate than the IRR's implicit assumption of reinvestment at the long-term average rate of return. The empirical application of the geometric mean formula is straightforward, and a method for systematically "reinvesting" all cash dividends, stock dividends, and the market value of rights is defined.

QUESTIONS AND PROBLEMS

3.1 Define the following terms:
  (a) time value of money
  (b) present value
  (c) future value
  (d) internal rate of return
  (e) net present value

3.2 Why is it necessary to assume a goal for the firm when applying capital budgeting methods?

3.3 Under what assumptions will the IRR and NPV methods rank all projects in the *same* order of priority?

3.4 "To facilitate comparisons, absolute magnitudes should always be reduced to pure numbers." What is your opinion of the above quotation?

3.5 "The problem of reinvestment rates can be avoided by considering only projects of the same duration." Is this statement true? Explain.

3.6 For each of the following investment projects, calculate:
  (a) the internal rate of return
  (b) the net present value using a 20% discount rate

	Cash Flow							
Year	0	1	2	3	4	5	6	7
Project A	−4,564	1,000	1,000	1,000	1,000	1,000	1,000	1,000
Project B	−2,000	512.8	512.8	512.8	512.8	512.8	512.8	512.8
Project C	−21,000	3,000	3,000	3,000	3,000	3,000	3,000	3,000

3.7 For each of the following three projects, calculate:
  (a) the internal rate of return
  (b) the net present value using a 16% discount rate

	Cash Flow				
Year	0	1	2	3	4
Project D	−800	350	350	200	123
Project E	−70	40	25	15	22
Project F	−20,000	2,000	8,000	14,000	4,466

3.8 Assume that you are confronted with the following three projects:

	Cash Flow					
Year	0	1	2	3	4	5
Project A	−1,000	100	100	100	100	1,100
Project B	−1,000	264	264	264	264	264
Project C	−1,000	—	—	—	—	1,611

(a) Calculate the net present value of each of the above projects, assuming a 10% discount rate, and rank the projects.

(b) Calculate the internal rate of return for each of the above projects and rank the projects.

(c) Calculate the net present value of each of the projects using a 6% discount rate and rank the projects.

(d) Calculate the net present value of each of the projects assuming a 15% discount rate and rank the projects.

(e) Compare and explain the rankings which you obtained in parts a–d above using a diagram which graphs the NPV as a function of the discount rate.

3.9 (1) The Bitter Almond Company was confronted with the following two *mutually exclusive* investment opportunities:

Year	0	1	2	3	4	5
Project A	−50,000	17,000	17,000	17,000	17,000	17,000
Project B	−32,000	12,000	12,000	12,000	12,000	12,000

(a) Calculate each project's net present value and internal rate of return. (Assume that the firm's cost of capital is 8%.)

(b) Which of the two projects would be chosen according to the IRR criterion? According to the NPV criterion?

(c) How can you explain the differences in rankings given by the NPV and IRR methods in this case?

(2) Another company in the industry was confronted by the following two mutually exclusive investment opportunities:

Year	0	1	2	3	4
Project C	−100	—	—	—	174.9
Project D	−100	120.0	—	—	—

(a) Calculate each project's net present value and internal rate of return. (Assume that this company's cost of capital is also 8%.)

(b) Which of the two projects would be chosen according to the NPV criterion? According to the IRR?

(c) How can you explain the difference in rankings in this case?

(3) In view of your answers to parts (1) and (2) above, which of the two methods, in your opinion, provides the *optimal* decision in each of the cases? Explain and defend your choice.

(4) How would you qualify your answers to parts (1)–(3) above in the absence of mutual exclusiveness, that is, if the projects were *independent*?

3.10 Having proven yourself to be a superior student (your choice of finance as a major being a case in point), Doe University offers you a choice between an outright gift of $1,000 or a $10,000 interest-free loan to be paid back in ten equal annual installments of $1,000 each.

(a) Which alternative would represent the optimal choice for you? Explain your decision.

(b) Under what circumstances would you reverse your choice? Be specific.

(c) Which alternative, the gift or the loan, do you think would be optimal from the standpoint of the university?

(d) Under what circumstances would both the university and the recipient of the money prefer the same alternative? Be specific.

QUESTIONS AND PROBLEMS

3.11 (1) Graph the NPV of the following four projects as a function of the discount rate. (Hint: calculate three points and draw the remaining segments of the curve in free-hand.)

		Cash Flow				
Year	0	1	2	3	4	5
Project A	−50	17	17	17	17	17
B	+50	−17	−17	−17	−17	−17
C	−100	20	20	20	20	20
D	0	5	5	5	5	5

(2) What is the IRR of each of the projects?

3.12 What are the most significant differences between capital investments and financial investments from the standpoint of the measurement of their profitability?

3.13 The following table sets out the annual adjusted rates of return on the stock of two hypothetical companies:

	Rates of Return	
	Company A	Company B
1966	−26	−18
1967	36	30
1968	−2	13
1969	15	1
1970	19	−3

(a) Calculate the arithmetic mean for each of the companies.

(b) Calculate the geometric mean for each of the two companies.

(c) Which calculation is the conceptually correct one to represent the average annual rate of return on a company's stock?

3.14 From the following data calculate the rate of return on AT&T common stock for the year 1967 (mid-January 1967 to mid-January 1968).

Cash Dividends ($ per share)	Ex-dividend Date	Share Price on 15th of Following Month (in dollars)
0.55	Feb. 24	$61\frac{5}{8}$
0.55	May 26	$56\frac{6}{8}$
0.55	Aug. 28	$53\frac{3}{8}$
0.60	Nov. 28	$49\frac{7}{8}$

Price at the beginning of the year (mid-Jan., 1967) was $55\frac{4}{5}$.
Price at the close of the year (mid-Jan., 1968) was $55\frac{2}{8}$.

3.15 From the following data calculate the rate of return on Colgate common stock for the year 1965.

Cash Dividends ($ per share)	Ex-dividend Date	Share Price on 15th of Following Month (in dollars)
0.30	Jan. 19	50
0.30	April 14	53
0.225	July 12	$30\frac{3}{8}$
0.225	Oct. 20	$28\frac{1}{8}$

On July 12 the company split its stock 3 for 2.
The prices of the company's stock at the beginning and end of the year were $51\frac{4}{8}$ and 28 respectively.

3.16 The following data pertain to the Komplex Corporation during the year 1970.

(a) Interim dividends of $1.50 and $0.60 per share were declared; the ex-dividend dates were February 28 and August 31, respectively.

(b) The company declared a 20% stock dividend in April (the ex-stock dividend date was April 15).

(c) In June the company split its stock 2 for 1.

(d) On October 25 the company issued rights; the allocation ratio was two old shares required to purchase one new share. The subscription price was $40 and on the day before the shares went ex-rights the market price of the old shares was $46. The rights were traded at $2 and the market price of the shares ex-rights was $44.

(e) The company's shares were traded at the following prices at selected dates during the year:

Date	Share Price
January 15, 1970	105
March 15, 1970	100
Sept. 15, 1970	50
January 15, 1971	40

(1) Calculate the unadjusted rate of return on Komplex common stock for 1970.

(2) Calculate the adjusted rate of return on Komplex common for 1970.

3.17 Comment on the following quotation taken from a news handout of Shrewd Investment Services Inc.: "IBM common stock does not represent a particularly good investment; the dividend is low and its price has been around 300 for the past ten years."

SELECTED REFERENCES

Alchian, A. A., "The Rate of Interest, Fisher's Rate of Return over Cost, and Keynes' Internal Rate of Return," *American Economic Review* (December 1955).

Bailey, M. J., "Formal Criteria for Investment Decisions," *Journal of Political Economy* (October 1959).

Bauman, W. S., "Investment Returns and Present Values," *Financial Analysts Journal* (November–December 1969).

Ben-Shahar, H., and Sarnat, M., "Reinvestment and the Rate of Return on Common Stocks," *Journal of Finance* (December 1966).

Bernhard, H. B., "Discount Methods for Expenditure Evaluation—A Clarification of Their Assumptions," *Journal of Industrial Engineering* (January–February 1962).

Bierman, H., and Smidt, S., *The Capital Budgeting Decision*, 2nd edition. New York: Macmillan, 1966.

Boulding, K., "The Theory of a Single Investment," *Quarterly Journal of Economics* (May 1935).

Brigham, E. F., and Pappas, J. L., "Rates of Return on Common Stock," *Journal of Business* (July 1969).

Dean, J., *Capital Budgeting*. New York: Columbia University Press, 1951.

Elton, E. J., "Capital Rationing and External Discount Rates," *Journal of Finance* (June 1970).

Fisher, L., "An Algorithm for Finding Exact Rates of Return," *Journal of Business* (January 1966).

———, "Some New Stock-Market Indexes." *Journal of Business* (January 1966).

Fisher, L., and Lorie, J. H., "Rates of Return on Investments in Common Stocks," *Journal of Business* (January 1964).

———, "Rates of Return on Investments in Common Stocks; The Year by Year Record, 1926–1965," *Journal of Business* (July 1968).

Hirshleifer, J., "On the Theory of Optimal Investment Decision," *Journal of Political Economy* (August 1958).

Lerner, E. M., and Rappaport, A., "Limit of DCF in Capital Budgeting," *Harvard Business Review* (September–October 1968).

———, and Carleton, W. T., *A Theory of Financial Analysis*. New York: Harcourt, Brace & World, 1966.

Lorie, J. H., and Savage, L. J., "Three Problems in Rationing Capital," *Journal of Business* (October 1955).
Lutz, F., and Lutz, V., *The Theory of Investment of the Firm*. Princeton, N.J.: Princeton University Press, 1951.
Mao, J. C. T., "An Analysis of Criteria for Investment Under Certainty: A Comment," *Management Science* (January 1967).
Merrett, A. J., and Sykes, A., *Capital Budgeting and Company Finance*. London: Longmans, Green, 1966.
Norstrum, C., "A Note on 'Mathematical Analysis' of Rates of Return Under Certainty," *Management Science* (January 1967).
Porterfield, J. T. S., *Investment Decisions and Capital Costs*. Englewood Cliffs, N.J.: Prentice-Hall, 1965.
Quirin, G. D., *The Capital Expenditure Decision*. Homewood, Ill.: Irwin, 1967.
Robinson, R., "The Rate of Interest, Fisher's Rate of Return over Costs and Keynes' Internal Rate of Return: Comment," *American Economic Review* (December 1956).
Samuelson, P. A., "Some Aspects of the Pure Theory of Capital," *Quarterly Journal of Economics* (May 1937).
Solomon, E., *The Theory of Financial Management*. New York: Columbia University Press, 1963.
Teichrow, D., Robichek, A. A., and Montabano, M., "Mathematical Analysis of Rates of Return Under Certainty," *Management Science* (January 1965).
———, "An Analysis of Criteria for Investment and Financing Decisions Under Certainty," *Management Science* (November 1965).
Weingartner, H. M., "Some New Views on the Payback Period and Capital Budgeting Decisions," *Management Science* (August 1969).
Weston, J. F., *The Scope and Methodology of Finance*. Englewood Cliffs, N.J.: Prentice-Hall, 1966.

Chapter IV
Valuation of Securities: Bonds and Preferred Stock

1. INTRODUCTION

This chapter is devoted to an examination of the principles underlying the valuation of fixed-income bearing securities—bonds and preferred stock. Chapter V analyzes the somewhat more complex case of common stock. We shall first generalize the rate of return concepts developed in the previous chapter to cover bonds and preferred stock. The special nature of the risks confronting the investor in fixed-income securities will then be discussed and the implications of these risks for investors will be spelled out in some detail with respect to the yield–maturity relationship for bonds. We conclude the chapter with a brief review of the special features often attached to bond or preferred stock issues, such as early redemption and convertibility to common stock.

2. ALTERNATIVE FORMULATIONS OF THE YIELD ON BONDS AND PREFERRED STOCK

2.1 THE RATE OF RETURN

The formula for computing the rate of return on common stock presented in Chapter III can readily be generalized to cover fixed-income bearing securities, and for that matter other financial assets as well. The application of the geometric mean rate of return to preferred stock requires no special treatment. As is true of a common stock, the rate of return on a preferred share in any particular year is given by the formula

$$i'_t = \frac{D_t + (P_t - P_{t-1})}{P_{t-1}}$$
$$= \frac{D_t + P_t}{P_{t-1}} - 1$$

where: i_t = the rate of return in period t
P_t = the share's market price at the end of period t
D_t = the cash dividend received in period t.

Since stock dividends, and rights, are usually not offered to preferred shareholders, no further adjustments are necessary and the rate of return on a preferred stock held over n years can be found by taking the geometric mean:[1]

$$\bar{i} = \sqrt[n]{\prod_{t=1}^{n}(1+i_t)} - 1$$

where: $\bar{i}$ = the geometric mean rate of return.

The rate of return on a bond in any given year can be calculated as a straightforward extension of the formula for a preferred share:

$$i'_t = \frac{C_t + P_t}{P_{t-1}} - 1$$

where: i'_t = the rate of return to an investor in a bond in period t
C_t = the interest coupon received in period t
P_t = the market price of the bond at the end of period t.

For investment periods in excess of one year the geometric mean formula is again applied:

$$\bar{i}' = \sqrt[n]{\prod_{t=1}^{n}(1+i'_t)} - 1$$

Thus the geometric mean rate of return can be applied to preferred stock and bonds as well as to common stock. It should be emphasized that when comparing the historical rates of return on bonds and stocks, the same formula, that is, the geometric mean, should be used for both. This cautionary note is introduced since we now turn our attention to an alternative, and much better known formula, for calculating the yield to maturity of a bond. The two should not be confused.

2.2 BOND YIELDS

The investor contemplating the purchase of a bond is often concerned with the rate of return which the bond offers if held to maturity, independent of fluctuations in the bond's price during the interim period. An insurance company, for example, is concerned with the *long-term* return which can be earned on bonds currently purchased, since the rate of return is an important

---

[1] See Chapter III.

2. ALTERNATIVE FORMULATIONS OF THE YIELD ON BONDS 101

factor influencing the terms which the company is able to offer new policy-holders; similarly, many investors contemplating the purchase of a bond are concerned with the yield such a bond affords if held to maturity. The rate of return, when a bond is held until redemption, is called its "yield to maturity" or "redemption yield," and is given by a simple application of the familiar formula for the internal rate of return:[2]

$$P_0 = \frac{C_1}{1+k'} + \frac{C_2}{(1+k')^2} + \cdots + \frac{C_n}{(1+k')^n} + \frac{R_n}{(1+k')^n}$$

$$= \sum_{t=1}^{n} \frac{C_t}{(1+k')^t} + \frac{R_n}{(1+k')^n}$$

where: C_t = the interest coupon in period t
P_0 = the current market price of the bond
R_n = the redemption value of the bond at maturity
k' = the yield to maturity of the bond.

In practice the calculation of yields to maturity is a relatively simple matter since detailed bond tables are available which eliminate all of the tedious arithmetic necessary to calculate the yield. Using the sample bond table pages given in Table IV-1 we can easily "calculate" the yield to

Years and months   TABLE IV-1

Yield	19–5	19–6	19–7	19–8	19–9	19–10	19–11	20–0
0.00	197.08	197.50	197.92	198.33	198.75	199.17	199.58	200.00
0.25	189.97	190.35	190.72	191.10	191.48	191.85	192.23	192.61
0.35	187.21	187.58	187.94	188.30	188.66	189.02	189.38	189.74
0.40	185.85	186.21	186.56	186.92	187.27	187.62	187.98	188.33
0.45	184.50	184.85	185.20	185.55	185.89	186.24	186.59	186.93
0.50	183.17	183.51	183.85	184.19	184.53	184.87	185.21	185.54
0.55	181.84	182.18	182.51	182.84	183.17	183.51	183.84	184.17
0.60	180.53	180.86	181.18	181.51	181.83	182.16	182.48	182.81
0.65	179.23	179.55	179.87	180.18	180.50	180.82	181.14	181.46
0.70	177.94	178.25	178.56	178.87	179.19	179.50	179.81	180.12
0.75	176.66	176.97	177.27	177.58	177.88	178.19	178.49	178.80
0.80	175.39	175.69	175.99	176.29	176.59	176.88	177.18	177.48
0.85	174.14	174.43	174.72	175.01	175.30	175.60	175.89	176.18
0.90	172.89	173.18	173.46	173.75	174.03	174.32	174.60	174.89
0.95	171.66	171.94	172.22	172.49	172.77	173.05	173.33	173.61
1.00	170.43	170.71	170.98	171.25	171.52	171.80	172.07	172.34
1.05	169.22	169.49	169.75	170.02	170.29	170.55	170.82	171.09
1.10	168.02	168.28	168.54	168.80	169.06	169.32	169.58	169.84
1.15	166.82	167.08	167.34	167.59	167.85	168.10	168.36	168.61
1.20	165.64	165.89	166.14	166.39	166.64	166.89	167.14	167.39

[2] See Chapter III.

Years and months TABLE IV-1 (Continued)

Yield	19–5	19–6	19–7	19–8	19–9	19–10	19–11	20–0
1.25	164.47	164.72	164.96	165.20	165.45	165.69	165.93	166.18
1.30	163.31	163.55	163.79	164.02	164.26	164.50	164.74	164.98
1.35	162.16	162.39	162.63	162.86	163.09	163.32	163.55	163.79
1.40	161.02	161.25	161.47	161.70	161.93	162.15	162.38	162.61
1.45	159.89	160.11	160.33	160.55	160.77	161.00	161.22	161.44
1.50	158.77	158.98	159.20	159.42	159.63	159.85	160.07	160.28
1.55	157.65	157.87	158.08	158.29	158.50	158.71	158.92	159.13
1.60	156.55	156.76	156.97	157.17	157.38	157.58	157.79	158.00
1.65	155.46	155.66	155.86	156.06	156.27	156.77	156.67	156.87
1.70	154.38	154.58	154.77	154.97	155.16	155.36	155.56	155.75
1.75	153.30	153.50	153.69	153.88	154.07	154.26	154.45	154.64
1.80	152.24	152.43	152.61	152.80	152.99	153.17	153.36	153.55
1.85	151.18	151.37	151.55	151.73	151.91	152.09	152.28	152.46
1.90	150.14	150.32	150.49	150.67	150.85	151.02	151.20	151.38
1.95	149.10	149.28	149.45	149.62	149.79	149.96	150.14	150.31
2.00	148.07	148.24	148.41	148.58	148.75	148.91	149.08	149.25
2.05	147.05	147.22	147.38	147.55	147.71	147.87	148.04	148.20
2.10	146.04	146.21	146.36	146.52	146.68	146.84	147.00	147.16
2.15	145.04	145.20	145.35	145.51	145.66	145.82	145.97	146.13
2.20	144.05	144.20	144.35	144.50	144.65	144.80	144.96	145.11
2.25	143.07	143.21	143.36	143.51	143.65	143.80	143.95	144.09
2.30	142.09	142.23	142.38	142.52	143.66	142.80	142.95	143.09
2.35	141.12	141.26	141.40	141.54	141.68	141.81	141.95	142.09
2.40	140.16	140.30	140.43	140.57	140.77	140.84	140.97	141.11
2.45	139.21	139.34	139.47	139.60	139.73	139.86	140.00	140.13
2.50	138.27	138.40	138.52	138.65	138.75	138.90	139.03	139.16
2.55	137.33	137.46	137.58	137.70	137.83	137.95	138.07	138.20
2.60	136.41	136.53	136.65	136.76	136.88	137.00	137.12	137.24
2.65	135.49	135.61	135.72	135.83	135.95	136.07	136.18	136.30
2.70	134.58	134.69	134.80	134.91	135.02	135.14	135.25	135.36
2.75	133.67	133.78	133.89	134.00	134.11	134.22	134.33	134.44
2.80	132.78	132.89	132.99	133.09	133.20	133.30	133.41	133.52
2.85	131.89	131.99	132.09	132.19	132.30	132.40	132.50	132.60
2.90	131.01	131.11	131.21	131.30	131.40	131.50	131.60	131.70
2.95	130.14	130.23	130.33	130.42	130.52	130.61	130.71	130.80
3.00	129.27	129.36	129.45	129.55	129.64	129.73	129.82	129.92
3.05	128.41	128.50	128.59	128.68	128.77	128.85	128.94	129.04
3.10	127.56	127.65	127.73	127.82	127.90	127.99	128.07	128.16
3.15	126.72	126.80	126.88	126.96	127.05	127.13	127.21	127.30
3.20	125.88	125.96	126.04	126.12	126.20	126.28	126.36	126.44
3.25	125.05	125.13	125.20	125.28	125.36	125.43	125.51	125.59
3.30	124.23	124.30	124.38	124.45	124.52	124.59	124.67	124.75
3.35	123.41	123.49	123.55	123.62	123.69	123.76	123.84	123.91
3.40	122.60	122.67	122.74	122.81	122.87	122.94	123.01	123.08
3.45	121.80	121.87	121.93	122.00	122.06	122.13	122.19	122.26
3.50	121.00	121.07	121.13	121.19	121.25	121.32	121.38	121.45
3.55	120.22	120.28	120.34	120.40	120.45	120.51	120.58	120.64
3.60	119.43	119.50	119.55	119.61	119.66	119.72	119.78	119.84
3.65	118.66	118.72	118.77	118.82	118.88	118.93	118.99	119.04
3.70	117.89	117.95	117.99	118.05	118.10	118.15	118.20	118.26

2. ALTERNATIVE FORMULATIONS OF THE YIELD ON BONDS   103

Years and months

Yield	19–5	19–6	19–7	19–8	19–9	19–10	19–11	20–0
3.75	117.13	117.18	117.23	117.28	117.32	117.37	117.43	117.48
3.80	116.37	116.42	116.47	116.51	116.56	116.61	116.65	116.70
3.85	115.62	115.67	115.71	115.75	115.80	115.84	115.89	115.94
3.90	114.88	114.92	114.96	115.00	115.05	115.09	115.13	115.18
3.95	114.14	114.18	114.22	114.26	114.30	114.34	114.38	114.42
4.00	113.41	113.45	113.49	113.52	113.56	113.60	113.64	113.78
4.05	112.68	112.72	112.76	112.79	112.82	112.86	112.90	112.94
4.10	111.97	112.00	112.03	112.06	112.10	112.13	112.17	112.20
4.15	111.25	111.29	111.32	111.34	111.38	111.41	111.44	111.47
4.20	110.55	110.58	110.60	110.63	110.66	110.69	110.72	110.75
4.25	109.84	109.88	109.90	109.92	109.95	109.98	110.01	110.04
4.30	109.15	109.18	109.20	109.22	109.25	109.27	109.30	109.33
4.35	108.46	108.49	108.51	108.53	108.55	108.57	108.60	108.62
4.40	107.78	107.80	107.82	107.84	107.86	107.88	107.90	107.93
4.45	107.10	107.12	107.14	107.15	107.17	107.19	107.21	107.23
4.50	106.42	106.45	106.46	106.47	106.49	106.51	106.53	106.55
4.55	105.76	105.78	105.79	105.80	105.82	105.83	105.85	105.87
4.60	105.10	105.11	105.12	105.13	105.15	105.16	105.18	105.19
4.65	104.44	104.46	104.46	104.47	104.48	104.50	104.51	104.57
4.70	103.79	103.80	103.81	103.82	103.83	103.84	103.85	103.86
4.75	103.14	103.16	103.16	103.17	103.17	103.18	103.19	103.20
4.80	102.50	102.51	102.52	102.52	102.53	102.53	102.54	102.55
4.85	101.87	101.88	101.88	101.88	101.88	101.89	101.90	101.91
4.90	101.24	101.25	101.25	101.25	101.25	101.25	101.26	101.27
4.95	100.61	100.62	100.62	100.62	100.62	100.62	100.62	100.63
5.00	100.00	100.00	100.00	99.99	99.99	99.99	100.00	100.00
5.05	99.38	99.38	99.38	99.37	99.37	99.37	99.37	99.38
5.10	98.77	98.77	98.77	98.76	98.76	98.75	98.75	98.76
5.15	98.17	98.17	98.16	98.15	98.15	98.14	98.14	98.14
5.20	97.57	97.57	97.56	97.55	97.54	97.54	97.53	97.53
5.25	96.97	96.97	96.96	96.95	96.94	96.93	96.93	96.93
5.30	96.39	96.38	96.37	96.36	96.35	96.34	96.33	96.33
5.40	95.22	95.21	95.20	95.18	95.17	95.16	95.15	95.14
5.50	94.07	94.06	94.05	94.03	94.01	94.00	93.99	93.98
5.60	92.95	92.94	92.91	92.89	92.88	92.86	92.85	92.84
5.70	91.84	91.82	91.80	91.78	91.76	91.74	91.72	91.71
5.75	91.29	91.27	91.25	91.23	91.21	91.19	91.17	91.15
6.00	88.62	88.60	88.56	88.54	88.51	88.49	88.46	88.44
6.50	83.58	83.55	83.51	83.47	83.44	83.40	83.37	83.34
7.00	78.93	78.90	78.85	78.80	78.76	78.72	78.68	78.64

maturity of a bond with, say, a 5% coupon and 20 years remaining to maturity. If the offering or market price is 100 (that is, 100% of face value) the yield is 5%. If the market price is above the face value of the bond, for example, 110, the yield can be found by running down the 20 year column of the appropriate page of the bond table until 110 is found and then glancing across to the left-hand column to find the yield. In this particular case the yield to maturity is approximately 4.25%.[3] Similarly, should the same bond be selling at a discount from face value, for example, $969.30 (96.93% of face value) the yield to maturity will be greater than the coupon yield in this instance 5.25%.

3. THE RISKS OF BONDS

It is convenient for our purposes to view the yield on bonds as being composed of two parts: the pure or certain rate of interest, reflecting the underlying forces of the economy as whole which determine the price of money *now* in exchange for money at some later date, plus a risk premium. The latter reflects at least three distinct types of risk:

> (a) Credit risk—the chance that the bond issuer will default on either the payment of interest and/or the redemption of principal.
>
> (b) Purchasing power risk—the risk of a decline in the "real value," that is, in the purchasing power, of the bond's interest and principal.
>
> (c) Interest rate risk—the risk of an increase in the market interest rate during the period in which a bond is held.

3.1 CREDIT RISK

A bond is in effect a legal commitment on the part of the bond issuer to make periodic payments of interest and principal to the bondholder. By its very nature, such an obligation raises the possibility that the issuer will default on one or more such payments; that is, the issuer either will be unable to make, or will be compelled to request a postponement of, the payment. By convention we ignore such possibilities in the case of government obligations, since a government cannot go bankrupt in terms of its own currency.[4] The latter qualification is necessary since foreign governments may find it impossible to meet their legal obligations to make the payments on dollar loans or loans in any currency other than their own. Thus with respect to

---

[3] The bond tables themselves are simply very elaborate present value tables which reflect the payment of interim interest and permit a very accurate calculation of the yield. If the exact bond price does not appear in the table, the correct yield can be found by interpolation.

[4] A sovereign government is not subject to *involuntary* insolvency in its own currency since the option of creating additional currency sufficient to meet its domestic obligations always exists.

3. THE RISKS OF BONDS

U.S. government bonds we shall ignore the possibility of default. This is equivalent to identifying the interest rate on U.S. government obligations of a given maturity as the pure rate of interest on such loans.

Agency Ratings

With regard to corporate bonds a significant credit risk often exists and the investor is confronted with the problem of assessing the probability of default of alternative investment opportunities and weighing them against the risk premium (higher yield) offered. Often the investor lacks the time, the inclination, or the ability to attempt an independent assessment of the investment quality of the myriad of corporate bonds available in the market. One way out of this dilemma is to consult one of the bond rating agencies, such as Moody's or Standard and Poor's, which regularly publish their evaluations of the quality of a firm's outstanding bonds. Moody's, for example, rates corporate bonds from Aaa, comprising "gilt edge" bonds of minimal credit risk, to C, which includes bonds of a speculative nature offering only minimal assurance that obligations will be successfully met in the future. Standard and Poor's uses the same principle but a slightly different notation, with AAA designating its highest rating.

Used as an initial screening device, the agency ratings have some obvious advantages, especially for the investor who is concerned with avoiding speculative securities in his bond portfolio. It is extremely unlikely that an independent analysis will transform a bond whose agency-rating is "speculative" into a "gilt-edge" or high quality bond. On the other hand, a high agency rating at time of issue does not constitute a guarantee that the bonds will retain their initial investment quality (and therefore, their rating) until redemption.[5]

Independent Analysis

Using the agency ratings as a starting point the analyst (or investor) can carry out an independent evaluation of the credit worthiness of the corporate securities in question. Essentially this requires an estimate of the probability of default on payments of either interest or principal. Unfortunately, the outside analyst is rarely in a position to acquire all of the data required for such an analysis, but even when limited to the ex-post data of firms' annual

---

[5] The interested reader should consult W. B. Hickman, *Corporate Bond Quality and Investors' Experience*, New York: National Bureau of Economic Research, 1958. For the period 1900–1943 Hickman showed that over 40% of the highest rated bonds and over 50% of those in the next three categories were downgraded subsequent to their issue. Of course it should be noted that Hickman's study reflects the Great Depression of the 1930s, which imparts an upward bias to the results.

balance sheets and income statements, some useful rule-of-thumb tests can be carried out. The results can then be used to effect interfirm comparisons at a given point of time, and intertemporal comparisons within a given firm.

Before attempting a quantitative analysis, attention should initially be directed to the bond indenture which sets out the detailed provisions of the bond issue. The issuing company can, and often does, enhance the investment quality of its bonds by introducing a number of protective provisions into the bond indenture.[6] Perhaps the best known means of modifying the risk of a bond issue is the inclusion of a "pledge of assets" clause in the indenture. Mortgage bonds, for example, have priority over other debtors with regard to the mortgaged assets. Risk may also be reduced by including a "negative pledge," for example a limitation on the creation of additional debt in general, or on the creation of additional debt with prior or equal status to the bonds in question. On the other hand, the investment quality of bonds can be reduced by issuing them as "subordinated debentures," that is, bonds which are placed in a secondary position with respect to otherwise equal debts. The latter provision is not uncommon in corporate reorganizations in which the firm's debtors have no recourse other than to accept the lesser of two evils—a subordinated position in the reorganized company or bankruptcy proceedings.

The "economics" of bankruptcy proceedings have led to a deemphasis of the various collateral provisions. The value of the pledged assets shows an unfortunate tendency to shrink drastically at the time of bankruptcy so that the holder of the defaulted bonds can rarely be compensated in full. Moreover, the assets of a modern corporation are often highly specific and the very fact of bankruptcy suggests that the present value of the future earnings that can be derived from the assets, and therefore, their value, is likely to be very low. But even in cases where a substantial proportion of the debt can be recovered, the legal processes are often prolonged over a number of years.

Recognition of the limited protection that asset pledges afford has led to the inclusion of clauses designed to protect the bondholder by means of restrictions placed on the corporation's activities subsequent to the bond issue. Thus, for example, restrictions may be placed on the size of dividend payments to the common stockholder if certain minimum standards regarding the size of earned surplus or working capital are not met. The indenture also sets out the method of redemption, for example, redemption of a fixed proportion of the issue each year, or the purchase on the open market of a

---

[6] The reader should be cautioned that the presence of such provisions does not guarantee strength, nor does their absence necessarily indicate weakness. On the contrary, very large corporations such as AT&T are often able to forgo many of the protective provisions without impairing the quality of the bond issue.

3. THE RISKS OF BONDS

fixed proportion of the issue each year, and so on. Here again, the indenture agreement may stipulate a change (presumably acceleration) of redemption schedules if certain conditions are not met. Similarly, conditions under which the bondholders are given control of the company may also be included.

Turning to the company's financial statements the analyst has recourse to a number of simple tests of the firm's ability to meet its financial obligations. Clearly, the number of permutations is quite large, but we shall restrict ourselves to the more widely used of the financial ratios. Perhaps the most popular measure of ability to pay is the *times interest earned ratio*, or *coverage ratio*:

$$\frac{\text{Earnings before Interest and Taxes}}{\text{Total Bond Interest}}$$

Thus for example if we assume the following hypothetical financial data:

> Earnings before Interest and Taxes $1,000,000
> Interest Payments 250,000

the times interest earned ratio is 4, in other words, the interest obligation is "covered" four times by pre-tax earnings. The problem is slightly more complicated if several classes of bonds (for example, senior bonds and a junior issue) are outstanding. Here care must be exercised to avoid misrepresenting the comparative strength of the two issues. In our example if we assume that the interest obligations were as follows:

> Interest on senior bonds $200,000
> Interest on junior bonds 50,000

the average ratio on all interest obligations is, as we have already seen, 4. If the inappropriate *prior deductions* method is employed we find that the coverage of the senior bonds, taken alone, is 1,000,000/200,000 = 5, but should we then deduct the senior interest from earnings the coverage of the remaining junior bonds becomes $800,000/50,000 = 16. Such an approach implies that the junior bonds are much better protected than the senior obligations. A more appropriate approach is to examine successively the coverage ratios of the senior bonds as above, followed by an examination of the coverage ratio of the *cumulative combination* of the senior and junior obligations. Thus in our example the coverage of the senior obligation is

$$\frac{\$1,000,000}{\$200,000} = 5$$

Using the cumulative method the coverage of the junior bonds is

$$\frac{\$1,000,000}{\$200,000 + 50,000} = 4$$

Since the firm incurs an obligation to redeem the principal of the bonds as well as to pay the interest, many analysts prefer to use a *total coverage ratio* or *burden coverage ratio*, which relates the firm's pre-tax earnings to the combined principal and interest payments:

$$\frac{\text{Earnings before Interest and Taxes}}{\text{Interest} + \text{Principal Payment}\,(1/1 - T)}$$

where T = the appropriate federal tax rate. The tax adjustment is necessary since the redemptions of principal, unlike the interest payments, are *not* deductible for tax purposes. Thus if we assume a 50% tax rate and annual principal payments of \$200,000, the amount of *pre-tax* earnings necessary to meet the redemption obligation is 200,000 $(1/1 - 0.50)$ = \$400,000, and the burden coverage ratio is

$$\frac{\$1,000,000}{\$250,000 + 400,000} \simeq 1.5$$

A similar line of reasoning applies to preferred dividend payments, which again are not deductible for tax purposes. Thus the effective burden of, for example, \$175,000 of annual preferred dividends in terms of pre-tax income is \$175,000 $(1/1 - 0.50)$ = \$350,000, and the burden coverage ratio becomes

$$\frac{\$1,000,000}{\$250,000 + \$400,000 + \$350,000} = 1$$

Of course this type of ratio analysis provides at best a rough rule of thumb calculation of the firm's ability to meet its fixed charges out of current income. A more comprehensive analysis would require an examination of the firm's cash and capital budgets, but these data are not generally available to the outside analyst. Moreover, no absolute standard is available to assess the coverage ratios. Thus we have no objective standard which can be used to determine the adequacy of a burden ratio of, say, 2 to 1 or 3 to 1.[7] However, where the ratios are available over a period of time, they can be usefully compared over time within the same company. And even when the time series is short, the results can be compared with other companies within the industry or with industry averages.

Similarly, ratio analysis can be applied to various other balance sheet items in order to get a rough idea of a firm's liquidity. Thus the firm's working capital (current assets minus current liabilities) can be examined

---

[7] Hickman's study for the National Bureau of Economic Research, *op. cit.*, does provide some basis for evaluating the adequacy of various average ratios with respect to the period 1900–1943.

over time and compared with that of other firms; the current ratio (current assets divided by current liabilities) also provides a rough measure of the firm's ability to pay its current debts out of its current assets. And finally, some idea can be gained of the protection afforded to holders of prior claims in case of insolvency by checking on the firm's capital structure; if a firm's equity comprises 75% of its total capitalization, the debtors are "protected" to the extent of a 75% fall in the value of the assets. But again the reader must be cautioned that assets have a disconcerting habit of shrinking drastically during liquidation.

3.2 PURCHASING POWER RISK

In addition to a premium to cover the financial risk of default, the yields on fixed-income securities also reflect the risk of a general rise in consumer prices during the lifetime of the contract. Such a premium becomes necessary since creditors (bondholders) suffer a real economic loss when consumer prices rise. Inflation reduces the purchasing power of the fixed nominal amounts (interest and return of principal) which the bondholder is entitled to receive; hence the need for a premium to induce him to give up present money in return for a promise to receive a fixed amount of future money.[8]

The role of purchasing power risk can be clarified by using the well known distinction between the "money" (nominal) and "real" rates of interest.[9] The former, as its name implies, measures the rate of interest in terms of money, while the latter measures the rate of interest in terms of the command over commodities, that is, in terms of the purchasing power of money. Unless the general price level remains stable during the duration of the loan, the two rates are not identical. Consider, for example, an investor who buys a newly issued bond for the sum of A dollars. For simplicity, we assume that the bond is issued for one year at a money rate of interest of i. Now let us

---

[8] When uncertainty regarding the purchasing power of money becomes very great, investors may become unwilling to acquire fixed-income bearing securities unless an explicit purchasing power guarantee is added to the contract. Thus the worldwide inflation during and after the Second World War brought forth a spate of investments whose interest and/or principal were linked to various price indexes. Such purchasing power guarantees have become quite common in Finland, Israel, and many other countries; see Marshall Sarnat, *The Development of the Securities Market in Israel*, Basel, Switzerland: Kyklos-Verlag, 1966, pp. 35–42.

[9] We owe this distinction to Irving Fisher, *The Rate of Interest*, New York: Macmillan, 1907. The algebraic formulation and discussion of the text are taken from Don Patinkin, "Secular Price Movements and Economic Development: Some Theoretical Aspects," in *The Challenge of Development*, edited by A. Bonné, Jerusalem: The Hebrew University, 1958, p. 28.

assume that the initial price level is equal to p, but that the price level at the end of the year is expected to be $(1 + g)p$, where $g =$ the rate of change of prices. In "real" terms the investor has given up A/p units of commodities in return for a promise to receive $(1 + i)A/(1 + g)p$ units at the end of the year, and the "real" rate of interest on the bond is given by:

$$1 + m = \frac{(1 + i)A/(1 + g)p}{A/p} = \frac{1 + i}{1 + g}$$

where m denotes the real rate of interest. By cross-multiplying this equation we obtain:

$$m = i - g - mg$$

which reduces to the following familiar form when m and g are small:

$$m \simeq i - g$$

Thus the real rate of interest can be approximated by deducting the expected increase in the general price level from the nominal rate of interest.

Consider the following simplified numerical example.

Let $A = \$100$
$p = 100$
$i = 10\%$
$g = 5\%$

In this example the investor loans \$100 at a nominal interest rate of 10%, and therefore expects a gross return of \$110 (principal plus interest) at the end of the year. However, if he anticipates an inflationary rise in prices, the \$110 at the end of the year will *not* represent a 10% increase in his command over commodities; the real rate of interest, given an expected rise in prices of 5%, is slightly less than 5%:

$$m = 0.10 - 0.05 - 0.0024 = 0.0476 = 4.76\%$$

If we consider a more extreme case, in which prices are expected to rise by 10%, the real rate becomes zero; and if the rate of price increase *exceeds* the money rate of interest, the real rate is negative; that is, the bondholder gives up *more* current purchasing power than he receives at the end of year. Thus if the general level of consumer prices is increasing the real rate is less than the money rate; conversely, when prices are decreasing the real rate exceeds the money rate.

Since individuals invest their savings to enhance their eventual command over consumer goods, strong expectations of inflation undermine the willingness to loan money (buy bonds) at a *given* nominal interest rate. As a result, bond prices will tend to fall and yields to rise until the investing public

3. THE RISKS OF BONDS

is offered a nominal interest return sufficiently high to ensure the desired real rate of interest. It is in this sense that the yields on fixed-income bearing securities reflect a purchasing power risk premium in addition to the previously discussed credit risk premium.

3.3 INTEREST RATE RISK

Now let us abstract from credit and purchasing power risks in order to isolate yet a third type of risk. If we glance back at the formula for yield to maturity we can readily verify that an inverse relationship exists between interest yields and bond prices. This relationship can best be seen by considering the rate of interest on a perpetuity, that is, a bond whose principal is not redeemable.[10]

$$P_0 = \frac{C}{1+k} + \frac{C}{(1+k)^2} + \frac{C}{(1+k)^3} + \cdots$$

$$= \sum_{t=1}^{\infty} \frac{C}{(1+k)^t}$$

This is an infinite geometric progression with the common factor $1/(1 + k)$. Summing the progression yields

$$P_0 = \frac{C}{1+k} \cdot \left[1 + \frac{1}{1+k} + \frac{1}{(1+k)^2} + \cdots \right]$$

$$= \frac{C}{1+k} \cdot \frac{1}{1 - \frac{1}{1+k}} = \frac{C}{k}$$

Transposing terms we derive the well known relationship for the yield of a nonredeemable bond:[11]

$$k = \frac{C}{P_0}$$

Given the coupon interest C, the yield k varies inversely with the bond's price; in other words, the higher the price the lower the yield and vice versa.

---

[10] Perhaps the best known example of a perpetuity is provided by the British government "consols" issued to finance the war against Napoleon.

[11] The same formula holds for a nonredeemable preferred stock as well:

$$k = \frac{D}{P_0}$$

where D denotes the annual dividend payment.

Since the interest coupon is fixed for the duration of the bond contract (in this particular case, forever) any fluctuations in the market's *required* yield will be reflected by changes in the price of the bond. For example, consider a 6% nonredeemable bond which was originally issued at a price of 100:

$$P = 100 = \frac{C}{k} = \frac{6}{0.06}$$

Now let us assume that for any number of reasons the market rate of interest on bonds of a similar type rises to 8%. Since the new bonds (which by definition are perfect substitutes for the outstanding bonds) are now being issued at 8%, investors will not agree to buy (or hold) the old bonds unless their yield is equalized to that of the new bonds, but this can be accomplished only if their price falls sufficiently to raise their yield to 8%:

$$k = 0.08 = \frac{6}{75}$$

In this instance the price will fall to $75. Similarly, should the market interest rate (on identical obligations) fall, for example, to 4%, the price of the outstanding bonds will rise to $150, at which price the yield on the old bonds is also 4%.

$$k = 0.04 = \frac{6}{150}$$

These results reflect the fundamental principle that in a perfectly efficient market identical products cannot sell at different prices. Of course in practice, tax considerations, transactions costs, and other imperfections may preclude the exact equalization of yields, but such deviations are usually small and do not obscure the fundamental price adjustment mechanism. In fact in the absence of the need to equalize yields we would not have an explanation of the observed fluctuations of the prices of bonds having no default risk. Thus a drastic fall in U.S. government bond prices does not reflect a weakening of confidence in the government's ability to meet its obligations, but rather a rise in market interest rates which, among other things, might reflect a strengthening of the government's anti-inflationary policy.

The inverse relationship between interest rates and bond prices is not without significance for both individual and institutional investors. Clearly a rise in interest rates implies the availability in the market of higher yields on bond investments. But as we have already noted, the rise in interest rates is not an unmixed blessing, since investors who hold a portfolio of previously issued bonds suffer a "loss" owing to the fall in the market price of the older bonds induced by the rise in interest rates. This loss takes the form of a realized capital loss in the event that the bonds are sold or of an "opportunity

3. THE RISKS OF BONDS

loss" of income in the event that the low yielding bonds are retained in the portfolio.

For convenience we have used the example of a nonredeemable bond to illustrate the inverse relationship between bond prices and interest yields, but the analysis can readily be generalized to include bonds of any maturity. A bond, in general, combines a series of future interest payments with the more remote payment of principal. Discounting this stream of payments to its present value, using the required market yield, we derive the price of the bond. But as the cash flow (interest and principal) is fixed for the lifetime of the bond, a rise (fall) in the required yield again implies, other things being equal, a fall (rise) in the bond's price. Put another way, a set of observed bond prices implies a set of interest yields; conversely, given the required market rates of interest we can derive the relevant set of prices.

However, once we consider bonds of differing maturities, another systematic relationship between bond prices and yields can be discerned. Although the inverse relationship between bond prices and yields holds for all maturities, the extent of the impact of a given change in market interest rates on bond prices depends on the maturity date. In general the induced price change will be greater, the longer the remaining duration of the bond. This relationship is illustrated in Table IV-2, which sets out the prices of a 6% coupon bond of varying maturities for alternative market rates. Note that the price of the bond equals 100 for all maturities when the relevant market rate is assumed to be 6%. However, should the rate of interest rise (fall), the differential fall (rise) in price is greatest for bonds of longer maturities. Thus a rise in interest rates to 8% induces a less than 2% fall in the price of a one year bond (from $100 to $98.15) as compared with a price drop of almost 20% (from $100 to $80.41) in the case of a 20 year bond. Conversely, the windfall gain in the event of a fall in interest rates is again greatest for the longer term bonds.

For the investor who desires to avoid the risk of loss—and bond investors are generally considered to be averse to risk—long-term bonds are considerably more vulnerable to the risk of a rise in interest rates than their short-term counterparts. This has some interesting implications for investment analysis. For example, if we define a liquid asset as one which can readily be converted into a *known* amount of money, we can identify two necessary conditions for liquidity:[12]

    (a) marketability, and
    (b) certainty of capital value—there must be only a minimal risk of capital loss.

---

[12] To the degree that liquidity is held to meet *nominal* obligations, purchasing power considerations can be ignored.

TABLE IV-2. Price of a one hundred dollar 6% coupon bond at alternative market rates of interest, by maturity* (in dollars)

Years to Maturity	Market Rate of Interest			
	4%	6%	8%	12%
1	101.97	100.00	98.15	94.66
2	103.82	100.00	96.40	89.84
3	105.55	100.00	94.86	85.61
4	107.28	100.00	93.37	81.83
5	108.91	100.00	92.06	78.32
8	113.50	100.00	88.48	70.21
10	116.27	100.00	86.56	66.10
15	122.21	100.00	82.85	59.17
20	127.14	100.00	80.41	55.22
30	134.55	100.00	77.44	51.63
40	139.56	100.00	76.15	50.56
50	142.30	100.00	75.50	50.12
∞	150.00	100.00	75.00	50.00

*Coupon Interest is assumed to be payable at end of the year.

The latter condition is equivalent to demanding that the asset be riskless, that is, that there be no risk of default, but as we have just seen, this also means that even with regard to such bonds only those of very short maturities can qualify as liquid assets.

4. THE TIME PATTERN OF YIELDS: THE YIELD CURVE

At any point in time the yields on bonds will differ chiefly for two reasons:

(a) differences in duration, and
(b) differences in the risk of default.

Abstracting from the latter we can concentrate on the yield–maturity relationship by considering bonds which are identical in every respect but

4. THE TIME PATTERN OF YIELDS: THE YIELD CURVE

maturity. The family of outstanding U.S. Treasury issues provides such a population for studying the time patterns of yields.[13]

At first glance it would appear that liquidity considerations alone should be sufficient to determine the yield–maturity relationship. Such an approach suggests that a "premium" will exist for giving up liquidity so that the yield on long-term bonds will be above the yield of shorter-term bonds. This "liquidity preference" explanation is often identified with the work of Keynes, who viewed the rate of interest as the "reward for parting with liquidity."[14] Equivalently, such an approach suggests that a graphic portrayal of the yield–maturity relationship for otherwise identical securities, at any given point of time, will result in a monotonically rising "yield curve." Such a curve is illustrated in Figure IV.1, and represents the hypothetical time structure of bond yields for a given class of bonds on a particular date.

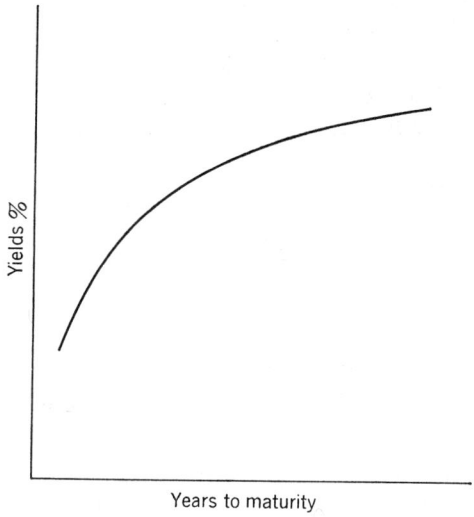

FIGURE IV.1.

[13] Strictly speaking, the yields on government securities of a given maturity provide a homogeneous population only when all the bonds are selling at par. Owing to the differential taxation of interest income and capital gains, the pre-tax yields of two bonds with the *same* post-tax yield will tend to differ where one of the bonds is selling at a discount from par. For an analysis of this tax effect and the bias which it introduces into the observed yield curve, see A. A. Robichek and W. D. Niebuhr, "Tax-Induced Bias in Reported Treasury Yields," *Journal of Finance* XXV (December 1970).

[14] J. M. Keynes, *The General Theory of Employment, Interest and Money*, New York: Harcourt, Brace, 1936, Chapter 13.

Years to maturity are measured along the horizontal axis and yield to maturity is measured in percentage along the vertical axis.

The simplified liquidity considerations which we have sketched above are, however, not sufficient in themselves to account for the time pattern of interest rates. Historically, three additional types of yield curves have been observed in the capital market. At various times during the past 70 years, the yield curve has been (a) monotonically decreasing—the yields on long-term maturities were *below* those of short-term maturities; (b) "humped"—the yield curve rises between short- and intermediate-term bonds and then declines for longer-term maturities; (c) stable—the yield curve remains flat as the yields on short- and long-term securities are the same. These three additional varieties of yield curve, decreasing, humped, and flat, are illustrated in Figure IV.2.

The yield curve is a simplified graphical representation of the yields of a given risk class of securities on a particular day. From time to time the yield curve may change, and in fact all of the types of yield curves illustrated in Figures IV.1 and IV.2 have been observed at one time or another. Figure IV.3 sets out the yield curves for corporate bonds which were calculated by David Durand for the first four decades of the century.[15] It is apparent from

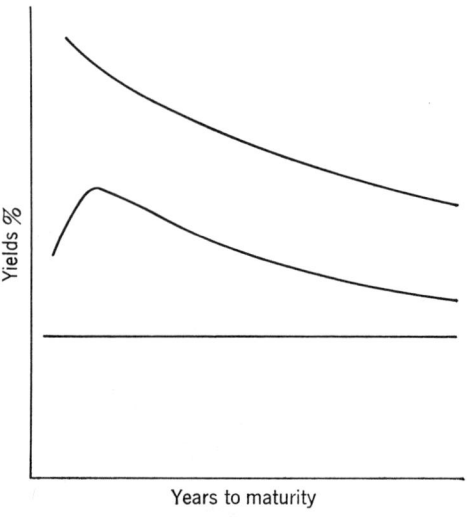

FIGURE IV.2.

the diagram that the upward sloping yield curve, which represents a situation in which long-term yields exceed short-term yields, cannot be considered to

[15] See D. Durand, *Basic Yields of Corporate Bonds 1900–1942*, Technical Paper No. 3, New York: National Bureau of Economic Research, June 1942.

4. THE TIME PATTERN OF YIELDS: THE YIELD CURVE ||||||||||||||||| 117

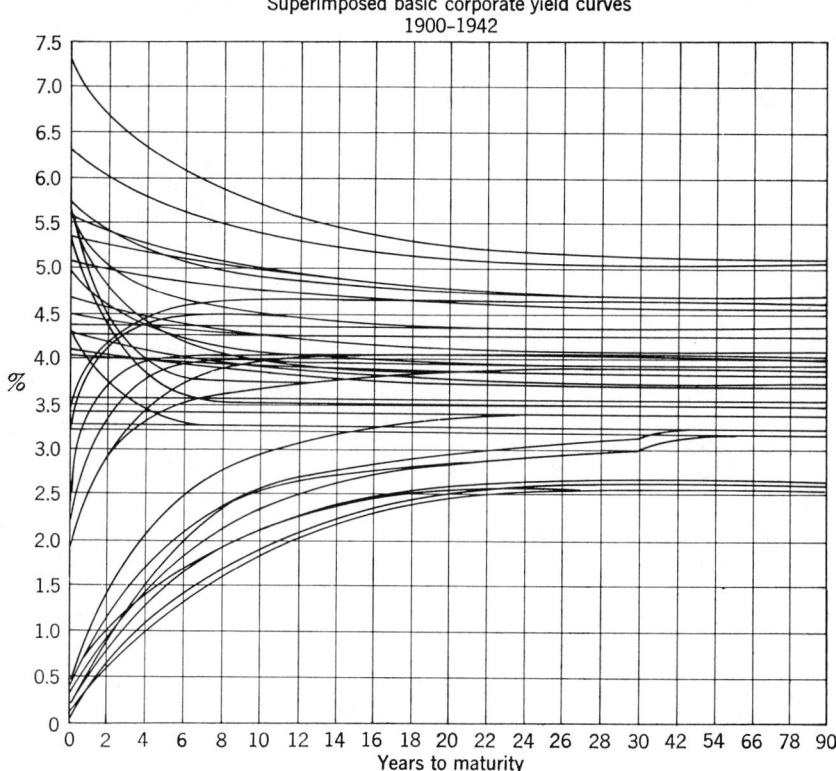

FIGURE IV.3. Source: David Durand, *Basic Yields of Corporate Bonds, 1900–1942*, National Bureau of Economic Research, Technical Paper 3, June, 1942.

constitute the "normal" relationship, at least from the statistical point of view; while it is true that for the period 1900–1960, for which data are available, yield curves have been on the average positively sloped, negatively sloped or humped curves have not been uncommon.[16] In general, short-term rates have tended to be high relative to long-term rates at the peaks of the business cycle, while the opposite relationship, that is, low short-term rates relative to long-term rates, has existed at cyclical troughs.[17]

Theory can be reconciled with these empirical findings, even within the

---

[16] See R. A. Kessel, *The Cyclical Behavior of the Term Structure of Interest Rates*, Occasional Paper No. 91, New York: National Bureau of Economic Research, 1965.
[17] *Ibid.*, p. 4.

framework of liquidity preference, by explicitly introducing expectations regarding the future level of interest rates. The so-called expectations hypothesis is especially popular among economists; well known variants have been expounded by Fisher, Keynes, Hicks, and Lutz.[18] In what follows we shall set out two highly simplified alternative views of expectations which can be used to reconcile the empirical evidence regarding the slope of the yield curve.[19]

To bring out the crucial role played by expectations let us make the following simplifying assumptions:

(a) Future short-term rates are known with certainty.

(b) There are no transaction costs of borrowing or lending.

(c) Lenders and borrowers enjoy complete shiftability among bonds of different maturities; that is, an investor is indifferent between the purchase of a ten year bond or ten purchases of one year bonds.

Under these assumptions the yield on all investments taken for a given period will be equalized, independent of whether we deal with an investment which is for the life of the period or a series of short-term investments repeated several times over the period in question. Competition in the market will ensure that under these assumptions the sum to which a dollar accumulates over n years at the long-term rate R_n must be equal to the future value which accumulates over n years using the short-term rates $r_1, r_2, \ldots, r_n$:

$$1 + R_1 = 1 + r_1$$
$$(1 + R_2)^2 = (1 + r_1)(1 + r_2)$$
$$\vdots$$
$$(1 + R_n)^n = (1 + r_1)(1 + r_2) \cdots (1 + r_n)$$

From these relationships we can derive the appropriate formula for the long-term rate.

Since investors must receive the same capital sum by accumulating two periods at the rate R_2 or one period at r_1 and a second period at the *forward*

---

[18] A convenient summary of the expectations hypothesis can be found in F. A. Lutz, *The Theory of Interest*, Dordrecht, Holland: D. Reidel Publishing Co., 1967, Chapter 17.

[19] For more detailed discussions of the expectations hypothesis see J. R. Hicks' classic analysis in his *Value and Capital*, 2nd ed., Oxford: Oxford University Press, 1953, Chapter 11; and B. G. Malkiel, "Expectations, Bond Prices, and the Term Structure of Interest Rates," *Quarterly Journal of Economics*, Vol. 76 (May 1962).

4. THE TIME PATTERN OF YIELDS: THE YIELD CURVE

rate r_2, the long-term rate is the geometric average of the relevant forward short rates:

$$R_1 = (1 + r) - 1$$
$$R_2 = \sqrt[2]{(1 + r_1)(1 + r_2)} - 1$$
$$R_3 = \sqrt[3]{(1 + r_1)(1 + r_2)(1 + r_3)} - 1$$
$$\vdots$$
$$R_n = \sqrt[n]{(1 + r_1)(1 + r_2)(1 + r_3) \cdots (1 + r_n)} - 1$$

Using this formula we can also infer the expected forward short-term rates from the existing long-term rates. For example, the expected short-term rate r_3 is derived as follows:

$$1 + r_3 = \frac{(1 + R_3)^3}{(1 + R_2)^2}$$

Viewing the long-term rate as an average of the expected short-term rates yields the following conclusions, which can help to reconcile the existence of the differing shapes of the yield curve discussed above.

(1) If the short-term rates are expected to remain unchanged, all long-term rates will equal the short-term rates.

(2) If at a given point in time the (geometric) average of the expected short-term rates up to the maturity date of the long-term bond is above the current short-term rate, the long rate will be above the short rate.

(3) If the (geometric) average of short rates increases as additional time periods are considered, (that is, $r_2 > r_1$, $r_3 >$ average r_1 and r_2, and so on) the yield curve will be monotonically increasing. If after a given period the future short rates remain unchanged, the yield curve will eventually flatten out.

(4) Conversely, if at a given moment, the (geometric) average of the expected short-term rates is below the current short-term rate, the long-term rate will be *below* the short-term rate, and by using a line of reasoning similar to that used in (3) above, the yield curve will be downward sloping, if the expected short-term rates are expected to fall.

Thus by introducing "expectations" all types of yield curve—upward sloping, stable, downward sloping, or for that matter any combination of the three, can be rationalized.[20]

---

[20] For a more detailed and critical evaluation of the expectations hypothesis see Lutz, *op cit*.

It should be noted that no automatic mechanism exists to equalize the rates themselves, but that such a mechanism does exist to keep them consistent. Thus, should the long-term rate exceed the average of expected future short-term rates, it would pay to borrow short and buy a long-term bond. But the increased demand for short-term loans would raise the short-term rate while the increased demand for long-term bonds would raise their price, thereby lowering the long-term yield, and the process would continue until the long-term rate equals the average of future expected short-term rates.

From the standpoint of investment analysis, the assumption that investors estimate short-term rates into the distant future is not intuitively appealing.[21] However, the expectations hypothesis can be restated in terms of future long-term rates in a manner which is consistent with the previous presentation.[22] According to this approach the short-term rate will lie below the long-term rate, on liquidity considerations, when the long-term rate is expected to remain stable. The difference between the two rates will be even greater when investors expect future long-term rates to rise, since they anticipate a future capital loss on long-term bonds currently acquired, and therefore demand an "additional" risk premium. Only when the current long-term rate appears abnormally high so that long-term rates are expected to fall in the future will the current short-term rate lie above the long-term rate. Such an approach combines liquidity preference and expectations considerations[23] and, in addition, provides a more appealing explanation of the term structure in which investors are assumed to have explicit expectations regarding future long-term rates.[24]

The yield curve is a subject of considerable theoretical appeal, but it is not without significance for the intelligent investor. An understanding of the forces which determine the term structure of interest rates goes a long way toward dispelling the popular belief that the investment in bonds is less risky than the investment in other securities. At a time of volatile changes in expectations, the magnitude of the changes in long-term bond prices can be (and has been) dramatic. Moreover, it is difficult to conjure up a field in which the professional analyst has a greater comparative advantage over his untutored counterpart. Intuition is simply not enough to explain what often appear to be bewildering changes in bond prices and yields.

---

[21] See D. G. Luckett, "Professor Lutz and the Structure of Interest Rates," *Quarterly Journal of Economics*, Vol. 73 (1959).
[22] Hicks, *op. cit.*, pp. 151–52.
[23] On the explanatory power of such a hypothesis, see Kessel, *op. cit.*
[24] For a verbal proof of the equivalence of the two approaches, see Lutz, *op. cit.*, p. 219.

5. OTHER FEATURES OF FIXED-INCOME SECURITIES

Several other characteristics of bonds and preferred stock are of special interest to investors. In particular, attention should be directed to specific provisions regarding early redemption and the possibility of conversion to other types of securities, both of which may materially affect our evaluation of bonds and preferred stock as investment media.[25]

5.1 RETIREMENT PROVISIONS

As we have already noted, the bond indenture sets out the method and timing of redemption payments. In the case of *serial bonds* a given amount of an issue matures periodically. For example, if we assume that $100 million of serial bonds were issued in 1970, 10% of the original issue ($10 million) might mature each year, commencing in 1980. Note that the average maturity of the bonds is 15 years, but by purchasing these bonds selectively, the investor can choose the exact maturity he desires. However, more often than not bonds mature on the same date but a *sinking fund* provision is included in the indenture, which stipulates that the issuing corporation will make periodic sinking fund payments for the purpose of retiring the bond issue. Many variants exist: the bonds to be retired may be purchased on the open market, drawn at random and purchased at a fixed "call" price, or the sinking fund may be left intact with a trustee until the final redemption date. In the case of early redemption, the actual bonds which will be retired often cannot be identified in advance. This can prove inconvenient to the investor, especially one who acting on his expectations of future interest rate movements, acquired the bonds to increase the average maturity of his bond portfolio, only to have them called for sinking fund redemption at a time when interest rates have fallen. This disadvantage may be more or less offset by the protection against default which the sinking fund affords.

In the case of preferred stock, a sinking fund appears to be of considerably more significance since in its absence a preferred stock is a perpetuity, that is, it has no redemption date. In effect, the sinking fund provision is tantamount to issuing redeemable preferred shares; depending on an investor's expectations regarding the course of future yields, such a feature may or may not

---

[25] We ignore voting rights, which are of paramount importance to those who seek effective control over a corporation but of only secondary interest to most investors.

be desirable. However the importance of the sinking fund feature has declined somewhat, since almost all firms issuing preferred stock now add a *call provision* to the preferred contract, as do many firms issuing bonds.[26]

5.2 CALL PROVISION

The call feature gives the company the right to repurchase its securities at a call price during all, or part, of the period that the bonds are outstanding. The call price itself is almost invariably fixed above par, with the price declining according to a scale, fixed in advance, as the maturity date approaches. Clearly the call privilege has value to the issuing company; should interest rates decline the company will be able to retire the older and presumably high interest bearing issue at a fixed price, using the proceeds of a new lower interest bearing issue for this purpose. The company's ability to take advantage of this privilege depends on the prices (yields) of the bonds, the call price, and the costs of flotation. Thus the value of the call privilege to the firm depends on its expectations regarding the direction and magnitude of future fluctuations of interest rates. The greater the expectation of a fall in interest rates, the greater the value the firm places on the call provision.[27]

Just as clearly the call privilege constitutes a disadvantage to investors, with the degree of disadvantage again depending on the call price, flotation costs, and the course of future interest rates. Given a fixed call price of for instance 106% of par value, there exists an upper limit to an investor's possible capital gain. No matter how steep the fall in interest rates, the market price of the bond cannot rise much above the call price of 106, since beyond that price (plus a premium to cover flotation costs) the company is likely to exercise its privilege of repurchasing the bonds at the call price of 106. Thus when interest rates are considered high (for example at cyclical peaks) the issuing firm will have to offer higher yields in order to induce investors to accept a given call privilege; similarly, institutional investors will press for higher call prices and/or for the deferment of the call privilege for a maximum number of years after issue.

---

[26] A recent study of 932 nonconvertible preferred issues during the period 1950–1965 showed that all 932 issues had some form of discretionary redemption provision. See D. E. Fischer and G. A. Wilt, Jr., "Non-Convertible Preferred Stock as a Financing Instrument 1950–1965," *Journal of Finance* XXIII (September 1968), p. 616.

[27] See G. Pye, "The Value of the Call Option of a Bond," *Journal of Political Economy* (April 1966).

5. OTHER FEATURES OF FIXED-INCOME SECURITIES

5.3 CONVERTIBILITY

In recent years a hybrid security—a bond or preferred stock which is convertible, at the option of the holder, into common stock—has become increasingly popular.[28] Numerous variants of convertible securities can be found, but typically the conversion feature gives the bondholder or preferred shareholder the privilege of converting his senior security into common stock under specific conditions, which are stipulated in advance. These conditions include:

> (a) the *conversion ratio*—the number of shares of common stock for which each bond (or preferred share) can be exchanged, and
>
> (b) the *conversion price*—the effective price paid for the common stock at the time of exchange.

In practice, the convertibility clause can be set out either in terms of the conversion ratio or in terms of the conversion price, since given the one, the second can be readily derived using the formula

$$\text{Conversion Price} = \frac{\text{Face Value of the Bond}}{\text{Number of Shares Received}}$$

Conversion terms are usually fixed for the duration of the bond; however, a rising scale of conversion prices is sometimes used. Similarly, provision is also made to adjust the conversion price (ratio) in the event of stock splits or rights offerings.[29] Almost invariably the conversion price is set above, and often considerably above, the current market price of the common stock so that the value of the conversion privilege depends on the future course of common stock prices.

Insight into the desirability of the investment in convertibles can be gained by first considering the motives of the issuing company. It appears that most companies issuing convertible securities have their eventual conversion into equity in mind. To such firms the convertibles represent an indirect raising of equity capital at tomorrow's prices since the conversion price becomes effective only after a rise in ths price of the common stock. This desire to raise equity capital manifests itself in the inclusion of a call provision in the

---

[28] See Robert R. McKenzie, "Convertible Securities 1956–1965," *Quarterly Review of Economics and Business* VI (Winter 1966); W. J. Baumol, B. G. Malkiel, and R. E. Quandt, "The Valuation of Convertible Securities," *Quarterly Journal of Economics* 80 (February 1966); and E. F. Brigham, "An Analysis of Convertible Debentures: Theory and Some Empirical Evidence," *Journal of Finance* 21 (March 1966).
[29] On the need for such adjustments, see Chapter II.

convertible contract. The call feature permits the company to force conversion once the price of the common has risen sufficiently to raise the conversion value of the convertibles above the call price. In the absence of the call feature, any capital gains accruing from the rise in common stock prices could be taken by selling the convertibles rather than converting them to common stock.

A less common motivation for the use of convertibles is the desire to add a "sweetener" to the firm's bonds. Some companies find it difficult to raise debt capital at reasonable terms unless they offer investors an additional inducement in the form of possible future capital gains. To this end a conversion clause may be added, or *warrants*, which grant the bondholder the option to purchase a given number of common shares at a fixed price, may be attached to the bonds. The warrants may be detachable, in which case they can be sold independently of the bond, or nondetachable, in which case the warrant can be detached from the bond only when the option is exercised. An expiration date for the option is also usually stipulated.

From the standpoint of the issuing firm it would appear that the higher the conversion (or option) price, the better. However the setting of conversion or option prices is a tricky business. For the company which issues convertibles in lieu of common stock, too high a conversion price may mean that the actual conversion of the bonds will be deferred for years. In the interim the firm loses a degree of financing freedom, since it is difficult to float additional convertibles, and even nonconvertible securities, while the old issue is still outstanding. Similarly, when used as a sweetener for a debt issue the terms of conversion, or the option price in the case of warrants, cannot be too remote from current reality if the sweetener is to have an effect on the required yield of the bonds.

From the standpoint of the investor a convertible bond or preferred share, or one with warrants attached, appears to offer "the best of all possible worlds." Such a bond, for example, combines the security and income stability of the debt contract with the speculative opportunities afforded by common stock. Thus should the price of the common rise above the bond's conversion price, the investor shares in the capital gain, but should the common fail to rise, he can always fall back on his bond.

The element of truth in this description lies in the fact that a convertible security does offer the investor a sort of hedge position between the risks of acquiring the common stock outright and the forgoing of such investment completely. Thus should the floor drop out from under the common stock and the value of the conversion privilege become zero, the convertible bond would still retain much, but not all, of its value as a straight bond. Security markets rarely offer something for nothing, and convertibles are no exception. One must presume that a convertible bond is issued at a higher price (that is, on a lower yield basis) than a comparable nonconvertible issue—the difference being the premium paid for the conversion feature. Thus should the value of the conversion right drop to zero, the investor will incur a capital loss, since the bond price will fall until it is selling on a yield basis which equals that of comparable nonconvertible bonds.

6. SUMMARY

This chapter has set out some of the basic considerations underlying the decision to invest in fixed-income securities—bonds and preferred stock. The formula for calculating the rate of return on common stock, presented in Chapter III, is generalized to cover preferred stock and bonds, and an alternative measure of return, yield to maturity, is introduced. The risks of investment in fixed-income securities are also analyzed, and the use of agency ratings and ratio analysis to evaluate credit—that is, default—risk is discussed. Attention is also directed to the purchasing power risk, stemming from possible rises in consumer prices, which attaches to fixed-income investments. Nominal and real interest rates are distinguished and the relationship between them is spelled out in some detail. Next the inverse relationship between bond prices and bond yields is presented within the context of an analysis of yet a third type of risk—the risk of a rise in interest rates.

The differential impact of given changes in market interest rates on the prices of bonds of varying maturities is pointed out, and the time pattern of interest rates is analyzed with the aid of the concept of a "yield curve." Such a curve is a simple graphical representation of the yields on a particular class of bonds of varying maturity on a particular date. Four types of yield curve are distinguished:

(a) monotonically increasing
(b) monotonically decreasing
(c) "humped"
(d) stable

These alternative shapes of the yield curve, all of which have been observed at one time or another, can be accounted for within the framework of "liquidity preference" by explicitly introducing investors' expectations regarding the future course of interest rates. Using this approach we conclude that:

(a) The short-term rate will lie below the long-term rate owing to liquidity considerations when the long-term rate is expected to remain stable.

(b) The difference between the two rates will be even greater should investors expect the long-term rate to rise, since this is tantamount to the expectation of a future capital loss on long-term bonds currently acquired.

(c) However, when future long-term rates are expected to fall, the current short-term rate can rise above the current long-term rate.

Several other features of bond indentures, or of preferred stock contracts, which are of interest to investors are also discussed. Attention is directed to retirement provisions, sinking fund payments, and the callability and convertibility features which are often attached to fixed-income securities and which are of significance for the investor.

QUESTIONS AND PROBLEMS

4.1 Distinguish between the rate of return to investors in bonds and the yield to maturity.

4.2 What are the relevant formulas for computing the yields on non-redeemable bonds and preferred stock?

4.3 What is the counterpart in a preferred stock of the "credit risk" of a corporate bond?

4.4 Define the following features of a bond indenture:

(a) pledge of assets

(b) "negative pledge"

(c) sinking fund provision

(d) call feature

4.5 Consider the case of an investor about to acquire a $1,000 one year bond, which for simplicity we assume pays interest on the last day of the year. The interest coupon on the bond is 5%. Assuming that the investor requires a 5% return *in real terms*, what price will he offer for the bond if he assumes that the consumer price level will be 3% higher at the end of the year? How does your answer change if we assume that he expects the price level to fall by 3%?

4.6 "A given set of observed interest yields implies a particular set of bond prices." Appraise this quotation.

4.7 If allowance is made for special features such as tax exemption, callability, convertibility, and so on, the yields on high grade corporate bonds usually change along with the change in the interest rate on government bonds of similar maturity. In the Great Depression of the early 1930s the prices of high grade corporate bonds fell while at the same time the prices of government bonds rose. How do you account for this phenomenon? Be specific.

4.8 "The fact that in recent years the yield on short-term government bonds has often been above the long-term rate is conclusive evidence that the liquidity premium in those years was negative." Do you agree? If not, can you offer an alternative explanation for the observed pattern of yields?

4.9 Given the following expected short-term rates:

$$r_1 = 5\%$$
$$r_2 = 6\%$$
$$r_3 = 8\%$$

What will be the price of a $100 5% coupon bond redeemable at the end of three years? (For simplicity assume that the annual interest payments are made on the last day of the year.) What forces exist in an efficient market which ensure that this price will in fact be determined?

4.10 From the information that the existing long-term rates for two and three year bonds are R_2 and R_3 respectively, can you infer the expected short rate for, say, the third year? (Hint: calculate the short-term yield, r_3, *in terms* of the two long-term rates.)

4.11 Explain why a yield curve which includes U.S. government bonds and municipal bonds will give biased results.

4.12 What is the "cost" to the investor of the convertibility feature of a bond or preferred stock?

4.13 How can the following be expected to affect an investor's "valuation" of a call feature, sinking fund provision, and convertibility to common stock provision of a bond:

    (a) he expects future interest rates to fall;
    (b) he expects interest rates to rise;
    (c) the consumer price level is expected to rise significantly.

SELECTED REFERENCES

Baxter, N. D., "Marketability, Default Risk, and Yields on Money Market Instruments," *Journal of Financial and Quantitative Analysis* (March 1968).

Buse, A., "Expectations, Prices, Coupons and Yields," *Journal of Finance* (September 1970).

Chen, A. H. Y., "A Model of Warrant Pricing in a Dynamic Market," *Journal of Finance* (December 1970).

Cohen, J. B., and Zinbarg, E. D., *Investment Analysis and Portfolio Management*. Homewood, Ill.: Irwin, 1967.

Freund, W. C., *Investment Fundamentals*. New York: American Bankers Association, 1966.

Graham, B.; Dodd, D. L.; Cottle, S., and Tatham, C., *Security Analysis*, 4th edition. New York: McGraw-Hill, 1962.

Grossman, H. I., "Risk Aversion, Financial Intermediation, and the Term Structure of Interest Rates," *Journal of Finance* (December 1967).

Hickman, W. B., *Corporate Bond Quality and Investors' Experience*. New York: National Bureau of Economic Research, 1958.

Hicks, J. R., *Value and Capital*, 2nd edition. Oxford: Oxford University Press, 1953.

Kessel, R. A., *The Behavior of the Term Structure of Interest Rates*, Occasional Paper No. 91. New York: National Bureau of Economic Research, 1965.

Keynes, J. M., *The General Theory of Employment, Interest and Money*. New York: Harcourt, Brace, 1936.

Lerner, E. M., and Carleton, W. T., *A Theory of Financial Analysis*. New York: Harcourt, Brace & World, 1966.

Lutz, F. A., "The Structure of Interest Rates," *Quarterly Journal of Economics* (1940–1941), reprinted in the American Economic Association, *Readings in the Theory of Income Distribution*, Philadelphia: Blakiston, 1949.

―――, *The Theory of Interest*. Dordrecht, Holland: D. Reidel, 1967.

Malkiel, B. G., "Expectations, Bond Prices, and the Term Structure of Interest Rates," *Quarterly Journal of Economics* (May 1962).

McKenzie, R. R., "Convertible Securities 1956–1965," *Quarterly Review of Economics and Business* (Winter 1966).

Meiselman, D., *The Term Structure of Interest Rates*. Englewood Cliffs, N.J.: Prentice-Hall, 1962.

Michaelsen, J. B., "The Term Structure of Interest Rates and Holding-Period Yields on Government Securities," *Journal of Finance* (September 1965).

Pease, F., "The Warrant—Its Power and Its Hazards," *Financial Analysts Journal* (Jan.–Feb. 1963).

Pilcher, J. C., *Raising Capital with Convertible Securities*. Ann Arbor, Michigan: Bureau of Business Research, University of Michigan, 1955.

Pye, G., "The Value of the Call Option of a Bond," *Journal of Political Economy* (April 1966).

———, "The Value of Call Deferment on a Bond: Some Empirical Results," *Journal of Finance* (December 1967).

Robichek, A. A., and Niebuhr, W. D., "Tax-Induced Bias in Reported Treasury Yields," *Journal of Finance* (December 1970).

Samuelson, P. A., "Rational Theory of Warrant Pricing," *Industrial Management Review* (Spring 1965).

Sarnat, M., *The Development of the Securities Market in Israel*. Basel, Switzerland: Kyklos-Verlag, 1966.

Sauvain, H., *Investment Management*, 3rd edition. Englewood Cliffs, N.J.: Prentice-Hall, 1967.

Shelton, J. P., The Relation of the Price of a Warrant to the Price of Its Associated Stock," *Financial Analysts Journal* (May–June and July–August 1967).

Soldofsky, R. M., "Ex Ante and Ex Post Yields on Bonds: Concepts and Measurements," *Mississippi Valley Journal of Business Economics* (Spring 1970).

Stevenson, R. A., "Retirement of Non-Callable Preferred Stock," *Journal of Finance* (December 1970).

Van Horne, J. C., "A Linear Programming Approach to Evaluating Restrictions Under Bond Indenture on Loan Agreements," *Journal of Financial and Quantitative Analysis* (June 1966).

———, *Financial Management and Policy*. Englewood Cliffs, N. J.: Prentice-Hall, 1968.

Chapter V
Valuation of Securities: Common Stocks

1. INTRODUCTION

The return on common stock is uncertain and can change from period to period; it is the size of the return and the degree of fluctuation (that is, risk) which together determine the value of a share of stock to the investor. In this chapter we shall examine a number of alternative approaches to the problem of evaluating common stocks: net asset value, present value of earnings, a variant of the capitalized earnings approach using price–earnings ratios, and present value of dividends.

We then analyze the impact of growth and a firm's capital structure on the valuation process. A final element, the interaction among the returns of the securities of various companies will be deferred to Part II which treats the important problems of risk diversification and portfolio selection.

2. THE NET ASSET VALUE APPROACH

Although it is by now a commonplace to emphasize that investors "buy future earnings," it is no less true to say that they also "buy the firm's net assets." Distrust of present value formulas, the quest for "objectivity," and perhaps even nostalgia lead some analysts to place greater emphasis on the asset value factor when evaluating the investment worth of a firm's common stock.[1]

---

[1] The asset value or net worth approach is especially prevalent when the equity of nonlisted, corporations is being valued. See B. Graham; D. L. Dodd; S. Cottle; and C. Tatham. *Security Analysis*, 4th ed., New York: McGraw-Hill, 1962, Chapter 41.

TABLE V–1. Selected balance sheet data for the Mobil Oil Corporation, as of December 31, 1968

1. Current Liabilities	1,686,107,000
2. Long-term Debt	748,447,000
3. Deferred Tax Credits	192,138,000
4. Reserves (insurance, employee benefits, etc.)	157,570,000
5. Minority Interest in Subsidiaries	15,792,000
6. Capital Stock	768,396,000
7. Capital Surplus	641,362,000
8. Retained Earnings	2,710,585,000
9. Less: Treasury Stock	(−48,563,000)
10. Total Balance Sheet	$6,871,834,000

Given the accounting identity between total assets–and–total liabilities and net worth, net assets (total assets minus total liabilities), by definition, are nothing more than total net worth. Net assets or net worth can be calculated from either the asset or liability sides of the balance sheet. Table V–1 presents data on the liabilities and net worth of the Mobil Oil Corporation. The company had in 1968 total assets of $6,871,834,000; from this figure we deduct liabilities (lines 1–5) of Table V–1, which leaves:

Capital Stock[2]	719,833,000
Capital Surplus	641,362,000
Retained Earnings	2,710,585,000
Net Assets (Net Worth)	$4,071,780,000

This figure represents the total *book value* of the assets accruing to the share holders at the end of 1968. And since the company's annual report for that year indicates that 101,258,000 shares of stock were outstanding at the end of the year, net assets per share can readily be calculated by dividing the number of shares into total net assets (net worth):

$$\frac{4,071,781,000}{101,258,000} = \$40.21 \text{ per share}$$

What significance can be attributed to the figure $40.21 per share? Does it represent the "value" of the share in some objective sense? In particular, if Mobil stock is selling for more than $40, are we justified in concluding that it is overpriced? On the other hand, what if the price of the stock is significantly below the book value; does it then represent a "bargain"?

[2] Net of treasury stock.

Unfortunately, an unequivocal answer cannot be given to either of these questions. In general, no systematic relationship between book value and market price can be established. The estimate of net assets per share reflects the accounting conventions used in drawing up the balance sheet, and as we have already pointed out in Chapter II, accounting practice deviates significantly from economic theory, so that there is little reason to suppose that an accounting valuation will have a meaningful relationship to an economic valuation of the same property. It is sufficient for this purpose to consider the use of historical costs in accounting. A plant which was erected five years ago, for example, which is valued on the books today at $50 million (net of accumulated depreciation) might be worth double that amount on the open market today, owing to inflation, rise in property values, changes in local taxes, or perhaps even because oil was found under the basement. But we have no guarantee that it is not worth half or even less than half of its book value, owing to innovations, a fall in property values, or the like.

Clearly the net book value of a firm does not measure its value as a going concern, but neither does it measure its "break up" value, or the realizable value of the assets in case of liquidation. Of course there are exceptions to the rule, and some companies have a high correlation between the current market values and book values of their assets. But even in such cases one must recall that the going concern value may well be higher. All of the firm's valuable assets do not always appear on the balance sheet—for example, management, accumulated know-how, or a ten year contract to supply widgets to General Motors. Conversely, not all of the assets which do appear on the balance sheet have value—for example, an inventory of buggy whips or of mini (midi?) skirts. Moreover, in a business firm the sum of the parts rarely equals the value of the enterprise taken as a whole.

Attempts to improve the asset valuation by substituting current replacement (market) costs for historical costs lead almost invariably to the concept of present value. Consider, for example, a prime asset of any oil company—its oil producing fields. What is the market value of the proven oil reserves, which by the way typically do *not* appear in the company's balance sheet? Surely the answer must be the capitalized value of the net income which can be derived from the field over its lifetime. This brings us back to the use of discounted future cash flows when measuring the value of the firm.

3. PRESENT VALUE OF EARNINGS

This approach is based on the valuation of future earnings rather than on existing assets. The analysis of past earnings per share carried out in Chapter II was designed to lay the groundwork for a forecast of future earning power.

Past trends must be analyzed for possible breaks and the analyst must decide to what extent (if any) these past trends can be extrapolated into the future as well. Formal statistical techniques such as regression analysis can be used to make quantitative estimates of future earnings, but the prognostication of a highly uncertain future is likely to remain an art, and a very demanding one at that, *independent* of the degree of statistical sophistication which is brought to bear. A number of vital factors will always be difficult to quantify: the likelihood of future innovations; entrance of new, and changes in strategy of existing, competitors; shifts in the overall climate of the economy, and so on. These considerations suggest that investors' forecasts of future events are to a large extent subjective, and will vary from individual to individual.

Despite these serious shortcomings, the earnings forecast is favored by many analysts who prefer an admittedly rough estimate of a theoretically more appropriate concept to the more concrete, but conceptually incorrect, asset value approach. But even if we assume that the investor has made his (objective or subjective) forecast of a firm's future earning power, this information is not sufficient to reach a conclusion regarding the desirability of investing in the firm's shares. A forecast of future profitability is a necessary, but not a sufficient, condition for reaching such a decision. The outlook for the firm's future earnings must be compared with, and weighed against, the relative price of the shares. There always exists (in theory at least) a price which is sufficiently high so as to offset even the most optimistic of forecasts. Moreover, a sufficiently low current price can make the shares of a company with the smallest of growth potentials appear to be a bargain. To illustrate this method of valuation, let us assume an investor, whose cost of capital equals k, is attempting to decide whether to invest in the stock of a particular company. As a first step he calculates the *adjusted* earnings per share over the past ten years, examines the stability of earnings and their growth, and on the basis of these findings and of an analysis of the company's outlook derives an estimate of future earnings per share. For convenience let us assume that the expected earnings are constant, and equal to E per year; that these earnings will be received on the last day of each year;[3] and that the earnings will continue indefinitely into the future. What is the value of such a share to this particular investor? Given his cost of capital of k, the present value of such a share of stock can be calculated as follows:

$$V = \frac{E}{1+k} + \frac{E}{(1+k)^2} + \cdots = \sum_{t=1}^{\infty} \frac{E}{(1+k)^t} \qquad (5.1)$$

where: $V =$ the present value of the earnings stream.

---

[3] A correction to reflect the intrayear timing of the earnings does not change any of the conclusions, but does complicate the mathematics. See Appendix V–1.

3. PRESENT VALUE OF EARNINGS

Equation (5.1) can be rewritten as an infinite geometric progression with a common term $\dfrac{1}{1+k}$:

$$V = \frac{E}{1+k}\left[1 + \frac{1}{(1+k)} + \frac{1}{(1+k)^2} + \cdots \right] \qquad (5.2)$$

Summing the geometric progression within the brackets yields

$$V = \frac{E}{1+k} \cdot \frac{1}{1 - \dfrac{1}{1+k}} = \frac{E}{k} \qquad (5.3)$$

Thus the expected stream of earnings, capitalized at the investor's cost of capital, measures the share's "intrinsic" value to him. Invoking the present value rule,[4] we find that if the share's market price P is below its intrinsic value V the investor should purchase the share, since the net present value of such an investment is positive ($V - P > 0$). On the other hand, if the share's market price is greater than its intrinsic value he should not make this investment, since its net present value is negative ($V - P < 0$).

Clearly, different investors can be expected to evaluate the investment differently. Some will decide to buy the stock while others will decide not to buy, or to sell it if they already own some. This differential behavior reflects two principal factors:

> (a) Different individuals have different costs of capital so that a calculation using one discount rate may result in a negative NPV while the use of another discount rate may give a positive NPV for the same expected earnings.
>
> (b) Even if both investors have the same cost of capital, differences in their estimates of the firm's profitability may result in different investment decisions.

We can illustrate the logic of the present value approach by taking a concrete (but very unrealistic) example. An examination of the annual report of a leading U.S. manufacturing corporation, which we shall call "National Planter," shows that its earnings per share were $2.69 in the year in question. At the same time the market price for a share of National Planter was $37.25. Assume that on the basis of an analysis of the company's

---

[4] See Chapter III.

TABLE V–2.

Intrinsic Value of Share (2.69/k)	Discount Rate (percentage)
53.80	5
37.25	7.22
26.90	10
17.94	15
13.45	20

outlook we reach the conclusion that this rate of profit will continue indefinitely. Does it pay to buy the shares of National Planter, given the market price of $37.25?

Clearly, the answer to the question depends on an investor's cost of capital. Table V–2 calculates the value of a share of National Planter stock, given the constant expected earnings of $2.69 per share, for a variety of alternative assumptions regarding the discount rate. If we abstract from all transaction costs and transfer taxes, only investors whose costs of capital are lower than 7.22% will find the investment attractive. For higher discount rates, the purchase price, $37.25, exceeds the value of the capitalized earnings.

4. PRAGMATIC VALUATION: USING PRICE–EARNINGS RATIOS

The most popular method of valuation in practice is a variant of the present value of earnings approach which uses a share's Price–Earnings Ratio (hereafter referred to as PER) as a measure of a stock's *relative* price.[5] The PER gives the price of a share of stock in terms of annual earnings, that is, the number of years' earnings which the price represents. Thus in a sense the PER is analogous to the popular payback calculation used by firms in their capital investment feasibility studies.

What is the relationship of the PER method of valuation to the present value of earnings approach, which was defined in the previous section? In the present value method we assumed that the investor's cost of capital is known, and given the appropriate discount rate we calculated the economic or intrinsic value of the share. The PER approach uses the same earnings

---

[5] Its popularity can be attested to by the fact that PER figures are regularly published by all of the leading reporting services, for example, Moody's, Standard and Poor's.

4. PRAGMATIC VALUATION: USING RATIOS

per share forecast in the numerator, but uses the observed market price and solves the equation for the discount rate r, that is, for the share's internal rate of return (IRR):

$$P = \frac{E}{1+r} + \frac{E}{(1+r)^2} + \cdots = \sum_{t=1}^{\infty} \frac{E}{(1+r)^t} \qquad (5.4)$$

The internal rate of return r can be interpreted as the required rate of return on the shares of this particular company. In this model the required rate of return is a sort of average of investors' opinions, since P is determined by the market, and therefore r, which is a function of P, also reflects some average of market forces.

Equation (5.4) can also be written as a geometric progression. Summing the progression yields

$$P = \frac{E}{r} \qquad (5.5)$$

or, transposing terms,

$$r = \frac{E}{P} \qquad (5.6)$$

As is true of the IRR in capital investment analysis, an investor whose cost of capital is lower than r will find the share attractive; if his cost of capital is greater than r he will not wish to invest in these shares. In the jargon of the market and of finance literature as well, it has become a tradition to use the reciprocal of Equation (5.6)—the price–earnings ratio rather than the earnings–price ratio:

$$\frac{1}{r} = \frac{P}{E} \qquad (5.7)$$

It follows from the previous discussion that the lower the PER, other things being equal, the more attractive is the stock. And the higher the PER, the less attractive is the stock. Thus the PER is like the price of any other commodity—the lower, the better. Here the "commodity" is earnings, and the less an investor has to pay to acquire a unit of earnings, the more attractive the proposition becomes.[6]

4.1 ADJUSTING THE PRICE–EARNINGS RATIO

As already noted, the PER is readily calculated from the earnings per share figure in a company's annual report and the share's price which can be

---

[6] This holds true for *nongrowth* stocks. See Section 7.

obtained in any daily newspaper. In Chapter II we discussed at some length the need to adjust the EPS figures when studying the trends in a company's profitability. This raises the question of the desirability of adjusting the PER figures for splits, stock dividends, rights, and new issues.

Let us start with splits, stock dividends, and the stock dividend component of a rights offering, all of which require the identical treatment when adjusting EPS. The case for adjusting the PER is somewhat different. Let us take a firm whose shares are selling at $10 and which earns $1 per share, and is expected to earn $1 per share indefinitely into the future. The PER is 10/1 and its IRR is 10%. Now let us assume that the company splits its stock 2 for 1 (or equivalently declares a 100% stock dividend) on the last day of the year. What is the expected effect on the price of the company's shares?

Since the split is a technical accounting transaction which does not affect the company's total profits, but doubles the number of shares outstanding, EPS will be exactly one-half its former figure, that is, $0.50. Nor do we expect the required rate of return, 10%, to change following the technical split. As a result the expected price of a share P' can be calculated as follows:

$$P' = \sum_{t=1}^{\infty} \frac{0.50}{(1.10)^t} = \frac{0.50}{0.10} = \$5 \tag{5.8}$$

Since the expected price also falls in proportion to the split, the new PER (5/0.50) remains unchanged at 10 to 1. Thus, unlike the EPS time series, there is no need (and in fact it would be an error) to adjust the PER figure for splits or stock dividends.[7] The same conclusion holds for the stock dividend component of a rights issue, which is fully equivalent to a stock dividend or a split.

What about the adjustment for a public issue (or the new issue component of a rights issue)? Assume that instead of the split, the company of our previous example issued new shares to the public at $10 per share, thereby *doubling* the number of shares outstanding. Let us further assume that the issue took place on the last day of the year. The PER before the issue was, as we have already seen, 10/1. What is the new PER after the issue? Since insufficient time has elapsed for the investments which are financed out of the new issue to produce any income, the EPS for the year drops from $1.00 to $0.50. There is no reason, however, to expect the market to react so unfavorably to the new issue as to cause the price to fall from $10 to $5. On the

---

[7] The available empirical evidence offers strong support for the contention that the technical effect of a split or stock dividend (given the income expectation) is neutral, that is, the share's market price adjusts downward on the ex-dividend (split) date in proportion to the stock dividend or split. See, for example, C. A. Barker, "Price Effects of Stock Dividend Shares, At Ex-Dividend Dates," *Journal of Finance* XIV (September 1959), pp. 373–78.

contrary, if investors were willing to take up the issue yesterday at $10 per share, it seems reasonable to assume that *today's* price will remain at $10. But in such an event the new PER becomes 10/0.50 = 20/1, in other words, a doubling of the PER relative to the previous day. Clearly, this type of fluctuation of the PER is technical and does not reflect underlying economic forces. For this reason, where the *timing* of a new stock issue makes it necessary, the PER should be adjusted in the same way as the EPS was adjusted in Chapter II.

5. THE PRESENT VALUE OF DIVIDENDS

A fourth method used for the valuation of shares is the present value of dividends approach. Here an investor evaluates a common stock on the basis of the prospective cash flow to the investor, the stream of dividends rather than the corporate earnings. (For the moment we shall assume that the investor holds the share indefinitely, that is, we ignore the possibility of selling the share on the market.)

As before, we shall denote net earnings per share (after deduction of depreciation, interest, and taxes) by E. Cash dividends will be denoted d, with the dividend in the first year given by

$$d_1 = (1 - b)E$$

where b is the proportion of earnings which the firm desires to reinvest ($0 \leq b \leq 1$). It is clear from this definition that if the firm follows a policy of reinvesting a fixed proportion of its annual earnings, dividend payments in the following years will *not* remain constant.[8] This can be seen from the following calculation of the earnings available for distribution in the second year, assuming that the firm earns a rate of return R on the reinvested portion of the previous year's earnings:

$$E + RbE = E(1 + Rb)$$

---

[8] The dividend growth model was originally developed by John B. Williams in *The Theory of Investment Value*, Cambridge, Mass.: Harvard University Press, 1938; a modified version was presented by Myron Gordon and Eli Shapiro in "Capital Equipment Analysis: The Required Rate of Profit," *Management Science* (October 1956). A much more detailed version of the model is given in M. Gordon, *The Investment, Financing and Valuation of the Corporation*, Homewood, Ill.: Irwin, 1962. Some of the more serious pitfalls of the model are analyzed by D. Vickers, "Profitability and Reinvestment Rates: A Note on the Gordon Paradox," *Journal of Business* (July 1966).

For an exposition of the continuous case, see Appendix V–2.

If the firm follows the assumed policy of paying out a *fixed* proportion $(1 - b)$ of its annual earnings as dividends, the dividend in the second year becomes

$$d_2 = (1 - b)E(1 + Rb)$$

where d_2 denotes the dividend paid in the second year. In the third year the earnings available for allocation equal the earnings of year 2 plus the earnings on the additional investments financed out of the retention of part of the previous year's earnings. Thus the level of earnings per share in the third year will be

$$E(1 + Rb) + bE(1 + Rb) \cdot R$$

which can also be written as

$$E(1 + Rb)(1 + Rb) = E(1 + Rb)^2$$

The dividend in the third year becomes

$$d_3 = (1 - b)E(1 + Rb)^2$$

Given the investment policy, the dividend will go on increasing from year to year, so that in general the dividend in the tth year will be:

$$d_t = (1 - b)E(1 + Rb)^{t-1}$$

Having identified the components of the dividend flow, we can compute the present value of the dividends for an investor whose required rate of return is equal to k:

$$P = \sum_{t=1}^{\infty} \frac{d_t}{(1 + k)^t} = \sum_{t=1}^{\infty} \frac{E(1 - b)(1 + bR)^{t-1}}{(1 + k)^t}$$

$$= E(1 - b) \sum_{t=1}^{\infty} \frac{(1 + bR)^{t-1}}{(1 + k)^t} \tag{5.9}$$

This is an infinite geometric progression with the common factor $(1 + bR)/(1 + k)$. Summing[9] the progression yields

$$P = (1 - b)E \cdot \frac{1}{1 + k} \left[1 + \frac{1 + bR}{1 + k} + \frac{(1 + bR)^2}{(1 + k)^2} + \cdots \right]$$

$$= (1 - b)E \cdot \frac{1}{1 + k} \cdot \frac{1}{1 - \frac{1 + bR}{1 + k}} = \frac{(1 - b)E}{k - bR} \tag{5.10}$$

$$P = \frac{(1 - b)E}{k - bR}$$

---

[9] Note that $(bR < k)$ constitutes a necessary condition for the convergence of the geometric progression. Since in general $b < 1$ (that is, dividends are paid) R could be greater or smaller than k.

5. THE PRESENT VALUE OF DIVIDENDS

Denoting bR by g for growth rate, and the first year dividend by d, we derive the familiar dividend model,

$$P = \frac{(1-b)E}{k-g} = \frac{d}{k-g}$$

Now let us examine the relationship of the dividend valuation model to the PER and present value of earnings formulas presented earlier. If we assume that the rate of return which the firm realizes on the reinvestment of its retained earnings is exactly the same as the investor's required rate of return, k can be substituted for R in Equation (5.10), which gives

$$P = \frac{(1-b)E}{k-bR} = \frac{(1-b)E}{k-bk} = \frac{(1-b)E}{(1-b)k} = \frac{E}{k} \qquad (5.11)$$

This is the same result which we obtained using the PER. This is a somewhat surprising result and its meaning can be clarified by considering a simple numerical example.

The PER and the present value of dividends approaches obviously give the same results in the trivial case of a firm which has a constant stream of earnings, all of which it pays out as dividends.[10] Under these conditions the earnings and dividend approaches are the same. Assume that EPS is expected to be \$6 indefinitely and the appropriate discount rate is 10%. This gives

$$P = \sum_{t=1}^{\infty} \frac{d}{(1+k)^t} = \sum_{t=1}^{\infty} \frac{E}{(1+k)^t} = 6 \sum_{t=1}^{\infty} \frac{1}{(1+0.10)^t} = \frac{6}{0.10} = \$60$$

Since the PER is then $60/6 = 10$ we also have

$$P = \frac{E}{r} = \frac{6}{0.10} = \$60$$

using the PER rule of thumb to evaluate the stock. But what happens should the firm decide to retain 50% of its earnings for investment in projects yielding a 10% return, thereby reducing the dividend payout ratio to 50% of earnings? Using the dividend model (Equation 5.10) the value of the stock is given by

$$P = \frac{(1-b)E}{k-bR} = \frac{(1-0.5) \cdot 6}{0.1 - (0.5 \cdot 0.1)} = \frac{3}{0.05} = \$60$$

This is precisely the case assumed in Equation (5.11) above, and we can see that the value of the stock does not change, when retained earnings are reinvested at the same rate that investors use to discount future returns. As

---

[10] Since there is no *net* investment, the assumption that the earnings stream will remain stable over time makes economic sense.

a result the PER provides a valid measure of a share's value in this case as well, which might be termed *neutral growth*. But what happens to the rule of thumb if we assume "profitable" growth, that is, if we assume investment of retained earnings at a rate of return which exceeds investors' discount rates $(R > k)$? For example, assume $k = 10\%$ as before, but $R = 12\%$.[11] The resulting valuation using the dividend model is

$$P = \frac{(1-b)E}{k - bR} = \frac{0.5 \cdot 6}{0.1 - (0.5 \cdot 0.12)} = \frac{3}{0.04} = \$75$$

Here investors' evaluations rise, and therefore if the market reacts to investors' expectations the price of the share will be \$75 rather than \$60. Note that the PER in this case is $P/E = 75/6 = 12\frac{1}{2}$ and its reciprocal is 8% as compared with 10% of the previous example. Thus, using the reciprocal of the PER to estimate the rate of return for a stock with "profitable" growth imparts a downward bias to the rate of return.

This cannot be rectified by the simple expediency of redefining the dividend growth model in terms of earnings. Such an approach "double counts" by considering both the increase in future earnings generated by the investment of part of current earnings as well as the current earnings themselves.

Consider the following example[12] of a firm which pays out all of its earnings as dividends:

$$P_1 = \frac{E}{1+k} + \frac{E}{(1+k)^2} + \frac{E}{(1+k)^3} + \cdots \quad (5.12)$$

Note that $E = d$ so that (5.12) represents both a dividend *and* an earnings model. Now assume that the firm forgoes its dividend in the first year and reinvests the proceeds at $R\%$. In subsequent years all earnings are again paid out as dividends. The dividend model now becomes

$$P_2 = \frac{0}{1+k} + \frac{E + RE}{(1+k)^2} + \frac{E + RE}{(1+k)^3} + \cdots$$

$$= \frac{0}{1+k} + \frac{E_2}{(1+k)^2} + \frac{E_2}{(1+k)^3} + \cdots \quad (5.13)$$

---

[11] There is no need to consider the case where $R < k$, since a firm will not knowingly invest in projects with an expected rate of return below the market discount rate, and will prefer to pay out all of the earnings as dividends.

[12] The example is taken from M. Gordon, "Optimal Investment and Financing Policy," *Journal of Finance* 18 (May 1963), pp. 264–72.

6. DIVIDEND POLICY AND VALUATION

and as required no increase in price takes place when $R = k$, since the following relationship holds:

$$\sum_{t=2}^{\infty} \frac{RE}{(1+k)^t} \lessgtr \frac{E}{1+k} \quad \text{as} \quad R \lessgtr k$$

Now let us write the "earnings" model for the same case. Clearly it must be the same as Equation (5.13). If we add the term $E/(1+k)$ we will be double counting the investment (that is, $E/1+k$) and the fruits of the investment $\sum_{t=2}^{\infty} [RE/(1+k)^t]$. Thus if we define the dividend and earnings approaches, taking into account the investment required to generate the future income stream, both approaches come to the same thing. One advantage of the dividend approach is that it focuses attention on the cash flow to the investor, and therefore is less likely to mislead the analyst. The earnings approach requires a sophisticated adjustment to avoid double counting and provides an intuitively less satisfying measure for investors. Concentrating attention on dividends, however, suggests the existence of a direct connection between the value of the firm and its dividend policy. To this question we shall now turn.

6. DIVIDEND POLICY AND VALUATION

We have seen above that the value of a company's stock is a function of the dividend stream. Can we also conclude that the value of the stock (P) is a function of the company's dividend policy? This is an important question from the investor's point of view as well as from the point of view of management which seeks the optimal dividend policy to maximize the value of the company. Let us analyze the above question under two alternative assumptions regarding the financing of investment projects.

No External Financing

To analyze the impact of the dividend policy, let us return to the approach which argues that a stock's price is equal to the present value of the cash dividends, that is,

$$P_1 = \frac{d_1}{1+k} + \frac{d_2}{(1+k)^2} + \cdots = \sum_{t=1}^{\infty} \frac{d_t}{(1+k)^t} \qquad (5.14)$$

where d_t denotes the cash dividend distributed in year t. Let us assume the company decides not to distribute a cash dividend in the first year but to reinvest d_1 for one year, distributing in the second year $d_2 + d_1(1+R)$; that is, the company increases its second year dividend by d_1 plus the one year return on this additional investment, Rd_1.

Obviously shifting the dividend from the first year to the second year constitutes a change in dividend policy. What is the impact of this change on the value of the company's stock? Again, the answer to this question depends on the assumed reinvestment rate R. The present value of cash dividends after the change in the dividend policy is given by

$$P_2 = \frac{0}{1+k} + \frac{d_2 + d_1(1+R)}{(1+k)^2} + \sum_{t=3}^{\infty} \frac{d_t}{(1+k)^t} \qquad (5.15)$$

Subtracting (5.14) from (5.15) we get the change in the value of the stock which results from the change in dividend policy.

$$P_2 - P_1 = \frac{d_1(1+R)}{(1+k)^2} - \frac{d_1}{1+k} = \frac{d_1}{1+k}\left(\frac{1+R}{1+k} - 1\right) = \frac{d_1}{(1+k)^2}(R-k)$$

If $R = k$ (that is, if the reinstatement rate R is equal to the market required rate of return k), then the change in dividend policy has no impact on the value of the stock since $P_2 - P_1 = 0$. On the other hand if $R > k$, the reinvestment of the first year "dividend," d_1, increases the value of the shares, and if $R < k$ it decreases their value.

Notice that if the firm decides to increase its investment, we must also have an induced change in the dividend policy since we assume no external financing. In this case dividend policy is *tied* to the investment policy, and apart from the special case where $R = k$, dividend policy has a direct impact on the valuation of common stock. Since the assumption of no external financing is unrealistic, let us relax this assumption and analyze the more general case where external, as well as internal, financing is available.

External Financing Is Available

Suppose now that the company can change its investment policy without affecting its dividend policy, that is, new investments can be financed by external funds. Under this condition, and assuming a perfect market, Miller and Modigliani (hereafter referred to as M & M) have shown that the price of a company's stock is independent of its dividend policy.[13] To prove this theorem we shall use the notation of the original M & M article.

Let: $d_j(t)$ = the dividend per share paid by firm j during period t, and
$P_j(t)$ = the price (ex any dividend in $t-1$) of a share of firm j at the start of period t.

---

[13] See M. H. Miller and F. Modigliani, "Dividend Policy, Growth and the Valuation of Shares," *Journal of Business* (October 1961).

6. DIVIDEND POLICY AND VALUATION   145

As we assume perfect certainty, the price of each share must be such that the rate of return $\rho(t)$ on every share will be the same over any given interval of time; that is,

$$\frac{d_j(t) + P_j(t+1) - P_j(t)}{P_j(t)} = \rho(t) \tag{5.16}$$

and $\rho(t)$ is independent of j. Hence

$$P_j(t) = \frac{1}{1 + \rho(t)} [d_j(t) + P_j(t+1)] \tag{5.17}$$

for each j.[14]

Market forces assure that the last two equations hold. If the rate of return on one firm's shares is lower than that of the other firm's shares, investors will sell the low return firm's shares and buy the higher return firm's shares, and this process will continue until $\rho_j(t) = \rho(t)$ for all j. To analyze the impact of dividend policy on stock valuation let us reformulate (5.17) in terms of the total value of the firm rather than in terms of an individual share. Without loss of generality we drop the subscript j and introduce the following additional notations: $n(t) =$ the number of shares of record at the start of t; $m(t+1) =$ the number of new shares sold during t at the ex-dividend closing price $P(t+1)$.

It is clear from these definitions that $n(t+1) = n(t) + m(t+1)$.

Let: $V(t) = n(t)P(t) =$ the total value of the enterprise, and
$D(t) = n(t)d(t) =$ the total dividends paid during t to shareholders of record at the start of t.

Using these symbols Equation (5.17) can be rewritten as

$$V(t) = \frac{1}{1+\rho(t)} [D(t) + n(t)P(t+1)]$$

$$= \frac{1}{1+\rho(t)} [D(t) + V(t+1) - m(t+1)P(t+1)] \tag{5.18}$$

Hence the current dividend $D(t)$, the terminal value $V(t+1)$, and the term $m(t+1)P(t+1)$ seem to be the factors which determine $V(t)$. As we assume that in the future the dividends are independent of the current dividend $D(t)$, and that they are known with certainty, we may conclude that $V(t+1)$ is

---

[14] One might add that M & M do not mention that $\rho(t)$ should be the riskless rate of return. But since they assume a perfect market and full certainty (and hence there is no need to distinguish between bonds and stocks) $\rho(t)$ is in effect identical with the riskless rate of interest.

also independent of the current dividend $D(t)$, but is dependent on future dividends.

Suppose now that the company decides to invest $I(t)$ dollars in year t. The company may finance this investment by reducing $D(t)$ or by raising external capital, thereby increasing $m(t)P(t+1)$. As we can see from Equation (5.18) the dividend policy decision affects the value of the firm $V(t)$ in two ways: (a) *directly* through $D(t)$, and (b) *indirectly* through $-m(t+1)P(t+1)$.

We shall now show that in a perfect market, dividend policy has no effect on $V(t)$ since these two factors exactly offset each other. The amount of outside capital required is given by:

$$m(t+1)P(t+1) = I(t) - [X(t) - D(t)] \qquad (5.19)$$

where $X(t)$ is the firm's total net profit for period t. That is to say, the investment $I(t)$ minus the retained earnings must be financed by external capital. Substituting (5.19) in (5.18) yields

$$V(t) = n(t)P(t) = \frac{1}{1+\rho(t)}[X(t) - I(t) + V(t+1)] \qquad (5.20)$$

Thus the value of the firm is a function of the earnings $X(t)$, investment $I(t)$, and $V(t+1)$, but not a function of the current dividend $D(t)$. But since $V(t+1)$ is a function of future dividends one might conclude that although $V(t)$ is not a function of $D(t)$ it is still a function of the dividend policy in the future. But we can repeat the same reasoning for $V(t+1)$ and show that this value is independent of $D(t+1)$ and similarly $V(t+2)$ is independent of $D(t+2)$ and so on. Therefore, $V(t)$ is independent of future dividends. In sum, the level of earnings $X(t)$ is the important variable which determines the value of the firm; dividend policy (in a perfect market) is irrelevant.

Of course capital markets, in reality, are sufficiently imperfect so as to preclude the treatment of dividend policy as a mere datum, and much time and effort are expended on dividend decisions by corporate managements. Considerable evidence exists that the typical corporation has a pronounced preference for a policy which ensures an orderly continuation of the dividend rate, once it has been established.[15] The increase in the dividend rate tends to lag significantly behind a rise in earnings, and management appears to be very reluctant to cut the dividend rate, even temporarily. This policy creates a dependence on outside financing in cases where retained earnings are insufficient to meet a company's capital requirements. Given the desire to

---

[15] See John Lintner, "Distribution of Incomes of Corporations Among Dividends, Retained Earnings and Taxes," *American Economic Review* XLVI (May 1956), pp. 97–113.

7. GROWTH STOCKS

maintain the dividend rate, management, in such cases, must turn to the capital markets for investment funds, and the raising of new capital is *not* without costs. But perhaps the most important effect of dividend policy in the real world is through its "informational content." The actual behavior of corporations is consistent with the view that changes in dividend policy have an "announcement effect" on the valuation of the firm's shares. Thus, in a world of uncertainty, should fluctuations in dividends have informational content for investors, the stability and growth rate of the dividend stream would become important variables affecting investors' evaluations of share prices.[16]

7. GROWTH STOCKS

As we have shown in the previous section the dividend and earnings valuation models give the same results if we assume investment of retained earnings at the market's required rate of return. In practice most corporations do reinvest part of their current earnings; the ratio of dividends to net earnings, or "payout ratio" as it is usually called, measuring the degree of retention. The higher the dividend payout ratio the lower the relative retention. This is illustrated in Table V–3, which shows the calculation of the payout ratios for three companies in 1968. Note the very different dividend policies of the three companies: IBM paid out one-third of its net earnings as dividends against a 60% payout for Coca-Cola and 72% payout ratio for Baltimore Gas and Electric.

In all three cases retention of earnings is significant, which forces the analyst to face the question of evaluating the expected return on the investments to be financed out of the retained earnings. For as we have already

TABLE V–3. Payout ratios for three U.S. Corporations, 1968

Company	Cash Dividends (thousands of $)	Net Earnings (thousands of $)	Payout Ratio (%) (1)/(2) = (3)
IBM	292,646	871,498	34
Coca-Cola	66,620	110,325	60
Baltimore Gas & Electric	27,894	38,666	72

---

[16] Similarly tax considerations and market imperfections must be taken into account when evaluating alternative policies.

TABLE V–4. Moody's common stock averages

Year	Composite Mkt. Price $ per sh.	Earnings $ per sh.	Price Earns. Ratio	Dividend $ per sh.	Yield %	Industrials Mkt. Price $ per sh.	Earnings $ per sh.	Price Earns. Ratio	Dividend $ per sh.	Yield %	Mkt. Price $ per sh.	Earnings $ per sh.	Railroads Price Earns. Ratio	Dividend $ per sh.	Yield %
1969	262.77	15.93	16.50	8.98	3.42	313.15	17.69	17.70	0.83	3.14	93.90	7.28	12.90	4.60	4.90
1968	264.62	15.60	16.96	8.53	3.22	315.86	17.63§	17.70	9.83	3.14	93.90	7.28	12.90	4.60	4.90
1967	246.54	14.18	17.39	8.26	3.35	290.05	15.76	18.40	9.03	3.11	95.91	6.74	13.82	4.62	4.82
1966	230.88	14.79	15.61	8.25	3.57	266.77	16.78	15.90	9.17	3.44	92.65	9.34	9.92	4.45	4.80
1965	250.31	14.30	17.50	7.65	3.06	284.32	16.42	17.31	8.48	2.98	95.06	8.16	11.65	4.09	4.30
1964	235.08	12.70	18.41	7.05	3.00	258.55	14.35	18.01	7.70	2.98	94.01	6.97	13.49	3.81	4.05
1963	202.32	11.19	18.08	6.42	3.17	218.24	12.43	17.55	6.98	3.20	78.49	6.29	12.48	3.50	4.46
1962	177.87	10.20	17.44	5.99	3.37	189.95	11.10	17.11	6.43	3.39	63.39	5.73	11.06	3.36	5.30
1961	185.66	8.87	20.91	5.70	3.07	199.90	9.61	20.80	6.07	3.04	68.26	3.94	17.32	3.37	4.94
1960	155.46	8.93	17.41	5.59	3.60	173.18	9.62	18.00	6.03	3.48	62.46	4.80	13.01	3.53	5.65
1959	163.47	9.08	18.00	5.41	3.31	186.26	9.85	18.91	5.81	3.12	74.11	6.01	12.33	3.42	4.61
1958	132.02	7.79	16.95	5.29	4.01	149.81	8.31	18.03	5.75	3.84	59.29	5.82‡	10.19	3.32	5.60
1957	125.46	9.10	13.79	5.43	4.33	143.65	10.27	13.99	5.91	4.11	59.51	6.79	8.76	4.03	6.77
1953	130.55	9.25	14.11	5.31	4.07	149.41	10.35	14.44	5.81	3.89	71.56	8.33	8.59	3.94	5.51
1955	117.36	9.39	12.50	4.75	4.05	130.66	10.51	12.43	5.13	3.93	70.21	8.51	8.25	3.43	4.89
1954	80.04	7.54	11.81	4.23	4.75	95.81	8.38	11.43	4.46	4.66	51.33	6.03	8.51	3.16	6.16
1953	72.81	7.25	10.04	4.00	5.49	76.05	7.71	9.86	4.19	5.31	47.48	8.08	5.88	3.06	6.44
1952	71.73	6.80	10.55	3.94	5.49	75.63	7.18	10.53	4.20	5.55	46.35	7.69	6.03	2.72	5.88
1951	66.98	6.80	9.85	4.09	6.11	70.72	7.37	9.60	4.44	6.28	40.72	6.66	6.11	2.56	6.29
1950	56.23	7.67	7.33	3.53	6.28	57.83	8.45	6.84	3.77	6.52	33.60	7.36	4.57	2.18	6.49
1949	46.68	5.94	7.86	3.09	6.62	46.88	6.60	7.10	3.19	6.80	28.55	3.67	7.78	2.41	8.44
1948	47.46	6.48	7.32	2.74	5.77	47.50	7.03	6.76	2.78	5.85	34.23	6.19	5.53	2.06	6.02
1947	46.46	4.93	9.24	2.38	5.12	46.10	5.32	8.67	2.33	5.05	31.22	4.22	7.40	1.92	6.15
1946	51.34	3.48	14.75	2.02	3.93	49.84	3.53	14.12	1.85	3.71	41.48	2.44	17.00	2.19	5.28
1945	46.02	2.97	15.49	1.92	4.17	43.94	2.72	16.15	1.75	3.98	39.94	4.36	9.16	2.19	5.48
1944	38.12	3.15	12.10	1.84	4.83	36.57	2.73	13.40	1.67	4.57	29.51	6.58	4.48	1.99	6.74
1943	35.36	3.10	11.41	1.73	4.89	34.18	2.40	14.24	1.55	4.53	25.75	8.86	2.91	1.77	6.87
1942	26.66	3.10	8.60	1.77	6.64	25.70	2.36	10.89	1.64	6.38	18.87	9.87	1.91	1.46	7.74
1941	30.50	3.17	9.62	1.90	6.23	28.70	2.95	9.73	1.81	6.31	19.91	5.00	3.98	1.28	7.74
1940	33.84	2.67	12.67	1.78	5.26	31.76	2.59	12.26	1.67	5.26	20.16	1.98	10.18	1.08	5.36
1939	35.72	2.23	16.02	1.48	4.14	34.12	2.17	15.72	1.31	3.84	20.90	0.90	23.22	0.76	3.64
1938	33.25	1.40	23.75	1.43	4.30	32.35	1.42	22.78	1.22	3.77	19.71	d1.29	—	1.00	5.07
1937	44.04	2.79	15.78	2.04	4.63	42.04	2.86	14.70	1.94	6.61	35.63	0.78	45.68	1.44	4.04
1936	45.41	2.57	17.67	1.59	3.50	42.40	2.49	17.03	1.43	3.37	38.88	1.75	22.22	1.06	2.74
1935	32.44	1.69	19.20	1.30	4.01	30.09	1.64	18.35	1.05	3.49	26.18	d0.02	—	1.03	3.93
1934	29.74	1.17	25.42	1.21	4.07	26.47	1.00	26.47	0.90	3.40	31.11	d0.15	—	0.91	2.93
1933	26.78	0.90	29.76	1.13	4.22	22.31	0.62	35.98	0.76	3.41	28.59	d0.14	—	0.72	2.52
1932	21.05	0.43	48.95	1.50	7.13	15.43	d0.02	—	1.09	7.06	19.47	d1.01	—	1.10	5.65
1931	40.82	1.55	26.34	2.42	5.93	29.99	0.85	35.28	1.84	6.14	51.83	1.48	35.02	3.85	7.42
1930	65.90	3.08	21.40	2.93	4.45	49.26	2.23	22.09	2.38	4.83	90.77	5.77	15.73	4.95	5.45
1929	86.00	4.91	17.52	2.89	3.36	65.45	4.02	16.28	2.47	3.77	109.82	9.38	11.71	4.76	4.36

	Utilities†				N.Y.C. Banks					P/C Insurance				
Year	Mkt. Price $ per sh.	Earnings $ per sh.	Price Earns. Ratio	Dividend $ per sh.	Yield %	Mkt. Price $ per sh.	Earnings $ per sh.	Price Earns. Ratio	Dividend $ per sh.	Yield %	Mkt. Price $ per sh.	Earnings $ per sh.	Price Earns. Ratio	Dividend $ per sh.	Yield %
1969	94.55	6.92	13.66	4.61	4.88	171.93	13.19	13.03	6.40	3.72	295.14	17.28	17.08	9.94	3.37
1968	101.87	6.67	14.75	4.50	4.58	171.22	12.96§	13.24§	5.82	3.40§	277.71	17.18	16.16	8.62	3.21
1967	101.87	6.67	15.27	4.34	4.26	138.29	11.59	11.93	5.35	3.87	225.28	15.32	14.70	7.82	3.47
1966	102.90	6.30	16.33	4.11	3.99	125.20	10.65	11.76	5.06	4.04	234.39	17.36	13.50	6.85	2.92
1965	117.08	5.92	19.78	3.86	3.30	147.14	9.81	15.00	4.90	3.93	231.01	7.58	30.48	6.33	2.74
1964	108.76	5.41	20.10	3.43	3.15	153.75	9.07	16.95	4.57	2.97	239.82	9.17	26.15	6.00	2.50
1963	102.79	4.99	20.60	3.21	3.12	141.60	8.19	17.29	4.46	3.15	233.08	7.84	29.73	5.84	2.51
1962	91.50	4.73	19.34	2.97	3.25	129.85	7.97	16.29	4.30	3.31	214.40	10.53	20.36	5.31	2.48
1961	90.55	4.33	20.91	2.81	3.10	132.33	7.89	16.77	4.21	3.18	224.26	8.13	27.22	5.18	2.31
1960	69.82	4.12	16.95	2.68	3.84	101.42	8.16	12.43	3.97	3.91	162.58	9.50	17.11	4.75	2.92
1959	66.35	3.82	17.37	2.61	3.93	103.00	7.23	14.25	3.82	3.71	159.18	9.11	17.47	4.29	2.70
1958	57.96	3.63	15.97	2.50	4.31	84.39	6.34	13.31	3.76	4.46	139.07	6.56	21.20	4.08	2.93
1957	49.42	3.41	14.49	2.43	4.92	76.13	5.95	12.01	3.61	4.74	125.26	3.69	33.95	4.01	3.20
1956	49.62	3.35	14.81	2.32	4.68	78.12	5.95	13.13	3.39	4.34	127.94	5.47	23.39	3.93	3.07
1955	49.24	3.21	15.34	2.21	4.49	78.85	5.28	14.93	3.19	4.05	136.35	7.13	19.12	1.49	2.56
1954	44.30	2.94	15.07	2.13	4.81	67.70	5.07	13.35	3.04	4.49	115.93	5.50	21.08	3.35	2.89
1953	37.80	2.78	13.60	2.01	5.32	63.60	4.93	12.90	2.83	4.45	92.93	7.16	12.98	3.10	3.34
1952	35.48	2.62	13.54	1.91	5.38	60.25	4.60	13.10	2.65	4.40	89.11	7.44	11.98	2.88	3.23
1951	32.55	2.44	13.34	1.88	5.78	56.38	3.94	14.31	2.64	4.68	79.94	5.73	13.95	2.73	3.42
1950	31.23	2.62	11.92	1.76	5.64	55.71	3.78	14.74	2.50	4.49	72.60	6.04	12.02	2.46	3.39
1949	28.37	2.36	12.02	1.66	5.85	51.00	3.69	13.82	2.36	4.63	63.10	7.84	8.05	2.06	3.26
1948	27.34	2.22	12.32	1.60	5.85	50.39	3.84	13.12	2.33	4.62	55.90	7.17	7.80	1.88	3.36
1947	29.53	2.16	13.64	1.56	5.28	51.96	3.69	14.08	2.32	4.46	52.56	4.34	12.11	1.88	3.58
1946	34.05	2.19	15.55	1.43	4.20	58.78	3.94	14.92	2.20	3.74	55.61	3.09	18.00	1.83	3.29
1945	26.29	1.72	15.28	1.30	4.94	59.84	3.95	15.15	2.00	3.34	48.70	2.72	17.90	1.62	3.33
1944	20.90	1.75	11.94	1.31	6.27	54.16	3.85	14.07	1.93	3.56	43.60	2.59	16.83	1.63	3.74
1943	18.87	1.55	12.17	1.28	6.78	47.77	3.51	13.61	1.94	4.06	43.55	3.38	12.88	1.69	3.88
1942	12.92	1.40	9.23	1.26	9.75	36.11	3.05	11.84	1.95	5.40	36.64	2.00	18.32	1.71	4.67
1941	18.16	1.59	11.42	1.44	7.93	43.92	2.87	15.30	2.07	4.71	39.34	3.01	13.07	1.64	4.17
1940	25.64	1.81	14.17	1.54	6.01	47.15	2.89	16.31	2.08	4.41	36.92	2.78	13.28	1.62	4.39
1939	28.02	1.82	15.40	1.48	5.28	47.18	2.73	17.28	2.08	4.41	36.06	2.48	14.54	1.49	4.13
1938	24.27	1.42	17.09	1.50	6.18	42.19	2.79	15.12	2.10	4.98	31.67	2.48	12.76	1.36	4.30
1937	33.08	2.06	16.06	1.74	5.26	61.09	3.26	18.74	2.12	3.47	35.13	2.67	13.18	1.33	3.78
1936	40.28	2.01	20.04	1.48	3.67	59.71	3.13	18.32	2.10	3.52	38.66	2.40	16.11	1.26	3.26
1935	27.20	1.54	17.66	1.32	4.85	47.93	3.13	15.31	2.24	4.67	33.72	2.89	11.67	1.24	3.68
1934	27.84	1.22	22.82	1.60	5.75	46.28	3.76	12.31	2.57	5.55	26.88	2.78	9.67	1.05	3.91
1933	34.37	1.56	22.03	1.95	5.67	43.62	4.07	10.72	2.62	6.01	20.10	1.89	10.63	1.04	5.17
1932	36.40	2.30	15.83	2.63	7.23	49.31	4.31	11.44	3.27	6.63	17.29	0.85	20.34	1.51	8.73
1931	69.80	3.80	18.37	3.47	4.97	91.26	5.20	17.55	4.26	4.67	34.54	2.01	17.18	2.19	6.34
1930	107.67	4.59	23.46	3.55	3.30	174.53	5.80	30.09	4.69	2.69	54.64	2.56	21.34	2.32	4.22
1929	133.20	5.07	26.27	2.71	2.03	306.11	7.45	41.09	4.87	1.60	74.54	3.78	19.72	2.15	2.88

* Each stock is weighted by the number of shares currently outstanding. In computing the averages, adjustments are made for all stock splits and stock dividends, so that the series are comparable throughout the period covered. Market prices, dividends and yields are annual averages of end-of-month figures.
† Does not include American Telephone & Telegraph, which is in the composite average, however.
‡ Includes $0.68 retroactive mail pay increase.
§ Revised.

SOURCE: *Moody's Public Utility Manual*, 1970, pp. 9–10.

shown, the PER rule of thumb can serve as an adequate measure of investment worth only for the case of neutral growth, that is, when $R = k$. Where R is expected to be greater than k we can take the expected growth into account by defining the dividend growth model.

7.1 THE IBM PARADOX

In 1969 the average price–earnings ratios for various industries ranged from 13 to 18 (see Table V–4). A calculation of the PER for IBM gives a figure of 40/1. The reciprocal of 40 gives an implied capitalization rate of 2.5%. Similarly the dividend yield, d/p was less than 1%, 0.84% in the same year. All of this suggests that IBM was badly overpriced relative to other stocks in 1968, and of course, in terms of *current* earnings it was. Current earnings, however, are not relevant, since this figure neither reflects the high rate of earnings retention nor the expected rate of return on the reinvested profits.

Clearly the investor's required rate of return on IBM stock was not 2.5% (nor was it less than 1%) since perfectly safe investments in short-term U.S. government bonds yielded a better return, at a much lower level of risk. How can we evaluate IBM stock, taking growth into account?

As a first step, we calculate adjusted EPS for IBM for the ten year period 1959–1968 (see Table V–5). Since the very name IBM has become almost synonymous with growth, it is no surprise to find that its growth rate was very high. Figure V.1 plots the EPS for the same period. There can be no doubt that the high rate of growth induced the price rise which resulted in the very high PER of 40/1.

TABLE V–5. Earnings growth of IBM, 1959–1968

Year	Adjusted EPS	Growth Rate (%)
1959	1.66	—
1960	1.93	16.2
1961	2.39	23.8
1962	2.85	19.2
1963	3.39	18.9
1964	4.00	18.3
1965	4.40	10.0
1966	4.71	7.0
1967	5.81	23.4
1968	7.71	32.7

7. GROWTH STOCKS

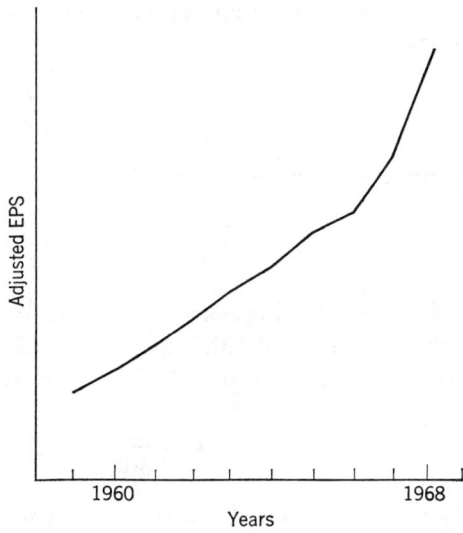

FIGURE V.1.

Since the growth rate has a cumulative effect on earnings, EPS can be estimated empirically from the following type of equation.

$$E_t = E_0(1 + g)^t \tag{5.21}$$

That is, the earnings per share in any year t is given by the EPS of the base year compounded at the growth rate over t years. To estimate the growth rate we take the logarithms of both sides of Equation (5.21), which gives

$$\log E_t = \log E_0 + t \log (1 + g) \tag{5.22}$$

This equation is linear in logarithms, with a slope equal to $\log (1 + g)$. A least-squares estimation of the slope gives $\log (1 + g) = 0.0690$; therefore, $g = 17.3\%$. Thus the estimated growth in EPS (and of dividends)[17] is 17.3% per year, as might be expected for a growth company such as IBM.

Now let us assume that we wish to estimate the investor's required rate of return in IBM shares. The naïve earnings model, which ignores growth, yields the illogical result

$$r = \frac{E_0}{P} = 2.5\%$$

[17] Assuming a *constant* payout ratio.

To estimate the required rate of return we can use the formula for a growth stock:

$$P = \frac{(1-b)E_0}{k-bR} = \frac{d_0}{k-g}$$

From this we derive

$$k = \frac{d_0}{P} + g$$

In 1968 IBM's dividend was $2.60 per share and on January 15, 1969 the price of a share of IBM stock was $308.75. Since g was estimated from the regression analysis to be 17.3%, we have

$$k = \frac{2.60}{308.75} + 0.173 = 0.181$$

That is, the required rate of return k was 18.1%.

Introducing the growth term resolves the IBM "paradox"; a required after-tax rate of return of 18.1% in 1968 is not unreasonable. Moreover, it is clear that investors bid up the price of IBM stock in anticipation of the return the company secures on its retained earnings.

Is it possible from the above data to estimate the profitability of IBM's investments? Recalling that g was estimated from the regression to be 17.3%, that by definition $g = bR$, and that by inspection $b = 60\%$ in the period in question, R can be estimated as follows:

$$g = bR$$
$$0.173 = 0.60R$$
$$R = \frac{0.173}{0.600} = 0.288 = 28.8\%$$

Thus the after-tax return on investments was 28–29% during the period. This suggests that IBM has consistently been able to earn "extraordinary" profits on its retained earnings. Of course the example is meant to be suggestive and does not represent a definitive analysis of IBM, but it does indicate the importance of introducing an explicit growth term when analyzing the profitability of the firm.

It is clear from the analysis that the accepted market rule of thumb, namely the price–earnings ratio, cannot be used to measure the relative prices of growth stocks. Moreover, since high growth is often accompanied by high risk as well, we shall see in Section 11 below that great care must be exercised when using the shortcut PER method of valuation.

8. FINANCIAL LEVERAGE

To this point we have assumed that the magnitude of the return on a firm's investments and the economic risk associated with them are fixed, and can be changed only should the firm alter its investment program. In this section we deal with an alternative means of influencing the financial risk associated with a firm's operations by means of changes in its capital structure. Here we take the investment program and the economic risk as given, and seek to determine the influence of changes in capital structure on the rate of return.

What effect does the introduction of fixed interest–bearing bonds (or preferred stock) have on the return to the shareholders and on the risk level of its common stock? To answer this question we start by considering a new company which faces a decision regarding its capital structure, that is, a decision with respect to the best debt–equity mix with which to finance its operations. For simplicity let us initially assume that there are only two mutually exclusive alternatives: (A) financing the firm with 100% equity, and (B) financing the firm with equal amounts of stock and bonds; and that there are no taxes levied on either the firm's income or the shareholders. Table V–6 sets out the relevant data for these two alternatives.

Since we are discussing two alternative financial plans for the same company, the operating income remains constant in both. Note also that the degree of economic risk attaching to these earnings must be the same in both alternatives. The net income in alternative B declines from $1,000 to $750 since (by assumption) 5% interest must be paid on the $5,000 of capital

TABLE V–6.

	Alternative A (100% equity)	Alternative B (50% bonds; 50% equity)
Net Operating Income (NOI)	$1,000	$1,000
Interest (5% on bonds)	——	250
Net Income (NI)	1,000	750
Capitalization:		
Stock	10,000	5,000
Bonds	——	5,000
Total Stocks and Bonds	10,000	10,000
Number of Shares	1,000	500
Earnings Per Share (EPS)	1.00	1.50

raised via bonds. But as fewer shares are issued in alternative B, earnings per share (EPS), which is the relevant return to the shareholders, rise in alternative B from $1.00 to $1.50. The change in EPS induced by the use of fixed payment securities to finance a company's operations is referred to as financial leverage; the bonds, in our example, serving as a lever, so to speak, which raises EPS for a given net operating income.[18] The reason for this is not hard to find: although the company pays out 5% interest on the bonds, it earns a return of 10% on the capital invested, thereby raising the return to the common shareholders. And if we introduce corporate taxes (say at the rate of 50%), net income will be reduced by one-half in both examples, and EPS (after taxes) will be $0.50 and $0.75 in alternatives A and B, respectively. The line of reasoning remains the same; although the firm pays out 5% on the bonds, the effective cost in terms of after-tax income is $(1-T)r$, where T denotes the tax rate and r the rate of interest. In our example, the after-tax cost of the debt capital is $(1-0.50)\cdot 05 = 0.025 = 2\frac{1}{2}\%$. Since the firm earns a net after-tax return of 5%, the leverage effect again results from the difference between the rate of outlay on the bonds and the rate of return earned by the company on the capital invested.

Note, however, that in the after-tax example cited, substituting a 5% preferred stock no longer creates a leverage effect. Since the *after-tax* "cost" of the preferred dividend is 5%, that is, just equal to the company's *after-tax* rate of return on invested capital, EPS after taxes is $0.50 in both cases:

	Alternative A	Alternative B
Net Income	$1,000	$1,000
Taxes	500	500
Net Income after Taxes	500	500
Preferred Dividend	—	250
Earnings Available for Common Shareholders	500	250
EPS	0.50	0.50
Number of Shares	1,000	500

Financial leverage is a two-edged sword. In the previous example we saw that the introduction of fixed interest–bearing securities in the capital structure can raise EPS, but upon reflection, it might in certain circumstances also decrease EPS. This possibility of *negative* leverage creates a new type of

---

[18] Since we are considering a case *without taxes*, substitution of a 5% preferred share for the bonds will result in the same leverage effect as the bonds.

8. FINANCIAL LEVERAGE

financial risk, in addition to the economic risk already inherent in the company's operations. How does negative leverage arise?

Surely, the firm does not *plan* to reduce EPS. The possible negative effects of leverage can be seen more clearly if we explicitly recognize that the firm's net operating income is a stochastic, or random, variable and not a constant, as might be inferred from Table V–6. (For simplicity only, we shall continue to use the example of a world with no taxes.) Although the company expects an average annual income of $1,000, this expectation is not held with certainty. In general earnings will fluctuate, so that in any given year the income from operations may be greater or less than $1,000. And of course there may also be some probability (presumably small) of incurring a loss in a particular year.

Table V–7 takes account of the possibility of fluctuations in net operating income (NOI) by calculating the EPS for both alternatives, over a wide range of possible levels of operating income. A glance at the data of Table V–7 shows that the financial leverage is positive (raises EPS) for NOI > $500, but is negative (decreases EPS) for cases in which NOI < $500. The leverage is neutral (leaves EPS unchanged) for the case in which NOI = $500. For NOI levels above $500, the firm earns a rate of return on capital invested in excess of the 5% paid to the bondholders, thereby raising EPS to the common shareholders; conversely, when operating earnings fall below $500 the firm earns less than 5% on assets, so the bondholders can be compensated only at the "expense" of the shareholders, and EPS declines.

TABLE V–7.

	Alternative A: 100% equity							
Net Operating Income (X)	1,500	1,250	1,000	750	500	250	0	−500
Interest	—	—	—	—	—	—	—	—
Net Income	1,500	1,250	1,000	750	500	250	0	−500
Number of Shares	1,000	1,000	1,000	1,000	1,000	1,000	1,000	1,000
Earnings per Share	1.50	1.25	1.00	0.75	0.50	0.25	0	−0.50
	Alternative B: 50% shares, 50% bonds							
Net Operating Income (X)	1,500	1,250	1,000	750	500	250	0	−500
Interest	250	250	250	250	250	250	250	250
Net Income	1,250	1,000	750	500	250	0	−250	−750
Number of Shares	500	500	500	500	500	500	500	500
Earnings per Share	2.50	2.00	1.50	1.00	0.50	0	−0.50	−1.50

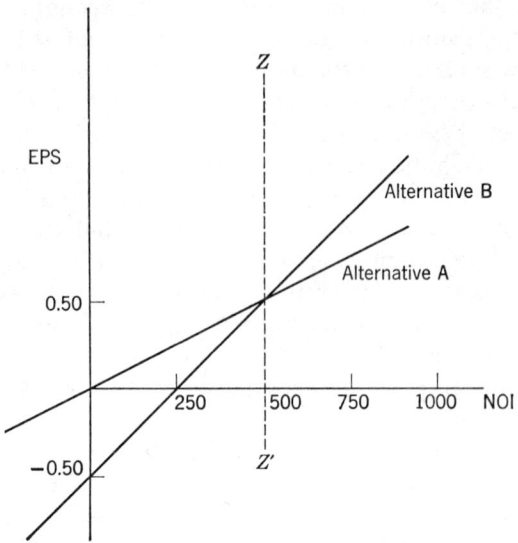

FIGURE V.2.

The differential impact of financial leverage is shown in Figure V.2, which graphs EPS as a function of NOI. The dashed line ZZ' divides the graph into two sections, all points to the right of this line representing positive leverage, and all points to the left representing negative leverage. Since risk is associated with the degree of fluctuation, the graph shows that the degree of financial risk associated with the mixed capital structure (Alternative B) is greater than that associated with the all equity structure (Alternative A). This is reflected in the steeper slope of line B, which shows that for a per unit change in NOI, the induced change in EPS is greater in the case of the levered capital structure. Despite the identical economic risk (we are making alternative assumptions about the financing of the *same* company) the introduction of leverage increases the fluctuations of EPS, which is a popular indicator of the risk associated with the investment in common stock.[19] Thus the risk incurred from an investment in the shares of the company when its capital structure is levered exceeds the risk associated with the unlevered capital structure.

This relationship can be seen even more clearly from Figure V.3, which plots the hypothetical fluctuations of EPS over time. The solid line, labeled

---

[19] The role of variability as an indicator of an investment option's risk is treated extensively in Part II.

9. LEVERAGE AND VALUATION

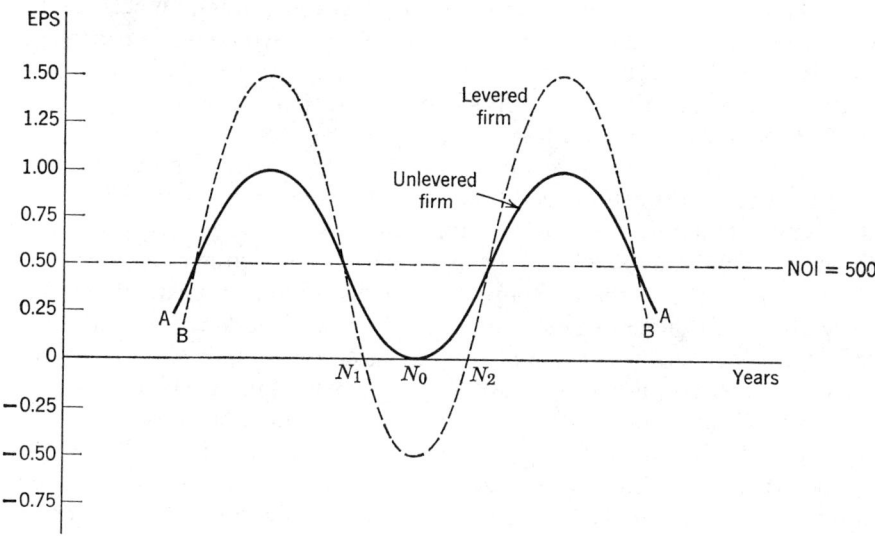

FIGURE V.3.

A, represents the assumed fluctuations when the company is financed solely by common stock; the dotted line, marked B, represents the fluctuations in EPS for the *same* operating incomes when the firm is financed by equal proportions of bonds and stock. Note that the introduction of leverage magnifies the variability of the income stream to the shareholders in both directions. (The guideline marked "NOI = 500" has been added to identify the points where the leverage changes from positive to negative.) Note also that while the firm never suffers an operating loss (we assume zero profits in only one year, point N_0 on the horizontal axis), when leverage is introduced, losses are incurred during the years N_1 to N_2.

9. LEVERAGE AND VALUATION

In the previous section we noted that financial leverage can be either positive or negative depending on the relationship between a firm's earnings on capital invested and the fixed obligation to pay interest to the bond holders. Where the former exceeds the latter we define the leverage effect as positive since EPS are increased; where the rate of return is less than the bond rate of interest, we define the leverage as negative since EPS is thereby decreased. Since a firm that does not succeed in earning a return in excess of the interest rate will not survive in the long run, financial leverage appears, on balance, to be positive in almost all instances. However, as we noted above, the increase in expected EPS has its "price"—the increased volatility of fluctuations in the income stream to the common shareholders, that is, an increase in the financial risk associated with the investment in the company's shares.

Since leverage increases expected return and risk simultaneously, the question arises of the net impact of the use of leverage on the market value of the company's shares. Can the investor profit from leverage? Before going into greater detail on the effect of changes in capital structure on the price of the common stock, we shall initially consider two simple, but extreme, cases.

The answer to the above question depends on the market's evaluation of the increase in return versus the increase in risk. For simplicity we continue to assume a world of no taxes. It will be instructive, at this stage, to examine two diametrically opposed approaches to the valuation problem: the capitalization of net operating income, or NOI method as it is usually called; and the NI method, which capitalizes a firm's net income.[20] The differences between the two methods can be illustrated by considering a firm which is financed partly by 4% bonds and partly by common stock. The net operating income of the firm is assumed to be $2,000,000. Table V–8 sets out the alternative valuations of the firm's common stock. In the NOI method the total value of the firm's securities is derived by capitalizing the net operating income at the assumed 10% market rate of discount.

$$V \equiv S + D = \frac{X}{k}$$

where: V = total market value of the firm's securities
S = market value of its common stock
D = market value of its bonds
X = net operating income
k = 10% market capitalization rate.

The market value of the equity,

$$S = \frac{X}{k} - D$$

is derived by subtracting the market value of the debt from the total value of the firm's securities.

---

[20] The terms *NI* and *NOI*, as well as the examples given in the text, are taken from the pioneering article by David Durand, "Cost of Debt and Equity Funds for Business: Trends and Problems of Measurement," in *Conference on Research on Business Finance*, New York: National Bureau of Economic Research, 1952, pp. 215–47.

9. LEVERAGE AND VALUATION

TABLE V–8.

	NOI Method		
	A	B	C
Net Operating Income	$2,000,000	$2,000,000	$2,000,000
Capitalization Rate (10%)	× 10	× 10	× 10
Total Market Value of Company	20,000,000	20,000,000	20,000,000
Total Market Value of Bonds	——	5,000,000	10,000,000
Total Market Value of Stock	20,000,000	15,000,000	10,000,000
Number of Shares	2,000,000	1,500,000	1,000,000
Value per Share	$10	$10	$10
	NI Method		
Net Operating Income	$2,000,000	$2,000,000	$2,000,000
Interest (4% on bonds)	——	200,000	400,000
Net Income	2,000,000	1,800,000	1,600,000
Capitalization Rate (10%)	× 10	× 10	× 10
Total Market Value of Stock	20,000,000	18,000,000	16,000,000
Total Market Value of Bonds	——	5,000,000	10,000,000
Total Market Value of Company	20,000,000	23,000,000	26,000,000
Number of Shares	2,000,000	1,500,000	1,000,000
Value per Share	$10	$12	$16

The essence of the NOI method is that the total value of the firm remains constant at $20,000,000 independent of its capital structure. For example, if the firm is financed by 2,000,000 shares of stock and no bonds (Alternative A), the total value of the firm is $20,000,000 and the value per share of common stock is $10. If it is financed with $10,000,000 in bonds (Alternative C), the total value of all securities (stocks and bonds) is still $20,000,000 and the value of the common stock ($20,000,000 less the value of the bonds) equals $10,000,000, or again $10 per share. This approach suggests that any increase in expected return induced by the leverage is exactly offset by the increase in risk to the common shareholder, so that the total value of the firm and the value of an individual share of common stock remain invariant.

In the NI method, the net income, rather than the net operating income, is capitalized to derive the total market value of the stock:

$$S = \frac{X - rD}{k}$$

Where: r denotes the rate of interest.

To this sum the market value of the bonds is added to derive the total market value of the firm's securities:

$$V = S + D = \frac{X - rD}{k} + D$$

Table V–8 clearly shows that by the NI method successive increases in the proportion of bonds in the capital structure *increase* the total value of the firm's common stock, that is, the price of a share of common stock rises from $10 in the unlevered case to $16 when $10,000,000 worth of bonds are used. In terms of our previous discussion, the NI method assumes no discount whatsoever for the financial risk incurred, and translates all increases in EPS into increases in the price of the common stock. The NOI method represents the other extreme and allows for no influence whatsoever of increases in EPS on the price of the shares, that is, it is assumed that the increased financial risk exactly offsets the increase in expected profitability.

These pre-tax relationships are summarized in Figure V.4, which provides a convenient diagrammatic representation of the two alternative methods of valuation. Note that both methods give the same valuation for the 100% equity capital structure. As bonds are introduced into the capital structure, the degree to which leverage increases the value of the firm depends on the

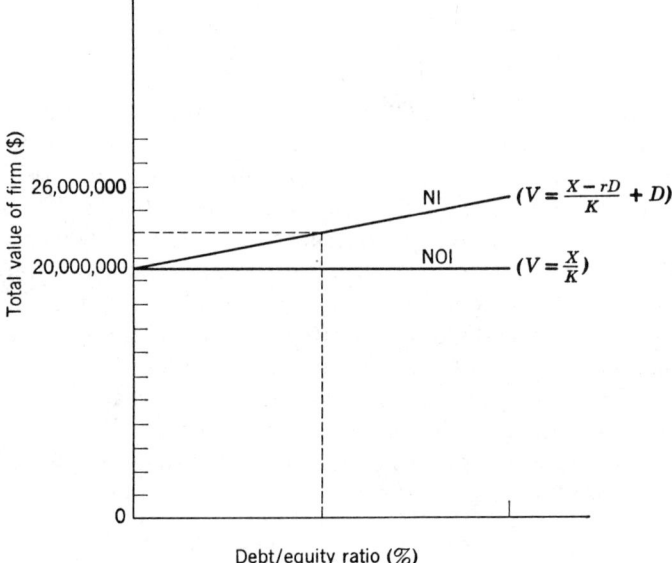

FIGURE V.4.

9. LEVERAGE AND VALUATION

TABLE V-9.

	A	B	C
1. Operating Income	$2,000,000	$2,000,000	$2,000,000
2. Interest	—	200,000	400,000
3. Taxable Net Income	2,000,000	1,800,000	1,600,000
4. Income Tax at 50%	1,000,000	900,000	800,000
5. Net Income after Taxes	1,000,000	900,000	800,000
6. Net Operating Income (line 5 + line 2)	1,000,000	1,100,000	1,200,000

proportion of bonds in the capital structure and the differential between the rate of return earned on total assets (k) and the rate of interest paid on the bonds (r). Other things being equal, the higher the proportion of debt and/or the greater the differential, the greater the leverage effect, that is, the steeper the NI line of Figure V.4. Clearly, many intermediate positions can be defined,[21] but the essence of the problems still hinges on our assumption regarding the market's appraisal of the financial risk created by leverage in relation to the increase in potential net earnings to shareholders.

Before turning to a more rigorous analysis of the relationship of capital structure to valuation, let us relax for a moment the assumption of no taxes. Table V-9 calculates the net operating income, *after taxes*, for the three alternatives given in Table V-8, assuming a 50% corporate income tax rate. While a strict application of the NOI method in a tax-free world suggests that no advantage can accrue to a firm which introduces debt into its capital structure, no question arises regarding the advantages of the use of debt, once taxes are allowed for. As can be seen from Table V-9, the NOI after taxes is an increasing function of the proportion of bonds in the capital structure, which also implies an increase in the value of the firm's common stock as the proportion of debt is increased.

The post-tax relationships between the value of the firm and its capital structure are shown in Figure V.5. Note that in sharp contrast to the pre-tax case, both the NI and NOI methods imply an increase in the total value of the firm as bonds are introduced into the capital structure, although the degree to which leverage increases value is considerably greater in the NI method than in the NOI method. However the introduction of taxes resolves all doubts as to the advantage of debt financing; under *both* the NOI and NI methods the value of the firm can be enhanced by the use of debt.

---

[21] For a stimulating discussion of some of the compromise positions between these two extremes, see Durand, *op. cit.*

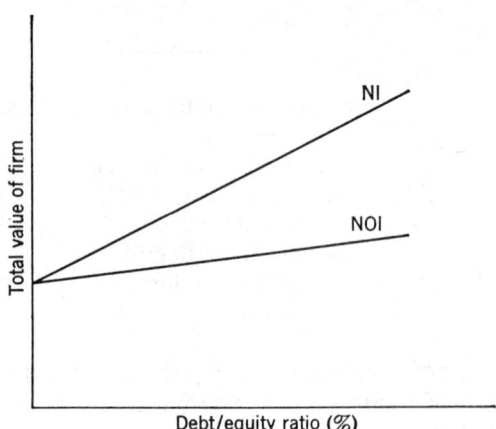

FIGURE V.5.

Thus the use of debt can potentially increase the value of the firm, independent of the valuation model, so long as interest is considered a deductible expense for tax purposes.[22]

10. THE MODIGLIANI AND MILLER ANALYSIS OF LEVERAGE AND VALUATION

The previous section set out two basic approaches to valuation, the Net Income method (NI) and the Net Operating Income method (NOI). Once risk is recognized it is clear that there probably has never been a proponent of the pure NI model which completely ignores the financial risk created by leverage. Although Durand preferred the NOI method, it was Modigliani and Miller who in a series of justly famous articles[23] provided a rigorous analysis of the NOI method. Their results can be summarized in two well known propositions relating to a firm's capital structure and the rate of return on its equity.[24]

---

[22] For a discussion of the factors which limit the use of debt in the capital structure, see Section 10.

[23] The original article, "The Cost of Capital, Corporation Finance, and the Theory of Investment," appeared in the *American Economic Review* XLVIII (June 1958), pp. 261–97.

[24] A third proposition, relating to the firm's cost of capital, is not germane to the present discussion.

10. ANALYSIS OF LEVERAGE AND VALUATION

Before examining these propositions a prefatory remark is called for. In their original 1958 article a set of very restrictive assumptions was required to establish the relationships between leverage and the value of a firm's shares. Subsequently, owing to further work, much of it by M & M themselves, it has been shown that the original propositions hold under far less severe assumptions than were originally thought necessary. Consequently we no longer need many of the implicit and explicit restrictions of the original paper, and shall replace them with the following two assumptions:

(a) Individuals can borrow or lend at the same market rate of interest as firms.
(b) There is no bankruptcy.

These two assumptions are sufficient to derive M & M's basic and most important first proposition.[25]

10.1 PROPOSITION I: CAPITAL STRUCTURE AND VALUATION

The Pre-Tax Analysis

M & M's first proposition states that the value of the firm is independent of its capital structure. In other words, a firm cannot increase its value by changing the ratio of debt to equity. To prove this statement let us define the following notations:

$V_U \equiv S_U =$ the market value of an unlevered firm's securities
$S_U =$ the market value of an unlevered firm's shares
$V_L \equiv S_L + D_L =$ the market value of a levered firm's securities
$S_L =$ the market value of a levered firm's shares
$D_L =$ the market value of a levered firm's bonds
$r =$ the interest rate
$X =$ net operating income, which is identical for both the levered and unlevered firms. This income stream is gross of interest payments (if any), but net of all other operating expenses.

Proposition I can be proved[26] by showing that if $V_U \neq V_L$, then it would be possible for holders of the shares of the overvalued firm to achieve a better investment combination by selling their shares and buying shares of the undervalued firm, and that this shift will continue until equilibrium is restored and $V_U = V_L$.

---

[25] See J. E. Stiglitz, "A Reexamination of the Modigliani–Miller Theorem," *American Economic Review* LIX (December 1969), pp. 784–93.
[26] The proof in the text is taken from F. Modigliani and M. H. Miller, "Reply to Heins and Sprenkle," *American Economic Review* LIX (September 1969), pp. 592–95.

TABLE V–10.

	Investment Required	Return Produced
1. Initial Position	αV_U	αX
2. Transaction		
a. Buy the fraction α of the shares in the levered firm	$\alpha S_L \equiv \alpha(V_L - D_L)$	$\alpha(X - rD_L)$
b. Buy the fraction α of the bonds of the levered firm	αD_L	$\alpha r D_L$
TOTALS	αV_L	αX

Consider an investor who holds a fraction α of the shares of the unlevered firm. His investment is $\alpha S_U \equiv \alpha V_U$ and his return is αX. If $V_U > V_L$, the investor can build a new portfolio which increases his return, without increasing his investment. Table V–10 describes the suggested transactions.

Before the change in the investment portfolio the investor received a return αX for an investment $\alpha S_U = \alpha V_U$. Following the change in the portfolio he still receives a return of αX, but his investment outlay is αV_L. Now, if we assume that $V_U > V_L$, it will be worthwhile to sell the shares of the unlevered firm and to use the proceeds of the sale to buy the stocks and bonds of the levered firm. But this process will tend to raise the market price of the levered firm's shares, while at the same time the price of the unlevered firm's shares will tend to fall. This can be expected to continue until $V_L = V_U$, at which time equilibrium will have been restored. When $V_U = V_L$ investors have no incentive to change their portfolios.

Let us now examine the reverse case, where $V_L > V_U$. In order to show that this inequality cannot hold in equilibrium, we shall assume that an investor holds a fraction α of the levered firm's stock. Hence his investment is $\alpha S_L \equiv \alpha(V_L - D_L)$ and his return equals $\alpha(X - rD_L)$. Table V–11 shows

TABLE V–11.

	Investment Required	Return Produced
1. Initial Position	$\alpha S_L \equiv \alpha(V_L - D_L)$	$\alpha(X - rD_L)$
2. Transaction		
a. Buy a fraction α of the shares of the unlevered firm	$\alpha S_U = \alpha V_U$	αX
b. Borrow αD_L on personal account	$-\alpha D_L$	$-\alpha r D_L$
TOTALS	$\alpha(V_U - D_L)$	$\alpha(X - rD_L)$

10. ANALYSIS OF LEVERAGE AND VALUATION

that if $V_L > V_U$, as assumed, the investor can gain by switching his investment from the levered firm to the unlevered firm. In this manner the investor still receives the same return $\alpha(X - rD_L)$ that he had before, but his investment is now $\alpha(V_U - D_L)$ rather than $\alpha(V_L - D_L)$. As long as $V_U < V_L$ it is worthwhile to shift to the shares of the unlevered firm, thereby obtaining the same stream of returns for less cost. By switching from the overvalued firm to the undervalued firm, market forces are again created which, in equilibrium, restore the equality $V_L = V_U$. To summarize, in equilibrium neither $V_L > V_U$ nor $V_L < V_U$ can persist and therefore U_L must equal V_U. This means that the value of the firm is *independent* of its capital structure, which is the proposition that we set out to prove.

It should be noted that we have assumed that the two firms are characterized by the same level of profitability (X) and by the same economic risk, and that they differ only in their capital structures. However, there is really no need to think about two firms at all; we seek to determine the impact of a change in the capital structure of a *given* firm on the value of its securities. Thus the relevant example would be to consider the same firm in two different hypothetical situations, rather than two different firms in a given time period. The use of two firms serves only as an expository device, and is not necessary for the argument.[27]

The Post-Tax Analysis

As we have already noted, a world with taxes constitutes the more important case for both the theory and practice of finance. Taking taxes into account, M & M show that the equilibrium value of the levered firm will be higher than that of the unlevered firm. The precise equilibrium relationship is given by

$$S_L + D_L \equiv V_L = V_U + TD_L$$

Thus a firm which takes advantage of the tax deductibility of interest payments can increase its value by levering its capital structure. This can be proved as follows: Denoting the corporate tax rate by T, the net income of the shareholders of the unlevered firm is $(1 - T)X$, while the net income to the shareholders of the levered firm is $(X - rD_L)(1 - T)$. Consider first the case where $S_L + D_L \equiv V_L > V_U + TD_L$, which implies that $S_L > V_U - (1 - T)D_L$. An investor who owns αS_L of the levered firm's shares can gain by making the portfolio switch that is spelled out in Table V–12.

---

[27] As Stiglitz, *op. cit.*, has shown, this enables us to dispense with the awkward device of postulating the so-called "equal risk classes" which plagued earlier proofs of the M & M propositions.

VALUATION OF SECURITIES: COMMON STOCKS

TABLE V-12.

	Investment Required	Return Produced
1. Initial Position	αS_L	$\alpha(X - rD_L)(1 - T)$
2. Transaction		
a. Buy a fraction α of the shares of the unlevered firm	$\alpha S_U \equiv \alpha V_U$	$\alpha X(1 - T)$
b. Borrow $\alpha(1 - T)D_L$ on personal account	$-\alpha(1 - T)D_L$	$-\alpha(1 - T)rD_L$
TOTALS	$\alpha[V_U - (1 - T)D_L]$	$\alpha(x - rD_L)(1 - T)$

The return to the investor, both before and after the transaction, is the same, and is given by $\alpha(X - rD_L)(1 - T)$. But by switching to the unlevered firm, and borrowing on personal account, his outlay is $\alpha[V_U - (1 - T)D_L]$, which by assumption is smaller than his previous outlay αS_L. Thus he can gain by selling the levered firm's shares and buying the unlevered firm's shares, so long as $V_L > S_U + TD_L$. Thus in equilibrium the last inequality cannot hold, and V_L must equal $V_U + TD_L$.

To complete the post-tax presentation, we must prove that $V_L < V_U + TD_L$ also cannot hold. Let us assume that an investor owns a fraction α of the unlevered firm's shares; that is, his investment outlay is $\alpha S_U \equiv \alpha V_U$ which affords him a return of $\alpha X(1 - T)$. But if the investor carries out the switch indicated in Table V-13, that is, selling the shares of the overvalued unlevered firm and purchasing the shares and bonds of the levered

TABLE V-13.

	Investment Required	Return Produced
1. Initial Position	$\alpha S_U = \alpha V_U$	$\alpha X(1 - T)$
2. Transaction		
a. Buy a fraction α of the shares of the levered firm	$\alpha S_L = \alpha(V_L - D_L)$	$\alpha(X - rD_L)(1 - T)$
b. Buy a fraction $\alpha(1 - T)$ of the bonds of the levered firm	$\alpha D_L(1 - T)$	$\alpha r D_L(1 - T)$
TOTALS	$\alpha(V_L - TD_L)$	$\alpha X(1 - T)$

10. ANALYSIS OF LEVERAGE AND VALUATION

firm, he can achieve the same level of return at a reduced investment outlay. And since this shift will be worthwhile as long as $V_L < V_U + TD_L$, forces are created which will restore the equality between V_L and $V_U + TD_L$ in equilibrium.

10.2 M & M's PROPOSITION II

Proposition II, which can be derived directly from the previous proposition, sets out the relationship between the yield on a firm's shares and its capital structure. In Chapter III the rate of return to investors was defined; Proposition II is spelled out in terms of the *company's* rate of return on its equity, rather than in terms of the investor's rate of return on his shares. This reflects the fact that in efficient capital markets, over a reasonably long period, a positive connection exists between a firm's rate of return and the rate of return which investors realize on its shares.

The Pre-Tax Analysis

From Proposition I we know that in equilibrium $V_L \equiv S_L + D_L = V_U$. Since the net operating income is X, the yield on equity of the unlevered firm is

$$Y_U = \frac{X}{V_U}$$

and the yield on the equity of the levered firm is

$$Y_L = \frac{X - rD_L}{V_L - D_L} = \frac{X - rD_L}{S_L} = \frac{X}{S_L} - \frac{rD_L}{S_L}$$

Multiplying and dividing the first term on the right-hand side by V_U, we get

$$Y_L = \frac{X}{V_U} \cdot \frac{V_U}{S_L} - \frac{rD_L}{S_L}$$

and by adding and subtracting $(X/V_U)(D_L/S_L)$ we obtain

$$Y_L = \frac{X}{V_U}\left(\frac{V_U}{S_L} - \frac{D_L}{S_L}\right) + \left(\frac{X}{V_U} - r\right)\frac{D_L}{S_L}$$

Since $V_U - D_L = S_L$ and $X/V_U = Y_U$ the above formula reduces to

$$Y_L = Y_U + (Y_U - r)\frac{D_L}{S_L}$$

Thus the rate of return on the equity of a levered firm (Y_L) is equal to the yield of an unlevered firm, Y_U, *plus* a risk premium $(Y_U - r)(D_L/S_L)$. The higher the proportion of debt in the capital mixture D_L/S_L, the greater an investor's risk, and hence the higher the required return on equity.

One can interpret the two pre-tax propositions as follows: by increasing the proportion of debt in its capital structure, the firm cannot affect its total value, and therefore no change occurs in its equity value (Proposition I). On the other hand, by Proposition II, increasing the proportion of debt in the capital structure increases the rate of return on the firm's equity (Y_L). When these two propositions are examined simultaneously, we can see that any change in the proportion of debt also changes investors' risk, and therefore their required return. Since these two influences exactly cancel one another, the value (price) of a firm's shares is invariant to leverage.

The Post-Tax Analysis

When taxes are introduced, Proposition I becomes

$$V_L = V_U + TD_L$$

and the yields on the unlevered and levered firm's shares are, respectively:[28]

$$Y_U^* = \frac{(1-T)X}{V_U}$$

$$Y_L^* = \frac{(1-T)(X - rD_L)}{V_L - D_L} = \frac{(1-T)(X - rD_L)}{S_L}$$

$$= \frac{(1-T)X}{S_L} - \frac{(1-T)rD_L}{S_L}$$

Multiplying and dividing the first term on the right-hand side of the latter by V_U, we have

$$Y_L^* = \frac{(1-T)X}{V_U} \cdot \frac{V_U}{S_L} - \frac{(1-T)rD_L}{S_L} = Y_U^* \frac{V_U}{S_L} - \frac{(1-T)rD_L}{S_L}$$

Now, if we add and subtract

$$\frac{Y_U^*(1-T)D_L}{S_L}$$

we obtain

$$Y_L^* = Y_U^* \left[\frac{V_U}{S_L} - \frac{(1-T)D_L}{S_L}\right] + Y_U^* \frac{(1-T)D_L}{S_L} - \frac{(1-T)rD_L}{S_L}$$

Since by Proposition I, $V_U - D_L + TD_L = S_L$, we get

$$Y_L^* = Y_U^* + (1-T)(Y_U^* - r)\frac{D_L}{S_L}$$

---

[28] After-tax yields are denoted by an asterisk.

10. ANALYSIS OF LEVERAGE AND VALUATION

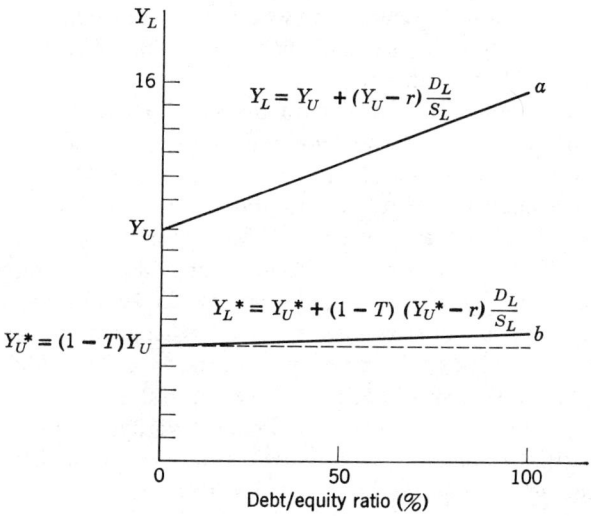

FIGURE V.6.

Thus the post-tax yield on the equity of the levered firm is equal to the post-tax yield on the unlevered firm *plus* a risk premium which is a function of the capital structure, the interest rate, and the corporate tax rate.

Proposition II, in both the pre-tax and post-tax cases, is represented graphically in Figure V.6. Line $Y_U a$ shows the required yield on equity as a function of the degree of leverage. The higher D_L/S_L, the higher the required yield. The slope of this line $(Y_U - r)$ represents the required risk premium when we change D_L/S_L by one unit.

Line $Y_U^* b$ shows the same relationship for the post-tax case. Since $(1 - T) < 1$ by definition, and $(Y_U^* - r) < (Y_U - r)$, the slope of line $Y_U^* b$ is smaller; that is, because of the tax advantage of debt, the required risk premium is much lower than in the pre-tax case. For example, assuming $Y_U = 10\%$, $r = 4\%$, and $T = 50\%$, the slope of line $Y_U a$ is 6% as compared with a slope of only $\frac{1}{2}\%$ for line $Y_U^* b$.

This completes the proof of the M & M propositions. In the after-tax case, as in the preceding pre-tax case, M & M have carried Durand's NOI model to its logical conclusions. Although the rigorous incorporation of risk in the leverage model greatly enhances our understanding of basic financial relationships, it leaves many important questions unresolved. In particular, the NOI model, in both the Durand and M & M versions, leads to a *corner solution* in the more important post-tax case, that is, a firm's *optimum* capital structure is comprised solely of bonds. This, of course, is an unsatisfactory result in the *positive* sense, since in reality business firms do not, and in fact cannot, achieve anywhere near that degree of leverage. Clearly, the analysis must incorporate additional risk variables if the degree of leverage is to be bounded.

In practice, a firm is confronted with steeply rising interest rates beyond fairly low levels of the debt–equity ratio, and both lenders and borrowers are sensitive to the possibility of "gamblers' ruin" or bankruptcy, both of which have been ruled out in the above analysis. Similarly the M & M proofs assume that the investor and the firm can borrow at the same interest rate. In effect this means that the investor will be indifferent between the leverage achieved by the firm and the so-called "homemade" leverage which he achieves by borrowing on his own account. Once again this reflects the absence of possible bankruptcy in the M & M model, for unless this assumption holds, considerations of limited liability will logically lead the investor to prefer corporate to homemade leverage. Thus to the degree that substantial differences in borrowing rates exist, which is tantamount to introducing *differential* financial risk into the model, one can expect a firm's optimal capital structure to fall far short of the corner solution. The actual degree of leverage used will reflect the particular firm's ability to absorb the financial risk inherent in the use of debt without incurring a penalty from the financial community in the form of increased interest rates and/or a fall in the price of the firm's stock.

11. PRICE–EARNINGS RATIOS AND FINANCIAL RISK

As we have previously seen, the PERs of growth and nongrowth stocks are not strictly comparable;[29] other things being equal, for higher growth rates we would expect higher price–earnings ratios. Similarly, care must be exercised when comparing the PERs of two different companies to take differential risks into account. Other things being equal, we expect high-risk stocks to have relatively low price–earnings ratios. Thus if a speculative mining stock has a PER of 5 while the shares of a bank are selling at a PER of 10, it is difficult to say that the mining stock has the lower relative price. Technically, the latter observed price is lower, but the differential risks between mining and banking are so great as to vitiate any conclusion drawn from such a comparison.

For this reason, almost all analysts are careful to compare the PERs of stocks *within* a given industry. The accepted procedure for standardizing risk differentials is to compare the PER of a given company with the average

---

[29] See Section 7.

11. PRICE–EARNINGS RATIOS AND FINANCIAL RISK

PER of the industry (see Table V–4). This represents a crude adjustment at best. Even a glance at Table V-4 suggests that the PER is a very unstable measure: the composite PER for all industries ranges from a high of 49 in 1932 to a low of 7.3 in 1948. In addition, this adjustment for risk ignores the interaction between the shares of different companies (and industries) which is vital for an evaluation of the risk of alternative investment portfolios.[30]

Despite all these shortcomings the use of price–earnings ratios, like the smile of the Cheshire cat, lingers on in the financial press and even in the more professional of financial journals, but strangely enough, the financial analysts have overlooked another important characteristic of the price–earnings ratio which stems from the analysis of capital structure and financial risk in Section 10. We turn now to an examination of the implications of the Modigliani and Miller analysis of capital structure, for the use of the PER rule of thumb.

The Pre-Tax Analysis

Following M & M, we shall initially assume a world with no taxes. In this case, their Proposition I states that the value of the firm is independent of its capital structure, so that

$$V_L \equiv S_L + D_L = V_U \equiv S_U$$

To examine the implications of this theorem for PER analysis, we have to calculate the expected prices and earnings per share for two firms which differ only in their capital structures.

For simplicity we assume that both the levered firm and the unlevered firm are of the same size and have issued the same number of shares, which we shall denote by n.[31]

Dividing each term in Proposition I by n, we get

$$\frac{S_L}{n} + \frac{D_L}{n} = \frac{S_U}{n}$$

or

$$P_L = P_U - \frac{D_L}{n}$$

---

[30] Part II of this book deals extensively with this problem.
[31] The value of the firm and therefore the value of its shares are determined independently of the number of shares outstanding. The firm can change the number of shares arbitrarily (by splits or stock dividends) without affecting the total market value of the shares.

where P_U is the price per share of the unlevered firm's stock and P_L is the price per share of the levered firm's stock.

Now let us examine the earnings per share of the two firms. For the unlevered firm, the earnings per share E_U are given by

$$E_U = \frac{X}{n}$$

where X denotes the total earnings of the unlevered firm. Similarly, the earnings per share of the levered firm, E_L, is given by

$$E_L = \frac{X - rD_L}{n} = \frac{X}{n} - \frac{rD_L}{n} = E_U - \frac{rD_L}{n}$$

where X denotes the total earnings before interest[32] and r denotes the interest rate, so that rD_L equals the interest outlay. The PER of the unlevered firm is

$$\text{PER} = \frac{P_U}{E_U}$$

The PER of the levered firm will be

$$\frac{P_L}{E_L} = \frac{P_U - \dfrac{D_L}{n}}{E_U - \dfrac{rD_L}{n}}$$

Dividing through by E_U we get

$$\frac{P_L}{E_L} = \frac{\dfrac{P_U}{E_U} - \dfrac{D_L}{nE_U}}{1 - \dfrac{rD_L}{nE_U}} \equiv \frac{\dfrac{P_U}{E_U} - a}{1 - ra}$$

where

$$a \equiv \frac{D_L}{nE_U} \geq 0$$

It can easily be shown that on the reasonable assumption that the anticipated return on the firm's operations exceeds the rate of interest, that is, $E_U/P_U > r$, the PER of the levered firm will be smaller than the PER of the unlevered

---

[32] As we have assumed that the firms are the same size, both have the same earnings before interest, which we denote by X.

11. PRICE–EARNINGS RATIOS AND FINANCIAL RISK   173

firm, that is, $P_L/E_L < P_U/E_U$.[33] We expect this assumption to hold since the risk involved in equity investments is higher than the risk involved in comparable bonds, so that the long-run average profit of the firm should be larger than the interest rate. Thus, if the financial risk which stems from financial leverage is taken into account, we expect a levered firm to have a lower PER than an unlevered firm, even if the two firms have the same economic risk and identical growth rates.[34] Moreover, we can be certain that the lower PER does not represent a "bargain" since given the assumption of perfect markets and no taxes, M & M have proved that a rational investor would be indifferent between two identical firms which differ only in their capital structures.

Post-Tax Analysis

Since in the long run we all pay taxes, let us examine the relationship between financial risk and the PER for the more realistic case where taxes are assumed to exist. Taking income taxes into account, M & M formulated the following relationship between the levered and unlevered firm:

$$V_L \equiv S_L + D_L = V_U + TD_L \equiv S_U + TD_L$$

where V_L, S_L, D_L, V_U, and S_U are defined as before and T denotes the tax rate. Assuming again that each firm has issued n shares, we can derive the relationship between the share prices of the two firms:

$$\frac{V_L}{n} \equiv \frac{S_L}{n} + \frac{D_L}{n} = \frac{V_U}{n} + \frac{TD_L}{n} \equiv \frac{S_U}{n} + \frac{TD_L}{n}$$

Hence

$$P_L = P_U - \frac{D_L(1-T)}{n} \qquad (5.23)$$

---

[33] From the assumption $E_U/P_U > r$ we derive $P_U/E_U < 1/r$. Alternatively, we can write

$$\frac{P_U}{E_U} = \frac{1}{r} - \delta \qquad (\delta > 0)$$

Substituting this expression for P_U/E_U in the equation of the text, we have

$$\frac{P_L}{E_L} = \frac{\frac{1}{r} - \delta - a}{1 - ra} = \frac{1}{r} - \frac{\delta}{1 - ra} < \frac{1}{r} - \delta = \frac{P_U}{E_U}$$

[34] In an empirical study of price–earnings ratios, Haskel Benishay has found a negative correlation between financial leverage (as measured by the debt–equity ratio) and the PER, a result which is consistent with our analysis. See his "Variability in Earning–Price Ratios of Corporate Equities," *American Economic Review* (March 1961), pp. 81–94.

174 VALUATION OF SECURITIES: COMMON STOCKS

The earnings per share of an unlevered firm are given by

$$E_U = \frac{(1-T)X}{n}$$

where X = the earnings before interest and taxes.

For the levered firm we have

$$E_L = \frac{(1-T)(X - rD_L)}{n} = \frac{(1-T)X}{n} - \frac{r(1-T)D_L}{n}$$

$$= E_U - \frac{r(1-T)D_L}{n} \quad (5.24)$$

From Equations (5.23) and (5.24) we can derive the relationship between the price–earnings ratios of a levered and an unlevered firm:

$$\frac{P_L}{E_L} = \frac{P_U - \frac{(1-T)D_L}{n}}{E_U - \frac{r(1-T)D_L}{n}} = \frac{\frac{P_U}{E_U} - \frac{(1-T)D_L}{nE_U}}{1 - \frac{r(1-T)D_L}{nE_U}} = \frac{\frac{P_U}{E_U} - b}{1 - rb}$$

where

$$b \equiv \frac{(1-T)D_L}{nE_U} \geq 0$$

If we make the reasonable assumption that $E_U/P_U \geq r$ (otherwise all investors would prefer to invest in bonds), it can again be shown that:[35]

$$\frac{P_L}{E_L} \leq \frac{P_U}{E_U}$$

Thus in the after-tax case as well, we expect that in equilibrium the PER of a levered firm will be lower than the PER of an otherwise identical unlevered firm, so that the PER cannot serve as an unequivocal measure of a share's relative price. In contrast to the pre-tax case, financial leverage does have an impact on share prices when taxes are taken into account, but the impact of leverage on earnings per share dominates, and as a result the PER is inversely related to financial leverage.[36] However, the difference between

---

[35] See note 33 on page 173.
[36] The pre-tax results follow directly from M & M's Proposition I; financial leverage increases earnings per share *without* changing share prices, therefore the PER must decline. The post-tax analysis is not quite so straightforward; leverage increases earnings per share as before, but it also causes share prices to rise so that without computations it is not clear which effect will be dominant.

the PERs stemming from a given difference in leverage will be smaller in the post-tax case.

This analysis is not complete because risk is multidimensional, in the sense that the risk of a given company depends on the interaction of its returns with those of other firms as well.[37] In Part II of the book we shall treat risk in the context of a portfolio, but this does *not* change the conclusions regarding the PER comparisons between companies having different capital structures.[38]

12. SUMMARY

This chapter analyzes four alternative approaches to security valuation: net asset value, present value of future earnings, the price–earnings ratio, and present value of future dividends.

The net asset value or balance sheet approach suffers from all of the shortcomings of the accounting conventions discussed in Chapter II. As a result, book value can be a very unreliable measure of economic value. In particular, it should be noted that not all a firm's assets appear on the balance sheet; moreover, "going concern" value is often different from the simple summation of the individual assets. Attempts to revalue a firm's assets on a current market value basis almost invariably require the discounting of future cash flows.

The present value of earnings approach is based on the discounting of a firm's future earnings rather than on its existing assets. By this method, the value of a firm's shares depends on the estimated future earnings and the capitalization rate applied by investors.

The most popular valuation method in practice is a variant of the earnings approach which uses the shares' price–earnings ratio (PER) as a measure of a stock's relative price. The PER is a shortcut rule of thumb; but its application and especially its interpretation present some very serious problems.

The final valuation method discussed is the present value of dividends approach. In this approach a common stock is evaluated on the basis of the

---

[37] Richard and Dorothy Bower found a negative correlation between the PER and a measure of the covariance of returns. This is as it should be, since the lower the covariance, the greater is the risk reduction stemming from a multisecurity portfolio. See R. S. Bower and D. H. Bower, "Risk and Valuation of Common Stock," *Journal of Political Economy* (May–June 1969), pp. 349–62, and Chapter X.

[38] R. S. Hamada, in "Portfolio Analysis, Market Equilibrium and Corporation Finance," *Journal of Finance* 24 (March 1969), pp. 13–31, has shown that M & M's proposition I holds for the mean-variance portfolio case. Thus the PER analysis, which depends only on that proposition, holds for this case as well.

cash flow to investors—the stream of dividends—rather than on the basis of corporate earnings.

The dividend and earnings models can be reconciled when the investment required to generate the future income stream is taken into account. But the use of a dividend model can be misleading in the sense that such a model, on the surface at least, appears to suggest a direct connection between dividend policy and the value of a firm's stock. This is true for the special case where no external financing of investment is permitted. In this case, increases in the level of a firm's investment imply decreases in dividends, and since investment (unless the rate of return equals the discount rate) affects value, dividend policy has a strong impact on share values. In the more general case, where external financing is permitted, Miller and Modigliani have demonstrated that in a perfect market dividend policy has no effect on stock values.

A growth term can readily be incorporated into the dividend valuation model. However, the explicit consideration of growth creates a serious problem for the use of the PER method. An analysis of the so-called "IBM paradox" clearly shows that the accepted market rule of thumb (the PER) should not be used to compare the stocks of firms which have significantly different growth rates.

This chapter also analyzes the influence of leverage on the value of a firm's equity, where the change in earnings per share (EPS) induced by the introduction of fixed interest–bearing obligations into the firm's capital structure is defined as financial leverage. In general, leverage causes an increase in the fluctuations over time of EPS, thereby increasing the relative financial risk of mixed capital structures.

The leverage effect can be positive or negative, depending on the relationship between the effective cost of the bonds (or preferred stock) and the rate of return which the company earns on its assets. Where the rate of return on assets exceeds the cost of financing, the leverage effect will be positive since EPS are increased; in the opposite case, the leverage is negative and EPS decline. Since firms must earn returns in excess of the interest rate in order to survive, we expect on balance that financial leverage will be positive.

Since leverage increases expected return and risk simultaneously, the question arises of the net impact of the use of leverage on the value of a company's shares. The answer hinges on the valuation model chosen, that is, on the income stream which is capitalized. Durand identifies two extreme positions: the NOI model capitalizes net operating income to determine the total market value of the firm's securities, and arrives at the market value of the equity by subtracting the market value of the debt; the NI model capitalizes net income to derive the market value of the equity, to which the the market value of the bonds is added to determine the total market value of the firm.

12. SUMMARY

The essence of the NOI method is that, in the absence of taxes, the total value of the firm is independent of its capital structure; that is, any increase in expected return engendered by the leverage is exactly offset by the increase in financial risk, so that the shareholder cannot benefit from the use of leverage. The NI method, on the other hand, assumes no discount whatsoever for the financial risk incurred and translates all of the increase in EPS engendered by the leverage into increases in the price of the common stock, thereby raising the total value of the firm. However when taxes are introduced, both the NOI and the NI models imply increases in the value of a firm's equity as the proportion of the debt in the capital structure is increased.

Since the pure NI method completely ignores risk, attention has been focused on the NOI model. Modigliani and Miller have provided a rigorous analysis of the NOI. Their results can be summarized in two pre-tax propositions:

(a) The first proposition states that the value of a firm is independent of its capital structure.

(b) The second proposition, derived from the first, sets out the (linear) relationship between the yield on a firm's shares and its capital structure.

The novelty of the M & M approach lies not in their conclusions (they are essentially the same as those of Durand's NOI model) but in the rigor with which the propositions are proved, thereby permitting an unequivocal conclusion in favor of the NOI method over the NI (and other) valuation models.

When taxes are introduced, M & M confirm the previous findings of Durand by rigorously proving that a firm which takes advantage of the tax deductibility of interest payments can increase the value of its equity by levering its capital structure. This is the most unsatisfactory part of the analysis. The NOI model, in both the Durand and M & M versions, leads to corner solutions of 100% bond financing in the relevant post-tax case, so that additional risk variables, which are exogenous to the model, must be introduced if the use of leverage is to be truncated.

When financial risk is explicitly taken into account the convention of standardizing the PER for risk by comparing it to the industry average is no longer acceptable. An extension of M & M's theorem regarding the relationship of the value of the firm to its capital structure shows that when the financial risk which stems from leverage is taken into account, a levered firm can be expected to have a lower PER than an unlevered firm, even if they have the same economic risk and identical growth rates. And this conclusion holds for *both* the pre-tax and post-tax cases.

This particular result holds for the more general analysis of a portfolio of securities as well. But we have now pushed the analysis of a single security about as far as it can go. Risk is multidimensional since the risk of one security depends, among other things, on its interaction with all other securities. But a full-scale attack on the portfolio problem requires an expanded arsenal and the forging of additional analytical tools. This is the task which we have set for Part II of this book, which is devoted to the theory of portfolio selection.

APPENDIX V-1
The Present Value of Earnings with Continuous Discounting

In the analysis of Chapter V we assume that the stream of receipts (outflow and inflow) occurs at the end of each year. In this case, using the earnings model, the value of the firm's stock is determined by

$$P = \sum_{t=1}^{\infty} \frac{E}{(1+k)^t} = \frac{E}{k} \qquad (5.1.1)$$

The purpose of this appendix is to derive a similar formula for the continuous case, that is, when we assume that the stream of receipts is continuous, and the net present value is determined by discounting these receipts continuously.

Suppose first that the firm receives E dollars at the beginning of a given year. What is the value of this sum at the end of the year? Using an annual calculation we get

$$E_1 = E_0(1+k) \qquad (5.1.2)$$

where E_1 is the value at the end of this year and k is the required rate of return, which for convenience in this appendix we call the interest rate. If we pay the interest m times a year, E_1 is given by

$$E_1 = E_0\left(1 + \frac{k}{m}\right)^m$$

Taking the limit of this term, where $m \to \infty$, we obtain

$$E_1 = E_0 e^k \qquad (5.1.3)$$

since $\lim_{m \to \infty} [1 + (k/m)]^m = e^k$ (where $e = 2.717\ldots$). Hence, the present value of E_1 (which is by definition equal to E_0) can be derived from (5.1.3):

$$E_0 = E_1 e^{-k} \qquad (5.1.4)$$

By the same token the future value of E_0 dollars t years from now is

$$E_t = E_0\left(1 + \frac{k}{m}\right)^{tm} = E_0\left[\left(1 + \frac{k}{m}\right)^m\right]^t = E_0 e^{kt} \qquad (5.1.5)$$

Hence the present value of E_t (discounted continuously) is

$$E_0 = E_t e^{-kt} \qquad (5.1.6)$$

If we have more than one receipt E_t, the discounted value of this stream of receipts is obtained by summing all the relevant terms given by (5.1.6.) But if we have a continuous stream of receipts E_t (for n years) this summation is given by the following integral:

$$PV = \int_{t=0}^{n} E_t e^{-kt}\, dt \qquad (5.1.7)$$

where PV denotes the present value of this stream of receipts.

If E_t is some constant number (E), and $n = \infty$ (5.1.7) is reduced to

$$PV = \int_{t=0}^{\infty} E e^{-kt}\, dt = E \int_{t=0}^{\infty} e^{-kt}\, dt = E\left[-\frac{e^{-kt}}{k}\right]_0^{\infty} = \frac{E}{k} \qquad (5.1.8)$$

Thus if we assume a stable stream of receipts (E), calculating the present value for the continuous case and for the discrete case yields similar results.

APPENDIX V-2

The Dividend Growth Model with Continuous Discounting

Assuming that the firm distributes a dividend d_0 in the first year and has an annual growth rate g, the value of the firm's stock (see Chapter V) is given by

$$P = \sum_{i=1}^{\infty} \frac{d_i}{(1+k)^i} = \sum_{i=1}^{\infty} \frac{d_0(1+g)^i}{(1+k)^i} = \frac{d_0}{k-g} \qquad (5.2.1)$$

Let us compute what P will be where the dividend growth and the discount process are carried out continuously. The dividend at the end of the first year is

$$d_1 = \lim_{m \to \infty} d_0 \left(1 + \frac{g}{m}\right)^m = d_0 e^g$$

Similarly, the dividend in year t is

$$d_t = d_0 e^{gt}$$

The discount value of d_t is

$$\lim_{m \to \infty} \frac{d_t}{\left(1 + \frac{k}{m}\right)^{mt}} = d_t e^{-kt}$$

Hence the present value of a stream of dividends which grows and is received continuously is

$$PV = \int_{t=0}^{\infty} d_t e^{-k} \, dt = \int_{t=0}^{\infty} d_0 e^{gt-kt} \, dt = \frac{d_0}{k-g} \qquad (5.2.2)$$

which is identical with the result given by (5.2.1).

QUESTIONS AND PROBLEMS

5.1 What are the major shortcomings of using the book value of net assets as a measure for the valuation of a firm's equity?

5.2 Define the present value of earnings approach to security valuation. Why does this method depend on investors' costs of capital?

5.3 What is the relationship between the present value of earnings and the price–earnings ratio methods of valuation?

5.4 Should the firm's price–earnings ratio be adjusted following a stock split or the payment of a cash dividend?

5.5 (a) Derive the dividend valuation model on the assumption that earnings are expected to increase at a given rate over time.
(b) How would you formulate the dividend valuation model for a case in which earnings are expected to increase for the next five years and to remain stable from the sixth year on?

5.6 What is the relationship between the dividend and earnings approaches to valuation?

5.7 How does dividend policy affect the value of the firm:

    a. in a perfect capital market
    b. in a less than perfect capital market

5.8 What is meant by the term *IBM paradox*.

5.9 Define "positive," "negative," and "neutral" financial leverage.

5.10 In what sense does the use of leverage increase a firm's risk?

5.11 Distinguish between the NOI and NI approaches to valuation. Which of the two methods is the more optimistic?

5.12 What do M & M mean by a "switch" and what role does switching play in their analysis of leverage?

5.13 Define and prove M & M's Proposition I in the absence of income taxes. How does the introduction of taxes affect this proposition?

5.14 Define and prove M & M's Proposition II in the absence of income taxes. What is the relationship of the pre-tax Proposition II to its post-tax counterpart?

QUESTIONS AND PROBLEMS

5.15 What is the relationship of the M & M analysis to that of Durand?

5.16 In what sense does the M & M analysis constitute a "corner solution" of the capital structure problem? Why is such a solution unsatisfactory?

5.17 What are the implications of the existence of differential growth rates and financial risk for the use of the PER in investment analysis?

SELECTED REFERENCES

Barker, C. A., "Price Effects of Stock Dividend Shares, At Ex-Dividend Dates," *Journal of Finance* (September 1959).
Bell, W. E., "The Price–Future Earnings Ratio," *Financial Analysts Journal* (August 1958).
Benishay, H., "Variability in Earnings–Price Ratios of Corporate Equities," *American Economic Review* (March 1961).
Bodenhorn, D., "On the Problem of Capital Budgeting," *Journal of Finance* (December 1959).
Bower, R. S., and Bower, D. H., "Risk and Valuation of Common Stock," *Journal of Political Economy* (May–June 1969).
Brigham, E. F., and Pappas, J. L., "Duration of Growth, Changes in Growth Rates, and Corporate Share Prices," *Financial Analysts Journal* (May–June 1966).
Durand, D., "Growth Stocks and the Petersburg Paradox," *Journal of Finance* (September 1957).
———, "The Cost of Capital, Corporation Finance, and the Theory of Investment: Comment," *American Economic Review* (September 1959).
Elton, E. J., and Gruber, M. J., "Marginal Stockholder Tax Rates and the Clientele Effect," *Review of Economics and Statistics* (February 1970).
Gordon, M., "Optimal Investment and Financing Policy," *Journal of Finance* (May 1963).
———, *The Investment, Financing and Valuation of the Corporation.* Homewood, Ill.: Irwin, 1962.
———, and Shapiro, E., "Capital Equipment Analysis: The Required Rate of Profit," *Management Science* (October 1956).
Graham, B.; Dodd, D. L.; Cottle, S.; and Tatham, C., *Security Analysis*, 4th edition. New York: McGraw-Hill, 1962.
Hamada, R. S., "Portfolio Analysis, Market Equilibrium and Corporation Finance," *Journal of Finance* (March 1969).
Heins, A. J., and Sprenkle, C. M., "A Comment on the Modigliani–Miller Cost of Capital Thesis," *American Economic Review* (September 1969).
Holt, C. C., "The Influence of Growth Duration on Share Prices," *Journal of Finance* (September 1962).

SELECTED REFERENCES

Hunt, P., "A Proposal for Precise Definitions of 'Trading on the Equity' and 'Leverage'," *Journal of Finance* (September 1961).

Lintner, J., "Dividends, Earnings, Leverage, Stock Prices and the Supply of Capital to Corporations," *Review of Economics and Statistics* (August 1962).

Lintner, J., "The Cost of Capital and Optimal Financing of Corporate Growth," *Journal of Finance* (May 1963).

Malkiel, B. G., "Equity Yields, Growth, and the Structure of Share Prices," *American Economic Review* (December 1963).

Mao, J. C. T., "The Valuation of Growth Stock: The Investment Opportunities Approach," *Journal of Finance* (March 1966).

McEnally, R. W., "The 'Information Effect' and Price–Earnings Ratios," *Mississippi Valley Journal of Business Economics* (Spring 1970).

McWilliams, J. D., "Prices, Earnings and P–E Ratios," *Financial Analysts Journal* (May–June 1966).

Miller, M. H., and Modigliani, F., "Dividend Policy, Growth, and the Valuation of Shares," *Journal of Business* (October 1961).

———, "Some Estimates of the Cost of Capital to the Electric Utility Industry, 1954–57," *American Economic Review* (June 1966).

Modigliani, F., and Miller, M. H., "The Cost of Capital, Corporation Finance, and the Theory of Investment," *American Economic Review* (June 1958).

———, "The Cost of Capital, Corporation Finance, and the Theory of Investment: Reply," *American Economic Review* (September 1959).

———, "Corporate Income Taxes and the Cost of Capital: A Correction," *American Economic Review* (June 1963).

———, "Reply to Heins and Sprenkle," *American Economic Review* (September 1969).

Molodovsky, N.; May, C.; and Chottiner, S., "Common Stock Valuation Principles, Tables and Application," *Financial Analysts Journal* (March–April 1965).

Molodovsky, N., "Recent Studies of P/E Ratios," *Financial Analysts Journal* (May–June 1967).

Nicholson, S. F., "Price–Earning Ratios," *Financial Analysts Journal* (July–August 1960).

Ophir, T. and Levy, H., "Modigliani and Miller's Cost of Capital: A Correction," *Research Report No. 1*, Department of Business Administration, The Hebrew University of Jerusalem, April 1969.

Robichek, A. A., and Myers, S. C., "Problems in the Theory of Optimal Capital Structure," *Journal of Financial and Quantitative Analysis* (June 1966).

Sarma, L. V. L. N., and Hanumanta Rao, K. S., "Leverage and the Value of the Firm," *Journal of Finance* (September 1969).

Schwartz, E., "Theory of the Capital Structure of the Firm," *Journal of Finance* (March 1959).

Soldofsky, R. M., "A Note on the History of Bond Tables and Stock Valuation Models," *Journal of Finance* (March 1966).

———, "Growth Yields," *Financial Analysts Journal* (September–October 1961).

Solomon, E., *The Theory of Financial Management*. New York: Columbia University Press, 1963.

Stiglitz, J. E., "A Re-examination of the Modigliani–Miller Theorem," *American Economic Review* (December 1969).

Vickers, D., "Profitability and Reinvestment Rates: A Note on the Gordon Paradox," *Journal of Business* (July 1966).

Wendt, P. F., "Current Growth Stock Valuation Methods: General Motors—An Illustration," *Financial Analysts Journal* (March–April 1965).

Williams, J. B., *The Theory of Investment Value*. Cambridge, Mass.: Harvard University Press, 1938.

PART II
PORTFOLIO SELECTION

Chapter VI
The Investment Decision Under Conditions of Uncertainty

1. INTRODUCTION

In Part I we reviewed the various methods used by investment analysts and advisers to estimate the prospective return on a company's securities. Clearly, the expectations of possible future gains must be based in part on more or less certain historical data of past performance and in part on forecasts of future events, which can usually be made only on a highly tentative basis. As a result, investors can rarely be thought of as having very precise expectations regarding the future returns to be derived from a particular investment option. In fact, if we abstract for the moment from the investment in short-term government and other low-risk debt instruments, the best that an investor can reasonably be expected to do is to make some estimate of the *range* of possible returns and of the relative chances of earning high or low returns on the investment.

Formally, we can distinguish three states of investors' expectations:[1] (a) certainty, (b) risk, and (c) uncertainty.

(a) *Certainty*. Strictly speaking, perfect certainty refers to cases where investors' expectations are *single-valued*; that is, the individual views prospective profits in terms of a particular outcome, and not in terms of a range of alternative possible returns. We shall also use the term *certainty* to describe those situations in which investors' expectations regarding future returns are bounded within a very narrow range. But do such investments exist in actual securities markets outside of the realm of textbooks? At first glance it may appear that no security yields a perfectly certain income stream, but on reflection several illustrations can be found. For example, short-term

---

[1] This tripartite distinction is associated with Professor Frank Knight; see his *Risk Uncertainty and Profit*, Boston and New York: Houghton Mifflin Company, 1921, Chapter VII.

Treasury bills permit the investor to calculate the exact return which he will receive upon redemption with what amounts to absolute certainty; we simply ignore the insignificant probability of a revolution or of a war which might destroy the existing monetary system. For the time being we also ignore the important question of inflation and its impact on the real return from investment, that is, on the return in terms of purchasing power. Similarly if we are willing to ignore the remote possibility of bankruptcy or financial default in such giants as General Motors and AT&T, the short-term notes of these companies can also be considered for all practical purposes as investments yielding safe returns.[2]

(b) *Risk*. The term *risk* will be used to describe an option whose return is not known with absolute certainty, but for which an array of alternative returns and their probabilities are known; in other words, for which the distribution of returns is known. The distribution may have been estimated on the basis of *objective* (either a priori or a postiori) probabilities, or on the basis of purely *subjective* probabilities.

An example of such a frequency distribution is given in Table VI–1, which sets out the historical record of rates of return for a hypothetical investment over the past 40 years. The data of Table VI–1 were then used to prepare the familiar histogram, shown in Figure VI.1. Historical data of this sort are

TABLE VI–1. An example of a frequency distribution of rates of return

Rates of Return (%)	Frequency (number of years)
−30.00 to −20.01	2
−20.00 to −10.01	3
−10.00 to −0.01	5
0.00 to 9.99	10
10.00 to 19.99	9
20.00 to 29.99	6
30.00 to 39.99	3
40.00 to 49.99	2
TOTAL	40

[2] We limit the discussion to short-term, (less than one year) bonds since in the longer run, fluctuations in interest rates may induce capital gains or losses, thereby changing the annual rates of return on such bonds. Needless to add, investors' expectations regarding future movements of interest rates are *rarely* single-valued.

1. INTRODUCTION

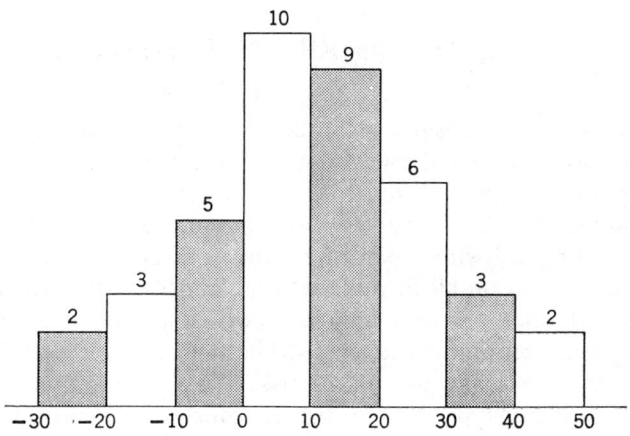

FIGURE VI.1.

often available for financial investments, and can be used to facilitate current investment decisions. But even where a long series of past rates of return is available the decision to invest remains complex. There often may be no reason why the future distribution of returns should resemble their distribution in the past, and before arriving at a decision all of the factors that might indicate future changes in the distribution must be carefully examined.

Even if the distribution can be expected to remain unchanged, realizing high returns (the right-hand side of the histogram) or negative returns (the left-hand side) in any particular year is largely a matter of luck. In other words, even if we knew that the past will be reproduced in the future, investing for one year is like drawing one observation from the distribution of a random variable. A positive probability of drawing an observation from the groups "−30 to −0.01" clearly exists, in which case we shall suffer a loss; nevertheless, if the distribution is expected to remain unchanged, we can be reasonably certain that losses will never exceed 30%, nor will profits exceed 50%, in any given year.

(c) *Uncertainty*. In this extreme case the possible range of returns is known but the probability of occurrence for each alternative is not. Of course, the borderline between uncertainty and risk is rather elusive; it is always possible to convert uncertainties into risks by introducing subjective probabilities. In the case of financial investment, probability beliefs are almost invariably subjective; therefore for the remainder of this book we shall use the terms *risk* and *uncertainty* interchangeably.

2. THE MAXIMUM RETURN CRITERION

Let us initially assume a constant investment period, for example, one year, and assume that the decision maker can choose only a single investment option.[3] What decision rule should the investor apply to choose the best alternative? To define the problem more precisely we shall assume that he is confronted with the five alternatives given in Table VI–2, that he has full information on all possible returns, and that their (objective or subjective) probabilities are also known. Two of the options (A and B) represent perfectly certain investments, while the other three alternatives (C, D, and E) entail varying degrees of risk. Such a situation is quite realistic: an investor can typically buy riskless short-term government bonds or deposit his money in a savings bank; alternatively, he can buy common stocks whose returns must be considered as highly uncertain random variables.

If the investor restricts himself to "safe" investments (options A and B), his choice is very simple. The only criterion required in this case is that of maximum return, and he will choose the alternative that offers the highest return at the end of the investment period. In our example he will choose option B, since B promises a 10% return as compared with the 8% offered by option A.

Such simple choice situations are hardly representative of a modern securities market; reality is much more complicated and for that matter much more interesting as well. Investors do not usually restrict themselves solely to safe prospects. A more realistic problem, therefore, is how to select the best option out of the five alternative choices A, B, C, D, and E. Can we still apply the maximum return criterion? Clearly we cannot do so without major qualifications. Whereas in the previous example of comparing only options A and B the returns were known with certainty (8% and 10%, respectively), we have no such knowledge regarding the other three options.

TABLE VI–2. Distribution of possible returns of five alternative investments*

A		B		C		D		E	
Return	Probability	Return	Probability	Return	Probability	Return	Probability	Return	Probability
8	1	10	1	−8	1/4	−4	1/4	−20	1/10
				16	1/2	8	1/2	0	6/10
				24	1/4	12	1/4	50	3/10

* To facilitate comparison, the returns are given in percentages.

[3] We defer discussion of the important portfolio problem to Chapters VIII and X below.

Suppose we try to compare options B and C: the return on B is 10%, but what return can we attribute to C? If we assume a negative return of −8%, B is clearly preferable; however, if we assume the return on C will be 16% or 24%, then it is equally clear that option C represents the better alternative. Since there is no a priori reason to single out any one of the three possible returns of option C, the maximum return criterion breaks down unless we restrict ourselves to the unrealistic (and trivial) problem of selecting investments under conditions of perfect certainty.

3. THE MAXIMUM EXPECTED RETURN CRITERION

To compare the desirability of alternative investments under conditions of uncertainty we must first devise a synthetic index which reflects the entire distribution of returns. One of the most popular solutions to this problem stipulates that decisions should be reached on the basis of an investment's *expected return*, where expected return is defined as the mean of the random variable distribution (in this case the returns) weighted by the probabilities of occurrence.[4] For example, if we consider option C in Table VI–2 the expected return can be calculated as follows:

$$\tfrac{1}{4} \cdot (-8) + \tfrac{1}{2} \cdot 16 + \tfrac{1}{4} \cdot 24 = 12$$

Similarly we can readily calculate the expected returns[5] for the other alternatives:

Option	Expected Return
A	8
B	10
C	12
D	6
E	13

Having calculated the expected returns for each of the five alternatives we can then choose that option with the highest expected return, in our example option E, whose expected return is 13%.

---

[4] Since we shall be calculating expected values quite often, a more formal definition may prove helpful. Let x be a discrete random variable with the probabilities $P(x)$. The expected value $E(x)$ is defined as follows:

$$E(x) = \sum_{x=-\infty}^{+\infty} x \cdot P(x).$$

For a more detailed discussion see the Statistical Supplement.

[5] In the special case of perfect certainty (options A and B) the expected return equals the actual return.

The principle of maximum expected value is deceptively simple. But is such a criterion appropriate for *all* types of investors? For example, can we expect all individuals, independent of their particular tastes, to prefer uncertain options such as C and E to an option such as B which offers a smaller, but more certain, return merely because the former have higher expected returns? Even if we restrict ourselves to a comparison of two uncertain alternatives, for example, C and E, similar problems arise. The maximum expected return criterion suggests that an option such as E should always be preferred to C since the former has a higher expected value. But option E does not dominate option C in every respect; the maximum loss that can be incurred if we choose C is 8%, while in option E we run the risk of losing as much as 20% of the investment.

3.1 THE ST. PETERSBURG PARADOX[6]

The shortcomings of the expected return criterion can perhaps be illustrated best by considering the classic problem known as the "St. Petersburg Paradox," which was first formulated in the eighteenth century by the Swiss mathematician Nicolas Bernoulli:[7]

> Peter tosses a coin and continues to do so until it should land "heads" when it comes to ground. He agrees to give Paul one ducat if he gets "heads" on the very first throw, two ducats if he gets it on the second, four if on the third, eight if on the fourth, and so on, so that with each additional throw the number of ducats he must pay is doubled. Suppose we seek to determine the value of Paul's expectation.[8]

In general, if "heads" first appears on the nth toss, the player is awarded a prize equal to 2^{n-1}. The size of the prize is uncertain, and depends on the results of each experiment, but when the coin lands "heads" for the first time the game is over, so that only one prize is awarded per game. Naturally,

---

[6] For a short history of the St. Petersburg Paradox, or the St. Petersburg Game as it is often called, see W. Fellner, *Probability and Profit*, Homewood, Ill.: Irwin, 1965.
[7] The first published analysis of the problem was written by Daniel Bernoulli (a younger cousin) during his stay in St. Petersburg as a visiting scholar (1725–1733), hence the name "St. Petersburg."
[8] The problem as formulated by Nicholas Bernoulli is quoted by Daniel Bernoulli in "Specimen Theoriae Novae de Mensura Sortis," *Papers of the Imperial Academy of Sciences in Petersburg*, Vol. V, 1738. An English translation, "Exposition of a New Theory on the Measurement of Risk," appears in *Econometrica* 22, No. 1, January 1954, pp. 23–36.

3. THE MAXIMUM EXPECTED RETURN CRITERION   195

the player would like "heads" to appear only after a long series of "tails," since this increases his prize.

What would be a fair price for Paul to pay for the opportunity to play such a game? If "heads" comes up on the first toss, the prize is one ducat; the probability of this outcome is 1/2 since there is an equal probability of obtaining either "heads" or "tails" when an unbiased coin is tossed. What is the probability of winning two ducats? This prize results should the coin land "heads" for the first time on the second toss. The probability of getting "tails" on the first toss is 1/2, and since the two tosses are *independent* events, the probability of getting "heads" on the second toss is also 1/2. The joint probability of the even TH is given by the product of the two probabilities:[9] $1/2 \cdot 1/2 = 1/4$. Theoretically the game can continue for a long time until the coin lands "heads" for the first time, but the probability of the game lasting for a great number of tosses is, of course, very small.

The principle of maximum expected return suggests that the game's expected value constitutes the maximum price for Paul to pay for this fair gamble. To facilitate the calculation of the expected value, we have set out the possible results of the coin tossing game in Table VI–3. If we denote the

TABLE VI–3. Summary of possible results of coin tossing experiment

Toss on Which "Heads" First Appears	Description of the Result*	Probability of the Result	Prize
1	H	1/2	1
2	TH	1/4	2
3	TTH	1/8	4
4	TTTH	1/16	8
.	.	.	.
.	.	.	.
n	$[(n-1)T]H$	$1/2^n$	2^{n-1}

* H signifies "heads"; T signifies "tails."

[9] Since the outcome of each toss is independent of the outcomes of the other tosses, $P(H \cap T) = P(H) \cdot P(T) = 1/2 \cdot 1/2 = 1/4$. See A. M. Mood and F. A. Graybill, *Introduction to the Theory of Statistics*, 2nd edition, New York: McGraw-Hill, 1963, p. 43, and the Statistical Supplement.

possible prize by x, the expected value (return) of the St. Petersburg game can be calculated as follows:[10]

$$E(x) = 1/2 \cdot 1 + 1/4 \cdot 2 + 1/8 \cdot 4 + 1/16 \cdot 8 + \cdots$$
$$= 1/2 + 1/2 + 1/2 + 1/2 + \cdots = \infty$$

Since there is no theoretical limit to the number of tosses, the mathematical expectation of the game is infinite; that is, invoking the principle of maximum return, Paul should be prepared to pay any sum, however large, for the opportunity to play the game!

Now assume that you are offered the opportunity to play such a game, of course in dollars rather than ducats. How much would you pay for the opportunity? An experiment conducted with a group of students revealed that most were prepared to pay only two or three dollars for a chance to play. A few were willing to pay as much as eight dollars but no one offered more than that. This contradiction between the amount that reasonable people are willing to pay for an opportunity to play the game and its infinite mathematical expectation constitutes the so-called "St. Petersburg Paradox," which troubled, and perhaps also entertained, some of the best mathematical minds of the eighteenth century.

Special interest attaches to the solutions proposed independently by the mathematician Daniel Bernoulli and by his contemporary Gabriel Cramer, who sought to resolve the problem by rejecting the principle of maximum expected return and substituting expected utility in its place. Their efforts constitute an important intellectual milestone leading to the modern theory of choice under conditions of uncertainty.

3.2 DANIEL BERNOULLI'S SOLUTION

Bernoulli's solution rests on the idea that individuals are concerned with the utility, rather than the money value, of the alternative prizes, and that the additional utility afforded by the additional money increments decreases as the money value of the prize is increased. The latter assumption is usually referred to by economists as the principle of diminishing marginal utility of money; it reflects the notion that initial sums of money are used to provide more basic needs. Thus while total utility is increased by successive increments to an individual's wealth, it increases at a diminishing rate.[11] The

---

[10] The expected return is calculated by first multiplying columns (3) and (4) of Table VI–3 and then summing the resulting products. It should also be noted that the probabilities of Table VI–3 add to 1; see note 13 on page 199.

[11] Mathematically diminishing marginal utility means that the second derivative of the utility function is negative.

3. THE MAXIMUM EXPECTED RETURN CRITERION

particular assumptions made by Bernoulli were that the utility of money is a *logarithmic* function of the size of the money prize and that the function is of the following form:[12]

$$U(x) = b \log \frac{x}{a} \qquad (6.1)$$

where: $U(x)$ is the utility derived from an amount of money x, and a and b are positive coefficients.

The logarithmic function embodies the notion that *equal proportionate* increases in wealth impart *equal absolute* additions to utility. This can be seen by considering two individuals with an initial wealth of $10 and $100 respectively. Let us assume that both investors have "Bernoulli" utility functions of the form $U(x) = b \log x/a$, and that we wish to increase their utilities by equal amounts. By how much must we increase each individual's wealth?

We first rewrite the utility function as follows:

$$U(x) = b \log \frac{x}{a} = b(\log x - \log a)$$
$$= b \log x - b \log a \qquad (6.2)$$

Table VI-4 sets out the answer to our problem using this utility function. Since $\log 10 = 1$ the utility of the first individual's initial wealth of $10 equals

$$U(10) = b \log 10 - b \log a$$
$$= b \quad - b \log a \qquad (6.3)$$

Similarly, the utility of the second individual's initial wealth of $100 is given by

$$U(100) = b \log 100 - b \log a$$
$$= 2b - b \log a \qquad (6.4)$$

---

[12] Bernoulli's function clearly incorporates the assumption of diminishing marginal utility. Since both a and b are assumed to be positive,

$$U(x) = b \log \frac{x}{a} = b \log x - b \log a$$

with the first derivative equal to

$$U'(x) = \frac{b}{x} \geq 0$$

That is, the function is monotonically *non*decreasing. This function's second derivative is negative (in the weak sense), that is, the marginal utility of money *decreases* as wealth is increased:

$$U''(x) = -\frac{b}{x^2} \leq 0.$$

For a discussion of derivatives and their use in financial analysis, see the Mathematical Supplement.

TABLE VI-4.

	Individual A	Individual B
Initial Wealth	10	100
Total Utility*	$b - b \log a$	$2b - b \log a$
Addition to Wealth	90	900
New Total Wealth	100	1,000
New Total Utility	$2b - b \log a$	$3b - b \log$
Addition to Utility Resulting from Increased Wealth	b	b

* $b \log \dfrac{x}{a} = b(\log x - \log a) = b \log x - b \log a.$

A comparison of Equations (6.3) and (6.4) shows that if we increase the wealth of the poorer individual by $90, that is, from $10 to $100, his total utility will increase by b units. (We simply subtract Equation (6.3) from Equation (6.4).) Now if we wish to increase the second individual's utility by an equal absolute amount, we must increase his wealth *in equal proportion*, that is, by $900 and not by $90. His new total wealth will then equal $1,000, with the following total utility:

$$U(1,000) = b \log 1,000 - b \log a$$
$$= 3b - b \log a \qquad (6.5)$$

Subtracting Equation (6.4) from Equation (6.5), we can verify that the wealthier individual's utility also increased by b units. In other words, the utility of an additional $900 to the wealthier individual equals the utility of the $90 added to the wealth of his poorer friend. This reflects the idea that the poorer individual has not yet fulfilled several basic requirements so that the marginal value to him of each incremental dollar is relatively higher.

Using this logarithmic function, Bernoulli argued that in determining the value of the St. Petersburg Game an individual would consider the *utility* afforded by the alternative prizes rather than their dollar amounts, and therefore the amount of money he would be prepared to pay for the opportunity to play the game depends on the game's *expected utility* and not on its expected money return. Let us denote the number of possible tosses before "heads" first appears by x (where $x = 1, 2, 3, \ldots$), and the utility derived from the prize awarded after x tosses by $U(x)$. Thus if "heads" appears after

3. THE MAXIMUM EXPECTED RETURN CRITERION

x tosses the money prize will be 2^{x-1}. The utility of this prize is given by

$$U(x) = b \log \frac{2^{x-1}}{a} = b \log 2^{x-1} - b \log a$$

$$= b[(x-1) \log 2 - \log a] \quad (6.6)$$

According to the principle of expected utility the individual will be willing to pay at most $EU(x)$ dollars (an amount equal to the game's expected utility) in order to participate:

$$EU(x) = \sum_{x=1}^{\infty} P(x)U(x) = \sum_{x=1}^{\infty} P(x)b[(x-1) \log 2 - \log a] \quad (6.7)$$

The probability of the game lasting for x tosses is $1/2^x$ so that

$$EU(x) = \sum_{x=1}^{\infty} \frac{1}{2^x} b[(x-1) \log 2 - \log a]$$

$$= b \sum_{x=1}^{\infty} \frac{x-1}{2^x} \log 2 - b \sum_{x=1}^{\infty} \frac{1}{2^x} \log a \quad (6.8)$$

However, since $\sum_{x=1}^{\infty} \frac{1}{2^x} = 1$, and $\sum_{x=1}^{\infty} \frac{x-1}{2^x} = 1$ as well,[13] we find that the expected utility of the game equals

$$EU(x) = b \log 2 - b \log a = b \log \frac{2}{a} \quad (6.9)$$

---

[13] The expression

$$\sum_{x=1}^{\infty} \frac{1}{2^x} = \frac{1}{2} + \frac{1}{4} + \frac{1}{8} + \cdots = \frac{\frac{1}{2}}{1 - \frac{1}{2}} = 1$$

Omitting the term $x = 1$ whose value is zero, the sum $\sum_{x=1}^{\infty} (x-1)/2^x$ can be expanded as follows:

$$\sum_{x=2}^{\infty} \frac{x-1}{2^x} = \frac{1}{4} + \frac{2}{8} + \frac{3}{16} + \frac{4}{32} + \cdots$$

which can be broken down into the sum of the following components:

$$\tfrac{1}{4} + \tfrac{1}{8} + \tfrac{1}{16} + \tfrac{1}{32} + \cdots = \tfrac{1}{2}$$
$$\tfrac{1}{8} + \tfrac{1}{16} + \tfrac{1}{32} + \cdots = \tfrac{1}{4}$$
$$\tfrac{1}{16} + \tfrac{1}{32} + \cdots = \tfrac{1}{8}$$
$$\tfrac{1}{32} + \cdots = \tfrac{1}{16}$$

Hence,

$$\sum_{x=1}^{\infty} \frac{x-1}{2^x} = \frac{1}{2} + \frac{1}{4} + \frac{1}{8} + \frac{1}{16} + \cdots = 1$$

But as Equation (6.2) above clearly shows, $b \log 2/a$ is also equal to the utility of \$2. It follows that an individual whose tastes are characterized by the Bernoulli utility function will pay \$2 at most to take part in the game. Alternatively, we can say that such an individual is indifferent between a perfectly certain promise of a gain of \$2 and the chance to play the game. Of course, if the individual is faced with a choice between playing the St. Petersburg Game or obtaining a perfectly certain income exceeding \$2 (say, \$3) he will prefer the second alternative even though the expected money return from the game is infinite! Thus by introducing the concept of expected utility and a logarithmic utility function Bernoulli resolved the paradox.

3.3 CRAMER'S SOLUTION

Gabriel Cramer, an equally famous eighteenth century mathematician, independently provided a somewhat similar solution to the paradox.[14] Like Bernoulli, Cramer resolved the paradox by introducing the mathematical expectation of utility in place of the expected money return. However, Cramer chose the following type of utility function to illustrate the principle of diminishing marginal utility of money:[15]

$$U(x) = \sqrt{x}$$

In other words, Cramer represented the gain in utility as being equal to the square root of the money gain. Using this utility function, the expected utility of the St. Petersburg Game becomes

$$EU(x) = \sum_{x=1}^{\infty} P(x)U(x) = \sum_{x=1}^{\infty} \frac{1}{2^x} \cdot \sqrt{2^{x-1}}$$

$$= \frac{1}{2} + \frac{\sqrt{2}}{4} + \frac{\sqrt{2} \cdot \sqrt{2}}{8} + \frac{\sqrt{2} \cdot \sqrt{2} \cdot \sqrt{2}}{16} + \cdots$$

$$= \frac{1}{2} \cdot \frac{1}{1 - \frac{\sqrt{2}}{2}} = \frac{1}{2 - \sqrt{2}}$$

---

[14] Cramer's solution was originally given in a letter which he wrote to Nicholas Bernoulli, and is quoted by Daniel Bernoulli in his celebrated paper.

[15] Like Bernoulli's, Cramer's utility function, $U(x) = \sqrt{x} = (x)^{\frac{1}{2}}$, is also monotonically nondecreasing in terms of x; that is, its first derivative is non-negative:

$$U'(x) = \tfrac{1}{2}(x)^{-\frac{1}{2}} \geq 0$$

The second derivative is negative (in the weak sense):

$$U''(x) = \tfrac{1}{2}(-\tfrac{1}{2})x^{-\frac{3}{2}} = -\tfrac{1}{4}(x)^{-\frac{3}{2}} \leq 0$$

Therefore this function also incorporates the assumption of diminishing marginal utility.

Thus the maximum price[16] that such an individual will be ready to pay in order to participate in the game is

$$\left(\frac{1}{2-\sqrt{2}}\right)^2 = (1.707)^2 = \$2.93$$

4. THE MODERN THEORY OF UTILITY

Although the expected utility hypothesis was first formulated over two hundred years ago, only comparatively recently was the deeper significance of this approach for decision making recognized. Bernoulli and Cramer were primarily interested in demonstrating the superiority of expected utility over expected monetary value. In particular, they showed that given the assumption of risk aversion (declining marginal utility of money), the expected utility approach can be used to resolve the St. Petersburg Paradox as well as to account for the willingness of people to purchase insurance policies with negative expected monetary values.

Not until the 1930s was the Bernoulli–Cramer analysis extended to the analysis of the general problem of choice under conditions of risk. In 1934 German mathematician Karl Menger demonstrated that unless the utility function is bounded, new paradoxes can be constructed which cannot be resolved by the use of expected utility.[17] For example, the Bernoulli solution breaks down[18] if we assume that the prize to be awarded when "heads" comes up on the nth toss is equal to e^{2^n}. Today, the modern theory of expected utility resolves this difficulty by assuming that the utility function is bounded.[19] However, what was to prove a more farreaching breakthrough was made by a brilliant young British logician, Frank Ramsey, in a paper published posthumously in 1931,[20] and independently in 1944 by John von Neumann and

---

[16] Cramer also presented an alternative solution. By assuming that beyond a very large possible gain the individual discounts the marginal utility of further gains to zero, the paradox can be resolved even if the utility function is linear (that is, if marginal utility is not diminishing) up to that point.
[17] Karl Menger, "Das Unsicherheitsmoment in der Wertlehre," *Zeitschrift fur National-ökonomie* 51, 1934.
[18] In this case the expected utility is given by $EU(x) = \sum_{x=1}^{\infty} (1/2^x)e^{2^x} = \infty$.
[19] See K. J. Arrow, *Aspects of the Theory of Risk-Bearing*, Helsinki, Yrjö Jahnssonin Säätiö, 1965.
[20] F. P. Ramsey, "Truth and Probability," in *The Foundations of Mathematics and Other Logical Essays*, London: K. Paul, Trench, Trusner and Co., 1931. For a sensitive appreciation of Ramsey, who died at the age of 26, see J. M. Keynes, *Essays in Biography*, London: Rupert Hart-Davis, 1951.

Oskar Morgenstern in their monumental work on the theory of games.[21] Ramsey, and later von Neumann and Morgenstern, were concerned to demonstrate the superiority of the expected utility hypothesis not only vis-à-vis expected monetary value but also with respect to other possible theories of behavior. They achieved this by providing a rigorous axiomatic justification for the use of expected utility to explain choices under conditions of uncertainty.

4.1 THE AXIOMATIC BASIS FOR EXPECTED UTILITY

Von Neumann and Morgenstern demonstrated that if a decision maker fulfills a number of reasonable consistency requirements, the expected utility hypothesis leads to optimal results under conditions of uncertainty. More specifically, they showed that utility can be introduced into decision problems in such a way that an individual who acts solely on the basis of expected utility is also acting in accordance with his true tastes. In this section we shall rough out the axiomatic foundations of the expected utility hypothesis.[22] A more rigorous presentation of the axioms and a proof that their fulfillment implies the optimality of the expected utility hypothesis is presented in Appendix VI–1 at the end of this chapter.

Let us assume that an individual is faced with alternative risky options (or alternative lotteries) A, B, and C, from which he has to choose one. If the following six axioms hold, his optimal choice will be given by that option which maximizes his expected utility:

Axiom 1: Any two alternatives are comparable, that is, the individual either prefers one to the other, or he is indifferent between them.

Axiom 2: Both the indifference and the preference relations are transitive. That is, if the individual prefers option A to option B and B to C then he also prefers A to C.

Axiom 3: Where a risky option has as one of its prizes another risky option, the first option is decomposable into its more basic alternatives. This can be clarified by considering the following example: Let Q be a lottery which includes two other lotteries L_1 and L_2 as prizes. (For example, Q is a roulette wheel whose prizes are national lottery tickets.)

$$Q = [qL_1, (1-q)L_2]$$

---

[21] See J. von Neumann and O. Morgenstern, *Theory of Games and Economic Behavior*, Princeton, N.J.: Princeton University Press, 3rd edition, 1953.

[22] Several axiomatic systems have been given; our presentation closely follows that of R. D. Luce and H. Raiffa, *Games and Decisions*. New York: Wiley, 1966.

4. THE MODERN THEORY OF UTILITY

and
$$L_1 = [P_1 A_1, (1 - P_1)A_2]$$
$$L_2 = [P_2 A_1, (1 - P_2)A_2]$$

where q is the probability of winning prize L_1, which is itself a lottery with a probability P_1 of winning prize A_1 and a probability $(1 - P_1)$ to win prize A_2. Similarly we define a second lottery, L_2. Now Axiom 3 asserts that lottery Q can be reduced to the more basic form

$$Q = [qL_1, (1-q)L_2] \sim \{q[P_1A_1, (1-P_1)A_2], (1-q)[(P_2A_1, (1-P_2)A_2]\}$$

or

$$(qL_1, (1-q)L_2) \sim (P^*A_1, (1-P^*)A_2)$$

where

$$P^* = qP_1 + (1-q)P_2$$

and the sign $\sim$ means "equivalent." That is, lottery Q can be reduced to a simple lottery, which includes as its prizes the possible outcomes A_1 and A_2.

Axiom 4: If an individual is indifferent between any two risky options, they are interchangeable as alternatives in any compound option. For example, assume the following lottery Q:

$$Q = (P_1 \cdot 1, P_2 \cdot 5, P_3 \cdot 10)$$

If the following relationship holds:

$$5 \sim (1/4 \cdot 1, 3/4 \cdot 6) = B$$

then

$$Q = (P_1 \cdot 1, P_2 \cdot 5, P_3 \cdot 10) \sim (P_1 \cdot 1, P_2[1/4 \cdot 1, 3/4 \cdot 6], P_3 \cdot 10) = Q_1$$

Thus the fourth axiom asserts that one can substitute B in lottery Q for 5, and so long as the individual is indifferent between the certainty of receiving 5 and the risky option represented by B, he will also be indifferent between Q and Q_1.

Axiom 5: If two risky options involve the same two alternatives, then the option in which the more preferred outcome has a higher probability of occurring is itself preferred. For example, if $Q = (1/4 \cdot 5, 3/4 \cdot 10)$ and $Q_1 = (1/2 \cdot 5, 1/2 \cdot 10)$, and if we assume that the individual prefers 10 to 5, then by Axiom 5 he also prefers Q to Q_1, since the probability of getting 10 in option Q is greater than in option Q_1. This assumption is usually referred to as the *monotonicity* axiom.

Axiom 6: If A is preferred to B and B to C then a lottery can be defined involving A and C which is indifferent to B. This is known in the literature as the *continuity* axiom. An example may help to clarify its meaning. Let us assume that an individual prefers $10 to $8 and $8 to $1. The continuity axiom asserts that there exists a probability P so that

$$P \cdot 10 + (1 - P) \cdot 1 \sim 8$$

where the sign $\sim$ again means equivalent.

If one is willing to accept the above six axioms then it can be shown that the optimal investment under conditions of uncertainty is that which affords the *maximum expected utility* (see Appendix VI-1). However, some criticisms have been raised: It can be argued (and often is) that in certain cases one or more of the axioms do not hold, and therefore the expected utility approach is not applicable. But despite the admitted fact that in certain choice situations the analysis may not be appropriate, we shall apply the expected utility hypothesis throughout the remainder of the book when analyzing investment decisions in securities markets. This, in turn, implies our acceptance of the consistency relationships set out in the above six axioms.[23]

4.2 THE MEANING OF UTILITY

Care must be exercised when interpreting the modern theory of utility. Although the von Neumann–Morgenstern analysis provides a logically consistent rationale for the use of expected utility as a guide for decision making under conditions of uncertainty, it should be noted that the meaning of the utility concept which is used to explain (or guide) choices under risk is limited. In the modern theory of utility, the preference axioms logically *precede* utilities, not the other way around. As a result there is no need to discuss the meaning of "underlying subjective utilities" since utilities are attached to alternative options to reflect the underlying preferences, not to account for them in any philosophical or psychological sense. Similarly, the numerical properties of the von Neumann–Morgenstern utility function are also limited. The class of admissible utility functions comprises only those which provide the same ranking of risky alternatives. Beyond this, no significance whatsoever can be attributed to the absolute magnitude of the utilities.

The class of utility functions which has the desired property of preserving the ranking of alternatives is composed of utility functions which are linear

---

[23] Needless to add, the acceptance of the axioms should not be interpreted in a normative sense. In particular we do not mean to imply that decisions *should* be consistent, but rather that investors' decisions can fruitfully be analyzed and explained on the assumption that investors act as if to maximize expected utility. We shall also present empirical evidence on the explanatory power of this assumption when applied to securities markets in Chapter VII.

4. THE MODERN THEORY OF UTILITY

TABLE VI-5.

	Option A			Option B			Option C		Option D	
Probability	1/4	1/4	1/2	1/4	1/4	1/2	1/2	1/2	2/3	1/3
Return	9	25	36	4	9	16	4	9	4	9
$U_1(x)$*	3	5	6	2	3	4	2	3	2	3
$U_2(x)$†	290	490	590	190	290	390	190	290	190	290
$U_3(x)$‡	−97	−95	−94	−98	−97	−96	−98	−97	−98	−97
$EU_1(x)$	5.00			3.75			2.50		2·33	
$EU_2(x)$	490.00			365.00			240.00		223.00	
$EU_3(x)$	−95.00			−96.25			−97.50		−97.67	

* $U_1(x) = \sqrt{x}$
† $U_2(x) = -10 + 100\sqrt{x}$
‡ $U_3(x) = -100 + \sqrt{x}$

functions of one another. Consider the three utility functions presented in Table VI-5:

$$U_1(x) = \sqrt{x};$$

$$U_2(x) = -10 + 100\sqrt{x}; \text{ and}$$

$$U_3(x) = -100 + \sqrt{x}.$$

As can be clearly seen from Table VI-5, the *absolute* magnitudes of the expected utilities of the four alternative investment options A, B, C, and D differ markedly depending on the utility function assumed. For example, using the first utility function, U_1, alternative A has an expected utility of 5, while using U_2 and U_3 results in expected utilities of 490 and −95, respectively, for the same investment option. However, Table VI-5 also clearly shows that the *ranking* of the four options remains invariant independent of the utility function assumed; thus option A is preferred tc B, B to C, and so on in all three cases, that is, for each of the utility functions U_1, U_2, and U_3.

These three functions differ only in origin and in the (positive)[24] unit of measure; the invariance of the preference ranking in our example is a special case of the following general theorem:

Theorem: *A von Neumann–Morgenstern utility function is defined up to a positive linear transformation.*

---

[24] Where utility is a negative function of income ($b < 0$), the preference ordering does *not* necessarily remain the same, see below.

This theorem states that the preference ordering of a group of alternative options will remain constant using the utility functions $U(x)$ or $U^*(x) = a + bU(x)$, independent of the value of a, so long as b is positive.[25]

The proof of this theorem is straightforward. Assume the following two alternatives:

	Option A		Option B	
x (return)	$P(x)$ (probability)	y (return)	$Q(y)$ (probability)
x_1	P_1	y_1	Q_1
.	.	.	.
.	.	.	.
.	.	.	.
x_n	P_n	y_m	Q_m

Now assume that for any general utility function U there also exists $EU(x) > EU(y)$; that is, option A is preferable to B. Let us now prove that if a utility function of the form $U^*(x)$, where $U^*(x) = a + bU(x)$ (and where $b > 0$) is used, there will necessarily exist $EU^*(x) > EU^*(y)$. In other words, substituting such a function does not change the preference ordering of the two options.

First we compute $EU^*(x)$:

$$EU^*(x) = \sum_{i=1}^{n} P_i U^*(x) = \sum_{i=1}^{n} P_i[a + bU(x_i)] = a\sum_{i=1}^{n} P_i + b\sum_{i=1}^{n} P_i U(x_i)$$

and since

$$\sum_{i=1}^{n} P_i U(x_i) = EU(x) \quad \text{and} \quad \sum_{i=1}^{n} P_i = 1$$

we obtain

$$EU^*(x) = a + bEU(x)$$

Similarly, for y

$$EU^*(y) = a + bEU(y)$$

As $b > 0$, it clearly follows that if $EU(x) > EU(y)$, then $EU^*(x) > EU^*(y)$.

---

[25] Thus despite the fact that numerical values are assigned to alternative outcomes, utilities are not cardinal utilities in the usual sense of the term.

5. ALTERNATIVE ATTITUDES TOWARD RISK

It will be convenient for the purposes of our analysis to be able to distinguish between two classes of investors: those who dislike risk, whom we shall call "risk averters"; and those who prefer risky prospects, whom we shall call "risk lovers." Suppose an individual is offered the opportunity of purchasing for $10 the following investment option:

End-of-Period Value	Probability
9	1/2
11	1/2

The expected end-of-period value of such an investment is $1/2 \cdot 9 + 1/2 \cdot 11 = 10$; that is, the expected value equals the initial purchase price. In other words, the net expected monetary return from this investment is zero.[26] Can an individual be expected to purchase such an option? Since we have rejected the principle of expected return and replaced it with the principle of expected utility, our answer depends on the individual's attitude toward risk, that is, on the degree to which he "likes" or "dislikes" to trade a safe prospect for an uncertain one.

Definition: An individual whose utility function is concave will be called a risk averter.[27]

A concave utility function, in addition to meeting the requirement that the first derivative be non-negative ($U'(x) \geq 0$), also has a negative second derivative ($U''(x) < 0$), that is, the marginal utility of money declines over the entire relevant range. Thus every risk averter will prefer a perfectly certain return to an equal, but uncertain, one. Taking our example, a risk-averse individual will not purchase the option, because in terms of utility the possible

---

[26] At this stage we are ignoring the discount factor, which is tantamount to assuming a very short investment period. For a more general formulation, taking the discount rate into account, see Chapter XII.

[27] A utility function is concave when for every two possible values x_1 and x_2 and for all $0 < \alpha < 1$ there exists

$$U[\alpha x_1 + (1 - \alpha)x_2] \geq \alpha U(x_1) + (1 - \alpha)U(x_2)$$

Graphically this means that a chord connecting points x_1 and x_2 will lie *below* the utility curve.

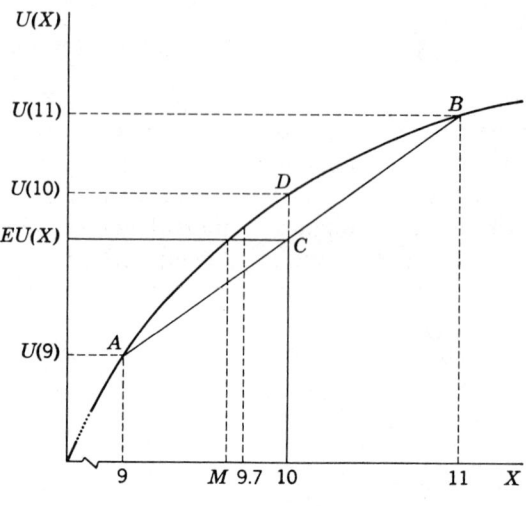

FIGURE VI.2.

loss of one dollar *more than offsets* the equal possible gain of one dollar. It follows that a risk averter is not a gambler, and in fact will never voluntarily enter a "fair" game of chance, that is one in which the expected prize equals the price of participation.[28]

This conclusion can be clarified by using a simple graphical device. Figure VI.2 sets out the same investment problem: the purchase for $10 of an investment option whose end-of-period value has an equal probability of being $9 or $11. The possible end-of-period values are set out along the horizontal axis and utility is measured along the vertical axis. The individual's utility function $U(x)$ is drawn in Figure VI.2 as a *concave* curve rising from the origin; this is tantamount to assuming that he is risk-averse.

The expected utility of the assumed investment option is

$$EU(x) = \tfrac{1}{2}U(9) + \tfrac{1}{2}U(11)$$

The expected utility is represented graphically by point C of Figure VI.2, the point at which a perpendicular rising from point 10 on the horizontal axis intersects the chord connecting A and B.[29] A glance at Figure VI.2 shows that the utility of the purchase price, $U(10)$, which corresponds to point D on the utility curve, is greater than the expected utility $EU(x)$ of the investment

---

[28] Our zero return investment option serves as a good proxy for such a gamble.
[29] For a general proof that point C represents the expected utility of such an option, see Appendix VI-2 at the end of this chapter.

5. ALTERNATIVE ATTITUDES TOWARD RISK 209

option, which corresponds to point C. Thus a risk-averse individual will not purchase an uncertain option whose expected value is equal to its purchase price, since the concavity of his utility function translates the *zero* monetary gain into a utility *loss*.

Now let us assume that the same individual is offered the same investment option, but at a lower price, say $9.70. The expected end-of-period value remains $10 so that the option has a positive expected return ($10 − 9.70). Will the individual purchase the option? Despite the lower price, Figure VI.2 clearly shows that he will *not* be willing to purchase the option since the utility of a perfectly certain sum of $9.70 exceeds the expected utility of the option (point C). How far must the price of the option fall before our risk-averse investor will be willing to acquire it? Again the answer can be readily inferred from Figure VI.2. The maximum price that he will be willing to pay is represented by point M on the horizontal axis.[30] At this price $U(M) = EU(x)$; the difference between 10 and M measures the "risk premium" required to induce the risk-averse individual to enter a fair gamble. At prices lower than M (points to the left of M on the horizontal axis) the investment option is attractive since it represents a gain in utility; conversely, at prices above M, as we have already seen, the option represents a loss of utility for the risk-averse investor.

Now let us turn our attention to a different class of possible investors—those optimistic fellows who have a preference, rather than an aversion, for risk. More formally, we shall define a risk lover as follows:

Definition: An individual whose utility function is convex[31] will be called a risk lover.

This requirement means that the second derivative of the utility function must be positive; that is, the marginal utility from each additional dollar *increases*. Unlike the previous case of risk aversion, a risk lover is by nature a gambler and will always prefer to enter a fair game of chance. It follows that such an individual will be willing to pay $10 (or perhaps even more) for the above mentioned option since it is equivalent to a fair gamble.

This result is illustrated in Figure VI.3, which sets out the relevant data for the same investment option along with a (convex) utility curve for a risk

---

[30] Strictly speaking, the prizes in all of the examples given in the text should be added to the individual's initial wealth; similarly, the price of the option should be deducted from his initial wealth. However, we defer consideration of an investor's wealth to chapter XII, thereby sacrificing at this stage accuracy for simplicity.

[31] A utility function is convex when for every pair of possible values of x_1 and x_2, and for all $0 < \alpha < 1$, there exists

$$U[\alpha x_1 + (1 - \alpha)x_2] \leq \alpha U(x_1) + (1 - \alpha)U(x_2)$$

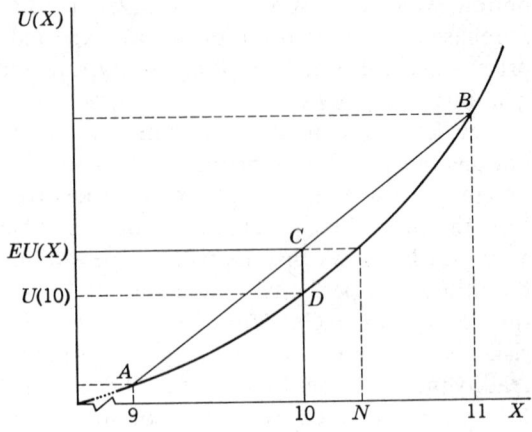

FIGURE VI.3.

lover. As before, point C on the chord connecting points A and B represents the expected utility $EU(x)$ of the risky investment option. In this case, however, $EU(x)$ is clearly greater than $U(10)$, which is represented by point D, and the risk lover will willingly purchase such an option for a price of $10. He will also gladly pay a lower price, but what is the *maximum* price that he will be willing to pay to acquire such an option? This price is represented by point N of Figure VI.3, since the utility of N dollars is equal to the expected utility of the investment option. Since $N > 10$, it also follows that a risk lover will not only accept a fair gamble, but will also be willing to accept (within limits) an "unfair" gamble as well; that is, he will be willing to pay more than the expected value for a chance of winning.

We shall now illustrate these same relationships by a numerical example. Table VI–6 sets out the end-of-period values and probabilities for another hypothetical investment option whose price is again $10. Clearly this option is again equivalent to a fair game of chance since its expected value equals its price:

$$E(x) = 7 \cdot 0.1 + 8 \cdot 0.2 + 9 \cdot 0.1 + 11 \cdot 0.5 + 13 \cdot 0.1$$
$$0.7 + \quad 1.6 + \quad 0.9 + \quad 5.5 + \quad 1.3 = 10$$

Table VI–6 also presents hypothetical utility schedules for two individuals, one of whom is assumed to be risk-averse while the second is assumed to have a preference for risk. As can be seen from the data of Table VI–6, higher levels of end-of-period value are accompanied by increases in total utility in both cases; that is, the utility functions' first derivatives are positive for both the risk averter and the risk lover. Note, however, that the "marginal"

5. ALTERNATIVE ATTITUDES TOWARD RISK

TABLE VI–6. Hypothetical utility schedules for a "risk lover" and a "risk averter"

Probability $P(x)$	End-of-Period Value (x)	Utility Schedule of Risk Lover $U(x)$	Utility Schedule of Risk Averter $U(x)$
0.1	7	5	5
0.2	8	6.1	6
0.1	9	7.3	6.9
0.0	10	8.6	7.7
0.5	11	10.0	8.3
0.0	12	13.0	8.8
0.1	13	18.0	9.0

utility (the change in utility per unit increase in end-of-period values) *decreases* for the risk averter and *increases* for the risk lover. Thus an increase in value from 7 to 8 increases the risk averter's utility by one unit ($6 - 5 = 1$), an increase from 8 to 9 raises utility by only 0.9 units, and so on. Conversely, an increase in value from 7 to 8 raises the risk lover's utility by 1.1 units ($6.1 - 5.0 = 1.1$), an increase from 8 to 9 raises utility by 1.2 units, and so on.

Now let us compute the expected utility of the option for the risk lover by multiplying the alternative end-of-period utilities by their respective probabilities[32] and summing the products:

$$
\begin{array}{lccccc}
U(x_i) & 5.0 & 6.1 & 7.3 & 10.0 & 18.0 \\
P(x_i) & 0.1 & 0.2 & 0.1 & 0.5 & 0.1 \\
U(x_i)P(x_i) & 0.50 & 1.22 & 0.73 & 5.00 & 1.80
\end{array}
$$

$$EU(x) = \sum U(x_i)P(x_i) = 9.25$$

Since the expected utility of the option is greater than the utility of its price

$$EU(x) = 9.25 > U(10) = 8.6$$

the risk lover will purchase such an option.

With respect to the risk averter, the calculation of expected utility is as follows:

$$
\begin{array}{lccccc}
U(x_i) & 5.0 & 6.0 & 6.9 & 8.3 & 9.0 \\
P(x_i) & 0.1 & 0.2 & 0.1 & 0.5 & 0.1 \\
U(x_i)P(x_i) & 0.50 & 1.20 & 0.69 & 4.15 & 0.90
\end{array}
$$

$$EU(x) = \sum U(x_i)P(x_i) = 7.44$$

---

[32] Note that the end-of-period values 10 and 12 both have zero probabilities.

In this case the utility of the price *exceeds* the expected utility of the investment option:

$$EU(x) = 7.44 < U(10) = 7.7$$

Therefore, the risk averter will not consider the option attractive.

6. THE SPECIAL CASE OF A LINEAR UTILITY FUNCTION

We have used the two hundred year old St. Petersburg Paradox and the modern theory of expected utility developed by von Neumann and Morgenstern to show that rational individuals select investments which maximize their expected utility rather than the expected monetary return. Despite this it appears that some individuals and investment companies follow a policy of maximizing expected income. The question arises whether such behavior is inherently "irrational"; more specifically, does such behavior *necessarily* constitute a contradiction of the von Neumann–Morgenstern dictum that a rational individual will reach his investment decision in accordance with the principle of maximum expected utility? With a little effort we can demonstrate that the maximization of expected return does not necessarily contradict the expected utility principle, and that such behavior can be explained as a *special* case of the utility hypothesis, one in which the decision maker's utility function is assumed to be linear.

Theorem: *When an individual's utility function is linear, that is, of the form $U(x) = a + bx$ $(b > 0)$, he will choose the investment that maximizes his expected return.*

In order to prove this theorem, let us consider an individual confronted by the following alternatives:

	Alternative A		Alternative B	
Return (x)	Probability $P(x)$	Return (y)	Probability $Q(y)$
x_1	P_1	y_1	Q_1
.	.	.	.
.	.	.	.
.	.	.	.
x_m	P_m	y_n	Q_n

where A and B represent two alternative options; $(x_1 \cdots x_m)$ and $(P_1 \cdots P_m)$ respectively denote the possible returns and probabilities of alternative A and

6. THE SPECIAL CASE OF A LINEAR UTILITY FUNCTION

$(y_1 \cdots y_n)$ and $(Q_1 \cdots Q_n)$ denote the returns and probabilities of alternative B. We also know that the following relationship must hold:

$$\sum_{i=1}^{m} P_i = \sum_{i=1}^{n} Q_i = 1$$

Let the price of option A be I_x and the price of B be I_y and assume that the individual's utility function is linear, that is, of the form $U(x) = a + bx$ (subject to the constraint that $b > 0$). We shall now show that such an individual's decision will be the same whether he chooses the option which maximizes his expected utility or the alternative which maximizes his expected net monetary return. To do this we must prove that if

$$EU(x - I_x) > EU(y - I_y)$$

then it also necessarily follows that

$$E(x) - I_x > E(y) - I_y$$

The expected utility of option x is defined as follows:

$$EU(x) = \sum_{i=1}^{m} P_i U(x_i - I_x)$$

Substituting the assumed *linear* utility function, this formula can be rewritten as

$$EU(x) = \sum_{i=1}^{m} P_i [a + b(x_i - I_x)]$$

$$= a \sum_{i=1}^{m} P_i + b \sum_{i=1}^{m} P_i x_i - b I_x \sum_{i=1}^{m} P_i$$

However, since $\sum_{i=1}^{m} P_i = 1$ and $\sum P_i x_i = E(x)$ by definition, the following equation results:

$$EU(x) = a + b[E(x) - I_x]$$

Similarly we obtain for alternative Y:

$$EU(y) = a + b[E(y) - I_y]$$

It is clear from these two equations that if the expected net return of X exceeds that of Y this also implies that the expected utility of X also exceeds that of Y, and vice versa, which is what we set out to prove.

This equivalence between the principle of maximum expected return and the assumption of a linear utility function can also be seen in Figure VI.4, which sets out a linear utility function for a hypothetical investor. Once again assume that the investor is offered the opportunity to purchase for $10 an option whose end-of-period value is expected to be $11 with a probability

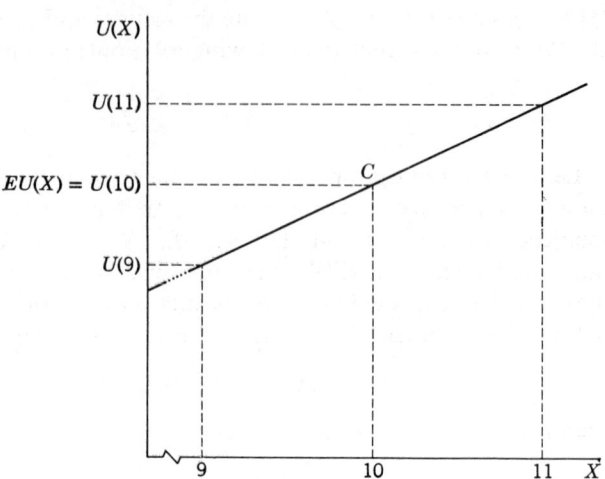

FIGURE VI.4.

of 1/2, or $9 with a probability of 1/2; that is, there is an equal probability of gaining a net return of $1 or suffering a net loss of $1. The expected utility of the option is

$$EU(x) = \tfrac{1}{2}U(9) + \tfrac{1}{2}U(11)$$

and as we have already shown, this value is given by point C of Figure VI.4. In this case

$$EU(x) = U(10)$$

and, given a price of $10, the investor is indifferent with respect to the option. The investor can be induced to acquire the option only if we assume a price lower than $10; conversely, he definitely will not purchase the option if we assume a price higher than $10. Since as we have already seen the net expected monetary value of this option is exactly zero at a purchase price of $10 (that is, it represents a fair gamble), we can state alternatively that such an individual will purchase a risky option *if and only if* its net expected return is positive.

Thus a linear utility function is appropriate for neither a risk lover nor a risk averter, but represents, so to speak, a borderline case between the two. A risk lover (with a convex utility function) will always be willing to enter a risky venture which is equivalent to a fair gamble, that is, whose net expected value is zero; a risk averter, on the other hand, will never accept such a risk. The investor with a linear utility function is *indifferent* to risk. He does not take the dispersion of outcomes into account when reaching his decision.

Thus, unlike the risk lover, he is unwilling to pay a premium to enter a fair game of chance; unlike the risk averter, he does not require a risk premium to induce him to enter such a game.

7. STATE-PREFERENCE THEORY

Typically the investment decision is characterized by the *certain* sacrifice of present resources for future *uncertain* benefits. In the remaining chapters of Part II we shall spell out a theory of investment choice under uncertainty in terms of expected returns and of the probability that the actual returns may differ from their expected values. In this section we shall present a brief review of an alternative approach which analyzes the investment decision under uncertainty in terms of the choice between consumption alternatives in different possible future "states of the world." Such a theory is usually referred to as the "time–state preference" or simply the "state-preference" approach to decision making problems.[33] Essentially this approach assumes that the evaluation of alternative investment options depends on the consumption opportunities in alternative possible states of the world. Thus a dollar's worth of return in one state (for example, prosperity) may not be the equivalent in terms of utility to an equal monetary return in a different state (depression).

Introducing the possibility that the utility of money differs in different states has some interesting implications for the analysis of investments in general and for the definition of risk in particular. To make the discussion manageable we shall consider a very restrictive case in which there exists only one present state (that is, the present is known with certainty); the future is represented by a single point in time (that is, we postulate a one-period model); and there are two *mutually exclusive* alternative states of the world, for example, war or peace. Table VI–7 presents a very simplified numerical example of this approach.[34] The individual is assumed to hold probability beliefs regarding the alternative states of the world (column 2). Applying

---

[33] State-preference theory has evolved from the pioneering work of K. J. Arrow, "The Role of Securities in the Optimal Allocation of Risk-bearing," *Review of Economic Studies* (April 1964); G. Debreu, *Theory of Value*, New York: Wiley, 1959; and J. Hirshleifer, "Investment Decision Under Uncertainty: Choice-Theoretic Approaches," *Quarterly Journal of Economics* (November 1965). A convenient review of much of the theory is given in A. A. Robichek, "Risk and the Value of Securities," *Journal of Financial and Quantitative Analysis* (December 1969).

[34] The numerical examples of Tables VI–7 and VI–8 and the textual discussion have been adapted from Robichek, *op. cit.*

TABLE VI–7. Value of a riskless option

State	Return Xi	Probabliity of State Ps	$Xi \cdot Ps$	Value of One Dollar in Alternative States Ys	$Xi \cdot Ps \cdot Ys$
1	1.00	0.3	0.30	0.70	0.21
2	1.00	0.7	0.70	0.98	0.686
			1.00		0.896

these probabilities to an option which yields $1 independent of which state occurs, yields the familiar result for a "riskless" security, namely, the expected return of such an option is also $1 (column 3). The state-preference approach is reflected in column 4, which sets out the value of $1 of return to the investor in each of the two possible states. Note that $1 of return is valued more in state 2 than in state 1, which might reflect the fact that the utility of real purchasing power in a depression, for example, is worth more to the individual than a corresponding unit of command over commodities during prosperity.[35] Applying this to our example of the "riskless" option gives a *subjective* value of 0.896 for the option which yields a return of $1 independent of the state of the world.

In the previous example we illustrated the valuation of a riskless option, that is, one that yields a given return with certainty. Table VI–8 sets out the

TABLE VI–8. Value of a risky option

State s	Return Xi	Probability of State Ps	$Xi \cdot Ps$	Value of One Dollar in Alternative States Ys	$Xi \cdot Ps \cdot Ys$
1	0.80	0.3	0.24	0.70	0.168
2	1.086	0.7	0.76	0.98	0.745
			1.00		0.913

[35] Alternatively it might reflect the correlation of the returns with the prices of the specific commodities which this particular investor desires to consume. See Y. Peles, "A Note on Risk and the Theory of Asset Value," *Journal of Financial and Quantitative Analysis* (January 1971).

relevant data for a "risky" option, the return on which is a random variable which depends on the state of nature that occurs. Again the expected value of this option is $1, but its subjective value to the investor is higher than in the previous case (0.913 as compared with 0.896), reflecting the fact that the second option offers the possibility of higher returns in state 2 when they are of most value to the investor.

Even this brief glimpse of the state-preference approach raises some very perplexing questions regarding the concept of risk, since the same option may be much more "risky" for one investor than for another[36] when the utility of wealth in alternative states is taken into account. In the extreme, this approach suggests that investment risk is unique to the individual; great care must be exercised when generalizing the analysis of risk options which was set out in the earlier sections of this chapter. Essentially, the previous approach is a special (degenerate) case of the state-preference approach—one in which a unique future state is postulated. Thus the utility of a given return at a given point of time may differ among investors depending on the shapes of their utility functions, but its utility for any *given* individual is assumed to be constant, independent of his consumption opportunities. The degree to which this admitted oversimplification of decision making behavior can provide a useful model for the analysis of investment decisions in security markets raises what is essentially an empirical question, which will be examined in the following chapter.

8. SUMMARY

The purpose of this chapter has been to set out the utility foundations of the theory of investment choice under conditions of risk or uncertainty. A risky (or uncertain) investment is defined as an option whose return is not known with absolute certainty, but for which an array of alternative returns and their (objective or subjective) probabilities are known. After a demonstration of the inappropriateness of the maximum return criterion for choices involving risk, the concept of expected value and its maximization was introduced. The shortcomings of the expected return criterion were then analyzed by considering the two hundred year old "St. Petersburg Paradox" and the solutions proposed by the eighteenth century mathematicians Daniel Bernoulli and Gabriel Cramer, both of whom attempted to resolve the paradox by substituting the principle of utility maximization for the principle of maximum money returns. Both the Bernoulli and the Cramer solutions

---

[36] We return to this problem, in a somewhat different context, in Chapter IX.

assume *concave* utility functions, that is, functions that incorporate the assumption of diminishing marginal utility of money.

Next, the modern theory of expected utility and its axiomatic basis, primarily associated with the work of von Neumann and Morgenstern, were introduced. The six axioms underlying the theory of expected utility were explained. A proof that their fulfillment implies the maximization of expected utility is given in Appendix VI–1. Some of the properties of the modern utility approach were then discussed. In particular it should be emphasized that a von Neumann–Morgenstern utility function is a tool of logical analysis far different from the concept of hedonist utility of classical economics. In the modern theory of utility, an option has a high utility *because* individuals prefer that option, and *not* the other way around. Similarly, the numerical properties of the utility function are limited. Although von Neumann and Morgenstern postulate a cardinal utility function, that is, one in which absolute numbers are assigned to alternative levels of utility, the utility function is defined up to a positive linear transformation. The class of admissible functions, therefore, includes only those which preserve the same *ranking* of risky alternatives; no other significance (psychological or philosophical) attaches to the magnitude of the utilities.

We next defined several alternative risk attitudes and a simple geometric apparatus for portraying them. We distinguished between three basic types of investors:

(a) risk averters—individuals with *concave* utility functions;
(b) risk lovers—individuals with *convex* utility functions; and
(c) risk-neutral individuals—individuals with linear utility functions.

The concept of utility frequently appears too theoretical, too complex, and perhaps too mathematical as well, to help the average investor or the proverbial widow of financial lore. However, this concept is nothing more than a generalization of the principle of expected return or of expected profits. The major difference is that the use of utility permits us to place differential weights on different money outcomes. According to the expected return principle, a loss of $100 with a probability of 1/10 is equivalent to a possible loss of $1,000 with a probability of 1/100. By introducing the concept of utility, we allow for those cases in which because of the size of the loss involved an investor may impute a much larger penalty to the chance of losing $1,000. In the special case of a linear utility function, we return to the principle of expected return.

The chapter concluded with a brief digression on state-preference theory, which introduces yet another dimension to the analysis: the differential value of a given return to an investor in different alternative states of the world.

A final caveat may be in order. The modern theory of utility does *not*

8. SUMMARY

imply that investors assign utilities to alternative choices, but rather that they act *as if* such calculations had been made. The abstract theory is designed to explain and predict complex behavior patterns, and with the advent of the electronic computer, to simulate choice situations. Gathering reliable information regarding investors' tastes and forecasting an uncertain future are likely to remain the central problems of investment analysis for some time to come. With this in mind, we turn in the next chapter to the problem of determining investors' attitudes toward risk in actual securities markets.

QUESTIONS AND PROBLEMS

6.1 Define the maximum expected return criterion. What is the major shortcoming of this criterion for decision making under conditions of risk?

6.2 Compare the Bernoulli and Cramer solutions to the St. Petersburg Paradox.

6.3 Resolve the St. Petersburg Paradox using a utility function other than the ones proposed by Bernoulli and Cramer.

6.4 In what sense do the von Neumann–Morgenstern Axioms "logically *precede*" the assignment of utilities?

6.5 Explain what is meant by a utility function which is defined up to a linear transformation. What is the significance of such a function for decision making?

6.6 Define the following terms:

   a. *risk averter*
   b. *risk lover*
   c. *risk neutrality*

6.7 "A risk averter will never enter a fair game of chance." Prove this statement graphically. In your answer indicate the "risk premium" necessary to induce him to agree to play.

6.8 "A risk-neutral investor, that is, one who has a linear utility function, makes his investment decisions in accordance with the principle of maximum expected return, *rather than with that of maximum expected utility*." Is this statement correct? Prove your answer.

6.9 Assume that an individual is confronted with the problem of choosing *one* of the following investment options:

Option A		Option B		Option C	
Probability	Return*	Probability	Return*	Probability	Return*
1/2	−10	5/8	−10	1/2	0
1/4	20	1/8	20	3/8	10
1/4	30	1/4	40	1/8	20

* per $100 invested.

QUESTIONS AND PROBLEMS

a. Which option will be chosen according to the principle of maximum expected return?

b. Which option will be chosen according to the maximum expected utility principle, using the following two alternative utility functions, $U_1(X)$ and $U_2(X)$:

Return (X)	$U_1(X)$	$U_2(X)$
−10	−100	−100
0	0	0
10	86	120
20	150	260
30	200	440
40	232	660

c. How does your answer to part (b) change if you assume that the individual has the following utility function:

$$U_3(X) = a + \frac{U_2(X)}{b} \quad \text{(where } b > 0\text{)}$$

Solve the problem numerically for the special case where $a = -10$ and $b = +10$, and explain your results.

d. Graph the above mentioned alternative utility functions, U_1, U_2, U_3, over the domain $(40 > X > -10)$ and indicate which of the functions represents a "risk averter" and which represents a "risk lover."

e. Why is it impossible for U_2 and U_3 to represent *different* risk attitudes?

f. Calculate the marginal utilities of money implied by U_1 and U_2. Show your calculations. Are these results consistent with your answer to part (d)?

6.10 An individual is offered a chance to choose between two alternative investment options, A and B.

Option A*		Option B†	
Probability	Return	Probability	Return
p	X_0	$P - q$	X_0
$1 - p$	$X_0 + \delta$	$2q$	$X_0 + \gamma$
		$1 - p - q$	$X_0 + \delta$

* (where $0 < p < 1$; $\delta > 0$).
† (where $0 < q < 1$; $0 < \gamma < \delta$).

a. Which option will be preferred by a risk lover? Support your conclusion by giving a numerical example. (Hint: Try a number of *different* convex utility functions and calculate the expected utility of the two options.)

b. Which option will be preferred by a risk averter?

6.11 Assume the following two investment options:

Option A		Option B	
Probability	Return	Probability	Return
1/2	2	1/2	8
1/2	10	1/2	20

a. Which of the two options will be chosen by an investor whose utility function is given by

$$U(X) = 1{,}000 + (X - 10)^3?$$

b. What is the maximum price that such an individual will be willing to pay for each option?

6.12 "A risk averter will always prefer a government bond to a common stock since the bond has less risk." What is your opinion of the above statement, assuming:

a. that the bonds are short-term.
b. that the bonds are long-term.

SELECTED REFERENCES

Alchian, A. A., "The Meaning of Utility Measurement," *American Economic Review* (March 1953).

Arditti, F. D., "Risk and the Required Return on Equity," *Journal of Finance* (March 1967).

Arrow, K. J., "Alternative Approaches to the Theory of Choice in Risk-Taking Situations," *Econometrica* (October 1951).

———, *Aspects of the Theory of Risk-Bearing*. Helsinki: Yrjo Jahnssonin Säätiö, 1965.

———, "The Role of Securities in the Optimal Allocation of Risk-Bearing," *Review of Economic Studies* (April 1964).

Bernoulli, D., "Exposition of a New Theory on the Measurement of Risk," *Econometrica* (January 1954).

Bierwag, G. O., and Grove, M. A., "Portfolio Selection and Taxation," *Oxford Economic Papers* (July 1957).

Borch, K., *The Economics of Uncertainty*. Princeton, N.J.: Princeton University Press, 1968.

———, "A Note on Utility and Attitudes to Risk," *Management Science* (July 1964).

Borch, K., and Mossin, J., *Risk and Uncertainty*, Proceedings of the Conference on Risk and Uncertainty of the International Economic Association. London: Macmillan, 1968.

Briscoe, G.; Samuels, J. M.; and Smyth, D. J., "The Treatment of Risk in the Stock Market," *Journal of Finance* (September 1969).

Debreu, G., *Theory of Value: An Axiomatic Analysis of Economic Equilibrium*. New York: Wiley, 1959.

Durand, D., "Growth Stocks and the Petersburg Paradox," *Journal of Finance* (September 1957).

Edwards, W., and Tversky, A., *Decision Making*. Harmondsworth, England: Penguin Books, 1967.

Ellsburg, D., "Classic and Current Notions of 'Measurable Utility'," *Economic Journal* (September 1954).

———, "Risk, Ambiguity and the Savage Axioms," *Quarterly Journal of Economics* (November 1961).

Fellner, W. J., *Probability and Profit*. Homewood, Ill.: Irwin, 1965.

Friedman, M., and Savage, L. J., "The Expected Utility Hypothesis and the

Measurability of Utility," *Journal of Political Economy* (December 1952).

Friedman, M., and Savage, L. J., "The Utility Analysis of Choices Involving Risk," *Journal of Political Economy* (August 1948).

Hakansson, N., "Friedman–Savage Utility Functions Consistent with Risk Aversion," *Quarterly Journal of Economics* (August 1970).

Hirshleifer, J., "Investment Decisions Under Uncertainty: Applications of the State-Preference Approach," *Quarterly Journal of Economics* (May 1966).

———, "Investment Decision Under Uncertainty: Choice-Theoretic Approaches," *Quarterly Journal of Economics* (November 1965).

Kaplansky, I., "A Common Error Concerning Kurtosis," *Journal of the American Statistical Association* (June 1945).

Keynes, J. M., *Essays in Biography* (new edition with three additional essays), edited by Geoffrey Keynes. New York: Horizon Press, 1951.

Knight, F. H., *Risk, Uncertainty and Profit*. Boston and New York: Houghton Mifflin, 1921.

Levy, H., "A Utility Function Depending on the First Three Moments," *Journal of Finance* (September 1969).

Luce, R. D., and Raiffa, H., *Games and Decisions*. New York: Wiley, 1957.

Markowitz, H. M., *Portfolio Selection*. New York: Wiley, 1959.

———, "The Utility of Wealth," *Journal of Political Economy* (1952).

Menger, K., "Das Unsicherheitsmoment in Der Wertlehre," *Zeitschrift Fur Nationalokonomie* 1934. (An English translation, "The Role of Uncertainty in Economics," appears in M. Shubik (editor), *Essays in Mathematical Economics in Honor of Oskar Morgenstern*. Princeton, N.J.: Princeton University Press, 1967.)

Miller, M. H., "Some Thoughts on Testing the Relation Between Risk and Return," unpublished paper (November 1965).

Mosteller, F., and Nogee, P., "An Experimental Measurement of Utility," *Journal of Political Economy* (October 1951).

Myers, S. C., "A Time–State-Preference Model of Security Valuation," *Journal of Financial and Quantitative Analysis* (March 1968).

Pratt, J. W., "Risk Aversion in the Small and in the Large," *Econometrica* (January–April 1964).

Raiffa, H., *Decision Analysis*. Reading, Mass.: Addison-Wesley, 1968.

Ramsey, F. P., "Truth and Probability," in *The Foundations of Mathematics and Other Logical Essays*. London: K. Paul, Trench, Trubner & Co., 1931.

Richter, M. K., "Cardinal Utility, Portfolio Selection and Taxation," *Review of Economic Studies* (June 1960).

SELECTED REFERENCES

Robichek, A. A., "Risk and the Value of Securities," *Journal of Financial and Quantitative Analysis* (December 1969).

Rosett, R. N., "Measuring the Perception of Risk," in *Risk and Uncertainty*, edited by Karl Borch and Jan Mossin. London: Macmillan, 1968.

Savage, L. J., *The Foundations of Statistics.* New York: Wiley, 1954.

Sharpe, W. F., "Risk Aversion in the Stock Market: Some Empirical Evidence," *Journal of Finance* (September 1965).

Shelly, M. W. II, and Bryan, G. L., eds., *Human Judgments and Optimality.* New York: Wiley, 1964.

von Neumann, J., and Morgenstern, O., *Theory of Games and Economic Behavior*, 2nd edition. Princeton, N.J.: Princeton University Press, 1947.

Yaari, M. E., "Convexity in the Theory of Choice Under Risk," *Quarterly Journal of Economics* (May 1965).

APPENDIX VI-1

Proof that the Expected Utility Principle Follows from the von Neumann-Morgenstern Axioms

The purpose of this appendix is to show that if an investor fulfills some consistency requirements (given in Chapter VI), he will carry out his decisions according to the expected utility rule. To prove this statement, let us assume that the investor is faced with the following two lotteries:

$$L_1 = (P_1 A_1, P_2 A_2 \cdots P_n A_n)$$
$$L_2 = (q_1 A_1, q_2 A_2 \cdots q_n A_n)$$
(1)

where: $A_i = $ a possible prize
$P_i = $ the probability of getting A_i under lottery L_1
$q_i = $ the probability of getting A_i under lottery L_2.

Obviously, $P_i \geq 0$, $q_i \geq 0$, and $\sum_{i=1}^{n} P_i = \sum_{i=1}^{n} q_i = 1$.
Without loss of generality, let us assume that[37]

$$A_1 \succ A_2 \succ A_3 \succ \cdots \succ A_n$$

where $\succ$ means preferable.

Using Axiom 6, we can find for each prize A_i a lottery A^* such that the investor will be indifferent between A_i and A_i^*, that is,

$$A_i \sim [u_i A_1, (1 - u_i) A_n] \equiv A_i^*$$

where $\sim$ means "equivalent" and u_i is some number. It is clear that if

$$A_i \succ A_j$$

---

[37] If this is not the case, we can always rearrange the prizes in such an order. See Axiom 1.

APPENDIX VI-1

we expect that $u_i > u_j$, since we have to give higher weight to A_1 under lottery A_i^* than under lottery A_j^*.[38]

By Axiom 4 we can substitute some A_i in L_1 and in L_2 for A_i^*. Since the preference and indifference relations are transitive (Axiom 2), we can continue this process serially till we get

$$L_1 = (P_1 A_1^*, P_2 A_2^*, \ldots, P_n A_n^*)$$
$$L_2 = (q_1 A_1^*, q_2 A_2^*, \ldots, q_n A_n^*) \qquad (2)$$

Hence we move from set of lotteries given by (1) to set of composite lotteries given by (2). Using Axiom 3, we can simplify (2) and express these lotteries by the following simple form:

$$L_1 = (\bar{P} A_1, (1 - \bar{P}) A_n)$$
$$L_2 = (\bar{q} A_1, (1 - \bar{q}) A_n) \qquad (3)$$

where:[39]

$$\bar{P} = P_1 u_1 + P_2 u_1 + \cdots + P_n u_n \quad \text{(Expected value of } u \text{ under } L_1\text{)}$$
$$\bar{q} = q_1 u_1 + q_2 u_2 + \cdots + q_n u_n \quad \text{(Expected value of } u \text{ under } L_2\text{)} \qquad (4)$$

As $A_1 \succ A_n$, by Axiom 5 (monotonicity)

$$L_1 \succ L_2 \quad \text{if and only if} \quad \bar{P} > \bar{q}$$

In conclusion, if Axioms 1 through 6 hold, then there are numbers (which we call utilities) u_i, associated with the prizes A_i, such that the lottery with the higher *expected value* of this number is preferred. That is to say, if $L_1 \succ L_2$, then we can assign a utility function u to this lottery such that

$$Eu(L_1) > Eu(L_2)$$

---

[38] Because of this relation we can assign the following values, which express A_i^* in probabilistic terms:

$$u(A_1) = u_1 = 1$$
$$u(A_i) = u_i \quad \text{where} \quad 0 < u_i < 1 \text{ for } i = 2, \ldots n - 1$$
$$u(A_n) = u_n = 0$$

There is no loss of generality since the utility function is determined up to a positive linear transformation (see Chapter VI). We can multiply each u_i by a positive number and add a constant number to each u_i without changing the preference order.

[39] Lottery L_1 can be written as follows:

$$L_1 = \{P_1[u_1 A_1, (1 - u_1) A_n], \ldots P_n[(u_n A_1, (1 - u_n) A_n]\}$$

Hence

$$L_1 = \left[\left(\sum_{i=1}^n P_i u_i \right) A_1, \left(1 - \sum_{i=1}^n P_i u_1 \right) A_n \right] = [\bar{P} A_1, (1 - \bar{P}) A_n]$$

Similarly, by changing q for P, L_2 is obtained.

APPENDIX VI–2

A Graphical Representation of Expected Utility

We prove in this appendix that if the investor is faced with outcome $\overline{OG}$ with probability α and outcome $\overline{OH}$ with probability $(1-\alpha)$ then the expected utility of this distribution is given by C, which represents the intersection

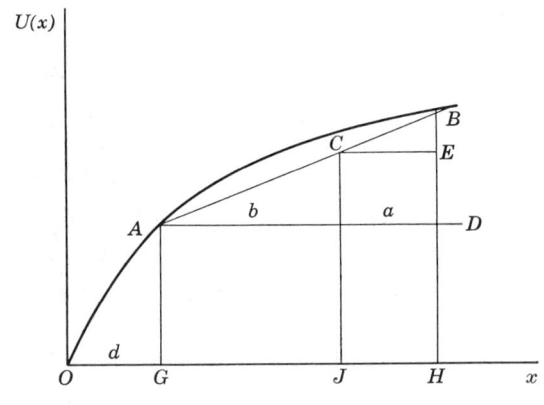

APPENDIX VI.2.

point between the perpendicular rising from point J and the chord connecting A and B, where point J represents the expected value of this distribution, that is

$$\overline{OJ} = \alpha\overline{OG} + (1-\alpha)\overline{OH} \qquad (1)$$

Proof: The expected utility is represented by a point between B and D, for example, point E. Hence

$$\overline{HE} = \alpha\overline{GA} + (1-\alpha)\overline{HB} \qquad (2)$$

where $\overline{HE}$ is the expected utility. Since $\overline{GA} = \overline{HD}$, (2) can be rewritten

$$\overline{HE} = \alpha\overline{HD} + (1-\alpha)\overline{HB} \qquad (2')$$

Subtracting $\overline{HD}$ from both sides we get

$$\overline{HE} - \overline{HD} = (1-\alpha)(\overline{HB} - \overline{HD}) \qquad (3)$$

APPENDIX VI-2

Hence
$$\alpha = \frac{\overline{HB} - \overline{HE}}{\overline{HB} - \overline{HD}}$$

Examining the triangle ABD it is clear that α can be rewritten as

$$\alpha = \frac{a}{a+b} \qquad (4)$$

Hence
$$1 - \alpha = \frac{b}{a+b}$$

It remains to show that using α, which is given by (4) in calculating the expected outcome, the expected value we get is equal to $\overline{OJ}$:

$$\text{Expected outcome} = \frac{a}{a+b}\overline{OG} + \frac{b}{a+b}\overline{OH}$$

$$= \frac{a}{a+b}d + \frac{b}{a+b}(a+b+d) = d+b = \overline{OJ}$$

Q.E.D.

Chapter VII
Alternative Shapes of the Utility Function

1. INTRODUCTION

In the previous chapter we saw that investment decisions under conditions of uncertainty can be explained by invoking the principle of expected utility. While it is true that in some cases rational investors will apply the principle of expected return, this is a special case of the expected utility principle, in which the investor's utility function is linear. Although the expected utility hypothesis provides a powerful tool for rationalizing investors' behavior, it does not, by itself, provide a divining rod for choosing the "best" option out of a group of alternative investments. Investment choice remains a very difficult problem in the absence of more precise knowledge regarding the shape of the investor's utility function (that is, of his tastes).

The need for additional information can be illustrated by means of the example given in Table VII–1, which sets out the end-of-period values of three alternative investments; for the sake of simplicity, we assume that all three have the same initial purchase price of $100. Let us suppose that an

TABLE VII–1.

Option A		Option B		Option C	
End-of-Period Value	Probability	End-of-Period Value	Probability	End-of-Period Value	Probability
95	1/2	85	1/2	70	1/2
105	1/2	100	1/4	130	1/2
		140	1/4		
$E(x_A) = 100$		$E(x_B) = 102.5$		$E(x_C) = 100$	

TABLE VII-2.

Option A			Option B			Option C		
x_A	$U(x_A)$	$P(x_A)$	x_B	$U(x_B)$	$P(x_B)$	x_C	$U(x_C)$	$P(x_C)$
95	119.49	1/2	85	118.44	1/2	70	116.73	1/2
105	120.48	1/2	100	120.00	1/4			
			140	123.66	1/4	130	122.8	1/2
	$EU(x_A) = 120.0*$			$EU(x_B) = 120.1*$			$EU(x_C) = 119.8*$	

* Expected utility has been calculated using the following function:

$$U(x) = 100 + 2\sqrt{x}$$

investor wishes to purchase one of these investment options, and we are given the task of recommending the "best" alternative. Let us further assume that the individual's utility function is known and is given by[1]

$$U(x) = 100 + 2\sqrt{x}$$

That is, we have complete information regarding his tastes. In this case all we have to do is calculate the expected utility of each of the alternatives, which has been done in Table VII-2. Option B has the highest expected utility, therefore the investor should choose this alternative. Thus, given *full* information regarding an investor's utility function, one can readily determine the most preferable alternative.

Unfortunately, however, an investment consultant is rarely in possession of such detailed information regarding an investor's tastes. Moreover, even the investor himself is often unable to articulate the rules that guide his own behavior, and thus he cannot provide reliable information as to his preferences. In cases where investors' tastes are not known with any degree of accuracy—and these represent the vast majority of cases—the investment analysis becomes more difficult since it must be made on the basis of *partial* information only.

To illustrate how partial information can be used to reach an investment decision, let us assume a case in which our knowledge is limited to the fact

---

[1] This utility function is appropriate for a risk averter, since there exist:

$$U'(x) = x^{-\frac{1}{2}} \geq 0 \quad \text{(for all } x \geq 0\text{), and}$$
$$U''(x) = -\tfrac{1}{2}x^{-\frac{3}{2}} \leq 0 \quad \text{(for all } x \geq 0\text{).}$$

The restriction of the analysis to $x \geq 0$ reflects the fundamental fact that the value of the option (for example, the price of a security) cannot fall below zero.

1. INTRODUCTION 233

that the investor is risk-averse. Thus all we know about the shape of his utility function is that the first derivative is non-negative, $U'(x) \geq 0$, and that the second derivative is negative, $U''(x) < 0$. The second condition indicates that the investor is a risk averter, because the marginal utility of money declines, that is, the value to him of each additional dollar decreases, as his wealth increases. Such information is clearly partial since it does *not* permit us to find the exact shape of the individual's utility function. The function might, for example, be $U(x) = \sqrt{x}$, or $U(x) = \log x$, or any other function that meets the above mentioned requirements regarding the first two derivatives. In effect, *any* concave utility function will do.

Is the partial information that the utility function is concave (that is, $U''(x) < 0$) sufficient to determine which of the three options given in Table VII-1 should be preferred? One thing is certain: option A is clearly preferable to option C since both have the same expected return while option C has a larger dispersion of outcomes. Since we know that a risk averter, other things being equal, dislikes dispersion, he will prefer the option with the more stable income flow. Graphically this is illustrated in Figure VII.1, which shows clearly that if $U(x)$ is a concave function then

$$EU(x_A) > EU(x_C)$$

and the investor will always prefer option A to option C. Thus his choice can be restricted to alternatives A and B. But which of these two alternatives is preferable for our risk-averse investor? The partial information we have on the shape of the utility functions is not sufficient to answer this question. True, option B has a greater dispersion of outcomes, but its expected return

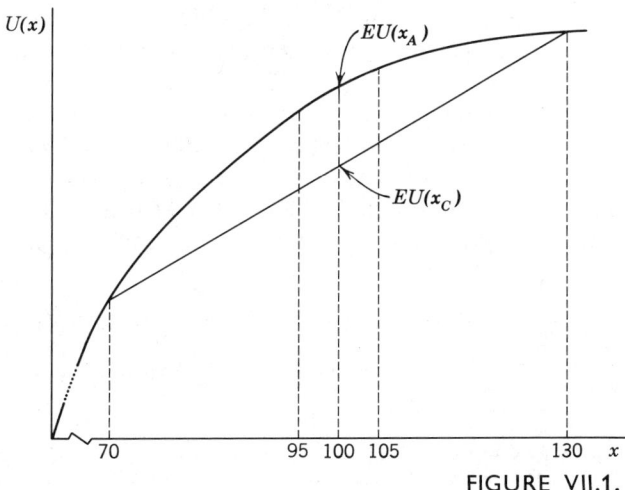

FIGURE VII.1.

TABLE VII-3.

Option A			Option B			Option C		
X_A	$U(x_A)$	$P(x_A)$	X_B	$U(x_B)$	$P(x_B)$	X_C	$U(x_C)$	$P(x_C)$
95	19.58	1/2	85	18.38	1/2	70	16.20	1/2
105	20.58	1/2	100	20.10	1/4			
			140	22.50	1/4	130	22.20	1/2
$EU(x_A) = 20.1^*$			$EU(x_B) = 19.8^*$			$EU(x_C) = 19.2^*$		

* Expected utility has been calculated using the following function:
$$U(x) = 100 + 300x - x^2 \text{ (for } x \leq 150\text{)}$$

is also higher than that of A. In this instance it is impossible to tell which of the two options is preferable, since some risk-averse investors might prefer option A, while other risk averters might conceivably prefer option B. For example, if an investor has a concave utility function of the form

$$U(x) = 100 + 2\sqrt{x}$$

he would prefer option B to option A, since the former has the higher expected utility (see Table VII–2). If, however, his utility function is concave, but of the form[2]

$$U(x) = 100 + 300x - x^2 \quad \text{(for } x \leq 150\text{)}$$

then option A has the higher expected utility,[3] as may again be seen in Table VII–3.

The conclusion to be drawn from this simplified example is that if we have a complete specification of the investor's utility function we can choose a single option unequivocally; but if we have only partial information (for example, on the general shape of the utility function) we can only reduce the opportunity set by eliminating those options which are inferior for the entire class of functions.[4] Thus partial information on an individual's utility function permits us to reduce the number of feasible options but typically does not permit an unequivocal recommendation of a particular alternative.

---

[2] The utility function $U(x) = 100 + 300x - x^2$ meets the requirements that $U'(x) \geq 0$ and that $U''(x) < 0$:
$$U'(x) = 300 - 2x \geq 0 \quad \text{(and therefore } x \leq 150\text{)}$$
$$U''(x) = -2 < 0$$

[3] Note that as we have already indicated, option C is not preferred in either case.
[4] Rules for reducing the opportunity set are set out in Chapter VIII.

Of course, the above example has been oversimplified. We dealt with only three alternatives in order to illustrate how partial information on individuals' tastes can be used to facilitate investment analysis. Our numerical example shows that with partial information on an investor's tastes we can divide all potential investments into two groups: one composed of those options which do not interest him, the second composed of all the options that he is likely to find profitable. We know that the rational investor will make his final choice from the second group, but we cannot specify what his exact choice will be. The ability to use partial information is not without economic significance. It should be emphasized that "search costs" can be minimized by an early elimination of nondesirable options, thereby enabling a proportionately larger expenditure on the analysis of the remaining smaller subset. No less important, knowledge of the factors which affect decision making under conditions of uncertainty is vital for our understanding of basic economic relationships. The structure of prices in financial markets, the financing of capital formation, and international capital movements all depend to a large extent on the decisions made by individual investors when choosing among risky alternatives.

As we have seen, the initial division into two groups depends on partial information regarding the general shape of investors' utility functions. This immediately raises the question of what assumptions can reasonably be made regarding the tastes of the investing public. Clearly, stronger assumptions regarding the shape of the utility function will enhance the selection process, that is, will reduce the size of the feasible subset.[5]

In a somewhat different context this question has received considerable attention from economic theorists who have attempted to rationalize individuals' behavior under conditions of uncertainty. We now turn our attention to two different approaches to the problem of inferring the shape of investors' utility functions under conditions of uncertainty.

2. THE FRIEDMAN–SAVAGE HYPOTHESIS

Perhaps the best known attempt to use utility analysis to explain individuals' choices under uncertainty was made by Friedman and Savage in their classic 1948 article.[6] Friedman and Savage were troubled by an apparent inconsistency in people's behavior: many people purchase insurance and also gamble, which would seem to imply a willingness to pay premiums for the

---

[5] See Chapter VIII.
[6] See Milton Friedman and Leonard J. Savage, "The Utility Analysis of Choices Involving Risk," *The Journal of Political Economy* LVI, No. 4, August 1948.

opportunity to avoid risk, in the first instance, and to undertake risk, in the second case. To remove the contradiction Friedman and Savage attempted to infer the shape of the utility function implied by the following simplified empirical evidence:[7]

1. Individuals always prefer higher to lower riskless income streams.
2. Many people in low income groups are willing to buy insurance.
3. Many people in low income groups are willing to buy lottery tickets.
4. Many people in low income groups purchase both insurance policies and lottery tickets.
5. Lotteries or raffles typically offer more than one prize.

What are the utility implications of the willingness to buy insurance? Consider an individual who is weighing the purchase of an insurance policy against fire loss. Assume that there exists a probability α that a fire will break out; if the individual fails to insure the property he will be left with a salvage value equal to I_1 in Figure VII.2. However, there is also a probability $(1 - \alpha)$ that no fire will break out, in which case the individual's property will be worth I_2 ($I_2 > I_1$). If the individual does *not* purchase the insurance

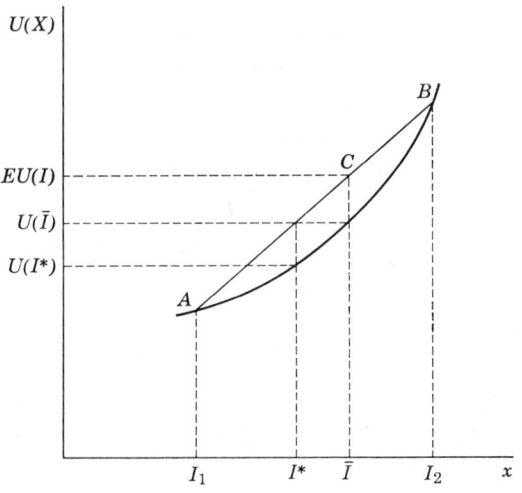

FIGURE VII.2.

[7] The following paraphrases Friedman and Savage, *op. cit.*

2. THE FRIEDMAN–SAVAGE HYPOTHESIS

policy his expected wealth will be $\bar{I}$, where

$$\bar{I} = \alpha I_1 + (1 - \alpha)I_2$$

Let us further assume that this individual is a risk lover, that is, he has a convex utility function. Will he be willing to take out fire insurance? The answer can be inferred from Figure VII.2, which sets out the relevant graphical analysis. If he does not take out insurance, his expected utility is

$$EU(I) = \alpha EU(I_1) + (1 - \alpha)EU(I_2)$$

which is represented in Figure VII.2 by point C, the intersection of the perpendicular originating from point $\bar{I}$ on the horizontal axis with the chord AB.[8] From Figure VII.2 we clearly see that the expected utility of the property value *without* insurance, $EU(I)$, exceeds the expected utility of $\bar{I}$, the maximum perfectly certain property value which an insurance company could offer. $\bar{I}$ is the maximum that an insurance company can offer; because due to the law of large numbers $\bar{I}$ is also the amount that the company will have to pay out on the average. In fact, since insurance companies must charge a commission to cover expenses and to earn a profit, the maximum *net* certain property value they can offer is actually lower than $\bar{I}$, say I^*. Since $I^* < \bar{I}$, clearly $U(I^*) < U(\bar{I})$ so that $EU(I) > EU(I^*)$; therefore an individual who is a risk lover will *not* purchase an insurance policy.

Can the purchase of insurance be rationalized by assuming risk aversion, that is, by assuming that the individual has a *concave* utility function? Figure VII.3 sets out such a function for our hypothetical property owner. As in the previous case, the expected property value without insurance is $\bar{I}$ where

$$\bar{I} = \alpha I_1 + (1 - \alpha)I_2$$

The expected utility without purchasing the policy is again given by

$$EU(I) = \alpha EU(I_1) + (1 - \alpha)EU(I_2)$$

that is, by point C in Figure VII.3. From the diagram we can see that if $U(x)$ is concave, that is, if the individual is a risk averter, he will prefer a perfectly certain property value, even if it is lower than $\bar{I}$.

Without insurance the property owner faces either an outcome of I_2 (with a probability of $1 - \alpha$) or of I_1 (with a probability of α). However since $U(\bar{I}) > EU(I)$, an individual with a concave utility function is vulnerable to risk, and therefore will prefer to "sell" this risk to the insurance company in return for a perfectly certain property value. Moreover, he will be willing to convert the risk-option $\alpha I_1 + (1 - \alpha)I_2$ into a perfectly certain value *lower*

---

[8] For a formal proof that point C represents $EU(I)$, see Appendix VI–2.

ALTERNATIVE SHAPES OF THE UTILITY FUNCTION

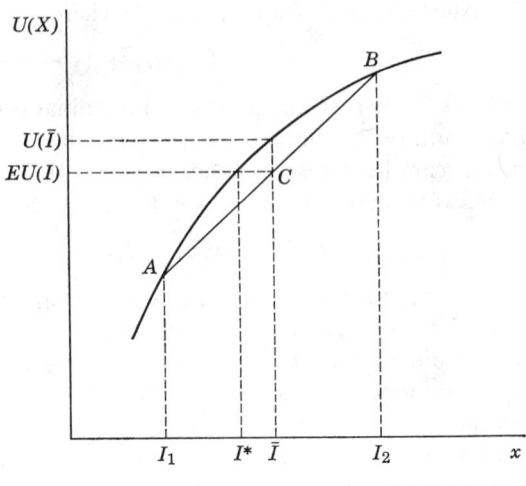

FIGURE VII.3.

than $\bar{I}$; in other words, he will be prepared to pay a premium to reduce his risk. The maximum risk premium that he will be willing to pay is given by $\bar{I} - I^*$ because

$$EU(I) \equiv \alpha U(I_1) + (1 - \alpha)U(I_2) = U(I^*)$$

If a higher premium is charged, thereby reducing the net property value below I^*, the individual will prefer the risk situation without insurance. Since members of low and medium income groups tend to purchase insurance, Friedman and Savage inferred that such individuals must have concave utility functions, that is,

$$U'(x) \geq 0; \quad U''(x) < 0$$

Let us see if we can use the same line of reasoning to account for the observed empirical fact that people in the low and medium income groups buy lottery tickets even though the expected prize (income) is lower than the price of the ticket. A risk averter will not enter a "fair" gamble, let alone a lottery which represents an "unfair" gamble. From this evidence, Friedman and Savage concluded that the utility function must have a convex segment in addition to its concave segment. In other words, to reconcile gambling and insurance an individual's utility function must have *both* a convex and a concave segment, as is shown in Figure VII.4.

Individuals located in the convex section, where $U''(x) > 0$, might purchase a lottery ticket even if the expectation of the prize is lower than the price of the ticket. An individual whose wealth places him on the intermediate

2. THE FRIEDMAN–SAVAGE HYPOTHESIS

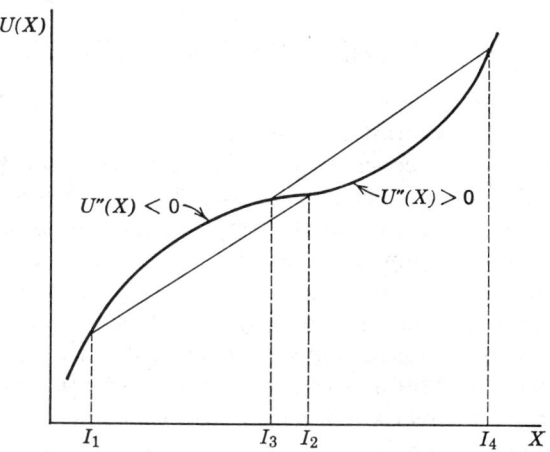

FIGURE VII.4.

section of the utility function would be willing to take out insurance *and* buy a lottery ticket simultaneously. If such an individual is confronted by the choice between the outcomes I_1 and I_2 he might conceivably desire to insure his property; if, however, he must choose between losing the price of a lottery ticket (reducing his wealth to I_3) with a probability of $(1 - \beta)$, or winning a large prize with a probability of β, thereby raising his wealth to I_4, the *same* individual will also be ready to purchase the lottery ticket. Since the modern theory of utility suggests that the behavior of individuals in choice situations dictates the form of the utility function, and not the other way around, Friedman and Savage concluded that the utility function must be wavelike, that is, it has both a concave and a convex segment.[9]

From the standpoint of investment analysis the Friedman and Savage results are rather negative, since apart from the trivial statement that $U'(x) \geq 0$, that is, that people prefer more to less wealth, no additional information can be gleaned regarding the shape of investors' utility functions. In particular we have no a priori grounds for determining whether the investor is a risk averter or a risk lover; therefore we cannot specify whether investors' utility functions are concave or convex, because the Friedman–Savage analysis suggests that these functions will have both concave and convex segments.

---

[9] From the additional empirical observation that lotteries typically offer more than one prize Friedman and Savage also showed that the convex segment would be truncated and followed by a second concave segment.

3. THE SUBJECTIVE UTILITY APPROACH

In sharp contrast to Friedman and Savage, a number of economists have argued that concave utility functions comprise the only form of function appropriate for economic theory.[10] These writers contend that in addition to the requirement that the first derivative be positive or zero (that is, that utility does not decrease with wealth) the second derivative of the utility function *must* be negative. Essentially, as we have already seen, such a function is appropriate for risk averters and can be rationalized by assuming that the marginal utility of money (like any other good) declines as wealth increases. But how can this hypothesis be reconciled with the empirical fact that in the real world many individuals purchase lottery tickets, that is, enter "unfair" gambles? On the surface such behavior would seem to contradict the concave utility assumption since, as we have seen, a risk averter is not even prepared to accept a fair gamble.

Friedman and Savage reconciled the coexistence of gambling and insurance by postulating that over some range the marginal utility of wealth increases, that is, that individuals' utility functions contain both concave and convex segments. An alternative explanation of such behavior can be had if one assumes a difference between the *objective* and *subjective* probabilities[11] which an individual attaches to the prizes. Yaari, for example, has hypothesized that subjective probabilities tend to be higher than objective probabilities when the latter are low, while they tend to be lower than high objective

---

[10] "If one draws the indifference curves which correspond to the Friedman and Savage hypothesis... one finds that in certain regions these indifference curves have 'wrong' curvatures. This fact is, of course, a cause for concern to the ordinalist just as it is to the cardinalist." M. Yaari, "Convexity in the Theory of Choice Under Risk," *Quarterly Journal of Economics* 75, No. 4, 1965, p. 281. See also J. Hirshleifer, "Investment Decision Under Uncertainty: Choice-Theoretic Approaches," *Quarterly Journal of Economics* 75, No. 4, 1965.

[11] For example, the probability of a die falling on any side is 1/6; this is the objective probability, since the die has six facets and is assumed to be balanced. When an individual bets on the fall of the die, however, he can attribute subjective probabilities to the results of different throws, such as:

Result of Throw	Objective Probability	Subjective Probability
1	1/6	1/12
2	1/6	1/12
3	1/6	4/12
4	1/6	1/12
5	1/6	1/12
6	1/6	4/12

3. THE SUBJECTIVE UTILITY APPROACH

probabilities. Such an assumption is sufficient to resolve the apparent contradiction in the observed behavior of individuals *without* recourse to the concept of increasing marginal utility of wealth, that is, without postulating the existence of a convex segment of the utility function.

To clarify this point, consider the following example. An individual is offered a lottery ticket for $10. One hundred tickets are to be sold so that the gross return from this lottery is $1,000 Assume that a single prize of $800 is offered on the winning ticket (that is, the sponsors of the lottery intend to earn a profit of $200). Since the probability of winning is 1/100, the expected value of the prize is $1/100 \cdot \$800 = \$8$. Let us further assume that our individual has an initial wealth of $110. When weighing the purchase of the lottery ticket he is in essence choosing between a perfectly certain income of $110 if he does not buy a lottery ticket, and the following distribution: $100, with a probability of 99/100, if he buys a losing ticket, and $900, with a probability of 1/100, should he buy the winning ticket (see Table VII–4). We now assume that the individual has a concave utility function, for example, $U(x) = \sqrt{x}$.[12] The utility of the perfectly certain income of $110 (alternative A in Table VII–4) is[13]

$$EU(x) = 1 \cdot \sqrt{110} = 10.49$$

His expected utility should he decide to buy the lottery ticket (alternative B in Table VII–4) is

$$EU(x) = 99/100 \cdot \sqrt{100} + 1/100 \cdot \sqrt{900} = 99/10 + 3/10$$
$$= \tfrac{102}{10} = 10.20$$

TABLE VII–4.

Alternative A		Alternative B	
Not to buy lottery ticket		To buy lottery ticket	
Income	Probability	Income	Probability
110	1	100	99/100
		900	1/100
$EU(x) = 10.49$*		$EU(x) = 10.20$*	

* Expected utility has been calculated using the following function:
$$U(x) = \sqrt{x}$$

---

[12] The function $U(x) = \sqrt{x}$ meets the requirement that $U'(x) \geq 0$ and $U''(x) \leq 0$, since $U'(x) = 1/2 x^{-\frac{1}{2}} \geq 0$ (for all $x \geq 0$) and $U''(x) = -1/4 x^{-\frac{3}{2}} \leq 0$ (for all $x \geq 0$).

[13] The expected utility of a given income $\bar{I}$ is simply the utility of that income:
$$EU(\bar{I}) = 1 \cdot U(\bar{I})$$

TABLE VII–5.

	Alternative A		Alternative B	
	Not to buy lottery ticket		To buy lottery ticket	
	Income	Subjective Probability	Income	Subjective Probability
	110	1	100	95/100
			900	5/100
	$EU(x) = 10.49$*		$EU(x) = 11.00$*	

*Expected utility has been calculated using the following function:

$$U(x) = \sqrt{x}$$

Since the expected utility of forgoing the lottery ticket exceeds that of its purchase (10.49 > 10.20), the risk-averse individual will not purchase the ticket. Although our example assumes a particular utility function, $U(x) = \sqrt{x}$, this conclusion is perfectly general and holds for all concave utility functions. In other words, if an individual is risk-averse and computes the expected utility using the objective probabilities (that is, the correct probabilities for a game of chance), he will never accept a gamble. If, however, the individual is an "optimist," and when weighing the purchase of the lottery ticket estimates his chances of winning at more than 1/100 (say 5/100), he might well buy a lottery ticket even though he is a risk averter.

Table VII–5 calculates the expected utility of the lottery using the individual's *subjective* probabilities. The expected utility of alternative A (not purchasing the ticket) remains 10.49, but the expected utility of alternative B (buying the lottery ticket) becomes

$$95/100 \cdot \sqrt{100} + 5/100 \cdot \sqrt{900} = 95/10 + 15/10 = 9.5 + 1.5 = 11.0$$

Since 11.0 > 10.49, our risk-averse individual using subjective probability will purchase the lottery ticket. Many other examples can be found in which a relatively small difference between the subjective and the objective probabilities convinces a risk averter to buy a lottery ticket which represents an "unfair" gamble using the objective probabilities.

We have illustrated the subjective utility approach using a specific utility function: $U(x) = \sqrt{x}$. Figure VII.5 presents the same analysis in a more general form. Assume that an individual is choosing between a perfectly certain income $\bar{I}$ if he forgoes the lottery and the distribution I_1 with a probability of α and I_2 with a probability of $(1 - \alpha)$, if he purchases the

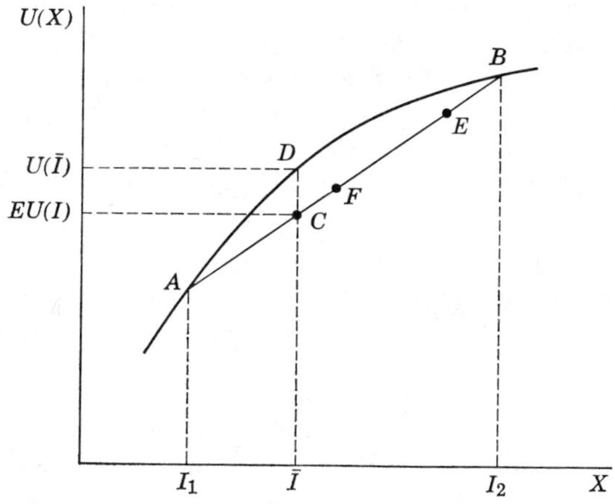

3. THE SUBJECTIVE UTILITY APPROACH 243

FIGURE VII 5.

lottery ticket. Let us further assume that the lottery represents a "fair" gamble so that

$$\bar{I} = \alpha I_1 + (1 - \alpha)I_2$$

As is clear from Figure VII.5, a risk averter will always prefer $\bar{I}$ to the lottery option since the expected utility of $\bar{I}$, point D, is greater than the expected utility following the purchase of the lottery ticket, point C.[14]

Let us now assume that the individual is an optimist, or else that for lack of accurate information he estimates his chances of winning the lottery at $1 - \beta$ where $(1 - \beta) > (1 - \alpha)$. Using the higher subjective probability, his expected utility after buying the ticket will be represented by a point higher than C on line AB of Figure VII.5, for example, point E; since E is higher than point D, purchasing the lottery ticket represents a higher level of utility than that associated with the steady income $\bar{I}$. As a result, the risk-averse individual will prefer the gamble, using the above mentioned subjective probabilities. Thus the existence of gambling can be rationalized *within* the framework of concave utility, or risk aversion.[15] We should hasten to add that assuming that the subjective probability of winning is higher than the

---

[14] The individual's expected utility is given by $EU(x) = \alpha U(I_1) + (1 - \alpha)U(I_2)$ which corresponds to point C in Figure VII.5.

[15] Nils Hakansson has shown that risk aversion might be consistent with a Friedman–Savage utility function even without introducing subjective probabilities. According to this approach the convex segment of the utility function is attributable to the convexity of the borrowing constraint. For more details on this approach see Nils Hakansson, "Friedman–Savage Utility Functions Consistent with Risk Aversion," *Quarterly Journal of Economics* (August 1970).

objective probability is not a *sufficient* condition to induce a risk-averse individual to purchase a lottery ticket. For example, should the subjective *expected* utility be represented by a point such as *F*, which while higher than *C* is lower than *D*, the individual will still prefer the perfectly certain alternative income *Ī*, and therefore will not buy the lottery ticket despite his optimistic subjective estimate of the probability of winning.

4. RISK ATTITUDES IN THE STOCK MARKET: SOME EMPIRICAL EVIDENCE

This section will be devoted to an empirical study of investors' behavior based on mutual fund returns. Before presenting our empirical findings and analyzing their implications regarding the shape of investors' utility functions, it may help to clarify the theoretical considerations underlying the regression analysis. For this purpose we shall assume the most general form of utility function, that is, we place no restrictions whatever on its shape beyond the usual stipulation that its first derivative be positive. Such a function can of course be concave or convex, or composed of any number of concave and convex segments.

Despite the almost complete lack of specific information regarding investors' tastes we can still apply utility analysis. When making his investment decision, the investor in risk assets is confronted by a probability distribution of possible returns and a market price for each alternative investment. His decision, strictly speaking, depends on all of the observations and the appropriate probabilities for each alternative distribution. Equivalently we can state that the investment decision will depend on *all* of the moments of the probability distribution, for if the investor knows all of the moments, he will generally know the exact features of the probability distribution.

To illustrate this claim, let us assume a general von Neumann–Morgenstern utility function $U(W + x)$, where x denotes a random variable, the return on investment; W is the investor's initial wealth; and U is a general function about which we know nothing except that its first derivative is positive.

Expanding this utility function in a Taylor series[16] around the point

---

[16] In certain circumstances the value of a function $f(t)$ around point a can be written as follows:

$$f(t) = f(a) + f'(a)(t-a) + [f''(a)/2!](t-a)^2$$
$$+ [f'''(a)/3!](t-a)^3 + \cdots + [f^n(a)/n!](t-a)^n + \cdots$$

For further details see the Mathematical Supplement and R. G. D. Allen, *Mathematical Analysis for Economists*, New York: St. Martin's Press, 1967, pp. 449–54.

4. RISK ATTITUDES IN THE STOCK MARKET

$(W + Ex)$ gives

$$U(W + x) = U(W + Ex) + U'(W + Ex) \cdot [W + x - (W + Ex)]$$
$$+ \frac{U''}{2!}(W + Ex) \cdot [W + x - (W + Ex)]^2$$
$$+ \frac{U'''}{3!}(W + Ex) \cdot [W + x - (W + Ex)]^3$$
$$+ \frac{U''''}{4!}(W + Ex) \cdot [W + x - (W + Ex)]^4 + \cdots$$

where Ex is the expected value of the random variable distribution, and the expression $U'(W + Ex)$ denotes the first derivative of the utility function at point $(W + Ex)$, $U''(W + Ex)$ denotes the second derivative at point $(W + Ex)$, and so on.

Since we have shown that a rational investor will select the investment option which maximizes his expected utility, we can write $EU(W + x)$ as follows:[17]

$$EU(W + x) = U(W + Ex) + \frac{U''}{2!}(W + Ex) \cdot \sigma^2$$
$$+ \frac{U'''}{3!}(W + Ex) \cdot \mu_3 + \frac{U''''}{4!}(W + Ex) \cdot \mu_4 + \cdots$$

where σ^2 is the variance of the distribution, μ_3 is the third central moment of the distribution defined as $E(x - Ex)^3$, that is, an index of the distribution's asymmetry; and μ_k is similarly defined as the central moment of the kth order: $\mu_k = E(x - Ex)^k$. In general, expected utility depends on all the moments of the probability distribution,[18] and to know if a particular moment is desirable or not one has to know the coefficient of this moment, that is, the appropriate derivative of the utility function at the point $(W + Ex)$.

Assuming that an individual is rational and always prefers more money to less, an increase in the expected return Ex, other things being equal, should also increase his expected utility. With respect to the other moments, no a priori determination can be made. For example, we do not know whether raising the variance (or some other higher order moment), while keeping the rest of the moments unchanged, is desirable to investors. Precise theoretical

---

[17] This is legitimate since the equation $E(\Sigma x_i) = \Sigma Ex_i$ always exists. In other words, the expectation of the sum of the random variables equals the sum of the expectations of these random variables.

[18] Requiring information regarding the distribution moments is equivalent to requiring detailed information on the distribution itself. See, for example, A. M. Mood and F. A. Graybill, *Introduction to the Theory of Statistics*, New York: McGraw-Hill, p. 117.

TABLE VII-6.

Period	Number of Years	Number of Mutual Funds
1956–67	12	86
1950–67	18	71
1946–67	22	58
1943–67	25	51

answers cannot be given to questions such as these, but we can test empirically the degree to which investments with greater variance afford higher average returns. Should this be the case the following interpretation may be given: investors are averse to variance, and therefore the higher an investment's variance the higher the return needed to compensate investors for the greater variance (risk).

To determine the impact of the distribution moments on expected utility a regression analysis was carried out for a sample of U.S. mutual funds. Data on rates of return were collected[19] for U.S. mutual funds during several subperiods from 1943 to 1967 (see Table VII–6). The rate of return to investors was calculated for each fund in each year, and a regression analysis was carried out for the four subperiods set out in Table VII–6 using the following regression equation:

$$\bar{X}_j = a + \sum_{i=2}^{n} b_i \mu_{ij}$$

where $\bar{X}_j$ is the mean rate of return to investors for the jth mutual fund; μ_{ij} denotes the ith moment of the distribution for the same fund, and n equals 20.[20] For example, μ_{22} denotes the variance of the mutual fund indexed as number 2 and μ_{32} denotes the indicator of asymmetry for the same fund.

The mean rate of return during the period, as well as the variance and the remaining 18 higher moments of the distribution of returns, were calculated for each period and for each mutual fund included in the regression. Of course the regression includes the *estimated* distribution moments, rather than the moments themselves, as explanatory variables. Clearly, the longer the period studied, the better will be the estimates of the distribution moments, but on the other hand, increasing the number of years also decreases the number of mutual funds available, thereby reducing the number of

---

[19] All of the data were obtained from the relevant annual editions of Arthur Wiesenberger and Company, *Investment Companies*.
[20] We examined the first 20 moments only because it appeared highly unlikely that any of the higher moments would prove significant.

4. RISK ATTITUDES IN THE STOCK MARKET

observations with which to estimate the regression coefficient. For this reason four alternative subperiods were used in the regression analysis.

The relationship of the distribution moments to investors' utility is derived from the regression analysis itself. Thus if a particular moment, for example the variance, is undesirable to most investors in mutual funds, we expect b_2 to be positive, that is, any increase in variance must be accompanied by a compensating increase in the average rate of return $\bar{X}$.[21]

The results of the analysis for the period 1946–1967 are summarized in Table VII–7; the results for the other periods (which are not essentially different) are given in Appendix VII–1 at the end of this chapter. Although the regression equations include 21 variables (that is, a constant and the first 20 moments of the distributions), only the variance and the third moment are significant in 1946–1967. For the period 1943–67, the fourth moment

TABLE VII–7. Analysis of regression results for the period 1946–67*

Source of Variance	Sum of Squares	Degrees of Freedom	Mean Squares	F	Critical Value (99%)	R^2
Due to Regression	544.3	2	272.2	162.3	$F \cdot 99 = 5.01$	0.86
Deviation from the Regression	92.2	55	1.7			

* Due to tolerance limit only two moments remain in the regression; that is, the contribution of the other 18 moments to the F value is negligible.

			The Significant Coefficients	
Variable	Coefficient	T Value		Critical Value (99%)
Constant	7.205	16.2		$t \cdot 99 = 2.40$
Variance	0.019	9.9		
Skewness	−0.000064	−8.4		

---

[21] In an unpublished paper on the relation between risk and return, M. H. Miller has pointed out that in cases where the random variables are identically distributed, this type of regression analysis can artificially produce significant statistical relationships between the first two moments of the distribution. Although the time distribution of mutual fund returns is not the same, we have (following a suggestion by Miller) carried out the regression analysis a second time using the geometric, rather than the arithmetic, mean. The results of this analysis are not materially different and fully corroborate the findings given in the text and in Appendix VII–1.

(kurtosis) is also significant, but the remaining higher moments are not significant in any of the time periods examined.

The percentage of the variance explained by the regression (R^2) is very high and ranges from 65% in 1956–67 to 94% for the years 1943–67. We can see that as the time period is increased, R^2 also increases; the most impressive result is the very high percentage of the explained variance for 1943–67 ($R^2 = 0.94$).

In all four regressions, the coefficient of the variance (b_2) is positive, and consequently we can conclude that investors are typically averse to variance. Since the magnitude of this coefficient lies between 0.02 and 0.03, this means that a 1% increase in the variance must be accompanied by an increase in the average rate return of 0.02 to 0.03%, in order to compensate the investor for the added variance.

The regression coefficient of the third moment (skewness) is negative in each of the four regressions, and in three of them this coefficient is also highly significant. This result suggests that the average investor in mutual funds likes positive asymmetry and avoids negative asymmetry. Thus increasing the skewness of the distribution *reduces* the required average return, since the investor feels compensated by the increased positive skewness, that is, by the small chance of obtaining a relatively high return.[22] The fourth moment, the kurtosis, is significant in only one of the four regressions, but even in this case the coefficient of this moment is very small.[23]

This empirical result has some theoretical support. Although expected utility is determined by the exact configuration of the distribution function, generally the first three or four distribution moments give most of the required information about the form of the distribution. In fact there exists a wide range of distributions for which the first four (or fewer) moments provide a complete specification of the shape of the probability function. Moreover, even experienced statisticians often find it difficult to interpret the meaning of higher moments. The first three moments represent a distribution's "location," its dispersion, and asymmetry, respectively; the additional information provided by the fourth, and higher, moments is not very clear[24] to the professional statistician, let alone to the uninitiated investor.

---

[22] This result can serve as a partial explanation of the behavior of people who participate in lotteries which typically have negative expected values but are characterized by high positive skewness. The preference for positive asymmetry was previously noted by F. D. Arditti, "Risk and the Required Return on Equity," *Journal of Finance* (March 1967).

[23] Moreover, even in this case, most of the "explained" variance stems from the first three moments; the addition of the fourth moment increases R^2 only slightly, from 0.92 to 0.94. This would seem to indicate that the first three moments are the main factors which determine investors' decisions.

[24] See I. Kaplansky, "A Common Error Concerning Kurtosis," *Journal of the American Statistical Association* 40 (June 1945), p. 259.

4. RISK ATTITUDES IN THE STOCK MARKET

4.1 IMPLICATIONS FOR UTILITY FUNCTIONS

Although decision making under uncertainty depends, in general, on all the moments of the distribution function, assuming a specific utility function allows us to concentrate on a subset of the distribution moments. For example, if we are willing to assume a quadratic utility function, investment decisions become a function of only the first two moments. The empirical analysis of mutual fund returns suggests that investors' decisions depend chiefly on the first three moments, or at most, on the first four moments of the distribution of returns. Of course this does not mean that all investors have cubic utility functions;[25] although the percentage of explained variance is relatively high, it is *not* 100%; moreover, the fourth moment is significant in one of the regressions. However, since some of the empirical results appear to approximate those which we would expect from a cubic utility function, it may be instructive to examine the implications of such an assumption.[26] A utility function which depends only on the first three moments *must* be of the following form:[27]

$$U(W + x) = a(W + x) + b(W + x)^2 + c(W + x)^3 + d$$

Expanding this function about the point W, we get

$$U(W + x) = U(W) + U'(W)x + \tfrac{1}{2}U''(W)x^2 + \tfrac{1}{6}U'''(W)x^3$$

After calculating the first three derivatives of U at the point W, and substituting these derivatives in the above equation, we get[28]

$$U(W + x) = a_1 x + b_1 x^2 + c_1 x^3 + d_1$$

---

[25] We are indebted to Nancy Jacob, who helped to clarify our thinking on this point.
[26] The cubic utility function is not bounded, so that in order to avoid the reintroduction of a variant of the St. Petersburg Paradox, we must assume that beyond a certain point (W_0) increments to wealth do not increase utility, that is, $U(W) = U(W_0)$ for all $W \geq W_0$.
[27] If we expand any utility function in a Taylor series it will always be dependent on *all* of the moments. However if the function is cubic, all of the derivatives of a higher order than three vanish, leaving only the first three moments.
[28] The parameters of this equation, $a_1, b_1, c_1,$ and d_1, are given by the following equations:

$$a_1 = a + 2bW + 3cW^2$$
$$b_1 = b + 3cW$$
$$c_1 = c$$
$$d_1 = aW + bW^2 + cW^2 + d$$

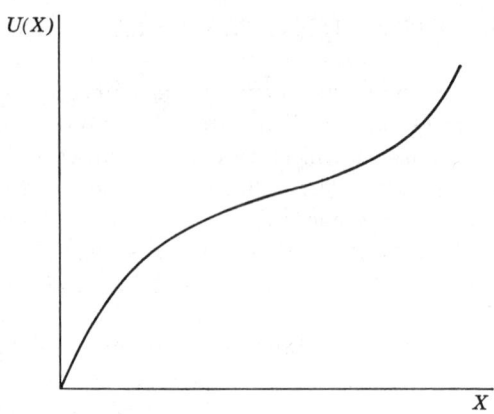

FIGURE VII.6.

This function must have *both* concave and convex segments.[29] Such a function is illustrated in Figure VII.6. From Figure VII.6 we can see that for low values of x the investor is a risk averter and therefore dislikes variance, but for relatively high values of x the investor becomes a risk lover, and consequently desires variance. This form of utility function is similar in many important respects to the one presented by Friedman and Savage; both of these utility functions have the property that they can reconcile the purchase of insurance contracts with gambling, without recourse to subjective utility since in both cases investors prefer positive asymmetrical distributions (like a lottery's) but dislike negative asymmetry, and therefore buy insurance policies.

Although a cubic utility function is appropriate for both risk lovers and risk averters, we can conclude from the empirical evidence that the influence of risk averters in the market for mutual funds shares is dominant. This conclusion stems from the fact that in each of the four regressions the coefficient of the variance is positive, that is, the average investor dislikes variance so that increasing the variance increases the required rate of return. Of course, this conclusion relates to the *average* investor and does not obviate the possibility that there are individual investors in this market who, in the relevant range, prefer a large variance.

---

[29] For a proof that a cubic utility function has both a concave and a convex segment, see Appendix VII–2.

It should also be noted that if $U(x)$ depends on the fourth moment as well, appropriate parameters can be found so that the utility function has both a concave and a convex segment in the relevant range.

5. SUMMARY

The primary purpose of this chapter has been to point out the crucial importance of the shape of the utility function for investment decisions. Two distinct hypotheses regarding the probable shape of an investor's utility function were discussed, and the results of an empirical investigation into investors' risk attitudes were presented.

The first hypothesis discussed was that associated with Friedman and Savage. These two writers attempt to reconcile the observed phenomenon that many individuals simultaneously purchase lottery tickets (or gamble) and take out insurance. The former action indicates that the individual is not risk-averse, since such an individual would never purchase a lottery ticket (or gamble). Taking out insurance, on the other hand, indicates that the individual *is* risk-averse; a risk lover would never agree to purchase an insurance contract to avoid a risk.

It follows, according to Friedman and Savage, that to remove the contradiction the utility function can be neither strictly concave nor strictly convex. They have shown that if the utility function has both a concave and a convex segment in the relevant range the apparent contradiction can be removed. In the concave range the individual willingly pays a risk premium (takes out insurance), while in the convex range the *same* individual buys lottery tickets (or gambles).

An alternative approach to the same problem suggests that individuals' utility functions are always concave, that is, universal risk aversion prevails. Whereas Friedman and Savage hypothesized that over some range the marginal utility of wealth increases, the alternative approach assumes diminishing marginal utility of wealth over the entire range. The undisputed empirical observations that many individuals simultaneously gamble and take out insurance are reconciled, in this alternative approach, by assuming that subjective and objective probabilities diverge. In particular it has been assumed that subjective probabilities exceed their objective counterparts when the latter are low. This assumption is sufficient to show that a risk-averse individual will also be willing, on occasion, to gamble or to purchase lottery tickets, without recourse to a convex segment of the utility function.

We next presented some empirical evidence on risk attitudes in the stock market. A regression analysis of mutual funds returns during the period 1943–67 gave the following results:

(1) Investors in mutual funds are, on the average, averse to variance: other things being equal, an increase in the variance of returns is

accompanied by an increase in the average annual returns to investors.

(2) The average mutual fund investor likes positive, and dislikes negative, asymmetry: he has a preference for even a small chance of obtaining an unusually high return.

(3) Mutual fund returns can be "explained," to a large extent, in terms of three moments, since in most of the regressions moments higher than the third order are not significant. In the one instance that the fourth moment is significant, most of the explained variability stems from the second and third moments.

Since a cubic utility function has both concave and convex segments, these results appear to lend some support to the Friedman–Savage hypothesis. On the other hand, the empirical analysis also shows that the influence of risk averters is dominant since increases in the variance are always accompanied by increases in the average rate of return. These results refer to mutual funds only, so that one cannot be certain that they hold true for all choice situations. With this in mind, we shall develop in the next chapter two different criteria for the analysis of choices involving risk—a general criterion which is appropriate for all types of utility functions (concave, convex, or both); and a risk-aversion criterion which assumes that all utility functions are concave.

QUESTIONS AND PROBLEMS

7.1 "The simultaneous existence of insurance companies and gambling dens indicates that many individuals do *not* have linear utility functions."

    a. Appraise the above quotation.
    b. How do Friedman and Savage account for this phenomenon?

7.2 Define the terms *subjective* and *objective probability*. How can these two concepts be used to rationalize the coexistence of risk aversion and gambling?

7.3 An individual with the utility function

$$U(X) = X^2$$

is known to be indifferent between two lotteries A and B. Each option costs $5 and offers the following prizes:

Option A		Option B	
Probability	Prize	Probability	Prize
1/2	95	1/2	70
1/2	105	1/2	Y

Given the above information, find the value of Y.

7.4 Mr. Horn, whose utility function is given by $U(X) = 100 + X^2$, is confronted with the following investments, A and B:

Investment A		Investment B	
Probability	Return	Probability	Return
1/2	0	1/2	0
1/2	20	1/2	40

Assuming that the price of A = $10 and the price of B = $20, will he purchase A? Will he also be willing to purchase B? Prove your answer.

7.5 "Security appraisal can be limited to the analysis of the first three moments of the probability distribution of returns."

    a. Define the first three moments and explain what information each conveys regarding the distribution.

    b. What empirical evidence can support the above quotation?

    c. What are the limitations of the available empirical evidence?

7.6 Is there any similarity between a cubic utility function and a Friedman–Savage utility function?

7.7 The Maxi Bus Company, which owns a fleet of 5,000 buses, does *not* insure its buses against theft, while the Mini Bus Company, which owns only 10 buses, does. Do these facts support the conclusion that the Maxi Bus Company is managed by risk lovers and the Mini Bus Company is run by risk averters?

7.8 "An insurance company is a 'risk lover' by definition since it is always willing to undetake the 'risks' which risk averters refuse to accept." What is your opinion of this statement?

SELECTED REFERENCES

See Chapter VI.

APPENDIX VII-1
Empirical Estimates of Risk Attitudes in the Stock Market, Selected Periods, 1943-67

APPENDIX TABLE VII-1. Regression results for selected subperiods, 1943-67

A. 1956-67*

Source of Variance	Sum of Squares	Degrees of Freedom	Mean Square	F	Critical Values (99%)	R^2
Due to Regression	403.9	6	67.3	24.5	$F \cdot 99 = 2.21$	0.65
Deviation from the Regression	216.9	79	2.7			

The significant coefficients†

Variable	Coefficient	T Value	Critical Value (99%)
Constant	5.576	6.2	
Variance	0.031	3.9	$t \cdot 99 = 2.36$

B. 1950-67*

Source of Variance	Sum of Squares	Degrees of Freedom	Mean Square	F	Critical Values (99%)	R^2
Due to Regression	425.2	6	70.9	49.6	$F \cdot 99 = 3.09$	0.82
Deviation from the Regression	91.5	64	1.4			

APPENDIX VII-1

The significant coefficients

Variable	Coefficient	T Value	Critical Value (99%)
Constant	6.929	7.6	$t \cdot 99 = 2.39$
Variance	0.034	2.8	
Skewness	−0.0012	−2.8	

C. 1943–67‡

Source of Variance	Sum of Squares	Degrees of Freedom	Mean Square	F	Critical Values (99%)	R^2
Due to Regression	2380.6	3	793.5	260.4	$F \cdot 99 = 4.22$	0.94
Deviation from the Regression	146.3	47	3.0			

The significant coefficients

Variable	Coefficient	T Value	Critical Value (99%)
Constant	13.692	22.163	$t \cdot 99 = 2.40$
Variance	0.022	16.197	
Skewness	−0.000279	−8.565	
Kurtosis	0.00046	4.766	

* Due to tolerance limit only six moments remain in the regression, that is, the contribution of the other fourteen moments to the F value is negligible.
† The coefficient of the third moment is negative but not significant; ($t = -0.081$).
‡ Due to tolerance limit only three moments remain in the regression, that is to say, the contribution of the other seventeen moments to the F value is negligible.

APPENDIX VII-2

The Shape of a Cubic Utility Function

In this appendix we shall prove that a third order polynominal utility function must include a concave section followed by a convex section, as drawn in Figure VII.6 of the text. Let us assume that $U(y)$ is a general third order polynomial of the form

$$U(y) = a_1 y + a_2 y^2 + a_3 y^3 + e \qquad (7.1)$$

As we know that $U(y)$ is determined up to a positive linear transformation[30] we may subtract e from Equation (7.1) and divide by a_1, thereby obtaining, without loss of generality, the following function:

$$U(x) = x + bx^2 + cx^3 \qquad (7.2)$$

where: $b = a_2/a_1$
$c = a_3/a_1$

Now making the conventional assumption that $U'(x) > 0$, we can write the first derivative as follows:

$$U'(x) = 3cx^2 + 2bx + 1 > 0 \qquad (7.3)$$

Since (7.3) is a quadratic equation, the inequality will hold only if both of the roots of (7.3) are imaginary, that is, if

$$(2b)^2 < 4 \cdot 3c \quad \text{or} \quad b^2 < 3c \qquad (7.4)$$

From Equation (7.4) we can see that c must be positive, which means that the sign of μ_3 is positive. A second result which can be derived from Equation (7.4) is that b may be negative as well as positive. Taking the second derivative of $U(x)$, we get

$$U''(x) = 6cx + 2b \qquad (7.5)$$

As c is positive, we can also determine that

$$U''(x) \leq 0 \quad \text{if} \quad x \leq -b/3c$$
$$U''(x) > 0 \quad \text{if} \quad x > -b/3c$$

---

[30] See J. von Neumann and O. Morgenstern, *Theory of Games and Economic Behavior*, 3rd edition. Princeton, N.J.: Princeton University Press, 1953.

APPENDIX VII-2

If $b < 0$, the utility function is concave for some positive values of x (as well as for all negative values of x). If $b > 0$, the utility function is concave only for negative values of x. We shall assume that $b < 0$ to allow risk aversion in the relevant range. Thus for small values of x (or large negative values of x), marginal utility is decreasing and $U(x)$ is concave—the individual is risk-averse for low levels of incomes or wealth, but for high returns he shows a preference for risk, that is, the marginal utility of money increases with income. Q.E.D.

Chapter VIII
The Efficiency Analysis of Investment Under Uncertainty

1. INTRODUCTION

In this chapter we shall develop appropriate investment criteria for the two alternatives discussed at the end of the previous chapter. We shall initially assume that no information whatsoever is available on the shape of the utility function: $U(x)$ can be concave at any place on the curve, but may also include one or more convex segments. Within this general framework we shall define an appropriate efficiency criterion which can be used to effect a preliminary screening of alternative investments. Next we shall assume the availability of additional information and develop an appropriate criterion for risk averters, that is, for the case in which utility functions are assumed to be concave. Intuitively it is almost obvious that the second criterion will permit us to make a more sensitive, but less general, selection since we not only assume that $U'(x) \geq 0$, but also that $U''(x) \leq 0$.

We then turn our attention to the important question of risk diversification and the building of investment portfolios. In particular we shall spell out, using the two newly developed efficiency criteria, the relationship between investors' tastes (utility functions) and the diversification of investments.

2. THE CONCEPT OF AN EFFICIENCY CRITERION

Before beginning the analysis, let us define a number of basic concepts which we shall be using throughout this and the next few chapters. An *efficiency criterion* is a decision rule for dividing all potential investment options into two mutually exclusive sets: an *efficient* set or group and an *inefficient* set or group. The former set contains all of the desirable alternatives for a particular class of investors. Utilizing the efficiency criterion we can be certain that all individuals belonging to the class being analyzed will make their final choice from the efficient group. Conversely, we can be equally certain that no individual having the assumed type of utility function will desire to choose an option from the inefficient set. Thus an efficiency criterion is a rule for effecting a preliminary screening of investments whereby we are able to reduce the number of relevant alternatives facing the particular class of investors by an initial elimination of all undesirable options.

The concept of an efficiency criterion is sufficiently important (and perhaps sufficiently vague as well) to warrant some clarification. Let us consider the following very unrealistic and very untypical criterion. Assume a class of investors ("the Plus Fivers") who will prefer a risky option X to a risky option Y *if and only if*

$$E(x) \geq E(y) + 5$$

Let us further assume that no additional information regarding investors' tastes (utility functions) is available, so that this is the sole criterion available to effect our initial screening. We shall now illustrate the use of this efficiency criterion on the following alternative investment options:

Option	Expected Return
x_1	9
x_2	10
x_3	3
x_4	6
x_5	11

Recall that our problem is to use the efficiency criterion to identify the efficient and nonefficient groups for our assumed "Plus Fiver" class of investors.

We start by comparing options x_1 and x_2. Since the expected return of the former, 9, is less than that of the latter, 10, x_1 is clearly *not* preferable to x_2. What about the reverse: perhaps x_2 is preferable to x_1 since it has the larger expected return. However, since our efficiency criterion requires a five-point spread between expected returns, a clear-cut preference cannot be established in this case either, and therefore we go on to compare x_1 and x_3:

$$E(x_1) > E(x_3) + 5, \quad \text{that is,}$$
$$9 > 3 + 5$$

In this case option x_1 with an expected return of 9 is clearly preferable to option x_3 whose expected return is only 3. Therefore option x_3 is relegated to the inefficient group since we can be absolutely certain that no "Plus Fiver"

2. THE CONCEPT OF AN EFFICIENCY CRITERION

will ever choose such an option as long as he has the alternative of choosing option x_1.

We go on to compare x_1 and x_4, but once again the required five-point spread between the expected returns does not obtain so neither x_1 nor x_4 is eliminated. This is also true for the comparison of x_1 and x_5 since the spread is only two points.

This does not complete the efficiency analysis. Since we must compare all possible pairs of investments, we go on to consider x_2. We have already compared x_2 with x_1, and since x_3 has already been eliminated from the efficient set[1] there is no need to compare x_2 and x_3. We go on to compare x_2 with x_4 and x_5, and the reader can verify that no elimination takes place. There now remains only one more comparison, that between x_4 and x_5. In this case the respective expected returns are 6 and 11, and

$$E(x_5) = E(x_4) + 5$$

Since our efficiency criterion is defined in terms of a five-point spread, option x_4 is eliminated from the efficient set.

Thus our hypothetical example results in the following partition: (a) an efficient set comprised of options x_1, x_2, and x_5; and (b) an inefficient set comprised of options x_3 and x_4. Without further information regarding their tastes we cannot be certain which alternative option a "Plus Fiver" will choose, but we may be absolutely certain that it will not be x_3 or x_4. Of course this particular division into efficient and inefficient groups is appropriate only for our "Plus Fiver" class of investors, but it does illustrate the general logic which underlies the efficiency analysis of investment choice.

In principle we can devise efficiency criteria for many other more meaningful classes of investors, for example risk averters, and by using such criteria identify the efficient subset of options out of which *all* risk averters will make their final choice. However, unless further information is available we cannot tell which of the options included in the efficient group will be selected. Moreover, there is no reason why all risk averters should necessarily select the same option from the group. It is possible (and in fact quite likely) that different individuals will choose different options, according to their individual preferences. Thus, even though we know that all of these investors have concave utility functions, the particular form of function may vary from individual to individual.

It is sufficient to consider the following forms, all of which can meet the risk aversion (concave) requirements:

$$U(x) = a\sqrt{x}; \qquad U(x) = ax + bx^2; \qquad U(x) = a \log x$$

---

[1] It is a matter of indifference whether a particular option is eliminated by more than one alternative.

Since the final choice among the efficient options will be made in accordance with the expected utility of the alternatives, it is possible, and in fact quite probable, that the option which maximizes expected utility for an investor with a quadratic utility function may differ from that option which maximizes the expected utility of a risk-averse individual with a logarithmic utility function.

An individual investor's final selection from the efficient group will be referred to as the *optimal investment*, that is, the option which maximizes that individual's expected utility. From this definition it is obvious that the optimal investment may vary from one investor to another depending on individual tastes. However it is also possible for several investors to choose the same optimal option.

To summarize, the investment decision among risky alternatives can be dichotomized into two steps: first, we reduce the number of investment alternatives by constructing an efficient set of options using an efficiency criterion appropriate for a given class of investors. Second, the individual makes his final choice in accordance with his own particular preferences. For the remainder of this chapter we shall be concerned with the first step, the construction of efficiency criteria for different classes of individual investors.

3. A GENERAL EFFICIENCY CRITERION (GC)

The degree to which an efficiency criterion can reduce the size of the efficient group depends on the amount of available information regarding the investors to be studied. Frequently, however, very little information is available regarding investors' tastes, and as a result, we must construct our efficiency criteria on the basis of investors' presumed, rather than observed, preferences. For example, a group of efficient options might be constructed on the assumption that investors' have logarithmic utility functions. Obviously, in this instance, our conclusions will be relevant only for those investors for which this assumption holds true. But when an efficiency criterion is based on the investors' assumed preferences, it is possible that few investors will fulfill the particular assumption that has been made. It is even possible that no investors have logarithmic utility functions. In this extreme case the whole exercise is pointless, for we have constructed a group of efficient portfolios based on an assumption which does not reflect investors' tastes, and therefore cannot be expected to explain their behavior. Clearly, the general validity and applicability of a criterion depend on the appropriateness of the underlying assumptions regarding investors' tastes.

3. A GENERAL EFFICIENCY CRITERION (GC)

In this section we shall try to devise an efficiency criterion of very broad applicability. We shall consider the most general case where investors are assumed to have no systematic preferences with respect to risk; no restrictions are placed on investors' utility functions beyond the reasonable assumption that they be nondecreasing with respect to returns, x. This means that the utility functions' first derivatives cannot be negative. This assumption, as we have already seen, is appropriate for risk lovers as well as for risk averters since the utility function can be either convex or concave. Moreover, in keeping with the Friedman–Savage hypothesis, an individual investor's utility function can have both convex and concave segments and still be included in this set. Our sole restriction is that investors behave consistently in the sense that, other things being equal, they must always prefer more money to less.

Now consider the two random variables x and y which represent the net returns from two investment options. Option x will be clearly preferable to option y *if and only if*

$$EU(x) > EU(y)$$

for every utility function belonging to the set. If the expected utility of option x is greater than that of option y, for all investors independent of their attitudes toward risk, we can also conclude that no investor whose utility function is included in the set of all nondecreasing functions will ever choose option y, that is, option y can safely be relegated to the nonefficient group. When option x eliminates another option y, using an efficiency criterion appropriate for a given class of investors, we shall say that x dominates y, and denote this by the symbol xDy.

In our example, xDy if and only if $EU(x) > EU(y)$. This result can be generalized by the following theorem:

Theorem: *Given two cumulative probability distributions*[2] *F and G an option F will be preferred over a second option G by the general criterion, independent of the concavity or convexity of the utility function, if $F(x) \leq G(x)$ for all values of x, on the condition that for at least one value of x the strong inequality, $F(x_0) < G(x_0)$, holds.*

The stipulation that the strong inequality must hold for at least one value of x is tantamount to the requirement that the two distributions *not* be identical. Without this restriction, it is conceivable that $F(x) = G(x)$ for every value of x, in which case the rational investor would be indifferent between the two options since they have identical probability distributions.

---

[2] For an explanation of cumulative probability distributions, see the Statistical Supplement at the end of the book.

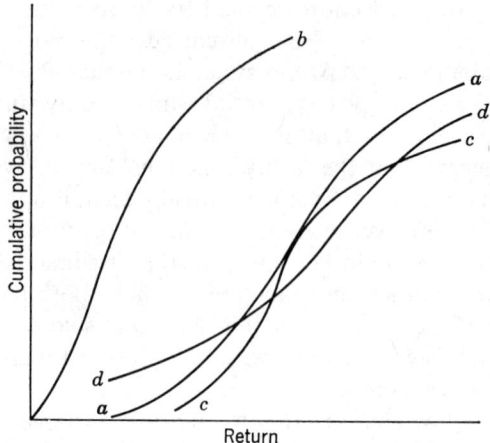

FIGURE VIII.1.

A formal mathematical proof that the General Criterion (hereafter referred to as GC) constitutes the appropriate efficiency criterion for all rational investors independent of their attitude toward risk is given in Appendix VIII–1. But the meaning of the GC can best be brought out by means of a simple graphical analysis. The GC is equivalent to the requirement that the two cumulative probability distributions do not intersect; a necessary and sufficient condition for one option to dominate another option, therefore, is that the cumulative probability distributions do not intersect. Thus the entire cumulative distribution of one option must lie to the right of the distribution of the second option.

Figure VIII.1 presents the cumulative distributions of four potential investment options: a, b, c, and d. Clearly option a dominates option b (aDb), since the *entire* cumulative distribution of investment a lies to the right of that of b, which means that the GC is fulfilled. If we denote the cumulative distribution of option a as $F_a(x)$ and that of b as $F_b(x)$, we can readily see from the diagram that for all values of x the relationship $F_a(x) \leq F_b(x)$ always holds. Similarly, options c and d are also preferable to option b since $F_c(x) \leq F_b(x)$ and $F_d(x) \leq F_b(x)$ for all values of x.[3] By the same token, we can see that option c is also preferable to option a. Although the two cumulative distributions have one section in common, there are other values of x (one would be sufficient) where distribution c lies to the right of

---

[3] To simplify the discussion in the text, we shall take for granted the stipulation that for at least one value of x the strong inequality must hold.

3. A GENERAL EFFICIENCY CRITERION (GC)

distribution a. Thus, over the entire range of x, the GC holds: $F_c(x) \leq F_a(x)$, and option c dominates option a. Distribution d, on the other hand, intersects both c and a, so that the GC does not hold between either d and c or d and a.

This presentation of the GC can also help to clarify some of the general concepts defined in the previous section of this chapter. We have used the GC, as formulated in the above theorem, in order to divide all potential options into two mutually exclusive groups: an efficient set comprising investments c and d and a nonefficient set comprising investments a and b. All the investment options of the efficient group need not be preferable to a given nonefficient investment, but it should be emphasized that every option included in the nonefficient group must be dominated by at least one preferable investment in the efficient group. From Figure VIII.1 we can readily verify that while option c dominates both of the inefficient options a and b, option d, which is also included in the efficient set, does *not* dominate option a. Similarly we can also verify from Figure VIII.1 that with respect to each of the options included in the efficient set, no preferred investment can be found in either the efficient or nonefficient groups.

3.1 AN INTUITIVE INTERPRETATION OF THE GENERAL CRITERION

We have defined the GC in terms of cumulative probability distributions and have stipulated that a prospect F dominates a prospect G if $F(x) \leq G(x)$. But this condition is equivalent to the requirement that the probability of receiving a return lower than some given amount, for example k, will always be *smaller* for option F than for option G. Thus since $F(k) \leq G(k)$, it follows that

$$P_F(x \leq k) \leq P_G(x \leq k)$$

where P denotes probability. This can be seen if we rewrite the GC as follows: For an option F to be preferred to an option G the following relationship must hold for all values of x:[4]

$$1 - F(x) \geq 1 - G(x)$$

The expression $1 - F(x)$ is equivalent to the probability of receiving a return which is *greater* than or equal to a given x. Thus for option F to dominate option G the probability of receiving a return greater than or equal to some level k must always be higher in option F than in option G. Since the chances of earning a higher return are *always* greater, option F will be preferred by risk averters and risk lovers alike.

---

[4] We defined the GC as $F(x) \leq G(x)$. If we multiply both sides of the inequality by -1 and add 1, we obtain $1 - F(x) \geq 1 - G(x)$.

3.2 THE CONCEPT OF AN OPTIMAL EFFICIENCY CRITERION

Now that we have clarified the meaning of an efficiency criterion and an efficient set, let us define the concept of an *optimal* efficiency criterion.[5]

Definition: An optimal efficiency criterion is one which, given the assumptions regarding investors' tastes, ensures a minimal efficient set.

In the previous section we developed a general efficiency criterion, $F(x) \leq G(x)$, which is appropriate for risk averters and risk lovers alike. Now let us assume that we are given another (arbitrary) efficiency criterion according to which an option F is preferable to an option G if and only if $F(x) + k \leq G(x)$ for all values of x, where k denotes any positive number, however small. This arbitrary criterion will be referred to as the "k" criterion and is illustrated graphically in Figure VIII.2, which sets out the cumulative probability distributions of four investment options, a, b, c, and d. Invoking the GC it is clear that investments c and d comprise the efficient set while options a and b are relegated to the nonefficient group. (Both c and d dominate options a and b.) Let us now examine the composition of the efficient group using the arbitrary "k" criterion. Since options c and d intersect there can be no doubt

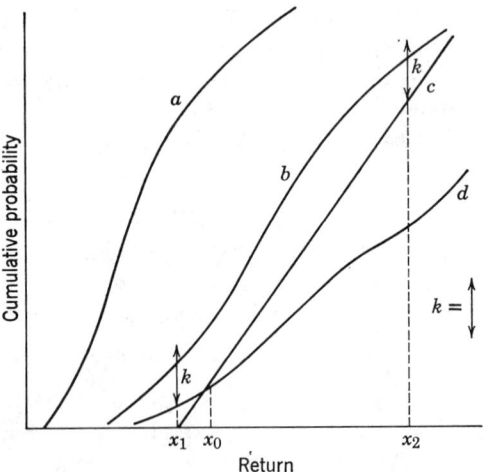

FIGURE VIII.2.

[5] Care should be taken not to confuse the *optimal efficiency criterion*, that is, the criterion which minimizes the efficient set for a given class of investors, with the *optimal investment option*, that is, the option which maximizes the expected utility of a particular investor. See page 264.

3. A GENERAL EFFICIENCY CRITERION (GC)

that they must be included in the efficient group; there exists a value of x for which the cumulative probabilities of these two options are equal so that the "k" criterion cannot hold. If we let x_0 denote the point of intersection of the two probability distributions, then

$$F_c(x_0) = F_d(x_0)$$

which also implies that

$$F_c(x_0) + k > F_d(x_0)$$

so that option c is *not* preferable to d. In similar fashion it can be shown that option d does not dominate option c according to the "k" criterion. At the same time a brief glance at Figure VIII.2 shows that according to the "k" criterion option b is also included in the efficient group, since it is dominated neither by option d nor by option c. The required inequality between b and d does not hold at point x_1, while the required inequality between option b and c does not hold at point x_2:

$$F_d(x_1) + k > F_b(x_1)$$

and

$$F_c(x_2) + k > F_b(x_2)$$

From the above we can conclude that while the GC efficient set comprises two investments, c and d, the "k" criterion's efficient set includes three investments, d, b, and c. Option a is not included in the efficient sets of either criterion.

What is the significant difference between the two criteria? Both are legitimate criteria for determining an efficient investment group. Moreover, if the "k" criterion holds for any two investment options, F and G, then the GC must also hold, since for all values of x

$$F(x) + k < G(x) \Rightarrow F(x) \leq G(x), \quad \text{since } k > 0$$

This means that any investment included in the GC efficient group is necessarily also included in the "k" criterion's efficient set. Hence there is no danger that GC efficient investments may be excluded. The obverse, however, does not necessarily hold: it is quite conceivable that the "k" criterion's efficient set may include "superfluous" investments, which from the given information on investors' preferences might have been eliminated. Thus in our example option b is included in the efficient group according to the "k" criterion, but is eliminated by the GC. Accordingly the general criterion is to be preferred over the arbitrary "k" criterion, since given the single assumption that investors prefer more to less wealth ($U'(x) \geq 0$) the GC reduces the efficient group of investments to the minimum.

This result can be generalized, and in Appendix VIII-1, at the end of this chapter, a formal proof is presented of the *optimality* of the GC. Any alternative criterion (for example, the "k" criterion) will be either too "poor" or too "rich" in efficient options. In the former case, a criterion may exclude options which are efficient, given the available information on investors' utility functions; in the latter instance, the criterion may include investments which should have been eliminated. The optimality of the GC can be clarified by considering a number of specific examples.

Example No. 1

Let us consider the two alternative investment options, A and B, presented in Table VIII–1.

A comparison of investments A and B clearly shows that option A is preferable, since option A offers an equal probability of double the returns from option B. This is equivalent to confronting an individual with the choice of betting on either of two unbiased roulette wheels, one of which pays the winner double the amount of the other for the same wager. Clearly all rational persons would choose to play on the roulette wheel having the equal probability of larger payoffs, represented by alternative A, since common sense alone suffices to tell us that this option is preferable.

Let us check to see if the GC reflects this common sense result, that is, if

$$F_A(x) \leq F_B(x)$$

for all values of x. The cumulative probability distributions appear in Table VIII–1, and these data are used to construct Table VIII–2, which sets out the relevant data for comparing the cumulative probability functions of the two options. The left-hand column of Table VIII–2 includes all attainable returns from options A and B as well as several values of returns which are *not* attainable in either of the options. The reader can verify that the cumulative probability distributions are not affected by considering the unattainable levels of returns. In other words, the cumulative probability distribution of a *discrete* random variable is a step function, remaining constant for those

TABLE VIII–1.

	Option A				Option B	
Probability (P)	Cumulative Probability F_A	Return (x)		Probability (P)	Cumulative Probability F_B	Return (x)
1/3	1/3	10		1/3	1/3	5
1/3	2/3	20		1/3	2/3	10
1/3	1	30		1/3	1	15

3. A GENERAL EFFICIENCY CRITERION (GC)

TABLE VIII-2.

Return	Cumulative Probability of Option B F_B	Cumulative Probability of Option A F_A	F_B Minus F_A
−5	0	0	0
0	0	0	0
5	1/3	0	1/3
7	1/3	0	1/3
10	2/3	1/3	1/3
12	2/3	1/3	1/3
15	1	1/3	2/3
17	1	1/3	2/3
20	1	2/3	1/3
22	1	2/3	1/3
25	1	2/3	1/3
28	1	2/3	1/3
30	1	1	0
35	1	1	0

values of x which have a zero probability and rising in jump fashion at those values of x for which the probability is positive.

From the right-hand column of Table VIII-2, we can see that $F_B(x) - F_A(x) > 0$ for all levels of x; alternatively we can write $F_A(x) \leq F_B(x)$. This can also be seen in Figure VIII.3, which plots the cumulative probability

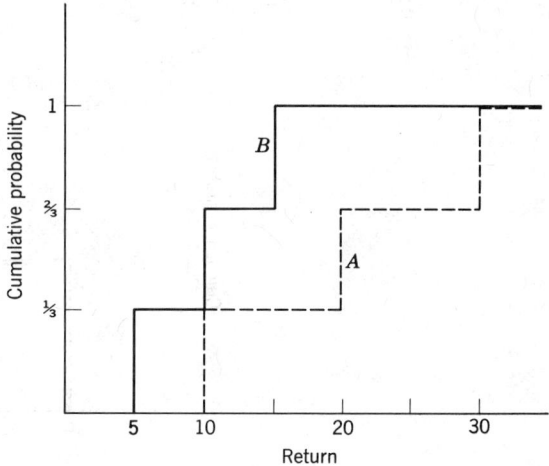

FIGURE VIII.3.

TABLE VIII-3.

	Option A		Option B
Probability (P)	Return (x)	Probability (P)	Return (x)
1/4	5	1/2	5
1/4	6	1/4	12
1/2	20	1/4	20

functions for the two options. The roulette wheel with the smaller returns is denoted by B and the other alternative by A. Since A lies to the right of B, the GC is fulfilled, and option A (the roulette wheel with the larger returns) is preferable to the first, independent of the shape of the utility function, which is as it should be.

Example No. 2

Since the roulette wheel example appears not only contrived but perhaps trivial as well, it might be argued that the general criterion is superfluous and that common sense alone will suffice. While this may be true for the roulette wheel, Table VIII-3 presents a less transparent example. In this example it is no longer intuitively obvious that one of the options should be preferred to the other. But as Figure VIII.4 clearly shows, option A fulfills the general criterion and represents the preferable alternative for all investors, independent of their attitudes toward risk.

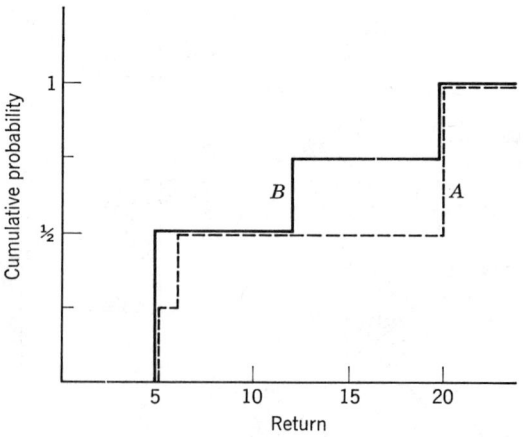

FIGURE VIII.4.

3. A GENERAL EFFICIENCY CRITERION (GC)

Example No. 3

Let us assume a third example which is much closer to reality. Table VIII–4 presents the annual *gross* returns to investors (per $100 of investment) for eight alternative investment options during the past eight years. These data were then used to calculate the expected net return for each option.[6]

The data are set out in terms of dollar returns rather than in percentages, since utility functions are defined in terms of absolute returns. In order to ensure comparability we calculate the return per $100 of investment.[7] Thus a return of 10% in a given year is entered in Table VIII–4 as a gross return of $110; a negative rate of return of −20% is entered as a gross return of $80.

In the absence of any additional information we shall assume that the investor attributes a probability of 1/8 to each of the past outcomes, which enables us to set out the cumulative probability distributions for each of the eight alternatives (see Table VIII–5). These distributions are plotted in Figure

TABLE VIII–4. Gross annual returns* for eight hypothetical investment options (in dollars)

Option/Year	1	2	3	4	5	6	7	8
1963	90	70	160	145	60	30	150	110
1964	110	90	170	145	60	80	170	140
1965	110	70	170	120	20	80	170	140
1966	110	90	170	190	40	30	160	160
1967	110	130	170	120	60	80	170	160
1968	90	70	170	145	70	140	170	160
1969	110	130	160	190	120	80	180	160
1970	110	70	170	145	70	30	170	160
Expected Return	5.00	−10.00	67.50	50.00	−37.50	−31.25	67.50	48.75

* The annual returns have been calculated per $100 of investment.

[6] For simplicity we use unadjusted historical data on the returns to investors to estimate the expected return. Clearly, an investment analyst might desire to change this expectation in keeping with his analysis of the company's prospects. Similarly a time period of eight years was chosen arbitrarily in order to illustrate the efficiency analysis.

[7] It should be recalled that we assume an efficient market in which an individual investor is fairly small relative to the market as a whole. As a result his sales and purchase orders do not affect securities' prices so that it makes no difference, institutional considerations aside, if we assume an investment of $100 or of $1,000.

274 III EFFICIENCY ANALYSIS OF INVESTMENT UNDER UNCERTAINTY

TABLE VIII–5. Cumulative probability distributions for eight hypothetical investment options*

Gross Return	F_1	F_2	F_3	F_4	F_5	F_6	F_7	F_8
20	0	0	0	0	1/8	0	0	0
30	0	0	0	0	1/8	3/8	0	0
40	0	0	0	0	2/8	3/8	0	0
60	0	0	0	0	5/8	3/8	0	0
70	0	4/8	0	0	7/8	3/8	0	0
80	0	4/8	0	0	7/8	7/8	0	0
90	2/8	6/8	0	0	7/8	7/8	0	0
110	1	6/8	0	0	7/8	7/8	0	1/8
120	1	6/8	0	2/8	1	7/8	0	1/8
130	1	1	0	2/8	1	7/8	0	1/8
140	1	1	0	2/8	1	1	0	3/8
145	1	1	0	6/8	1	1	0	3/8
150	1	1	0	6/8	1	1	1/8	3/8
160	1	1	2/8	6/8	1	1	2/8	1
170	1	1	1	6/8	1	1	7/8	1
180	1	1	1	6/8	1	1	1	1
190	1	1	1	1	1	1	1	1

* The symbol $F_i (i = 1, 2, \ldots, 8)$ denotes the cumulative probability distribution of the ith investment option.

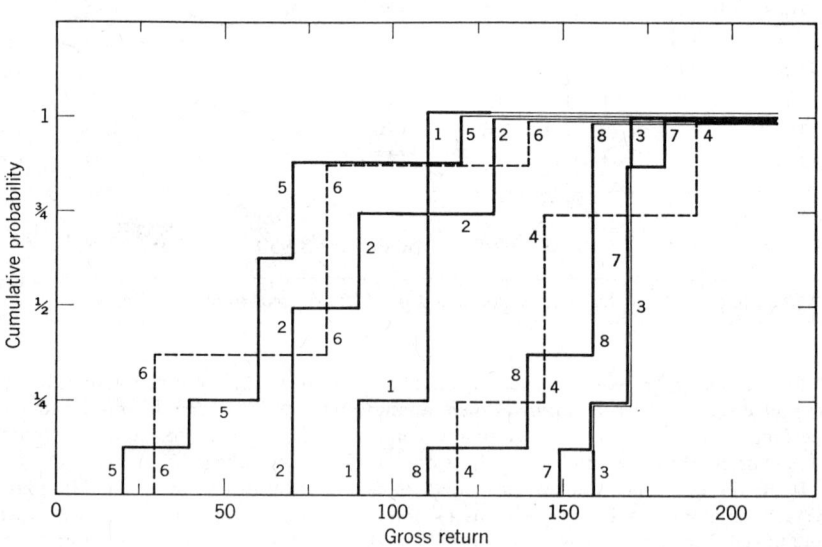

FIGURE VIII.5.

3. A GENERAL EFFICIENCY CRITERION (GC)

VIII.5. Applying the GC to the diagram we find that investment options 3, 4, and 7 comprise the efficient set. All the other options do not fulfill the GC and can be relegated to the inefficient group. For example, option 8 is eliminated by option 7, which dominates it.

Given the assumption that investors prefer more to less wealth, and without stipulating whether they are risk averters or risk lovers, we have reduced the feasible set to the above three options. In other words, all investors, irrespective of the shape of their utility functions, will make one of these efficient alternatives their final, or optimal, choice. The particular option chosen depends on an investor's tastes (utility function). In Table VIII–6 we have calculated the expected utility for each of the three efficient investments[8] using the following utility function:

$$U(x) = 100 + 100 \log x$$

The maximum expectation is that of option 3 (expected utility = 322.38), which is the optimal investment for all investors having the specified utility function.

TABLE VIII-6. Annual gross returns, utilities, and expected utilities of three efficient options

Option No. 3		Option No. 4		Option No. 7	
Utility	Return	Utility	Return	Utility	Return
320.41	160	316.14	145	317.61	150
323.04	170	316.14	145	323.04	170
323.04	170	307.92	120	323.04	170
323.04	170	327.88	190	320.41	160
323.04	170	307.92	120	323.04	170
323.04	170	316.14	145	323.04	170
320.41	160	327.88	190	325.53	180
323.04	170	316.14	145	323.04	170
$EU(x_3) = 322.38$		$EU(x_4) = 317.02$		$EU(x_7) = 322.34$	

* Utilities were calculated using the following utility function:
$$U(x) = 100 + 100 \log x$$

---

[8] There is no need to calculate the expected utility of the inefficient options since each of their expectations is, by definition, below the expectation of at least one of the efficient options.

276 III EFFICIENCY ANALYSIS OF INVESTMENT UNDER UNCERTAINTY

TABLE VIII-7. Annual gross return, utilities, and expected utilities of three efficient options*

Option 3		Option 4		Option 7	
Utility	Return	Utility	Return	Utility	Return
266	160	220.25	145	235	150
299	170	220.25	145	299	170
299	170	154.00	120	299	170
299	170	371.00	190	266	160
299	170	154.00	120	299	170
299	170	220.25	145	299	170
266	160	371.00	190	334	180
299	170	220.25	145	299	170
$EU(x_3) = 290.75$		$EU(x_4) = 241.38$		$EU(x_7) = 291.25$	

* Utilities were calculated using the following utility function:

$$U(x) = 10 + \frac{1}{100} x^2$$

To demonstrate the dependence of *optimal* investment choice on the shape of utility functions we have recalculated the expected utilities of the three efficient options using a different utility function:

$$U(x) = 10 + \frac{1}{100} x^2$$

Table VIII-7 sets out the relevant data using this utility function. In this case option 7 is the optimal investment, that is, the alternative which maximizes expected utility.

3.3 THE RELATIONSHIP OF THE GENERAL CRITERION TO THE FIRST TWO DISTRIBUTION MOMENTS

One of the most important characteristics of an investment option's probability distribution is the expected return, or the first central moment of the distribution. When we refer to an investment's "profitability" we almost invariably have the expected return in mind. We turn now to the relationship of the GC to the expected return.

As we have already proved, an investment option F dominates an alternative option G, by the General Criterion, *if and only if* the following relation-

3. A GENERAL EFFICIENCY CRITERION (GC)

ship between their cumulative probability distributions holds:

$$F(x) \leq G(x)$$

The economic interpretation of this theorem is straightforward: for the family of all monotonically *nondecreasing* utility functions, fulfillment of this criterion implies the following as well:

$$E_F U(x) > E_G U(x)$$

Thus if an option dominates another option by the GC, the expected utility of the former exceeds that of the latter for *all* investors, irrespective of their attitudes toward risk. The emphasis here is on *all* investors; the relationship *must* hold for all nondecreasing utility functions, independent of their shape. Thus, if we recall that the linear utility function $U(x) = x$ is also monotonically nondecreasing, the above mentioned relationship between the GC and expected utility holds for the relationship between their expected returns as well:

$$E_F(x) > E_G(x)$$

that is, the expected return of F must exceed that of G.

A necessary condition for one option to be preferred to a second option by the GC is that the expected return of the preferred option be greater than the expected return of the second. This can be confirmed by looking at Table VIII–4. For every nonefficient option (investments 1, 2, 5, 6, and 8) there corresponds an efficient option (investments 3, 4, and 7) which has a higher expected return.

The question which arises almost immediately is whether a similar systematic relationship can be found between the variances of the returns. Consider the three investment options given in Table VIII–8; their cumulative probability distributions are drawn in Figure VIII.6. From the diagram it is clear that, by the GC, investment B dominates investment C, and option A

TABLE VIII–8.

Option A		Option B		Option C	
Probability $P(x_A)$	Return x_A	Probability $P(x_B)$	Return x_B	Probability $P(x_C)$	Return x_C
1	10	1/2 1/2	6 18	1/2 1/2	3 9
$E(x_A) = 10$ Var $(x_A) = 0$		$E(x_B) = 12$ Var $(x_B) = 36$		$E(x_C) = 6$ Var $(x_C) = 9$	

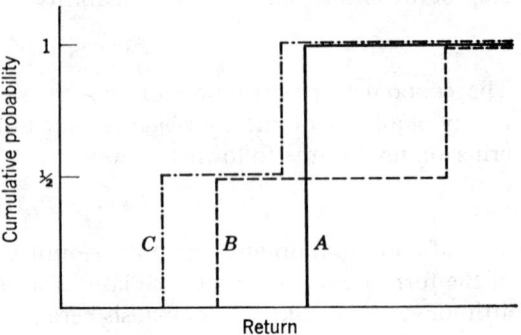

FIGURE VIII.6.

also is preferable to option C. The expected return of C is lower than the expectation of both A and B, as required. With respect to the variance, however, no systematic relationship can be found: the variance of option A is smaller than that of option C, while the variance of B is greater than that of C. Thus, unlike the expected return, no necessary condition for dominance can be found regarding the second central moment, the variance. It follows that investments' expected returns, and not their variance, play the crucial role in determining efficiency by the GC.

An intuitive explanation for this phenomenon is not difficult to find. When defining the GC we assumed that investors prefer more to less wealth, and therefore that they prefer higher expected returns. On the other hand we did *not* specify investors' attitudes toward risk. The variance is an indicator of dispersion, and therefore an investor, other things being equal, will prefer a high variance if he is a risk lover, while a risk averter will prefer investments with a lower variance. Since the GC was designed to find the efficient set for risk lovers and risk averters alike, the variance does not play a clear-cut role in determining the preference ordering in this most general case.[9]

4. A RISK AVERSION CRITERION

As we pointed out in Chapter VII, there are two somewhat conflicting views regarding the shape of investors' utility functions. According to many economists an individual's utility function is necessarily concave, while

---

[9] We shall see that even if all investors are risk averters the variance still plays only a limited role in determining dominance.

4. A RISK AVERSION CRITERION

according to others (in particular Friedman and Savage) it may contain convex as well as concave segments. In the preceding section we have presented a general efficiency criterion which corresponds to the Friedman–Savage view that the utility function may take any form provided only that the first derivative be non-negative. In this section we shall present an optimal efficiency criterion for those cases where investors are known to be risk averters. This means that in addition to the basic requirement that $U'(x) \geq 0$ we also require that $U''(x) \leq 0$, that is, that the second derivative be less than (or equal to) zero.

Even if we had decisive theoretical and empirical evidence in support of the claim that utility functions generally contain convex sections with positive second derivatives, it would still pay to develop additional efficiency criteria for specific subgroups of investors. This point will become clear if we consider the following simple example. Let us assume that there are a million investors in the securities market; let us further assume that there is unequivocal proof that among them are risk lovers as well as risk averters, so that it cannot be presumed that an efficiency criterion which assumes concave utility functions will be appropriate for all investors. Clearly, it is the GC which provides an optimal universally applicable criterion. But should a significant percentage of the investors, for example 70%, be risk averters an additional screening using the risk aversion criterion can further reduce the relevant subset of efficient options, if not for all investors at least for a significant subgroup (700,000 in our hypothetical example).

Two things should be emphasized:

(a) In developing additional criteria we do not mean to imply that the GC should be replaced. On the contrary, it almost invariably pays to make an initial screening using the GC to eliminate options which are inefficient for *all* investors.

(b) The stronger assumptions which underly the risk aversion criterion will enable us to make a more sensitive preselection of investment options so that the efficient subset for risk averters can be expected to be smaller, and in most cases substantially smaller, than the efficient set derived using the GC.[10]

If we again denote the cumulative probability distributions of two *different* investment options by F and G, the Risk Aversion Criterion (RAC) can be defined as follows:

Theorem: *A necessary and sufficient condition for an option F to be preferred over a second option G by all risk averters is that the following relationship*

---

[10] The relative ability of these and other criteria to reduce the efficient set is tested empirically in Chapter XII below.

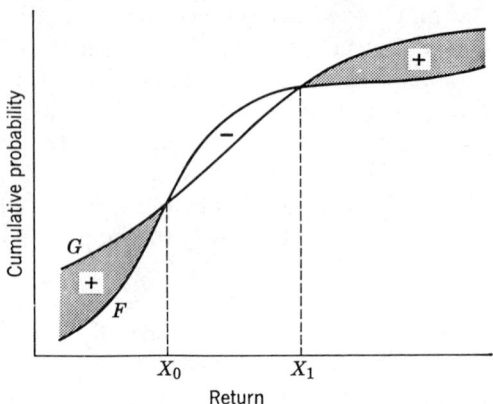

FIGURE VIII.7

hold for all x:

$$\int_{-\infty}^{x} [G(t) - F(t)]\, dt \geq 0$$

with the strong inequality holding for at least some x_0.[11]

The meaning of the RAC can readily be verbalized if we consider the two investment options F and G whose (continuous) cumulative probability distributions are drawn in Figure VIII.7. According to the RAC, the cumulative probability distributions may intersect, but the *cumulative difference* between G and F must remain non-negative over the entire domain of x. In Figure VIII.7 the differences between the two distributions are marked with a plus sign where $G > F$, since the contribution to the integral is positive; and with a minus sign where $F > G$, since over this range the contribution to the integral is negative. A glance at the diagram shows that over the entire range of returns the *cumulative* area between the two distributions always remains positive so that the RAC is fulfilled and option F dominates option G (FDG) for all risk averters. This is true since up to x_0 the distribution of G lies above that of F and therefore the area under G exceeds the area under F. And while it is true that for the range $x_0 < x < x_1$ F lies above G, the preceding shaded area marked with a plus sign is greater

---

[11] A formal mathematical proof of the optimality of the Risk Aversion Criterion is given in Appendix VIII-2 at the end of the chapter. Thus, given the information that $U'(x) \geq 0$ and $U''(x) \leq 0$, no criterion can be developed to further reduce the subset of efficient investments resulting from a screening using the RAC without making additional assumptions regarding investors' utility functions and/or the probability distributions of returns.

4. A RISK AVERSION CRITERION

TABLE VIII-9.

	Option F			Option G	
Return	Probability	Cumulative Probability	Return	Probability	Cumulative Probability
1	1/4	1/4	1/2	3/16	3/16
2	1/4	1/2	3/2	3/16	6/16
			5/2	4/16	10/16
9	1/4	3/4	7/2	3/16	13/16
10	1/4	1	9/2	3/16	1

than the area marked with a minus sign. Since beyond x_1 G again exceeds F, the cumulative shaded areas *always* exceed the areas marked with a minus sign over the entire domain of x.

Before we examine the general characteristics of the RAC let us apply it to the specific numerical example given in Table VIII-9. From the data of this table we have computed the cumulative probability distributions for the two alternatives; these distributions are plotted in Figure VIII.8. Since the two distributions intersect, both F and G are included in the efficient set of the GC. But if we invoke the RAC, option F is clearly preferable to option G since the cumulative first difference between the two distributions is always non-negative. It is clear by inspection that the cumulative shaded area for which $G(x) > F(x)$ always exceeds the cumulative area for which $F(x) > G(x)$ over the entire domain of x. In other words, the cumulative area under G is always greater than the cumulative area under F.

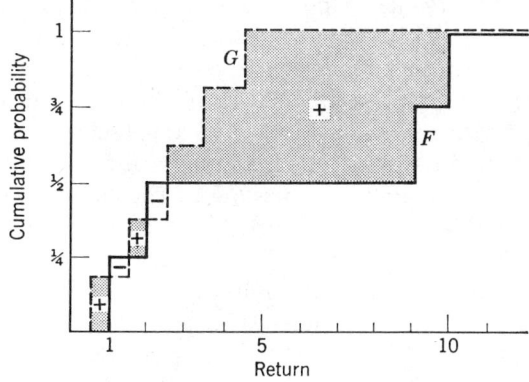

FIGURE VIII.8.

TABLE VIII-10. Cumulative area under F and G of Figure VIII.8

Return	Cumulative Area under G	Cumulative Area under F	The Areas under G − F
0	0	0	0
1/2	0	0	0
1	3/32	0	3/32
1 1/2	6/32	4/32	2/32
2	12/32	8/32	4/32
2 1/2	18/32	16/32	2/32
3	28/32	24/32	4/32
3 1/2	38/32	32/32	6/32
4	51/32	40/32	11/32
4 1/2	64/32	48/32	16/32
5	80/32	56/32	24/32
5 1/2	96/32	64/32	32/32
6	118/32	72/32	46/32
7	150/32	88/32	62/32
8	182/32	104/32	78/32
9	214/32	120/32	94/32
10	246/32	144/32	102/32
11	278/32	176/32	102/32

Of course it may not always be an easy matter to verify the dominance of one option over another by inspection, especially in cases where the probability distributions intersect a number of times. In such instances the area under the cumulative probability distributions can be calculated, as has been done in Table VIII-10. Up to a return of $\frac{1}{2}$, the area under both the distributions (value of the integrals) is zero, as can readily be verified from Figure VIII.8. Up to a return of 1, the cumulative area under G is given by the first shaded rectangle marked with a plus sign. This rectangle has a base equal to 1/2 and a height (probability) equal to 3/16; therefore the area of the rectangle equals 3/32. The area under F up to the same point is still zero. Up to a return of 1-1/2, an identical rectangle is added under G, so that the cumulative area becomes 6/32. The cumulative area under F up to a return of 1-1/2 is given by a rectangle with a base of 1/2 and a height (probability) of 1/4; its area equals $1/8 = 4/32$. Thus the *difference* between the cumulative areas under G and F up to a return of 1 is equal to 3/32; up to a return of 1-1/2 the area under G exceeds that under F by 2/32, and so on for all possible values of return. A glance down the right-hand column of Table VIII-10 verifies that the cumulative area under G always exceeds that under F at all possible levels of return, and therefore F dominates G by the RAC.

4. A RISK AVERSION CRITERION 283

4.1 SOME BASIC PROPERTIES OF THE RISK AVERSION CRITERION

As was true for the GC, a necessary condition for the dominance of an option F over an option G by the RAC is that the expected return of F be greater than, or equal to, the expected return of G. We have shown that FDG implies that

$$E_F U(x) > E_G U(x)$$

for *all* concave utility functions.[12] However, since the linear utility function $U(x) = X$ is also concave, in the weak sense, it follows that

$$E_F(x) > E_G(x)$$

is a necessary condition for dominance if the RAC is to have the assumed degree of generality.

Here again relative profitability plays a crucial role in determining the preference ordering. But despite the underlying assumption of risk aversion, a similar systematic preference for a smaller variance *cannot* be established. This contention can be illustrated by the example of the two options whose cumulative probability distributions are plotted in Figure VIII.9. F represents an option having some dispersion, while G represents an option offering a perfectly certain return (return x_0 with a probability of 1). The latter's variance, of course, is zero by definition. However, it is clear from Figure VIII.9 that the option having the larger variance (option F) dominates option G by the RAC since the cumulative area under G exceeds the cumulative

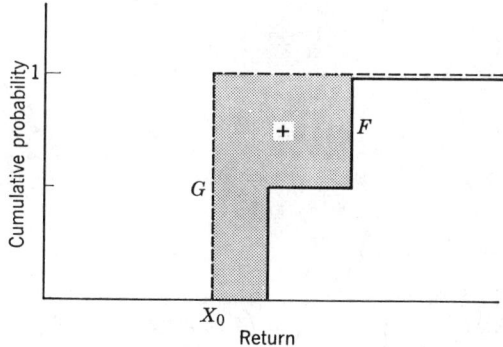

FIGURE VIII.9

---

[12] See Appendix VIII-2; for a proof of the special case in which the cumulative distributions intersect only once, see Appendix VIII-3.

284 III EFFICIENCY ANALYSIS OF INVESTMENT UNDER UNCERTAINTY

area under F at all levels of return: Thus, despite the assumption of risk aversion, the efficient set using the RAC does not necessarily exclude investments having a relatively high variance.

Another important property to be determined is the relationship of the RAC to the GC.

Theorem: *The RAC efficient set is of necessity a subset of the GC efficient set.*

In other words all the investments included in the RAC efficient set are also included in the GC efficient set. But the reverse does not hold true; not all the options which are GC efficient need be RAC efficient. As a result the RAC efficient set cannot be larger (and is usually much smaller) than the GC efficient set.

To prove the above theorem it is sufficient to show that if F dominates G by the GC, F also dominates G by the RAC. Thus if an option G is eliminated by the GC it cannot be included in the RAC efficient set. A simple and straightforward proof can be given with the aid of Figure VIII.10. For any option F to be preferred over another option G using the GC the two cumulative probability distributions *cannot* intersect, and F must lie to the right of G. But as the diagram clearly shows, if this is true the RAC, which is defined in terms of the first difference between G and F, must also hold.[13]

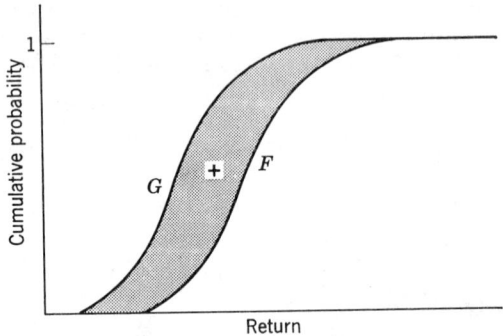

FIGURE VIII.10.

---

[13] If FDG by the General Criterion then, for all values of x, $F(x) \leq G(x)$ or $G(x) - F(x) \geq 0$. Since this expression cannot be negative it follows that for all values of x the following must also hold:

$$\int_{-\infty}^{x} [G(t) - F(t)]\, dt \geq 0$$

that is, FDG also by the Risk Aversion Criterion.

5. EFFICIENCY CRITERIA AND DIVERSIFICATION

Since there may exist other options which are *not* eliminated by the GC (for example those which intersect option *F*) but which can be eliminated by the RAC, the latter criterion provides the smaller efficient set.

5. EFFICIENCY CRITERIA AND DIVERSIFICATION

So far our illustrations of the efficiency analysis of choice under conditions of uncertainty have been based on the assumption that the investor must select one of several alternative investments. These alternatives, in turn, have been referred to as investments, options, securities, or portfolios. In practice the investor is usually faced with the problem of building an investment *portfolio* out of all the available potential securities. Of course, he may decide to put all of his eggs in one basket, that is, to buy a single security, or he may diversify his investment by purchasing a portfolio composed of several securities. The essence of the problem can best be seen by considering the simplified example set out in Table VIII–11, which assumes that an individual is confronted with the alternative of investing either in security A, in security B, or in a portfolio, C, made up of equal proportions of A and B.

Let us assume that our potential investor has $100 at his disposal. If he chooses to invest the entire $100 in security A, he will have an equal probability of earning a net return of either $3 or $4. If he places all of his money in security B he will be faced with an equal probability of earning either $1 or $6. Let us see what happens should he choose to diversify his investment by building a portfolio (C) comprised of equal amounts of A and B. In this case the investor receives the return on $50 of A plus the return on $50 of B.

TABLE VIII–11. Percentage returns on three alternative options

Security A			Security B			Portfolio C*		
Probability	Cumulative Probability	Return	Probability	Cumulative Probability	Return	Probability	Cumulative Probability	Return
1/2	1/2	3.0	1/2	1/2	1.0	1/4	1/4	2.0
						1/4	1/2	2.5
1/2	1	4.0	1/2	1	6.0	1/4	3/4	4.5
						1/4	1	5.0

* The return of Portfolio C = 1/2 the return on *A* plus 1/2 the return on *B*.

Depending on which alternative return is realized on each of the two securities, the possible returns on the portfolio are $2, $2.50, $4.50 or $5.00.

What are the chances of earning each alternative return? The answer depends on the statistical relationship between the two distributions. Solely for the sake of convenience, let us assume in this instance that the return distribution of security A is statistically *independent* of the distribution of security B. In that case the probability of realizing each of the four possible returns on the portfolio is calculated by multiplying the individual probabilities for each component return. Thus the probability of realizing the combination of $3 on A and $1 on B is given by

$$1/2 \cdot 1/2 = 1/4$$

Similarly, the probability of realizing each of the other three possible combinations is also 1/4 (see Table VIII–11).

Can we apply our two efficiency criteria to these three alternatives, even though one of them is a portfolio? Since a portfolio of securities, like a single security, is also characterized by a probability distribution of possible returns, the efficiency analysis we presented above is perfectly general and can be applied with equal validity to single investment options or to portfolios comprising two or more securities.

The cumulative probability functions of our three alternatives, security A, security B, and portfolio C are set out in Figure VIII.11. From the diagram it is clear that the cumulative distributions of securities A and B intersect, so that neither fulfills the general criterion, and a clear-cut preference ordering cannot be established. Since distribution C, representing the composite portfolio, also intersects both distributions A and B, all three alternatives,

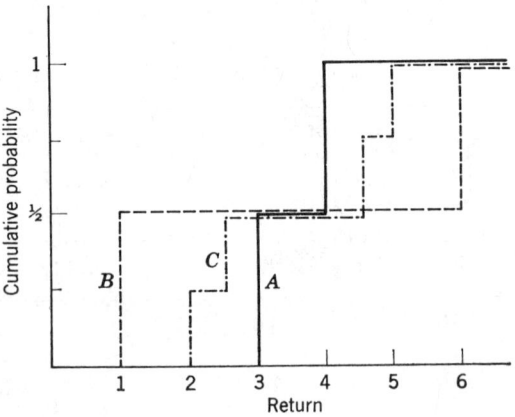

FIGURE VIII.11.

5. EFFICIENCY CRITERIA AND DIVERSIFICATION

TABLE VIII-12.

Return	Cumulative Area under A	Cumulative Area under B	Cumulative Area under C	B Minus A	B Minus C	C Minus A
1.0	0	0	0	0	0	0
2.0	0	1/2	0	1/2	1/2	0
2.5	0	3/4	1/8	3/4	5/8	1/8
3.0	0	1	3/8	1	5/8	3/8
4.0	1/2	1 1/2	7/8	1	5/8	3/8
4.5	1	1 3/4	1 1/8	3/4	5/8	1/8
5.0	1 1/2	2	1 1/2	1/2	1/2	0
6.0	2 1/2	2 1/2	2 1/2	0	0	0

A, B, and C are included in the GC efficient set. Thus it cannot be stipulated that all investors, independent of their attitudes toward risk, will tend to diversify their securities investment; using the GC, the efficient set includes both single security investments as well as the portfolio.

Let us now see whether the additional information that investors are risk averters can help us to establish a clear-cut preference for a mixed portfolio. To do this we calculate the cumulative areas under each of the three distributions (Table VIII-12) and apply the RAC. Comparing the portfolio C with security B we find that CDB so that alternative B can be eliminated. But going on to a comparison of C with security A, we find that ADC, and the portfolio C is eliminated leaving A as the only efficient investment for all risk averters.

Since the single security A dominates portfolio C, it might seem to follow that risk averters generally will not diversify their investments. But this is not true. If we vary the investment proportions of the portfolio we can always find at least one mixed portfolio which is RAC efficient. As both securities have the same expected return (3.5%), combining the two securities in the portfolio in varying proportions will not change the portfolio's expected return, which remains invariant at 3.5%. However, it does change the variance. If we choose the porportions of A and B which *minimize* the portfolio variance, 25/26 of A and 1/26 of B, the probability distribution changes (see Table VIII-12a). The reader can verify that security A does not dominate the portfolio C so that both A and C are included in the RAC efficient set.

If we compare the results of applying the RAC with the previous results of applying the GC to the same three alternatives the following conclusions can be reached.

TABLE VIII-12a. Portfolio C'

Probability	Cumulative Probability	Return*
1/4	1/4	76/26
1/4	1/2	81/26
1/4	3/4	101/26
1/4	1	106/26

* The return of Portfolio $C' = 25/26 \times$ the return on A plus $1/26 \times$ the return on B.

(a) Applying the RAC reduces the GC efficient set. In our last example, all three alternatives are GC efficient but only two options, A and C, are RAC efficient, while in the previous example of equal proportions only one option (A) was RAC efficient.

(b) The assumption of risk aversion ($U''(x) \leq 0$) is *not* sufficient to ensure that all diversified investments will invariably dominate a single asset option. In our example, the single security A is preferable to the two security (equal proportions) portfolio C for all risk averters. The reason for this is not difficult to find. The expected returns on each security and on the portfolio are the same—3.5% in all three cases. And although the portfolio decreases the dispersion of returns relative to security B, the portfolio dispersion still *exceeds* that of security A, which accounts for A's dominance.

(c) Changing the investment proportions (25/26 of A and 1/26 of B), we found that both option A and the portfolio C' are included in the RAC efficient set. Thus some risk averters can be expected to choose the portfolio, but there can be no guarantee that others will not prefer the single security option to the mixed portfolio.

Let us consider a different example. Assume that an investor is confronted with two *identical* securities, A and B, and a portfolio, C, comprised of equal proportions of A and B. Can an investor be expected to diversify his investments in this case, that is, will he prefer the portfolio? Table VIII-13 sets out

TABLE VIII-13.

Security A		Security B		Portfolio C	
Probability	Return	Probability	Return	Probability	Return
1/2	2	1/2	2	1/4	2
1/2	4	1/2	4	1/2	3
				1/4	4

5. EFFICIENCY CRITERIA AND DIVERSIFICATION 289

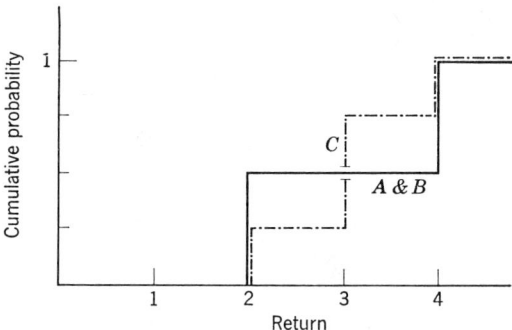

FIGURE VIII.12.

the relevant data for these three options on the assumption that the returns on the securities are statistically independent. The resulting cumulative probability distributions are drawn in Figure VIII.12. Note that since A and B are identical, their cumulative distributions are also identical and the investor is indifferent between them.

A glance at the data of Table VIII–13 is sufficient to show that the portfolio has the same expected return as the individual securities, while the dispersion about the mean has been reduced. But since distribution C intersects both A and B, all three alternatives—the two identical securities and the composite portfolio—are included in the GC efficient set. Once again we can conclude that diversification will not necessarily be preferred by all investors, independent of their attitudes toward risk. Now let us apply the RAC. Figure VIII.12 shows that the area under the cumulative distributions of A or B always exceeds the area under the distribution of the portfolio C. Therefore, in this case, *all* risk averters will prefer the portfolio to an investment in *either* of the (identical) securities.

In both of the preceding examples we assumed that the returns on investments A and B were statistically independent. Let us now take an extreme example where two distributions are assumed to have perfect *negative* statistical interdependence (see Table VIII-14) so that by diversifying into a portfolio of two securities, the variance of returns can be reduced to zero and perfectly certain returns assured. Given the *negative* interdependence, a portfolio comprised of 50% of A and 50% of B offers a perfectly certain return of 3. If security B yields a return of 2 the portfolio return equals $1/2 \cdot 2 + 1/2 \cdot 4 = 3$; if the return on B should be 4 the portfolio return is again 3, since

$$1/2 \cdot 4 + 1/2 \cdot 2 = 3$$

Figure VIII.13 presents the cumulative distributions of securities A and B and portfolio C. (Note that as before, A and B have identical cumulative

TABLE VIII-14.

	Security B		Security A	
Returns	Probability	Returns	Conditional Probability
2	1/2	$\begin{pmatrix} 2 \\ 4 \end{pmatrix}$	0 1
4	1/2	$\begin{pmatrix} 2 \\ 4 \end{pmatrix}$	1 0

probability distributions.) Once again the distributions intersect so that invoking the GC, the portfolio with a perfectly certain return of 3 does *not* dominate the two securities, each of which has a risky expected return also equal to 3. The explanation is not difficult to find. Since the GC is appropriate for risk lovers as well as risk averters, the reduction in variance, inherent in the portfolio, is not a desirable characteristic for the former class of investors.

If we apply the RAC to the same sample, it is clear from Figure VIII.13 that the areas under each of the identical securities A and B exactly equal the area under the portfolio distribution C. But since the distributions of A and B intersect distribution C from the left, the RAC criterion is fulfilled; the cumulative area under A (or B) is always greater than, or equal to, the cumulative area under C over the entire domain of returns. Thus CDA and CDB for this extreme case of negative interdependence, and *all* risk averters

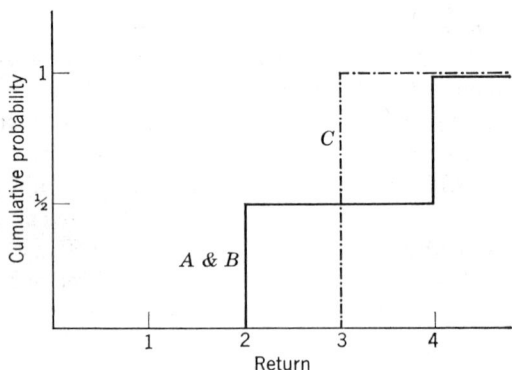

FIGURE VIII.13.

will prefer the portfolio with the stabilized return. In sum, while the assumption of negative interdependence does not change our conclusions regarding the GC, it does strengthen the tendency of risk averters to diversify their investments.[14]

6. SUMMARY

The choice among risky investment options by the individual may be regarded as a two-step procedure: first, the investor chooses the efficient set, independent of his tastes or preferences; second, he chooses the optimal portfolio from the efficient set. In the first stage, on the basis of highly general information on a given group of investors, all potential investment options are divided into two groups: an efficient set and an inefficient set. The partition is effected by applying an efficiency criterion which is appropriate for a given class of investors. Using such a decision rule, we can be certain that all individuals belonging to the class in question will make their final choice out of the efficient group. In the second stage, the investor, in accordance with his tastes, chooses the optimal option out of the efficient set, namely, that alternative which maximizes his expected utility.

Two efficiency criteria, the General Criterion (GC) and the Risk Aversion Criterion (RAC) are defined in this chapter. The GC places no restrictions on the form of the utility function beyond the usual requirement that it be nondecreasing. Thus this criterion is appropriate for risk averters and risk lovers alike since the utility function may contain concave as well as convex segments. Owing to its generality, the GC permits a preliminary screening of investment options which eliminates those options which no rational investor (independent of his attitude toward risk) will ever choose.

The RAC is the appropriate efficiency criterion for all risk averters. Here we assume the utility function to be concave. This criterion is based on stronger assumptions, and therefore it permits a more sensitive selection of investments. On the other hand, the RAC is applicable to a smaller group of investors. The RAC efficient set is of necessity a subset of the GC efficient set; this means that all of the options included in the RAC efficient set are also included in the GC efficient set, but not necessarily vice versa.

Both the GC and RAC are optimal, in the sense that given the assumptions regarding investors' tastes (utility functions), their application ensures a *minimal* efficient set.

An analysis of these two criteria shows that an investment option's expected return plays a crucial role in determining the preference ordering.

---

[14] A much stronger case for diversification can be made when the number of securities is increased. See Chapter X.

The role of an investment's variance, on the other hand, is less clear; under both criteria an option F may be preferred to an option G even though G has the lower variance.

When the two criteria are applied to the problem of building a portfolio comprising more than one security a clear preference for risk diversification *cannot* be established for all investors using the GC. This is as it should be since the stabilization of the income stream is *not* a desirable characteristic for risk lovers. A risk averter, on the other hand, usually will prefer to diversify his investments by building a portfolio, thereby reducing the variance of the returns. This preference for a portfolio holds true both for the case where the returns of the various securities are statistically independent and *a fortiori* for the case where they are negatively interdependent.

QUESTIONS AND PROBLEMS

8.1 Define the following concepts:
   a. efficiency criterion
   b. General Efficiency Criterion (GC)
   c. Risk Aversion Criterion (RAC)
   d. efficient set

8.2 Distinguish between the concepts of an optimal investment option and an optimal efficiency criterion.

8.3 "The General Criterion and the Risk Aversion Criterion are *mutually exclusive* methods for screening investment options." Appraise this statement.

8.4 What is the relationship (if any) of the GC and RAC to investment options' expected returns? What is their relationship to the variance of the distribution of returns?

8.5 What is the relationship between the GC and RAC *inefficient* sets?

8.6 It is often said that "diversification always pays." Do you agree?

8.7 In what sense can investment decisions be thought of as comprising a "two-step" procedure?

8.8 Consider the following five investment options:

A		B		C		D		E	
Probability	Return*	Probability	Return*	Probability	Return*	Probability	Return*	Probability	Return*
1/4	20	1/2	5	1/4	15	3/4	15	1/4	10
3/4	30	1/2	30	3/4	40	1/4	25	1/4	15
								1/4	20
								1/4	30

* All the returns of each of the five options are given per $100 of outlay.

   a. Which of these options will be included in the GC efficient set?
   b. Prove your answer graphically.

8.9 Consider the following five investment options:

A		B		C		D		E	
Prob-ability	Return	Prob-ability	Return	Prob-ability	Return	Prob-ability	Return	Prob-ability	Return
1/2	10	1/3	10	1/2	5	1/2	12	1/4	6
1/2	20	1/3	15	1/4	6	1/2	20	3/4	40
		1/3	30	1/4	8				

* All returns are per $100 of outlay.

    a. Which options comprise the GC efficient set?
    b. Which options are included in the RAC efficient set?
    c. Prove your answers to parts (a) and (b) graphically.

8.10 Distinguish between an option's (density) probability distribution and its *cumulative* probability distribution.

8.11 Assume that we are using the following *arbitrary* and therefore *non-optimal* efficiency criterion:

FDG if and only if $F(X - 5) \leq G(X)$ for every X;
where $F(X_0 - 5) < G(X)$, for some X_0.

    a. Calculate the efficient set using this criterion. (Use data of Problem 8.8.)
    b. Prove that this criterion is *not* optimal for investors where the one restriction on utility is that the function be nondecreasing ($U'(x) > 0$). (Hint: Find a specific nondecreasing utility function and show that the optimal project, using this function, is eliminated by the arbitrary efficiency criterion. Use the data of Question 8.8.)
    c. Calculate the efficient set (for the data of Question 8.9) using the following arbitrary criterion:

FDG if $F(X) + 1/2 < G(X)$ for every value X

    d. Compare and explain your answer in parts (d) and (a) with your answer in 8.8 (GC) above.

8.12 "If FDG by the GC then necessarily FDG by the RAC." Prove this statement.

8.13 "The GC is the best of all the efficiency criteria since it does not require strong assumptions regarding investors' preferences." Appraise.

8.14 Prove that the GC always results in a *smaller* efficient set than does the following criterion:

FDG if for every X, $F(X) + \delta \leq G(X)$ (where $\delta > 10$)

(Hint: Use numerical examples to prove your answer.)

SELECTED REFERENCES

Cramer, H., *Mathematical Methods of Statistics*. Princeton, N.J.: Princeton University Press, 1946.
Feller, W., *An Introduction to Probability Theory and Its Application*. New York: Wiley, 1965.
Hadar, J., and Russell, W. R., "Rules for Ordering Uncertain Prospects," *American Economic Review* (March 1969).
Hanoch, G., and Levy, H., "Efficient Portfolio Selection with Quadratic and Cubic Utility," *Journal of Business* (April 1970).
———, "The Efficiency Analysis of Choices Involving Risk," *Review of Economic Studies* (July 1969).
Levy, H., and Sarnat, M., "Portfolio Selection and Investors' Utility: A Graphical Analysis," *Applied Economics* (June 1970).
Markowitz, H. M., "Portfolio Selection," *Journal of Finance* (March 1952).
———, *Portfolio Selection*. New York: Wiley, 1959.
Massé, P., *Optimal Investment Decisions: Rules for Action and Criteria for Choice*. Englewood Cliffs, N.J.: Prentice-Hall, 1962.
Quirk, J. P., and Saposnik, R., "Admissibility and Measurable Utility Functions," *Review of Economic Studies* (October 1962).
Richter, M. K., "Cardinal Utility, Portfolio Selection and Taxation," *Review of Economic Studies* (June 1960).

APPENDIX VIII-1

Proof of the General Criterion[15]

Before proving that the General Criterion is an optimal efficiency criterion, given the assumption $U'(x) \geq 0$, we shall prove the following lemma:

Lemma 1: Let G, F be two (cumulative) distributions, and $U(x)$ a non-decreasing function, with finite values for any finite x; then

$$Eu = E_F u(x) - E_G u(x) = \int_{-\infty}^{\infty} [G(x) - F(x)]\, du(x)$$

if the limit exists.[16]

Proof: By definition.[17]

$$\Delta Eu = \int_{-\infty}^{\infty} u\, dF - \int_{-\infty}^{\infty} u\, dG \qquad (8.1.1)$$

Integrating (1) by parts gives

$$\Delta Eu = \int_{-\infty}^{\infty} d(u \cdot F) - \int_{-\infty}^{\infty} F\, du - \int_{-\infty}^{\infty} d(u \cdot G) + \int_{-\infty}^{\infty} G\, du$$

$$= \int_{-\infty}^{\infty} d[u \cdot (F - G)] + \int_{-\infty}^{\infty} (G - F)\, du$$

---

[15] This theorem has been proved by Quirk and Saposnik for the discrete case and by Hadar and Russell, and by Hanoch and Levy for the general (continuous) case. However, in this appendix we use the formulation of the latter.
[16] The integrals throughout are Stieltjes–Lebesgues integrals, ranging on all real values of x, unless specified otherwise; see Cramer, p. 62.
[17] The arguments in the functions appearing in integrals are omitted in cases where no misunderstanding can arise.

To show that the first term on the right vanishes, we define a sequence of functions $u_n(x)$ converging to $u(x)$:

$$u_n(x) = \begin{pmatrix} u(-n) & \text{for} & x < -n \\ u(x) & \text{for} & -n \leq x \leq n \\ u(n) & \text{for} & x > n \end{pmatrix}$$

$$\int_{-\infty}^{\infty} d[u(F-G)] = \lim_{n \to \infty} \int_{-\infty}^{\infty} d[u_n(F-G)]$$
$$= \lim_{n \to \infty} \{u(n)[F(\infty) - G(\infty)] - u(-n)[F(-\infty) - G(-\infty)]\}$$
$$= \lim_{n \to \infty} \{u(n) \cdot 0 - u(-n) \cdot 0\}$$

Hence $\Delta Eu = \int_{-\infty}^{\infty} (G-F)\, du$, if the integral exists. Q.E.D.

The optimal criterion for FDG is given in Theorem 1.

Theorem 1: *Let F, G, and u, be as in Lemma 1. A necessary and sufficient condition for FDG is: $F(x) \leq G(x)$ for every x, and $F(x_0) < G(x_0)$ for some x_0.*

Proof: (a) The sufficiency follows immediately from Lemma 1. $G - F \geq 0 \Rightarrow \int_{-\infty}^{\infty} (G-F)\, du \geq 0$ when u is nondecreasing. If $(G(x_0) - F(x_0)) > 0$, due to the right continuity of F and G, there is an interval $x_0 \leq x \leq x_0 + \beta$ where $G(x) - F(x) > 0$. To show that there exists some u_0 for which $\Delta Eu_0 > 0$, choose $u_0(x)$ as follows:

$$u_0(x) = \begin{pmatrix} x_0 & \text{for} & x \leq x_0 \\ x & \text{for} & x_0 \leq x \leq x_0 + \beta \\ x_0 + \beta & \text{for} & x > x_0 + \beta \end{pmatrix}$$

Then $u_0 \in U$, and

$$\int_{-\infty}^{+\infty} (G-F)\, du = \int_{x_0}^{x_0+\beta} (G-F)\, dx > 0$$

(b) The necessity is proved similarly.

If, for some x_1, $G(x_1) - F(x_1) < 0$, there is an interval $[x_1, x_1 + \varepsilon]$, where $G(x) - F(x) < 0$; choose:

$$u_1(x) = \begin{pmatrix} x_1 & \text{for} & x \leq x_1 \\ x & \text{for} & x_1 \leq x \leq x_1 + \varepsilon \\ x_1 + \varepsilon & \text{for} & x \geq x_1 + \varepsilon \end{pmatrix}$$

Then

$$\int_{-\infty}^{\infty} (G-F)\, du_1 = \int_{x_1}^{x_1+\varepsilon} (G-F)\, dx < 0$$

In addition, if $F(x) = G(x)$ for all x, then:

$$\int_{-\infty}^{\infty} (G - F)\, du = 0 \text{ for all } u \quad \text{Q.E.D.}$$

The interpretation of this criterion is straightforward: F dominates G if for every value x, the probability of getting x or less is smaller (or equal) with F than with G. This also means that $1 - F \geq 1 - G$, or that the probability of getting more than x is higher with F than with G, for every x. Hence, the cumulative probability distribution F is a shift downward (or to the right) of the distribution G. Whenever the two cumulative distributions intersect, they cannot dominate one another: that is, one can find one utility function u where $\Delta Eu > 0$, and another function v where $\Delta Ev < 0$ (where both u and v are nondecreasing).

APPENDIX VIII-2
Proof of the Risk Aversion Criterion[18]

Theorem 2: Let F and G be two (cumulative) distributions. A necessary and sufficient condition for FDG, for every $u(x)$ which is nondecreasing and concave, is $\int_{-\infty}^{x} [G(t) - F(t)]\, dt \geq 0$ for every x, and $G \neq F$ for some x_0. That is, the accumulated area under G should not be less than the area under F, below any real value of x (and F and G are distinct).

Proof: (a) The necessity of the condition follows again from Lemma 1 above. Suppose, for some x_0, $\int_{-\infty}^{x_0} (G - F)\, dt < 0$. Define $u_2(x)$ as follows:

$$u_2(x) = \begin{pmatrix} x & \text{for} & x \leq x_0 \\ x_0 & \text{for} & x \geq x_0 \end{pmatrix}$$

Now, $u_2(x)$ is in U_1, since it is nondecreasing and concave, but $\Delta E u_2 = \int_{-\infty}^{\infty} (G - F)\, du_2 = \int_{-\infty}^{x_0} [G(t) - F(t)]\, dt < 0$, by assumption. Again, $F = G$ for all x implies $\Delta E u = 0$ for all u. Therefore, the condition is indeed necessary.

(b) The proof of sufficiency is somewhat more involved. Define two characteristic functions

$$I_A(x) = 1; \quad I_B(x) = 0, \quad \text{when } G(x) \geq F(x)$$
$$I_A(x) = 0; \quad I_B(x) = 1, \quad \text{when } G(x) < F(x)$$

---

[18] This theorem has been proved by Hadar and Russell, Hanoch and Levy, and Rothchild and Stiglitz. We use in this appendix the version of Hanoch and Levy. For more details see G. Hanoch and H. Levy, "The Efficiency Analysis of Choices Involving Risk," *Review of Economic Studies* (July 1969), pp. 338–41.

It is interesting to note that similar ideas (though in a different context) were developed by Blackwell in two articles which appeared in 1950 and 1953. However, Blackwell deals with comparisons of experiments rather than comparison of different options. For more details see D. Blackwell, "Comparison of Experiments," *Proceedings of the Second Berkeley Symposium on Mathematical Statistics and Probability*, University of California Press, 1951; and D. Blackwell, "Equivalent Comparisons of Experiments," *Annals of Mathematical Statistics* (June 1953).

And define a transformation Tx by the following equation:[19]

$$\int_{-\infty}^{Tx} I_A(t) |G - F| \, dt = \int_{-\infty}^{x} I_B(t) |G - F| \, dt \qquad (8.2.1)$$

Since

$$\lim_{x \to -\infty} \int_{-\infty}^{x} |G - F| \, dt = 0$$

we have

$$\int_{-\infty}^{x} (G - F) \, dt = \int_{-\infty}^{x} I_A(t) |G(t) - F(t)| \, dt - \int_{-\infty}^{x} I_B(t) |G(t) - F(t)| \, dt$$

which is non-negative, by assumption. The first term on the right is a non-decreasing function of x, hence the equality (8.2.1) may be maintained only if $Tx \leq x$, for all x. One can verify that Tx is almost everywhere continuous and differentiable, and that $T'(x) \geq 0$ (that is, Tx is nondecreasing).

Differentiating Equation (8.2.1), which holds for all x, one gets:

$$I_A(Tx) |G(Tx) - F(Tx)| \, T'(x) = I_B(x)[G(x) - F(x)] \qquad (8.2.2)$$

for almost all x.

We shall now prove that $\int_{t \leq x} [G(t) - F(t)] \, du(t) \geq 0$ for all x.

$$\int_{t \leq x} (G - F) \, du(t) = \int_{t \leq x} I_A |G - F| \, du(t) - \int_{t \leq x} I_B |G - F| \, du(t) \qquad (8.2.3)$$

Substituting (8.2.2) in the integrand of the second term, we get

$$\int_{t \leq x} (G - F) \, du(t) = \int_{t \leq x} I_A |G - F| \, du(t)$$
$$- \int_{t \leq x} I_A(Tt) |G(Tt) - F(Tt)| \, T'(t) \, du(t)$$

Consider now the second term on the right. Remembering that the integrand is non-negative, we get

$$\int_{t \leq x} I_A(Tt) |G(Tt) - F(Tt)| \, T'(t) \, du(t)$$
$$\leq \int_{t \leq x} I_A(Tt) |G(Tt) - F(Tt)| \, du(Tt)$$

since $Tt \leq t$, and $u(t)$ is concave.

---

[19] For simplicity we assume that there is only one value $T(x)$ for every x. However, if for a given interval the two cumulative distributions F and G coincide, we might find a set of values $T(x)$ which fulfill Equation (8.2.1). In this case some modifications in the proof are called for, but the results of the theorem remain unchanged.

APPENDIX VIII-2

A change of variable in the last term, $Z = Tt$, gives

$$\int_{z \leq Tx} I_A(Z) |G(Z) - F(Z)| \, du(Z)$$

so that, collecting this result back in (8.2.3)

$$\int_{t \leq x} (G - F) \, du > \int_{t \leq x} I_A |G - F| \, du - \int_{t \leq Tx} I_A |G - F| \, du$$

$$= \int_{Tx \leq t \leq x} I_A |G - F| \, du(t) \geq 0 \quad \text{since } Tx \leq x$$

Now, the non-negativity of ΔEu follows, since

$$\Delta Eu = \int_{-\infty}^{\infty} (G - F) \, du = \lim_{x \to \infty} \int_{t \leq x} [G(t) - F(t)] \, du(t) \geq 0$$

for all concave u.

And since $F = G \Rightarrow \int_{-\infty}^{\infty} (G - F) \, du = 0$, we need $F \neq G$ for some x_0, to assure that $\Delta Eu > 0$ for some u. Q.E.D.

APPENDIX VIII-3
Proof of the Risk Aversion Criterion When the Cumulative Distributions Intersect Only Once

Theorem 3:[20] Let F, G be two distributions with mean value u_1, u_2 respectively, such that for some $x_0 < \infty$, $F \leq G$ for $x \leq x_0$ (and $F < G$ for some $x_1 < x_0$) and $F \geq G$ for some $x \geq x_0$, then FDG (for concave utility functions) if and only if $u_1 \geq u_2$.

Proof: (a) If $u_1 \geq u_2$ we have, by applying the lemma of Appendix VIII-1 to the case $u(t) = t$,

$$u_1 - u_2 = \int_{-\infty}^{\infty} (G - F)\, dt = \int_{-\infty}^{x_0} (G - F)\, dt - \int_{x_0}^{\infty} |G - F|\, dt \geq 0$$

Therefore $\int_{-\infty}^{x} (G - F)\, dt \geq 0$ for all x, and by Theorem 2, FDG.

(b) If $u_1 < u_2$

$$u_1 - u_2 = \int_{-\infty}^{x_0} (G - F)\, dt - \int_{x_0}^{\infty} |G - F|\, dt < 0$$

Hence, for some $x_2 > x_0$,

$$\int_{-\infty}^{x_2} (G - F)\, dt = \int_{-\infty}^{x_0} (G - F)\, dt - \int_{x_0}^{x_2} |G - F|\, dt < 0$$

whereas for x_0 we have $\int_{-\infty}^{x_0} (G - F)\, dt > 0$ and the condition of Theorem 2 (Appendix VIII–2) does not hold for all x. That is, neither F nor G dominates the other for all concave utilities. Q.E.D.

---

[20] This proof appeared originally in G. Hanoch and H. Levy "The Efficiency Analysis of Choices Involving Risk," *Review of Economic Studies* (July, 1969), p. 371.

Chapter IX
The Mean-Variance Criterion

1. INTRODUCTION

As far back as the eighteenth century Bernoulli and Cramer reached the conclusion that decisions under conditions of uncertainty could not be made solely on the basis of expected (mean) returns.[1] Subsequently, various economists have tried to evaluate investments with the aid of two (or more) indicators based on the distribution of returns. Generally one index reflects the profitability of the investment while the other is based on the dispersion of the distribution of returns and reflects the investment's risk. The most common profitability index used is the expected return, that is, the mean of the probability distribution of returns; the risk index is usually based on the variance of the distribution, its range,[2] and so on.

Tobin[3] and Markowitz[4] base their theory of investment choice under conditions of uncertainty on the mean and variance of the distributions of returns, and Markowitz has developed a mean–variance model for the selection of portfolios. According to this approach investors desire high returns but are averse to a high variance, which is taken as the indicator of an investment's risk. The Markowitz–Tobin analysis remains the cornerstone of much of the work in the field of investment analysis. It also has provided the basis for several extensions to other problems which involve risky decisions.[5]

---

[1] See Chapter VI, Section 3.
[2] The range is defined as the difference between the highest and lowest values of the random variable. See P. G. Hoel, *Introduction to Mathematical Statistics*, New York, Wiley, 1966, p. 78.
[3] Tobin, J., "Liquidity Preference as Behavior Towards Risk," *Review of Economic Studies* 26, (February 1958); and "The Theory of Portfolio Selection" in F. H. Hahn and F. P. R. Brechling, eds. *Theory of Interest Rates*, New York, Macmillan, 1965.
[4] H. M. Markowitz, "Portfolio Selection," *Journal of Finance* 6 (March 1952); and *Portfolio Selection*, New York, Wiley, 1959.
[5] For example, the mean–variance model has been successfully applied to the problem of determining equilibrium prices in the securities market. See Chapter XIII.

2. THE NATURE OF INVESTMENT RISK

Before turning to a detailed description of the mean–variance portfolio selection model we shall present a brief review of the literature on the nature of investment risk. Numerous economists have identified investment risk with the dispersion of returns. Keynes, for example, identifies the risk involved in an investment with the possible deviations from the average return. According to Keynes, an individual who invests in an asset whose returns have a widely dispersed distribution must be given a "risk cost," a premium to compensate him for the risk taken.[6]

Like Keynes, Hicks[7] also identifies the variance of returns with risk. Hicks emphasizes the fact that the greater the dispersion of returns (for a given level of expectation), the less attractive is the investment. Nevertheless, Hicks also emphasizes that when returns are uncertain the third moment of the distributions, the index of asymmetry, may also be a significant factor affecting investors' decisions.

Although Marschak[8] maintains that decision making under conditions of risk should reflect *all* the moments of the distribution, he also notes that in many cases two moments, "the mathematical expectation and the coefficient of variation," will suffice. In other words, Marschak, too, identifies (in some cases) investment risk with the variance, or rather the coefficient of variation.[9]

Domar and Musgrave, on the other hand, identify the risk involved in making an investment under conditions of uncertainty with the possibility of sustaining a loss, and therefore suggest that investors should measure risk solely on the basis of that possibility:

> Of all possible questions which the investor may ask, the most important one, it appears to us, is concerned with the probability of actual yield being less than zero, that is, with the probability of loss. This is the essence of risk.[10]

These two authors developed a quantitative index of risk affected both by the probability of getting a result less than zero, and by the size of the possible loss. Thus they emphasize the negative segment of the probability

---

[6] See J. M. Keynes, *The General Theory of Employment Interest and Money*, London, Macmillan, 1937.
[7] J. R. Hicks, *Value and Capital*, 2nd ed., London: Oxford University Press, 1946.
[8] J. Marschak, "Money and the Theory of Assets," *Econometrica* 6 (October 1938).
[9] The coefficient of variation is defined as the standard deviation divided by the mean.
[10] E. Domar and R. A. Musgrave, "Proportional Income Taxation and Risk Taking," *Quarterly Journal of Economics* LVII (May 1944).

2. THE NATURE OF INVESTMENT RISK

distribution, and according to their model, a larger dispersion per se does not necessarily involve a greater risk.

Baumol[11] is another author who argues that variance per se does not indicate risk. According to Baumol, risk mainly reflects the possibility that the random variable may take on extremely low values. If the expected return from an investment is high, relative to its standard deviation, Baumol suggests that the spread between the expected return and k times the standard deviation ($Ex - k\sigma$) be taken as the risk index,[12] since the probability that a random variable will have a value lower by k standard deviations from its mean is bounded (by Chebyshev's Inequality) to $1/k^2$.[13]

Even from this brief survey we can see that while there is no unanimity of opinion regarding risk, it is often identified with one of the measures of dispersion of the distribution of returns. In what follows we shall see whether it is possible to find a universally applicable quantitative risk index by invoking the expected utility hypothesis. Such an approach implies that the choice among risky alternatives is a function of investment options' expected utility.

Let us assume that an individual is faced with the distribution of a random variable (return) x which can take on only two values, x_1 and x_2 with the probabilities p_1 and p_2 ($p_2 = 1 - p_1$), respectively. The expected value of this distribution is given by

$$Ex = p_1 x_1 + p_2 x_2$$

The expected utility is

$$EU(x) = p_1 U(x_1) + (1 - p_1) U(x_2)$$

This distribution is plotted in Figure IX.1.

Let us further assume that the individual is a risk averter[14] and can sell this distribution, thereby converting it into a perfectly certain income (for example, by purchasing an insurance policy). How much will the individual be ready to pay to transform the random variable x into a riskless alternative? Since he reaches his decision according to the principles of expected utility, he will be ready to pay as a premium any sum equal to or smaller than R in Figure IX.1. R represents the maximum premium because such a premium does not change the individual's expected utility.[15] Thus one way to measure the magnitude of risk inherent in a particular distribution of returns is to

---

[11] W. J. Baumol, "An Expected Gain–Confidence Limit Criterion for Portfolio Selection," *Management Science* 10 (October 1963).
[12] For a more detailed analysis of the properties of this criterion see Chapter XI.
[13] See Chapter XI and the Statistical Supplement.
[14] Therefore the utility function in Figure IX.1 is drawn concave downward.
[15] See Chapter VI, Section 5.

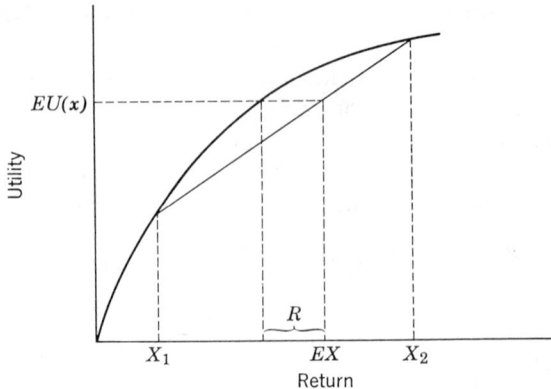

FIGURE IX.1.

estimate the size of the premium that an individual is prepared to pay in order to shift this risk to someone else. The higher the maximum risk premium he is willing to pay, the greater is the risk.

Let us now assume that there is another investment option (distribution) y, with a different expected return, as well as a different dispersion, from that of x. We proceed in the same manner and ask how much the individual will be ready to pay in order to burden someone else with the risk. If the risk premium that he is willing to pay is higher than that for x, we can conclude that the risk of y is greater than the risk of x. (The reader should note that this does not mean that x is preferable to y or vice versa; here we have isolated the risk aspect, while other important factors that affect the final decision are ignored.) As far as any *individual* investor is concerned, we can, in principle, array the risks in descending order by attaching to each random variable a quantitative index that reflects the risk it imposes on the investor. But can the above analysis be generalized for all investors? Since there is every reason to believe that individuals have widely differing tastes, this quantitative index cannot be generalized, even for the subclass of risk averters. This will become apparent when we consider the following example. Suppose that two risk-averse investors face the same choice between two random variables, x and y, whose utility functions are drawn in Figure IX.2 and are marked U_1 and U_2, respectively.

How will these two investors evaluate the risks involved in each of the investments? The investor whose utility function is given by U_1 is ready to pay a premium of "a" in order to shift the risk of x to someone else, but he is not willing to pay anything for shifting the risk of y (the utility function is linear in the relevant range). For this investor, therefore, the risk involved

3. THE MEAN-VARIANCE CRITERION (MVC)

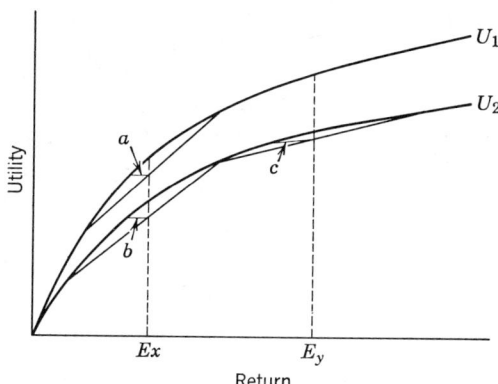

FIGURE IX.2.

in x is greater than the risk involved in y. On the other hand, the investor whose utility function is marked U_2 is ready to pay a premium of "b" to avoid the risk of x, but an even higher premium, "c," to avoid the risk of y. Thus to the second investor y is the riskier alternative.

From this example we can conclude that, in general, a universally applicable *quantitative* risk index cannot be found. While individuals may impute a quantitative measure of risk to each investment alternative, these measures typically will differ from individual to individual. When isolating efficient options, we are interested in selecting a set of efficient investments which is appropriate for a given class of investors. But as we have seen in the above example, even where two investors are known to be risk averters a unique quantitative index can not be found to reflect the riskiness of investments for all investors of this class.

Despite these conceptual difficulties, attempts have been made to identify risk with a particular measure of dispersion. In the following section we shall consider what is undoubtedly the best known attempt to solve this problem—the identification of risk with the *variance* of the distribution of returns. We shall then go to determine the exact conditions under which the use of the variance as a risk index and the use of the mean–variance criterion as an investment decision rule are justified.

3. THE MEAN–VARIANCE CRITERION (MVC)

The efficiency analysis presented in the previous chapter, using the General Criterion (GC) and the Risk Aversion Criterion (RAC), requires, as we have seen, full knowledge of the distribution of returns for each investment option (portfolio) being considered. A striking advantage of the mean–variance model is that the investment analyst can confine himself to the first two distribution moments—the expected (mean) return and the variance (or standard deviation)—of each option being considered.[16] This constitutes a significant advantage and perhaps accounts for the fact that the Mean–Variance Criterion (hereafter referred to as MVC) is by far the most widely known efficiency criterion for investment analysis.

The MVC can be defined as follows: An option x dominates (is preferred to) an option y, by the MVC, if and only if

$$Ex \geq Ey$$
$$Var(x) \leq Var(y)$$

on the condition that at least one of the strong inequalities holds.[17] This means that an option x dominates an option y if its expected return is greater than (or equal to) that of y, while its variance is smaller than (or equal to) the variance of y. The expected return is taken as an indicator of the investment's profitability; the variance serves as an indicator of its risk.

The MVC can also be defined in two other equivalent (and perhaps more familiar) forms

$$Ex \geq Ey; \quad Var(x) < Var(y)$$
$$Ex > Ey; \quad Var(x) \leq Var(y)$$

This alternative notation clearly shows that $Ex \geq Ey$ constitutes a *necessary* condition for option x to dominate option y. This is the same necessary condition which we found in the GC and the RAC. Here, however, there also exists a clear-cut requirement regarding the variance; for x to dominate y, by the MVC, it is also necessary that $Var(x) \leq Var(y)$. According to the RAC and the GC, as we have seen in Chapter VIII, x can dominate y even though the variance of x is greater than that of y.[18]

To illustrate the use of the MVC in efficiency analysis, let us consider the

---

[16] The use of the Mean–Variance Criterion for portfolio selection is analyzed in detail in Chapter X.

[17] The variance of x is usually denoted by $Var(x)$, but for the sake of brevity, the accepted mathematical notation σ^2 will also be used.

[18] We shall show below that the MVC can be reformulated to allow for the case in which xDy even if $Var(x) > Var(y)$. See Section 5.

3. THE MEAN-VARIANCE CRITERION (MVC)

following five investment options.

Option	x_1	x_2	x_3	x_4	x_5
Expected Return	10	8	9	11	12
Variance	10	11	10	12	11

We begin the analysis by comparing option x_1 with option x_2 as follows

$$Ex_1 = 10 > 8 = Ex_2$$
$$Var\,(x_1) = 10 < 11 = Var\,(x_2)$$

The MVC is satisfied, and therefore $x_1\,Dx_2$. Accordingly, x_2 is relegated to the inefficient set. Comparing options x_1 and x_3 we find that

$$Ex_1 > Ex_3$$
$$Var\,(x_1) = Var\,(x_3)$$

Again x_1 is dominant, and x_3 can also be eliminated from the efficient set. We go on to compare x_1 and x_4 and find that

$$Ex_1 = 10 < 11 = Ex_4$$
$$Var\,(x_1) = 10 < 12 = Var\,(x_4)$$

This means that while the expected return of x_4 is greater than that of x_1, which is considered to be to the investor's advantage, the variance of returns of option x_4 exceeds that of option x_1, which is considered to be to the investor's disadvantage. Thus we are unable to say whether x_1 is preferable to x_4, and both investments must, for the time being at least, be retained in the efficient set. Similarly, a comparison of options x_1 and x_5 fails to establish a clear-cut preference between them, so that x_5 is also retained, for the time being, in the efficient set.

Since options x_2 and x_3 nave already been eliminated, we go on to compare x_4 and x_5 and find

$$Ex_5 = 12 > 11 = Ex_4$$
$$Var\,(x_5) = 11 < 12 = Var\,(x_4)$$

Here again the MVC is satisfied so that investment x_5 dominates investment x_4. As we have already seen, x_1 does *not* dominate x_4, but since another option can be found in the efficient group (x_5) which is preferable to investment x_4, the efficient group is further reduced by the elimination of x_4. There are thus only two investments left in the efficient set: options x_1 and x_5. This set cannot be further reduced since, by the MVC, x_1 does not dominate

x_5 nor does x_5 dominate x_1. The inefficient group includes three investments: x_2, x_3, and x_4.

A look at the relevant data shows that option x_3 is preferable to investment option x_2 since

$$Ex_3 = 9 > 8 = Ex_2$$
$$Var\,(x_3) = 10 < 11 = Var\,(x_2)$$

Does this really matter? Hardly. Any analysis of priorities *within* the inefficient group is a barren exercise, for the partition into two subsets, an efficient and an inefficient one, means that every investor who acts in accordance with the MVC will make his final selection from the efficient group. Since it is clear that he will never willingly choose any of the options included in the inefficient group, the order of priorities within that group is of no consequence, and can safely be ignored.

Before we examine the utility assumptions which underly the MVC, the reader should note that this criterion can be formulated in terms of either the variance or the standard deviation without affecting the results, because if the variance of an option x is greater (less) than the variance of an option y this also implies that the standard deviation of x is greater (less) than the standard deviation of y, and vice versa. The use of the variance, rather than the standard deviation, has no significance beyond the mathematical convenience of being able to dispense with the use of somewhat awkward square roots.

4. THE UTILITY FOUNDATIONS OF THE MVC

Efficiency criteria are generally based on certain underlying assumptions regarding investors' tastes. In constructing the GC we made only one assumption: that every investor always prefers more to less wealth ($U'(x) \geq 0$). In the RAC it was further assumed that the marginal utility of money declines ($U''(x) \leq 0$). In addition to these two assumptions, the MVC places further restrictions on the shape of investors' utility functions and/or the shape of the distribution of returns. These additional assumptions make a more effective criterion which tends to reduce the size of the efficient set, but they also mean that the criterion is appropriate for a smaller class of investors, or for a restricted class of options.

The MVC provides a relevant decision rule in the following two cases:

(a) *Quadratic utility functions.* In this case investors' utility functions are assumed not only to be concave ($U''(x) \leq 0$) but also to be of a specific type, that is, of the form

$$U(x) = a + bx + cx^2$$

4. THE UTILITY FOUNDATIONS OF THE MVC   311

Given this assumption, Tobin and Markowitz have shown that the MVC provides an appropriate decision rule, but several serious objections have been raised regarding the assumption of quadratic utility; moreover, it can be shown that the MVC does not provide an *optimal* criterion, in the sense that a modification of the MVC reduces the efficient set without additional information.[19]

(b) *Concave utility functions.* This assumption, which as we have already shown is tantamount to assuming general risk aversion, provides an economically more meaningful case. The efficient set generated under this assumption is relevant for a broad class of investors—all those who are averse to risk. However, it should be noted that under this assumption the MVC does *not* apply to all types of return distributions. Where risk aversion is assumed the random variables must belong to the same family of distributions with two parameters, each of which is an independent function of the mean and the variance.

Theorem IX–1: *Let x and y denote two random variables representing the returns on two alternative investment options; $F(x)$ and $G(y)$ denote the cumulative probability distributions; and (μ_x, σ_x) and (μ_y, σ_y) the expected returns and standard deviations of the two distributions. Now, given that $\mu_x \geq \mu_y$ and that x and y belong to the same family of (independent) two-parameter distributions,[20] then if the cumulative distributions G and F intersect, a necessary and sufficient condition for dominance is that $\sigma_x \leq \sigma_y$.*

A detailed proof of this theorem is given in Appendix IX–1 at the end of the chapter. Here we shall deal with its significance and implications for financial analysis.

Since the normal distribution is perhaps the most important of the (independent) two-parameter distributions, let us initially examine the workings of the MVC in relation to normal distributions. Consider two investment options, x and y, whose returns are distributed normally, and assume investors' utility functions to be concave. Given these assumptions, can the dominance of one of the alternatives be established using the MVC?

Distributions x and y are two-parameter distributions since a normal distribution depends on two parameters only—the mean and the variance.[21] Moreover, the two parameters in a normal distribution are independent of

---

[19] For these reasons we defer the discussion of the quadratic utility case to Chapter XI.
[20] The two parameters must be independent functions of the mean and the variance respectively; see Appendix IX–1. However, to simplify the discussion we refer to such distributions in the text as "two-parameter distributions."
[21] Knowledge of the mean and the variance of a normal distribution is tantamount to having a complete specification of the distribution.

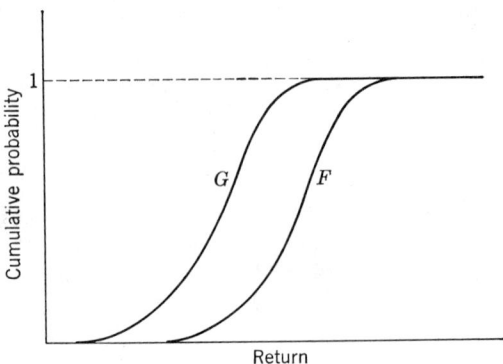

FIGURE IX.3.

each other; this means that one parameter can be varied without varying the other, that is, the mean can be changed without affecting the variance, or alternatively, the variance can be changed without affecting the mean.[22] However the condition that the two distributions intersect is not necessarily satisfied; for example, if the variances of the two distributions are identical ($\sigma_x^2 = \sigma_y^2$) the distribution with the higher mean is shifted to the right so that the two cumulative distributions do *not* intersect.

Two such normal distributions are presented in Figure IX.3: Distribution F has a higher mean than distribution G, but an identical variance. Does F dominate G for every concave utility function? Clearly F dominates G according to the General Criterion since F lies wholly to the right of G.[23]

---

[22] It is sometimes thought that if a distribution is symmetric and biparametric this constitutes a sufficient condition for the MVC to be optimal. Yet for many symmetric distributions, which are members of a two-parameter family, the mean and the variance are both functions of the two parameters. Since the independence condition is not fulfilled, the MVC is not applicable. For example, when x has a log-normal distribution (that is, log x is normal with parameters μ, σ, we have $Ex = e^{\mu+\sigma^2/2}$; $Var(x) = e^{2\mu+\sigma^2} \cdot (e^{\sigma^2} - 1) = (Ex)^2 \cdot (e^\sigma - 1)$. In this case one cannot find two independent parameters which are functions of the mean and the variance, respectively, and it can be shown that the MVC does not hold for this case.

[23] Notice that although F and G do not intersect, the density functions f and g do intersect (diagram).

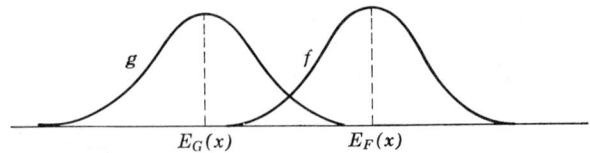

4. THE UTILITY FOUNDATIONS OF THE MVC

This means that F dominates G for any nondecreasing utility function so that it should also be dominant for all concave functions. But is it also dominant according to the Mean–Variance Criterion? Since distribution F lies wholly to the right of distribution G, then of necessity $E_F(x) > E_G(y)$. Since we also assumed that $\sigma_F^2(x) = \sigma_G^2(y)$, F dominates G also according to the MVC. Thus in this example F dominates G, by the MVC, even though the two distributions do *not* intersect, so that the requirement that the cumulative probability functions intersect appears to be redundant. And in fact it is redundant if we restrict ourselves to options whose returns are normally distributed. In such cases the MVC applies even if F and G do *not* intersect.

It should be recalled, however, that we have formulated the MVC in very general terms so that it will be appropriate for all risk averters on the condition that the distribution of returns belongs to an (independent) two-parameter set of distributions. Such a distribution need not be a normal one: consider the two alternative options in Table IX–1 whose cumulative probability distributions are drawn in Figure IX.4. In this example, FDG for all nondecreasing utility functions (since the entire function F is shifted to the right of function G) so that F is also certainly dominant for the subset of all concave functions as well. But when we compare the means and variances of the two options (Table IX–1) we find that

$$E_F(x) = 25 > 14 = E_G(x)$$
$$Var_F(x) = 25 > 16 = Var_G(x)$$

Thus the MVC is not satisfied and the dominance of F over G cannot be determined by this rule, although option F clearly fulfills the General Criterion (Figure IX.4). The reason for this paradoxical result is that not all of the requirements of Theorem IX–1 hold in this example. Although F and G are both members of an (independent) two-parameter family of distributions, their cumulative probability distributions do *not* intersect. And while

TABLE IX–1.

	Option F		Option G
Return	Probability	Return	Probability
20	1/2	10	1/2
30	1/2	18	1/2
	$E_F(x) = 25$		$E_G(x) = 14$
	$Var_F(x) = 25$		$Var_G(x) = 16$

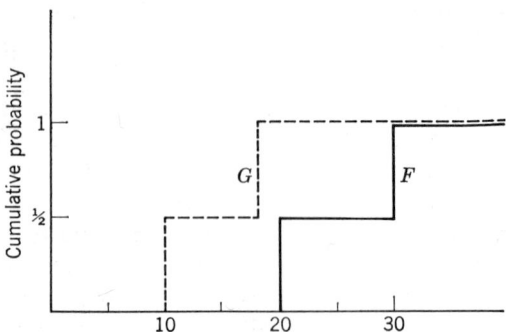

FIGURE IX.4.

the intersection requirement, as we have seen, is redundant with respect to normal distributions, it constitutes a *necessary* condition when the MVC is extended to (independent) two-parameter distributions in general.

Since the MVC depends only on the expected return and the variance of the distribution it appears not implausible that this criterion is appropriate for all symmetrical distributions since the third moment (skewness), which is usually relevant for decisionmaking under uncertainty, is zero in such distributions. Table IX–2 and Figure IX.5 present a counter-example which shows that symmetrical distributions of returns, in themselves, do not ensure consistently acceptable results using the MVC.

A glance at Table IX–2 suffices to show that, invoking the MVC, option F dominates option G since their expected values are the same (zero in this case) while F has the lower variance (0.5 as compared with 0.8). However when the cumulative probability distributions of the two options are plotted

TABLE IX–2.

Option F		Option G	
Return	Probability	Return	Probability
−1	1/4	−2	0.1
0	1/2	0	0.8
1	1/4	2	0.1
$E_F(x) = 0$		$E_G(x) = 0$	
$Var_F(x) = 0.5$		$Var_G(x) = 0.8$	

5. THE TWO-STAGE CRITERION (TSC)

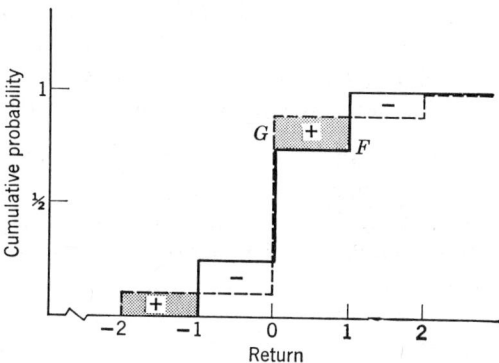

FIGURE IX.5.

as has been done in Figure IX.5, we see that F does *not* dominate G by the RAC, and therefore it will not be consistently preferred by all risk-averse investors, the MVC result notwithstanding. Thus the MVC does not ensure an optimal efficient set even if we assume symmetrical distributions of returns.[24]

5. THE TWO-STAGE CRITERION (TSC)

As we have seen from the above analysis, even when the returns of the alternative investment options have a two-parameter distribution, the MVC provides an optimal criterion which ensures a minimal efficient group only if all of the alternative cumulative return distributions intersect. Where some of the distributions do not intersect, the MVC is not optimal, since it is possible to find an alternative criterion which can reduce the efficient set.

The Two-Stage Criterion (hereafter referred to as TSC) is an optimal criterion, incorporating both the GC and the MVC. Using this criterion, the efficient set is derived in two stages: a preliminary screening of proposals using the GC followed by a second stage in which the MVC is applied to the GC efficient group. This modification of the MVC provides an optimal decision criterion for all risk averters.

---

[24] It should be noted that in this example the distributions are *not* two, but three, parameter distributions so that not all of the requirements of Theorem IX-1 are fulfilled. The point being made, however, is that contrary to what common sense would seem to imply, the assumption of symmetrical distributions is not *in itself* a sufficient condition to ensure the relevance of the MVC. For this purpose, the three-parameter example given in the text is appropriate.

Theorem IX–2: *If the distribution of returns of each of the alternative investment options belongs to the same family of (independent) two-parameter distributions, the two-stage criterion (TSC) is the optimal efficiency criterion for all investors having concave utility functions.*[25]

To avoid an unnecessarily complex mathematical presentation, we can prove this theorem by a simple extension of the proof of Theorem IX–1. Appendix IX–1 presents a formal proof that the MVC is optimal, provided all the cumulative distributions of returns intersect. The initial screening using the GC systematically eliminates *all* distributions which do not intersect; in the second stage the MVC is applied to the GC efficient subset. Since the MVC is optimal for intersecting distributions, and all nonintersecting distributions have already been eliminated by the GC, the resulting efficient set is optimal.

To clarify the use of the TSC let us consider the five investment options whose distributions of returns are set out in Table IX–3. In this particular example all of the options have distributions which are uniformly distributed with the two parameters α and β.[26] Applying the MVC to this example, we can eliminate only one alternative—in this case option E, since option D has both a higher expected return and a lower variance than option E. None of the others can be eliminated by the mean–variance rule so that the MVC efficient set comprises four options: A, B, C, and D.

---

[25] See the qualification in note 20 on page 311.

[26] If a random variable, x, is distributed uniformly with parameters α and β [$x \sim U(\alpha, \beta)$], the density function $f(x)$ is given by

$$f(x) = \begin{pmatrix} \dfrac{1}{\beta - \alpha} & \alpha \leq x \leq \beta \\ 0 & \text{otherwise} \end{pmatrix}$$

The cumulative distribution $F(x)$ is

$$F(x) = \begin{pmatrix} 0 & x \leq \alpha \\ \dfrac{x - \alpha}{\beta - \alpha} & \alpha < x \leq \beta \\ 1 & x > \beta \end{pmatrix}$$

For such distributions the return and variance are defined as follows:

$$E(x) = \frac{\alpha + \beta}{2}$$

$$\text{Var}(x) = \frac{(\beta - \alpha)^2}{12}$$

See, for example, A. Hald, *Statistical Theory with Engineering Applications*, New York, Wiley, 1952, pp. 93 and 100–108.

5. THE TWO-STAGE CRITERION (TSC)

TABLE IX-3.

| | \multicolumn{5}{c}{Options} | | | | |
	A	B	C	D	E
Parameter α	9	13	10	25	17
Parameter β	10	15	20	40	47
$E(x)$	9.5	14.0	15.0	32.5	32.0
$Var(x)$	0.088	0.38	8.33	18.75	75.00

Now let us apply the TSC to the same problem. Figure IX.6 sets out the cumulative probability distributions of the five options of our previous example. In the first stage we effect an initial screening using the GC. As both D and E lie wholly to the right of A, B, and C, the latter three options can be eliminated from the efficient set. Thus the GC efficient group includes only options D and E. In the second stage we apply the MVC to the GC efficient set and find that it can be further reduced since investment option D dominates option E by the MVC. This eliminates option E, leaving the TSC efficient set consisting of only a single investment option, D.[27]

As can be seen from this example only the intersecting distributions D and E remain in the efficient group once the GC has been applied. The question arises as to the appropriateness of this procedure. For example, option A was eliminated in the first stage by the GC. Essentially this means that option

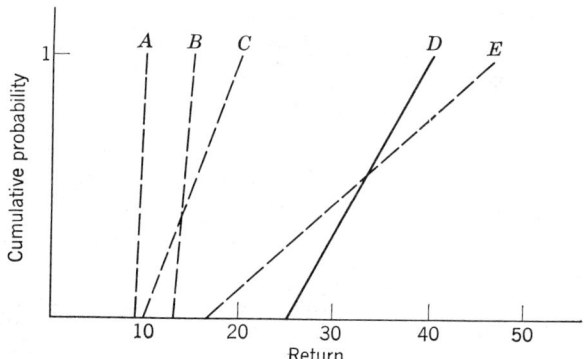

FIGURE IX.6.

[27] The optimality of the two-stage procedure can be confirmed by applying the RAC to Figure IX.6, which results in the same efficient set.

318 |||||||||||||||||||||||||||||||||||||||||||||||| THE MEAN-VARIANCE CRITERION

A was ignored when the MVC was applied, in the second stage, to the GC efficient set. Conceivably it could be argued that some risk-averse investors, having concave utility functions, might have preferred to choose option A, yet such a possibility was ignored when applying the MVC.

If such a contention were true then the TSC clearly would not be optimal. But as we already have shown in Chapter VIII, the GC is an optimal criterion for all investors *independent* of the shape of their utility functions. In particular, it is appropriate for risk averters as well as risk lovers. Thus the prior elimination of option A in the initial stage is appropriate, since we can be certain that no risk averter will ever choose option A so long as he has the alternative of choosing either option D or E. Thus there is no need to *reconsider* an option like A when applying the MVC in the second stage.

6. A GRAPHICAL REPRESENTATION OF THE MEAN–VARIANCE CRITERION

In contrast to the GC and RAC, the MVC is by its very nature two-dimensional so that the efficiency analysis using this criterion readily lends itself to graphical representation. In Figure IX.7, the vertical axis denotes expected return while the horizontal axis measures the standard deviation (or variance) of the returns. Given its expected return and standard deviation, any investment option can be represented by a point on such a plane and the set of all potential options can be enclosed by an envelope curve such as the one shown in Figure IX.7. The MVC rule can now be applied to this set of potential options to isolate the set of efficient investments. Using the MVC, only the options comprising the northwest segment AB of the envelope curve are efficient; the remaining portion of the envelope curve and all of the options included in the interior of the circle are inefficient by the MVC. The

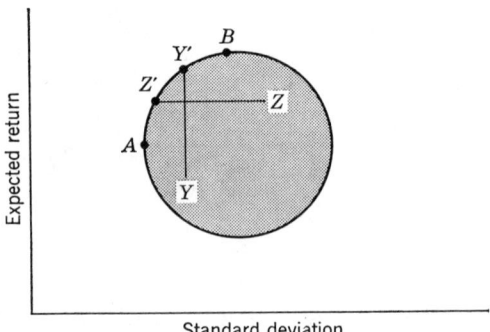

FIGURE IX.7.

6. REPRESENTATION OF THE MEAN-VARIANCE CRITERION   319

locus of efficient points AB will also be referred to as the efficiency frontier.[28]

To prove this, consider an interior and therefore inefficient point such as Z in Figure IX.7. From point Z draw a horizontal line to an efficient point Z' on the efficiency frontier. Clearly point Z' is preferable to point Z since for the same expected return it has a lower standard deviation (variance). Similarly, we can draw a vertical line from an inefficient point such as Y to the point Y' on the efficiency locus. Once again the point on the efficiency locus Y' clearly dominates the interior point Y since the former represents a higher expected return for a given standard deviation (variance). If this experiment is repeated for all possible points, the efficiency locus AB will be generated.[29]

[28] The efficiency frontier is often drawn on a diagram whose axis has been reversed, that is, one in which the vertical axis denotes the standard deviation and the horizontal axis the expected return. In such a case, the efficiency locus AB is a mirror image of Figure IX.7 of the text and is located in the southeast segment of the envelope curve.

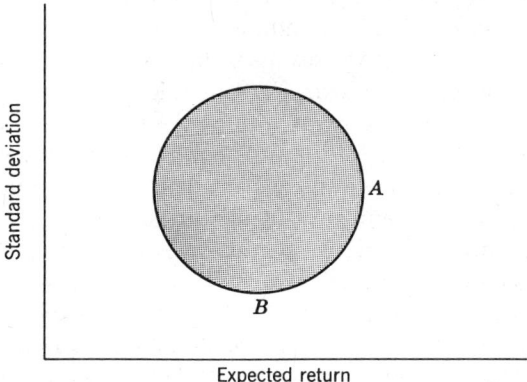

[29] Frequently the number of alternative investment options from which the individual is required to choose is not infinite so that not every point on the locus AB of Figure IX.7 may represent an actual investment opportunity. Thus an investment with the expected

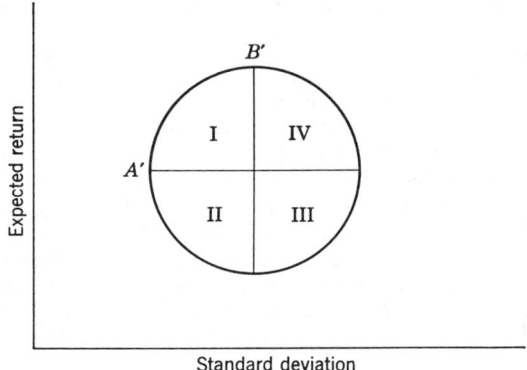

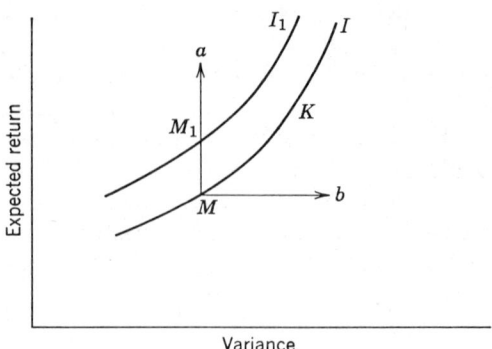

FIGURE IX.8.

To complete the graphical representation of investment choice we must first introduce the concept of an indifference curve. We know that an investor who uses the MVC increases his utility, both when expected return is increased or variance is decreased. For example, whenever an option such as M in Figure IX.8 is replaced by an alternative located in the direction of the arrow marked "a" the investor's utility is increased, since every movement along the line Ma raises the expected return without altering the variance. Similarly any movement in the direction of arrow "b" reduces the investor's utility, since the variance of the investment is thereby increased without any change in the expected return, which is clearly to the investor's disadvantage. Since any movement in the direction of arrow "b" reduces the investor's utility while any movement in the direction of arrow "a" increases his utility, a point can be found between "a" and "b" (say, K) at which the investor's utility is neither increased nor decreased. If we substitute option K for option M both the mean and the variance are increased, but since by assumption the investor's utility remains unchanged, the increased mean is exactly offset by the increased variance, so that the investor is indifferent to

---

return and standard deviation represented by point Y' might not exist. Nevertheless, we can still show that all the efficient options are located on the locus AB. For this purpose let us divide the circular set of all potential options into four quarter sections, I, II, III, and IV. It is clear from the diagram that option A' dominates all investments in quadrants II and III since it has a lower variance and a higher (or equal) expected return. Similarly option B' dominates all options in quadrants III and IV since it has a lower standard deviation and a higher (or equal) expected return. Now, if there are any efficient options in quadrant I they are located, by definition, on the locus $A'B'$. Thus even if the population is finite, for every inefficient option there exists at least one dominant point on the efficiency locus.

6. REPRESENTATION OF THE MEAN-VARIANCE CRITERION 321

the choice between these two investments. Other combinations of expected return and variance can also be found which leave the investor indifferent, that is, with the same utility which he derived from option M.[30] In principle all such combinations can be plotted along an "indifference curve" such as MI in Figure IX.8. If we start with a point such as M_1, we can repeat the process and generate still another indifference curve $M_1 I_1$, and so on until an entire indifference map is constructed which represents the investor's tastes.

The indifference curves in Figure IX.8 rise from left to right which indicates that the risk-averse investor must be compensated with a higher expected return as the variance increases. The curves are drawn convex downward on the assumption that additional increments of variance require increasingly larger increments of expected return to compensate the individual. Another property of the indifference map is that the indifference curves *cannot* intersect.[31]

An investor's final choice out of the efficient set depends on his tastes. In accordance with the expected utility hypothesis he will choose that option

---

[30] The investor's indifference curve is a continuous curve and is constructed independently of the actual investment projects available to the investor. Clearly, there may be no potential options having the variances and means represented by points such as K and M, but from the fact that both these points lie on the same indifference curve we can deduce that had such investments been available, the investor would have been indifferent to the choice between them.

[31] This can be proved as follows: Let the two indifference curves I and I_1 intersect at point R. Since R and R_1 are located on the same indifference curve (I), the individual must be indifferent between them. R_2 and R also lie on one indifference curve (I_1) so that the individual is also indifferent between these two alternatives. It follows that the individual must also be indifferent between R_1 and R_2, but this contradicts the mean–variance principle since R_2 has both a higher mean and a lower variance than R_1, and therefore represents a higher level of utility.

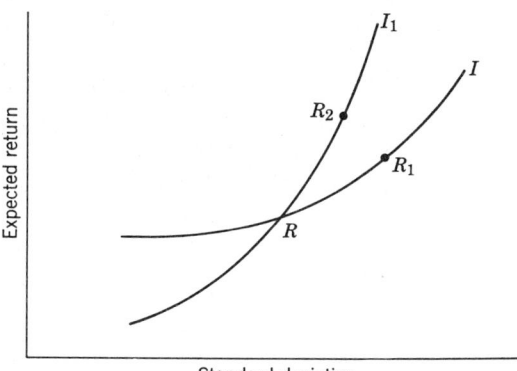

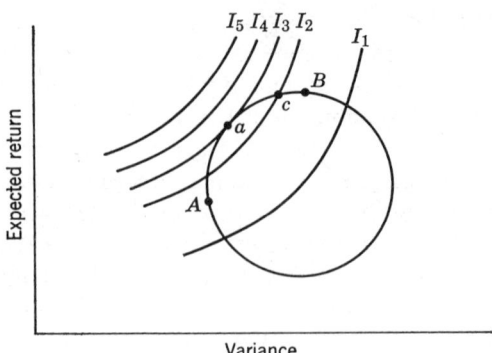

FIGURE IX.9.

which allows him to reach the highest indifference curve, for the higher the curve, the higher his utility. Figure IX.9 superimposes the individual's indifference map on the opportunity set of investments. The investor would prefer an option which would allow him to reach indifference curve I_5, but no attainable investment option of this kind exists (indifference curve I_5 does not intersect or touch the opportunity set). The best that he can do, given the potential options, is to choose option a out of the efficiency set AB, that is, the option which is tangent to indifference curve I_3. Since no other choice will permit him to reach a higher level of utility, option a is the investor's *optimal* choice, the one which maximizes his utility. Should he choose another alternative out of the efficient set, say point c, his utility will fall since this option permits him to reach indifference curve I_2, which represents a lower level of utility.

Can we infer from this analysis that no investor will ever prefer option c or that option a represents the optimal choice for all risk-averse investors? Since the shape of the indifference curves varies from one investor to the next it is quite conceivable that a second investor may have indifference curves, representing his individual preferences, which are tangent to the efficient set at point c rather than at point a. In fact, depending on the slope of the curves, any investment option on the efficient locus AB may be the optimal investment for a particular investor. This is illustrated in Figure IX.10, which sets out the indifference curves of two different individuals.[32] It should be noted that while both the investor whose optimal portfolio is

---

[32] The intersection of the indifference curves of two *different* individuals does *not* contradict our previous proof that the indifference curves of the *same* individual cannot intersect. See note 31 on page 321.

7. REPRESENTATION OF THE TWO-STAGE CRITERION

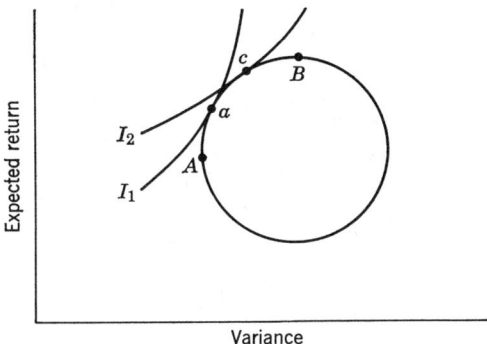

FIGURE IX.10.

represented by point a and the one whose optimal portfolio is represented by c regard a high variance of the returns as a disadvantage, they do *not* attach the same weight to this factor. The indifference curve of the investor who selects option a (I_1) is steeper than that of the investor who prefers investment c (I_2). This means that when the variance is increased by one unit, the former investor (I_1) requires a greater increase in expected return to offset the increased variance. For him, a higher variance represents a greater drawback than it does for the investor with the I_2 indifference curve. The latter individual is more willing to accept a greater variance, and therefore chooses option c, which has a higher variance (and a higher return) than point a.[33]

7. A GRAPHICAL REPRESENTATION OF THE TWO-STAGE CRITERION

A somewhat similar graphical apparatus can be used to analyze the properties of the TSC and its relationship to the MVC. This is of particular interest since, as we have already demonstrated, the TSC constitutes an optimal efficiency criterion while the popular MVC does not. Thus it is sometimes possible to reduce the MVC efficient set without additional assumptions regarding investors' tastes or the distribution of returns.

Figure IX.11 sets out the familiar diagram of the opportunity set of investment options. As before, segment AB of the envelope curve represents

---

[33] It should be noted that the first investor (I_1) would also be willing to accept the level of variance represented by point c if sufficient compensation in the form of an increase in expected return could be had. Since none of the potential options provides such a return, this investor settles for a smaller return with less variance.

324 THE MEAN-VARIANCE CRITERION

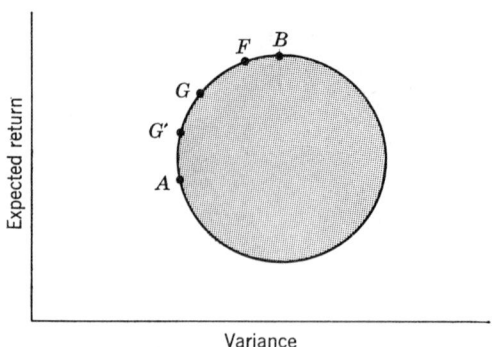

FIGURE IX.11.

the efficiency locus using the MVC. What is the composition of the efficient group using the TSC? Since, in general, the TSC efficient set constitutes a subset of the MVC efficient set, it is clear that *all* the investments which are efficient using the TSC must be located on the locus of MVC efficient investments, *AB*.

Consider, for example, the investment options whose cumulative probability distributions are drawn in Figure IX.12. Let's initially restrict our attention to just two of them—*F* and *G*. *F* has both a higher expected return and a higher variance than *G* so that both options are included in the MVC efficient set. But it is clear that *F* dominates *G* by the GC so that a two-stage application of the GC and MVC will eliminate *G* from the TSC efficient set. Returning for the moment to Figure IX.11, we see that both *F* and *G* are located, as they should be, on the MVC efficient locus *AB*.

Does the fact that *G* has been eliminated from the TSC efficient group imply that all of the options located on the segment *AG*, that is, below *G*, should

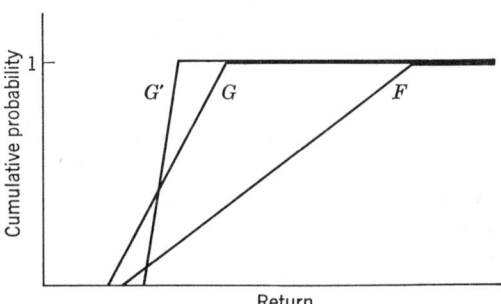

FIGURE IX.12.

8. EVIDENCE ON TWO-PARAMETER DISTRIBUTIONS 325

also be excluded from the efficient set? The following example shows that no such general rule can be established.

Consider the three options whose means and variances are represented by points F, G, and G' of Figure IX.11. All three are included in the MVC efficient set and therefore are located on the locus of efficient points AB. Let us now assume that their returns are uniformly distributed and that their cumulative distributions have the form given in Figure IX.12. By construction

$$E_{G'}(x) < E_G(x) < E_F(x)$$
$$Var_{G'}(x) < Var_G(x) < Var_F(x)$$

Therefore point G' lies below point G and point G lies below point F in Figure IX.11. As we have previously noted, FDG by the GC, so that using the TSC, G is eliminated from the efficient group. On the other hand, F does not dominate G' by the GC since their two cumulative distributions intersect, so even though G' is located below G in Figure IX.11 it remains in the TSC efficient set.

Thus it may be concluded that while the TSC may eliminate some of the MVC efficient investments, no systematic rule can be formulated as to the particular section of the efficiency locus which will be cut off. A second conclusion is that no indifference curve will be tangent to any of the eliminated points since they represent inefficient investments for risk averters and risk lovers alike. Thus the investor can always increase his utility by moving to another point which is included on the TSC efficiency locus.

8. SOME EMPIRICAL EVIDENCE ON TWO-PARAMETER DISTRIBUTIONS

In this chapter we have shown that the MVC provides a relevant criterion for risk averters (concave utility functions) if the distributions of returns belong to an (independent) two-parameter family.[34] This restriction necessarily limits the generality of the MVC where the distributions of returns are known to be of a different form. For example, the criterion cannot be used to explain the behavior of individuals who purchase lottery tickets or take out insurance since in these cases the higher moments of the distribution are also significant.

There is some indirect evidence, however, which leads us to presume that a significant proportion of investment choice can be explained by the mean–variance model. As we have already noted, risk-averse individuals tend to

---

[34] The discussion of the MVC and quadratic utility is deferred to Chapter XI.

TABLE IX-4.

Period	1943-67	1946-67	1950-67	1956-67	1958-67
No. of Years	25	22	18	12	10
No. of Funds	52	60	76	86	149
No. of Observations	1,300	1,320	1,368	1,032	1,490

diversify their holdings; that is, they build portfolios of a number of securities. Moreover, mutual funds make relatively large portfolios, of hundreds of individual securities, readily available even to the small investor. To the degree that the returns of the individual securities are independent of one another, the return on relatively large portfolios should approximate a normal distribution.[35]

Although we do not know whether the returns on individual securities are independent, we can adopt an indirect approach and examine the rate of return to investors in mutual fund shares. Table IX-4 summarizes the number of funds and the time periods covered in the empirical study.[36] As the observations from which the empirical distributions have been constructed are *annual* rates of return, the number of observations for each period is obtained by multiplying the number of funds by the number of years covered.

The hypothesis tested is that all these observations constitute a sample drawn from a normal distribution. For instance, in the period 1958-67 there were 149 mutual funds for which data on rates of return were available, so it is assumed that during these years 1,490 observations were drawn from the normal population. Before this hypothesis can be tested, however, some standardization is required. All mutual funds do not follow the same investment policy. Thus some funds invest most of their assets in growth stocks while others invest their assets in a balanced portfolio of more conservative securities. More speculative stocks usually yield higher returns but they also have higher standard deviations. Accordingly, even if the hypothesis that

---

[35] This follows directly from the Central Limit Theorem:

Let $f(x)$ denote the density function of a random variable with an expected value equal to μ and a variance equal to σ^2 ($\sigma^2 < \infty$). If $\bar{x}_n$ denotes the mean of a sample of size n drawn from this distribution then the random variable $(\bar{x}_n - \mu)/\sigma/\sqrt{n}$ will approximate a normal distribution with an expected value of zero, and a variance of unity, on the condition that n is sufficiently large. For a more precise formulation of this theorem, see A. M. Mood and F. A. Graybill, *op. cit.*, pp. 149-53.

[36] All data on rates of return were obtained from various annual editions of Arthur Wiesenberger, *Investment Companies*.

8. EVIDENCE ON TWO-PARAMETER DISTRIBUTIONS 327

the rates of return are distributed normally were correct, it still might be rejected, since owing to differences in investment policy, the annual observations are drawn from a number of normal distributions having different parameters. To bring the distributions to a common basis the annual rates of return were standardized as follows:

$$Z_i = \frac{x_i - \bar{x}}{s}$$

where: $\bar{x}$ = estimated mean return of a mutual fund over the period studied
x_i = the fund's rate of return in year i
s = estimated standard deviation of the distribution[37]
Z_i = the standardized rate of return in year i.

After computing Z_i for each one of the funds, in each of the periods, the histograms describing the distribution of all the values of Z_i for the aggregate population of mutual funds were constructed.[38] These histograms are given in Figures IX.13 through IX.17.

On the same diagrams we have also plotted the standard normal curve. An examination of each of the diagrams shows that in all five periods the empirical distribution (histogram) approximates a normal distribution. This is also confirmed by a statistical test which shows that the hypothesis that the rates of return are distributed normally cannot be rejected.[39] Thus the distribution of returns to investors in mutual fund shares is approximately

---

[37] This was derived by the formula

$$S^2 = \sum_{i=1}^{n} \frac{(x_i - \bar{x})^2}{n - 1}$$

[38] Theoretically we should have deducted the actual mean μ from each mutual fund and divided the result by the standard deviation of the population σ_i; since these data were not available estimates of σ_i and μ_i were used. The error introduced by using estimates rather than the actual parameters becomes smaller, the greater the number of years covered.

[39] For this purpose the Kolmogorov–Smirnov test was used. The precise hypotheses tested were H_0: the adjusted return distribution is a standard normal distribution; H_1: the adjusted return distribution is not a standard normal distribution. The main results can be summarized as follows:

Period	Value of Statistic in Sample	Critical Value ($\alpha = 5\%$)
1943–67	0.07264	0.2067
1946–67	0.08127	0.2260
1950–67	0.07868	0.2067
1956–67	0.06924	0.1917
1958–67	0.06340	0.1917

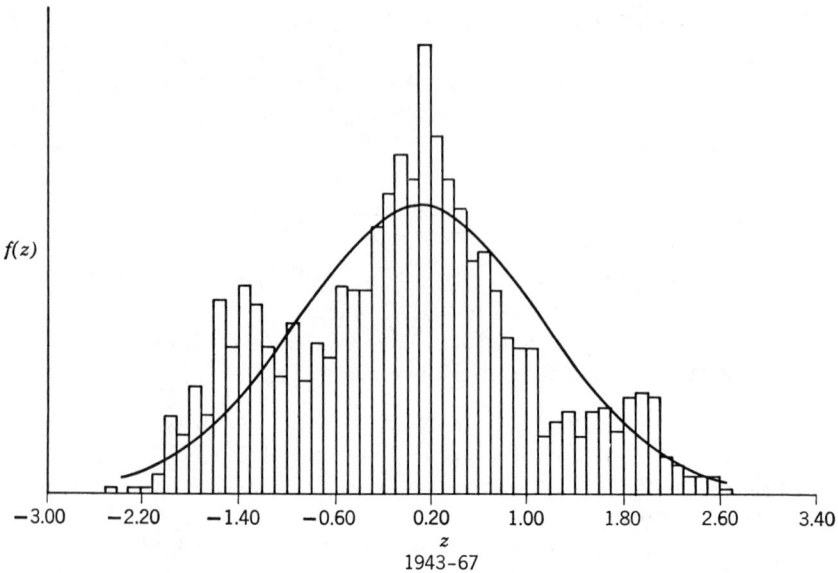

FIGURE IX.13.

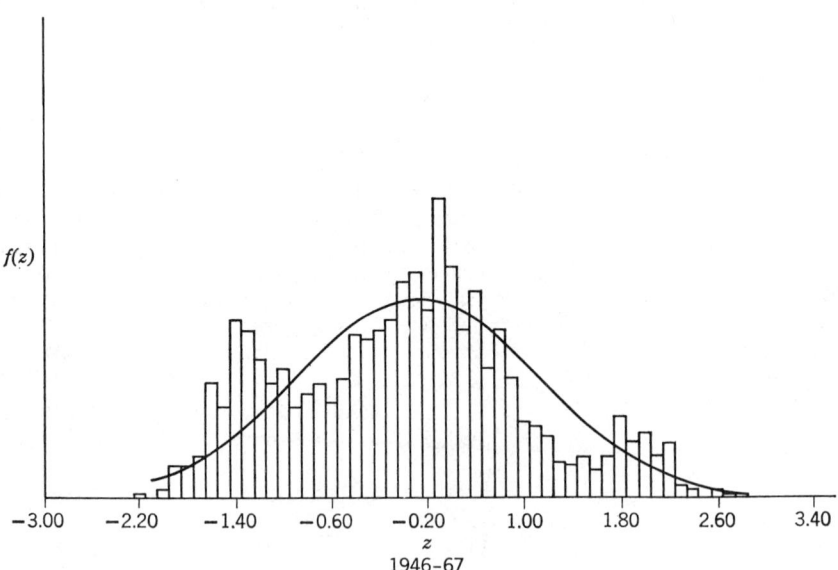

FIGURE IX.14.

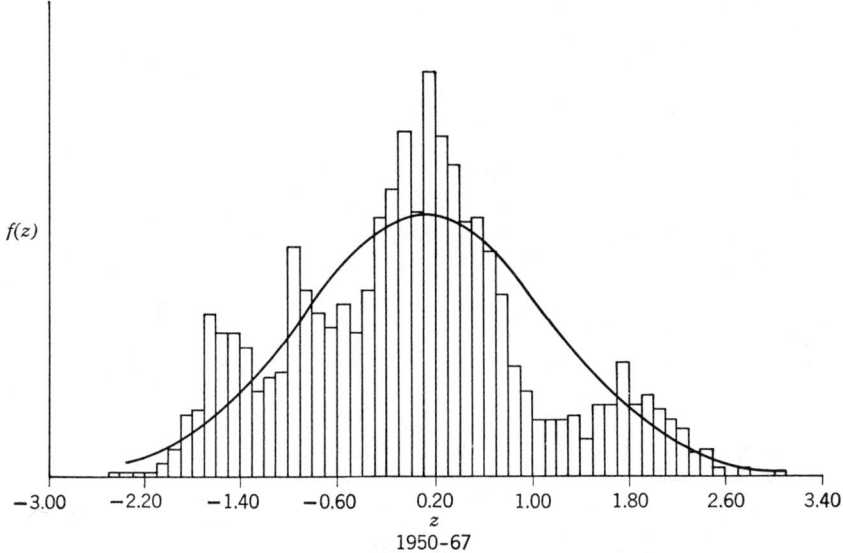

FIGURE IX.15.

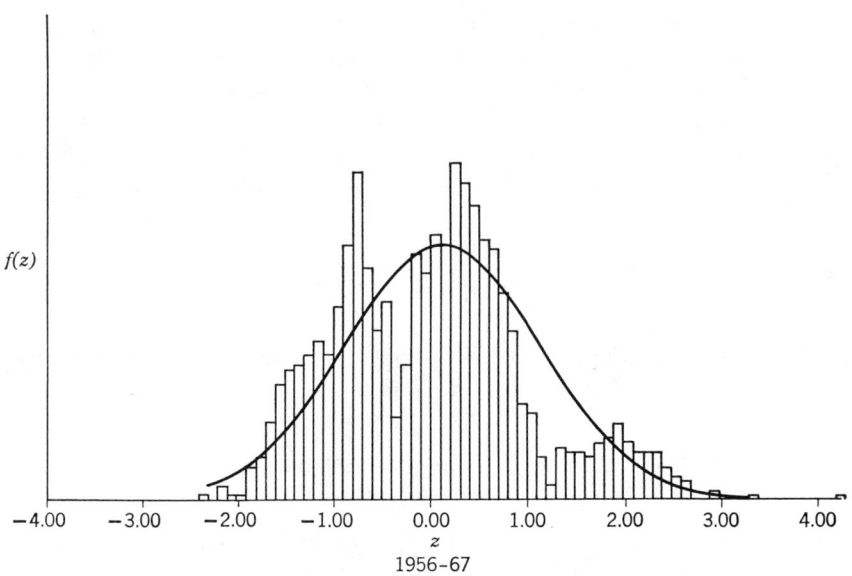

FIGURE IX.16.

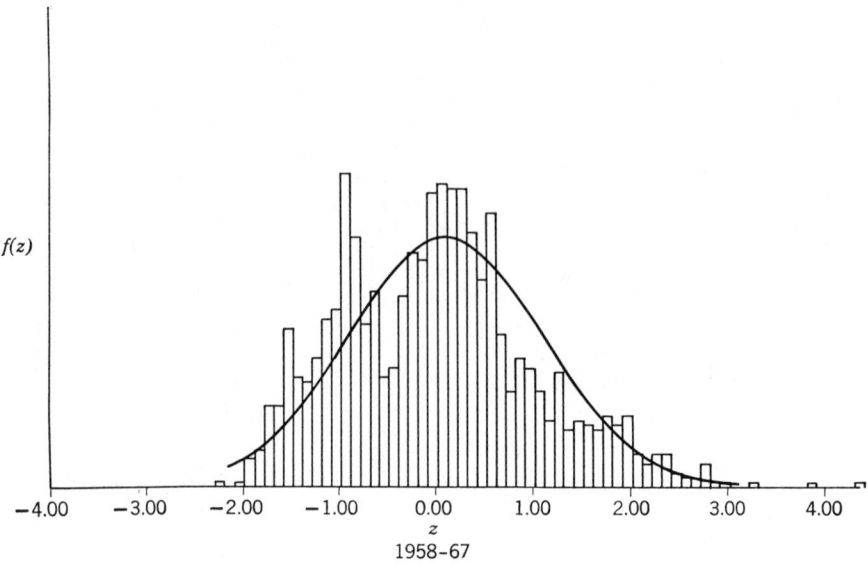

FIGURE IX.17.

normal,[40] and since such a distribution depends only on two (independent) parameters—the mean and variance—the MVC provides an appropriate criterion for this important segment of the securities market. Moreover, to the extent that mutual funds provide a relevant proxy for investment portfolios in general, the statistical evidence strongly suggests that the MVC can provide an effective decision rule for most risk-averse investors as well as a relevant model for studying investment behavior under conditions of risk.

9. SUMMARY

The efficiency analysis presented in Chapter VIII required detailed knowledge of the distribution of returns for every potential investment option. In this

---

[40] That the distributions are not perfectly normal is already clear from the statistical tests carried out on the same data in Chapter VII, which showed the third moment to be significant in most cases.

These results do *not* rule out the possibility that the underlying distributions belong to a more general class of distributions which includes the normal as a special case. See, for example, Eugene F. Fama, "The Behavior of Stock-Market Prices," *Journal of Business* (January 1965), pp. 34–105, and the references cited.

9. SUMMARY

chapter we have set out, and critically examined, the mean–variance efficiency analysis, developed by Markowitz and Tobin, which allows the investment analyst to confine himself to the first two moments of the distribution—the expected (mean) return and the variance (standard deviation). The Mean–Variance Criterion (MVC) states that an option x dominates (is preferred to) an option y, if and only if

$$E_x \geq E_y \quad \text{and} \quad Var(x) \leq Var(y)$$

on the condition that at least one of the strong inequalities holds.

The MVC is, by far, the most popular rule for investment analysis. Its widespread appeal lies in its simplicity; given the objective, or subjective, estimate of the probability distribution of returns, the mean and the variance are easily calculated. Moreover, the underlying logic of a decision rule, based solely on these two moments, is readily comprehended and lends itself to graphical representation.

Because of its simplicity, however, the MVC is not always valid and should not be applied indiscriminately in investment analysis. In this chapter we have examined the conditions under which the use of the MVC provides an optimal efficiency criterion for risk averters (concave utility functions). Under this assumption it should be noted that the MVC is not appropriate unless further restrictions are placed on the form of the distributions of return. In particular, the distributions must be members of the same (independent) two-parameter set, and the cumulative probability distributions of all the options must intersect. If the latter condition does not hold the MVC must be restricted to cases where the returns are normally distributed.

Alternatively, the MVC can be modified so as to ensure a minimal efficient set. The two-stage criterion (TSC), which incorporates both the General Criterion (GC) and the MVC, provides such an optimal criterion for all risk averters. Using this criterion, a preliminary screening of options using the GC is followed by a second stage in which the MVC is applied to the GC efficient set.

The above mentioned restrictions on the form of the distribution of returns reduce the generality of the MVC. However, the tendency of risk averters to diversify their investments suggests that the MVC may provide a relevant decision model for a significant proportion of investment choice; to the degree that the returns of individual securities are independent of one another, the returns on relatively large portfolios should approximate a normal distribution.

Since many investors diversify their investments by means of mutual funds, an empirical study of the distribution of the rates of return on mutual fund shares was carried out for various periods during the years 1943–67. The statistical analysis showed that the mutual fund returns are distributed approximately normally so that the MVC provides an appropriate criterion for this important (and growing) segment of the market. And to the degree that mutual funds provide a good proxy for portfolios in general, the MVC is likely to provide an effective tool for analyzing investment decisions.

With this in mind we shall turn our attention in the next chapter to the application of the mean–variance analysis to portfolio selection.

QUESTIONS AND PROBLEMS

9.1 The "risk premium," that is, the maximum amount that an individual is prepared to pay to convert a random distribution into a perfectly certain income, measures the degree of risk associated with such a distribution for all investors.

    a. Is this statement correct?
    b. Prove your answer graphically using a hypothetical numerical example.

9.2 Define the Mean–Variance Criterion (MVC). How do you account for its popularity?

9.3 What are the exact conditions for which the MVC provides an *optimal* efficiency criterion for *all risk averters*?

9.4 What are the necessary conditions for which the MVC provides an optimal efficiency criterion for all risk averters, if the distributions of returns are assumed to be normal?

9.5 Define the Two-Stage Criterion (TSC). What is its relationship to the MVC?

9.6 Define and graph the MVC "efficiency locus."

9.7 Draw the appropriate indifference curves in the mean–variance plane for the following types of individuals:

    a. A risk averter.
    b. A risk lover.
    c. An investor who will *never* take a risk.
    d. A risk-neutral investor.
    e. Can the indifference curves of a risk lover and a risk averter intersect?
    f. Can the indifference curves of two risk averters intersect?
    g. Can the indifference curves of the same individual intersect?

    Prove your answer.

9.8   a. What is the significance for the MVC of the empirical evidence on the form of mutual funds distributions?
    b. Do mutual funds constitute an appropriate subject for such a test?

9.9 Assume four investment options with the following relationships between their expected returns Ex_i and their standard deviations σ_i:

$$Ex_1 < Ex_2 < Ex_3 < Ex_4, \quad \text{and} \quad \sigma_1 < \sigma_2 < \sigma_3 < \sigma_4$$

that is, all four options are MVC efficient. It is claimed that *all* risk-neutral investors will choose option 4.

    a. Is this claim correct?
    b. If it is, does it contradict the MVC rule? Explain.
    c. Does such a result contradict the von Neumann–Morgenstern expected utility theorem? Explain.

9.10 The following table gives the annual return per dollar invested of four mutually exclusive investment options during the years 1965–70:

	A	B	C	D
1965	20	22	6	10
1966	40	21	8	12
1967	30	18	5	18
1968	22	16	4	20
1969	36	20	6	15
1970	46	22	10	14

Using these historical data,

    a. Calculate the expected returns and standard deviations of each of the investments.
    b. Define the efficient and inefficient sets.

9.11 For the following data:

| A | | B | | C | | D | |
Return	Probability	Return	Probability	Return	Probability	Return	Probability
18	7/8	10	1/4	15	3/4	5	1/2
26	1/8	30	3/4	24	1/4	25	1/2

    a. Graph the cumulative probability distribution of each of the options.
    b. Find the MVC efficient set.
    c. Find the TSC efficient set.

9.12 "The TSC reduces the MVC efficient set by systematically eliminating options with low variance." Appraise this statement and support your conclusions by giving appropriate numerical examples.

9.13   a. In general, is the MVC efficient set a subset of the RAC efficient set?

        b. When the distributions of return are two-parameter distributions, is the MVC efficient group a subset of the RAC efficient group?

SELECTED REFERENCES

Adler, M., "On Risk-Adjusted Capitalization Rates and Valuation by Individuals," *Journal of Finance* (September 1970).

Arditti, F. D., "Risk and the Required Return on Equity," *Journal of Finance* (March 1967).

Arrow, K. J., "Aspects of the Theory of Risk Bearing," Helsinki: Yrjo Jahnssonin Saatio, 1965.

Baumol, W. J., "An Expected Gain–Confidence Limit Criterion for Portfolio Selection," *Management Science* (October 1963).

Bierman, H., Jr., "Risk and the Addition of Debt to the Capital Structure," *Journal of Financial and Quantitative Analysis* (December 1968).

Borch, K., "A Note on Uncertainty and Indifference Curves," *Review of Economic Studies* (January 1969).

Clarkson, G. P., *Portfolio Selection: A Simulation of Trust Investment.* Englewood Cliffs, N.J.: Prentice-Hall, 1962.

Cohen, K. J., and Elton, E. J., "Inter-Temporal Portfolio Analysis Based on Simulation of Joint Returns," *Management Science* (September 1967).

Domar, E. and Musgrave, R. A., "Proportional Income Taxation and Risk Taking," *Quarterly Journal of Economics* (May 1944).

Farrar, D. E., *The Investment Decision Under Uncertainty.* Englewood Cliffs, N.J.: Prentice-Hall, 1962.

Feldstein, M. S., "Mean–Variance Analysis in the Theory of Liquidity Preference and Portfolio Selection," *Review of Economic Studies* (January 1969).

Freimer, M., and Gordon, M. J., "Investment Behavior with Utility a Concave Function of Wealth," in Karl Borch and Jan Mossin, eds., *Risk and Uncertainty.* New York: St. Martin's Press, 1968.

Hakansson, N. H., "Risk Disposition and the Separation Property in Portfolio Selection," *Journal of Financial and Quantitative Analysis* (December 1969).

Hald, A., *Statistical Theory with Engineering Applications.* New York: Wiley, 1952.

Hanoch, G., and Levy, H., "Efficient Portfolio Selection with Quadratic and Cubic Utility," *Journal of Business* (April 1970).

———, "The Efficiency Analysis of Choices Involving Risk," *Review of Economic Studies* (July 1969).

SELECTED REFERENCES   337

Hanssman, F., "Probability of Survival as an Investment Criterion," *Management Science* (September 1968).

Hastie, K. L., "The Determination of Optimal Investment Policy," *Management Science* (August 1967).

Hester, D. D., and Tobin, J., *Risk Aversion and Portfolio Choice*. New York: Wiley, 1967.

Hicks, J. R., *Value and Capital*, 2nd edition. Oxford: Oxford University Press, 1946.

Joyce, J. M., and Vogel, R. C., "The Uncertainty in Risk: Is Variance Unambiguous?" *Journal of Finance* (March 1970).

Keynes, J. M., *The General Theory of Employment, Interest and Money*. London: Macmillan, 1937.

Latané, H. A., "Investment Criteria—A Three-Asset Portfolio Balance Model," *Review of Economics and Statistics* (November 1963).

Latané, H. A., and Tuttle, D. L., "Criteria for Portfolio Building," *Journal of Finance* (September 1967).

Levy, H., and Hanoch, G., "Relative Effectiveness of Efficiency Criteria for Portfolio Selection," *Journal of Financial and Quantitative Analysis* (March 1970).

Levy, H., and Sarnat, M., "A Note on Indifference Curves and Uncertainty," *Swedish Journal of Economics* (September 1969).

———, "Alternative Efficiency Criteria: An Empirical Analysis," *Journal of Finance* (December 1970).

———, "Two-Period Portfolio Selection and Investors' Discount Rates," *Journal of Finance* (June 1971).

———, "A Note on Portfolio Selection and Investors' Wealth," *Journal of Financial and Quantitative Analysis* (December 1970).

Levy, R. A., "Yield Risk Measurement of the Performance of Common Stock," *Journal of Financial and Quantitative Analysis* (March 1968).

Lintner, J., "Security Prices, Risk and Maximal Gains from Diversification," *Journal of Finance* (December 1965).

Markowitz, H. M., "Portfolio Selection," *Journal of Finance* (March 1952).

———, *Portfolio Selection*. New York: Wiley, 1959.

Marschak, J., "Money and the Theory of Assets," *Econometrica* (October 1938).

Michaelsen, J. B., and Goshay, R. C., "Portfolio Selection in Financial Intermediaries: A New Approach," *Journal of Financial and Quantitative Analysis* (June 1967).

Mood, A. M., and Graybill, F. A., *Introduction to the Theory of Statistics*, 2nd edition. New York: McGraw-Hill, 1963.

Naslund, B., and Whinston, A., "A Model of Multi-period Investment under Uncertainty," *Management Science* (January 1962).

Pratt, J. W., "Risk Aversion in the Small and in the Large," *Econometrica* (January–April 1964).
Pyle, D. H., and Turnovsky, S. J., "Safety-First and Expected Utility Maximization in Mean–Standard Deviation Portfolio Analysis," *Review of Economics and Statistics* (February 1970).
Renshaw, E. F., "Portfolio Balance Models in Perspective: Some Generalizations that can be derived from the Two-Asset Case," *Journal of Financial and Quantitative Analysis* (June 1967).
Roy, A. D., "Safety First and the Holding of Assets," *Econometrica* (July 1952).
Samuelson, P. A., "General Proof that Diversification Pays," *Journal of Financial and Quantitative Analysis* (March 1967).
———, "Efficient Portfolio Selection for Pareto–Levy Investments," *Journal of Financial and Quantitative Analysis* (June 1967).
Schrock, N. W., "Asset Choice under Uncertainty with Borrowing Introduced," *Journal of Financial and Quantitative Analysis* (March 1967).
Sharpe, W. F., "A Simplified Model for Portfolio Analysis," *Management Science* (January 1963).
———, "Capital Asset Prices: A Theory of Market Equilibrium Under Conditions of Risk," *Journal of Finance* (September 1964).
———, "Portfolio Analysis," *Journal of Financial and Quantitative Analysis* (June 1967).
———, *Portfolio Theory and Capital Markets*. New York: McGraw-Hill, 1970.
Soldofsky, R. M., "Yield–Risk Performance Measurements," *Financial Analysts Journal* (September–October 1968).
Soldofsky, R. M., and Biderman, R., "Yield–Risk Measurement of the Performance of Common Stocks," *Journal of Financial and Quantitative Analysis* (March 1968).
Soldofsky, R. M., and Miller, R. L., "Risk–Premium Curves for Different Classes of Long-Term Securities 1950–1966," *Journal of Finance* (June 1969).
Tobin, J., "Liquidity Preference as Behavior Towards Risk," *Review of Economic Studies* (February 1958).
———, "The Theory of Portfolio Selection," in F. H. Hahn and F. P. R. Brechling, eds., *Theory of Interest Rates*. New York: Macmillan, 1965.
Wallingford, B. A., "A Survey and Comparison of Portfolio Selection Models," *Journal of Financial and Quantitative Analysis* (June 1967).

APPENDIX IX-1

Proof of the Optimality of the Mean-Variance Criterion for the Case of Concave Utility[41]

The purpose of this appendix is to show that if distributions F and G belong to the same two-parameter family and F and G intersect, the Mean–Variance Criterion provides an optimal decision rule for all risk averters ($U''(x) < 0$).

Let $F(x)$ and $G(y)$ be two distinct distributions with means μ_1 and μ_2, and variances σ_1^2, σ_2^2, respectively, such that $F(x; \mu_1, \sigma_1) = H[(x - \mu_1)/\sigma_1; 0, 1]$ $G(y; \mu_2, \sigma_2) = H[(y - \mu_2)/\sigma_2; 0, 1]$. Hence $F(x) = G(y)$, for all x and y which satisfy $(x - \mu_1)/\sigma_1 = (y - \mu_2)/\sigma_2$. Let $\mu_1 \geq \mu_2$, and $F(x_1) > G(x_1)$, for some x_1 (that is, $F(x)$ and $G(x)$ intersect). Then FDG (F dominates G) for all concave $u(x)$, if and only if $\sigma_1^2 \leq \sigma_2^2$. That is, F and G belong to the same family of distributions, with two parameters which are independent functions of μ and σ^2, respectively. In that case, $Z = (x - \mu)/\sigma$ is distributed identically with mean 0 and variance 1 (according to $H(Z; 0, 1)$), for both F and G. In these limited cases, when the two distributions $F(x)$ and $G(x)$ intersect (so that the General Criterion does not apply) the mean–variance criterion is both necessary and sufficient for efficiency. The proof is an immediate application of Theorem 3 of Appendix VIII-3.

Proof: if $\sigma_1 = \sigma_2 = \sigma$; and $\mu_1 > \mu_2$: for all x, $(x - \mu_1)/\sigma < (x - \mu_2)/\sigma$; thus $F(x) \leq G(x)$ for all x, and there is no intersection point. F dominates G by the General Criterion (if $\mu_1 = \mu_2$, F and G are identical).

If $\sigma_1 \neq \sigma_2$, we have an intersection point at x_0, where

$$\frac{x_0 - \mu_1}{\sigma_1} = \frac{x_0 - \mu_2}{\sigma_2} \quad \text{or:} \quad x_0 = \frac{\mu_2 \sigma_1 - \mu_1 \sigma_2}{\sigma_1 - \sigma_2}$$

The case $\sigma_1 \neq \sigma_2$ can be decomposed to the following two alternatives: (a) If $\sigma_1 > \sigma_2$, then for $x < x_0$, $(x - \mu_1)/\sigma_1 > (x - \mu_2)/\sigma_2$, and $F(x) \geq G(x)$

---

[41] This proof appeared originally in G. Hanoch and H. Levy, "The Efficiency Analysis of Choices Involving Risk," *Review of Economic Studies* (July 1969), p. 343.

($F > G$ for some x); and for $x \geq x_0$, $(x - \mu_1)/\sigma_1 \leq (x - \mu_2)/\sigma_2$, and $F(x) \leq G(x)$. Thus the condition of Theorem 3 of Appendix VIII–3 is not satisfied, and F cannot dominate G.

(b) If $\sigma_1 < \sigma_2$, then for $x < x_0$ we have $(x - \mu_1)/\sigma_1 < (x - \mu_2)/\sigma_2$, and $F \leq G$; for $x > x_0$ $(x - \mu_1)/\sigma_1 > (x - \mu_2)/\sigma_2$ and $F \geq G$. Since $F < G$ for some x (given that $\mu_1 \geq \mu_2$), F dominates G by Theorem 3 of Appendix VIII–3.

Chapter X

The Mean-Variance Criterion and Portfolio Selection

1. INTRODUCTION

Most investors do not fail to heed the warning implicit in the by now rather shopworn adage, "Don't put all your eggs in one basket."[1] As a result, the typical investor tends to diversify his risk by building a portfolio which includes two or more risk assets, for example, common stocks and one or more cash assets such as cash itself and bonds. The exact composition of the portfolio depends, of course, on the investor's goals (retire at forty, send Junior to college, and so on) and on his attitude toward risk. In this chapter we shall develop appropriate tools, based on the MVC, for the graphical analysis of the portfolio selection problem.

2. THE INVESTMENT IN LIQUID ASSETS

Both individual as well as institutional investors tend to hold a proportion of their assets in cash. The holding of money or "near money" reflects current needs for liquidity and/or anticipated requirements in the not distant future. However, very often cash assets are held over and beyond the amounts needed to meet those needs; these assets should be considered as an "investment," that is as an integral part of the individual's or firm's investment portfolio.

Given the need to hold cash assets, let us turn our attention to the problem

---

[1] The statement in the text is appropriate for risk averters; an appropriate corollary for a risk lover might be, "Put all your eggs in one basket, but keep your eye on the basket."

of determining the ratio of actual cash to other liquid assets. For our purpose we define a liquid (or near money) asset as one which can be readily converted to cash without incurring significant losses, for example, a *short-term* government bond, savings account, or the like. Since the return on investments in bonds is positive while investments in idle cash yield no return whatsoever,[2] it seems on the surface rather unreasonable for any firm or individual to hold cash in view of the convenient alternative of buying government bonds or some other liquid asset which provides a positive return. However, if we apply the portfolio principle to the problem it can be shown, following Tobin, that the MVC implies a liquid portfolio comprising cash as well as bonds.[3]

Consider an individual who wishes to hold one dollar in liquid form and must now decide on the proportions to hold in cash and in government bonds. Although the government regularly meets its obligations to pay interest and/or to pay the principal upon redemption, and the bonds can be readily converted into cash in the market, these assets are not riskless even if we explicitly assume that the government cannot go bankrupt. The reason for this is that in addition to the perfectly certain interest (redemption) payments, the investor faces the probability of incurring a capital gain or loss as a result of fluctuations in the bond's market price. The price of the bond may fluctuate, independent of any default risk, as a function of changes in the market rate of interest. Take, for example, a government bond which was issued at par (100) and carries a 5% annual interest coupon. After a while, because of changed market conditions, a new series of 6% bonds (of similar maturity) is issued. Clearly, all rational investors will prefer the 6% to the 5% bond since they are perfect substitutes. Because of the drop in demand, the price of the 5% bond will fall, and will continue to fall until it reaches a level which offers the potential purchaser a 6% yield, that is, the new current market rate.[4] Conversely, should the market rate fall below 5%, a capital gain will be incurred on the old bond. Thus the problem of determining the ratio of bonds (which carry a degree of risk) to riskless cash is analogous to a portfolio problem and can be treated as a special case of risk diversification.

---

[2] The analysis to be presented is perfectly general and its validity does not depend on the assumption that cash earns a zero return, so that any fixed positive return can be substituted without affecting the conclusions.

[3] We shall use the term *bonds* throughout as a convenient reference to all interest-bearing liquid assets.

[4] The percentage fall in price required to equate the yields depends on the length of time to maturity. Roughly speaking, the longer the maturity the greater the fall in price; hence the requirement that liquid reserves be held in *short-term* bonds. For a more detailed discussion of the relationship between interest rates and bond prices, see Chapter IV.

2. THE INVESTMENT IN LIQUID ASSETS

To show this let us first define the following symbols:

$r =$ the interest paid on bonds, per dollar invested
$g =$ the capital gain or loss
$x = r + g =$ the total return on bonds

We also assume that g is a random variable with a given variance σ_g^2 and an expected return equal to zero, that is, on the average capital gains are expected to cancel capital losses.

$A_1 =$ the proportion invested in cash
$A_2 =$ the proportion of the liquid reserve invested in bonds

so that by definition $A_1 + A_2 = 1$

$E(x) =$ the expected return on the combined portfolio of cash and bonds

$\sqrt{Var(x)} \equiv \sigma_x =$ the standard deviation of the portfolio

Should the individual desire to invest the entire liquid reserve in bonds, his expected return is given by[5]

$$E(x) = E(r + g) = E(r) + E(g) = r + 0 = r \qquad (10.1)$$

The variance of the returns to an investor who puts all his reserve into bonds is[6]

$$Var(x) = Var(r + g) = Var(r) + Var(g) + 2\,Cov(rg) \qquad (10.2)$$

---

[5] Equation (10.1) is based on the well known theorems that

(a) the expected value of the sum of two random variables is equal to the sum of their individual expected values;
(b) the expected value of a constant number (a degenerate random variable) equals the number itself.

See W. Feller, *An Introduction to Probability Theory and its Applications*, 2nd edition, New York, Wiley, 1965, pp. 207-9.

[6] $Var(r + g) = E[(r + g) - E(r + g)]^2$
$= E[(r - Er) + (g - Eg)]^2$
$= E[(r - Er)^2 + (g - Eg)^2 + 2(r - Er)(g - Eg)]$
$= E(r - Er)^2 + E(g - Eg)^2 + 2E(r - Er)(g - Eg)$
$= Var(r) + Var(g) + 2\,Cov(rg)$

where 2 *Cov* (*rg*) should be read as twice the covariance between r and g. However, since r is constant, *Var* $(r) = 0$ and therefore, *Cov* $(rg) = 0$:[7]

$$Var\ (x) = Var\ (g) \qquad (10.3)$$

or, alternatively in terms of the standard deviation:

$$\sigma_x = \sigma_g \qquad (10.3')$$

Thus an individual who invests his entire reserve in bonds obtains an expected return of r with a standard deviation of σ_g. Should he decide to leave all his reserve in cash, he obtains an expected return of zero and a standard deviation of zero. Now, invoking the MVC, which of these extremes is preferable? Since both the standard deviation and the expected return of the bond portfolio exceed those of the cash alternative, neither alternative dominates by the MVC. In other words both the 100% cash option and the 100% bond option are MVC efficient.

Between these two extremes, there is an infinity of alternative investment options which are all included in the MVC efficient set. To demonstrate this let us assume that an individual decides to invest his liquidity reserve in the proportions: A_1 in cash and A_2 in bonds. The return on the total portfolio, x, can be written as

$$x = A_2(r + g) + A_1 \cdot 0 = A_2(r + g) \qquad (10.4)$$

so that the expected return equals[8]

$$Ex = E[A_2(r + g)] = A_2 E(r + g) = A_2 r \qquad (10.5)$$

and the variance of the portfolio is[9]

$$Var\ (x) = Var\ [A_2(r + g)] = A_2^2\ Var\ (r + g) = A_2^2\ Var\ (g) \qquad (10.6)$$

or alternatively in terms of the standard deviation:

$$\sigma_x = A_2 \sigma_g \qquad (10.7)$$

---

[7] For a more detailed discussion of the concepts of variance and covariance see Feller, *op. cit.*, pp. 213–19 and the Statistical Supplement, pp. 588–92.

[8] In addition to the theorem

$$E(x_1 + x_2) = E(x_1) + E(x_2)$$

we now use the additional theorem

$$E(ax) = aE(x)$$

where a is any constant. *Ibid*, p. 208.

[9] Here we use the rule that

$$Var\ (ax) = a^2\ Var\ (x)$$

where a is any constant. *Ibid*, p. 214.

2. THE INVESTMENT IN LIQUID ASSETS   345

This can be rewritten as

$$A_2 = \frac{\sigma_x}{\sigma_g} \qquad (10.8)$$

Substituting Equation (10.8) into Equation (10.5) above, the expected return on the portfolio of cash and bonds equals

$$E(x) = \frac{r}{\sigma_g} \cdot \sigma_x \qquad (10.9)$$

This is a linear equation and since r and σ_g are constant parameters (that is, exogenous data obtained or estimated by the investor), the straight line represents an infinity of alternative combinations of portfolio expected returns and standard deviations (Ex, σ_x) which face the investor. Each alternative (portfolio) represents a different proportion (A_2) invested in bonds.[10] All the possible combinations are set out along the line ab in Figure X.1. Line ab, which we shall refer to as the transformation line, has a slope equal to r/σ_g. At point a, the standard deviation (and therefore also the variance) equals zero. This means that the entire liquid reserve has been invested in cash. At point b, the expected return and the standard deviation are r and σ_g respectively, which means that all the liquid assets have been invested in bonds. Each point on the transformation line between a and b represents a different combination of cash and bonds. Each of these combinations constitutes an efficient portfolio, since there is no other combination on the

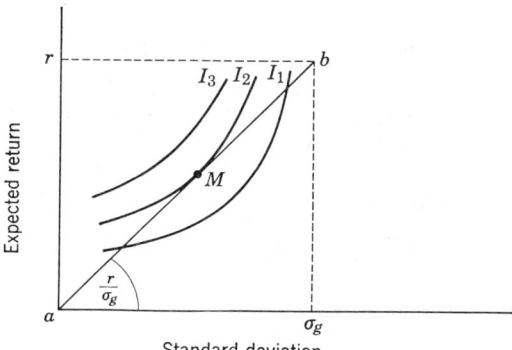

FIGURE X.1.

[10] A glance at Equations (10.5) and (10.7) will confirm this.

transformation line that is preferable according to the MVC. Thus we have an infinity of efficient portfolios.[11]

If we now superimpose the investor's indifference map on Figure X.1 we see that point M represents the optimal combination of cash and bonds, this being the point of tangency between the transformation line and indifference curve I_2 which represents the highest attainable level of utility. As the indifference curve generally is tangent to the transformation line at some intermediate point between a and b, rather than at either corner, it appears that investors typically will hold part of their investment in liquid assets in cash, even though the return on cash holdings is nil.

The intuitive explanation for the willingness to hold cash is that although the return on the investment in cash is zero, the risk involved is also zero. The expected return on a bond, on the other hand, is positive, but an investor who holds a bond for a given period (for example, one year) may incur a capital loss, so that even the "safest" bond carries some degree of risk. Generally investors are not willing to risk all of their liquid reserves, and as a result prefer to hold part of their liquid assets in cash to reduce the overall risk.

To clarify our thinking let us consider the hypothetical example of an investor who has a liquid reserve of \$1,000 which he wants to hold partly in bonds and partly in cash. Let us further assume that bonds yield 10% interest, and that the capital gain on bonds constitutes a random variable (g) with a mean of 0 and a standard deviation $\sigma_g = 0.04$ (4%). The investor is assumed to be a risk averter and his subjective preferences (indifference curves) regarding the trade-off between expected returns and the standard deviation (variance) of returns are specified by the following relationship:

$$E(x) = a + 40\sigma_x^2 \qquad (10.10)$$

Now let us find the optimal combination of bonds and cash for our hypothetical investor. We already know that the optimum solution will be given by the point of tangency between one of the investor's indifference curves and the transformation line. Since at the point of tangency the slopes of the two curves are equal, we can solve our problem analytically by equating the first derivatives of the indifference curves and of the transformation line.

Equation (10.10) represents the indifference relationship. Taking its first derivative, we get

$$\frac{\partial E(x)}{\partial \sigma_x} = 80\sigma_x \qquad (10.11)$$

---

[11] Obviously the possibilities of dividing one dollar into bonds and cash are not unlimited, but this amount was taken only for the sake of convenience. When larger amounts of money are concerned the number of alternative combinations is very large, and for our purposes can be considered infinite.

2. THE INVESTMENT IN LIQUID ASSETS

Equation (10.9) specifies the transformation line; differentiating this equation and taking its first derivative, we get

$$\frac{\partial E(x)}{\partial \sigma_x} = \frac{r}{\sigma_g} \qquad (10.12)$$

To find the optimal solution, the point at which the slopes of the two curves are equal, we set their first derivatives equal to one another:

$$80\sigma_x = \frac{r}{\sigma_g} \qquad (10.13)$$

Solving this equation explicitly for σ_x yields

$$\sigma_x = \frac{r}{80\sigma_g} \qquad (10.14)$$

If we substitute the assumed values for r and σ_g (0.10 and 0.04 respectively), Equation (10.14) can be solved numerically:

$$\sigma_x = \frac{0.10}{80 \cdot 0.04} = \frac{5}{160} = 0.0312$$

From Equation (10.8) we know that

$$A_2 = \frac{\sigma_x}{\sigma_g} = \frac{0.0312}{0.04} = 0.78$$

Thus the optimal portfolio includes $780 in bonds and $220 in cash. And from Equation (10.5) we can find the expected return on this portfolio:

$$E(x) = A_2 \cdot r = 0.78 \cdot 0.10 = 0.078$$

That is, the expected return is 7.8%.

Now let us see how the proportions of bonds and cash vary as we change the interest rate on bonds. Assume a lower rate of interest, say 9%. From Equation (10.9):

$$E(x) = \frac{r}{\sigma_g} \cdot \sigma_x = \frac{0.09}{0.04} \sigma_x = 2.25(\sigma_x)$$

From the tangency condition we can solve for σ_x:

$$\sigma_x = \frac{r}{80\sigma_g} = \frac{0.09}{80 \cdot 0.04} = 0.02812$$

The proportion held in bonds, A_2, equals

$$A_2 = \frac{\sigma_x}{\sigma_g} = \frac{0.02812}{0.04} = 0.703$$

MEAN-VARIANCE CRITERION AND PORTFOLIO SELECTION

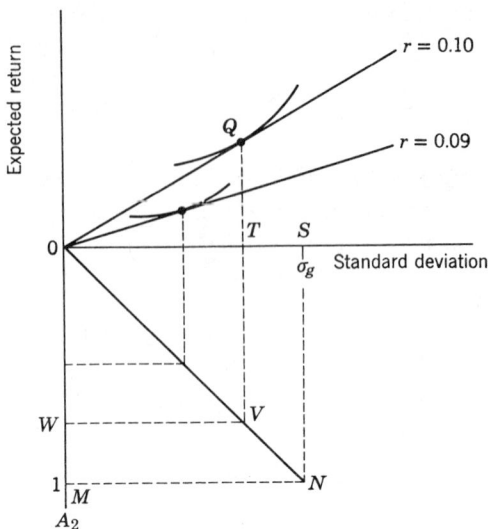

FIGURE X.2.

In this case the investor reduces the share of assets invested in bonds to $703; the remaining $297 is held in cash. This result represents the special case where the substitution effect (the bonds' variance remains fixed while the expected return is decreased, which makes them a less attractive investment) outweighs or is reenforced by the income effect.

The same result can be derived graphically. Figure X.2 reproduces Tobin's familiar expected return—standard deviation diagram.[12] A_2 (the proportion invested in bonds) is marked in a negative direction on the vertical axis, the maximum possible value of A_2 being 1. Through point M (where $A_2 = 1$) a horizontal line MN is drawn. Point σ_g is specified at the appropriate point on the horizontal axis, and through it a vertical line SN is drawn. Point N is then connected to the origin of the axes, whereby line ON is obtained. The transformation line is determined by the relationship

$$E(x) = \frac{r}{\sigma_g} \cdot \sigma_x$$

and is represented diagrammatically by a straight line rising from the origin; the slope of the line increases as r is increased (or σ_g is decreased).

[12] See J. Tobin, "Liquidity Preference As Behavior Towards Risk," *Review of Economic Studies* 1958.

3. PORTFOLIOS OF TWO SECURITIES

The point of tangency between the transformation line and an indifference curve, point Q of Figure X.2, uniquely determines both the expected return and the standard deviation of the portfolio. Let us now drop a vertical line from point Q which meets line ON at point V. Through V pass a horizontal line VW to the vertical axis. The segment OW on the vertical axis measures the optimal proportion of bonds, the optimal proportion of cash being $1 - OW$. With the aid of this diagram we can also determine appropriate values of $E(x)$, σ_x, and A_2 for various interest rates (and standard deviations) on bonds. The lower the interest rate the smaller the slope of the transformation line; the line for a 9% interest rate lies below the 10% line in Figure X.2, and therefore is tangent to a lower indifference curve. The corresponding change in σ_x, $E(x)$, and A_2 can be read off as before. And as we have already noted, in this particular case all three decrease for the lower interest rate.

3. PORTFOLIOS OF TWO SECURITIES

Let us now assume that the investor is confronted with two risky securities (A and B) and that he has the opportunity of investing either in one or in the other, or diversifying his investment by building a portfolio which includes both securities. To analyze the motives underlying the portfolio decision it will be convenient to adopt the following notation: Let

x_1 and $x_2 = $ random variables denoting the return on one dollar invested in securities A and B respectively

$E(x_1) \equiv \mu_1 = $ the expected return on security A

$E(x_2) \equiv \mu_2 = $ the expected return on security B

$\sqrt{Var(x_1)} \equiv \sigma_1 = $ the standard deviation of returns for security A

$\sqrt{Var(x_2)} \equiv \sigma_2 = $ the standard deviation of returns for security B

$p_1 = $ the proportion invested in A

$p_2 = $ the proportion invested in B

Since $p_1 + p_2 = 1$, it is evident that if $p_1 = 1$ (or $p_2 = 1$) the portfolio includes only one security. On the other hand, where $0 < p < 1$, the investor has diversified his portfolio to include both securities. The portfolio return is given by

$$x = p_1 x_1 + p_2 x_2$$

The expected return on the portfolio is[13]

$$E(x) = p_1 E(x_1) + p_2 E(x_2)$$

---

[13] See note 8 on page 344.

or, in abbreviated form,
$$\mu = p_1\mu_1 + p_2\mu_2 \tag{10.15}$$

The variance of the portfolio returns is[14]
$$Var(x) = p_1^2 \, Var(x_1) + p_2^2 \, Var(x_2) + 2p_1p_2 \, Cov(x_1x_2)$$

Let us now write the variance of the portfolio in the more usual form:
$$\sigma^2 = p_1^2\sigma_1^2 + p_2^2\sigma_2^2 + 2p_1p_2 \, Cov(x_1x_2)$$

For the time being we shall assume that there is no correlation between the returns to the investor from these two securities, that is, that $Cov(x_1x_2) = 0$. (This assumption will be relaxed later in the chapter). If the returns of the two securities are not correlated then the variance of the portfolio becomes
$$\sigma^2 = p_1^2\sigma_1^2 + p_2^2\sigma_2^2 \tag{10.16}$$

As may be seen from Equations (10.15) and (10.16) the investor may choose various combinations of expected returns and variances (standard deviations), depending on the proportions in which he includes the two securities in his portfolio. For instance, if $p_1 = 1$ (and therefore $p_2 = 0$) Equation (10.15) becomes
$$Ex = 1\mu_1 + 0\mu_2 = \mu_1$$

and Equation (10.15) becomes
$$\sigma^2 = 1^2\sigma_1^2 + 0^2\sigma_2^2 = \sigma_1^2$$

Thus, when $p_1 = 1$ the entire portfolio is concentrated in security A and the expected return and variance of returns of the portfolio are identical to the expectation and variance of security A. Similarly, if $p_2 = 1$ (and therefore $p_1 = 0$) the expected return of the portfolio will be μ_2 and the variance of the returns σ_2^2. For all other combinations of p_1 and p_2, however, different values of μ and σ^2 will be obtained.

---

[14] $Var \, x = E(x - Ex)^2 = E[(p_1x_1 + p_2x_2) - (p_1\mu_1 + p_2\mu_2)]^2$
$= E[(p_1x_1 - p_1\mu_1) + (p_2x_2 - p_2\mu_2)]^2 = E[(p_1x_1 - p_1\mu_1)^2$
$\quad + (p_2x_2 - p_2\mu_2)^2 + 2(p_1x_1 - p_1\mu_1)(p_2x_2 - p_2\mu_2)]$
$= Var(p_1x_1) + Var(p_2x_2) + 2p_1p_2 \, Cov(x_1x_2)$
$= p_1^2\sigma_1^2 + p_2^2\sigma_2^2 + 2p_1p_2 \, Cov(x_1x_2)$

See also note 6 on page 343.

The coefficient of correlation between x_1 and x_2 is defined as follows:
$$R = \frac{Cov(x_1x_2)}{\sigma_1\sigma_2}$$

Hence $Cov(x_1x_2) = R\sigma_1\sigma_2$ and $\sigma_x^2 = p_1^2\sigma_1^2 + p_2^2\sigma_2^2 + 2p_1p_2 \cdot R\sigma_1\sigma_2$.

3. PORTFOLIOS OF TWO SECURITIES 351

To find out how the investor selects his optimal portfolio (the optimal combination of p_1 and p_2) let us first consider the factors that influence his decision. Since it is assumed that this decision is made according to the MVC[15] it is clear that his utility level is determined by only two parameters, which are also the sole factors that determine his decision. These parameters are the expected return and the variance of returns of the portfolio. We shall initially analyze the effect of each of these parameters separately and then examine their combined effect.

Let us start with the effect of the expected return, disregarding the variance; that is, we assume that the investor's goal is to select that portfolio which maximizes the expected return. It is clear that if this is the investor's objective he will prefer to put all his money into a single security, the one with the highest return. Thus, if $\mu_1 > \mu_2$ he will choose $p_1 = 1$ and $p_2 = 0$; but if $\mu_2 > \mu_1$ he will choose $p_2 = 1$ and $p_1 = 0$.[16] This result can be illustrated graphically with the aid of a simple device which we will need throughout the remainder of the chapter.

First let us rewrite Equation (10.15) as follows:

$$p_1 = \frac{\mu}{\mu_1} - \frac{\mu_2}{\mu_1} p_2$$

This is a linear equation, with μ/μ_1 as the constant and with a negative slope equal to $-(\mu_2/\mu_1)$. Since μ_1 and μ_2 are constants there are three variables p_1, p_2, and μ whose interrelationship we wish to determine. If in the above equation we substitute a given value, for example 5, for μ, then the linear equation gives us all the combinations of p_1 and p_2 with an expected return equal to 5. If instead we substitute $\mu = 10$, then we have all the combinations of p_1 and p_2 which produce an expected return of 10. This means that every line consists of the various combinations of p_1 and p_2 which produce a given expected return. We shall call these lines *iso-return* lines. A family of three such lines is given in Figure X.3. The larger the expected return which is inserted in the equation the higher the iso-profit line. From the diagram, it is clear that we assume $Ex_3 > Ex_2 > Ex_1$ since the iso-profit line which represents a return of Ex_3 lies above the line which represents Ex_2, and so on.

These lines are parallel since the slope of line μ_2/μ_1 is not affected by changes in μ. It is also clear from the diagram that in this case the absolute value of the slope is greater than 45°, so that in this particular example

---

[15] For the sake of simplicity it is assumed that all the cumulative return distributions intersect so that the MVC is optimal, and will give the same results as the TSC.
[16] For the sake of simplicity we have excluded the possibility that $\mu_1 = \mu_2$. In such a case the investor would be indifferent to the choice between securities, since all combinations provide the same return.

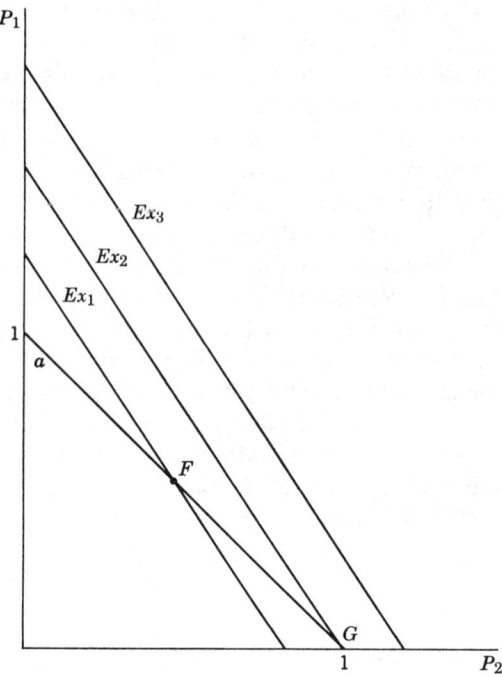

FIGURE X.3.

$\mu_2 > \mu_1$. Obviously the investor will desire to reach the highest possible iso-return line, but he cannot invest without limit because of his budget constraint. Such a budget line (aG) has been drawn in Figure X.3. Since we assumed an investment of one dollar and the investor cannot invest more than 100% of his dollar the constraint takes the form $p_1 + p_2 = 1$, which can be rewritten as $p_1 = 1 - p_2$. This is a linear equation with a 45° slope. The investor who desires to maximize his expected return will try to reach the highest iso-return line, given the constraint that $p_1 + p_2 = 1$. This means that not all the p_1 and p_2 combinations on a line are open to the investor; for example, he cannot select a combination located on Ex_3 without violating his budget constraint since on that line $p_1 + p_2 > 1$. Nor will he choose the combination represented by point F, whose expected return is Ex_1, since he can increase his return (reach a higher iso-return line) by choosing investment G, whose expected return is Ex_2. At point G the expected return is maximized since the budget constraint does not cross or touch a higher iso-return line. As may be seen from Figure X.3, the portfolio that maximizes the investor's expected return (point G) lies on the horizontal axis,

3. PORTFOLIOS OF TWO SECURITIES

which means that $p_1 = 0$ and $p_2 = 1$, so that the investor places all of his funds in security B since it has a higher expected return than security A.

Conversely, if we assume $\mu_2 < \mu_1$, then the slope of the iso-return lines will be less than 45°. A family of iso-return lines which reflects this assumption is drawn in Figure X.4. As could be expected, in this case the introduction of the budget constraint results in a corner solution (point G) on the vertical, rather than on the horizontal, axis. At this point, $p_1 = 1$ and $p_2 = 0$, which means that the investor maximizes his return by placing all of his funds in security A.

It follows from the graphic analysis that an investor who wants to maximize the expected return of his portfolio, independent of all other factors such as the risk involved, will invariably invest all of his funds in the security that offers the maximum return. This conclusion also holds for cases in which he has the opportunity of investing in more than two securities.

Let us now make the alternative extreme assumption that the investor wants to minimize the variance (risk) of the portfolio returns, without regard to the expected return. Here we have the diametrically opposite approach to the one described previously. In the present case all that matters is the risk involved in the investment. In Equation (10.16) we have seen that the variance of the portfolio, assuming zero correlation between the returns from the two securities, is given by

$$\sigma^2 = p_1^2 \sigma_1^2 + p_2^2 \sigma_2^2$$

If we divide both sides of the equation by σ^2 we obtain

$$1 = p_1^2 \frac{\sigma_1^2}{\sigma^2} + p_2^2 \frac{\sigma_2^2}{\sigma^2} \tag{10.17}$$

$$1 = \frac{p_1^2}{a_1^2} + \frac{p_2^2}{a_2^2} \tag{10.18}$$

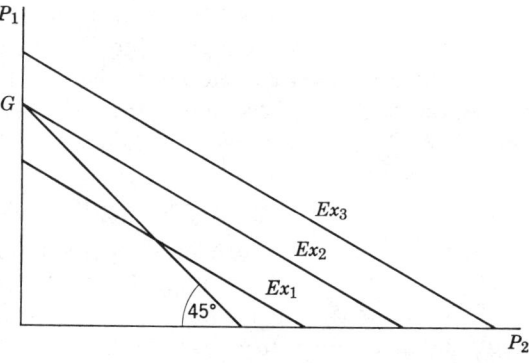

FIGURE X.4.

MEAN-VARIANCE CRITERION AND PORTFOLIO SELECTION

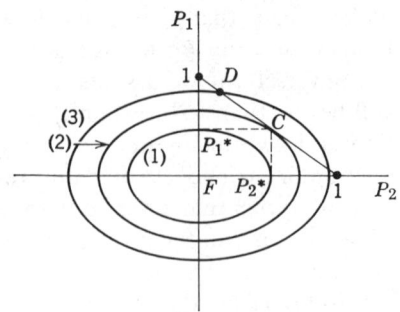

FIGURE X.5.

where

$$a_1 = \frac{\sigma}{\sigma_1}; \quad a_2 = \frac{\sigma}{\sigma_2}$$

Now, (10.18) is the equation of an ellipse having its center at zero, with the parameters a_1 and a_2. Since σ_1 and σ_2 are given constants, a_1 and a_2 are determined by σ. Any increase in σ increase both a_1 and a_2. When we insert a particular value of σ in Equation (10.18) a_1 and a_2 are also determined, so that we can derive all the combinations of p_1 and p_2 which are located on this ellipse. All the combinations of p_1 and p_2 located on the same ellipse represent alternative combinations of securities A and B, whose variance is constant and equal to the value of σ which was inserted in Equation (10.18). Obviously, for each different value of σ which is inserted in Equation (10.18) a different ellipse is derived.

Figure X.5 presents a family of such elipses. Since each ellipse represents a constant level of variance we shall call them *iso-variance* curves. A glance at Equation (10.18) will suffice to show that the parameter a_1 determines the length of the vertical axis. If we set $p_2 = 0$, Equation (10.18) reduces to $a_1 = p_1$. Similarly if we set p_1 equal to zero, this equation reduces to $a_2 = p_2$, that is, the parameter a_2 determines the length of the horizontal axis. The greater the distance of the ellipse from the origin, the higher the variance; thus Figure X.5 has been constructed on the assumption that

$$\sigma_{(3)}^2 > \sigma_{(2)}^2 > \sigma_{(1)}^2$$

As was true for the iso-return lines, the iso-variance lines also cannot intersect since a single point on the diagram cannot represent two different levels of portfolio variance. Again, as in the case of the iso-return lines, not every combination of investments on the ellipse obeys the budget constraint that $p_1 + p_2 = 1$. At point F, for example, $p_1 = 0$ and $p_2 = 0$; the portfolio

3. PORTFOLIOS OF TWO SECURITIES

variance is also zero at this point. Thus one sure way of minimizing variance is simply to abstain from purchasing securities. As we are interested in the behavior of those individuals who have decided to invest in the securities market we shall confine ourselves to cases where $p_1 + p_2 = 1$. This constraint indicates that the investor has a fixed sum of money at his disposal, and our problem is to determine the manner in which he allocates the sum between two given (risky) securities. Let us then, on the same diagram, draw the line representing the budget constraint, which as we see is tangent to ellipse (2) at point C.[17] Any point of intersection between an ellipse and the budget line represents an attainable portfolio since the budget constraint is satisfied. Thus point D represents one such portfolio, but as this point is located on ellipse (3) the investor will prefer portfolio C on ellipse (2), as the variance of this portfolio is smaller. The variance can be minimized, given the constraint, by finding that portfolio which is tangent to the budget line, point C in our example. Thus the proportions p_1 and p_2 at point C represent the *optimal* portfolio for an investor who desires to *minimize* the variance at all costs.[18]

Unlike the case of the maximizer of returns, who puts all his money in one security, the risk minimizer diversifies his investment by building a portfolio which includes both securities. This is clear, since at the optimal point C,

---

[17] Since there exists an infinity of ellipses corresponding to the infinite values of σ that can be plugged into Equation (10.18), an ellipse can always be found which is tangent to a straight line.

[18] The optimal proportions p_1^* and p_2^* can be found as follows:

From Equation (10.16) we know that $\sigma^2 = p_1^2 \sigma_1^2 + p_2^2 \sigma_2^2$.
It is further given that $p_1 + p_2 = 1$.
Hence $\sigma^2 = p_1^2 \sigma_1^2 + (1 - p_1)^2 \sigma_2^2 = p_1^2 \sigma_1^2 + (1 + p_1^2 - 2p_1)\sigma_2^2$
$= p_1^2(\sigma_1^2 + \sigma_2^2) - 2p_1 \sigma_2^2 + \sigma_2^2$

Differentiating this equation and setting its first derivative equal to zero, we obtain

$$\frac{\partial \sigma^2}{\partial p_1} = 2p_1(\sigma_1^2 + \sigma_2^2) - 2\sigma_2^2 = 0$$

That is,

$$p_1 = \frac{\sigma_2^2}{\sigma_1^2 + \sigma_2^2}$$

$$p_2 = 1 - p_1 = \frac{\sigma_1^2 + \sigma_2^2 - \sigma_2^2}{\sigma_1^2 + \sigma_2^2} = \frac{\sigma_1^2}{\sigma_1^2 + \sigma_2^2}$$

which means that the optimal investment proportions are

$$p_1^* = \frac{\sigma_2^2}{\sigma_1^2 + \sigma_2^2} \; ; \quad p_2^* = \frac{\sigma_1^2}{\sigma_1^2 + \sigma_2^2}$$

See Figure X.5.

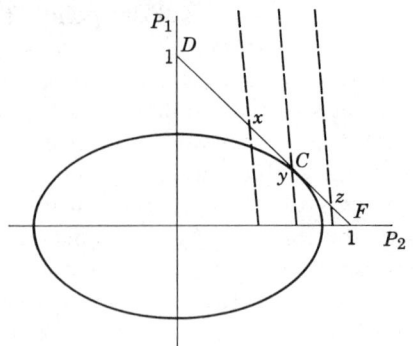

FIGURE X.6.

both p_1^* and p_2^* are less than unity. Thus, despite the fact that we have assumed a mean variance model, diversification can be identified solely with one parameter, the variance associated with the investment.

In both of the above examples we adopted an extreme position of stipulating either an absolute preference for expected return or an absolute preference for stability of returns. On these assumptions we were able to derive the optimal investment proportions without much difficulty. However, if we introduce the more realistic assumption that an investor chooses his portfolio on the basis of both the expected return and the variance of the returns, the optimal investment proportions *cannot* be determined unless further information is available on the investor's tastes. This problem is illustrated in Figure X.6, which sets out the iso-variance ellipse which is tangent to the budget line DF, as well as a family of (dashed) iso-return lines. (In this example the iso-return lines have a slope greater than 45° so that $E(x_2) > E(x_1)$.)

Proposition: All portfolios which are efficient by the mean–variance criterion lie on the segment CF of the budget line.

Since all attainable portfolios (combinations of p_1 and p_2) must lie on the budget line DF, the above proposition states that all attainable portfolios can be divided into two mutually exclusive subsets: an efficient set represented by segment CF and an inefficient set represented by segment DC of Figure X.6.

To prove this proposition we shall choose an arbitrary point on segment DC and show that it represents a portfolio which is inefficient by the MVC. Consider, for instance, point x on line DC. This point represents an inefficient option since the attainable portfolio represented by point y is preferable to it: point y lies on a higher iso-return line than point x so that y represents

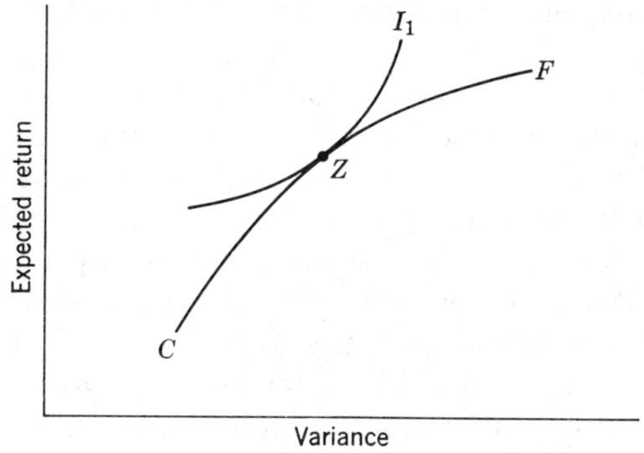

3. PORTFOLIOS OF TWO SECURITIES   357

FIGURE X.7.

a portfolio with a higher profit. Now if we draw an imaginary ellipse through point x, it lies outside the ellipse passing through point y, so that point y represents a portfolio with both a higher expected value and a lower variance than those of point x. Thus portfolio y dominates portfolio x by the MVC. Similarly it can be shown that all other points on section DC represent inefficient portfolios. The efficient set is represented by section CF. As we move from point y to some point on this segment, say point z, both the expected returns and the variance increase so that both portfolios are included in the efficient group. Note that point z represents a higher iso-return and also a higher variance. Similarly it may be shown that all other points on segment CF are included in the MVC efficient group.[19]

The set of efficient portfolios can also be presented on the perhaps more familiar mean–variance plane. Every point on section CF denotes given proportions (p_1, p_2) of securities A and B. Using these proportions the expected return can be computed from Equation (10.15) and the variance can be computed from Equation (10.16) for every point on CF. The resulting combination of expected return and variance can then be plotted on a diagram whose vertical axis measures expected return and whose horizontal axis measures the variance, as has been done in Figure X.7.

As we already noted in Figure X.6, both the expected return and the variance increase as we move from C to F; as a result the locus of efficient portfolios in Figure X.7 rises from left to right. Since point C was on the innermost iso-variance curve it is located on the extreme left of the efficiency locus of Figure X.7. Similarly option F, which was on the highest iso-return

---

[19] However, unless all of the requirements regarding the MVC are met, a preliminary screening using the General Criterion may reduce the efficient set by eliminating some of the points on segment CF.

358 |||||||| MEAN-VARIANCE CRITERION AND PORTFOLIO SELECTION

line, lies at the right-hand end of the efficiency locus, and so on for all of the remaining points. Examination of the efficient set shows it to contain numerous mixed portfolios, containing various proportions of both securities A and B as well as one portfolio consisting of security B alone (at point F). On the other hand the option of investing solely in security A, the security with the lower expected return, is excluded from the efficient set.

The optimal investment can be selected from the efficient set only if we add information regarding the individual investor's preferences. An investor whose indifference curve is represented by indifference curve I_1, for instance, will choose portfolio z, the point of tangency between the efficiency locus CF and the indifference curve I_1. Since with one exception all the infinity of points on the efficiency curve represent mixed portfolios of varying proportions of both securities, almost every (risk-averse) investor will diversify his investment to include both securities.

To summarize, assuming that investors desire to maximize expected returns, without regard to the variance, they will tend to place all their investment funds in a single security—the one with the highest expected return. On the other hand, if we assume that investors are interested *exclusively* in minimizing the variance of returns, without regard to expected returns, they will diversify their investment by building a portfolio which includes the two securities in fixed proportions, namely, the proportions represented by point C in Figure X.6. When it is assumed that investors take both the expected return and the variance into account, they are still almost certain to diversify their investments, but in this case the proportions selected by different investors are no longer constant, and depend on the investors' individual preferences.

In Figure X.6 the iso-return lines are drawn steeper than the slope of the budget line, on the assumption that $E(x_2) > E(x_1)$. Accordingly, a portfolio consisting exclusively of security B is included in the efficient group, while the option of investing exclusively in security A is excluded. However, if we

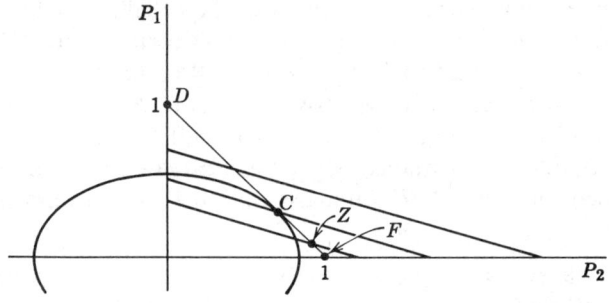

FIGURE X.8.

assume that $E(x_2) < E(x_1)$ these results are reversed: an investment consisting solely of security A is included in the efficient set and that consisting solely of security B is excluded. Similarly, the efficient set is represented by the upper segment CD of the budget line; see Figure X.8. Point Z, for example, now represents an inefficient portfolio since point C has a higher expected return (being located on a higher iso-return line) and a smaller variance (being located on a lower iso-variance curve) and therefore dominates point Z. Similarly it can be shown that investment C dominates all other portfolios represented by points on section CF, thereby eliminating them from the efficient set.

4. A THREE-SECURITY PORTFOLIO

We shall now extend the analysis to include the possibility of investing in three securities—A, B, and C. For convenience we use the same notation as before except that the subscript 3 will be used, when necessary, to identify the third security. Again we set a limit on the amount invested and require that $p_1 + p_2 + p_3 = 1$; so that the problem is how to allocate a given sum of money among the three securities.

The expected return on a portfolio is given by:

$$Ex = p_1 Ex_1 + p_2 Ex_2 + p_3 Ex_3$$

or

$$Ex = p_1 Ex_1 + p_2 Ex_2 + (1 - p_1 - p_2) Ex_3$$

Hence

$$Ex = p_1(Ex_1 - Ex_3) + p_2(Ex_2 - Ex_3) + Ex_3 \quad (10.19)$$

This equation can also be written in the following form:

$$p_1 = \frac{(Ex_3 - Ex)}{Ex_3 - Ex_1} + \frac{Ex_2 - Ex_3}{Ex_3 - Ex_1} \cdot p_2 \quad (10.20)$$

This means that on the plane $(p_1 p_2)$ Equation (10.19) and therefore also Equation (10.20) is represented by a straight line having the slope

$$\frac{Ex_2 - Ex_3}{Ex_3 - Ex_1}$$

For example, if $Ex_1 = \$7$, $Ex_2 = \$4$, $Ex_3 = \$6$, then

$$p_1 = \frac{(6 - Ex)}{6 - 7} + \frac{4 - 6}{6 - 7} \cdot p_2 = \frac{(6 - Ex)}{-1} + 2p_2$$

The location of the line is determined by the size of Ex and its slope, which is $+2$.

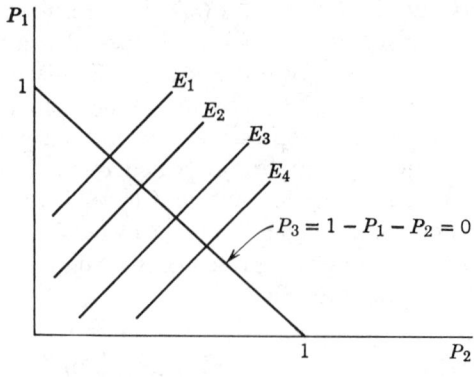

FIGURE X.9.

A family of such iso-return lines labeled E_1, E_2, and so on is given in Figure X.9. Obviously an infinity of such lines can be drawn, depending on the level of expected return assumed. The higher the expected return, the higher the iso-return line, that is, line E_1 represents a higher return than E_2 and so on. Moving along an iso-return line in a northeasterly direction, p_1 and p_2 increase while p_3 decreases.

Let us now see how the iso-variance curves can be represented on this plane. First let us find the variance of the returns:[20]

$$Var\ x = Var\ (p_1 x_1 + p_2 x_2 + p_3 x_3) = p_1^2 \sigma_1^2 + p_2^2 \sigma_2^2 + p_3^2 \sigma_3^2$$
$$+ 2 p_1 p_2 \sigma_1 \sigma_2 R_{12} + 2 p_1 p_3 \sigma_1 \sigma_3 R_{13} + 2 p_2 p_3 \sigma_2 \sigma_3 R_{23}$$

Let us now substitute $p_3 = 1 - p_1 - p_2$, which yields the following:

$$\sigma^2 = p_1^2 \sigma_1^2 + p_2^2 \sigma_2^2 + (1 - p_1 - p_2)^2 \sigma_3^2 + 2 p_1 p_2 \sigma_1 \sigma_2 R_{12}$$
$$+ 2 p_1 (1 - p_1 - p_2) \sigma_1 \sigma_3 R_{13} + 2 p_2 (1 - p_1 - p_2) \sigma_2 \sigma_3 R_{23}$$

By opening the brackets and collecting terms we obtain the following equation:

$$\sigma^2 = p_1^2 (\sigma_1^2 - 2 \sigma_1 \sigma_3 R_{13} + \sigma_3^2) + p_2^2 (\sigma_2^2 - 2 \sigma_2 \sigma_3 R_{23} + \sigma_3^2)$$
$$+ 2 p_1 p_2 (\sigma_1 \sigma_2 R_{12} - \sigma_1 \sigma_3 R_{13} - \sigma_2 \sigma_3 R_{23} + \sigma_3^2)$$
$$+ 2 p_1 (\sigma_1 \sigma_3 R_{13} - \sigma_3^2) + 2 p_2 (\sigma_2 \sigma_3 R_{23} - \sigma_3^2) + \sigma_3^2 \quad (10.21)$$

[20] The coefficient of correlation is defined as follows:

$$R_{x_1 x_2} = \frac{Cov\ (x_1 x_2)}{\sigma_1 \cdot \sigma_2}$$

Hence $Cov\ (x_1, x_2) = R \sigma_1 \cdot \sigma_2$ so that instead of $2 p_1 (1 - p_1) Cov\ (x_1, x_2)$ we can write $2 p_1 (1 - p_1) R \cdot \sigma_1 \sigma_2$.

4. A THREE-SECURITY PORTFOLIO   361

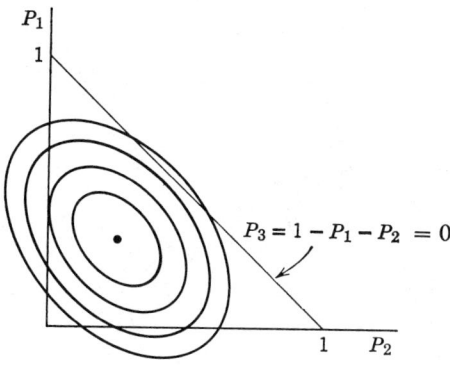

FIGURE X.10.

This equation describes an ellipse on the (p_1, p_2) plane.[21] The greater the diameter of the ellipse, the higher the variance it represents. A family of such iso-variance curves is given in Figure X.10. The point at the center of the ellipse may or may not represent an attainable portfolio. The set of attainable portfolios is represented by all the points within the triangle formed by the vertical axis, the horizontal axis, and the budget line, $p_3 = 1 - p_1 - p_2 = 0$. For the sake of simplicity we have assumed that the center of the ellipse represents an attainable combination, and therefore it has been drawn within the triangle.

Figure X.11 sets out the iso-return lines, iso-variance curves, and the triangle of attainable points. The iso-return line E_5 is tangent to the iso-variance curve V_2 at point K. Line E_4, which represents a higher expected return, is tangent to the iso-variance line V_3 at point D, which represents a smaller variance than line V_2. This means that a movement from K to D increases the expected return while the variance goes down. If we apply the MVC, the portfolio represented by point D is preferable to that represented by point K. Line E_3 passes through point C where the variance of returns is

---

[21] The equation is not elliptical if and only if one or more of the following conditions hold:

  (a) the variance of the variable $(x_1 - x_3)$ equals 0; $\sigma_1^2 - 2\sigma_1\sigma_3 + \sigma_3^2 = 0$
  (b) the variance of the variable $(x_2 - x_3)$ equals 0; $\sigma_2^2 - 2\sigma_2\sigma_3 + \sigma_3^2 = 0$
  (c) the random variables $(x_1 - x_3)$ and $(x_2 - x_3)$ have a correlation of $+1$ or -1

The mathematical analysis is the same whether one or more of these conditions are fulfilled. For the sake of convenient graphical representation it was assumed in this chapter that none of the conditions applies.

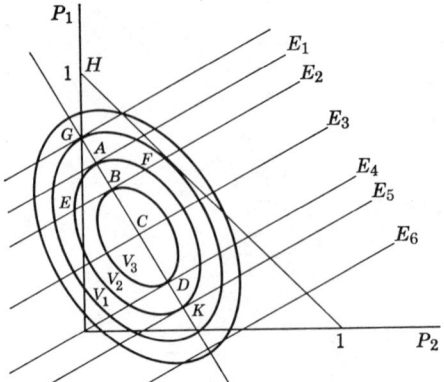

FIGURE X.11.

zero, and by an analogous argument we can show that the portfolio represented by piont C is preferable to that represented by D. However, this is not the case for points C and B. At point B the expected return is higher than at point $C(E_2 > E_3)$ but the variance is also higher. Thus the portfolios represented by C and B are both MVC efficient. Similarly, all of the portfolios (points) along the segments CG and GH are efficient, while all of the other attainable points are inefficient, using the mean–variance rule. For example, at point F (and at point E) the expected return is E_2 and the variance is V_2. If instead we substitute point B, the variance is decreased while the expected return remains constant. Thus point F (and point E) represent inefficient options.

As in the two security case, the efficiency curve can be plotted on an

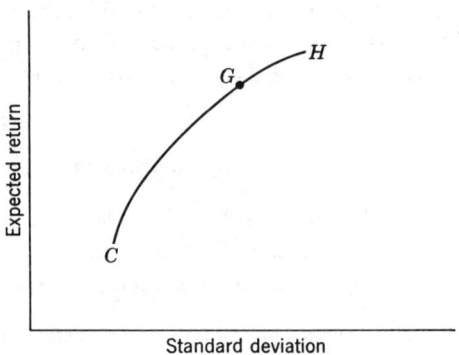

FIGURE X.12.

5. THE GAINS FROM DIVERSIFICATION

expected return–variance plane by determining the expected return and standard deviation for each point on the segments CG and GH, and transposing them to a diagram such as Figure X.12.

5. THE GAINS FROM DIVERSIFICATION

As we have just seen, the desire to stabilize the income stream is a *sine qua non* for investment diversification. However, some degree of stabilization can be achieved, without impairing the expected return. We can illustrate this proposition by means of simple example of two securities. Let us assume that we have two identical securities, A and B, whose distribution of returns (per $100 invested) is given in Table X–1. Now consider an investor with $100 at his disposal who must decide whether to buy one (or both) of these securities.

If he invests the entire amount in a single security he has a 50% chance of losing $20 and a 50% chance of gaining $30. His expected gain is $5, with a variance of 625. Now what will he earn should be decide to invest $50 in A and $50 in B?

TABLE X–1.

Security A		Security B	
Return	Probability	Return	Probability
−20	1/2	−20	1/2
+30	1/2	+30	1/2
$Ex_A = 5$		$Ex_B = 5$	
$Var\, x_A = 625$		$Var\, x_B = 625$	

The answer depends on the statistical relationship between the two distributions. Let us initially assume that the returns from the two securities are statistically independent of each other.[22] Accordingly, the probability of obtaining any given pair of returns from investments A and B is the product of their individual probabilities. For example, the joint probability that the return on *both* securities will be −20 in any given year is $1/2 \cdot 1/2 = 1/4$, so that the investor has a 25% chance of losing $20.

Using this approach we calculate the probability distribution of returns for

---

[22] That is, the correlation between the returns from the two securities is zero.

TABLE X-2.

Return	Probability
−20	1/4
+5	1/2*
+30	1/4

$E(x) = +5$
$\text{Var}(x) = 312.5$

* The probability of earning $5 results from a 1/4 chance that A will lose $20 while B earns $30 or from a 1/4 probability that A will earn $30 while B loses $20. Since the two alternatives are independent events, the probability of earning $5 equals $1/4 + 1/4 = 1/2$.

a mixed portfolio which includes securities A and B in equal proportions (see Table X-2). The expected return on the portfolio is $5, that is, the same return as that of each of the identical securities, but the variance is considerably reduced. Instead of the two extreme results (+30 and −20) attainable from the investment in a single security, the portfolio provides an intermediate result (+5) as well. Thus the portfolio reduces the dispersion of the distribution of returns, and the chances of suffering a major loss (−20) are reduced from a probability of 1/2 for the single security to a probability of only 1/4 for the mixed portfolio. However, in all fairness, it should also be noted that the chances of making a big profit (+30) are also reduced from 1/2 to 1/4. But since the investor who makes his selection using the MVC is assumed to be a risk averter, his expected utility is increased when the dispersion of returns is reduced, as long as the expected return remains unchanged.

In this example we have demonstrated how the investor can increase his expected utility by diversifying his investments when the returns to the investor from the securities in question are assumed to be statistically independent. In practice, however, the returns on the individual securities are not necessarily statistically independent, but as long as they are not *perfectly* correlated the risk-averse investor can gain from diversification. The size of his gain depends on the degree of the statistical interdependence among the returns on different securities and on the number of securities over which he can spread his risk. The lower the interdependence (or the higher the negative interdependence) among the returns and the greater the number of securities over which he is able to diversify his portfolio, the more he stands to gain from diversification.

6. THE IMPACT OF INTERDEPENDENCE ON THE GAINS FROM DIVERSIFICATION

To analyze the effect of the various relationships that may exist between the returns of different securities, let us assume that we have two securities, A and B, the expected returns and standard deviations of which are (μ_1 and σ_1) and (μ_2 and σ_2) respectively. These two points are plotted in Figure X.13, where A represents (μ_1, σ_1) and B represents (μ_2, σ_2). Should the individual diversify his investment by purchasing a proportion p_1 of security A and a proportion p_2 ($p_2 = 1 - p_1$) of security B, the expected return on this portfolio is equal to

$$\mu = p_1\mu_1 + (1 - p_1)\mu_2 \tag{10.22}$$

with a variance of

$$Var(x) = p_1^2\sigma_1^2 + (1 - p_1)^2\sigma_2^2 + 2p_1(1 - p_1)\,Cov(x_1, x_2) \tag{10.23}$$

where the random variables x_1 and x_2 denote the returns on securities A and B, respectively. Equation (10.23) can also be written as follows:

$$Var(x) = p_1^2\sigma_1^2 + (1 - p_1)^2\sigma_2^2 + 2p_1(1 - p_1)R\sigma_1\sigma_2 \tag{10.24}$$

where R denotes the coefficient of correlation between the returns of the two securities.

Let us now examine the effects of combining the two securities in a portfolio, under varying assumptions regarding the coefficient of correlation R. When $R = 0$ the transformation curve, which represents the pairs of expected return and variance which result from combining the two securities in all possible proportions, has the form of the locus ACB of Figure X.13. This curve has its minimum variance (standard deviation) at point C. All the portfolios (points) on curve ACB correspond to the different proportions in

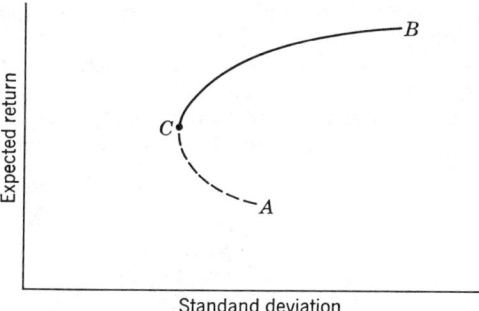

FIGURE X.13.

which the amount invested is divided between the two securities. The dashed segment AC is irrelevant, since these portfolios are inefficient.[23]

The degree to which a two-security portfolio reduces the variance of returns depends on the degree of correlation between the returns of the securities. To quantify this relationship we assume the following expected returns and variances for two securities A and B:

$$\mu_1 = 10 \qquad \mu_2 = 20$$
$$\sigma_1^2 = 100 \qquad \sigma_2^2 = 900$$

The expected returns and variances for portfolios of varying proportions and for four alternative assumptions regarding the correlation among returns are given in Table X–3. The data clearly show that by diversifying his investment an investor can reduce the variance of returns. Moreover, the lower the coefficient of correlation, the greater the reduction in variance.[24]

[23] The statement can readily be proved by examining the following diagram.

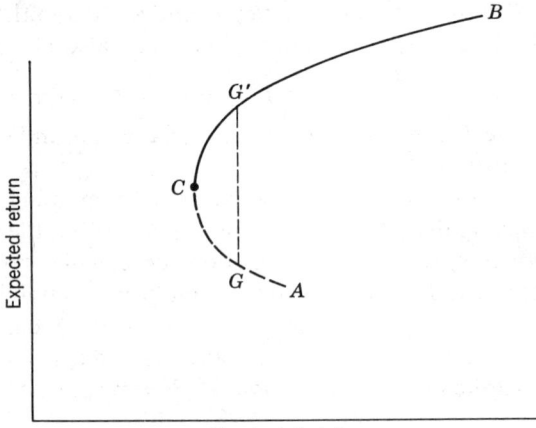

For every point on section AC a corresponding point which is preferable can be found on section BC. For example, point G' dominates G since it has a higher mean and an equal variance. Therefore, section AC represents inefficient portfolios which will never be chosen by a rational investor.

[24] If we choose the proportions p_1 and p_2 which minimize the variance, in this case $p_1 = 3/4$ and $p_2 = 1/4$, and assume $R = -1$, the portfolio variance is reduced to zero:

$$\begin{aligned}\sigma^2 &= p_1^2\sigma_1^2 + p_2^2\sigma_2^2 - 2p_1p_2\sigma_1\sigma_2 \\ &= 9/16 \cdot 100 + 1/16 \cdot 900 - 2 \cdot 3/4 \cdot 1/4 \cdot 10 \cdot 30 \\ &= \frac{900 + 900 - 1800}{16} = 0\end{aligned}$$

This portfolio corresponds to the point on the $R = -1$ transformation locus which is tangent to the vertical axis in Figure X.14.

6. INTERDEPENDENCE ON GAINS FROM DIVERSIFICATION

TABLE X–3.

Proportion of Portfolio Invested in Security A	Expected Return on Portfolio*	Variance of Returns for Alternative Coefficients of Correlation†				
		$R = +1$	$R = +1/2$	$R = 0$	$R = -1/2$	$R = -1$
0	20	900	900	900	900	900
1/5	18	676	628	580	532	484
2/5	16	484	412	340	268	196
3/5	14	324	252	180	108	36
4/5	12	196	148	100	52	4
1	10	100	100	100	100	100

* The mean is independent of R, and is obtained from the formula

$$Ex = p_1 Ex_1 + p_2 Ex_2$$

† The formula for the variance is

$$\operatorname{Var}(x) = p_1^2 \sigma_1^2 + p_2^2 \sigma_2^2 + 2 p_1 p_2 R \sigma_1 \sigma_2$$

This inverse relationship between the degree of correlation and the degree of variance reduction can be seen even more clearly in Figure X.14, which presents a family of transformation curves for varying assumptions regarding the correlation coefficient. Diversification can always reduce variance except in the extreme case where the returns are perfectly correlated ($R = +1$). On such an assumption the transformation curve reduces to a

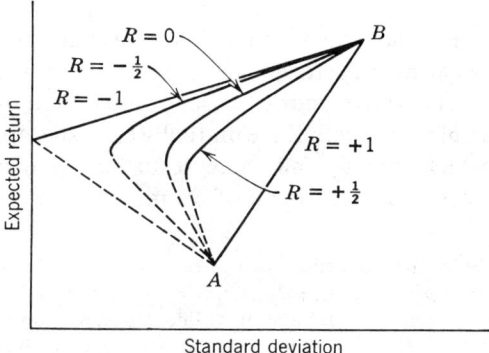

FIGURE X.14.

straight line joining points AB.[25] As the correlation coefficient is reduced to $+1/2$, 0, and $-1/2$ the transformation curve bulges out farther and farther to the left, and if we were to superimpose a set of indifference curves on the same plane, we could readily see that the risk-averse investor reaches higher levels of utility, the smaller the coefficient of correlation. And this conclusion holds for all degrees of correlation (positive, negative, or zero) except for the limiting case of perfect positive correlation. It should also be noted that in the case of perfect negative correlation between the returns of the two securities, the transformation curve will at one point be tangent to the vertical axis, which means that there exists a portfolio which can completely eliminate the variance. Of course, the final decision to choose the minimum variance portfolio or some other point on the curve depends on individual tastes (that is, on the slope of the indifference curves).

7. THE NUMBER OF SECURITIES AND THE GAIN FROM DIVERSIFICATION

To see the relationship between the number of securities included in the portfolio and the gain from diversification, let us assume that we now have three securities, A, B, and C, the price of each of which is \$100. The expected return and variance of each of these securities are given in Table X–4.

TABLE X–4.

	Security		
	A	B	C
Expected Return	10	20	30
Variance of Returns	100	900	2,500

For the sake of convenience we shall assume zero coefficients of correlation between the returns of each pair of securities.

The three-security case is illustrated in Figure X.15. The investor is confronted with three mutually exclusive alternatives: (a) invest in a portfolio which includes all three securities; (b) confine himself to a two-security portfolio; (c) put all of his money into a single security.

---

[25] In the particular case where $R = +1$ the variance of the portfolio is given by $\sigma^2 = p_1^2\sigma_1^2 + p_2^2\sigma_2^2 + 2p_1p_2\sigma_1\sigma_2 = (p_1\sigma_1 + p_2\sigma_2)^2$, and hence $\sigma = p_1\sigma_1 + p_2\sigma_2$. The last equation describes a straight line connecting points A and B. In the other extreme case where $R = -1$, the portfolio variance is given by $\sigma^2 = p_1^2\sigma_1^2 + p_2^2\sigma_2^2 - 2p_1p_2\sigma_1\sigma_2 = (p_1\sigma_1 - p_2\sigma_2)^2$. The investment proportions which minimize the variance are given by $p_1/p_2 = \sigma_2/\sigma_1$. In this case the variance of the portfolio is equal to zero, and hence curve AB is tangent to the vertical axis.

7. SECURITIES AND GAIN FROM DIVERSIFICATION 369

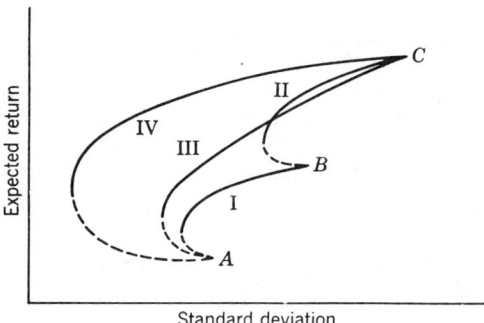

FIGURE X.15.

Curve I in Figure X.15 represents the transformation curve of portfolios comprised of differing proportions of securities A and B; curve II and curve III are the relevant transformation curves for portfolios which include securities B and C, and securities A and C, respectively. Curve IV represents the transformation curve for portfolios which include all possible combinations of all three securities. In that case the investor is offered an additional degree of freedom, and is in a better position to reduce the variance for any given expected return, that is, curve IV lies to the left of other three curves. This additional possibility for diversifying his investment can only increase, and not decrease, an investor's utility, since he still remains free to put his money into only two of the three securities.

Table X-5 gives numerical examples which show that for a given expected return one can always find a portfolio which includes all three securities that reduces the variance of returns without at the same time reducing the expected return. And although we confine ourselves to only three examples, to illustrate the advantages the investor derives from diversification, it should be obvious that an infinity of three-security portfolios can be found which are preferable to a given portfolio consisting of only two securities.

It would seem to follow that investors who select their portfolios according to the MVC should tend to include a considerable number of securities in their portfolios. In practice, however, the degree of diversification is often limited, for one or more of the following reasons:

(a) Sometimes an investor has only a relatively small amount of money at his disposal. Diversifying over a large number of stocks would mean investing very small amounts in each share, which usually involves excessive brokerage commissions and other costs. Moreover it may sometimes be physically impossible, as it would require buying fractions of stocks.

(b) An individual investor may find it difficult and expensive to keep track of a large number of securities; even a cursory check of the

TABLE X–5*.

Proportions Invested in Two-Security Portfolios	Expected Returns	Variance of Returns	Proportions Invested in Three-Security Portfolios	Expected Returns	Variance of Returns
$p_1 = 2/5$ $p_2 = 3/5$ $p_3 = 0$	16	340	$p_1 = 3/5$ $p_2 = 1/5$ $p_3 = 1/5$	16	172
$p_1 = 2/5$ $p_2 = 0$ $p_3 = 3/5$	22	916	$p_1 = 3/10$ $p_2 = 2/10$ $p_3 = 1/2$	22	670
$p_1 = 0$ $p_2 = 7/10$ $p_3 = 3/10$	23	616	$p_1 = 1/10$ $p_2 = 5/10$ $p_3 = 4/10$	23	576

* The expected return for a three-security portfolio is calculated from the following formula:

$$Ex = p_1 Ex_1 + p_2 Ex_2 + p_3 Ex_3$$

The variance is given by

$$Var\ (x) = p_1^2 \sigma_1^2 + p_2^2 \sigma_2^2 + p_3^2 \sigma_3^2 + 2p_1 p_2 R_{12} \sigma_1 \sigma_2 + 2p_1 p_3 R_{13} \sigma_1 \sigma_3 + 2p_2 p_3 R_{23} \sigma_2 \sigma_3$$

When $R = 0$ for each pair of securities the last three expressions are each equal to zero.

financial statements of a large number of companies is likely to prove a difficult and tedious task for the individual investor.

Thus individual investors often restrict themselves to a relatively small number of individual securities, and seek greater diversification by purchasing shares in mutual funds or investment companies. These institutions pool the funds of many individual investors and thus are able to achieve a high level of diversification. The typical mutual fund often holds the stocks of more than 500 different companies; they are also in a better position to allocate the necessary resources for data collection and financial analysis required to manage such a portfolio.[26]

8. THE EFFICIENCY FRONTIER—THE GENERAL CASE

So far we have illustrated the advantages an investor can derive from diversification, by means of examples where the investment is spread over two (or three) securities. In actual fact thousands of individual securities are traded

[26] A more detailed evaluation of mutual fund performance is given in Chapter XIV.

8. THE EFFICIENCY FRONTIER—THE GENERAL CASE

on the stock exchange and the investor has to decide which of them to include in his portfolio and in what proportions. To illustrate the general problem of generating the locus of efficient portfolios when the number of securities is very large, let us assume n securities, where x_i is a random variable denoting the return on the ith security; $0 \leq p_i \leq 1$ denotes the proportion of the portfolio invested in that security; and μ_i and σ_i denote the expected return and the standard deviation of the ith security.

Let us now determine the proportions $(p_1 \cdots p_n)$ which ensure that a portfolio will be efficient. For any proportions $p_1 \cdots p_n$ that we select, the expected return of the portfolio μ is given by

$$\mu = \sum_{i=1}^{n} p_i \mu_i \qquad (10.25)$$

while the variance of returns, σ^2, equals[27]

$$\sigma^2 = \sum_{i=1}^{n} p_i^2 \sigma_i^2 + 2 \sum_{i=1}^{n} \sum_{\substack{j=1 \\ j>i}}^{n} p_i p_j \, Cov\,(x_i, x_j) \qquad (10.26)$$

Since $Cov\,(x_i, x_j) = R_{ij}\sigma_i\sigma_j$ Equation (10.26) can also be written as follows:

$$\sigma^2 = \sum_{i=1}^{n} p_i^2 \sigma_i^2 + 2 \sum_{i=1}^{n} \sum_{\substack{j=1 \\ j>i}}^{n} p_i p_j R_{ij} \sigma_i \sigma_j \qquad (10.27)$$

where R_{ij} devotes the coefficient of correlation between the returns of securities i and j.

By definition, the portfolio will be efficient if there exists no other having the same expected return and a lower variance of returns.[28] To determine the

---

[27] σ^2 is obtained as follows (by definition):

$$\sigma^2 = E\left[\sum_{i=1}^{n} p_i x_i - \sum_{i=1}^{n} p_i \mu_i\right]^2 = E[\sum_{i=1}^{n} (p_i x_i - p_i \mu_i)]^2$$

$$= E\left[\sum_{i=1}^{n} (p_i x_i - p_i \mu_i)^2 + 2 \sum_{i=1}^{n} \sum_{\substack{j=1 \\ j>i}}^{n} (p_i x_i - p_i \mu_i)(p_j x_j - p_j \mu_j)\right]$$

$$= E\left[\sum_{i=1}^{n} p_i^2 (x_i - \mu_i)^2 + 2 \sum_{i=1}^{n} \sum_{\substack{j=1 \\ j>i}}^{n} p_i p_j (x_i - \mu_i)(x_j - \mu_j)\right]$$

$$= \sum_{i=1}^{n} p_i^2 \sigma_i^2 + 2 \sum_{i=1}^{n} \sum_{\substack{j=1 \\ j>i}}^{n} p_i p_j \, Cov\,(x_i, x_j)$$

[28] An alternative definition is that a portfolio is regarded as efficient if there is no other portfolio having a higher expected return and the same variance of returns.

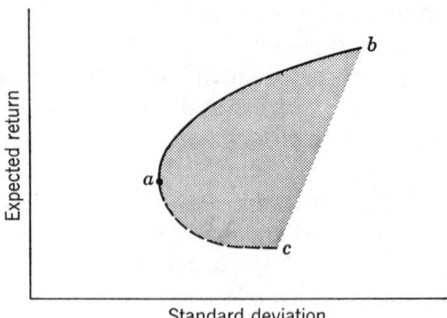

FIGURE X.16.

efficient set we must accordingly find those investment proportions $(p_1 \cdots p_n)$ which minimize the variance for a given expected return. The same constraint $\sum_{i=1}^{n} p_i = 1$ that applied in the case of a two- or three-security portfolio also applies in the general case.

The optimal proportions are obtained by differentiating the following function, C:

$$C = \sum_{i=1}^{n} p_i^2 \sigma_i^2 + 2 \sum_{i=1}^{n} \sum_{\substack{j=1 \\ j>i}}^{n} p_i p_j R_{ij} \sigma_i \sigma_j$$

$$+ \lambda_1 \left(1 - \sum_{i=1}^{n} p_i\right) + \lambda_2 \left(\mu - \sum_{i=1}^{n} p_i \mu_i\right) \quad (10.28)$$

where λ_1 and λ_2 are Lagrange multipliers.[29]

Functions C has $n + 2$ unknowns: $p_1 \cdots p_n, \lambda_1, \lambda_2$. If we now differentiate C with respect to p_i, λ_1, and λ_2, and equate the first derivatives to zero, we derive $n + 2$ equations which provide us with a solution for the $n + 2$ unknowns of equation C. Using this technique we can determine the minimum variance for any value of expected returns which we plug into Equation (10.28), subject to the constraint that $\sum_{i=1}^{n} p_i = 1$. The constraint ensures that we deal only with attainable investments, eliminating, for instance, portfolios comprised of securities whose total value exceeds the funds at our disposal.

To determine the set of efficient portfolios, in practice, recourse must be had to an electronic computer since the number of calculations rapidly

---

[29] For an explanation of the Lagrange multipliers and their use in finding constrained minima and maxima, see R. G. D. Allen, *Mathematical Analysis for Economists*, London: Macmillan, 1950 and the Mathematical Supplement at the end of the book.

9. SUMMARY

increases as the number of securities increases. Using standard techniques of quadratic programming, the set of equations can be solved with relative ease on existing computers. Using this method different values of μ are inserted in Equation (10.28) and the vector of investment proportions $(p_1, \ldots, p_n)$ which minimize the portfolio variance for any given expected return is determined[30].

In the multi-dimensional case, as in the case of two securities, the efficient set of portfolios can be represented by an envelope curve, such as *ab* in Figure X.16. The efficient portfolios lie only on segment *ab*, since for every portfolio on segment *ac* another dominant portfolio can be found on section *ab*. All points located to the right of the envelope curve are obviously inefficient, some of these points representing portfolios which include all n securities while others represent partial portfolios or individual securities.

9. SUMMARY

Both individual and institutional investors tend to diversify risk by building portfolios which include a number of common stocks as well as cash and bonds. The purpose of this chapter has been to present a graphical analysis of the portfolio selection process based on the Mean–Variance Criterion (MVC).

The first asset combination considered was a portfolio comprising cash and bonds. Despite the fact that cash earns no return, the MVC implies the existence of a mixed portfolio which includes both bonds and cash. This follows from the fact that even a bond without financial risk generates a probability distribution of returns, because of possible fluctuations in the market rate of interest. Should the interest rate rise (fall), the investor in an existing bond will incur a capital loss (gain) in addition to earning the fixed rate of interest. Thus the rate of return (interest plus capital gains or losses) must be treated as a risk asset, which permits an investor to reduce the dispersion of returns by diversifying his liquid assets in a portfolio which includes cash as well as bonds.

The second case discussed is that of an investor who is confronted with two risky securities. Two alternatives are assumed to be open to him: either to invest all of his funds in one of the two securities, or to diversify his investment by building a portfolio which includes both. In effect, the investor may choose various combinations of expected returns and variances, depending on the proportions in which he includes the two securities in his portfolio.

---

[30] The use of this technique is illustrated in Part III.

An investor who desires to maximize the expected return of his portfolio, independent of all other considerations, will invariably invest all of his funds in the security which offers the maximum return. Investors who wish to minimize risk, independent of all other considerations, always diversify their investments by building a portfolio which includes both securities, in fixed proportions. Thus, in the two-parameter M–V model, diversification can be identified solely with one parameter, the variance of returns. When it is assumed that investors take both the expected return and the variance into account, they are still almost certain to diversify their investments, but the proportions selected by different investors are not constant and depend on their individual preferences. These conclusions hold for the three-security portfolio case as well.

The gains from such diversification were then examined for a risk-averse investor. Such an individual can increase his expected utility by diversifying his investments as long as the returns on the individual securities are not perfectly correlated. The size of the gain depends on the degree of statistical interdependence among the returns and on the number of securities over which he can spread the risks. The lower the positive correlation (or the greater the negative correlation) among the returns, and the larger the number of securities over which he may diversify his portfolio, the greater the gains from diversification. It should also be noted that in the case of perfect negative correlation between the returns of two securities there exists a portfolio which will completely eliminate the variance.

Although the greater the number of securities included in a portfolio, the lower the variance, institutional restrictions and costs limit the size of actual portfolios. For these reasons many small investors seek diversification by means of mutual funds which pool the resources of many individual investors. We defer the analysis of the diversification effected through mutual fund portfolios to Part III.

QUESTIONS AND PROBLEMS

10.1 Define and graph the efficiency locus for the two-asset case of bonds and cash.

10.2 Why is an individual willing to hold part of his liquid reserve in the form of cash?

10.3 "An investor who ignores risk will diversify his portfolio; an investor who ignores the portfolio's expected return will diversify his portfolio." What is your opinion of these two statements? Support your answer with a graphical presentation.

10.4 "Bonds should not be included in the risk portfolio." Appraise.

10.5 Given the following two securities A and B:

	A	B
$E(x)$	10	20
$Var(X)$	5	40

(a) Will an individual (using the MVC) ever concentrate all of his investment in security A?
(b) Will he ever concentrate all of his investment in security B?

10.6 Define the following concepts:
  (a) transformation line
  (b) iso-variance curve
  (c) iso-return line
  (d) variance of a security
  (e) variance of a portfolio

10.7 What is the connection between the gains from diversification and the correlation among the returns of securities?

10.8 What is the relationship between the number of available securities and the gains from diversification? Does this have any implications for the small investor?

QUESTIONS AND PROBLEMS

10.9 Assume that an individual is confronted with the following mutually exclusive alternatives:

(1) Invest $10,000 in security A.
(2) Invest $10,000 in security B.
(3) Invest $10,000 in a portfolio which includes these two securities in any desired proportions.

The market price of each security is $1.00 and their expected returns are
(1) security $A = \$0.20$ per share
(2) security $B = \$0.40$ per share

Also assume that the individual invests *all* of the $10,000.

(a) Construct a diagram which shows the proportion invested in each security on the assumption that the investor reaches his decision *solely* on the basis of expected return.

(b) Now assume that you are given the following additional information:
$$Var\ (x)\ \text{of security}\ A = 0.1$$
$$Var\ (x)\ \text{of security}\ B = 0.3$$

The correlation among returns of A and $B = 0$.
What proportion of the $10,000 will the individual invest in each of the securities, assuming that he reaches his decision solely on considerations of minimum variance, that is, he ignores expected return?

(c) Answer part (b) on the assumption that the correlation among returns equals $+1$. How do you account for the differences in your answers to parts (b) and (c)?

(d) Now assume that the investor reaches his decision by considering *both* the return and variance of the securities:

(1) Construct and explain the locus of efficient portfolios facing the investor.

(2) Indicate on a diagram the inefficient alternatives facing the individual. Explain why these alternatives are *not* efficient.

(3) Can you unambiguously determine the proportion invested in each security? If your answer is yes, what are the optimal proportions; if your answer is no, what information do you require in order to determine the proportions of investment.

QUESTIONS AND PROBLEMS

10.10 Assume that four securities have an *equal probability* of earning the following rates of return:

	A	B	C	D
	40	−16	60	5
	−10	50	−30	5
	20	−12	120	5
	−6	22	−40	5

(a) Assuming that the investor is constrained to a single security portfolio, what are the MVC efficient options? Draw the efficiency locus for this case.

(b) Answer part (a) assuming that the investor can also build portfolios which include two securities in equal proportions.

(c) Draw the efficiency locus for a case in which the investor is also permitted to construct portfolios which include three securities in equal proportions.

(d) Redraw the three efficiency curves of parts (a), (b), and (c) on one diagram. Explain your results.

SELECTED REFERENCES

See Chapter IX.

Chapter XI
The Mean–Variance Criterion and Quadratic Utility*

1. INTRODUCTION

In Chapters IX and X the Mean–Variance Criterion (MVC) was analyzed on the assumption that investors' utility functions are concave. With respect to this assumption, which is equivalent to assuming risk aversion, the necessary and sufficient conditions for the optimality of the MVC relate to the form of the distribution of returns. Alternatively, the modified Two-Stage Criterion can be used to ensure optimality. In this chapter we shall critically evaluate a third attempt to ensure the optimality of the MVC, the assumption of a quadratic utility function.

2. THE MEANING OF QUADRATIC UTILITY

One of the primary advantages of assuming concave utility is that such a function can readily be given an economic interpretation in terms of risk aversion. The case for a quadratic utility function is less clear. As we have already seen, the MVC is based exclusively on the first two moments of the distribution of returns: the expected return and the variance. A quadratic utility function is the only function which depends solely on the first two moments of the distribution of returns.[1] Technically, a general quadratic

---

* The contents of this chapter are not necessary for comprehending the rest of the book, and can be skipped by the general reader.

[1] Although expected utility depends, in general, on all the moments of the distribution of returns, in the case of the quadratic utility function all of the higher derivatives vanish, leaving only the first two. For the mathematical method of demonstrating this, see Chapter VII, Section 4.

utility function can be written as a second degree polynomial of the following form:

$$U(x) = a + bx + cx^2$$

where x is a random variable denoting the return on investment, and a, b, and c are coefficients. The coefficients a and c can take on any value, positive or negative, but b must be positive if the function is to fulfill the requirement that the first derivative be non-negative:

$$U'(x) = b + 2cx \geq 0$$

Inserting the value $x = 0$ into this equation (which is legitimate, since we do not exclude the possibility of zero returns at some level of probability), we find that b must be positive.[2]

Since the utility function is defined up to a linear transformation (see Chapter VI), we can deduct the constant a and divide through by b without changing the investor's preference order. This yields

$$U(x) = x + \beta x^2$$

where $\beta = c/b$. The exact configuration of the quadratic function depends on the value of β, which can be either positive or negative.

2.1 β LESS THAN ZERO

Let us first consider the case where β is negative; the resulting quadratic utility function is drawn in Figure XI.1. The equation for this function, as we have already shown, is

$$U(x) = x + \beta x^2$$

which has the following two derivatives:

$$U'(x) = 1 + 2\beta x \geq 0$$

$$U''(x) = 2\beta < 0$$

Since we have assumed that $\beta < 0$, the second derivative is also negative, which is equivalent to assuming that the marginal utility for money declines; as can be recalled from the discussion in Chapter VI, the graph of such a function is concave. However, only part of the curve of Figure XI.1 is

---

[2] From the condition that $U'(x) \geq 0$, we can infer only that b must also be non-negative ($b \geq 0$), but despite this we shall assume $b > 0$. We eliminate the possibility of $b = 0$ because in such an event, the investor either prefers both a high return and a high variance (if $c > 0$), or has an aversion to both (where $c < 0$). In both instances these results are inconsistent with the MVC.

2. THE MEANING OF QUADRATIC UTILITY 381

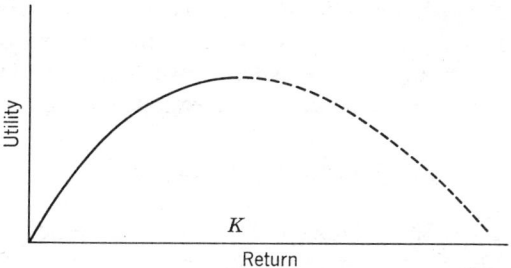

FIGURE XI.1.

relevant; the declining part of the function which is shown by the dotted line must be ignored in decision making problems since it does not fulfill the basic non-negativity constraint on the first derivative. (Beyond the point of inflection, the first derivative is negative.) The relevant range of the quadratic function (where $\beta < 0$) must be restricted, therefore, to the following values of x:

$$x \leq \frac{1}{-2\beta} \equiv K$$

Since β is negative, $1/-2\beta$ must be positive. For the sake of convenience, we shall denote $1/-2\beta$ by K; the quadratic utility function is appropriate only over the domain $x \leq K$ (where $K > 0$). Other values of K are not economically relevant, since in this range additional money increments decrease utility, and this contradicts the basic assumption that an investor is rational and, therefore, prefers more money to less. Thus, use of the quadratic utility function is restricted to a limited range of values, which greatly detracts from its usefulness.

The quadratic utility function is appropriate only for relatively low returns (those below K), which precludes its use for many types of investments, especially those which like lotteries have some very high values of x, albeit with low probabilities of occurrence. This is a very serious drawback since we do not have the option of assuming that some decisions will be reached using a quadratic function while others (those where $x > K$) will be governed by some other function.

Of course it might be argued that since higher values of K shift the point of inflection to the right, the value of K can always be set sufficiently high as to permit the analysis of all possible returns. However, since we have defined $K \equiv 1/-2\beta$, raising K is tantamount to lowering β. Therefore as K grows very large (approaches infinity) β becomes very small (approaches zero); at the limit, the quadratic function reduces to the linear function $U(x) = x$, since βx^2 vanishes. This, of course, may not be acceptable since the linear function represents an investor who is neutral, rather than averse, to risk. Nor is this the only shortcoming of the quadratic utility function: Pratt[3] and Arrow[4] have shown that a quadratic utility function implies ever increasing absolute risk aversion,[5] which contradicts common experience.

2.2 β GREATER THAN ZERO

These shortcomings of the quadratic function cannot be avoided by assuming that β is positive, rather than negative. If $\beta > 0$ the second derivative is positive:

$$U''(x) = 2\beta > 0$$

and therefore the utility function is *convex* throughout. In this case the non-negative restriction is given by

$$U'(x) = 1 + 2\beta > 0$$

And since $\beta > 0$, the relevant range of x is restricted to

$$x > \frac{-1}{2\beta} \equiv K$$

and K is *negative*. This can be seen even more clearly in Figure XI.2, which plots the quadratic utility function on the assumption that β is positive.[6]

---

[3] See J. W. Pratt, "Risk Aversion in the Small and the Large," *Econometrica* 32 (January–April 1964), pp. 122–36.

[4] K. J. Arrow, *Aspects of the Theory of Risk Bearing*, Helsinki, Yrjö Jahnssonin Säätiö, 1965.

[5] Absolute risk aversion, $r(x)$, is defined as $r(x) = -U''(x)/U'(x)$. When the utility function is quadratic we find that the larger the value of x, the higher the degree of risk aversion; the first two derivatives of the quadratic function are

$$U'(x) = 1 + 2\beta x$$
$$-U''(x) = -2\beta$$

so that the measure of absolute risk aversion equals

$$r(x) = \frac{-U''(x)}{U'(x)} = \frac{-2\beta}{1 + 2\beta x}$$

Taking the first derivative of this function, we see that risk aversion rises, because

$$r'(x) = \frac{4\beta^2}{(1 + 2\beta x)^2} > 0$$

[6] The function is a parabola with its minimum point at $K = x = -1/2\beta$. If we set x equal to zero, we see that the utility function passes through the origin:

$$U(0) = 0 + \beta(0)^2 = 0$$

3. THE MEAN-VARIANCE CRITERION

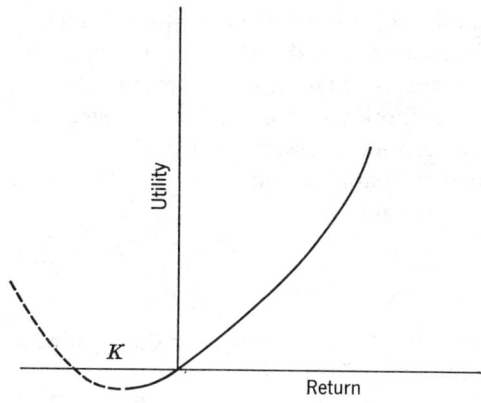

FIGURE XI.2.

This function is convex in the relevant range, that is for values of x greater than K, and is appropriate for risk lovers. And while it can be used to analyze investment options with high degrees of asymmetry, such as a lottery, the convex utility function does not jibe with everyday experience. In particular it cannot account for the phenomenon of insurance, and it stands in contradiction to the empirical evidence on risk aversion in securities markets (see Chapter VII). For this reason we shall ignore the possibility that the utility function is convex and restrict our discussion of the quadratic function to the case where $\beta < 0$ and $U''(x) < 0$.

3. THE MEAN-VARIANCE CRITERION FOR THE CASE OF QUADRATIC UTILITY

The shortcomings of the quadratic utility assumption are so serious (and so well known as well) that one might assume that it should simply be dropped from consideration. Indeed, there is much to be said for this approach! Despite this, almost all of the relevant literature in economics and finance assumes a quadratic utility function.[7] This reflects both the mathematical

---

[7] See, for example, Markowitz (1959), *op cit.;* Tobin (1958), *op. cit.;* W. Fellner, *Probability and Profit*, Homewood, Ill., Irwin, 1965; M. Hamburg and W. F. Matlock, "Maximizing Insurance Buyers' Utility," *Management Science* 14 (February 1968); M. K. Richter, "Cardinal Utility Portfolio Selection and Taxation," *The Review of Economic Studies* XXVII (June 1960); D. D. Hester, and J. Tobin, *Risk Aversion and Portfolio Choice*, Cowles Foundation Monograph 19, New York, Wiley, 1967. Also J. Mossin, "Security Pricing and Investment Criteria in Competitive Markets," *American Economic Review* LIX (December 1969).

convenience of using this particular type of function and the fact that a quadratic utility function which depends only on the first two moments of the random variable distribution fits so well with the MVC, which is defined in terms of these same two moments.

To show the connection between the MVC and the quadratic utility function let us assume a distribution of returns x_i with (subjective or objective) probabilities equal to P_i. The expected return and variance of this distribution are

$$Ex = \sum p_i x_i \tag{11.1}$$

$$Var(x) = \sum P_i(x_i - Ex)^2 = \sum P_i x_i^2 - (\sum P_i x_i)^2 \tag{11.2}$$

Assuming that β is negative the quadratic utility function has the following form:

$$U(x) = x + \beta x^2 \tag{11.3}$$

Since the investor maximizes expected utility, we calculate the expectation of (11.3) as follows:

$$\begin{aligned} EU(x) &= \sum P_i U(x_i) = \sum P_i(x_i + \beta x_i^2) \\ &= \sum P_i x_i + \beta \sum P_i x_i^2 \\ &= Ex + \beta Ex^2 \end{aligned}$$

From Equation (11.2) we see that

$$Ex^2 = \sigma^2(x) + (Ex)^2 \tag{11.4}$$

and therefore the expected utility is a function of the first two moments of the distribution of returns:

$$EU(x) = Ex + \beta(Ex)^2 + \beta\sigma^2(x) \tag{11.5}$$

Since β is negative, the above function clearly shows that the investor is averse to variance; that is, other things being equal, the higher the variance, the lower the investor's expected utility. Will the investor always prefer a high expected return? The answer is not immediately evident from the above equation, since the sign of the expression $Ex + \beta(Ex)^2$ is not clear because β is negative. To answer this question we first differentiate the utility function with respect to Ex and determine its sign:

$$\frac{\partial EU(x)}{\partial Ex} = 1 + 2\beta Ex \tag{11.6}$$

This expression must be positive since we have assumed the first derivative of the quadratic utility function to be non-negative. Thus for all possible values of x there exists

$$U'(x) = 1 + 2\beta x \geq 0 \tag{11.7}$$

4. THE QUADRATIC UTILITY CRITERION (QUC)

Multiplying Equation (11.7) by $p(x)$ (the probability of obtaining x) does not affect the inequality, and therefore we can write

$$1 \cdot p(x) + 2\beta p(x) x \geq 0 \qquad (11.8)$$

Summing all the x observations does not affect the inequality either (because we are adding only positive values).

$$1 \cdot \sum p(x) + 2\beta \sum p(x) x = 1 + 2\beta Ex \geq 0 \qquad (11.9)$$

Since we must have at least one value for x for which $1 + 2\beta x_i > 0$,[8] we can conclude that $1 + 2\beta Ex > 0$. Thus for a given variance, the higher the expected return, the greater the investor's expected utility.

In sum, the quadratic function implies an increase in investors' utility if either the expected return (for a given variance) is increased or the variance (for a given expected return) is decreased. This is in accordance with the popular interpretation of the MVC, where expected returns represent an investment's profitability and the variance its risk. Therefore an investor with a quadratic utility function who is confronted with two options x and y which fulfill the conditions for MVC dominance—$Ex \geq Ey$ and $Var(x) \leq Var(y)$ (with at least one of the strong inequalities holding)—will invariably prefer x to y. This is always true since for such an investor the higher returns or lower variance of x represents a higher level of utility.

4. THE QUADRATIC UTILITY CRITERION (QUC)

Within the confines of the quadratic utility assumption, and *without* recourse to additional information, we can improve the MVC, that is, define an alternative criterion which reduces the efficient subset.

Let us assume that an investor is choosing between two options, x and y, whose expected returns and variances are known. This is precisely the information needed to apply the MVC. Following Equation (11.5) we calculate the investor's expected utility from options x and y, respectively:

$$EU(x) = Ex + \beta(Ex)^2 + \beta\sigma_x^2 \qquad (11.10)$$

$$EU(y) = Ey + \beta(Ey)^2 + \beta\sigma_y^2 \qquad (11.11)$$

Let us assume that $Ex \geq Ey$. To determine which option is preferable we deduct (11.11) from (11.10); if the difference is positive this indicates that x

---

[8] We require this since should $U'(x) = 0$, for all values of x, the utility function is linear and parallel to the horizontal axis. This is an irrelevant case, since with such a function the investor's utility is independent of his income.

dominates y because $EU(x) - EU(y) > 0$; if the difference is negative, option y dominates.[9] Now let us assume that the difference was found to be positive, and therefore x is the preferable option. The following inequality must exist:

$$EU(x) - EU(y) = (Ex - Ey) + \beta[(Ex)^2 - (Ey)^2] + \beta(\sigma_x^2 - \sigma_y^2) > 0 \quad (11.12)$$

Dividing all the arguments by a positive number does not change the inequality, so we can obtain

$$\frac{1}{-\beta}(Ex - Ey) - [(Ex)^2 - (Ey)^2] - (\sigma_x^2 - \sigma_y^2) > 0 \quad (11.13)$$

(The reader should remember that $\beta < 0$ and therefore $-\beta > 0$.)

Recalling the definition, $-(1/2\beta) = K$, we have $-(1/\beta) = 2K$. Substituting $2K$ for $-(1/\beta)$ in Equation (11.13) gives

$$2K(Ex - Ey) - [(Ex)^2 - (Ey)^2] - (\sigma_x^2 - \sigma_y^2) > 0 \quad (11.14)$$

By factoring the second expression we find that $(Ex)^2 - (Ey)^2 = (Ex - Ey)(Ex + Ey)$; substituting this result in Equation (11.14) and putting $(Ex - Ey)$ before the brackets we obtain

$$(Ex - Ey)[2K - (Ex + Ey)] - (\sigma_x^2 - \sigma_y^2) > 0 \quad (11.15)$$

which can also be written as

$$2(Ex - Ey)\left[K - \frac{Ex + Ey}{2}\right] - (\sigma_x^2 - \sigma_y^2) > 0 \quad (11.16)$$

In other words, if an option x dominates an option y, Inequality (11.16) must hold.

Looking back at Figure XI.1 we can see that K is defined to be larger than all observations of the distributive of returns; it immediately follows that $K > Ex$ and $K > Ey$ so that $K > (Ex + Ey)/2$ and therefore the bracketed expression of (11.16) is positive.

If the MVC conditions for dominance hold—

$$Ex \geq Ey$$
$$\sigma_x^2 \leq \sigma_y^2$$

Inequality 11.16 also must hold. What if the MVC conditions do *not* hold? Can we be certain that the dominance of one of the options cannot be established?

---

[9] We arbitrarily assumed $Ex \geq Ey$. However, if $Ey \geq Ex$ we simply reverse the process and deduct Equation (11.10) from Equation (11.11) and the same conclusions apply.

4. THE QUADRATIC UTILITY CRITERION (QUC)

We can see from Inequality (11.16) that a preference relationship can sometimes be established, even though the MVC conditions do not hold, and therefore that the MVC efficient group can be reduced without additional information. Let us use the findings to define an optimal criterion for the quadratic utility case.

Let us assume that (11.16) exists, and that $Ex \geq Ey$. We say nothing about the variances at this stage. Substituting Ex for K in (11.16), we derive the following expression:

$$2(Ex - Ey)\left[Ex - \frac{Ex + Ey}{2}\right] - (\sigma_x^2 - \sigma_y^2) \quad (11.17)$$

If (11.17) is positive (11.16) must also be positive, since the expression within the brackets in (11.16) includes K rather than Ex, and K is greater than Ex by definition, and we may conclude that x dominates y. Thus option x dominates option y if $Ex \geq Ey$ and (11.17) is positive:

$$2(Ex - Ey)\left[Ex - \frac{Ex + Ey}{2}\right] - (\sigma_x^2 - \sigma_y^2) > 0 \quad (11.18)$$

This expression, in turn, can be simplified to

$$(Ex - Ey)^2 - (\sigma_x^2 - \sigma_y^2) > 0 \quad (11.19)$$

Using this result we now define the Quadratic Utility Criterion (QUC), which is an improved version of the MVC for the quadratic utility case. According to the QUC an option x dominates an option y if the following two relationships hold:

$$Ex \geq Ey \quad (11.20)$$
$$(Ex - Ey)^2 - (\sigma_x^2 - \sigma_y^2) > 0 \quad (11.20')$$

It is clear from these two expressions that if the MVC is fulfilled ($Ex \geq Ey$; $\sigma_x^2 \leq \sigma_y^2$), the QUC conditions must also exist. If an option is MVC inefficient, of necessity it is also QUC inefficient. But we can readily demonstrate that not all MVC efficient options are also QUC efficient, that is, there is a possibility of reducing the MVC effect set. Consider the example of the following two investment options:

	Option X	Option Y
Expected Return	10	5
Variance	12	10

Both these investments are included in the MVC efficient set since $Ex > Ey$ and $\sigma x > \sigma y$. However, if we invoke the QUC, we find that x dominates y, because $Ex > Ey$ and (11.20′) also holds:

$$(10 - 5)^2 - (12 - 10) = 25 - 2 = 23 > 0$$

In sum: when we assume quadratic utility it is possible to reduce the MVC efficient subset solely on the basis of the first two moments of the distribution of returns. This is precisely the same information required by the MVC.[10] Thus the MVC is not an optimal criterion, even for the quadratic utility case, since its efficient set is not the minimal one. The MVC, as we have seen, constitutes a sufficient, but not a necessary, condition for preference, and therefore may result in a subset which is "too rich" in efficient options. The QUC provides an improved criterion for the quadratic utility case. This criterion generates a set of efficient options which is a subset of the MVC efficient set so that it cannot be larger than the MVC efficient group, while sometimes it may reduce the size of the efficient set without additional information on the distribution of returns.

5. THE EXPECTED GAIN–CONFIDENCE LIMIT CRITERION (EGC)

Despite its widespread use, the indiscriminate application of the MVC as a decision rule may lead to unreasonable results. To eliminate paradoxical cases, Baumol, in a very well known article,[11] formulated an alternative criterion, the "Expected Gain–Confidence Limit Criterion" (hereafter referred to as the EGC or the "Baumol" criterion). Table XI-1 reproduces Baumol's numerical example. According to the MVC both options would be included in the efficient set, since $Ey < Ex$, but $\sigma_y^2 < \sigma_x^2$. But Baumol argues that the variance (or standard deviation) cannot in itself serve as a measure of risk. An investor is averse to variance because a high variance means the possibility of a high deviation from the mean return, and a downward deviation leads to losses. From statistical theory, we know that the probability that an investor's return will be lower than k standard deviations below the expected return is bounded by $1/k^2$, so that the larger k, the lower this

---

[10] If additional information is available, even more effective criteria can be constructed; and the more information available (for example, the index of asymmetry and so on), the smaller the efficient subset. Improved criteria for different levels of information are described in G. Hanoch and H. Levy, "Efficient Portfolio Selection with Quadratic and Cubic Utility," *The Journal of Business* 43 (April 1970), pp. 181–89.

[11] See W. J. Baumol, "An Expected Gain–Confidence Limit Criterion for Portfolio Selection," *Management Science* 10 (October 1963).

5. EXPECTED GAIN–CONFIDENCE LIMIT

TABLE XI-1.

	Option y	Option x
Expected Return (E)	8	15
Standard deviation (σ)	2	4
$E + \sigma$	10	19
$E - \sigma$	6	11

probability.[12] To illustrate: In the example given in Table XI-1 the standard deviation of option x is 4, higher than the standard deviation of option y (2). The expected return of option x is far higher than that for investment y, so that

$$Ex - \sigma_x = 11 \qquad Ey - \sigma_y = 6$$

Furthermore

$$Ex - 2\sigma_x = 7 \qquad Ey - 2\sigma_y = 4$$

so that even if the return from option x should deviate downward by two standard deviations, the return on x still exceeds the return on option y, for a similar deviation of 2σ. However, if we choose a sufficiently large number of standard deviations, say 10, the result will be reversed,

$$Ex - 10\sigma_x = -25 \qquad Ey - 10\sigma y = -12$$

The basic argument put forward by Baumol is that the probability of obtaining such a large deviation is negligible and can be ignored. Suppose we have two normal distributions; the probability of obtaining a deviation of 2 standard deviations, or more, below the mean is 2.275%, and the probability of a deviation of 3 standard deviations is only 0.135%. Baumol suggests that a lower limit that depends on k be set, and that the possibility that returns may deviate by more than $k\sigma$ below the mean should be ignored. This is the essence of the EGC, which states that an option x is preferable to an option y if

$$Ex \geq Ey$$

and

$$Lx = Ex - k\sigma_x \geq Ey - k\sigma_y = Ly$$

---

[12] By Chebyshev's Inequality,

$$Pr\{|x - Ex| \geq k\sigma\} \leq \frac{1}{k^2}$$

Thus the probability of a particular observation being greater than k standard deviations cannot exceed $1/k^2$. See, for example, D. A. S. Fraser, *Statistics: An Introduction*, New York, Wiley, 1960, p. 99 and the statistical supplement at the end of the book.

where Lx and Ly represent the "Lower Limits" of possible returns for x and y, respectively. For a given k, the lower limit L serves as the indicator of an option's risk—the higher the limit, the lower the risk. Thus the EGC rejects the variance as a risk index and replaces it with a composite measure which reflects the expected return as well as the dispersion. According to this approach, many options with a relatively high variance will still be relatively safe as long as their expected returns are sufficiently high, given the intuitively appealing assumption that investors are sensitive to losses in excess of some absolute limit. Using this criterion, and assuming $k = 2$, we can readily see that option x of our example dominates option y, by the EGC, although the MVC is unable to discriminate between these two investments, both of which are included in the MVC efficient set.[13]

5.1 THE RELATIONSHIP OF THE EGC TO OTHER EFFICIENCY CRITERIA

The EGC efficient set is a subset of the MVC efficient set. In order to demonstrate this let us assume that two options, x and y, fulfill the MVC conditions:

$$Ex \geq Ey \quad \text{and} \quad \sigma_x \leq \sigma_y$$

Since k is a positive number, the EGC conditions must also hold:

$$Ex - k\sigma_x \geq Ey - k\sigma_y$$

However, the relationship is not symmetrical. Fulfillment of the EGC conditions does not necessarily imply the fulfillment of the MVC conditions, which we have already demonstrated in the above numerical example for the assumption that $k = 2$.

The essence of the EGC is a further reduction of the MVC subset of efficient options. But on reflection not every reduction of the efficient group is desirable. This can be seen by considering the two cases for which the MVC provides a relevant decision rule.

(a) *Concave Utility Functions.* As was proved in Chapter IX, the MVC provides an optimal decision rule for all risk averters if the distributions of returns belong to an independent two-parameter family and all the cumulative probability distributions intersect. In cases where they do not intersect the TSC (which first applies the GC) provides the optimal criterion. Since both of these efficient sets are *optimal*, any further reduction using the EGC is

---

[13] For an alternative but somewhat similar criterion, see A. Roy, "Safety First and the Holding of Assets," *Econometrica* 20 (July 1952), pp. 431–49.

5. EXPECTED GAIN–CONFIDENCE LIMIT

undesirable, since options which might be chosen by some risk averters will be excluded.

(b) *Quadratic Utility Functions.* In this case the MVC is *not* optimal, and as we already have shown the QUC provides the optimal criterion for this case. The QUC requires, in addition to $Ex \geq Ey$,

$$(Ex - Ey)^2 - (\sigma_x^2 - \sigma_y^2) > 0 \tag{11.20'}$$

The EGC requires, in addition to $Ex \geq Ey$,

$$Ex - k\sigma_x > Ey - k\sigma_y \tag{11.21}$$

Both these criteria reduce the MVC efficient set, but not to the same extent. Factoring the expression $(\sigma_x^2 - \sigma_y^2)$, transposing terms, and dividing by $Ex - Ey$, Inequality (11.20') becomes

$$(Ex - Ey) > \frac{(\sigma_x + \sigma_y)}{Ex - Ey}(\sigma_x - \sigma_y) \tag{11.20''}$$

and the EGC conditions can be reformulated as

$$(Ex - Ey) > k(\sigma_x - \sigma_y) \tag{11.21'}$$

Thus the EGC and the optimal QUC are identical only if

$$k = \frac{\sigma_x + \sigma_y}{Ex - Ey} \tag{11.22}$$

For other values of k we may obtain an EGC efficient set that differs from the QUC set. And since the QUC is an optimal criterion the EGC will be optimal only for the value of k given in (11.22).[14]

5.2 THE EGC AND THE EFFICIENCY FRONTIER

The EGC, as we have seen, reduces the MVC efficient subset, but the question arises which options are eliminated. Figure XI.3 sets out the locus of MVC efficient points by the curve cbd;[15] this curve is a graphical representation of

---

[14] We might also note that there is no unique method for determining the value of k. Just how small is a probability that can be ignored? This depends on the personal tastes of the investors and it is quite likely that different individuals will choose different values of k. Thus each investor constructs his own particular efficient set, which vitiates the basic idea underlying the efficiency analysis.

[15] Figure XI.3 follows Baumol's practice and measures the standard deviation along the vertical axis and the return along the horizontal axis.

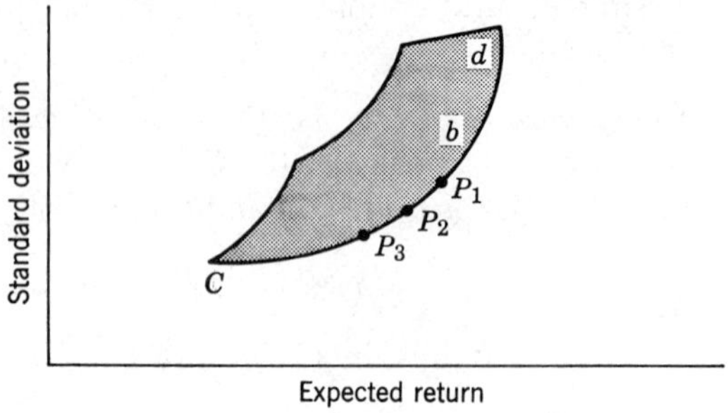

FIGURE XI.3.

the following functional relationship: $\sigma = f(E)$. Substituting this function in Baumol's "lower confidence limit" condition, we have

$$L = E - k\sigma = E - kf(E) \tag{11.23}$$

Now consider two portfolios, A and B, where

$$E(x_A) > E(x_B)$$

In order for both portfolios to be included in the EGC efficient set the following inequality must hold:[16]

which means that
$$L_A < L_B$$

$$\frac{\partial L}{\partial E} < 0$$

Differentiating (11.23) we find

$$\frac{\partial L}{\partial E} = 1 - kf'(E) < 0 \tag{11.24}$$

Hence

$$f'(E) > \frac{1}{k} \tag{11.25}$$

This implies that the EGC efficient set includes only that segment of the MVC efficiency locus for which (11.25) holds. For example, assume that points p_1, p_2, and p_3 (of Figure XI.3) represent slopes of 1, 1/2, and 1/3 respectively. If we set $k = 1$, the EGC efficiency locus is given by the segment p_1bd; similarly, setting $k = 2$ gives an efficient locus of p_2bd, while if

---

[16] Otherwise, portfolio A dominates portfolio B, and the latter is eliminated from the EGC efficient set.

6. A COMPARISON OF ALTERNATIVE EFFICIENCY CRITERIA

$k = 3$ the EGC efficiency frontier becomes p_3bd. As $k \to \infty$, the EGC efficient set approaches the MVC efficient set cbd.

In sum, the EGC systematically reduces the lower tail of the MVC efficiency locus. As k increases, the EGC gives higher and higher weights to the standard deviation (since $L = E - k\sigma$), and the EGC and MVC efficient sets become identical.

6. A COMPARISON OF ALTERNATIVE EFFICIENCY CRITERIA: AN EXAMPLE

To illustrate the differences in the compositions of the efficient subsets of the three criteria presented in this chapter (MVC, EGC, and QUC) let us consider the example of an investor who is confronted with the eight portfolios whose expected returns and standard deviations are set out in Table XI-2.

Applying the MVC, we find that portfolios 1, 2, 4, 5, 6, and 8 are included in the efficient set, while 3 and 7 are relegated to the inefficient group. Thus portfolio 2 dominates (and therefore eliminates) portfolio 3, since the first has both a higher expected return and a lower standard deviation. Similarly, portfolio 4 dominates portfolio 7.

Which of these same eight portfolios is efficient according to the EGC? We shall carry out this calculation for three alternative assumptions: (a) $k = 1$; (b) $k = 2$; (c) $k = 10$. We know that the EGC efficient set of portfolios (for each value of k) is a subset of the MVC efficient set. Since portfolios 3 and 7 are eliminated by the MVC we can restrict ourselves to a comparison of the remaining six portfolios, the data for which are given in Table XI-3.

Recalling the EGC conditions

$$Ex \geq Ey$$

and

$$Ex - k\sigma_x \geq Ey - k\sigma_y$$

TABLE XI-2.

	Portfolios							
	1	2	3	4	5	6	7	8
Expected Return	8	10	6	12	18	13	10	7
Standard Deviation	2	4	7	5	12	10	10	1

TABLE XI-3.

	1	2	4	5	6	8
E	8	10	12	18	13	7
σ	2	4	5	12	10	1
$E - \sigma$	6	6	7	6	3	6
$E - 2\sigma$	4	2	2	−6	−7	5
$E - 10\sigma$	−12	−30	−38	−102	−87	−3

(with at least one strong inequality holding), the data of Table XI-3 show that for $k = 1$ the efficient set includes only two portfolios: 4 and 5; for $k = 2$ four portfolios are included: 1, 4, 5 and 8; and where $k = 10$ the EGC set is the same as the MVC set, that is, all six portfolios are included: 1, 2, 4, 5, 6, and 8.

This result can be generalized as follows: when $k \to \infty$, the EGC and MVC provide identical decision rules; the smaller the value of k, the smaller the EGC efficient relative to the MVC set; when $k = 0$, the second EGC condition becomes identical with the first, and the EGC efficient set is reduced to a single portfolio, the one with the highest expected return.

Now let us examine the composition of the QUC efficient set. Again this will be a subset of the MVC group so that our attention can be restricted to the six portfolios included in the MVC efficient set.

Recalling the QUC requirements:
$$Ex \geq Ey$$
and
$$(Ex - Ey)^2 - (\sigma_x^2 - \sigma_y^2) > 0$$
we find that comparing portfolios 1 and 2,
$$(10 - 8)^2 - (16 - 4) = 4 - 12 < 0$$
Comparing portfolios 1 and 4,
$$(12 - 8)^2 - (25 - 4) = 16 - 21 < 0$$
Comparing portfolios 1 and 5,
$$(18 - 8)^2 - (144 - 4) = 100 - 140 < 0$$
Comparing portfolios 1 and 6,
$$(13 - 8)^2 - (100 - 4) = 25 - 96 < 0$$
Comparing portfolios 1 and 8,
$$(8 - 7)^2 - (4 - 1) = 1 - 3 < 0$$

Since none of the five portfolios dominates portfolio 1, the latter is included in the QUC efficient set. Comparing portfolio 2 with all the others we find:

Portfolios 2 and 4 $(12 - 10)^2 - (25 - 16) = 4 - 9 < 0$

Portfolios 2 and 5 $(18 - 10)^2 - (144 - 16) = 64 - 128 < 0$

Portfolios 2 and 6 $(13 - 10)^2 - (100 - 16) = 9 - 84 < 0$

Portfolios 2 and 8 $(10 - 7)^2 - (16 - 1) = 9 - 15 < 0$

Thus portfolio 2 is also included in the QUC efficient set. Comparing portfolio 4 with the remaining portfolios we find:

Portfolios 4 and 5 $(18 - 12)^2 - (144 - 25) = 36 - 119 < 0$

Portfolios 4 and 6 $(13 - 12)^2 - (100 - 25) = 1 - 75 < 0$

Portfolios 4 and 8 $(12 - 7)^2 - (25 - 1) = 25 - 24 = 1 > 0$

Portfolio 4 dominates portfolio 8, thereby eliminating portfolio 8 from the efficient group. Finally, comparing portfolios 5 and 6 we find:

$$(18 - 13)^2 - (144 - 100) = 25 - 44 < 0$$

Thus, the QUC efficient set includes five portfolios: 1, 2, 4, 5, and 6. Portfolio 8, which was included in the MVC efficient set, is eliminated by the QUC without additional information, since a rational investor, having a quadratic utility function, will always prefer portfolio 4 to portfolio 8. Neither does the EGC provide an optimal criterion: when k was set equal to 1 or 2, the EGC efficient set is too small, and eliminates portfolios which could well prove optimal for some quadratic utility functions. Moreover, when $k = 2$, not only are some efficient portfolios excluded, but portfolio 8, which is not QUC efficient, is included in the EGC efficient set.

7. SUMMARY

A quadratic utility function of the general form $U(x) = a + bx + cx^2$, is the only function which depends solely on the first two moments of the distribution of returns. Since the MVC is also a function of the first two moments, many economists have assumed quadratic utility when analyzing portfolio problems.

The quadratic function has several serious drawbacks. The assumption of quadratic utility is appropriate only for relatively low returns, which precludes its use for many types of investments. Moreover, Arrow and Pratt have shown that a quadratic utility function implies ever increasing absolute risk aversion, which contradicts everyday experience. (Attempts to avoid these problems by constraining the values of the coefficients of the function so that it is convex, rather than concave, in the relevant range are not satisfactory since a convex utility function contradicts the empirical evidence on risk aversion in the stock market.)

The great popularity of a quadratic type of function among researchers can be attributed only to its mathematical convenience and the fact that the quadratic utility assumption fits so well with the MVC. The quadratic utility function implies an increase in investors' utility if either the expected return (given the variance) is increased, or the variance (given the expected return) is decreased. This is in accordance with the intuitive interpretation of the MVC, namely, that expected returns represent an investment option's profitability and the variance its risk.

Within the confines of the quadratic utility assumption, the MVC is not an optimal efficiency criterion. Without recourse to additional information on the distribution of returns, an alternative criterion can be defined which reduces the MVC efficient set for all quadratic utility functions. The optimal Quadratic Utility Criterion (QUC) can be defined as follows: An option x dominates an option y, by the QUC, if

$$E_x \geq E_y$$

and

$$(E_x - E_y)^2 - (\sigma_x^2 - \sigma_y^2) > 0$$

We have shown that if an option is QUC efficient, of necessity, it is also MVC efficient, but that not all MVC efficient options are also QUC efficient, and therefore there exists a possibility of reducing the MVC efficient set. Thus in the quadratic utility case, the MVC constitutes a sufficient, but not a necessary, condition for dominance.

Baumol, in a well known article, has attempted to improve on the MVC by formulating an alternative criterion, the "Expected Gain–Confidence Limit Criterion" (EGC). Baumol argues that the variance (standard deviation) in itself cannot serve as a measure of risk, and should be replaced by a composite measure which reflects the expected return as well as the dispersion. The EGC is defined as follows: an option x dominates an option y, by the EGC, if

$$E_x \geq E_y$$

and

$$L_x = E_x - k\sigma_x \geq E_y - k\sigma_y = L_y$$

where L_x and L_y represent "lower confidence limits" of possible returns. For a given k, the confidence limit is the measure of an option's risk; the higher the limit, the lower the risk. According to this approach many options with relatively high variances may still be relatively attractive if their expected returns are sufficiently high.

7. SUMMARY

The EGC efficient set is a subset of the MVC efficient set. However the relationship is not symmetrical; fulfillment of the EGC conditions does not necessarily imply the fulfillment of the MVC conditions. Thus the essence of the EGC is a further reduction of the MVC subset of efficient options. In particular, the EGC systematically reduces the lower tail of the MVC efficiency locus. But not all of these reductions are desirable, and in general, the EGC does not constitute an optimal efficiency criterion.

QUESTIONS AND PROBLEMS

11.1 (a) Can a quadratic utility function of the form $U(X) = X - (1/20)X^2$ be used to explain investors' decisions where a typical investment option has the following distribution of returns? Explain.

Return	Probability
−2	9/10
30	1/10

(b) What is your answer using the following utility function: $U(X) = X + 2X^2$

(c) Using the above example, determine the permissible values of β in the general quadratic utility function

$$U(X) = X + \beta X^2$$

(d) How does your answer to (c) change if, in addition, we assume risk aversion?

11.2 An investor with the utility function $U(X) = X + \beta X^2$ is confronted with the following two options:

	A	B
$E(X)$	10	12
$Var(X)$	9	0

Which option will be chosen if we assume $\beta = 8$? which option will be chosen if we assume $\beta = -1$?

11.3 Given the following investment options:

	X	Y
$E(X)$	20	10
$Var(X)$	12	10

(a) Does XDY by the MVC?
(b) Does XDY by the QUC?

11.4 "The EGC is optimal if a preliminary screening is carried out using the GC." Appraise.

11.5 What is the relationship of the EGC efficient set to the MVC efficient set?

11.6 Prove that the QUC efficient set is a subset of the MVC efficient set.

11.7 "A preliminary screening using the RAC ensures that the EGC efficient set is optimal." Appraise.

SELECTED REFERENCES

See Chapter IX.

Chapter XII
Investors' Wealth, the Discount Rate, and the Relative Effectiveness of Efficiency Criteria

1. INTRODUCTION

In the previous four chapters a number of efficiency criteria, or decision rules, were defined. These criteria are designed to divide all potential investment options (individual securities as well as all attainable portfolio combinations) into two mutually exclusive sets: a subset of efficient options, out of which all investors (of a particular class) will invariably make their optimal choices; and an inefficient subset, which includes those options that are dominated by at least one of the efficient securities or portfolios. Thus, efficiency analysis is concerned with isolating the efficient subset of portfolios for all investors of a specified class.

The appropriateness of a particular criterion can be judged at two distinct levels:

(a) The class of investors for whom a particular criterion is appropriate can be examined; here the relevant questions relate to the utility assumptions underlying the analysis and the degree of comparability *within* the class. In particular, our assumptions must be carefully examined to ensure that the decision rule in question holds for *all* members of the class. In the next two sections of this chapter we shall critically examine the assumptions which have been made regarding initial wealth and the timing of future returns.

(b) The degree to which a given decision rule reduces the set of attainable options can be examined. This is an empirical question designed to test the size of the efficient sets which results from the preliminary screening of alternative investment options using each of the efficiency criteria. To the degree that a criterion does not significantly reduce the size of the set, investment analysis is not facilitated, and the criterion's contribution is negligible. Section 4 is devoted to an empirical analysis of relative effectiveness.

2. INVESTORS' WEALTH

All the efficiency criteria presented in this book are based on the distributions of anticipated future outcomes, or on the first two moments of these distributions. In order to simplify the analysis, the criteria have been defined in terms of a random variable x which denotes the money returns from a given option. This is tantamount to ignoring the possible influence of investors' wealth on investment decisions.

However, if an efficiency criterion is to be meaningful, it must hold for all investors within a particular class. If an option x dominates an option y, by the Risk Aversion Criterion for example, the dominance must hold for *all* risk-averse investors, *independent of their wealth*. But the latter requirement raises a thorny question. It is almost intuitively obvious that an investor whose initial wealth w equals $1,000 may not consider an additional dollar of income to be as important as will an investor whose initial wealth is only $100. Clearly the "poor" man may be expected to place a somewhat higher value on the additional dollar since it represents, to him, a 1% increase in his wealth.[1] This possibility is *not* reflected in an efficiency criterion based on returns. Since the money returns represent increments (or decrements) to individual's wealth, which typically varies from individual to individual, the additional utility afforded by the random variable x must be measured in terms of $U(w + x)$ rather than in terms of $U(x)$, where U denotes the utility function and w the investor's initial wealth.

The purpose of this section is to show that under reasonable conditions, the composition of the efficient sets generated by the various criteria is independent of investors' wealth, which greatly enhances the usefulness of the analysis. In simple terms it means that if Henry Ford and the authors are both risk-averse (have concave utility functions), the RAC efficient set is appropriate for all, despite the rather appalling differences in their initial wealth.

[1] See Chapter VI.

2. INVESTORS' WEALTH

2.1 WEALTH AS A NONSTOCHASTIC VARIABLE

To simplify the analysis let us *initially* assume that investors' wealth is not a random variable. This means that while different investors may have different initial wealth positions, their wealth is known with certainty, and therefore is single-valued. In this case determining the preference order between any two options x and y requires the comparison of $EU(w + x)$ with $EU(w + y)$ and not $EU(x)$ and $EU(y)$ as was done in the previous chapters. But if w is *not* a random variable, adding the term w to the random variables x and y shifts the cumulative distributions at every coordinate, so that the relationship between the two distributions does not change. Since the GC and the RAC are defined solely in terms of the relationship between the cumulative probability distributions, it follows that the efficient set is the same whether or not initial wealth is considered. The reason for this is that while wealth may vary from investor to investor, as long as it is not a random variable, wealth is a constant for *each* individual. If one option dominated a second option by either the GC or RAC before, the addition of a constant to an individual's utility function leaves the relationship unchanged. Since this holds for one investor, by repeating the experiment, we can readily see that it holds for all investors.

Let us illustrate this result by considering the two options set out in Table XII–1. Even a cursory glance at the data shows that option F is dominant, using the GC. Now assume that a particular investor has an initial wealth w_1. Table XII–2 sets out the relevant data for this case. Once again it is clear that option F continues to dominate by the GC, since the addition of w_1 only shifts the distributions at every coordinate. Thus if they did not intersect before wealth was considered, taking *nonstochastic* wealth into account cannot change this result. If we now consider a second investor with a wealth of $w_2 \neq w_1$, we can repeat the experiment with the same results, and so on for the class of all investors.

The same conclusions hold for the RAC since shifting the cumulative probability distributions by a constant amount leaves the relationship

TABLE XII–1.

Option F		Option G	
Probability	Return	Probability	Return
1/2	10	1/2	5
1/2	20	1/2	10

TABLE XII-2.

	Option F		Option G	
	Probability	Return	Probability	Return
	1/2	$w_1 + 10$	1/2	$w_1 + 5$
	1/2	$w_1 + 20$	1/2	$w_1 + 10$

between the areas under the curves (integrals) unchanged as well. Nor does the addition of a nonstochastic wealth term have any effect on the efficient sets generated by the Mean–Variance or Quadratic Utility criteria. This can be illustrated for the MVC. Let us assume that an option x dominates an option y by the MVC so that the following holds:

$$E(x) \geq E(y)$$
$$Var\ (x) \leq Var\ (y)$$

What happens if we incorporate the investor's initial wealth w? Clearly, adding the same term to each side of an inequality leaves the inequality unchanged so that if

$$E(x) \geq E(y)$$

this implies

$$E(x + w_1) \geq E(y + w_1)$$

and if $Var\ (x) \leq Var\ (y)$ this implies $Var\ (x + w_1) \leq Var\ (y + w_1)$. The same can be shown for the Quadratic Utility Criterion.

2.2 WEALTH AS A STOCHASTIC VARIABLE

Unfortunately, the demonstration that the efficiency criteria hold up even if nonstochastic wealth is considered is, on reflection, not very convincing. The major criticism that can be leveled relates to the assumption that wealth is a single-valued variable. There can be little doubt that investors' wealth should be considered a random variable, since wealth represents the present value of incomes from all sources: wages, interest, dividends, rent, and so on. And as the income components are not known with certainty, neither is their present value. Wealth, therefore, must be treated (as we have already treated investment returns) as a stochastic variable.

Fortunately, it can be shown that given the assumption that w and x (or y) are independent random variables, all four efficiency criteria are valid, independent of investors' wealth. A formal mathematical proof is given in

2. INVESTORS' WEALTH

TABLE XII-3.

Option x		Option y	
Probability	Return	Probability	Return
1/2	10	1/2	4
1/2	20	1/2	8

Appendices XII–1 and XII–2; here we shall confine ourselves to a demonstration that the efficient set generated by the GC remains invariant with respect to wealth, even when wealth is considered to be a random variable.

Consider any investor who must choose between the investment options set out in Table XII–3. It is clear, by inspection, that option x dominates option y by the General Criterion, since $F(x) \leq G(y)$ for all values of x and y. This means that all investors, both risk-averse and risk lovers, will always prefer option x to option y.

But does this conclusion hold, independent of an investor's initial wealth? Consider an investor with an initial wealth w which is given by the following probability distribution:

$P(w)$	w
1/2	1000
1/2	2000

To determine the effects of introducing wealth on the efficiency analysis we recalculate the probability distributions of our two options in terms of $(w + x)$ and $(w + y)$. This has been done in Table XII–4. Since we assume independence between w and x and between w and y, the joint probability of receiving any particular combination of wealth and return is given by the product of the individual probabilities. And as all of the individual probabilities are equal to 1/2 in this example, the joint probabilities are given by $1/2 \cdot 1/2 = 1/4$. The cumulative probability distributions, taking wealth into account, are drawn in Figure XII.1. An examination of Figure XII.1

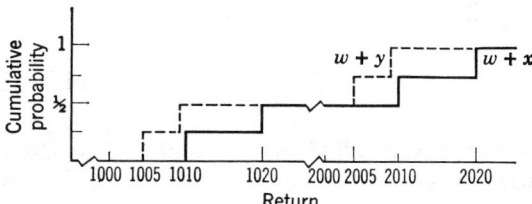

FIGURE XII.1.

TABLE XII-4.

Option x*

Return (x)	Probability $p(x)$	Wealth (w)	Probability $p(w)$	$w + x$	$p(w + x)$
10	1/2	1,000	1/2	1,010	1/4
		2,000	1/2	2,010	1/4
20	1/2	1,000	1/2	1,020	1/4
		2,000	1/2	2,020	1/4

Option y*

Return (y)	Probability $p(y)$	Wealth (w)	Probability $p(w)$	$w + y$	$p(w + y)$
4	1/2	1,000	1/2	1,004	1/4
		2,000	1/2	2,004	1/4
8	1/2	1,000	1/2	1,008	1/4
		2,000	1/2	2,008	1/4

* The probabilities $p(w + x)$ and $p(w + y)$ reflect the assumption of independence between x and w, and between y and w.

and Table XII-4 confirms that the introduction of the random variable wealth leaves the efficiency analysis unchanged, and option $w + x$ dominates option $w + y$. This result holds over the entire range of possible values for initial wealth. Since this holds for other criteria as well (see Appendix) we may conclude that given the intuitively plausible assumption of statistical independence between initial wealth and returns, the efficiency analysis of Chapters VIII through XI is valid for all investors, independent of their wealth.

3. DISCOUNTING INVESTMENT RETURNS

In Part I we pointed out the need to discount all future returns to a common basis if the time value of money was to be taken into account. But despite the fact that all of the efficiency criteria which were developed in previous chapters deal with two-period investment options, they completely ignore the

3. DISCOUNTING INVESTMENT RETURNS

element of timing, and therefore they neglect the possible impact of the discount rate on the composition of the efficient set.

Strictly speaking, such an approach is appropriate when choosing among alternative prospects if there is no lag between the time the decision is made and the time the rewards are received, for example, in the case of a lottery. But financial investment differs from the purchase of a typical lottery ticket in at least one important respect: although the investment decision also can be set out as a two-period decision—period one in which the investment is made, and period two in which the investor sells his portfolio and receives his return (profit or loss)—the time which elapses between the two periods can be short (a day or a week) or as long (one or more years) as the problem calls for.[2] Because of this time lag, an appropriate discount rate must often be applied to the alternative outcomes before a decision can be reached. Thus where the time lag is significant, the distributions (moments) should be compared only after discounting every possible return.

In the efficiency analysis of investment decisions, we have implicitly assumed that the probability distributions of returns in period two are the same for all investors. Thus all investors of a given class choose their efficient subsets from the same set of future distributions. As a result, if a prospect F dominates a prospect G by one of the efficiency criteria, it follows that every investor who fulfills the relevant assumptions of the efficiency criterion will prefer F to G. However, investors with different time values of money use different discount rates, and therefore in general are confronted with different sets of discounted distributions. Thus it appears plausible that an individual investor might have a subset of efficient options which is a function of his particular discount rate. But should this be the case, the concept of an efficient set would lose most of its meaning, and the generality of the efficiency analysis would be impaired.

The following example may help to clarify the problem. Let us assume that investors are considering two options, F and G, whose probability distributions of *undiscounted* returns in the second period are given in Table XII–5. We define

$$\alpha_i \equiv \frac{1}{1 + k_i}$$

where k_i denotes the appropriate discount rate for investor i. In the undiscounted case where $\alpha = 1$ ($k = 0$), the distributions of returns given in Table XII–5 are *identical* for all investors, and therefore if F dominates G,

---

[2] Most empirical studies assume a holding period of one year. See, for example, M. C. Jensen, "Problems in Selecting Security Portfolios," *Journal of Finance* (May 1968); and W. F. Sharpe, "Mutual Fund Performance," *Journal of Business* (January 1966).

TABLE XII-5.

Prospect F		Prospect G	
Return	Probability	Return	Probability
10	1/2	−10	1/3
20	1/2	0	1/3
		+30	1/3

by one of the efficiency criteria it follows that every investor who fulfills the relevant assumptions of the efficiency criterion will prefer F to G. However, investors with different discount rates, in general, are confronted with different sets of discounted distributions, since the discounted distributions depend on the discount factor, which can vary from investor to investor.[3] For example, assuming $\alpha_1 = 0.9$ and $\alpha_2 = 0.8$ results in the two alternative sets of discounted distributions given in Table XII-6. The reader should note that the investor whose discount factor is $\alpha_1(0.9)$ is faced with a set of probability distributions which differs from that faced by the investor whose discount factor is $\alpha_2(0.8)$.

Fortunately, it can be shown that the efficient sets generated by all the efficiency criteria discussed in this book are *invariant* to changes in the discount rate, so there is no need to consider the distributions of discounted

TABLE XII-6.

Option F		Option G	
Return	Probability	Return	Probability
		$\alpha_1 = 0.9$	
9	1/2	−9	1/3
18	1/2	0	1/3
		27	1/3
		$\alpha_1 = 0.8$	
8	1/2	−8	1/3
16	1/2	0	1/3
		24	1/3

[3] Differences in discount rates may arise from imperfections in the capital market, for example, where significant differences exist between borrowing and lending rates.

3. DISCOUNTING INVESTMENT RETURNS

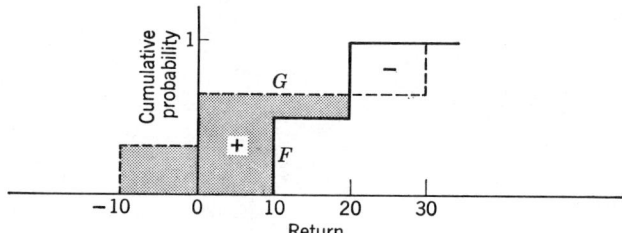

FIGURE XII.2.

returns. Once again this greatly enhances the generality of the efficiency analysis since the criteria can be applied to all investors, independent of their discount rates.

A formal proof of the invariance of the efficient subsets with respect to the discount rate is given in Appendix XII–3; here we shall confine ourselves to the example given in Tables XII–5 and XII–6. The cumulative frequency distributions of *undiscounted* returns (computed from the data of Table XII–5) are drawn in Figure XII.2. Since the distributions intersect, both of the options are GC efficient. An examination of the areas between the distributions, however, clearly shows that option F dominates option G by the RAC, that is, for all risk averters. In Figures XII.3 and XII.4 we plot the cumulative probability distributions of *discounted* returns (from Table XII–6) using two different discount factors: $\alpha_1 = 0.9$ and $\alpha_2 = 0.8$. An examination of the diagrams shows that the introduction of different discount rates does not affect the conclusions: both options are GC efficient while option F dominates G by the RAC, independent of the discount rate assumed.[4]

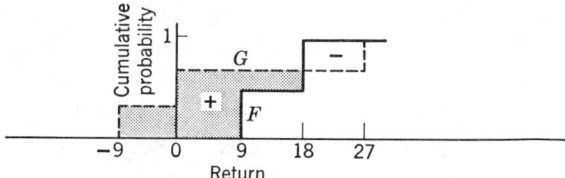

FIGURE XII.3.

---

[4] These conclusions hold for the MVC and QUC also (see Appendix XII–3). It should be noted that the invariance theorems of Appendix XII–3 relate to two-period investments only, and not to multiperiod investments in general. However, no restriction is placed on the length of the period which can be as short (one day, week, or month) or as long (one or more years) as the problem requires.

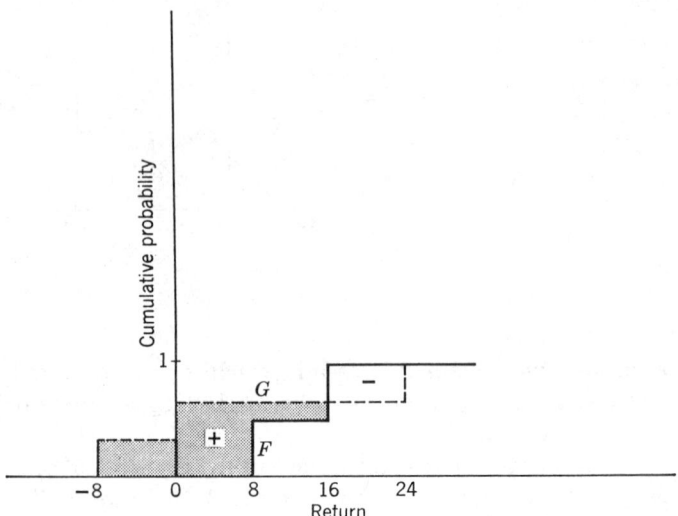

FIGURE XII.4.

4. RELATIVE EFFECTIVENESS OF ALTERNATIVE EFFICIENCY CRITERIA

The size of the efficient set generated by the various criteria is related to the assumptions made with respect to investors' utility functions: the stronger the utility restrictions, the smaller the number of portfolios included in the efficient set. Thus the General Criterion, which is appropriate for both risk lovers and risk averters, will generate a larger efficient set (out of a given group of potential options) than the RAC, MVC, or TSC, since the latter criteria all assume risk aversion. Similarly the QUC, which assumes a very special form of risk aversion—a quadratic utility function—can be expected to result in an even smaller subset than the MVC. While the inverse relation between the size of the efficient subset and the strength of the assumptions regarding utility does not require (and in fact is not amenable to) empirical verification, since it is a logical deduction from a valid theory, considerable interest attaches to the degree in which alternative criteria affect the size of the efficient set. This quantitative aspect, that is, the relative size of the efficient set under alternative decision rules and utility specifications, constitutes an important empirical question.

Clearly, there exists a trade-off between the loss of generality, as stronger and stronger assumptions are introduced, and the reduction of the efficient set. At one and the same time, the analyst and researcher seek criteria with

4. EFFECTIVENESS OF ALTERNATIVE EFFICIENCY CRITERIA

TABLE XII-7. Number of mutual funds included in samples, by time periods

	1946–67	1956–67	1958–67
Growth Funds	8	20	44
Diversified Common Stock Funds	29	37	50
Balanced Funds	16	22	26
Income Funds	4	7	17
Specialized Funds	1	1	12
TOTAL	58	87	149

Source: Arthur Wiesenberger and Co., *Investment Companies*, annual editions.

the broadest possible applicability, but which generate a minimum number of efficient portfolios. But these goals are contradictory, in the sense that efforts to reduce the size of the efficient subset entail restriction of the generality of the efficiency analysis.

If it is to be useful an initial screening using the GC must eliminate a significant number of alternatives while the restriction of further analysis to risk averters (using one of the other criteria) can be justified only if a further significant reduction in the size of the efficient subset takes place. The purpose of this section is to present an empirical test of the size and composition of the efficient sets generated by the five criteria discussed in the previous chapters: the General Criterion (GC); Risk Aversion Criterion (RAC); Mean–Variance Criterion (MVC); Two-Stage Criterion (TSC); and Quadratic Utility Criterion (QUC).

The empirical analysis of the relative effectiveness of the five efficiency criteria is based on mutual fund data. Mutual funds comprise a particularly appropriate subject for the purposes of such a test: an individual mutual fund provides an excellent analogue for a particular portfolio of securities; data on the return to investors in mutual fund shares is readily available;[5] and these data are available for a relatively large group of funds over a 20-year period. Moreover, mutual funds constitute the investment medium through which a significant proportion of investors seek to diversify their holdings.

The sample of funds employed is summarized in Table XII-7. The distribution of the returns was estimated for each mutual fund on the basis

---

[5] The annual rates of return for each mutual fund were taken from Wiesenberger, *op. cit.* These returns reflect the assumption that all dividends (capital gains and/or current income) are reinvested.

of its past performance during three time periods: 1946–67, 1956–67, and 1958–67. Within each time period the sample population is exhaustive, and includes all funds for which data are available over the entire time period. Recourse was had to three successively shorter time periods in order to increase the size of the population from 58 for the period 1946–67 to 149 for the years 1958–67. Thus, while for the shorter time periods each distribution is estimated on the basis of fewer observations, more funds become available for comparison.

In generating the efficient subset for each of the efficiency criteria the following general method was used. The historical data on the distributions of returns were used to estimate the first two distribution moments: mean and variance. The distributions were reordered by increasing mean returns, $\bar{x}_1 < \bar{x}_2 < \cdots < \bar{x}_k$, and the distribution having the highest mean, F_k, was compared with the distribution having the lowest mean, F_1, where $F_1, \ldots, F_k$ denote the cumulative probability distributions from which the means were calculated. If F_k was found to dominate F_1 (that is, the expected utility of F_k exceeds that of F_1 for every utility function in the assumed class of functions), F_1 was eliminated from the efficient subset.[6] F_k was then compared with F_2, and so on, until the list was exhausted. This procedure was then successively repeated, with the distribution F_i ($i < k$) having the highest mean of the remaining distributions (that is, distributions not eliminated in the first round) being compared with all other remaining distributions whose means are less than $\bar{x}_i$.

This procedure results in efficient subsets which cannot be reduced further by additional comparisons only if the efficiency criteria are transitive. A proof of the transitivity of each of the criteria is given in Appendix XII–4, but the importance of this property can be illustrated by a simple hypothetical example. The efficiency criteria are based on pairwise comparisons of the following type: option A is compared with an option B, and if A dominates B by that criterion, B is eliminated from the efficient set. Option A is then compared with option C, and for example if A does *not* dominate C, both A and C are retained in the efficient set. We do not go on to compare B and C, for once an option has been eliminated from the efficient set, it is also eliminated from all the remaining pairwise comparisons. However, in the absence of transitivity, an eliminated option such as B could still conceivably dominate an efficient option such as C. The transitivity of all five criteria ensures that if A dominates B and A does not dominate C, B cannot possibly dominate C, which effectively eliminates the need for any additional comparisons.

Table XII–8 presents the results of the application of the five efficiency

---

[6] F_1 can not dominate F_k since $\bar{x}_1 < \bar{x}_k$. See Chapter VIII.

4. EFFECTIVENESS OF ALTERNATIVE EFFICIENCY CRITERIA

TABLE XII-8. Number of mutual funds included in the efficient sets by criterion for selected time periods 1946–67

	Total Population	General Criterion (GC)	Risk Aversion Criterion (RAC)	Mean–Variance Criterion (MVC)	Two-Stage Criterion (TSC)	Quadratic Utility Criterion (QUC)
			1958–67			
Growth Funds	44	40	14	10	10	10
Diversified Common Stock Funds	50	26	2	2	2	2
Balanced Funds	26	7	—	6	3	6
Income Funds	17	10	1	3	2	3
Specialized Funds	12	6	1	—	—	—
TOTAL	149	89	18	21	17	21
			1956–67			
Growth Funds	20	17	7	7	7	7
Diversified Common Stock Funds	37	26	3	—	—	—
Balanced Funds	22	16	6	7	7	7
Income Funds	7	2	—	—	—	—
Specialized Funds	1	1	—	—	—	—
TOTAL	87	62	16	14	14	14
			1946–67			
Growth Funds	8	8	4	3	3	3
Diversified Common Stock Funds	29	26	6	4	4	4
Balanced Funds	16	13	7	5	5	5
Income Funds	4	2	—	—	—	—
Specialized Funds	1	1	—	—	—	—
TOTAL	58	50	17	12	12	12

criteria to the mutual fund returns for each of the subperiods.[7] The GC was not a very effective tool for selection in the longest period considered, only 8 (about 15%) of the funds being eliminated by this criterion for the years 1946–67; but when the number of funds is increased, that is, in the shorter periods, the GC becomes more effective and 30% of the funds in 1956–67 and 40% of the funds for the years 1958–67 were eliminated despite the fact that no assumptions are made regarding investors' risk attitudes.

When the assumption of risk aversion is introduced (the RAC), the number of funds remaining in the efficient set is greatly reduced in each time period, with the proportionately greatest reduction again coming in the shortest period, 1958–67. For this period the RAC eliminates almost 90% of the total population, and the efficient set includes only 18 funds.

Perhaps the most interesting result can be seen by comparing the efficiency

---

[7] The detailed compositions of the efficient sets under each of the efficiency criteria for the period 1958–67 are given in Appendix XII-5.

of the popular MVC with that of the RAC. Although the use of the MVC reduces the size of the efficient subset in two of the time periods, the MVC efficient sets are only slightly smaller than the RAC efficient sets. In fact, in one period (1958–67) the MVC results in a slightly larger subset (21 funds) than that of the RAC (18 funds). The TSC, which first applies the General Criterion, reduces the efficient set to 17 funds.

With regard to the two longer periods surveyed, the TSC and MVC give identical results. This follows from the fact that the longer the period in question, the better the estimate of the distribution of returns. And as we have already pointed out in Chapter IX, mutual fund returns tend to approximate a normal distribution. Thus for the two longest periods, the MVC efficient set is optimal, and therefore equals the TSC efficient set. In all three periods, the QUC and MVC efficient sets are identical. Moreover, the QUC efficient subsets are not significantly smaller than the efficient sets generated by the RAC, which suggests that the strong assumption of quadratic utility can be dropped without greatly impairing the effectiveness of the analysis.

As is true of the size of the efficient subsets, the compositions of these sets under the MVC and RAC are also roughly similar in each of the longer periods; nine funds (out of a maximum possibility of twelve) are in both sets for the period 1946–67 and eleven funds (out of a maximum possibility of fourteen) are included in both efficient sets for the period 1956–67. The relevant figures for the period 1958–67, however, are twelve out of a maximum possibility of twenty-one. The data also show that all the efficient sets generated by the five criteria include a disproportionate share of "growth funds,"[8] but this is especially pronounced for the periods 1958–67 and 1956–67.

5. SUMMARY

This chapter critically examined the assumptions regarding initial wealth and the discounting of future returns which underlie the efficiency criteria developed in Part II, and also presented the results of an empirical analysis of the relative effectiveness of the various criteria.

All of the efficiency criteria discussed in Chapters VIII–XI are defined in terms of a random variable x which denotes the money returns from a given option. This is tantamount to ignoring the possible influence of investors' wealth on investment decisions. Since the money returns represent increments to individual's wealth, this chapter examined the influence on the efficiency criteria of adding a wealth term w to investors' utility functions.

---

[8] The classification of funds appears in Wiesenberger, *op. cit.*, and is based on the declared policy objectives of the funds themselves.

5. SUMMARY

It was shown in Section 2 that if initial wealth is statistically independent of the returns from investments, the efficiency analysis is valid for all investors, independent of their wealth. This means that if one option dominates a second option by one of the efficiency criteria, for example the RAC, defining the utility function in terms of $U(w + x)$ rather than of $U(x)$ does *not* affect the preference relationship. (Appendix XII–1 and Appendix XII–2 present formal proofs of this independence theorem for each of the various criteria.)

Despite the fact that all the efficiency criteria deal with two-period investment options (period one in which the investment is made, and period two in which the returns are realized), the time value of money is ignored. Thus none of the criteria applies an appropriate discount rate to the returns. Section 3 examined the impact of the discount rate on the composition of the efficient sets.

Although investors with differing time values of money are, in general, confronted with different sets of cumulative probability distributions of *discounted* returns, it was shown that the efficient sets generated by the efficiency criteria are *invariant* to changes in the discount rate. Thus there is no need, in the two-period case, to consider the distributions of discounted returns; this property greatly enhances the generality of the analysis since the efficiency criteria can be applied to all investors of a class, independent of their discount rates. A formal proof that the efficient sets are independent of the discount rate is given in Appendix XII–3.

The size of the efficient subset generated by the various criteria is related to the assumptions made with respect to investors' utility functions: the stronger the utility restrictions, the smaller the number of portfolios included in the efficient set. In Section 4 an empirical analysis of the size of the efficient subsets for five criteria—GC, RAC, MVC, TSC, and QUC—was presented. The empirical analysis was based on the returns to investors in mutual funds during three time periods, 1946–67, 1956–67, and 1958–67. The GC proved effective only in the two shorter periods, eliminating 30% and 40% of all the funds in 1956–67 and 1958–67, respectively. When the assumption of risk aversion was introduced (the RAC) the number of efficient funds was greatly reduced in each time period, and for the shortest period considered, 1958–67, the RAC eliminated almost 90% of the total population, generating an efficient subset which included only 18 out of a total of 149 mutual funds. It is also noteworthy that the QUC and MVC efficient sets are identical, and moreover are not significantly smaller than the RAC efficient sets. This suggests that the strong assumption of quadratic utility can be replaced by the theoretically more appropriate assumption of risk aversion, without greatly impairing the effectiveness of the efficiency analysis.

QUESTIONS AND PROBLEMS

12.1 "There appears to be no intuitively satisfying reason why one should be able to construct efficiency criteria which are *independent* of investors' initial wealth since a rich man is inherently more capable of bearing risk than is a poor man, and therefore will prefer to accept greater risks even though both men are risk-averse." Critically examine and appraise this argument.

12.2 Under what assumptions can the efficient sets be considered independent of initial levels of investors' wealth? Does your conclusion hold for the *optimal* portfolio as well? Explain.

12.3 Using a graph of a hypothetical utility function, give an example of a case in which the optimal investment decision depends on wealth. (Hint: Use a Friedman–Savage utility function.)

12.4 Can you think of cases in which the returns on alternative investments are correlated with initial wealth?

12.5 What is meant by the statement that the efficient sets are independent of the discount rate?

12.6 Does an individual's *optimal* investment choice depend on the discount rate? Explain your answer using numerical examples.

12.7 You are asked to test the effectiveness of the efficiency criteria empirically. Assuming that data on mutual funds are *not* available, how can you conduct the test? Be specific. Why do individual shares constitute an inappropriate choice for such a test?

SELECTED REFERENCES

See Chapter IX.

# APPENDIX XII-1

Proof that the General and Risk Aversion Criteria are Independent of Initial Wealth

We shall prove first that under the assumption that w and x (or y) are *independent* variables, both the General and the Risk-Aversion efficiency criteria are valid, independent of investors' wealth.

Let us denote by x and y the returns from two prospects being compared. If x dominates y by either the GC or RAC then the following inequality:

$$EU(x) \geq EU(y) \tag{12.1.1}$$

must hold for every utility function belonging to a particular class.[9] We must now prove that if Equation (12.1.1) holds then the following equation:

$$EU(w + x) \geq EU(w + y) \tag{12.1.2}$$

must also hold, where w is now defined as a *random variable*. Equation (12.1.2) can be rewritten as follows:

$$\int_w \int_x f(w, x) U(w + x)\, dx\, dw \geq \int_w \int_y f(w, y) U(w + y)\, dy\, dw \tag{12.1.3}$$

Given the assumption that w and the prospects' returns are independent variables, we can substitute $f(w)f(x)$ for $f(w, x)$ and $f(w)f(y)$ for $f(w, y)$ in (12.1.3) and get

$$\int_w f(w) \left[\int_x f(x) U(w + x)\, dx \right] dw \geq \int_w f(w) \left[\int_y f(y) U(w + y)\, dy \right] dw \tag{12.1.4}$$

---

[9] In the case of the General Criterion this class is the set of all utility functions; in the case of the Risk Aversion Criterion it is the set of all concave utility functions.

The terms in brackets are the expected utilities for a given value of w, and (12.1.4) is equivalent to the following inequality:

$$\int_w f(w)[E_x U(w + x)/w]\, dw \geq \int_w f(w)[E_y U(w + y)/w]\, dw \quad (12.1.5)$$

As we have already pointed out, if w is *not* a random variable then $EU(x) \geq EU(y) \Leftrightarrow EU(w + x) \geq EU(w + y)$, and therefore for each given w, the following relationships must hold:

$$EU(x) \geq EU(y) \Leftrightarrow E_x U(w + x)/w \geq E_y U(w + y)/w \quad (12.1.6)$$

Now if (12.1.1) holds, (12.1.6) must hold, and as (12.1.5) is nothing but a weighted average of terms like those being illustrated in the right side of (12.1.6), (12.1.5) must also hold. Q.E.D.

APPENDIX XII-2

Proof that the MVC and QUC are Independent of Initial Wealth

We shall now prove that given the assumption that w and x (or y) are independent variables, the Mean–Variance Criterion (MVC) and the Quadratic Utility Criterion (QUC) are invariant with respect to changes in investors' wealth, w.

a. Mean–Variance Criterion

The expected value and the variance of $(w + x)$ and $(w + y)$ are given by

$$E(w + x) = Ew + Ex$$
$$E(w + y) = Ew + Ey \qquad (12.2.1)$$
$$Var(w + x) = Var(w) + Var(x) + 2\,cov(wx)$$

Since w and x and w and y are independent, $cov(wx) = cov(wy) = 0$; hence

$$Var(w + x) = Var(w) + Var(x)$$
$$Var(w + y) = Var(w) + Var(y) \qquad (12.2.2)$$

From these equations it is clear that

$$E(x) \geq E(y) \Leftrightarrow E(w) + E(x) \geq E(w) + E(y) \Leftrightarrow E(w + x) \geq E(w + y)$$
$$Var(x) \leq Var(y) \Leftrightarrow Var(w) + Var(x) \leq Var(w) + Var(y)$$
$$\Leftrightarrow Var(w + x) \leq Var(w + y)$$

b. Quadratic Utility Criterion

$(w + x)$ dominates $(w + y)$ according to this rule, if $E(w + x) > E(w + y)$ and if (12.2.4) holds:

$$[E(w + x) - E(w + y)]^2 - [Var(w + x) - Var(w + y)] > 0 \qquad (12.2.4)$$

APPENDIX XII–2

Expanding (12.2.4) we get

$$= [E(w) + E(x) - E(w) - E(y)]^2 - [Var(w) + Var(x) - Var(w) - Var(y)]$$
$$= [E(x) - E(y)]^2 - [Var(x) - Var(y)] > 0$$

since

$$E(x) \geq E(Y) \Leftrightarrow E(w + x) \geq E(w + y)$$

We can conclude that if $(w + x)$ dominates $(w + y)$, by the above criterion, then y also dominates x, and vice versa.

APPENDIX XII–3

Proof that the Efficiency Criteria are Independent of the Discount Rate

We shall now prove that the efficient sets generated by the efficiency criteria are invariant to changes in the discount rate.

Theorem 1: *Prospect $F(x)$ dominates prospect $G(x)$ by the General Efficiency Criterion if and only if prospect $F(\alpha_i x)$ dominates prospect $G(\alpha_i x)$, that is to say:*

$$F(x) \leq G(x) \text{ for every value } x \Leftrightarrow F(\alpha_i x) \leq G(\alpha_i x) \text{ for every value } \alpha_i x, \quad (1)$$

where $F(\alpha x)$ and $G(\alpha x)$ denote the cumulative distributions of discounted returns, and $\alpha_i \equiv 1/(1 + k_i)$, k_i being the appropriate discount rate for investor i.

Proof: Let us assume first that $F(x) \leq G(x)$ and $F(x_0) < G(x_0)$ for some x_0. This inequality can be written explicitly as follows:

$$P_F(X \leq x) \leq P_G(X \leq x) \text{ for every value of } x, \text{ and}$$
$$P_F(X \leq x_0) < P_G(X \leq x_0) \text{ for some value } x_0. \quad (2)$$

Now, if (2) holds, then (3) must also hold:

$$P_F(\alpha_i X \leq \alpha_i x) \leq P_G(\alpha_i X \leq \alpha_i x) \text{ for every value } \alpha_i x, \text{ and}$$
$$P_F(\alpha_i X \leq \alpha_i x_0) < P_G(\alpha_i X \leq \alpha_i x_0) \text{ for some value } \alpha_i x_0. \quad (3)$$

Hence

$$P_F(\alpha_i X \leq \alpha_i x) = F(\alpha_i x), \qquad P_G(\alpha_i X \leq \alpha_i x) = G(\alpha_i x)$$

and consequently

$$F(\alpha_i x) \leq G(\alpha_i x), \text{ for every value } \alpha_i x \text{ and}$$
$$F(\alpha_i x_0) < G(\alpha_i x_0) \text{ for some value } \alpha_i x_0$$

APPENDIX XII-3

Theorem 2: *Prospect $F(x)$ dominates prospect $G(x)$ by the Risk Aversion Criterion if and only if prospect $F(\alpha_i x)$ dominates prospect $G(\alpha_i x)$, that is,*

$$\int_{-\infty}^{t} [G(x) - F(x)]\, dx \geq 0 \quad \text{for every value } t$$
$$\Leftrightarrow \int_{-\infty}^{u} [G'(y) - F'(y)]\, dy \geq 0 \quad \text{for every value } u \tag{4}$$

and if $G(x_0) \neq F(x_0)$ for some value x_0, then $G'(y_0) \neq F'(y_0)$ for some value y_0, where F and G denote the original distributions and F' and G' denote the distributions of discounted returns.

Proof: The relationship between the original distributions F and G, and the discounted distributions F' and G', can be formulated as follows:

$$F(z) = P(X \leq z)$$
$$F'(z) = P(\alpha_i X \leq z) = P\left(X \leq \frac{z}{\alpha_i}\right) = F\left(\frac{z}{\alpha_i}\right)$$

Similarly

$$G'(z) = G\left(\frac{z}{\alpha_i}\right)$$

Now if F dominates G, we have

$$\int_{-\infty}^{t} [G(x) - F(x)]\, dx \geq 0 \quad \text{for every value } t, \text{ (and } F \neq G \text{ for some value)} \tag{5}$$

Let us define a transformation $Z = \alpha_i x$, (and hence $dz/\alpha_i = dx$). Equation (5) will have the following transformed form:

$$\frac{1}{\alpha_i} \int_{-\infty}^{\alpha_i t} \left[G'\left(\frac{z}{\alpha_i}\right) - F\left(\frac{z}{\alpha_i}\right) \right] dz \tag{5'}$$

but as $G(z/\alpha_i) = G'(z)$ and $F(z/\alpha_i) = F'(z)$, one can summarize the result in (5) and (5') as follows:

$$\int_{-\infty}^{t} [G(x) - F(x)]\, dx = \frac{1}{\alpha_i} \int_{-\infty}^{\alpha_i t} [G'(z) - F'(z)]\, dz \tag{6}$$

As $1/\alpha_i$ is a positive number, it is clear that the left-hand term $\int_{-\infty}^{\alpha_i t} [G'(z) - F'(z)]\, dz$ must also be non-negative[10] for every value $\alpha_i t$, that is, if

---

[10] If the left-hand term in (6) is strictly positive (that is, $G(x_0) \neq F(x_0)$ for some value x) then the right-hand term in (6) must also be positive (that is, $G'(z_0) \neq F'(z_0)$ for some term z_0).

F dominates G by the Risk Aversion Criterion then F' dominates G', and vice versa.[11]

Theorem 3: $F(x)$ dominates $G(x)$ according to the Mean-Variance Criterion if and only if $F(\alpha_i x)$ dominates $G(\alpha_i x)$.

Proof: The proof is straightforward: $F(x)$ dominates $G(x)$ if

$$E_F(x) \geq E_G(x)$$
$$Var_F(x) \leq Var_G(x) \tag{7}$$

Similarly $F(\alpha_i x)$ dominates $G(\alpha_i x)$ if

$$E_F(\alpha_i x) \geq E_G(\alpha_i x)$$
$$Var_F(\alpha_i x) \leq Var_G(\alpha_i x) \tag{8}$$

Since α_i is a constant, (8) can be written as follows:

$$\alpha_i E_F(x) \geq \alpha_i E_G(x)$$
$$\alpha_i^2 Var_F(x) \leq \alpha_i^2 Var_G(x) \tag{9}$$

Obviously, if (7) holds, (9) holds, and vice versa.

Theorem 4: $F(x)$ dominates $G(x)$ according to the QUC if and only if $F(\alpha_i x)$ dominates $G(\alpha_i x)$ by this criterion.

Proof: $F(x)$ dominates $G(x)$ if

$$E_F(x) \geq E_G(x)$$
$$[E_F(x) - E_G(x)]^2 - [Var_F(x) - Var_G(x)] \geq 0 \tag{10}$$

Similarly $F(\alpha_i x)$ dominates $G(\alpha_i x)$ if

$$E_F(\alpha_i x) \geq E_G(\alpha_i x)$$
$$[E_F(\alpha_i x) - E_G(\alpha_i x)]^2 - [Var_F(\alpha_i x) - Var_G(\alpha_i x)] \geq 0 \tag{11}$$

As α_i is a constant, (11) can be written as follows:

$$\alpha_i E_F(x) \geq \alpha_i E_G(x)$$
$$\alpha_i^2 \{[E_F(x) - E_G(x)]^2 - [Var_F(x) - Var_G(x)]\} \geq 0 \tag{12}$$

Obviously, if (10) holds, (12) holds, and vice versa.[12]

[11] When $t \to \infty$, $\alpha_i t \to \infty$, and the ratio between the total area under $(G' - F')$ to the total area under $(G - F)$ is given by the discount factor α_i:

$$\alpha_i = \frac{\int_{-\infty}^{+\infty} [G'(z) - F'(z)]\,dz}{\int_{-\infty}^{+\infty} [G(x) - F(x)]\,dx}$$

[12] All four invariance theorems are valid for two-period investments, and cannot be extended automatically to the multiperiod case.

APPENDIX XII-4
Proof that the Efficiency Criteria are Transitive

The purpose of this appendix is to show that the efficiency criteria described in Chapter XII are transitive.

a. The General Criterion

We have to prove that if $F\ D\ G$ and $G\ D\ G'$ then $F\ D\ G'$.

Proof: Since $F\ D\ G$ and $G\ D\ G'$ we have

$$F(x) \leq G(x)$$
$$G(x) \leq G'(x)$$

and hence

$$F(x) \leq G(x) \leq G'(x)$$
$$F(x) \leq G'(x)$$

Q.E.D.

b. Risk Aversion Criterion

We have to prove that if $F\ D\ G$ and $G\ D\ G'$ by the RAC then $F\ D\ G'$.

Proof: It is given that

$$\int_{-\infty}^{x} [G(t) - F(t)]\, dt \geq 0 \quad \text{for all values of } x$$

$$\int_{-\infty}^{x} [G'(t) - G(t)]\, dt \geq 0 \quad \text{for all values of } x$$

Hence

$$\int_{-\infty}^{x} [G'(t) - F(t)]\, dt = \int_{-\infty}^{x} \{[G'(t) - G(t)] + [G(t) - F(t)]\}\, dt$$

$$= \int_{-\infty}^{x} [G'(t) - G(t)]\, dt + \int_{-\infty}^{x} [G(t) - F(t)]\, dt \geq 0$$

Since the two terms on the right side of the last equation are non-negative, $\int_{\infty}^{x} [G'(t) - F(t)] \, dt \geq 0$, that is, $F \, D \, G'$. Q.E.D.

c. Mean–Variance Criterion

Proof: If we assume that $X \, D \, Y$ and $Y \, D \, Y'$ by the Mean–Variance rule, the following inequalities hold:

$$EX \geq EY; \quad EY \geq EY'$$
$$\text{Var } X \leq \text{Var } Y; \quad \text{Var } Y \leq \text{Var } Y'$$

Hence

$$EX \geq EY \geq EY'$$

That is,

$$EX \geq EY'$$

and similarly

$$\text{Var } X \leq \text{Var } Y \leq \text{Var } Y'$$
$$\text{Var } X \leq \text{Var } Y'$$

Q.E.D.

d. Quadratic Utility Criterion

Assume that $\mu_x > \mu_y > \mu_{y'}$. Since $X \, D \, Y$ and $Y \, D \, Y'$ the following inequalities hold:

$$(\mu_x - \mu_y)^2 - (\sigma_x^2 - \sigma_y^2) > 0 \tag{1}$$

$$(\mu_y - \mu_{y'})^2 - (\sigma_y^2 - \sigma_{y'}^2) > 0 \tag{2}$$

We have to prove that $X \, D \, Y'$, that is,

$$(\mu_x - \mu_{y'}) - (\sigma_x^2 - \sigma_{y'}^2) > 0$$

Summing Equation (1) and (2) above we get

$$(\mu_x - \mu_y)^2 + (\mu_y - \mu_{y'})^2 - (\sigma_x^2 - \sigma_{y'}^2) > 0 \tag{3}$$

Let us expand the term $(\mu_x - \mu_{y'})^2$ as follows:

$$(\mu_x - \mu_{y'})^2 = [(\mu_x - \mu_y) + (\mu_y - \mu_{y'})]^2$$
$$= (\mu_x - \mu_y)^2 + (\mu_y - \mu_{y'})^2 + 2(\mu_x - \mu_y)(\mu_y - \mu_{y'}) \tag{4}$$

Plugging this result into (3) we obtain

$$(\mu_x - \mu_{y'})^2 - (\sigma_x^2 - \sigma_{y'}^2) - 2(\mu_x - \mu_y)(\mu_y - \mu_{y'}) > 0 \tag{5}$$

Since $(\mu_x - \mu_y)(\mu_y - \mu_{y'}) \geq 0$ by assumption, then if (5) holds (6) must hold:

$$(\mu_x - \mu_{y'})^2 - (\sigma_x^2 - \sigma_{y'}^2) > 0 \tag{6}$$

Hence $X \, D \, Y'$. Q.E.D.

APPENDIX XII–5
Composition of the Efficient Sets of Mutual Funds, Based on 1958–67 Data

TABLE XII–5.1. Mutual funds* included in the general criterion's efficient set, 1958–67

Affiliated Fund
American Mutual Fund
Associated Fund Trust
Axe-Houghton Fund A
*Axe Houghton Stock Fund
Axe Science Corp.
Century Shares Trust
Channing Balanced Fund
Channing Growth Fund
Channing Income Fund
*Channing Special Fund
Chemical Fund
Colonial Fund
Colonial Growth Shares
Composite Fund
Decatur Income Fund
Delaware Fund
de Vegh Mutual Fund
Diversified Growth Stock Fund
Diversified Investment Fund
Dividend Share
*Dreyfus Fund
Eaton & Howard Stock Fund
Energy Fund
Equity Fund
Fidelity Fund
Florida Growth Fund
Franklin Custodian—Common Stock
Franklin Custodian—Income Series

Fund of America (1960)
Fundamental Investors
*Guardian Mutual Fund
Imperial Capital Fund
*Insurance Investors Fund
*Investment Company of America
Investors Variable Payment Fund
Investors Mutual
*Istel Fund
*Johnston Mutual Fund
Keystone (S–3) Growth Common
Keystone (K–2) Growth Fund
Keystone (S–2) Income Common
Keystone International Fund
*Keystone (S–4) Lower Priced Common
Knickerbocker Fund
Knickerbocker Growth Fund
Lexington Research Investing Corp. (1959)
Liberty Fund (1967)
Life & Growth Stock Fund
Life Insurance Investors
Mass. Investors Growth Fund
McDonnell Fund
*Morton (B.C.)—Growth Series
Mutual Investing Foundations MIF Fund
*National Investors Corporation

* Funds marked with the sign * are also efficient using the Risk Aversion Criterion.

TABLE XII–5.1. (Continued)

National Securities—Dividend Series	Steadman Science & Growth Fund
National Securities—Income Series	Stein Roe & Farnham Balanced Fund
National Securities—Growth Stocks	Teachers Association Mutual Fund
New England Fund (1966)	Technology Fund
Northeast Investors Trust	Templeton Growth Fund
Philadelphia Fund	Texas Fund
Pine Street Fund	United Accumulative Fund
Pioneer Fund	United Income Fund
*Price (T. Rowe) Growth Stock Fund	United Science Fund
*Puritan Fund	*Value Line Fund
*Putnam Growth Fund	Value Line Income Fund
Scudler, Stevens & Clark Common	*Value Line Special Situation Fund
*Securities Fund	Vanderbilt Mutual Fund (1964)
Shareholders' Trust of Boston	Wall Street Investing Corp.
Southwestern Investors	Washington Mutual Investors Fund
State Street Investment Corp.	*Winfield Growth Fund
Steadman Fiduciary Investment Fund	Wisconsin Fund

TABLE XII–5.2. Mutual funds* included in the efficient sets of the risk aversion criterion and mean–variance criterion

RAC	MVC[1]
Axe Houghton Stock Fund	*Channing Special Fund
Channing Special Fund	*Dreyfus Fund
Dreyfus Fund	*Investment Company of America
Guardian Mutual Fund	*Johnston Mutual Fund
Investment Company of America	Keystone (K–1) Income Fund
Istel Fund	*Keystone (X–4) Lower-Priced Common
Johnston Mutual Fund	Massachusetts Fund
Keystone (S–4) Lower Priced Common	*Morton (B.C.)—Growth Series
	Nassau Fund
Morton (B.C.)—Growth Series	*New England Fund
National Investors Corporation	*Northeast Investors Trust
Price (T. Rowe) Growth Stock Fund	*Price (T. Rowe) Growth Stock Fund
Puritan Fund	*Puritan Fund
Putnam Growth Fund	*Putnam Growth Fund
Securities Fund	*Securities Fund
Value Line Fund	*Southwest Investors
Value Line Special Situation Fund	*Stein Roe & Farnham Balanced Fund
Winfield Growth Fund	*Value Line Special Situation Fund
American Business Shares	*Winfield Growth Fund
*Channing Balanced Fund	

* Funds marked with an asterisk are included in the efficient set of the Two-Stage Criterion.
[1] The Quadratic Utility Criterion efficient set includes the same 21 funds as the MVC efficient set.

Chapter XIII
Price Determination in the Stock Market

1. INTRODUCTION

In the preceding five chapters we presented a number of efficiency criteria which can be used to analyze investment decisions under uncertainty, and the gains from risk diversification. In essence, these chapters spell out a normative theory of investment behavior; for a variety of assumptions regarding investors' utility functions (tastes), the theory sets out the optimal patterns of investment choice. In this chapter the *normative* theory will be applied to a *positive* problem: the analysis of the set of relative prices of securities in the stock market, particular attention being given to the demand and supply of securities and the way in which they interact to determine equilibrium prices.

2. SOME SIMPLIFYING ASSUMPTIONS

A modern securities market is an awesome mechanism incorporating thousands of decision variables, and therefore any attempt to gain insight into the workings of such a market requires a high degree of abstraction. Clearly, the model cannot be exhaustively descriptive in any meaningful sense; in fact, such a model would be utterly useless except, perhaps, as a monument to Milton Friedman's justly famous essay.[1] But granted that

---

[1] Milton Friedman, "The Methodology of Positive Economics," in *Essays in Positive Economics*, Chicago, University of Chicago Press, 1953, pp. 3–43.

simplifying assumptions are required, the choice of a particular set of assumptions regarding investors' behavior is crucial for both the explanatory and predictive powers of the model. The stronger the assumptions governing individuals' investment choices, the sharper the conclusions regarding the market; but the less general the results, and therefore the greater the danger that the model will not accord with the phenomena that it is designed to explain.

In what follows we shall take as our starting point the pioneering model developed by Sharpe and Lintner.[2] The Sharpe–Lintner capital market model represents an extension of the basic Markowitz–Tobin mean–variance portfolio selection analysis in which the variance (or the standard deviation) serves as the risk indicator. As we have seen (in Chapter X), the use of the mean–variance criterion to characterize investors' behavior implies a set of relatively strong assumptions: investors in securities are risk-averse (have concave utility functions) and the distributions of returns approximate a normal distribution.[3]

Although it is true that with regard to portfolios which include only a small number of different securities the distribution of portfolio returns is likely to deviate significantly from the normal, it can be argued that investors in a competitive capital market tend to include a large number of individual securities in their portfolios, so that the portfolio returns will tend to approximate a normal distribution. The empirical analysis of mutual funds returns lends some support to this contention.[4] Another reason for choosing the mean–variance model is pedagogical: the available alternatives are much more complex and place heavier demands on a student's mathematical abilities.[5] Since mathematical sophistication is not a free good, the trade-off between loss of generality and the simplification of the analysis leads us to prefer the mean–variance model despite its admitted shortcomings.[6]

---

[2] W. F. Sharpe, "Capital Asset Prices: A Theory of Market Equilibrium Under Conditions of Risk," *Journal of Finance* (September 1964), pp. 425–42; and J. Lintner, "Security Prices, Risk and Maximal Gains from Diversification," *Journal of Finance* (December 1965), pp. 587–615.
[3] Because of its logical deficiencies we ignore the alternative of assuming that investors' tastes are characterized by quadratic utility functions; see Chapter XI.
[4] See Chapters IX and XII.
[5] The distributions could be assumed to be symmetrical and to belong to a stable class of *Paretian* distributions. This is a much broader class which includes the normal distribution as a special case. See E. F. Fama, "Portfolio Analysis in a Stable Paretian Market," *Management Science* (January 1965), pp. 404–19.
[6] It might also be noted that all the market equilibrium models are basically similar so that having mastered one, the reader should be reasonably well prepared to go on to the alternative models.

3. SINGLE-STOCK PORTFOLIOS WITH LENDING   431

In addition to the underlying assumption that investors are risk-averse and select their portfolios by the MVC, we shall also assume that the capital market is perfect, which implies the following conditions:

(1) The market comprises many buyers and sellers of securities, none of whose transactions is large enough to affect the prices in the market, and all of whom have an equal opportunity to invest.

(2) There are no transaction costs or transfer taxes, nor is there an income or capital gains tax.

(3) All investors have all relevant information regarding alternative investments, and there are no costs involved in obtaining this information. All investors, therefore, have the same expectations[7] regarding the expected returns and variances of all the alternative investment options.

(4) All investors can borrow or lend any amount in the relevant range without affecting the interest rate. The borrowing rate equals the lending rate and is the same for all investors both large and small, institutional and individual.

(5) There is a given uniform investment period for all investors; this means that all decisions are taken at a particular point in time, and all investments are held for the same period.

Before turning to the analysis of equilibrium prices in the stock market, one possible objection should be noted explicitly. The very essence of a securities market is that prices fluctuate continuously; in more technical jargon, there is no equilibrium in such a market, or if there is, it is never reached! This would seem to vitiate the use of equilibrium models as a tool for explaining relative prices in such a market. In this context it may be well to recall Boulding's famous analogy drawn from dog racing, where the dogs go around the track chasing a mechanical rabbit. Equilibrium is reached should a dog catch the rabbit, but barring failures in the electric power supply, this *never* happens. However, knowledge of the existence of the rabbit is of paramount importance when attempting to explain or predict the otherwise rather peculiar behavior of the dogs.

3. SINGLE-STOCK PORTFOLIOS WITH LENDING OR BORROWING

Let us start the analysis with the most simple case imaginable: investors restrict their portfolios to the shares of one company and to bonds. Thus the

---

[7] This assumption can be relaxed without changing the conclusions of the analysis. See Appendix XIII-4.

individual invests part of his wealth in a common stock and lends (buys bonds) with the remainder; or he may use all his wealth to buy the common stock and borrow (issue his own bonds) to finance additional stock purchases, that is, he builds a "levered" portfolio. To further simplify matters we shall assume that the rate of return (interest) on bonds and loans is riskless and *perfectly certain*, while the return on the common stock is uncertain, and therefore constitutes a stochastic variable.

Let x = a random variable denoting the net return per dollar invested in the common stock
Ex = the expected return
σ_x = the standard deviation of returns
r = the *riskless* lending rate (the rate of return on bonds) = the borrowing rate

The expected return and standard deviation of the common stock can be shown as a point on the familiar M–V plane; see point A in Figure XIII.1. Similarly, the riskless interest rate r is shown as a point on the vertical axis of the same diagram. (Note that for all points on the vertical axis, $\sigma = 0$.)

Consider an investor with an initial wealth of w. If he invests all his wealth in (riskless) bonds the expected return and standard deviation of the bond portfolio will be

$$Ey = wr; \quad \sigma_y = 0$$

where y denotes the return on the portfolio. Alternatively, if he invests all his wealth in the common stock A, the return on the portfolio is $y = xw$, and the expected return and standard deviation of the all-equity portfolio becomes

$$Ey = wEx; \quad \sigma_y = w\sigma_x$$

Of course the investor is also free to choose any combination which he desires of bonds (loans) and stock A. Thus he may invest any proportion of

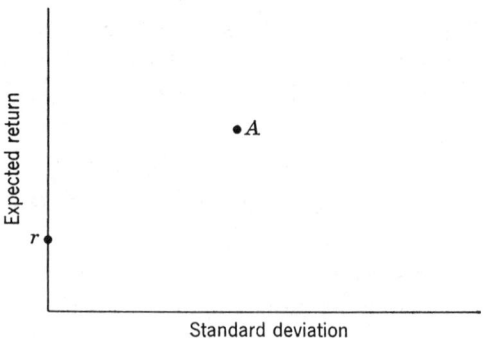

FIGURE XIII.1.

3. SINGLE-STOCK PORTFOLIOS WITH LENDING

his wealth p in bonds and $(1 - p)$ in the stock, on the constraint that $p \leq 1$. The return on the portfolio in this general case can be written as follows:

$$y = pwr + (1 - p)wx \tag{13.1}$$

Note that we put an upper bound on the proportions invested in bonds and stock, $p \leq 1$. This is the familiar constraint that an individual cannot invest more than 100% of his wealth. However we do *not* place a lower bound of $p \geq 0$, and, therefore, p can take on negative, as well as positive, values. If p is positive, this means that the individual invests part of his wealth in bonds. Where $p = 1$ all the wealth is invested in bonds and nothing $(1 - p = 1 - 1 = 0)$ is invested in the stock. Where $p = 0$, the opposite holds: nothing is invested in bonds and all the wealth $(1 - p = 1 - 0 = 1)$ is invested in the stock. Negative values of p represent cases in which an individual borrows money (at the interest rate r) to invest in stock. For example, an initial wealth of $100 and $p = 0.25$ denotes the case of a mixed portfolio composed of $25 in bonds and $75 in stock; the return on the portfolio is $r \cdot 25 + x \cdot 75$. Now consider a case where for the same initial wealth p is negative, for example, $p = -0.5$. Here the individual borrows $50 on which he *pays* interest, but the levered stock portfolio now exceeds the investors' initial wealth: $(1 - p)w = [1 - (-0.5)]100 = \$150$.

The expected return and standard deviation of a portfolio which includes any combination of stocks or bonds (loans) are given by the following two equations:

$$Ey = pwr + (1 - p)wEx \tag{13.2}$$

$$\sigma_y = (1 - p)w\sigma_x \tag{13.3}$$

The reader should note that in the equation of the standard deviation the argument pwr vanishes, since it is a perfectly certain sum, and therefore has a zero variance.

The more an investor borrows in order to finance his purchases of common stock, the higher the expected return (the risky expected return Ex is, by assumption, higher than the riskless rate of interest r), but the greater the risk (standard deviation) as well. This relationship between the expected return and standard deviation can be made explicit by a little algebraic manipulation. Dividing both sides of Equation (13.3) by σ_x yields

$$(1 - p)w = \frac{\sigma_y}{\sigma_x} \tag{13.4}$$

Removing the parenthesis and transposing terms:

$$pw = w - \frac{\sigma_y}{\sigma_x} \tag{13.5}$$

Now substituting the right-hand sides of Equations (13.4) and (13.5) into Equation (13.2), we find[8]

$$Ey = rw + \frac{Ex - r}{\sigma_x} \sigma_y \tag{13.6}$$

Equation (13.6) represents the relationship between expected return and standard deviation for any portfolio, that is, it represents the attainable combination of Ey and σ_y for all possible combinations of stocks and bonds (loans). This equation is linear,[9] so that all of the attainable combinations of Ey and σ_y lie along a straight line.

Within the confines of a "one-stock" model it is also easy to determine the "price" or premium which an investor puts on a unit of risk. When we increase a portfolio's standard deviation by one unit, the investor requires an addition to his expected return equal to $(Ex - r)/\sigma_x$ to compensate him for the additional risk incurred. Conversely, when he adds bonds to his portfolio, thereby reducing the portfolio's standard deviation, he is willing to forgo $(Ex - r)/\sigma_x$ units of expected return per unit of reduction in the standard deviation.

To facilitate a graphical presentation of this relationship between the expected return and risk (Equation 13.6), let us assume an initial wealth of one dollar. The assumption $w = 1$ is made for convenience, and does not affect the generality of the analysis.[10] The transformation line ra of Figure XIII.2 represents all the attainable combinations of expected return and standard deviation which an investor can secure by altering the proportions of his portfolio. The intercept on the vertical axis represents a portfolio invested solely in bonds ($Ey = r$; $\sigma_y = 0$); point A represents the expected return and standard deviation for a 100% equity portfolio. All the intermediate points on the transformation line represent the risk–return characteristics for mixed portfolios which combine stock A and bonds in varying

---

[8] Substituting (13.4) and (13.5) into (13.2) yields

$$Ey = r \left(w - \frac{\sigma_y}{\sigma_x} \right) + Ex \frac{\sigma_y}{\sigma_x}$$

Removing the parentheses we have

$$Ey = rw - r\frac{\sigma_y}{\sigma_x} + Ex \frac{\sigma_y}{\sigma_x} = rw + (Ex - r)\frac{\sigma_y}{\sigma_x}$$

[9] Of the form $Ey = a + b\sigma_y$ where

$$a = rw$$

$$b = \frac{Ex - r}{\sigma_x}$$

[10] By setting $w = 1$, we can easily convert the returns which are given in absolute terms in the equations into percentages.

3. SINGLE-STOCK PORTFOLIOS WITH LENDING

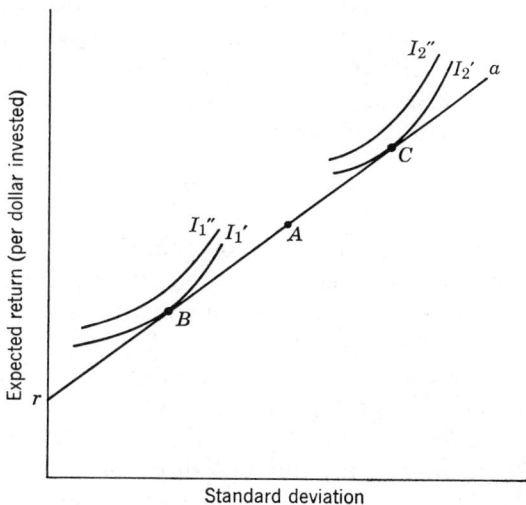

FIGURE XIII.2.

proportions. Since $Ex > r$ by assumption (otherwise no risk averter would be willing to invest in common stock A, whose returns are uncertain), the transformation line rises in a northeasterly direction. The slope of this line $(Ex - r)/\sigma_x$ is equal to the difference between the expected return on the stock of company A and the riskless interest rate divided by the risk associated with the investment in A. This is the price or premium which investors place on the risk associated with investments in this particular company.

All the points along the transformation line represent efficient portfolios, since between any two points on the line the following relationships hold:

$$E_2 > E_1$$
$$\sigma_2 > \sigma_1$$

Thus the MVC is fulfilled for all points and the MVC efficiency locus, in this case, is given by the transformation line itself.

How does the investor choose his portfolio from among the efficient alternatives, that is, how does he allocate his initial wealth between stocks and bonds? As we noted in Chapter X, the answer to this question depends on the individual's preferences. To illustrate this, the indifference maps of *two different* individuals are drawn in Figure XIII.2. (Recall that along each curve in the set expected utility is held constant and that higher curves (in a northwesterly direction) represent higher levels of utility, and therefore more desirable risk–return combinations.) The investor whose preferences are represented by the indifference curves marked I_1', I_1'' will choose a portfolio with the risk–return characteristics associated with point B (the point of tangency between the transformation line and his indifference curve). The optimal portfolio for the second investor is given at point C of Figure XIII.2.

The optimum portfolio for every investor must satisfy the following (tangency) relationship:

$$\frac{\partial Ey}{\partial \sigma_y} = \frac{Ex - r}{\sigma_x}$$

Thus at the optimum the investor's subjective trade-off between return and risk must be equal to the objective risk–return trade-off provided by the market. The latter is measured by the slope of the transformation line, or "market line" as it is often called.

Since the optimum portfolio depends on individual preferences, its composition can be expected to differ from investor to investor. Thus a point like B on the segment rA of the market line represents an optimal portfolio which includes a proportion of bonds as well as a proportion of the stock. Point C, on segment Aa, represents the optimal solution for an investor who borrows to build a levered portfolio, that is, who borrows to finance his stock purchases. In the more familiar terms of the market, the points along the segment Aa of the market line represent equity portfolios bought "on margin." The further we move along the segment in a northeasterly direction, the *smaller* the margin provided by the investor's own funds and the larger the proportion of the portfolio which is financed out of loans. Put another way, p is negative along the segment Aa and positive along the segment rA. At point A, $p = 0$, and the investor who chooses such a portfolio neither borrows nor lends.

3.1 CHOOSING AMONG ALTERNATIVE SINGLE-STOCK PORTFOLIOS

Until now we have limited the investor's choice to a single stock or a combination of that stock with bonds (loans). While retaining the single stock constraint, let us permit the investor to choose the company in whose stock he wishes to invest. To keep the problem manageable let us further assume that there are five such alternatives, and that their risk–return characteristics are given by the five points A, B, C, D, and E of Figure XIII.3. (All the returns are given per dollar of investment to facilitate the comparison among the alternatives.) Before deciding on the proportions of his wealth to be invested in stocks or bonds, the investor must first choose the *particular* stock in which to invest. (Remember, we still do not allow him to buy the stock of more than one company.) From the diagram it is clear that he will not choose D or E, because B, for example, which has a higher expected

3. SINGLE-STOCK PORTFOLIOS WITH LENDING 437

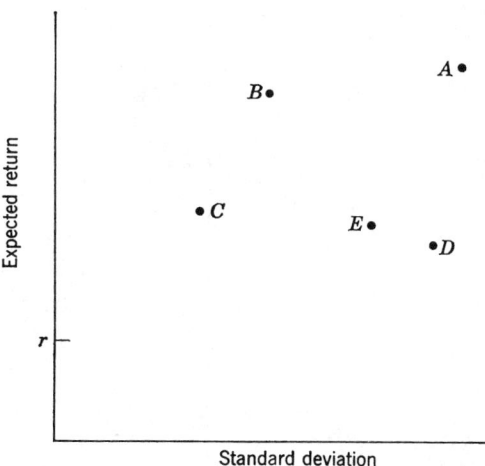

FIGURE XIII.3.

return and lower risk, dominates both D and E. Therefore there are three candidates, A, B, and C, since these three stocks fulfill the MVC efficiency conditions:

$$E_A > E_B > E_C$$
$$\sigma_A > \sigma_B > \sigma_C$$

Although the MVC cannot distinguish between these three alternatives, all of which represent efficient options, the possibility of borrowing or lending (buying bonds) allows the investor to make a choice among these alternatives, without recourse to his indifference map. Let us assume a borrowing (or lending) rate equal to r. To compare the three alternatives, we have drawn in Figure XIII.4 a transformation line from point r on the vertical axis through each of the points A, B, and C. Each of these lines represents all the risk–return combinations which can be obtained from alternative combinations of the stock of a particular company and bonds (loans): the mixed stock–bond portfolios lie on the segments rA, rB, and rC respectively; the levered portfolios lie along the segments Ca_1, Aa_2, and Ba_3. Since the stock of company B lies on the highest transformation line (ra_3) of Figure XIII.4, it is clear that an investor who has the opportunity of borrowing or lending at the rate r should choose stock B when making his final portfolio decision, since a mixed (or levered) portfolio which includes B rather than A or C allows him to reach a higher level of utility. This can be confirmed from Figure XIII.4, which superimposes an investor's preference map on the transformation lines and shows that the tangency with the highest indifference

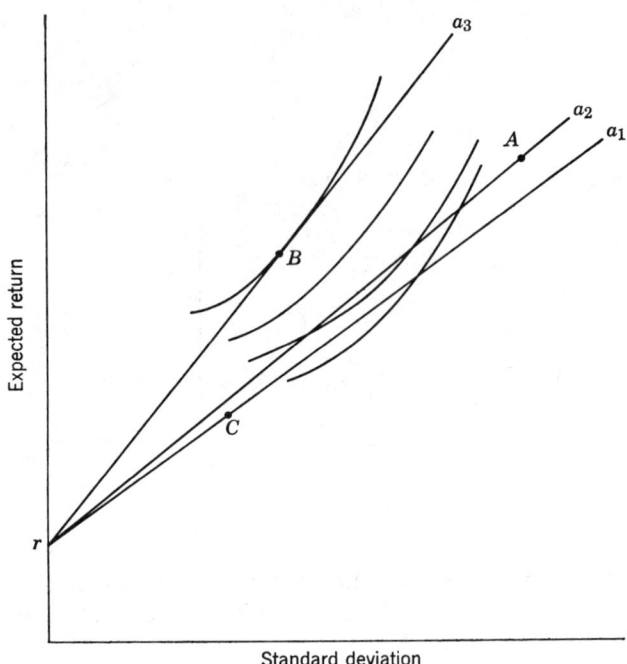

FIGURE XIII.4.

curve will be along line ra_3, which is the same conclusion we reached by examining the transformation lines themselves *without* recourse to the indifference curves!

As we have seen, it is the option of borrowing or lending which permits us to distinguish among the three alternatives. This result holds even for the investor who chooses not to borrow or lend. In fact, the indifference curves of Figure XIII.4 have been drawn so that the optimum portfolio is represented by point B. This point represents a portfolio consisting only of stock B; the investor neither borrows nor buys bonds. But even in this limiting case we were able to establish the dominance of B over A and C (without recourse to his subjective preferences) simply by assuming that the investor has the *opportunity* of borrowing or lending.

In sum, the investment process has been dichotomized as follows:

(1) Choosing the stock to be included in the portfolio, independent of the investor's subjective tastes
(2) Choosing the optimal proportion of bonds (loans) and stock, in accordance with the investor's tastes

3. SINGLE-STOCK PORTFOLIOS WITH LENDING   439

The first stage corresponds to finding the stock which lies along the highest transformation (market) line; the second stage corresponds to finding the tangent between the transformation line and the investor's indifference map. It is only at this stage that *subjective* preferences are relevant.

3.2 EQUILIBRIUM IN THE STOCK MARKET: SINGLE-STOCK PORTFOLIOS AND A UNIQUE INTEREST RATE

It is clear from the previous discussion that the possibility of borrowing or lending allows us to reduce the efficient set of alternative stocks to a single stock. Together with this, a large (strictly speaking infinite) family of efficient portfolios, alternative proportions of bonds (loans) and stock, is created. Similarly, we can conclude that in the single stock case, and for a given interest rate, all investors will wish to choose the same stock—in our example that of company B. As a result of the increased demand for stock B, its price can be expected to rise, thereby lowering the expected return to investors. Conversely, the lack of demand for the shares of the other companies (A and C in our example) will lead to a fall in their prices, thereby raising their expected returns. This process will continue until all the shares lie along the same market line, at which time the investor will be indifferent among them. This is the essence of the market equilibrium process in the single-stock portfolio case.

Let us examine the process a bit more carefully with the aid of some algebra. The following notation will be used:

x = a random variable denoting the operating income of company B
$\bar{x}$ = the expected operating income of company B
V = the market value of the company's securities (stocks and bonds)
D = the market value of its bonds
$S_1 = V - D$ = the market value of its stock
Ex_1 = the expected return on the stock

The return on the company's shares is given by

$$\frac{x - rD}{V - D} = \frac{x - rD}{S_1} \tag{13.7}$$

and their expected return is

$$Ex_1 = \frac{\bar{x} - rD}{V - D} = \frac{\bar{x} - rD}{S_1} \tag{13.8}$$

To calculate the standard deviation of the returns, we first note that (13.7) can be rewritten as follows:

$$\frac{x - rD}{S_1} = \frac{x}{S_1} - \frac{rD}{S_1} = \frac{1}{S_1} \cdot x - \frac{rD}{S_1}$$

Since the expressions $1/S_1$ and rD/S_1 are constants, the standard deviation equals

$$\sigma_1 = \frac{1}{S_1} \sigma(x) = \frac{\sigma(x)}{S_1} \qquad (13.9)$$

Now let us assume that the increase in the demand for the shares of B raises their price at the rate g, so that the new market value of shares becomes $S_2 = S_1(1 + g)$, where $g > 0$. What will be the new expected return Ex_2 and standard deviation σ_2?

$$Ex_2 = \frac{\bar{x} - rD}{S_2} = \frac{\bar{x} - rD}{S_1(1 + g)} = \frac{Ex_1}{(1 + g)} \qquad (13.10)$$

that is, the expected return is decreased at the rate g, and

$$\sigma_2 = \frac{\sigma(x)}{S_2} = \frac{\sigma(x)}{S_1(1 + g)} = \frac{\sigma_1}{1 + g} \qquad (13.11)$$

That is, the standard deviation also falls at the rate g.

These results are illustrated graphically in Figure XIII.5, which reproduces the market lines of Figure XIII.4.[11] The starting point is again point B, which represents the initial expected return–standard deviation combination of the shares of company B; as we have seen the induced rise in price of B causes both its expected return and standard deviation to fall at the same rate. This is shown in the diagram as a downward movement along the ray OB. As B moves toward the origin the slope of the relevant market line also declines. Thus the dashed market line ra' which connects the rate of interest with B' (the new risk–return combination of B after the price rise) has a smaller slope than ra_3. The opposite holds true for A and C. For example, the fall in the price of C raises its expected return and standard deviation; this is shown as an *upward* movement along the ray OCC', which *raises* the slope of the relevant market line (for stock C). This process continues (for A as well) until all three shares (B', A', C') lie along the *same* market line ra' in Figure XIII.5. At the new risk–return combinations, B', A', and C', investors are indifferent as to which share they hold, since all three now lie

---

[11] The market line for A has been omitted to avoid confusion.

3. SINGLE-STOCK PORTFOLIOS WITH LENDING

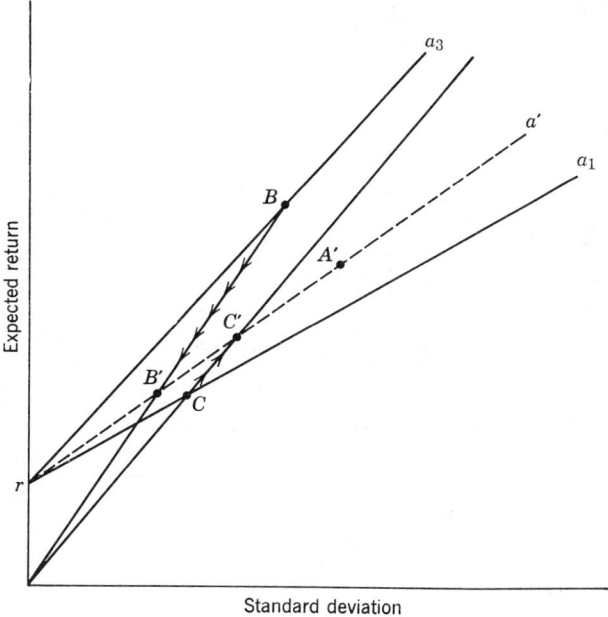

FIGURE XIII.5.

along the same market line and therefore afford *all* investors with an equal opportunity of maximizing their utilities. Should the price of any of the shares fall, thereby raising its expected return and standard deviation, it will lie on a new market line with a higher slope. But such an investment will now be so desirable that an increase in demand will be engendered, thereby raising its price until the previous equilibrium is restored.[12] Conversely, a rise in price (fall in return) will make the share an undesirable investment, calling forth a rush of sales and thereby lowering the price (raising the return) until the previous equilibrium price is again restored.

3.3 THE CASE OF MULTIPLE INTEREST RATES

The results of the previous section depend on the assumption that all investors can borrow or lend at the same interest rate. In this section we relax the assumption of a unique interest rate, and assume that the borrowing rate r_2

---

[12] For the sake of simplicity we ignore any possible effects of the dynamic process on the final equilibrium position itself.

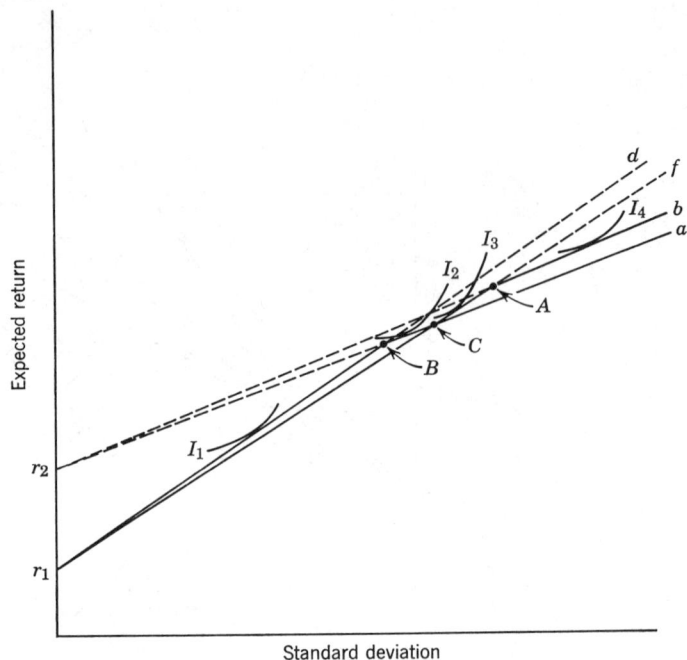

FIGURE XIII.6.

is higher than the lending rate[13] (the rate on bonds) r_1. However, each of these two rates is the same for all borrowers and lenders, respectively. In this case, different individuals will generally prefer to invest in the shares of different companies; moreover, the set of efficient portfolios will not lie along the same market line.

Consider the case of the shares of two companies, whose risk–return characteristics are given by points A and B in Figure XIII.6. The attainable combinations of expected return and standard deviation from mixed (or levered) portfolios which include stock A are given by the solid market line r_1Ab. The dashed line r_2A is not relevant since between r and A the market line is comprised of mixed portfolios of the stock A and bonds, and the latter require the use of the (by assumption) lower *lending* rate. Thus the relevant market line is r_1A. (Similarly the relevant line for B is r_1B and not the dashed line r_2B.) Beyond points A and B the investor builds a levered

---

[13] The borrowing rate cannot be set lower than the lending rate, for in such a case utility maximization implies borrowing infinite amounts of money which are in turn invested in bonds.

4. MULTIPLE-STOCK PORTFOLIOS

equity portfolio so that the borrowing rate, r_2, applies. The relevant market line for A is the solid line Ab, and Ba is the relevant line for stock B. Thus, where the borrowing and lending rates differ, the market transformation lines are kinked; the left-hand side, representing mixed portfolios, uses the lower lending rate and the right-hand side, representing levered portfolios, uses the borrowing rate.

The only *attainable* combinations lie along the solid market lines r_1B and r_1AB; the dashed lines of Figure XIII.6 represent unattainable risk–return combinations. For example, the dashed line Af assumes that an investor can lever his portfolio of A by borrowing at the rate r_1, but this is not possible since the borrowing rate is, by assumption, r_2 which is higher than r_1. Therefore feasible levered portfolios of A lie along the lower market line Ab. In sum, all of the dashed lines Af, Bd, r_2A, and r_2B represent nonattainable combinations and should be ignored. Two segments, r_1C and Ca, represent *inefficient* portfolios; the portfolios along r_1BC dominate those along r_1C, and CAb dominates Ca. (Note that C represents the point of intersection of two market lines and not necessarily the stock of a third company.)

The mixed and levered portfolios which are both attainable and efficient lie along a composite market line which includes four segments: r_1B, Bc, CA, and Ab. Clearly, there is no reason to suppose that all investors will choose the same portfolio. Figure XIII.6 also sets out the indifference curves of four hypothetical investors, each of whose curves is tangent to a different segment of the composite market line:

> Investor I_1 chooses a mixed portfolio of B and bonds;
> Investor I_2 chooses a levered portfolio of B;
> Investor I_3 chooses a mixed portfolio of A and bonds;
> Investor I_4 chooses a levered portfolio of A.

4. MULTIPLE-STOCK PORTFOLIOS

Now let us apply the same type of market equilibrium analysis to the more realistic case where investors can include in their portfolios as many shares of stock as they like, of as many companies as they like. The previous case considered, where investors included the shares of only a single company, is a special case in which the number of companies, n, was taken equal to 1. What are the optimal investment proportions in the general unconstrained case? Will the investor include only one company in his optimum portfolio or will he diversify his portfolio to include the shares of many companies?

4.1 A GRAPHICAL ANALYSIS

To answer these questions,[14] we shall approach the problem initially by means of a simplified graphical presentation. Assume a market comprised of the shares of five companies: A, B, C, D, and E. Figure XIII.7 sets out the risk–return characteristics of each of these shares; the shaded area represents the various combinations of two or more of the shares, in portfolios of differing proportions. Consider an investor who restricts himself to a portfolio which includes only shares of A and E: the transformation curve I,[15] connecting points A and E, represents all the attainable risk–return combinations from this two-share portfolio, with each point on the curve representing a different set of investment proportions. Note that only the solid part of the curve represents efficient portfolios; the dashed part of the curve represents inefficient combinations. Similarly, transformation curve II is the appropriate curve for portfolios which include various proportions

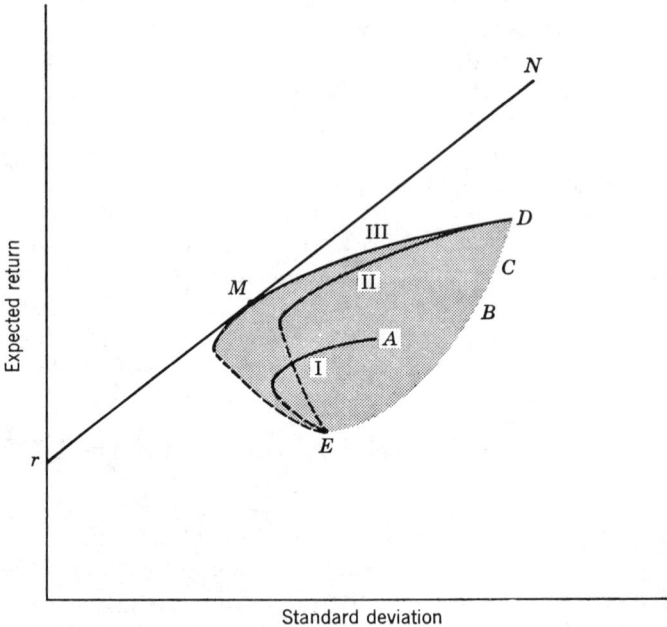

FIGURE XIII.7.

[14] The connection between the optimal multi-stock investment portfolios and equilibrium share prices is analyzed in Section 6.
[15] On the shape of the transformation curve and its relationship to the correlation between the returns of the shares, see Chapter X.

4. MULTIPLE-STOCK PORTFOLIOS

of D and E. Clearly, curves could also be generated for other two-share combinations or for portfolios which include three, four, or more shares. If we relax all constraints and permit the investor to build his portfolio as he wishes, choosing any proportion of all the five shares assumed to comprise the market, the envelope curve of the five-share portfolios will lie to the left of the transformation curves of the constrained portfolios which include the securities of four or fewer companies. The transformation curve for the unconstrained five-share case is given by curve III of Figure XIII.7. This curve sets out all of the combinations of expected return and standard deviation which can be obtained by freely building a pure equity portfolio using all of the available stocks in the market. For graphical convenience only we assume a market which includes the shares of only five companies. The shaded area to the right of the transformation curve III, which includes all of the constrained curves, represents portfolios which are inefficient relative to the portfolios on the solid part of curve III. Here again the lower, dashed, part of the curve is also inefficient since these portfolios are dominated by the upper segment of curve III.

Now let us assume that the investor can borrow or lend (buy bonds) at the rate r. (Note that we have returned to the assumption of a perfect market in which the borrowing and lending rates are the same.) Thus in Figure XIII.7 the market line which rises from the interest rate r on the vertical axis, and which is tangent to transformation curve III at point M, sets out all the alternative combinations of the pure equity portfolio M with bonds (up to point M on the rM line, and levered by loans beyond point M). Point M represents the risk–return characteristics of the market portfolio which has *optimal* proportions of the five stocks. This portfolio is optimal, since given the option of borrowing or lending at rate r, portfolio M permits the investor to reach the highest market line, thereby permitting him to reach the highest possible indifference curve. Note that the optimal pure equity portfolio, represented by point M, has the property of maximizing the angle formed when a straight line is drawn from point r to any point on the transformation curve. Thus the line rM has the highest possible slope of any market line drawn to any point on the transformation curve.

If the indifference curve of an investor is tangent to point M, this individual invests all of his wealth in equities.[16] Of course, the indifference curves of many investors will not be tangent to point M. Tangency solutions which lie on the segment rM represent mixed stock and bond portfolios; those which occur on the segment MN represent levered portfolios, that is, a pure equity portfolio financed in part by loans. However it must be emphasized that all

---

[16] A point of tangency (or corner solution) will always exist since the indifference curves of a risk averter must be concave upward. For a proof of this proposition see Appendix XIII-2.

investors have one important characteristic in common. Whether he chooses a pure equity, mixed, or levered portfolio, an investor who chooses to invest in equities *invariably* builds a portfolio which has the optimal proportions represented by point M. Hence the proportions of each stock in the equity portion of the portfolios of *all* investors are the same, independent of their individual tastes; that is, despite the differences in tastes all individuals will diversify the equity portion of their portfolios in the same proportions among the individual stocks. Differences in individual tastes are operative only in determining the proportion of bonds (loans) which the investor buys (takes). The indifference curves enter the analysis only *after* the optimal proportions of the equity portfolio (represented by point M) have been established, and serve to determine the tangency point with the market line rMN, but do *not* alter the tangency of the market line with point M itself. It is this property of a perfect market (that the equity portfolios of all individuals include the same available common stocks, and in the same proportions) which permits us to aggregate individuals' demands for stocks into a market demand function.

These results are a special case of Tobin's "separation theorem,"[17] which dichotomizes the investment process into two separate stages: (1) finding the proportions of the optimal risk portfolio; (2) choosing the mix between the risk assets and bonds (loans).[18]

As we have seen, all investors hold the same proportions of the same stocks in their portfolios. This raises two questions: which stocks are held, and in what proportions? The answer to the first question is straightforward. In a perfect market, in which all lenders and borrowers face the same (riskless) interest rate, the equity portfolios of all investors include the same stocks, independent of their tastes. Thus if a particular stock is not included in portfolio M, no investor holds it. But if no investor will desire to hold a stock, its price will fall, thereby raising its return, until it becomes sufficiently attractive to be included in portfolio M. It follows that in equilibrium, *all* available common stocks will be included in the risk portfolios of *all* investors.

4.2 THE OPTIMAL INVESTMENT PROPORTIONS

To answer the second question, relating to the proportions in which the stocks are included in M, we must analyze the process by which the optimal

---

[17] See Tobin (1958), *op. cit.*
[18] In general the risky portfolio (point M) also includes risky bonds since a bond with a positive standard deviation should be treated as a stock. For simplicity we shall use the terms *equity*, *risk*, and *market portfolio* interchangeably, although the reference is to all relevant risk assets.

4. MULTIPLE-STOCK PORTFOLIOS

point M is derived. Let Ex_0 and σ_{x_0} denote the expected return per dollar invested and standard deviation of *any* equity portfolio; they are given by the following formulas:

$$Ex_0 = \sum_{i=1}^{n} p_i Ex_i$$

$$\sigma_{x_0} = \sqrt{\sum_{i=1}^{n} p_i^2 \sigma_i^2 + 2 \sum_{\substack{i=1 \\ j>i}}^{n} p_i p_j \sigma_{ij}}$$

where: p_i = the proportion of an investor's wealth invested in the ith common stock
  n = the number of different stocks available in the market
  σ_i^2 = the variance of returns (per dollar invested) in the ith security
  Ex_i = the expected return (per dollar invested) in the ith security.
  σ_{ij} = the covariance between securities i and j.

Note that since this formula holds for any portfolio, the investment proportions p_i need not be optimal. The second expression in the formula for the portfolio standard deviation represents the covariance between all pairs of stocks; thus it reflects the correlation between the fluctuations in the returns of the two stocks from period to period.

In general $\sum_{i=1}^{n} p_i \neq 1$, that is, the investment proportions will not add up to one dollar[19] since the investor may also buy bonds or borrow. When the latter possibilities are taken into account the investment proportions (including bonds or loans) must add to 1: $\sum p_i + p_r = 1$, where p_r denotes the proportion invested in bonds or loans. If the investor borrows, $p_r < 0$ and $\sum p_i > 1$; if the investor buys bonds, $p_r > 0$ and $\sum p_i < 1$; and if the investor neither borrows nor lends, $p_r = 0$ and $\sum p_i = 1$. The latter possibility represents the special case where the indifference curve is tangent to the market line at point M itself.

Recalling our discussion of Figure XIII.7, the problem confronting the investor is how to choose a point (Ex_0, σ_0) on the transformation curve so that the market line connecting it to point r on the vertical axis forms a maximum angle α, thereby permitting him to reach the highest possible indifference curve. In analytical terms, the investor must find the vector of investment proportions p_i which maximizes the following expression:[20]

$$tg\alpha_i = \frac{Ex_0 - r}{\sigma_{x_0}} = \frac{\sum_{i=1}^{n} p_i Ex_i - r}{\sqrt{\sum_{i=1}^{n} p_i^2 \sigma_i^2 + 2 \sum_{\substack{i=1 \\ j>i}}^{n} p_i p_j \, Cov\,(x_i x_j)}} \tag{13.12}$$

[19] For mathematical convenience the analysis is carried out in terms of "per dollar invested."
[20] For details of this approach see Lintner (1965), *op. cit.*

448 ⦀⦀⦀⦀⦀⦀⦀⦀⦀⦀⦀⦀ PRICE DETERMINATION IN THE STOCK MARKET

Portfolio M (Ex_m; σ_m) in the example given in Figure XIII.7 maximizes this expression, and therefore represents the optimum portfolio. The proportions of this portfolio are the optimal investment proportions for all investors.[21]

Note again that in terms of the separation theorem we are discussing stage one in which the optimal *equity* portfolio is determined, that is, we are locating the optimal point on the transformation curve and *not* the tangent of the transformation curve to an indifference curve.

4.3 OPTIMAL INVESTMENT PROPORTIONS: AN ALTERNATIVE APPROACH*

Additional insight into the optimization process can be gained by considering an alternative method whereby we differentiate Equation (13.13) below with respect to p_i in order to find the optimal investment proportions. Let us start by defining the expected return Ex and standard deviation σ_x of an investor's *overall* portfolio of equities *and* bonds (loans):

$$Ex = \sum_{i=1}^{n} p_i Ex_i + \left(1 - \sum_{i=1}^{n} p_i\right) r$$

$$\sigma_x = \sqrt{\sum_{i=1}^{n} p_i^2 \sigma_i^2 + 2 \sum_{\substack{i=1 \\ j>i}}^{n} p_i p_j \, Cov\,(x_i x_j)}$$

Clearly the inclusion of riskless bonds (loans) influences, and therefore appears in, the formula of the expected return. However, including the bonds (loans) does *not* affect the standard deviation of the overall portfolio since the variance of a perfectly certain income r is zero. Hence the covariance of the bonds with the stocks is also zero.

Now let us define the function C, as follows:

$$C = \sigma_x + \lambda \left[Ex - \sum_{i=1}^{n} p_i Ex_i - \left(1 - \sum_{i=1}^{n} p_i\right) r \right] \quad (13.13)$$

where λ = a Lagrange multiplier.

The problem is to determine the vector of investment proportions which minimizes the overall portfolio standard deviation for all values of Ex, the

---

* The mathematical techniques used in this section are discussed in the Mathematical Supplement; the general reader, however, may prefer to skip this section entirely.

[21] Equation (13.12) is formulated in terms of an investor who desires to invest *one dollar* among the various alternative securities. However, it can be shown that these results also hold (that is, $tg\alpha_i$ does not change) for the general case in which Z dollars are invested. See Appendix XIII–1.

4. MULTIPLE-STOCK PORTFOLIOS

expected return on the mixed or levered portfolio. This is tantamount to finding the market line rN of Figure XIII.7 since by definition the market line represents the efficient set of alternatives facing the investor. Thus, each point on the line represents the overall portfolio (equities plus bonds or loans) which minimizes the variance, given the expected return. The market line can be determined analytically by differentiating Equation (13.13) with respect to each p_i and with respect to the Lagrange multiplier λ, and setting the first derivatives equal to zero. This yields a set of $n + 1$ equations.[22] The set has a solution since it includes $n + 1$ equations for the $n + 1$ unknowns $(p_1, \ldots, p_n, \text{ and } \lambda)$. Solving the set we derive the proportions $p_1 \cdots p_n$ (and of course $1 - \sum p_i$ as well), which minimize the variance for a given level of expected return. By varying the level of return we can generate the entire market line. In the special case of $p_r = 0$, the solution set gives the optimal investment proportions of the pure equity portfolio represented by point M of Figure XIII.7.

Now let us turn to the economic interpretation of the Lagrange multiplier λ. By some algebraic manipulation, the optimal[23] values can be expressed as:[24]

$$\sigma_{x_m} = \lambda(Ex_m - r) \qquad (13.15)$$

$$\frac{1}{\lambda} = \frac{Ex_m - r}{\sigma_{x_m}} \qquad (13.16)$$

As we have already seen, the expression $(Ex_m - r)/\sigma_{x_m}$ defines the slope of the market line (rN of Figure XIII.7). The reciprocal of the Lagrange Multiplier $1/\lambda$ measures the price of a unit of risk, that is, the required

---

[22]
$$\frac{\partial C}{\partial p_1} = \tfrac{1}{2}(\sigma^2 x)^{-\tfrac{1}{2}} \left[2p_1 \sigma_1^2 + 2 \sum_{j=2}^{n} p_j \text{ Cov }(x_1, x_j) \right] - \lambda(Ex_1 - r) = 0$$

$$\frac{\partial C}{\partial p_2} = \tfrac{1}{2}(\sigma^2 x)^{-\tfrac{1}{2}} \left[2p_2 \sigma_2^2 + 2 \sum_{\substack{j=1 \\ j \neq 2}}^{n} p_j \text{ Cov }(x_2, x_j) \right] - \lambda(Ex_2 - r) = 0$$

$$\vdots \qquad \qquad \vdots \qquad \qquad \vdots \qquad \qquad (13.14)$$

$$\frac{\partial C}{\partial p_n} = \tfrac{1}{2}(\sigma^2 x)^{-\tfrac{1}{2}} \left[2p_n \sigma_n^2 + 2 \sum_{j=1}^{n-1} p_j \text{ Cov }(x_n, x_j) \right] - \lambda(Ex_n - r) = 0$$

$$\frac{\partial C}{\partial \lambda} = Ex_0 - \sum_{i=1}^{n} p_i Ex_i - \left(1 - \sum_{i=1}^{n} p_i\right) r = 0$$

[23] Optimal values of a variable will be designated hereafter either by the subscript m or by an asterisk.
[24] For the derivation of Equations 13.15 and 13.16, see Appendix XIII–5.

increase in expected return when one unit of risk (where the risk is denoted in terms of the standard deviation) is added to the portfolio. Since the larger the number of different shares which are available in the market, the greater are the opportunities to reduce risk, the entire efficient set (market line) will shift to the left as the market grows. Thus for a given interest rate, the price of unit of risk (slope of the market line) will be higher, other things being equal, in larger markets.

Similarly, we can derive the following optimum equilibrium condition which must hold for every investor in the market:[25]

$$\frac{1}{\lambda} \cdot \frac{\partial \sigma_{x_m}}{\partial p_i} = Ex_i - r \qquad (13.17)$$

This can be verbalized as follows: Investors will increase their holdings of a particular common stock up to the point where the value of that stock's marginal contribution to the portfolio's total standard deviation equals its risk "premium," that is, the difference between its expected rate of return and the riskless interest rate. This is the equilibrium condition for investors when risk is measured in terms of the standard deviation.

---

[25] This can be derived by rewriting Equations (13.14) as follows:

$$\begin{aligned}
\frac{\partial C}{\partial p_1} &= \frac{\partial \sigma_{x_m}}{\partial p_1} - \lambda(Ex_1 - r) = 0 \\
\frac{\partial C}{\partial p_2} &= \frac{\partial \sigma_{x_m}}{\partial p_2} - \lambda(Ex_2 - r) = 0 \\
&\quad \cdot \qquad \cdot \qquad \cdot \qquad \cdot \\
&\quad \cdot \qquad \cdot \qquad \cdot \\
&\quad \cdot \qquad \cdot \qquad \cdot \\
\frac{\partial C}{\partial p_n} &= \frac{\partial \sigma_{x_m}}{\partial p_n} - \lambda(Ex_n - r) = 0
\end{aligned} \qquad (13.18)$$

or alternatively:

$$\begin{aligned}
\frac{1}{\lambda} \frac{\partial \sigma_{x_m}}{\partial p_1} &= Ex_1 - r \\
\frac{1}{\lambda} \frac{\partial \sigma_{x_m}}{\partial p_2} &= Ex_2 - r \\
&\quad \cdot \quad \cdot \quad \cdot \\
&\quad \cdot \quad \cdot \\
\frac{1}{\lambda} \cdot \frac{\partial \sigma_{x_m}}{\partial p_n} &= Ex_n - r
\end{aligned} \qquad (13.19)$$

5. THE RELATIONSHIP OF EXPECTED RATE OF RETURN TO RISK

Let us now turn to the question of determining the relationship between an individual share's expected return and its risk. We recall, in this context, that risk reflects not only the standard deviation of returns on the share itself but also the covariance with the returns of all other shares in the market. In the previous section the relationship between a share's expected return and its contribution to the total risk of the optimal portfolio was stated in terms of the standard deviation. For mathematical convenience we shall now use the variance to indicate risk, but this does *not* change the optimal solution (13.14).

Since this set of equations, from which we derived the equilibrium conditions for the individual investor, must hold simultaneously for all investors, independent of their tastes, we can also use Equations (13.14) to derive the general relationship among the expected returns of all shares and their risk. The risk–return relationship for any share i is usually formulated in terms of the following equation[26]

$$Ex_i = r + \frac{Ex_m - r}{\sigma_m^2} \, Cov\,(x_i, x_m) \qquad (13.20)$$

[26] See, for example, Lintner *op. cit.*; Sharpe *op. cit.*; and Fama *op. cit.* Equation (13.20) can be derived from the previous analysis as follows: From Equations (13.14) we know that the following relationship always exists so clearly it must also hold for the optimum:

$$\frac{\partial \sigma_x}{\partial p_i} = \frac{1}{2\sigma_m} \left[2p_i \sigma_i^2 + 2 \sum_{\substack{j=1 \\ j \neq i}}^n p_j \, Cov\,(x_i, x_j) \right]$$

$$= \frac{1}{\sigma_m} \left[p_i \sigma_i^2 + \sum_{\substack{j=1 \\ j \neq i}}^n p_j \, Cov\,(x_i, x_j) \right] \qquad (13.21)$$

Substituting (13.21) and (13.16) into (13.17) we have

$$Ex_i = r + \frac{Ex_m - r}{\sigma_{x_m}} \left[p_i \sigma_i^2 + \sum_{\substack{j=1 \\ j \neq i}}^n p_j \, Cov\,(x_i, x_j) \right] \cdot \frac{1}{\sigma_m} \qquad (13.22)$$

However, since by definition

$$x_m = \sum_{i=1}^n p_i x_i \qquad (13.23)$$

$$Cov\,(x_i, x_m) = Cov\left(x_i, \sum_{i=1}^n p_i x_i\right) = p_i \sigma_i^2 + \sum_{\substack{j=1 \\ j \neq i}}^n p_j \, Cov\,(x_i, x_j) \qquad (13.24)$$

Substituting (13.24) for the square-bracketed term of (13.22) yields the desired relationship of (13.20):

$$Ex_i = r + \frac{Ex_m - r}{\sigma_5^2} \, Cov\,(x_i, x_m)$$

where x_m and Ex_m denote, respectively, the returns and expected returns of the optimal equity portfolio whose proportions are fixed for all investors. This portfolio, which we shall call the "Market Portfolio," corresponds to point M of Figure XIII.7. The equilibrium relationship of risk (variance) to return which is given in Equation (13.20) must hold for *every* security in the market.

6. EQUILIBRIUM IN THE STOCK MARKET

We now turn to the problem of deriving the equilibrium conditions for the market as a whole. As a first step let us define some basic aggregate relationships.

Since every investor holds the same proportions of all available shares in his optimal portfolio, the following relationship must hold:

$$Sp_i^* = V_{i0} \tag{13.25}$$

where: S = total capital invested in the market
p_i^* = proportion of share i in the optimal portfolio
V_{i0} = market value of the i shares outstanding in the base period 0.

It follows from (13.25) that

$$p_i^* = \frac{V_{i0}}{S} \tag{13.26}$$

But since the total capital invested by all investors in all shares must equal the total market value of all outstanding shares, we have

$$S = \sum_{i=1}^{n} V_{i0} = T_0 \tag{13.27}$$

where T_0 denotes the market value of all shares, that is, the size of the market.

It follows that if the market is to clear, the relative share of any given security in the optimal portfolio must be proportional to its relative weight in the market

$$p_i^* = \frac{V_{i0}}{S} = \frac{V_{i0}}{T_0} \tag{13.28}$$

And since we are analyzing the optimal unlevered pure-equity portfolio these proportions must also add to one.

$$\sum_{i=1}^{n} p_i^* = \frac{\sum_{i=1}^{n} V_{i0}}{T_0} = \frac{\sum_{i=1}^{n} V_{i0}}{\sum_{i=1}^{n} V_{i0}} = 1 \tag{13.29}$$

6. EQUILIBRIUM IN THE STOCK MARKET

Since we have been assuming that all investors have the same expectations[27] regarding the returns on the various securities, they also have the same estimate of the market value of each of the shares at the end of the period, V_{i1}. And as Ex_i are determined in equilibrium in accordance with Equation (13.29), the prices of securities will adjust themselves during the investment period so that the following relationship holds for every security:

$$Ex_i = \frac{V_{i1} - V_{i0}}{V_{i0}} \qquad (13.30)$$

Given the expectations of investors, the value of V_{i0} which fulfills the condition of Equation (13.30) is the aggregate equilibrium value of the i shares outstanding in the base period. But any change in V_{i0} also induces changes in the variance of the shares, and therefore in all the covariances of the set of Equations (13.14) as well. Moreover, although we assume that all investors have the same expectations regarding V_{i1} these expectations are *not* single-valued. Let's denote the *estimated* variance of the aggregate value of the ith security by $\bar{\sigma}_i^2$. The variance and covariance per dollar invested can be written as follows:

$$\sigma_i^2 = \frac{\bar{\sigma}_i^2}{V_{i0}^2} \qquad (13.31)$$

$$Cov(x_i, x_j) = \frac{\bar{\sigma}_{ij}}{(V_{i0} \cdot V_{j0})} \qquad (13.32)$$

Using these definitions the following relationship can be derived:

$$[V_{i1} - (1+r)V_{i0}] = \frac{Ex_m - r}{\sigma_m^2} \cdot \frac{1}{T_0}\left[\bar{\sigma}_i^2 + \sum_{\substack{j=1 \\ j \neq i}}^{n} \bar{\sigma}_{ij}\right] \qquad (13.33)$$

Equation (13.33) represents the market equilibrium conditions when all investors have the same estimates of $\bar{\sigma}_i^2$, $\bar{\sigma}_{ij}$, and V_{i1} (and therefore of Ex_m, σ_m, and T_0 as well). Should V_{i0} deviate from its value in (13.33) the prices of securities will adjust until equilibrium is restored. Similar equations can be derived for each of the n securities comprising the market. Solving the set of

---

[27] Similar conclusions can be reached if we relax the assumption of full agreement. See Appendix XIII-4.

equations simultaneously and dividing through by the number of shares, we derive the set of equilibrium prices for all the securities.[28]

From (13.33) we can also derive the equilibrium market value for the aggregate shares of any company i,

$$V_{i0} = \frac{V_{i1} - \frac{Ex_m - r}{\sigma_m^2} \cdot \frac{1}{T_0}\left[\bar{\sigma}_i^2 + \sum_{\substack{j=1 \\ j \neq i}}^{n} \bar{\sigma}_{ij}\right]}{1 + r} \qquad (13.36)$$

The expression $(Ex_m - r)/\sigma_m^2 \cdot 1/T_0$ is the price of a unit of risk in terms of the variance rather than of the standard deviation. If we invest T_0 dollars rather than one dollar (that is, the aggregate amount invested in the market in all securities), the optimum portfolio values become $T_0 Ex_m$ and $T_0^2 \sigma_m^2$. In this case we multiply the numerator and denominator of the expression $(Ex_m - r)/\sigma_m^2$ by T_0 (which does not change its value) and rewrite (13.36) as follows:

$$V_{i0} = \frac{V_{i1} - \frac{T_0(Ex_m - r)}{T_0 \sigma_m^2} \cdot \frac{1}{T_0}\left[\bar{\sigma}_i^2 + \sum_{\substack{j=1 \\ j \neq i}}^{n} \bar{\sigma}_{ij}\right]}{1 + r} \qquad (13.37)$$

or

$$V_{i0} = \frac{V_{i1} - \frac{T_0 Ex_m - T_0 r}{T_0^2 \sigma_m^2}\left[\bar{\sigma}_i^2 + \sum_{\substack{j=1 \\ j \neq i}}^{n} \bar{\sigma}_{ij}\right]}{1 + r} \qquad (13.38)$$

---

[28] Let us take one of the equations out of the set (13.14′) of Appendix XIII–5:

$$\lambda(Ex_i - r) = \frac{1}{\sigma_m}\left[p_i \sigma_i^2 + \sum_{\substack{j=1 \\ j \neq i}}^{n} p_j \, \text{Cov}\,(x_i, x_j)\right]$$

Substituting the appropriate expression for Ex_i, σ_i, and $\text{Cov}\,(x_i, x_j)$ we get

$$\lambda\left[\frac{V_{i1} - V_{i0}}{V_{i0}} - r\right] = \frac{1}{\sigma_m}\left[\frac{V_{i0}}{T_0} \cdot \frac{\bar{\sigma}_i^2}{(V_{i0})^2} + \sum_{\substack{j=1 \\ j \neq i}}^{n} \frac{V_{j0}}{T_0} \cdot \frac{\bar{\sigma}_{ij}}{V_{i0}, V_{j0}}\right] \qquad (13.34)$$

Multiplying both sides of Equation (13.34) by V_{i0} and cancelling terms yields

$$\lambda[V_{i1} - (1+r)V_{i0}] = \frac{1}{T_0 \sigma_m}\left[\bar{\sigma}_i^2 + \sum_{\substack{j=1 \\ j \neq i}}^{n} \bar{\sigma}_{ij}\right] \qquad (13.35)$$

And recalling that by Equation (13.16) $(1/\lambda) = (Ex_m - r)/\sigma_m$ must hold in equilibrium, this becomes Equation (13.33) of the text.

The equilibrium conditions in terms of individual share prices are given in Appendix XIII–3.

which reduces to

$$V_{i0} = \frac{V_{i1} - \gamma\left[\bar{\sigma}_i^2 + \sum_{\substack{j=1\\j\neq i}}^{n}\bar{\sigma}_{ij}^2\right]}{1+r} \qquad (13.39)$$

and therefore

$$\frac{V_{i1} - V_{i0}}{V_{i0}} = r + \frac{\gamma\left[\bar{\sigma}_i^2 + \sum_{\substack{j=1\\j\neq i}}^{n}\bar{\sigma}_{ij}^2\right]}{V_{i0}} \qquad (13.40)$$

where γ denotes the price of a unit of risk in terms of *variance*[29] when the total amount invested in the market is taken into account. It should also be noted that the present value of a share is equal to its "certainty equivalent" value at the end of the period discounted at the riskless pure rate of interest (see Equation (13.36)). Equation (13.40) represents the basic equilibrium conditions of a perfect securities market and can be verbalized as follows: In equilibrium, security prices adjust to the point where the prospective rate of return to investors in every security is just equal to the riskless rate of interest *plus* a risk premium which reflects not only that security's risk but its total contribution to the risk of the optimum portfolio as well.

7. SUMMARY

The preceding five chapters spelled out a normative theory of investment behavior. In this chapter the normative theory was applied to the positive problem of explaining equilibrium prices in the securities market. A model, based on the work of Sharpe and Lintner, was developed on the following assumptions:

> (a) investors are risk-averse and choose their portfolios by the Mean–Variance Criterion.
> (b) securities are traded in a perfect market.

The first case considered is an example in which investors are constrained to portfolios which include the shares of one company and/or riskless bonds (or loans). The relationship between the expected return and the standard deviation of such portfolios is linear, with a slope $(E_x - r)/\sigma_x$. The slope of the linear transformation line measures the "price" of a unit of risk, that is, the number of units of expected return which an investor is willing to forgo

---

[29] See Lintner *op. cit.*

per unit reduction in the standard deviation. And the transformation line itself constitutes the MVC locus of efficient portfolios. The optimal portfolio is given by the tangency of the transformation line to the investor's indifference curve.

When the option of borrowing or lending at a riskless interest rate is introduced the investment process can be dichotomized as follows:

> (1) Choosing the risky security which is to be included in the portfolio, independent of the investor's tastes;
> (2) Choosing the optimal proportions of riskless bonds (loans) and of risky securities, in accordance with the investor's tastes.

The first stage corresponds to finding the stock which lies on the highest transformation line; the second stage corresponds to finding the tangent between the transformation line and the investor's indifference curve. Where investors are constrained holding single-stock portfolios, the prices of shares will adjust so that all the shares (potential single-stock portfolios) lie along the same transformation line. This result, however, does not hold for an imperfect market in which the lending rate differs from the borrowing rate.

In an unconstrained perfect market, where investors can include in their portfolios as many securities of as many companies as they wish, the proportion of each security in the risky portion of the portfolios of *all* investors is the same, independent of their individual tastes. Thus all investors will diversify the equity portions of their portfolios in the *same* proportions among the individual stocks; differences in individual tastes serve only to determine the proportion of riskless bonds (loans) which the investor buys (takes). It is this property of a perfect market which permits us to aggregate the individuals' demands for securities into a market demand function. Since all investors hold the same proportions of the same stocks in their portfolios, it can also be shown that the optimal portfolio includes *all* available stocks. And since the larger the number of available stocks, the greater are the opportunities to reduce risk, the entire market line shifts to the left, thereby permitting investors to reach higher indifference curves.

It also follows that, for a given interest rate, the price of a unit of risk (slope of the market line) will be higher in larger markets. The optimum market equilibrium condition states that all investors will increase their holdings of a particular security up to the point where the value of the security's marginal contribution to the portfolio's total variance equals its "risk premium," that is, the difference between its expected rate of return and the riskless interest rate.

QUESTIONS AND PROBLEMS

13.1 What are the assumptions underlying a perfect capital market? How would you go about testing the realism of these assumptions?

13.2 It has been said that the prices of risky alternatives are determined in a perfect capital market *as if* there were only one investor. Do you agree? Explain.

13.3 Assume a perfect capital market in which investors are constrained to building single-stock risk portfolios; that borrowing or lending at a riskless interest rate is possible; and that in *equilibrium* the following relationship between two risky securities i and j holds:

	Share i	Share j
Expected Return (%)	0.18	0.25
Standard Deviation (%)	0.08	0.12

(a) What is the riskless rate of interest in this market?

(b) Assume that the investor is confronted with two mutually exclusive alternatives:
    A portfolio of $900 worth of the security i;
    A portfolio of $600 worth of security j plus $300 in riskless bonds.
Which of these two alternatives will he prefer?

(c) Now assume that the investor can choose either portfolio "A" ($900 worth of i) or another portfolio made up of security i and bonds, or a levered portfolio of security i (that is, security i plus loans). If the investor prefers portfolio "A" what can you infer about his indifference curves?

13.4 Assume the following data:
$$\text{borrowing rate} = 8\%$$
$$\text{lending rate} = 4\%$$

and that there are only two risky stocks A and B in the market, with the following expected returns and standard deviations:

	A	B
Expected Return	18	12
Standard Deviation	20	10

Consider the case of an investor with \$100 who is constrained to a single-stock portfolio plus bonds (or loans).

(a) What is the maximum amount that the investor will borrow in order to build a levered portfolio of stock B?

(b) What is the maximum amount which will be invested in bonds when constructing a mixed portfolio of bonds and stock A?

13.5 Assume a case in which all investors are constrained to single-stock portfolios plus bonds (or loans); the riskless interest rate is 6%; and the market is *not* in equilibrium. The following data refer to the three stocks, A, B, and C, which comprise the market:

	A	B	C
Expected Return	10	20	30
Standard Deviation	20	60	40

Compare the equilibrium prices of each of these stocks with their initial prices; that is, determine whether the price rises, falls, or remains the same during the equilibrating process.

13.6 Derive the market's price for a unit of risk reduction, when investors are constrained to single-stock portfolios and bonds (loans).

13.7 Define the "market line" for the case of single-stock and multiple-stock portfolios (a) when the borrowing rate equals the lending rate, (b) when the borrowing and lending rates differ.

13.8 In what sense does a perfect capital market dichotomize the investment process?

13.9 What are the theoretical considerations which lend support to the contention that in a perfect market the returns on the optimal portfolio will tend to approximate a normal distribution?

13.10 What is the general equilibrium relationship between risk (variance) and return which must hold for every risk asset in a perfect market?

QUESTIONS AND PROBLEMS

13.11 Do you expect that in an efficient market every stock will have the same risk premium? Explain. How would you change your answer if we substitute "diversified portfolio" for "stock"?

13.12 Assume that an investor whose indifference curves in the (μ, σ) expected return–standard deviation plane are given by the equation

$$\mu = a + 2\sigma$$

wishes to invest $1,000 in a portfolio which includes one stock. The rate of interest on riskless bonds (r) is 5% and the expected return and standard deviation of the single stock are 0.12 and 0.07, respectively.

(a) Is the investor risk-averse?

(b) What are the optimal investment proportions for a portfolio composed of the stock and bonds, on the assumption that the investor invests all of the $1,000 in the portfolio?

(c) What would be your answer to parts (a) and (b) if the investor's indifference curves were given by the relationship:

$$\mu = a + 0.5\sigma$$

(d) What would be your answer to parts (a) and (b) if the following equation described the investor's indifference curves:

$$\mu = a + 20\sigma^2$$

SELECTED REFERENCES

Bierwag, G. O., and Grove, M. A., "On Capital Asset Prices: Comment," *Journal of Finance* (March 1965).
Bower, D. H., and Bower, R. S., "Test of a Stock Valuation Model," *Journal of Finance* (May 1970).
Diamond, P. A., "The Role of a Stock Market in a General Equilibrium Model with Technological Uncertainty," *American Economic Review* (September 1967).
Fama, E. F., "The Behavior of Stock Market Prices," *Journal of Business* (January 1965).
———, "Risk, Return and Equilibrium: Some Clarifying Comments," *Journal of Finance* (March 1968).
Friedman, M., *Essays in Positive Economics*. Chicago: University of Chicago Press, 1953.
Lintner, J., "The Aggregation of Investors' Diverse Judgments and Preferences in Purely Competitive Security Markets," *Journal of Financial and Quantitative Analysis* (December 1969).
———, "The Market Price of Risk, Size of Market and Investor's Risk Aversion," *Review of Economics and Statistics* (February 1970).
———, "Security Prices, Risk and Maximal Gains from Diversification," *Journal of Finance* (December 1965).
Litzenberger, R. H., "Equilibrium in the Equity Market Under Uncertainty," *Journal of Finance* (September 1969).
Lorie, J. H., "Some Comments on Recent Quantitative and Formal Research on the Stock Market," *Journal of Business* (January 1966).
Mandelbrot, B., "The Variation of Certain Speculative Prices," *Journal of Business* (October 1963).
Moore, B. J., *An Introduction to the Theory of Finance: Assetholder Behavior Under Uncertainty*. New York: The Free Press, 1968.
Mossin, J., "Equilibrium in a Capital Asset Market," *Econometrica* (October 1966).
Pogue, J. A., "An Extension of the Markowitz Portfolio Selection Model to Include Variable Transactions' Costs, Short Sales, Leverage Policies and Taxes," *Journal of Finance* (December 1970).

SELECTED REFERENCES

Pye, G., "Portfolio Selection and Security Prices," *Review of Economics and Statistics* (February 1967).

Renwick, F. B., "Economic Growth and Distributions of Change in Stock Market Prices," *Industrial Management Review* (Spring 1968).

———, "Theory of Investment Behavior and Empirical Analysis of Stock Market Price Relatives," *Management Science* (September 1968).

Sharpe, W. F., "Capital Asset Prices: A Theory of Market Equilibrium Under Conditions of Risk," *Journal of Finance* (September 1964).

———, *Portfolio Theory and Capital Markets*. New York: McGraw-Hill, 1970.

Tobin, J., "Liquidity Preference as Behavior Towards Risk," *Review of Economic Studies* (February 1958).

APPENDIX XIII-1
Proof that Optimal Investment Proportions are Independent of the Scale of Investment

The purpose of this appendix is to show that the optimal investment proportions are independent of the scale of investment. We have seen that the optimal proportions per dollar invested are given by the set of proportions which maximizes the following expression:

$$tg\alpha = \frac{Ex - r}{\sigma x} = \frac{\sum_{i=1}^{n} P_i Ex_i - r}{\sqrt{\sum_{i=1}^{n} P_i^2 \sigma_i^2 + 2 \sum_{\substack{i=1 \\ j>i}}^{n} P_i P_j \, Cov\,(x_i x_j)}} \qquad (13.1.1)$$

where Ex and σx are the expected return and standard deviation of a given portfolio, and r is the interest rate.

Suppose that we diversify Z dollars in the same proportions as above, that is, the return on the portfolio is given by

$$P_1 Z X_1 + P_2 Z X_2 + \cdots + P_n Z X_n \qquad (13.1.2)$$

and hence the expected return and the standard deviation of the new portfolio are

$$EZX = \sum_{i=1}^{n} P_i Z X_i = Z \sum_{i=1}^{n} P_i X_i = ZEX \qquad (13.1.3)$$

Similarly,

$$\sigma(ZX) = Z\sigma_x \qquad (13.1.4)$$

Since the maximum risk-free return is Zr, the slope of the new market line is given by

$$tg\alpha = \frac{ZEX - Zr}{Z\sigma_x} = \frac{EX - r}{\sigma_x}$$

That is, the slope is determined independently of the amount invested and hence the optimal proportions are independent of the scale of the investment.

APPENDIX XIII-2

The Shape of Investors' Indifference Curves

We shall show that a risk averter's indifference curve is necessarily concave upward and a risk lover's indifference curve is necessarily concave downward. We shall prove the above relationship for two alternatives: (a) two parameter distributions, and (b) quadratic utility functions.

a. Two-parameter Distributions

The expected utility is given by

$$EU(x) = \int_{-\infty}^{\infty} U(x)f(x:\mu, \sigma)\, dx \qquad (13.2.1)$$

where x is the random variable (return) and (μ, σ) are the parameters of the distribution.

After normalizing the random variable we obtain $Z = (x - \mu)/\sigma$. Hence $x = \mu + z\sigma$ where the expected value and the variance of z are 0 and 1 respectively. Plugging these results into (13.2.1), we get

$$EU(x) = \int_{-\infty}^{\infty} U(\mu + z\sigma)f(z; 0, 1)\, dz \qquad (13.2.2)$$

By definition, an indifference curve is a locus of points (μ, σ) along which the expected utility is constant, that is, all the points (μ, σ) which yield

$$C = \int_{-\infty}^{\infty} U(\mu + z\sigma)f(z: 0, 1)\, dz \qquad (13.2.3)$$

where C is a given constant.

Differentiating (13.2.3) with respect to σ gives

$$0 = \int_{-\infty}^{\infty} U'(\mu + z\sigma)\left[\frac{d\mu}{d\sigma} + z\right] f(z: 0, 1)\, dz$$

Hence

$$\frac{d\mu}{d\sigma} = \frac{-\int_{-\infty}^{\infty} ZU'(\mu + z\sigma)f(z: 0, 1)\, dz}{\int_{-\infty}^{\infty} U'(\mu + z\sigma)f(z: 0, 1)\, dz} \qquad (13.2.4)$$

Since $\mu + z\sigma = x$, we get from (13.2.4)

$$\frac{d\mu}{d\sigma} = \frac{-\int_{-\infty}^{\infty} ZU'(x)f(z; 0, 1)\,dz}{\int_{-\infty}^{\infty} U'(x)f(z; 0, 1)\,dz} \qquad (13.2.5)$$

We can determine the sign of the slope of the investor's indifference curve ($d\mu/d\sigma$) by examining Equation (13.2.5). $U'(x)$ is the marginal utility of return, and therefore this term is non-negative everywhere. Hence the denominator of (13.2.5) is positive. The numerator can be rewritten as follows:

$$-\int_{-\infty}^{\infty} ZU'(x)f(z; 0, 1)\,dz$$
$$= -\left[\int_{-\infty}^{0} ZU'(x)f(z; 0, 1)\,dz + \int_{0}^{\infty} ZU'(x)f(z; 0, 1)\,dz\right] \qquad (13.2.6)$$

Now, if the investor is a risk averter ($U''(x) < 0$), the values of $U'(x)$ in the range $(-\infty, 0)$ are higher than the appropriate values in the range $(0, +\infty)$ and hence the numerator of (13.2.5) is positive, that is, we can determine that for risk averters $\partial\mu/\partial\sigma > 0$. Similarly, for risk lovers (13.2.6) is negative (since $U''(x) > 0$) and hence $\partial\mu/\partial\sigma < 0$. Similarly in case that $U''' < 0$ the curvature of the indifference curve is concave. To prove this, suppose that (μ, o) and (μ', o') are on the same indifference curve. Is ($\frac{\mu+\mu'}{2}$, $\frac{o+o'}{2}$) on the same indifference curve or on a higher or lower one? If $U''' < 0$, it is on a higher indifference curve, which implies that indifference curves of risk-averters are indeed concave upward. If $U''' < 0$ we get,

$$\tfrac{1}{2} U (\mu+oZ) + \tfrac{1}{2} \tfrac{1}{2} U (\mu'+o'Z) < U \frac{\mu+\mu'}{2} + \frac{o+o'}{2}Z)$$

Consequently, the expected utility of ($\frac{\mu+\mu'}{2}$, $\frac{o+o'}{2}$) is greater than the expected utility for either (μ, o) or (μ', o') which implies that the indifference curves of risk averters are indeed concave. By analogy if $U''' > 0$, the indifference curves are convex.

b. Quadratic Utility Function

We have seen in Chapter XI that the expected utility for the quadratic case is given by

$$EU(x) = EX + \beta(EX)^2 + \beta\sigma^2 \quad \text{(see Equation 11.5)} \qquad (13.2.7)$$

where $\beta > 0$ for risk averters and $\beta < 0$ for risk lovers.

Differentiating (13.2.7) with respect to σ, and treating $EU(x)$ as a constant, we obtain

SHAPE OF INVESTORS' INDIFFERENCE CURVES

$$0 = \frac{dEX}{d\sigma} + \beta 2\sigma + \beta \frac{d(EX)^2}{d\sigma}$$

For convenience let us denote EX by μ.

$$0 = \frac{d\mu}{d\sigma} + \beta 2\sigma + \beta \frac{d\mu^2}{d\sigma} \qquad (13.2.8)$$

Since

$$\frac{d\mu^2}{d\sigma} = \frac{d\mu^2}{d\mu} \cdot \frac{d\mu}{d\sigma} = 2\mu \frac{d\mu}{d\sigma}$$

we get from (13.2.8)

$$0 = \frac{d\mu}{d\sigma}(1 + 2\mu\beta) + 2\beta\sigma \qquad (13.2.9)$$

and the slope of the indifference curve is given by

$$\frac{d\mu}{d\sigma} = \frac{-2\beta\sigma}{1 + 2 \cdot \mu\beta}$$

For risk averters we have $\beta < 0$ and $x < -(1/2\beta)$ (see Chapter XI). Since $x < -(1/2\beta)$ for every x, we can conclude that $\mu < -(1/2\beta)$, hence $d\mu/d\sigma > 0$. Similarly, for a risk lover $\beta > 0$ and $x > -(1/2\beta)$ [hence $\mu > -(1/2\beta)$], that is, $d\mu/d\sigma < 0$. Taking the second derivative of the above term, it can easily be seen that this derivative is positive for risk averters and negative for risk lovers. Q.E.D.*

---

* The proof follows that of Tobin, 1958. *op. cit.*

APPENDIX XIII–3
Equilibrium Prices in a Perfect Securities Market

In Chapter XIII we analyzed the aggregate equilibrium market values of a company's stock. In this appendix we give the same equilibrium results but in terms of price per share rather than in terms of the aggregate value.

Let us define the following notation:

N_i = the number of shares of firm i
P_{i1} = the expected price of the share at the end of the investment period
P_{i0} = the equilibrium price
σ_i = the expected variance of the value of the share at the end of the investment period
σ_{ij} = the expected covariance of the value of a share of firm i and a share of firm j

Hence the aggregate value of the stock is given by

$$V_{i1} = N_i P_{i1} \tag{13.3.1}$$

$$V_{i0} = N_i P_{i0} \tag{13.3.2}$$

Similarly the variance (σ_i^2) and the covariance (σ_{ij}) in terms of aggregate values are given by

$$\sigma_i^{*2} = N_i^2 \sigma_i^2 \tag{13.3.3}$$

$$\sigma_{ij}^{*} = N_i N_j \sigma_{ij} \tag{13.3.4}$$

The equilibrium equation given in Chapter XIII is

$$V_{i0} = \frac{V_{i1} - \gamma\left[\sigma_i^{*2} + \sum_{\substack{i=1 \\ j>i}}^{n} \sigma_{ij}^{*}\right]}{1 + r} \tag{13.3.5}$$

Substituting (13.3.1), (13.3.2), (13.3.3), and (13.3.4) in (13.3.5) we obtain

$$N_i P_{i0} = \frac{N_i P_{i1} - \gamma \left[N_i^2 \sigma_i^2 + \sum_{\substack{i=1 \\ j>i}}^{n} N_i N_j \sigma_{ij} \right]}{1 + r} \quad (13.3.6)$$

Reducing by N_i, the equilibrium market value in terms of individual shares is obtained:

$$P_{i0} = \frac{P_{i1} - \gamma \left[N_i \sigma_i^2 + \sum_{\substack{i=1 \\ j>i}}^{n} N_j \sigma_{ij} \right]}{1 + r} \quad (13.3.7)$$

Thus the end-of-period variance is weighted by the number of shares outstanding. This weighted average ensures that the aggregate value of a company's stock is independent of stock splits.*

---

* The proof follows that of Lintner, *Journal of Finance*, 1965, *op. cit.*

APPENDIX XIII-4

The Effects of Investors' Expectations on Equilibrium Prices in the Securities Market

Assuming full agreement among investors about securities' prices in the future, we analyzed in Chapter XIII the forces which determine equilibrium prices. In this appendix we shall show that similar conclusions can be reached even when we relax the assumption of full agreement. When investors assign different probability distributions to the end-of-period values of the same stock, we say that there is disagreement among investors. In this case the equilibrium value of the company's stock is a function of the weighted averages of the various estimates of the end-of-period variances, expected returns, and covariances.

Assuming agreement we find that in equilibrium the price of the ith company's share is given by

$$(1 + r)P_{i0} = P_{i1} - \gamma \left[N_i \sigma_i + \sum_{\substack{j=1 \\ j \neq i}}^{n} N_j \sigma_{ij} \right] \quad \text{(see Appendix XIII-3)} \quad (13.4.1)$$

If investors' judgments differ, the kth investor will be in equilibrium if the market price P_{i0} is such that (13.4.1) holds in terms of his estimates of P_i, σ_i, and σ_{ij}. Hence for the kth investor the following equation must hold:

$$P_{i1(k)} - (1 + r)P_{i0} = \gamma_k \left[N_{i(k)} \sigma^2_{i(k)} + \sum_{\substack{j=1 \\ j \neq i}}^{n} N_{j(k)} \sigma_{ij(k)} \right] \equiv \gamma_k 0_k \quad (13.4.2)$$

where the index k denotes the kth investor's estimates and $\gamma_k \equiv A_k/B_k$, where A_k is defined as the aggregate excess dollar return of the investor's portfolio, and B_k is defined as the variance of the end-of-period values of his portfolio. For simplicity we also denote by 0_k the entire term in the right-hand side of (13.4.2).

Using this definition of γ_k we get from (13.4.2)

$$B_k [P_{i1(k)} - (1 + r)P_{i0}] = A_k 0_k \quad (13.4.3)$$

INVESTORS' EXPECTATIONS ON EQUILIBRIUM PRICES

Summing (13.4.3) for all investors in the market we get

$$\sum_k B_k P_{i1(k)} - (1+r)P_{i0} \sum_k B_k = \sum_k A_k 0_k \qquad (13.4.4)$$

Hence,

$$(1+r)P_{i0} = \frac{\sum_k B_k P_{i1(k)}}{\sum_k B_k} - \frac{\sum_k A_k 0_k}{\sum_k B_k} \qquad (13.4.5)$$

since

$$\frac{\sum_k A_k 0_k}{\sum_k B_k} = \frac{\sum_k A_k}{\sum_k B_k} \cdot \frac{\sum_k A_k 0_k}{\sum_k A_k} = \gamma \frac{\sum_k A_k 0_k}{\sum_k A_k}$$

(γ is the excess dollar return of the total market portfolio divided by its variance. See Chapter XIII.)

We obtain from (13.4.5)

$$(1+r)P_{i0} = \frac{\sum_k B_k P_{i1(k)}}{\sum_k B_k} - \gamma \frac{\sum_k A_k 0_k}{\sum_k A_k} \qquad (13.4.6)$$

Equation (13.4.6) is very similar to the equilibrium equation when we assume that the investor's judgments of the end-of-period values do not differ (see Equation (13.4.7)). γ is identical in both cases and the only difference is that the end-of-period prices as well as the risk of each share of Equation (13.4.6) are weighted averages of the various estimates of the investors.*

---

* The proof follows that of Lintner, *Journal of Finance*, 1965, *op. cit.*

APPENDIX XIII–5

Derivation of the Equilibrium Risk-Return Trade-off in a Perfect Market

The purpose of this appendix is to derive Equations (13.15) and (13.16) of the text from the set of Equations (13.14). First we rewrite the set (13.14):

$$\frac{\partial C}{\partial p_1} = \tfrac{1}{2}(\sigma^2 x)^{-\frac{1}{2}}\left[2p_1\sigma_1^2 + 2\sum_{j=2}^{n} p_j\,Cov\,(x_1, x_j)\right] - \lambda(Ex_1 - r) = 0$$

$$\frac{\partial C}{\partial p_2} = \tfrac{1}{2}(\sigma^2 x)^{-\frac{1}{2}}\left[2p_2\sigma_2^2 + 2\sum_{\substack{j=1 \\ j\neq 2}}^{n} p_j\,Cov\,(x_2, x_j)\right] - \lambda(Ex_2 - r) = 0$$

$$\vdots \qquad\qquad\qquad\qquad\qquad\qquad\qquad\qquad (13.14)$$

$$\frac{\partial C}{\partial p_n} = \tfrac{1}{2}(\sigma^2 x)^{-\frac{1}{2}}\left[2p_n\sigma_n^2 + 2\sum_{j=1}^{n-1} p_j\,Cov\,(x_n, x_j)\right] - \lambda(Ex_n - r) = 0$$

$$\frac{\partial C}{\partial \lambda} = Ex_0 - \sum_{i=1}^{n} p_i Ex_i - \left(1 - \sum_{i=1}^{n} p_i\right)r = 0$$

Cancelling out the number "2" in the first n equations of (13.14) and transposing terms yields the following set of equations:

$$\frac{1}{\sigma_x}\left[p_1\sigma_1^2 + \sum_{j=2}^{n} p_j\,Cov\,(x_1, x_j)\right] = \lambda(Ex_1 - r)$$

$$\frac{1}{\sigma_x}\left[p_2\sigma_2^2 + \sum_{\substack{j=1 \\ j\neq 2}}^{n} p_j\,Cov\,(x_2, x_j)\right] = \lambda(Ex_2 - r)$$

$$\vdots \qquad\qquad\qquad\qquad\qquad\qquad\qquad\qquad (13.14')$$

$$\frac{1}{\sigma_x}\left[p_n^2\sigma_n^2 + \sum_{j=1}^{n-1} p_j\,Cov\,(x_n, x_j)\right] = \lambda(Ex_n - r)$$

RISK-RETURN TRADE-OFF IN A PERFECT MARKET

Multiplying the first equation by p_1; the second equation by p_2 and so on for the remaining equations gives the following:

$$\frac{1}{\sigma_x}\left[p_1^2\sigma_1^2 + \sum_{j=2}^{n} p_1 p_j \, Cov\,(x_1, x_j)\right] = \lambda(p_1 Ex_1 - p_1 r)$$

$$\frac{1}{\sigma_x}\left[p_2^2\sigma_2^2 + \sum_{\substack{j=1 \\ j\neq 2}}^{n} p_2 p_j \, Cov\,(x_2, x_j)\right] = \lambda(p_2 Ex_2 - p_2 r)$$

$$\vdots \qquad\qquad\qquad\qquad \vdots \qquad\qquad\qquad\qquad \vdots \qquad\qquad (13.14'')$$

$$\frac{1}{\sigma_x}\left[p_n^2\sigma_n^2 + \sum_{j=1}^{n-1} p_n p_j \, Cov\,(x_n, x_j)\right] = \lambda(p_n Ex_n - p_n r)$$

Summing all of the equations of (13.14'') we have

$$\frac{1}{\sigma_x}\left[\sum_{i=1}^{n} p_i^2\sigma_i^2 + \sum_{\substack{i=1 \\ j\neq i}}^{n} p_{ij}\,Cov\,(x_i, x_j)\right] = \lambda\left[\sum_{i=1}^{n} p_i Ex_i - \sum_{i=1}^{n} p_i r\right] \quad (13.15)$$

The expression within the square brackets on the left-hand side of Equation (13.15) is simply the variance $\sigma^2 x$ so that (13.15) reduces to

$$\sigma_x = \lambda\left[\sum_{i=1}^{n} p_i Ex_i - \sum_{i=1}^{n} p_i r\right] \quad (13.16)$$

We can add and subtract the expression $p_r r$ without changing the equation, which gives

$$\sigma_x = \lambda\left[\sum_{i=1}^{n} p_i Ex_i + p_r r - r\left(\sum_{i=1}^{n} p_i + p_r\right)\right]$$

Since, by definition,

$$\sum_{i=1}^{n} p_i + p_r = 1$$

and

$$Ex = \sum_{i=1}^{n} p_i Ex_i + p_r r$$

the optimal values can be written as

$$\sigma_{xm} = \lambda(Ex_m - r)$$

or

$$\frac{1}{\lambda} = \frac{Ex_m - r}{\sigma_{xm}}$$

PART III
APPLICATIONS OF PORTFOLIO THEORY

Chapter XIV
The Assessment of Portfolio Performance

1. INTRODUCTION

The theory of portfolio selection which was expounded in Chapters VI through XII of the book offers normative rules for the diversification of risk assets; the market equilibrium model of Chapter XIII, which was derived from the normative theory, provides a positive explanation and interpretation of the structure of prices and returns in the capital market. Of course, these two aspects of the theory of portfolio balance are closely interrelated and to a large extent overlap. Normative rules designed to maximize investors' wealth inevitably depend on the positive forces which determine the prices of risk assets in the market. The structure of prices, in turn, cannot be explained without taking individuals' normative portfolio decisions into account. In this and the following two chapters we shall put both the normative and positive aspects of the theory through their paces. In this chapter the portfolio model is used to assess the performance of mutual funds and to test the degree to which efficiency criteria, based on realized returns, can be used to facilitate current investment decisions. Taking mutual funds as a proxy for portfolios in general we shall attempt to "explain" the risk–return pattern of mutual fund returns during the period 1946–69. These results, in turn, will be used to account for the rapid growth of this type of investment medium. To accomplish this, several measures of portfolio performance will be introduced and the market model of Chapter XIII will be modified slightly to take into account the major type of imperfections which exist even in the most efficient of security markets. Since our theory is based on *expected* variables, and therefore relates to the future, we next direct our efforts to a test of the ability of the various efficiency criteria used in this book to *predict* the future *on the basis of past data* on risk and return. The results of these tests are then analyzed against the background of the so-called "Random Walk" theory of security prices. We conclude the chapter with a few brief remarks regarding the implications and significance of portfolio theory for investment analysis.

2. MEASURING THE INVESTMENT PERFORMANCE OF MUTUAL FUNDS

Mutual funds, or open-end investment companies as they are often called, pool the resources of many individuals and invest them in a diversified portfolio of securities. Unlike other financial intermediaries such as insurance companies and pension funds, which invest in securities as a means to meet assumed liabilities or risks, investing itself is the primary function of mutual funds. The latter provide their participating members with a *direct* investment experience in securities, that is, one which directly reflects the changes in capital values and income of a portfolio of securities.[1] Although differences exist among the individual funds, an open-end investment company has two distinguishing characteristics:

> (a) Participating shares in the mutual funds are continuously offered to the public at a price which reflects the value of the underlying assets at the time of sale. Hence the term *open-end*.

> (b) The fund is obligated to redeem or repurchase all shares presented at a price based on the net asset value per share at the time of redemption.

Mutual funds provide a convenient and very popular investment medium, especially for the small investor. During the past two decades the rate of growth of U.S. mutual funds' assets outstripped that of insurance companies, saving deposits, and U.S. Government Saving Bonds.[2] Moreover, this phenomenon has not been limited to the United States: as Table XIV-1 shows, the relative increase in mutual funds' assets during the period

---

[1] For an excellent analysis of mutual funds' activities, see Investment Company Institute, *Management Investment Companies*, Englewood Cliffs, N.J.: Prentice-Hall, 1963. Comprehensive annual surveys are available in Arthur Wiesenberger & Co., *Investment Companies*, annual editions.
[2] See R. E. Greely, "What's Happening to Mutual Fund Management Companies," *Financial Analysts Journal* (Sept.–Oct. 1967), p. 79.

2. INVESTMENT PERFORMANCE OF MUTUAL FUNDS

TABLE XIV-1. End-of-year assets of open-end investment companies 1965-68 (in millions of dollars)

	1965	1966	1967	1968	Average Annual Growth Rate (percentage)
Near East, Far East, and Africa	1,361	2,548	2,954	3,590	38
Europe	3,503	3,595	4,853	6,692	24
North America (excl. U.S.A.)	1,963	2,237	2,906	3,450	20
South America	31	37	38	58	23
Total All Countries (excl. U.S.A.)	6,858	8,417	10,751	13,790	26
U.S.A.	35,220	34,829	44,701	52,677	14

SOURCE: *Mutual Fund Fact Book*, 1969.

1965-68 was even greater outside the United States (average annual growth rate equal to 26%) than was true for U.S. mutual funds (average annual growth rate equal to 14%). By the end of 1968, almost 53 billion dollars had been invested in mutual funds in the United States,[3] while mutual fund assets outside of the United States had reached the 14 billion dollar mark.

2.1 THE BENCHMARKS OF MUTUAL FUND PERFORMANCE

Mutual funds often have varying objectives, and as a result the funds' investment policies also tend to differ. Funds which emphasize capital gains attempt to invest mainly in growth stocks, while funds which emphasize current income tend to build more balanced portfolios. But despite these differences, some investment objectives and policies are common to all (or almost all) of the funds. For example, all mutual funds typically attempt

> (a) to increase returns through professional investment analysis, and by taking full advantage of scale economies in the management of the portfolio;
>
> (b) to decrease investment risk by diversifying the portfolio.

---

[3] Following the stock market decline, U.S. mutual fund assets had shrunk to $43 billion by the end of 1969.

When deciding between the alternatives of investing in mutual fund shares or directly in common stocks, investors must first weigh the degree to which the funds have succeeded in achieving these two common objectives against the expenses (usually in the form of a loading charge) incurred in providing the professional management.

Professional investment management, scale economies, and management expenses are all factors which are reflected in the rate of return a fund earns on its investments. If a fund's mean rate of return is higher than the rate of return earned by an investor who randomly diversifies his stock market investments, one might conclude that the mutual fund has succeeded in achieving the first of its main objectives, that is, increasing the average rate of return to investors. However, the second common objective of mutual funds, decreasing risk, is not reflected in the average rate of return earned by mutual fund investors, but rather in the *variability* of the annual rates of return. Fluctuations of the rate of return can be measured by the standard deviation of the rate of return; the smaller the standard deviation, the more stable the series of returns, and consequently the lower the risk associated with such investments. Thus, to evaluate the investment performance of mutual funds, we require two variables: the mean rate of return and the standard deviation associated with these returns.

To evaluate a particular mutual fund's performance we shall compare the fund's average rate of return and risk with the average rate of return and risk of investments randomly chosen from the stock market, that is, with an *unmanaged* portfolio. The accepted way to carry out such an evaluation is to compare the mutual fund's average return and variability with the average return and variability of a general index such as Dow-Jones or Standard & Poor. For this purpose we shall use Standard & Poor's 500 Stock Index as our proxy for an unmanaged portfolio. Price and dividend data for the Standard & Poor's Index are readily available, and we have computed the annual rates of return (dividends plus the change in the Index) for the period 1946–69. This series of annual rates of return was then used to compute the average rate of return and variability (standard deviation) for an "unmanaged" portfolio. The rate of return and variability for such investments are represented by the point marked "$S\&P$" in Figure XIV.1; the average return and variability (risk) for an unmanaged portfolio during the period were 12.0% and 16.3% respectively.

By passing vertical and horizontal dashed lines through point $S\&P$, Figure XIV.1 has been divided into four zones marked I, II, III, and IV. Now if we calculate the average rate of return and variability for an individual mutual fund, that fund's performance can be represented by a point in one of these four zones. Should a fund's average return and variability be given by

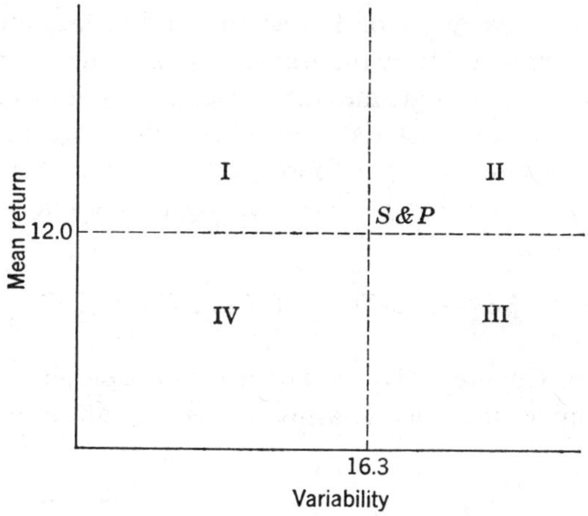

3. ALTERNATIVE MEASURES OF INVESTMENT PERFORMANCE

FIGURE XIV.1.

a point in zone I, one can safely conclude that this particular mutual fund outperformed an unmanaged portfolio, since all points in zone I represent higher returns and lower variability than the Standard & Poor's benchmark. On the other hand, if a fund has a combination of mean return and variability represented by a point in zone III, the unmanaged portfolio is clearly superior since point $S\&P$ has a higher return and lower risk than all points in zone III. The case is much less clear-cut, however, with respect to funds whose rate of return–risk characteristics place them in either of zones II or IV: a point in zone II represents a higher return, but also a higher risk, than an unmanaged portfolio, while points in zone IV have a lower risk, but also a lower return, than the randomly chosen portfolio.

Unfortunately most mutual funds have risk–return combinations represented by points in zones II or IV, and consequently the analysis must be further refined if conclusions are to be reached regarding the funds' relative performance.

3. ALTERNATIVE MEASURES OF INVESTMENT PERFORMANCE

Basing their research on the Sharpe–Lintner security market model (see Chapter XIII), several researchers have suggested alternative measures of portfolio performance. Although these measures differ from one another they are very closely related,[4] and in fact they represent a common attempt to reduce the two-parameter risk–return dimension of investment performance to a single measure which incorporates considerations of return with an adjustment for risk. In what follows we shall confine our attention to two measures of portfolio performance: (a) Sharpe's reward-to-variability ratio, and (b) Treynor's characteristic line.

3.1 REWARD-TO-VARIABILITY RATIO

In Chapter XIII we noted that the slope of the market line uniquely determines the price of a unit of risk for all investors in a perfect capital market:

$$\frac{Ex_m - r}{\sigma_{x_m}}$$

where: Ex_m = the expected return of the market portfolio
r = the riskless rate of interest
σ_{x_m} = the standard deviation of returns of the market portfolio.

A similar relationship can be defined for *any* portfolio i:

$$\frac{Ex_i - r}{\sigma_{x_i}}$$

For empirical work we plug in the estimates of these parameters: the actual observed average rate of return, the pure interest rate, and the standard deviation of returns. Sharpe calls this ratio "reward-to-variability" (R/V) and has suggested its use as an indicator of past performance of portfolios[5] in general and of mutual funds in particular.[6] Figure XIV.2 illustrates the

---

[4] On the formal relationship of the performance measures formulated by Jensen, Sharpe, and Treynor see Irwin Friend and Marshall Blume, "Measurement of Portfolio Performance Under Uncertainty," *American Economic Review* LX (September 1970).
All three performance indicators were first applied to the problem of evaluating the investment performance of mutual funds. See W. F. Sharpe, "Mutual Fund Performance," *Journal of Business* 39 (January 1966); J. Treynor, "How to Rate Management Investment Funds," *Harvard Business Review* 43 (Jan.–Feb. 1965); and M. C. Jensen, "The Performance of Mutual Funds in the Period 1945–1964," *Journal of Finance* 23 (May 1968).
[5] Reward-to-variability should not be used to measure the performance of inefficient portfolios or individual securities.
[6] Arditti, who extends Sharpe's reward-to-variability index, suggests, a performance index which takes into account the portfolio skewness. For more details see F. D. Arditti, "Another Look at Mutual Fund Performance," *Journal of Financial and Quantitative Analysis* (June 1971).

3. ALTERNATIVE MEASURES OF INVESTMENT PERFORMANCE   481

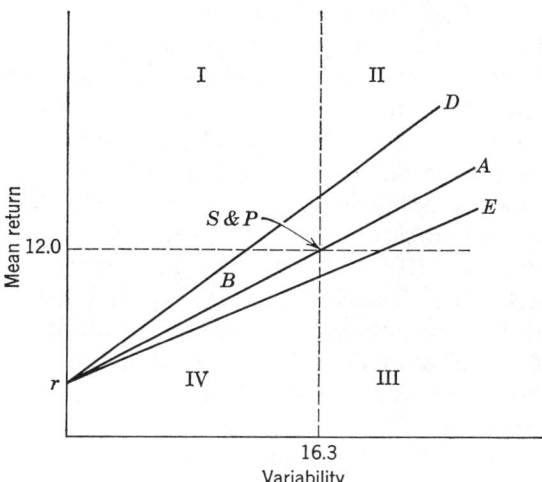

FIGURE XIV.2.

application of the R/V performance indicator. An investment in *riskless* bonds is represented by point r in Figure XIV.2; a portfolio comprising a cross section of randomly chosen stocks is again represented by point $S\&P$. The straight line connecting point r and point $S\&P$ represents the set of all attainable combinations of bonds with an unmanaged equity portfolio. For example, point B on this line, which lies halfway between point r and point $S\&P$, represents the risk–return characteristics of a portfolio equally divided between the riskless bonds and equities. Points on the continuation of the line from $S\&P$ to A represent levered portfolios, that is, attainable risk–return combinations for the investor in an unmanaged portfolio who borrows money at the riskless rate r.

Let us now assume that we wish to compare the performance of mutual funds, or portfolios, represented by points such as D and E in Figure XIV.2 with the unmanaged portfolio. Clearly, if the line passing from r through point D, which represents all attainable combinations of that mutual fund's shares with bonds, lies above the line rA we can conclude that the performance of mutual fund D is superior to that of the unmanaged portfolio, since all points on the line rD represent a higher return for a given risk when compared with the line rA. On the other hand, in cases such as E, where the line rE lies below rA, we can conclude that an investment in the unmanaged portfolio is preferable to an investment in mutual fund E. Thus the slope of the line connecting the mutual fund (portfolio) with the riskless rate, which by definition is the R/V ratio, provides a convenient measure of the performance of mutual funds (portfolios). Larger slopes, that is, higher R/V ratios, indicate better investment performance, since investors can reach higher levels of expected utility the greater the slope of the transformation line connecting the riskless rate and the point representing the risk–return characteristics of the mutual fund. In a reasonably efficient market we expect all highly diversified portfolios (and mutual funds comprise an excellent proxy for such portfolios) to cluster in a random fashion along the estimated market line, in our example the line connecting r and point $S\&P$ in Figure XIV.2. A mutual fund, or portfolio, which deviates significantly below the market line indicates a case of inadequate risk–return performance, and a rational mean–variance investor would not consciously choose such a fund or portfolio since he could improve his position by investing in a randomly diversified portfolio such as the one represented by point $S\&P$ of Figure XIV.2.

3.2 VOLATILITY AND THE CHARACTERISTIC LINE

As Sharpe and others have pointed out, the R/V ratio constitutes an appropriate measure of performance for efficiently diversified portfolios but should not be applied to single securities or small portfolios. For this purpose Treynor has suggested an alternate performance indicator based on *volatility* rather than on *variability* which is appropriate for both individual securities and portfolios. The concept of volatility can be explained by introducing the notion of a *characteristic line*.

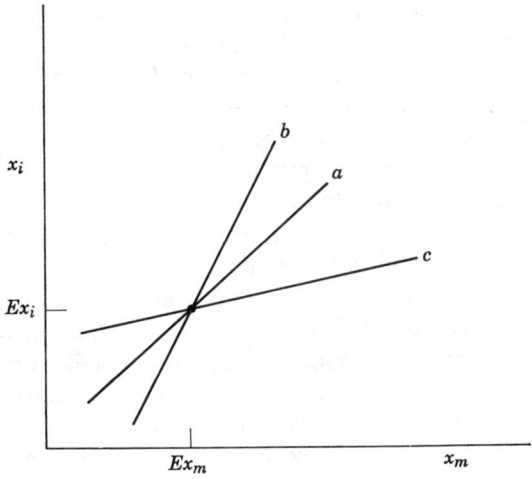

FIGURE XIV.3.

3. ALTERNATIVE MEASURES OF INVESTMENT PERFORMANCE

The characteristic line of a particular security i (or mutual fund i) is defined as the regression line between x_i and x_m, where x_i and x_m denote the returns of the ith security (mutual fund) and of the market portfolio, respectively. Three examples of possible characteristic lines are drawn in Figure XIV.3. The slope of the regression line, β_i, is a measure of the relationship between the change in x_i following a change in x_m. Treynor calls this relationship *volatility*. If $\beta_i = 1$ (line a of Figure XIV.3) a 1% increase (decline) in the return of the market portfolio is accompanied by a 1% increase (decline) in the return of security (mutual fund) i. If β_i is greater than 1 (line b of Figure XIV.3) i is more volatile than the market portfolio, that is, it is an "agressive" security which rises faster than the average during a bull market, but also falls more than the average during a bear market. Using the same type of reasoning, a security (portfolio) having a characteristic line with a slope of *less* than 1 (line c of Figure XIV.3) represents a "defensive" security (portfolio), that is, one which rises more slowly than the average during a rising market, but also falls less than the average in a declining market.[7]

3.3 SYSTEMATIC AND UNSYSTEMATIC RISK

Having defined volatility as the slope of the characteristic line, let us now determine the relationship of the characteristic line to the market equilibrium relationship between risk and return. In Chapter XIII, Equation (13.20), we found that the following equilibrium condition holds simultaneously for every security in the market, independent of investors' tastes:

$$Ex_i = r + \frac{Ex_m - r}{\sigma_m^2} Cov(x_i x_m)$$

where x_m, Ex_m, and σ_m^2 denote the returns, expected return, and variance of the market portfolio, Ex_i denotes the expected return of security i, and $Cov(x_i x_m)$ is the covariance between x_i and x_m. Since by definition the slope of the regression line x_i and x_m is

$$\beta_i = \frac{Cov(x_i, x_m)}{\sigma_m^2}$$

the equilibrium condition can be expressed in terms of the volatility, β_i:

$$Ex_i = r + (Ex_m - r)\beta_i$$

---

[7] A "super" defensive stock, that is, one which has negative correlation with the market portfolio, would have a characteristic line with a negative slope. Of course, such securities are hard to come by.

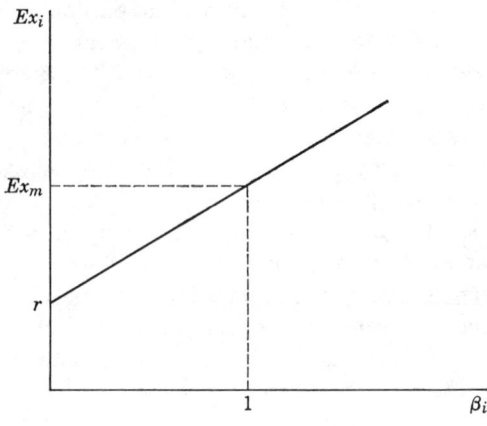

FIGURE XIV.4.

The linear relationship of expected return to volatility is drawn in Figure XIV.4. Note that the higher a security's volatility, the higher is its expected return in equilibrium. If $\beta_i = 1$, that is, is the individual security's volatility is equal to that of the market portfolio, $Ex_i = Ex_m$. If $\beta_i = 0$ (that is, if the security returns do not fluctuate), then its expected return equals the riskless rate r; for $\beta_i > 1$ the expected return of the security will exceed the expected return of the market portfolio. If all securities were "correctly" priced their expected returns would satisfy the equilibrium condition, and therefore all would lie along the rising line of Figure XIV.4.

The empirical counterpart of Figure XIV.4 can be estimated by regressing the historical returns of a security, portfolio, or mutual fund (x_i) on the market return (x_m), using a regression equation of the form

$$x_{i(t)} = \alpha + \beta_i x_{m(t)} + e_{(t)} \tag{14.1}$$

where the subscripts i and t denote the ith security examined and the year, respectively; and $e_{(t)}$ denotes the deviation of the observed return in year t from the regression line. The hypothetical scatter diagram of such an analysis is set out in Figure XIV.5, with each point representing a particular combination of (x_i, x_m) which obtained in a given year. Note that where x_i and x_m are perfectly correlated, $e_{(t)}$ will be zero in each year, and all the points of Figure XIV.5 would lie along the regression line.

Taking the variance of both sides of Equation (14.1) we obtain:[8]

$$\sigma_{x_i}^2 = \beta_i^2 \sigma_m^2 + \sigma_e^2 \tag{14.2}$$

[8] Equation (14.2) also includes the term $Cov\,(x_{m(t)}, e_{(t)})$, but this expression, by definition, is equal to zero.

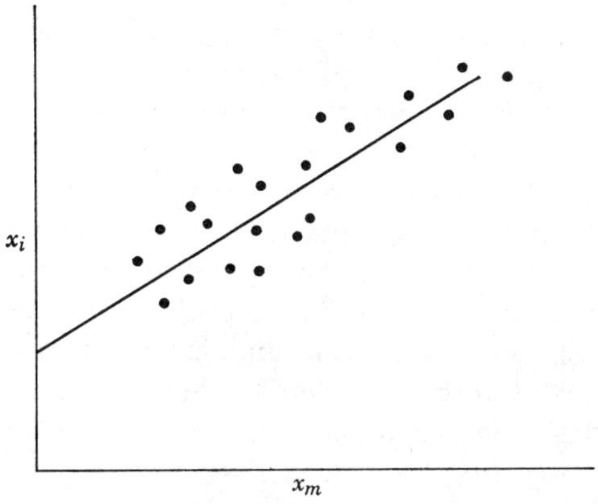

4. ALTERNATIVE MEASURES OF INVESTMENT PERFORMANCE

FIGURE XIV.5.

A glance at Equation (14.2) suffices to show that the total risk of a security (portfolio) can be divided into two components:

(1) $\beta^2 \sigma_m^2$—systematic or undiversifiable risk, that is, the risk which is associated with market fluctuations; and

(2) σ_e^2—nonsystematic or diversifiable risk, that is, that portion of the risk which can be eliminated by combining the security in a diversified portfolio. This nonsystematic risk is represented by the variance around the regression line.

For normal securities whose returns are positively correlated with the market, $[R(x_i, x_m) > 0]$, the following relationship holds:[9]

$$\sigma_e^2 / \sigma_{x_i}^2 = 1 - R^2$$

[9] Recalling that

$$\beta_i = \frac{Cov\ (x_i x_m)}{\sigma_m^2}$$

Equation (14.2) of the text can be rewritten as

$$\sigma_{x_i}^2 = \frac{[Cov\ (x_i x_m)]^2\ \sigma_m^2}{\sigma_m^2 \sigma_m^2} + \sigma_e^2$$

Dividing both sides by $\sigma_{x_i}^2$ we get

$$1 = \frac{[Cov\ (x_i x_m)]^2}{\sigma_m^2 \sigma_{x_i}^2} + \frac{\sigma_e^2}{\sigma_{x_i}^2}$$

and since

$$\frac{[Cov\ (x_i x_m)]^2}{\sigma_m^2 \sigma_x^2} = R_{x_i x_m}^2$$

where $R_{x_i x_m}$ denotes the coefficient of correlation between x_i and x_m, we derive

$$\frac{\sigma_e^2}{\sigma_{x_i}^2} = 1 - R^2$$

When $R^2 = 1$, the nonsystematic risk is zero and there remains only the systematic or nondiversifiable portion of the variance. We define such a portfolio as being "efficiently diversified" since further diversification will not reduce its risk.[10] The variance about the regression line, σ_e^2, or the nonsystematic component of total risk, can be eliminated by further diversification, so that this component vanishes when the portfolio is efficiently diversified.

The ratio $\sigma_e^2/\sigma_{x_i}^2$ also serves as an indicator of the desirability of diversification. If this ratio is zero for a given security or portfolio, all diversifiable risk has already been eliminated, so that further diversification cannot reduce risk. On the other hand, when the ratio is positive, further diversification is desirable to eliminate the remaining nonsystematic risk. The closer the ratio is to unity, the greater the potential gains from diversification. In practice, the gains from risk diversification appear to be substantial; in an empirical study[11] of 63 stocks, Benjamin King found that for the period 1927–60 only about half of the variance of the returns on these stocks could be attributed to market fluctuations, the remaining 50% representing nonsystematic—that is, diversifiable—risk. For the subperiod 1952–1960, the proportion of the variance which is explained by market factors is only 30%; hence the diversifiable risk component in those years comprised 70% of the total variance, which constitutes a rather strong prima facie case for diversification.

3.4 TREYNOR'S PERFORMANCE INDICATOR

Whereas Sharpe takes the reward-to-variability as his performance indicator, Treynor replaces the standard deviation of the R/V ratio with volatility:

$$\frac{Ex_i - r}{\beta_i}$$

thereby deriving a performance measure which is appropriate for single securities and partially diversified portfolios, as well as for fully diversified portfolios. Using this measure, the performance of a security is judged by its deviation from the equilibrium relationship (characteristic line) implied by its volatility or systematic risk. Thus the Treynor index is set out in terms of

---

[10] Note that even when $R^2 = 1$ the security's (portfolio's) variance can be greater or smaller than the market portfolio's variance. For example, an "aggressive" security (portfolio) may have a beta coefficient greater than 1, while $R_{x_i x_m}^2 = 1$; such a security (portfolio) will be more volatile than the market portfolio.

[11] B. F. King, "Market and Industry Factors in Stock Price Behavior," *Journal of Business* 39 (January 1966).

4. EMPIRICAL RESULTS OF MUTUAL FUND PERFORMANCE

the differential return $(Ex_i - r)$ per unit of systematic risk, β[12]. This measure is appropriate since, as we have shown in Chapter XIII, the market risk premium is a function of the systematic, or nondiversifiable, portion of the risk, no premium being expected on that portion of a security's risk which is diversifiable.

4. SOME EMPIRICAL RESULTS OF MUTUAL FUND PERFORMANCE

Numerous empirical studies of mutual funds' returns, using the above mentioned performance indicators, have been carried out in recent years. Despite the fact that different samples and varying time periods are used, all of the researchers have concluded that mutual funds' managements are unable to "outguess" the market, and as a result, the funds do not outperform an unmanaged portfolio.

William Sharpe[13] analyzed the returns of 34 mutual funds for the period 1954–63 using the R/V reward-to-variability ratio. His results varied from 0.78 to 0.43; the relevant ratio for the Dow-Jones Industrial Average was 0.633 for the same time period. The average R/V ratio for the funds was considerably lower than that of the Dow-Jones index, and only eleven funds outperformed the "index," while 23 mutual funds had R/V ratios which were lower than the ratio for the Dow Jones index.

To check the stability of these findings, a replication of the Sharpe study was carried out for the 56 mutual funds for which data are available over the period 1946–69. The average returns for these funds are plotted against their variability in Figure XIV.6, which also includes the estimated "market line" for the Standard & Poor's 500 Stock Index, assuming a riskless interest rate of $3\frac{1}{2}\%$. The scatter diagram clearly shows that taken as a group the mutual funds failed to outperform the unmanaged portfolio. The R/V ratios of the funds ranged from a low of 0.31 to a high of 0.75; only 18 out of the 56 funds included in the study "outperformed" the S&P index.[14] These

---

[12] Jensen *op. cit.* uses a similar indicator, taking the differential return itself as the measure of the deviation from the equilibrium relationship. For an alternative approach to the problem of comparing the risk–return characteristics of securities, see Nancy Jacob, "The Measurements of Market Similarity for Securities Under Uncertainty," *Journal of Business* 43 (July 1970), pp. 328–40.

[13] *Journal of Business, op. cit.*

[14] Because most mutual funds diversified their portfolios over 100 or more stocks, the reward-to-variability ratio constitutes an appropriate measure of performance. Substitution of the Treynor index based on volatility does not change these results; the rank correlation coefficient between the R/V ratio and the Treynor index is 0.927.

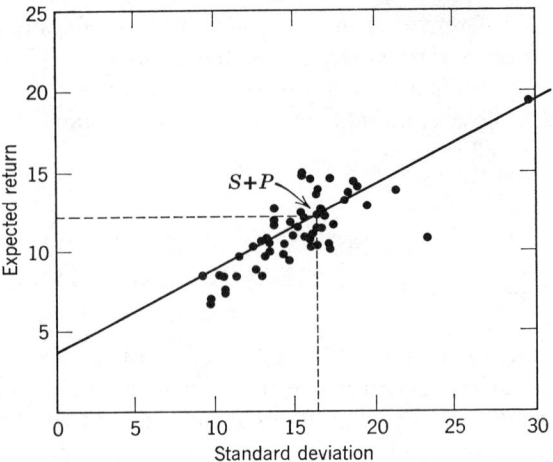

FIGURE XIV.6.

results reflect the rates of return to investors *before* deducting the loading charges of the mutual funds. When expenses are deducted, the mutual funds, taken as a group, actually did worse than the unmanaged portfolio.

These conclusions have also been corroborated by Treynor and Mazuy,[15] who used the characteristic line method to study the performance of 57 mutual funds during the years 1953–62. These authors conclude that with one exception mutual fund managers were not able to predict the major swings in the market. Jensen[16] in a comprehensive study of 115 mutual funds during the period 1945–64 also concludes that professional investment management has been unable to consistently pick a better cross section of stocks than can be obtained by mere chance. Thus mutual funds were unable to outperform a simple "buy the market and hold" strategy. This conclusion holds even when management expenses are not deducted from the funds' returns.

All of the studies in question do indicate that the funds have been efficient in risk diversification, and therefore provide a socially desirable service. The statistical evidence, however, strongly suggests that in theory at least an equal measure of diversification could have been achieved by investing in a randomly chosen cross section of common stocks.

---

[15] Jack L. Treynor and Kay K. Mazuy, "Can Mutual Funds Outguess the Market?" *Harvard Business Review* 44 (July–August 1966).
[16] *Journal of Finance, op. cit.*

5. MUTUAL FUND PERFORMANCE IN AN IMPERFECT SECURITIES MARKET

As we have just seen, most attempts to evaluate empirically the performance of mutual funds support the contention that the funds, taken as a group, are unable to outguess the market; and as a result, investors would be equally well off to invest their savings in a randomly chosen sample of common stocks. Despite this rather gloomy evaluation, mutual funds, as evidenced by their growth rates, have continued to comprise one of the most popular, if not the most popular, of investment media. The extraordinary growth of mutual funds is, to say the least, hardly accounted for by the empirical evidence on mutual funds' performance. On the contrary, the 53 billion dollars invested in U.S. mutual funds at the end of 1968 appears to be paradoxical, given the empirical findings.

In view of the above evidence, how can one account for the widespread appeal of mutual funds as an investment medium? This apparent paradox between the performance record and the popularity of mutual funds can be resolved if we recall that securities are traded in a *less than perfect* market. The empirical evaluations invariably compare mutual fund performance with a benchmark provided by some general index of common stocks (Standard & Poor, Dow Jones, and so on). On reflection, such an alternative is not available to most investors. Unless he has unusual resources at his disposal, an individual cannot invest in the shares of 500 companies, although he can easily purchase the shares of mutual funds whose assets include the shares of 500, or more, corporations. Of course it might be argued that a random sample of shares would suffice to approximate the risk–return characteristics of the index. However, even such an approach implies the purchase of the shares of a dozen or more companies. If we remind ourselves that a portfolio comprising one share of AT&T and one share of IBM entails an outlay of several hundred dollars, the number of investors for whom even a two- or three-share portfolio represents the maximum attainable alternative to mutual fund shares is considerable.

Thus, for many investors the fact that a portfolio comprising a large enough sample of shares will approximate the risk–return characteristics of the Standard & Poor's Index is simply not relevant. It is only under the assumption of a perfect securities market, with infinite divisibility of investments, that the degree of diversification implied by the use of a stock index becomes possible. A more realistic approach is to recognize that because of market imperfections and the indivisibility of investments the relevant alternative confronting most investors in mutual fund shares is to invest

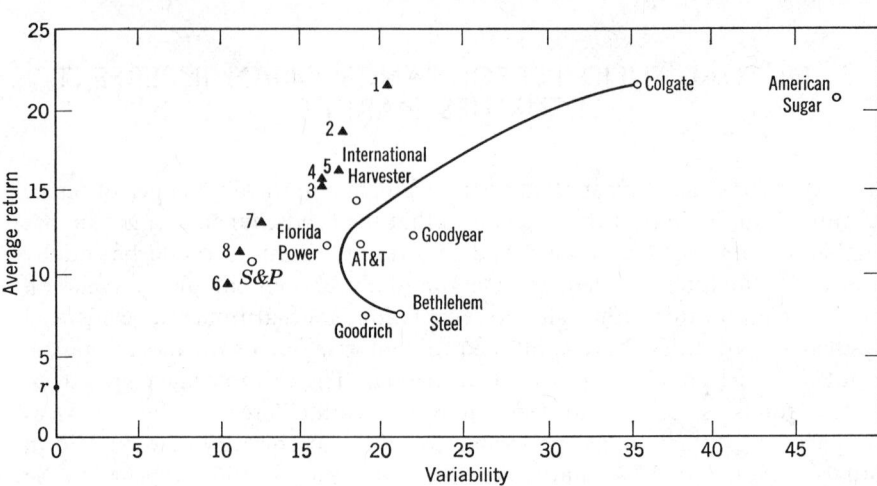

FIGURE XIV.7. Key: 1. American Investors Fund. 2. Dreyfus Fund. 3. Fidelity Fund. 4. Washington Mutual Investors Fund. 5. Axe-Houghton Fund A. 6. Investors Mutual. 7. Financial Industrial Income Fund. 8. Northeast Investor Fund.

directly in a small portfolio of individual shares, rather than in the S&P Index.

To illustrate such an approach the risk–return characteristics of eight mutual funds and of the shares of eight well known corporations for the period 1958–68 have been set out in Figure XIV.7.[17] If an imaginary line is drawn from point r (the riskless interest rate) through the S&P point on the diagram, the eight mutual funds tend to cluster closely along this line. This indicates that the Funds' performance approximates, but does not significantly exceed, the performance of the S&P index, which corroborates the much more comprehensive evidence of Sharpe, Treynor and Mazuy, and of Jensen. But if we recall that the investor cannot "buy the index," more appropriate comparisons can be devised. If imaginary lines are drawn from point r to the 16 points representing the funds and the individual shares, one can readily see that mutual funds almost invariably represent preferable alternatives to the investment in individual shares.

Now let us assume that the investor is prepared to diversify his investment in the shares of two companies. If we choose the example of Colgate and

---

[17] The sample includes two growth funds, two diversified common stock funds, two balanced funds, and two income funds. The reader should also note that the rate of return and standard deviation of return for the Standard & Poor's 500 Stock Index were 10.6% and 11.7% respectively for the period 1958–68.

6. PREDICTIONS OF PERFORMANCE FROM PAST DATA

Bethlehem Steel an envelope curve can be constructed which represents the risk–return characteristic for all possible combinations of the two shares into a single portfolio (see Figure XIV.7). Since this curve lies *below* the lines which connect point *r* with each of the mutual funds, every individual would prefer an investment in one of the mutual funds to an investment in this particular two-share portfolio.

Similar exercises can be carried out to compare mutual fund investments with other two-share combinations, with three-share portfolios, and so on. This constitutes not only a legitimate, but also the only relevant, approach for investors who are constrained to purchase a small number of shares. Because of the indivisibility of investment in an imperfect market, it would be perfectly rational for such investors to buy mutual fund shares even if the funds' performance was significantly inferior to that of the S&P Index. It is this role of providing a "second-best" but attainable alternative which perhaps explains the failure of the negative empirical appraisals to have any perceptible influence on the small investor's penchant for mutual funds, both in the United States and abroad.

In sum, even if we fully accept the view that mutual funds typically show no better results than could be obtained from a randomly chosen unmanaged portfolio, we do not necessarily have to accept the "normative" inferences regarding the desirability of investing in mutual funds shares which are often drawn from the "positive" evidence. A theoretically appropriate case for the investment in mutual funds can still be made once the implicit assumption that securities are traded in a perfect market is relaxed.

6. PREDICTIONS OF PERFORMANCE FROM PAST DATA

As we noted in the introduction to this chapter, the two-parameter security market model, and the portfolio theory on which it is based, are set out in terms of "expected" or *ex-ante* variables. These variables relate to the shapes of the probability distributions of future returns on securities, to their expected values, to their variances, and to the possible interaction among security returns, that is, to their covariances as well. Very little has been said, however, about the way in which investors reach their probability beliefs regarding future returns. In fact in all of our illustrations we have implicitly assumed that past or *ex-post* data on security (mutual fund) returns can serve as a benchmark for the efficiency analysis which we have expounded. But before examining the ability of various efficiency criteria to predict future performance on the basis of past data, let us digress for a moment on a subject of much heated, albeit often unnecessary, controversy—the theory of random walks.

6.1 THE RANDOM WALK HYPOTHESIS

One of the chapters of a recent bestseller written by a very knowledgeable member of the Wall Street community is entitled "What the Hell Is a Random Walk?"[18] The answer is something like this: the random walk approach to security markets asserts that the period-to-period price changes of a security are statistically *independent*, or very nearly so. If this hypothesis holds, the price movements of securities will follow what statisticians call a "random walk."[19] The reader may be tempted to ask, "What the hell is all the fuss about?" But to answer this question we must first examine the hypothesis more carefully, and in particular we must derive its implications for investment analysis and portfolio selection.

Random walk theorists usually take as their starting point the model of an efficient securities market in which a relatively large number of investors, traders, and speculators compete in an attempt to predict the course of future prices. Moreover, it is further assumed that current information relevant to the decision making process is readily available to all at little or no cost. If we "idealize" these conditions and assume that the market is *perfectly* competitive then common stock prices at any given point of time would reflect the market's evaluation of all currently available information. In such ideal markets, prices would change solely as new, hitherto unavailable information becomes known. And unless the new information is distributed over time in a nonrandom fashion, and we have no reason to presume this, price movements in a perfect market will be statistically independent of one another.

It is an important property of such a market that the analysis of current or past prices can tell us *nothing* about the future, that is, future price changes, which are randomly associated with past and present prices, *cannot* be forecast on the basis of historical time series of price movements. Stock prices "have no memory," so that one might do as well flipping a coin as spending time analyzing past price movements or patterns of past price levels.[20]

---

[18] "Adam Smith," *The Money Game*, Chapter 11. London: Michael Joseph, 1969.
[19] The literature on the subject of random walks is voluminous: an excellent nontechnical introduction to the subject is provided by Eugene F. Fama, "Random Walks in Stock Market Prices," *Financial Analysts Journal* 21 (Sept.–Oct. 1965). A comprehensive compilation of the pioneering articles on the subject is available in Paul H. Cootner, *The Random Character of Stock Market Prices*, Cambridge: M.I.T. Press, 1964.
[20] Paul H. Cootner, "Stock Prices: Random vs. Systematic Changes," *Industrial Management Review* 3 (Spring 1962). Cootner goes on to stress in this article that stock prices do *not* conform to a pure random walk because of the differential cost of information available to "professionals" who specialize in the market.

6. PREDICTIONS OF PERFORMANCE FROM PAST DATA

Although diligent scholars have, as usual, been able to trace the beginnings of the random walk literature back to the turn of the century,[21] it was not until the 1950s and the first half of the 1960s that the hypothesis was subjected to a series of comprehensive tests. The interpretation of the results of these often highly sophisticated statistical tests is of course a rather subjective matter. On the whole, it appears safe to conclude that the case for *complete independence* of past and future stock prices has *not* been established. This is not particularly surprising since such a result merely confirms that real-world securities markets depart from the "ideal." However an important result of these studies was to show that although the departures from independence are statistically significant, the degree of dependence between future and past price changes is negligible, that is, the serial correlation coefficients are small and account for only a minor fraction of the observed current price variation.

This result led to tests of alternative trading rules; for example, one such rule states that if a security's price rises by 5% buy and hold it until its price moves down by 5% from the previous high, at which time it is sold and a "short" position is taken in the stock until the price again rises by 5% from the previous low, at which time the short position is covered and the security is again purchased. Such a rule is called a "5% filter." Comprehensive tests of such rules using varying "filters" and price data have been carried out;[22] the positive dependence of successive daily price changes again manifests itself in these tests, and as a result trading rules can be devised which outperform on the average a simple "buy and hold" strategy. However, these "improved" rules invariably require very small filters (0.5 to 1.5%) and generate such a large number of hypothetical transactions that the "trading profits" are wiped out by even the smallest of trading costs. Thus the existence of dependence per se does not necessarily contradict the premise of an efficient market, that is, one in which current prices reflect all available information. In such a market investors cannot "profit" from an analysis of past trends and prices, and as we have just seen, this does not necessarily require a *pure* random walk model in which price movements are completely independent. Small degrees of dependence are of little consequence, so long as they cannot be translated into systematic increases in investors' returns.[23]

[21] L. Bachelier, *Theorie de la Speculation*, Paris: Gauthier-Villars, 1900. Reprinted in Cootner (1964).
[22] See, for example, Cootner, *op. cit.* (1964).
[23] This conclusion follows from the work of Benoit Mandelbrot, "Forecasts of Future Prices, Unbiased Markets and Martingale Models," *Journal of Business* 39 (January 1966); and Paul Samuelson, "Proof that Properly Anticipated Prices Fluctuate Randomly," *Industrial Management Review* 6 (Spring 1965). A strong case for this approach is made in a comprehensive review article by E. Fama, "Efficient Capital Markets: A Review of Theory and Empirical Work," *Journal of Finance* 25 (May 1970).

6.2 IMPLICATIONS FOR INVESTMENT ANALYSIS

By this time the reader must be wondering why the antiseptic and rather esoteric random walk theory should produce perceptible rises in blood pressure in the vicinity of Broad and Wall Streets. The answer lies in the implications of this approach for respected, and often highly influential, segments of the financial community.

Let us start with the "tape readers," "chart watchers," "Dow Theorists," and other practitioners of the art of analyzing past patterns of stock market prices, or "technical analysis" as it is often called. Technical analysis includes a bewildering number of variants, but all proponents of such an approach to investment analysis believe to a greater or lesser degree that a study of past price behavior can provide useful insights into the future. In the extreme, the pure tape reader or chartist depends *solely* on the tape or on the patterns which appear on his charts of the historical prices of a particular stock or of a general stock index. For this by no means uninfluential group of analysts,[24] the random walk theory which suggests that patterns of past prices are of little or no significance, representing, so to speak, statistical noise rather than harbingers of the future, constitutes a challenge to their very existence. Whether the random walk or efficient markets approach to security prices will lead to the "euthanasia" of the technical analyst is a matter for conjecture. Based on personal experience, it is often very difficult to convince people using arguments which are basically statistical in nature.

The random walk theory and its weaker counterpart, the efficient market assumption, also have important implications for a second class of investment analysts, the so-called "fundamentalists" who analyze the economic environment and the performance of stocks to isolate those stocks which are underpriced.[25] In a perfect (or near perfect) market, prices at any point in time reflect all available information, and therefore will deviate only randomly from their intrinsic or true values. Competition among investors will quickly eliminate any systematic deviations of stock prices from the "best estimate" of their intrinsic values. It follows that in such a market the return to traditional security analysis will not deviate significantly from zero, that is, no amount of manipulation and analysis of current and past data can

---

[24] An informative, entertaining, but perhaps biased description of the work of some prominent technical analysts is given in two articles by Daniel Seligman: "Playing the Market with Charts," *Fortune*, LXV (February 1962), and "The Mystique of Point and Figure," *Fortune*, LXV (March 1962), both of which are reprinted in H. K. Wu and A. J. Zakon, *Elements on Investments*, New York: Holt, Rinehart & Winston, 1965.

[25] See Chapter V.

6. PREDICTIONS OF PERFORMANCE FROM PAST DATA   495

significantly increase investment returns. Of course, the intrinsic values of stocks will change as new information becomes available, but unless the market is markedly inefficient, the adjustment process will be too rapid to permit investors to derive benefits from the new information. In such a market monopolistic access to information *prior* to its becoming generally available is a necessary condition for systematically improving investment returns, and the acquiring of such information is usually considered the province of "insiders" rather than of security analysts.

As we have just seen, considerable evidence exists that the stock market is sufficiently efficient to preclude the generation of significant increases in expected returns from an analysis of past data. Moreover, as we noted in Section 4, at least one class of professional analysts for whom data are available, the professional managers of mutual funds, appears to be unable to outperform a simple random buy and hold strategy. However in contrast to the "chartists," the security analysts do provide a socially desirable service, since taken as a group they are part of the mechanism which quickly and efficiently eliminates systematic deviations of stock prices from their estimated intrinsic values.

6.3 IMPLICATIONS FOR PORTFOLIO THEORY

Finally we might ask what are the implications of the random walk hypothesis and the efficient markets assumption for portfolio theory. The random walk model and portfolio analysis are not mutually exclusive alternatives. More specifically, the random walk approach does not assert that past data are of no value when estimating the distribution of returns,[26] but only that the sequence in which past returns are observed is of no significance when estimating distributions of future returns. Nor does the efficient market assumption vitiate portfolio theory. On the contrary, the mean–variance market model of Chapter XIII was based explicitly on the assumption of a perfect market. Thus many portfolio theorists, as well as the proponents of random walk models, support the hypothesis that empirically valid explanations can be derived from the assumption that securities are traded in perfect or near perfect markets. In fact, a number of well known scholars appear to reside simultaneously in both camps. This is not too surprising, once we recall the central role which risk diversification plays in portfolio theory. On reflection, the importance of risk reduction is in no way diminished by the fact that predictions of expected returns cannot be systematically improved; in fact, in such a market, diversification remains one of the few meaningful activities an analyst can pursue.

[26] See Fama (1970), p. 387.

7. PREDICTING PORTFOLIO PERFORMANCE

As we have seen, the fact that mutual funds appear to be unable to outperform the market is consistent with the random walk or efficient markets hypotheses. We turn now to a somewhat different, but related, question. Taking mutual funds as proxies for portfolios in general, to what extent can *ex-post* data on efficiency be used to predict efficiency in the future? More specifically, what is the connection, if any, between the efficient sets of two successive periods?

Table XIV–2 sets out the size composition of the efficient sets using the five efficiency criteria defined in Part II: General Criterion (GC), Risk Aversion Criterion (RAC), Mean–Variance Criterion (MVC), Two-Stage Criterion (TSC), and Quadratic Utility Criterion (QUC). For this purpose the returns of the 56 mutual funds which were in continuous operation over the period 1946–69 comprise the sample population. Using data on returns for the periods 1946–57 and 1958–69, the efficient sets were calculated for each of the two periods (columns 1 and 2 of Table XIV–2); the efficient sets in each period were then compared to determine the number of mutual funds which were included in the efficient sets of *both* periods (column 3 of Table XIV–2).

The results of this examination were then used to construct Table XIV–3. Column (1) of this table sets out the probability of picking an efficient

TABLE XIV–2. Number of mutual funds included in efficient sets for selected efficiency criteria in the years 1946–57 and 1958–69

Efficiency Criterion	No. of Funds in Efficient Set		No. of Funds Included in Both Sets
	1946–57 (1)	1958–69 (2)	(3)
General Criterion	38	48	33
Risk Aversion Criterion	12	13	5
Mean–Variance Criterion	9	9	2
Two-Stage Criterion	9	9	2
Quadratic Utility Criterion	8	9	1

Addendum: Total population = 56 mutual funds.

7. PREDICTING PORTFOLIO PERFORMANCE

TABLE XIV-3. Probability of predicting efficient mutual funds in the period 1958-69 from 1946-57 data, by selected efficiency criteria (percentage)

Efficiency Criterion	Probability Based on Previous Period's Data (1)	Probability of Random Choice (2)
General Criterion	87	86
Risk Aversion Criterion	42	23
Mean–Variance Criterion	22	16
Two-Stage Criterion	22	16
Quadratic Utility Criterion	12.5	16

mutual fund when the decision is based on past data. The relevant estimate for each efficiency criterion is derived by dividing column (3) of Table XIV-2 by column (1) of the same table. Thus, with respect to the GC, an investor who based his estimates of GC efficiency for the period 1958-69 on the *past* performance of the mutual funds during 1946-67, would have predicted efficiency with a probability of 87% (33 ÷ 38 = 0.87); that is, in 33 out of 38 chances, the funds chosen on the basis of past performances proved to be GC efficient in the later period as well.

At first glance this result is very impressive. However on reflection it does not necessarily mean that predictions based on past data are superior to simple random choice. This becomes clear when we examine the probability of picking efficient funds *at random*—column (2) of Table XIV-3. In our example of the GC, there was a probability of 86% (48 ÷ 56 = 0.86) of choosing GC efficient mutual funds at random. To determine the degree to which past data can be used to *improve* decision making, we must compare columns (1) and (2) of Table XIV-3. In only one instance, the case of the RAC, was the probability of choosing efficient funds increased significantly (from 23% to 42%); and in one instance, the QUC, using past data reduced the probability below that of simple random choice.

The reasons for this moderately indifferent performance of the efficiency criteria can be found by reexamining the data for Table XIV-2. With the exception of the GC the composition of the efficient sets over time was not stable enough to derive predictions materially better than simple random choice. However, in the case of the GC, the efficient set in the second period, 1958-69, was so large that despite the stability of composition of the initial

TABLE XIV–4. Average annual rates of return during 1958–69 of mutual funds included in efficient sets as estimated from current and past data (percentage)

Efficiency Criterion	Rates of Return for Efficient Sets Estimated from 1958–69 Data (1)	Rates of Return for Efficient Sets Estimated from 1946–57 Data (2)
General Criterion	10.6	10.6
Risk Aversion Criterion	11.1	10.4
Mean–Variance Criterion	10.9	10.3
Total Population*	10.2	10.2

* Average annual rate of return in 1958–69 for the 56 mutual funds in operation over the entire period 1946–69.

efficient set over time, random choice alone provided such excellent results that it could not materially be improved upon.[27]

However, even a moderate degree of success in improving predictions could conceivably translate itself into very significant increases in the return on investment. To this question we now turn. Table XIV–4 sets out the average annual rates of return for the period 1958–69 of the mutual funds included in the GC, RAC, and MVC efficient sets as estimated from current and past data, as well as the rate of return during this same period for the 56 mutual funds which comprise our total population. The ten-year average rates of return were computed by taking the geometric means of the annual rates for each individual fund;[28] the averages for the various groups were computed by taking the arithmetic average of the mean rates of the funds included in the set in question.

The average rate of return for 1958–69 for the entire sample population (56 funds) was 10.2%. Column 1 of Table XIV–4 clearly shows that this rate of return could have been improved upon rather substantially if investors could successfully predict the composition of the efficient sets *in advance*. The average annual rate of return for the funds included in the GC efficient set is 10.6%, while the relevant figures for the RAC and MVC efficient sets are 11.1% and 10.9% respectively. These results, however, provide little comfort for the investor who is faced with the problem of predicting the

[27] This also proved true when alternative time periods were examined.
[28] See Chapter III.

7. PREDICTING PORTFOLIO PERFORMANCE 499

efficient sets. Column 2 of Table XIV-4 sets out the average annual rates of return for the efficient sets during 1958–69, when the composition of the sets themselves is estimated from the *ex-post* data of 1946–57. Clearly, the RAC and MVC criteria do not provide a very significant improvement over the rate of return which could have been realized by choosing randomly among the funds. The rates of return on the RAC and MVC efficient sets (estimated from past data) are 10.4 and 10.3% respectively, which represents a very modest improvement over the average for the population as a whole, 10.2%. This result again reflects the lack of stability over time in the composition of the RAC and MVC efficient sets.

A somewhat different picture emerges with respect to the GC. As we have already noted, the composition of the set is much more stable over time, but random choice provides almost as good a prediction of the composition of this set (see Table XIV-3). However, the average annual rate of return for the GC efficient set, as estimated from past data, is significantly higher than the rate of return for the sample population as a whole: 10.6% as compared with 10.2%. Thus with regard to this criterion at least, efficiency analysis based on data of the previous ten years does significantly outperform a random buy and hold strategy. And unlike the random walk tests, this improvement in investment performance does *not* require additional transaction costs. Thus, on the whole, estimating efficient sets using relatively long series of past data appears potentially rewarding, that is, the market may be sufficiently imperfect[29] to allow investors to earn a positive return on the preliminary screening of inefficient portfolios. But we hasten to add that mutual funds may not be representative of portfolios in general, and one ten-year test is certainly not exhaustive. Much work remains to be done. However, by now the reader should be prepared to join in the task. The next step is up to him.

---

[29] In the sense that a sufficient number of mutual funds were mispriced in terms of available information to permit a profitable screening of the inefficient funds.

QUESTIONS AND PROBLEMS

14.1 Distinguish between a closed-end and open-end investment company. What are the investment objectives of an open-end investment company?

14.2 Define "reward to variability" and "reward to volatility" (i.e., Treynor's performance indicator). Which of these indices provides the more general measure of performance?

14.3 Define "systematic" and "nonsystematic" risk.

14.4 "The higher a security's variance the higher its expected return." Appraise.

14.5 The volatilities of four shares in a perfect market are as follows:

$$\beta_A = -1; \quad \beta_B = 0; \quad \beta_C = 1; \quad \beta_D = 2$$

Assume that the market is in equilibrium; that the riskless interest rate is 5 per cent; and that the expected return, and standard deviation of the "market portfolio" are 13% and 8%, respectively. Calculate the expected return on shares A, B, C, and D.

14.6 How can you account for the popularity of mutual funds despite the fact that they do not outperform the general index so that an individual investor could do equally as well, if not better, by choosing randomly among the alternative securities available in the market.

14.7 "In a perfect market there is no need for mutual funds." Appraise.

14.8 Mutual Fund "A" earned the following rates of return during the last decade:

1961	1962	1963	1964	1965	1966	1967	1968	1969	1970
+3.8	−14.1	+22.5	−12.1	+26.6	+11.7	+28.1	−12.5	+53.5	+20.7

Now assume that the mutual fund is considering the possibility of including security B in its portfolio. Security B had the following rates of return during the past decade.

1961	1962	1963	1964	1965	1966	1967	1968	1969	1970
+10.0	+15.3	0.0	+7.6	−17.4	−15.9	−22.3	0.0	−1.0	−4.5

For simplicity, assume that including the additional share does *not* affect the fund's expenses. Does it pay the fund to include the share in its portfolio?

QUESTIONS AND PROBLEMS 501

Assume that the riskless rate of interest is 4%, and base your answer on the assumption that the *expost* returns reflect expected return. Assume that Mutual Fund "A" represents the market portfolio.

14.9 What are the expected returns of two securities whose volatilities are zero and less than zero, respectively? Assuming that the riskless rate of interest is 5% and that the expected return on the security with zero volatility is 9%, is the market in equilibrium?

14.10 What is the hypothesis of the random walk theory? What are the implications of this theory for:

(a) technical analysis
(b) security analysis
(c) portfolio analysis.

SELECTED REFERENCES

Alexander, S. S., "Price Movement in Speculative Markets: Trends or Random Walk," *Industrial Management Review* (May 1965).
Altman, E. I., and Schwartz, R. A., "Common Stock Price Volatility Measures and Patterns," *Journal of Financial and Quantitative Analysis* (January 1970).
Arditti, F. D., "Another Look at Mutual Fund Performance," *Journal of Financial and Quantitative Analysis* (June 1971).
Baumol, W. J., "Mathematical Analysis of Portfolio Selection: Principles and Application," *Financial Analysts Journal* (September–October 1966).
Blume, M. E., Portfolio Theory: A Step Toward its Practical Application," *Journal of Business* (April 1970).
Bower, R. S., and Wippern, R. F., "Risk–Return Measurement in Portfolio Selection and Performance Appraisal Models: Progress Report," *Journal of Financial and Quantitative Analysis* (December 1969).
Breen, W., and Savage, J., "Portfolio Distribution and Tests of Security Selection Models," *Journal of Finance* (December 1968).
Carlson, R. S., "Aggregate Performance of Mutual Funds 1948–1967," Journal of *Financial and Quantitative Analysis* (March 1970).
Cohen, K. J., and Pogue, J. A., "An Empirical Evaluation of Alternative Portfolio Selection Models," *Journal of Business* (April 1967).
Cootner, P. H., *The Random Character of Stock Prices*. Cambridge: M.I.T. Press, 1964.
———, "Stock Prices: Random vs. Systematic Changes," *Industrial Management Review* (Spring 1962).
Dietz, P. O., *Pension Funds—Measuring Investment Performance*. New York: Columbia University and The Free Press, 1966.
Dryden, M. M., "Filter Tests of U.K. Share Prices," *Applied Economics* (January 1970).
Evans, J. L., "An Analysis of Portfolio Maintenance Strategies," *Journal of Finance*, (June 1970).
———, "The Random Walk Hypothesis, Portfolio Analysis and the Buy-and-Hold Criterion," *Journal of Financial and Quantitative Analysis* (September 1968).
Evans, J. L., and Archer, S. H., "Diversification and the Reduction of Dispersion: An Empirical Analysis," *Journal of Finance* (December 1968).

SELECTED REFERENCES

Fama, E. F., "Efficient Capital Markets: A Review of Theory and Empirical Work," *Journal of Finance* (May 1970).

———, "Random Walks in Stock Market Prices," *Financial Analysts Journal* (Sept.–Oct. 1965).

———, "Risk and the Evaluation of Pension Fund Performance," in *Measuring the Investment Performance of Pension Funds for the Purpose of Inter-Fund Comparison*. Park Ridge, Ill.: Bank Administration Institute, 1968.

Fama, E. F., and Blume, M. E., "Filter Rules and Stock-Market Trading," *Journal of Business* (January 1966).

Fisher, L., and Lorie, J. H., "Some Studies of Variability of Returns on Investments in Common Stocks," *Journal of Business* (April 1970).

Fried, J., "Forecasting and Probability Distributions for Models of Portfolio Selection," *Journal of Finance* (June 1970).

Friend, I., and Blume, M. E., "Measurement of Portfolio Performance Under Uncertainty," *American Economic Review* (September 1970).

Friend, I., and Vickers, D., "Portfolio Selection and Investment Performance," *Journal of Finance* (September 1965).

Friend, I.; Brown, F. E.; Herman, E. S.; and Vickers, D., *A Study of Mutual Funds*. Washington, D.C.: U.S. Government Printing Office, 1962.

Gaumnitz, J. E., "Appraising Performance of Investment Portfolios," *Journal of Finance* (June 1970).

Horowitz, I., "A Model for Mutual Fund Evaluation," *Industrial Management Review* (Spring 1965).

———, "The 'Reward-to-Variability' Ratio and Mutual Fund Performance," *Journal of Business* (October 1966).

Jensen, M. C., "The Performance of Mutual Funds in the Period 1945–1964," *Journal of Finance* (May 1968).

———, "Risk, the Pricing of Capital Assets, and the Evaluation of Investment Portfolios," *Journal of Business* (April 1969).

Jensen, M. C., and Bennington, G. A., "Random Walks and Technical Theories: Some Additional Evidence," *Journal of Finance* (May 1970).

King, B., "Market and Industry Factors in Stock Price Behavior," *Journal of Business* (January 1966).

Latané, H. A., and Young, W. E., "Test of Portfolio Building Rules," *Journal of Finance* (September 1969).

Levy, H., and Sarnat, M., "Investment Performance in an Imperfect Securities Market and the Case for Mutual Funds," *Financial Analysts Journal*, in press.

Levy, R. A., "Conceptual Foundations of Technical Analysis," *Financial Analysts Journal* (July–August 1966).

Lorie, J. H., "Some Comments on Recent Quantitative and Formal Research on the Stock Market," *Journal of Business* (January 1966).

Mandelbrot, B., "Forecasts of Future Prices, Unbiased Markets and Martingale Models," *Journal of Business* (January 1966).

Mao, J. C. T., "Essentials of Portfolio Diversification Strategy," *Journal of Finance* (December 1970).

Niederhoffer, V., "The Predictive Content of First-Quarter Earnings Reports," *Journal of Business* (January 1970).

Renshaw, E. F., "The Random Walk Hypothesis, Performance Management, and Portfolio Theory," *Financial Analysts Journal* (March–April 1968).

Renwick, F. B., "Asset Management and Investor Portfolio Behavior: Theory and Practice," *Journal of Finance* (May 1969).

——, "Theory of Investment Behavior and Empirical Analysis of Stock Market Price Relatives," *Management Science* (September 1968).

Roberts, H. V., "Stock Market 'Patterns' and Financial Analysis: Methodological Suggestions," *Journal of Finance* (March 1959).

Samuelson, P. A., "Proof That Properly Anticipated Prices Fluctuate Randomly," *Industrial Management Review* (Spring 1965).

Sharpe, W. F., "Mutual Fund Performance," *Journal of Business* (January 1966).

——, *Portfolio Theory and Capital Markets*. New York: McGraw-Hill, 1970.

Smith, K. V., and Tito, D. A., "Risk–Return Measures of Ex Post Portfolio Performance," *Journal of Financial and Quantitative Analysis* (December 1969).

Stevenson, R. A., and Bear, R. M., "Commodity Futures: Trends or Random Walks?" *Journal of Finance* (March 1970).

Treynor, J. L., "How to Rate Management Investment Funds," *Harvard Business Review* (Jan.–Feb. 1965).

Treynor, J. L., and Mazuy, K., "Can Mutual Funds Outguess the Market?" *Harvard Business Review* (July–August 1966).

Treynor, J. L.; Priest, W. W., Jr.; Fisher, L.; and Higgins, C. A., "Using Portfolio Composition to Estimate Risk," *Financial Analysts Journal* (September–October 1968).

Wallingford, B. A., "A Survey and Comparison of Portfolio Selection Models," *Journal of Financial and Quantitative Analysis* (June 1967).

Chapter XV
Two Studies in Corporate Diversification: Conglomerate Mergers and Multiperiod Capital Investments

1. INTRODUCTION

In this chapter portfolio theory is applied to problems involving less than perfect markets: the analysis of risk diversification by means of conglomerate mergers, and the analysis of capital budgeting decisions involving combinations of multiperiod risky investments.

2. CONGLOMERATE MERGERS

From the second half of the 1950s the United States has witnessed its third large-scale wave of merger activity. The two earlier movements occurred at the turn of the century and during the 1920s, and were considerably smaller both in terms of number of firms acquired and of assets involved. They also differed significantly with respect to type of merger.

The first great merger wave, which reached its peak during the years 1898 to 1902, was characterized by the *horizontal* type of merger, in which one firm acquires another firm that produces (or sells) an identical product or close substitute. Such mergers represent the combination of direct competitors, and the earliest merger movement is associated with the drive for monopoly and the creation of the "Great Trusts."[1]

The second wave of mergers, which took place during the 1920s, was characterized by the *vertical* type of merger, in which one company acquires the stock or assets of one of its suppliers or customers. In this type of merger a company seeks to strengthen its position, not by eliminating competition, but rather by acquiring control over the sources of its raw materials and/or the purchasers of its products. The overt motivation for this type of merger is the securing of economies in production, merchandizing, and management. However, such combinations may also increase a firm's market power along with the achievement of the above economies.

The most recent wave of merger activity has been marked by the emergence of a new type of company, the so-called "conglomerate firm."[2] As opportunities for horizontal and vertical mergers have become limited (often by law) the conglomerate type of merger, in which there are no discernible economic relationships between the activities of the parties to the merger, has become increasingly popular. In 1959 and 1960 about one-third of all corporate mergers appear to have been of the inter-industry or conglomerate type; by 1966 the proportion of conglomerate mergers was estimated to have risen to 70%,[3] ranging from the pure conglomerate mergers between firms which produce totally dissimilar goods or services through a variety of mixed conglomerate combinations involving various degrees of horizontal or vertical economic relationships.

The rapid rise of the interindustry conglomerate giant and the growing tendency for conglomerate mergers to displace the horizontal and vertical combinations treated in most economics textbooks raise questions which are difficult to answer within the traditional framework of the theory of the firm. At least since Adam Smith's discovery of the economies inherent in an eighteenth century pin factory, the virtues of specialization have comprised a central tenet of economic theory. But despite an almost all-pervasive trend toward increasing specialization in economic life, the recent spate of conglomerate mergers appears to have repealed Adam Smith's dictum regarding the benefits of specialization.

---

[1] In a sense this wave reached its culmination in 1901 with the formation of the United States Steel Corporation, the so-called "merger of mergers."
[2] A far from exhaustive list of diversified conglomerates includes Textron, Litton Industries, Ling–Temco–Vought, Gulf & Western, International Telephone & Telegraph, Teledyne, Glen Alden, and Signal Oil.
[3] See, for example, E. F. Renshaw, "The Theory of Financial Leverage and Conglomerate Mergers," *California Management Review* (Fall 1968), pp. 79–84.

2. CONGLOMERATE MERGERS

That horizontal and vertical mergers can potentially produce real economic gains is nowhere denied; in fact, the central problem of antitrust policy stems from the possible existence of economies strong enough to offset the socially unacceptable features of some mergers. Expansion through merger may create significant economies of scale in production, research, distribution, and management; but the economic case for a conglomerate merger is somewhat less clear. Much of the traditional analysis relating to the possible creation of economies of scale is not relevant for the pure conglomerate. If such economies are created by a merger then some significant degree of interrelationship between inputs, production facilities, or marketing channels must have existed prior to the acquisition, which means that the merger was not of the purely conglomerate type. Nevertheless, mergers between totally unrelated enterprises not only take place, but the pursuit of diversification has become, in recent years, almost a cult.[4]

2.1 THE PORTFOLIO ANALYSIS OF CONGLOMERATE DIVERSIFICATION

The portfolio theory set out in Part II provides an alternative approach to conglomerate growth by treating the diversification inherent in a conglomerate-type acquisition as a special case of the general theory of diversification and portfolio selection. The essence of this approach is that a merger between *unrelated* firms can help stabilize overall corporate profits since the standard deviation of the combined profits stream will be reduced following the combination of statistically independent or negatively correlated income streams.[5] Moreover, this "diversification effect" occurs even in a purely conglomerate type of merger, that is, one in which the aggregate profits of the acquiring and acquired firms are *not* increased following the merger.

Let us assume such a merger between two completely unrelated companies. In the absence of synergistic[6] effects, the postmerger return to shareholders in

---

[4] The extreme argument in favor of conglomerate growth has been articulated by one of the managers of Gulf & Western Industries. See D. N. Judelson, "A Philosophy for a Conglomerate Company," *Business Horizons* (June 1968), pp. 5–13. For the "antidote" see J. Dean and W. Smith, "The Relationships Between Profitability and Size," in W. W. Alberts and J. E. Segall, eds., *The Corporate Merger*, pp. 3–22, Chicago and London, The University of Chicago Press, 1966.

[5] Strictly speaking, this reduction occurs so long as the income streams are *not* perfectly correlated. See Chapter X.

[6] The term *synergism* (or *synergistic growth*) refers to situations where the sum of the parts after the merger is greater than the sum of the individual contributions. This has also been termed the $2 + 2 = 5$ effect. See J. F. Weston, "Determination of Share Exchange Ratios in Mergers," in Alberts and Segall, *op. cit.*, p. 130.

the new firm will be the weighted average of the returns of each of the individual firms making up the merger.

$$z = wx_1 + (1 - w)x_2 \qquad (15.1)$$

where: z = a random variable denoting the postmerger return to shareholders of the new firm
x_1 and x_2 = random variables denoting the return to shareholders of the two individual firms, in the absence of the merger
w = the relative size of the first firm
$1 - w$ = the relative size of the second firm

The expected return after the merger (μ_z) equals the weighted average of the expected returns (μ_1 and μ_2) of the individual firms making up the merger.

$$\mu_z = w\mu_1 + (1 - w)\mu_2 \qquad (15.2)$$

The postmerger total variance (σ_z^2) becomes

$$\sigma_z^2 = w^2\sigma_1^2 + (1 - w)^2\sigma_2^2 + 2w(1 - w)\,Cov\,(x_1 x_2) \qquad (15.3)$$

Since we are assuming the absence of perfect correlation between the returns of the individual firms, the total postmerger variance is lower than the simple sum of the individual variances. And as we have also assumed that the expected return after the merger is a weighted average of the individual returns, the risk–return characteristics of the new firm represent an "efficient" combination, that is, one for which total risk has been reduced with no change in the level of return. It would appear to follow that the shares of the new firm should sell at a premium vis-à-vis the weighted sum of the premerger prices of the individual firms. However, such a premium will *not* be forthcoming in a perfect capital market because the superior risk–return combination (σ_z^2, μ_z) could have been achieved by investors, even in the absence of the merger, by combining the individual shares in a portfolio in the proportions w and $1 - w$.

Thus, despite the stabilizing diversification effect, a conglomerate merger per se does not necessarily create opportunities for risk diversification over and beyond what was possible to individual (and institutional) investors prior to the merger. In a perfect capital market, the premerger equilibrium prices of the shares would reflect the possibility of all such combinations, and therefore no increase in the combined market value of the two firms after the merger has been effected is to be expected, or in fact, is even possible.[7]

---

[7] A proof of the "neutrality" of a pure conglomerate merger is given in Appendix XV–1.

2. CONGLOMERATE MERGERS

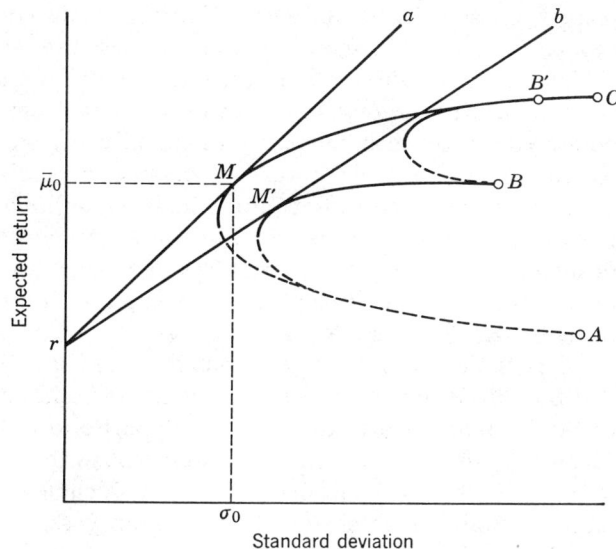

FIGURE XV.1.

This proposition is illustrated in Figure XV.1. For simplicity, and without loss of generality, we assume a securities market in which the shares of only three companies are traded.[8] *AMC* is the familiar envelope curve of efficient combinations of the three companies (*A*, *B*, and *C*) assumed to comprise the market; the market opportunity line *ra* rising from the riskless rate of interest, *r*, reflects the assumption that lending or borrowing at the rate *r* can take place. The slope of line *ra* which equals $(\bar{\mu}_0 - r)/\sigma_0$ (where $\bar{\mu}_0$ denotes the expected return on the optimum unlevered portfolio and σ_0 denotes the standard deviation of this portfolio) uniquely determines the market value of a unit of risk, that is, the measure of the trade-off between expected return and risk, for *all* investors independent of their tastes. As a result, the proportions of investment in each share included in portfolio *M* are optimal for every investor in the market.[9] Since it can be shown (see Appendix XV-1) that a pure conglomerate merger does not alter the optimum proportions of investment in the various shares, point *M* represents both the premerger and postmerger equilibrium share portfolio in a perfect market. Thus, where economies of scale and complementaries (synergism) are not

---

[8] The use of three rather than *N* companies does not impair the generality of the argument since the third company's shares can be thought of as representing the "rest of the world".
[9] See Chapter XIII.

present, the stabilization of the profit stream, induced by the merger, cannot produce a clear-cut economic gain in a perfect capital market.

Given the neutrality of conglomerate mergers in a perfect capital market, we now turn to the possible influence of market imperfections on the economic effects of such mergers. In practice investors do not include all security issues in their portfolios because of indivisibilities, differential transactions costs, cost of acquiring information, and difficulties of keeping track of numerous investments. For simplicity we shall assume that for all, or some, of the above reasons, an investor confines his portfolio to two shares only, A and B. The impact of such restrictions on optimal portfolios can again be seen in Figure XV.1.

All possible efficient combinations of A and B lie on the envelope curve $AM'B$, with M' on this curve representing the optimum portfolio, given the constraint that the investor restricts his portfolio to these two shares only. The new optimum share portfolio is tangent to the market opportunity line rb which lies below the ra line. Thus all attainable positions under the two-share constraint are inferior to the three-share case, and represent a reduction of utility to the investor.

Despite the two-share constraint, the investor, following a merger of companies B and C, can invest in all of the shares of the market, that is, in the new merger $(B + C)$ and in company A. To determine whether the merger has improved the investor's position, we first find the combination of shares B and C that the merger permits the investor to add to his portfolio. This combination lies on the envelope curve $BB'C$ which is constructed with no special restriction on the proportions of investment in shares B and C. But after the merger the proportions of B and C are fixed, and the envelope curve $BB'C$ reduces to a point, such as B'. The postmerger point B' has the characteristic that the ratio $P_B/P_C = w/(1 - w)$, that is, the merger creates a new composite share, with fixed proportions which reflect the relative size of the two companies making up the merger.

Following the merger the investor can combine shares B' and A when constructing his portfolio. A new envelope curve representing the efficient combinations of share A and the "composite" merger share B' is formed. If the new envelope curve crosses the rb market opportunity line the investor will have improved his position, that is, he will be able to reach a higher level of utility along a market opportunity line which lies to the left of rb. Thus, unlike the case of the perfect market, the conglomerate merger in an imperfect market does allow a degree of additional diversification which the investor hitherto could not effect for himself because of the two-share constraint, and this added degree of freedom may, as we have seen, translate itself into an economic gain for the investor. But on reflection it is equally clear that the investor may *not* gain, and in fact may even lose, from this type

2. CONGLOMERATE MERGERS

of merger—for while gaining the additional degree of freedom to invest *indirectly* in the shares of company C, he has lost the option of investing *directly* in the shares of B. Thus, should the new envelope curve lie below the line rb, the new equilibrium position will represent a loss of utility to the investor following the merger.[10]

2.2 CAPITAL COSTS

A stronger case for conglomerate mergers can be made when economies in capital costs are considered. Large firms have better access to the capital markets and also enjoy significant cost savings when securing their financing needs; for example, substantial economies of scale exist in the new issues market.[11] These cost savings presumably reflect, at least in part, the reduction in lenders' risk achieved through diversification. This can be illustrated by explicitly considering the possibility of financial failure and bankruptcy. If we assume that in any given year (or run of years) there exists for each individual firm some positive probability of suffering losses large enough to induce financial failure, it can readily be shown that the joint probability of such an event is reduced by a conglomerate merger. Clearly, the possibility that the critical level of losses will occur simultaneously for each of the component companies making up the merger is less (and often very much less) than the individual probabilities.

The capital cost economies are, of course, a special case of the general stabilizing diversification effect induced by the combination of other than perfectly correlated income streams in a conglomerate merger. But in this instance the diversification can be expected to create a true economic gain to the shareholders because the combination of the financial resources of the two firms making up the merger reduces lenders' risk, while combining each of the individual shares of the two companies in investors' portfolios does not. Since in this case capital market diversification is no longer a perfect substitute for corporate diversification, the latter provides a source of net gain to investors.

Although in general increasing the size of the firm may create financial advantages, the full measure of these capital cost savings will be realized only when a large diversified conglomerate absorbs a relatively small firm. The

---

[10] The possibility of loss assumes that the fixed proportions of B and C represented by the merger are, in this instance, sufficiently different from the preferred combination to allow the loss of "B" to completely offset the gains from adding "$B + C$" to the portfolio. In this context it should be emphasized that in an imperfect capital market the composition of the optimum share portfolio is not necessarily the same for all investors.

[11] See Securities and Exchange Commission, *Cost of Flotation of Corporate Securities, 1951–1955*, Washington D.C., U.S. Government Printing Office, June 1957.

differential between the capital costs of large and small firms declines rapidly except in the case of small firms.[12] With respect to larger firms it should be noted that after a point an individual firm may be sufficiently large (and even diversified) to have reduced financial risks to insignificant levels. Clearly the inclusion of such firms in a large conglomerate cannot be expected to engender further significant decreases in capital costs or the probability of bankruptcy.

3. CAPITAL INVESTMENTS

A second area in which the mean–variance portfolio selection model can be usefully applied is that of the firm's capital investment decisions. In the traditional theory of capital budgeting under certainty firms are assumed to accept (reject) those projects whose net present values are positive (negative) when discounted at the firm's opportunity cost of capital. In the real world, however, capital investment decisions almost invariably involve the evaluation of combinations of investments whose cash flows are not known with certainty. This immediately suggests the need to analyze capital budgets using *two* parameters to represent expected return and risk.

Since capital budgeting deals with multiperiod investments, some of which constitute mutually exclusive alternatives, expected net present values must be substituted for the expected returns of the financial portfolio selection model,[13] and by analogy, the variance of net present value is used as the risk indicator.[14]

3.1 THE VARIANCE AS A MEASURE OF RISK IN CAPITAL BUDGETING

The use of the variance as a measure of risk when dealing with multiperiod capital investments raises some thought-provoking questions:

(a) How should the variance *within* years be handled? Should the measure of risk reflect the sum of the annual variances or an average annual figure?

(b) How should we account, in the case of multiperiod investments, for the fact that risks are incurred in different years?

(c) What should be done about the variability between projects

---

[12] See D. F. Turner, "Conglomerate Mergers and Section 7 of the Clayton Act," *Harvard Law Review* 78 (May 1965), p. 1338.

[13] On the need to use present values when evaluating the investment in physical assets, see Chapter III.

[14] For an early application of expected NPV and the variance of NPV to capital budgeting, see F. S. Hillier, "The Derivation of Probabilistic Information for the Evaluation of Risky Investments," *Management Science* 9 (April 1963), pp. 443–57.

3. CAPITAL INVESTMENTS

which arises from differences in the levels of each year's average return; that is, how should the variance *between* years be handled?

To simplify the analysis we shall assume investment projects involving an immediate cash outlay followed by positive net cash flows in each of two subsequent years. Given this assumption, the expected net present value of an investment proposal is defined as the sum of the present values of the expected net cash flows in the first and second years, *less* the initial investment outlay:

$$E(NPV) = \alpha EX_1 + \alpha^2 EX_2 - I_0 \qquad (15.4)$$

where: EX_1 = the expected value of the net cash flow in the first year
EX_2 = the expected value of the net cash flow in the second year
I_0 = the initial investment outlay
$\alpha = 1/(1+r)$ = a coefficient for capitalizing cash flows over time, where r denotes the riskless interest rate.
$E(NPV)$ = the expected net present value.

Given the assumption that the net cash flow of the second year is statistically *independent* of the first year's outcome we define the variance of net present value as follows:

$$\sigma^2 = \sum_i \sum_j p_i p_j [\alpha X_i + \alpha^2 X_j - I_0 - (\alpha EX_1 + \alpha^2 EX_2 - I_0)]^2 \qquad (15.5)$$

where: x_i = a random variable denoting the net cash flow in year 1, with a probability of occurrence = P_i
x_j = a random variable denoting the net cash flow in year 2, with a probability of occurrence = P_j.

Equation (15.5) shows that the variance of net present value depends on all possible combinations of cash flows in years 1 and 2 multiplied by their probability of occurrence, which equals the product $P_i P_j$ in the case of independence. This formula can be rewritten as[15]

$$\sigma^2 = \alpha^2 \sigma_1^2 + \alpha^4 \sigma_2^2$$
$$= \frac{\sigma_1^2}{(1+r)^2} + \frac{\sigma_2^2}{(1+r)^4} \qquad (15.6)$$

---

[15] Rearranging terms, Equation (15.5) can be rewritten as follows:

$$\sigma^2 = \sum_i \sum_j P_i P_j [\alpha(X_i - EX_1) + \alpha^2(X_j - EX_2)]^2$$
$$= \alpha^2 \sum_i \sum_j P_i P_j (X_i - EX_1)^2 + \alpha^4 \sum_i \sum_j P_i P_j (X_j - EX_2)^2$$
$$+ 2\alpha^3 \sum_i \sum_j P_i P_j (X_i - EX_1)(X_j - EX_2)$$

But given the assumption of independence, the last expression disappears, leaving:

$$\sigma^2 = \alpha^2 \sum_i P_i (X_i - EX_1)^2 \sum_j P_j + \alpha^4 \sum_j P_j (X_j - EX_2) \sum_i P_i$$

and since $\sum_i P_i = \sum_i P_j = 1$, this equation reduces to Equation (15.6) of the text.

which can be generalized for investment proposals of any duration:

$$\sigma^2 = \sum_{t=1}^{n} \frac{\sigma_t^2}{(1+r)^{2t}} \qquad (15.7)$$

where: n = the project's duration in years
σ_1^2 = the variance of the cash flow distribution in year 1
σ_2^2 = the variance of the cash flow distribution in year 2.

Given the assumption of statistical independence, the total variance of net present value is equal to the discounted sum of the annual variances. Thus the overall measure of risk depends on the *time-adjusted* risks incurred in each year, with the discounting of all annual risks to their present values serving to make the expected risks of more distant years comparable to those of earlier years. This can be illustrated by considering the following case of a firm confronted by two investment proposals, A and B, each having the same expected net present value but different time patterns of *undiscounted* annual variances:

	σ_1^2	σ_2^2	σ^2
Project A	1	3	4
Project B	3	1	4

In the absence of discounting, the firm would be indifferent regarding these two "equal risk" projects despite the fact that Project A defers the larger risk to the second year. The discounting of annual variances (inherent in the variance of net present value calculation) ensures that the time pattern of risk will be taken into account, and in this particular example Project A would be preferred since its total *discounted* variance is smaller than that of Project B, at all positive discount rates.

The only peculiarity in this formulation of the "riskiness" of multiperiod investment projects stems from the exponents applied to the discount rate. Thus, in apparent contradiction to received capital budgeting doctrine, the discount factor of the first year is equal to $1/(1+r)^2$ rather than $1/(1+r)$, while the discount factor for year 2 is raised to the fourth power rather than to the second power. This anomaly arises because we have taken the variance, rather than the standard deviation, as the measure of dispersion. An alternative would be to set out the measure of risk directly in terms of the discounted standard deviation rather than the variance, thereby obtaining the appropriate measures of risk, $\sigma_1/(1+r)$ and $\sigma_2/(1+r)^2$ in the first and second year respectively. But since the variance provides a mathematically (and statistically) more convenient variable, we raise these expressions to

3. CAPITAL INVESTMENTS

TABLE XV-1.

	I_0	First Year		Second Year	
		X_i	P_i	X_j	P_j
Project A	-1	1	1/2	1	1/2
		3	1/2	3	1/2
Project B	-1	1	1/2	9	1/2
		3	1/2	11	1/2

their second power which results in the measures of dispersion given in Equation (15.6).

As can be seen from Equation (15.6), the total variance of net present value depends on the variability of possible outcomes *within* each year, but is completely independent of the variance *between* years. Thus the variance which arises from shifts in the expected cash flow over time is *not* a factor influencing this measure of risk. This can be illustrated by examining the numerical example given in Table XV-1. In this example the annual variance of both projects, in both years, is equal to one. Assuming a capitalization rate of r the total variance of net present value for both projects is equal to $1/(1 + r)^2 + 1/(1 + r)^4$. Since the *intra*-year variances are the same (equal to *one* in each year) for both projects, the total risk incurred in each project is also considered to be equal, despite the additional upward shift of Project B's distribution in the second year.

At first glance the failure to reflect the variance *between* years, along with the variance *within* each year, would appear to be a serious shortcoming of the variance of net present value as an indicator of risk. On further reflection, however, it is clear that while upward or downward shifts of the cash flow distribution in any particular year must affect a project's expected value, they do not necessarily affect its risk characteristic. Again this can be illustrated by the numerical example given in Table XV-1. Ignoring the common capitalization factor, Project A has a maximum net cash flow of 5 and a minimum of 1; the relevant figures for Project B are 13 and 9. As can be seen from these calculations, one can increase expected profitability (net present value) by shifting from Project A to Project B, but such a shift does *not* involve any change in risk (that is, change in the dispersion of outcomes). Since risk is measured by the variance from expected net present value, each of these projects carries the same risk index, independent of the upward shift of Project B's expected receipts in the second year. Far from being a shortcoming, the neglect of such shifts by the variance of net present value measure

TABLE XV-2.

	Initial Investment Outlay	First Year		Second Year	
		X_i	P_i	X_j	P_j
Project A	I_0	10	1/2	10	1/2
		30	1/2	30	1/2
Project B	I_0^*	10	1/2	—	—
		30	1/2	—	—

of risk is conceptually correct, these shifts properly affecting a project's profitability but not its risk index.

As we have already noted, the variance of net present value reflects the discounted sum of the annual variances, and not the average annual variance. With the aid of the numerical example given in Table XV–2, it can be shown that the measure of dispersion based on the sum of the annual variances, rather than the annual average, provides the more appropriate risk indicator. Let us assume a set of initial investment outlays for the two projects which equate their net present values. This, of course, implies $I_0 > I_0^*$. Which project involves the most risk? If we measure risk by the variance of net present value, that is, by the discounted sum of the annual variances, project B is less risky since its variance is smaller than that of project A. The variance of project A, whose total variance reflects the sum of two equal annual variances, is given by

$$\frac{\sigma^2}{(1+r)^2} + \frac{\sigma^2}{(1+r)^4} = \frac{100}{(1+r)^2} + \frac{100}{(1+r)^4} > \frac{100}{(1+r)^2}$$

However the result is reversed, and Project A becomes less risky than Project B, when the average annual variance is used as a risk indicator:

$$\frac{1}{2}\left[\frac{100}{(1+r)^2} + \frac{100}{(1+r)^4}\right] < \frac{100}{(1+r)^2}$$

Clearly, the *sum* of the variances provides the more appropriate measure or risk, since Project A affords the same net present value as Project B, but requires the firm to sustain a given degree of risk for *two* years. Thus the sum of the variances gives the intuitively appealing result that, *other things being equal*, the longer the duration of the project, the greater the risk incurred.

Given the assumption of statistical independence between the cash flows of the various projects over time, the total variance of expected net present

3. CAPITAL INVESTMENTS

value is equal to the discounted sum of the annual variances, and has the following properties:

(a) This measure of risk depends on the variance of possible outcomes *within* each year, but is completely independent of the variance *between* years.

(b) The annual variances are discounted to their present values, thereby making the risks of more distant years comparable to those of earlier years.

When the assumption of independence is dropped, the variance of net present value includes, in addition to the individual annual variances, an expression which reflects the degree of dependence between the annual cash flows of each individual project as well as between the annual cash flows of the various projects.

To show this let us examine the components of the variance of net present value for the case of two projects, each of which has a duration of two years. To simplify the notation, we shall define the following four indices to be applied to the cash flows and probabilities of the two projects in each of the two years:

$i =$ an index for the first project in year 1
$j =$ an index for the first project in year 2
$g =$ an index for the second project in year 1
$h =$ an index for the second project in year 2

We also define the following:

$EX_1, \sigma_1^2 =$ the expected value and variance of the *first* project's net cash flow in year 1

$EX_2, \sigma_2^2 =$ the expected value and variance of the *first* project's net cash flow in year 2

$EX_3, \sigma_3^2 =$ the expected value and variance of the *second* project's net cash flow in year 1

$EX_4, \sigma_4^2 =$ the expected value and variance of the *second* project's net cash flow in year 2

Using this notation, we write the total variance of both projects as follows:

$$\sigma^2 = \sum_i \sum_j \sum_g \sum_h P_i P_{g/i} P_{j/ig} P_{h/ijg} [\alpha x_i + \alpha^2 x_j + \alpha x_g + \alpha^2 x_h$$
$$- (\alpha EX_1 + \alpha^2 EX_2 + \alpha EX_3 + \alpha^2 EX_4)]^2 \quad (15.8)$$

where: $P_{g/i} =$ the conditional probability of outcome g for the second project in year 1, given the outcome i of the first project in year 1

$P_{j/ig} =$ the conditional probability of outcome j for the first project in year 2, given the outcome i of the first project in year 1 and the outcome g of the second project in year 1

$P_{h/ijg}$ = the conditional probability of outcome h for the second project in year 2 given the outcomes i, j, and g.

Equation (15.8) reflects the fact that every possible total net present value for the two-project "portfolio" is given by the sum of four observations, each of which is taken from one of the four indexed frequency distributions. The overall probability for the occurrence of any particular combination of cash flows, i, j, g, and h, is given by the multiple product $P_i P_{g/i} P_{j/ig} P_{h/ijg}$. These conditional probabilities reflect the general case in which interdependence is permitted between *all* combinations of the four random variable distributions.

The second and third terms of this multiple product respectively reflect the possible dependence between the cash flows of the two products in the first year and the possible interdependence between the cash flow of the first project in the second year and the first-year cash flows of both projects; the final term reflects the possible dependence of the second project's cash flow in year 2 on each of the other three outcomes: its own cash flow in the first year and the cash flows of the other project in each of the two years. Thus the conditional probability in the two project–two year cash flow case is given by the probability of getting any particular series of outcomes from the distributions x_i, x_j, x_g, and x_h.

After rearranging terms and simplifying, Equation (15.8) can be rewritten as

$$\sigma^2 = \alpha^2 \sigma_1^2 + \alpha^2 \sigma_3^2 + \alpha^4 \sigma_2^2 + \alpha^4 \sigma_4^2$$
$$+ 2\alpha^3 \sigma_{ij} + 2\alpha^3 \sigma_{gh} + 2\alpha^2 \sigma_{ig} + 2\alpha^4 \sigma_{jh} + 2\alpha^3 \sigma_{ih} + 2\alpha^3 \sigma_{jg} \qquad (15.9)$$

Thus, in general, the total variance of net present value reflects the sum of the individual variances for each project in each year plus an expression of interdependence based on every possible combination among the firm's indexed distributions i, j, g, and h. This measure reflects both the interdependence between years and the interdependence between projects, with each expression discounted at the midpoint between its two components.[16]

3.2 THE PORTFOLIO ANALYSIS OF CAPITAL INVESTMENTS

As we have just seen, a multiperiod capital investment analogue to the M–V securities portfolio model is provided by the expected net present value and the variance of NPV. The use of the former has been recommended because

---

[16] Conceptually, the same equations can be generalized for n projects over T years, but as the number of projects and/or years is increased the calculation of the variance rapidly becomes complex.

3. CAPITAL INVESTMENTS

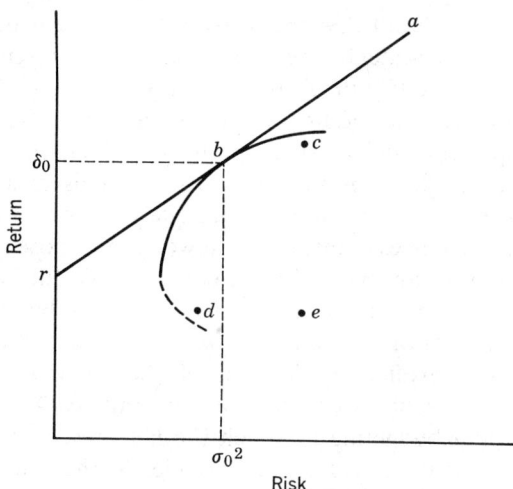

FIGURE XV.2.

of problems engendered by the existence of mutually exclusive investment options; and the latter, as we have shown, provides an appropriate measure of risk. Given these measures of return and risk for each investment alternative, the capital budgeting problem can be analyzed using the Markowitz–Tobin portfolio selection model. As is true of the individual investor in securities, the firm is faced with the problem of choosing an optimal combination (portfolio) of projects out of the subset of efficient combinations (portfolios); and because of possible covariance between the cash flows of new investment proposals and those generated by existing projects, the combinations should include existing as well as proposed investments.[17]

The subset of such efficient investment combinations facing the firm is illustrated by the familiar envelope curve in Figure XV.2. All of the remaining interior combinations should not be chosen since they represent inefficient options, in the sense that the firm can always improve its position (increase return with no increase in risk, or reduce risk without sacrifice of return) by choosing a different combination on the efficiency locus.[18]

---

[17] The need to include the firm's current operations is emphasized by J. Van Horne, "Capital Budgeting Decisions Involving Combinations of Risky Investments," *Management Science* 13 (October 1966), pp. B–84 to B–92.

[18] In the case of the business firm the efficiency frontier may not be continuous owing to the indivisibility of investment projects. It should also be noted that a point on the efficiency curve *cannot* include more than one project out of a set of mutually exclusive alternatives.

If we recall that the distribution of the expected income stream accruing to shareholders reflects the past and present capital investment projects undertaken by the firm, the market model of Chapter XIII can be used again to determine the firm's optimal capital budget. The line *ra* of Figure XV.2 represents the market opportunity line, the slope of which measures the market price of a unit of risk.[19] This measure of the trade-off between expected return and risk is uniquely determined for *all* investors, independent of differences in taste. When we superimpose such a line on Figure XV.2, the point of tangency with the curve of efficient investment combinations (point *b*) represents the optimal investment combination for the firm, namely, that combination which maximizes the value of the owners' equity.

The explicit application of the M–V criterion to capital expenditure decisions has some far-reaching implications for the received doctrine of capital budgeting in which the net present values of *individual* projects are used as the key decision variable. If the firm is confronted with projects of varying risk, the M–V model suggests that the optimal portfolio (point *b* of Figure XV.2) might have been achieved by combining two projects having the characteristics of points *c* and *d* in Figure XV.2, the first project having a higher expected return than δ_0 and a higher variance than σ_0^2, the second project having an expected return lower than δ_0, and also a variance lower than σ_0^2.

Thus the explicit application of the M–V framework to the capital budgeting problem immediately suggests the possibility that situations may arise in which it pays the firm to accept a low-risk project even though its net present value is *negative* when discounted at the rate δ_0 that is the firm's average cost of capital (for example, a project of the type represented by point *d* in Figure XV.2). At first glance this result seems startling, but on further reflection it can readily be explained. Most firms holding low-risk assets such as bonds would find the net present value of such investments negative when discounted at the firm's opportunity cost of capital, since the latter reflects the average risk of the firm, and is therefore higher (usually substantially higher) than the interest rate on bonds.

The appropriateness of the net present value rule becomes even more dubious once we recognize the possibility of statistical interdependence between the cash flows of the various investment projects. In such circumstances it may pay to accept a project with a negative net present value even

---

[19] The alternative of using the point of tangency between an indifference curve and the efficiency locus should not be applied to problems of capital budgeting since a firm's shareholders typically have different utility functions (indifference curves). Such a procedure also implicitly assumes that investors cannot lend or borrow. See Chapter XIII.

3. CAPITAL INVESTMENTS 521

though its variance is *higher* than σ_0^2. (Such a project is represented by point *e* in Figure XV.2.) Clearly, the negative covariance of such a project with the other proposals might conceivably be sufficient to combine with them into an "efficient" combination. Of course, if the firm was faced with the problem of choosing only *one* project, an alternative with the risk–return characteristics denoted by point *e* would be rejected by the M–V rule since it represents an inefficient alternative as compared with point *d*.

The importance of recognizing the correlations among investment opportunities is almost intuitively obvious. Numerous examples of risk-reducing combinations of investments can be found: manufacturers of machine tools and other highly cyclical products often tend to diversify into consumer goods to help stabilize the income stream; risk reduction, as we have seen, provides one of the explanations for the recent spate of conglomerate mergers.

The application of a single-valued risk-adjusted discount rate to all individual projects represents a sort of rule-of-thumb solution, and cannot be defended on theoretical grounds. Such a procedure assumes that the individual characteristics of the alternative projects do *not* change the average risk level of the firm. This is tantamount to assuming the absence of covariance effects. However, where the firm must choose among investment opportunities with risk characteristics which materially change the average risk level of the firm, both the optimal investment mix and the appropriate discount rate must be simultaneously determined. A way out of this impasse can be found, however, by dichotimizing the decision process:

> (a) In the first stage the future cash flows of all projects are reduced to a common denominator by calculating their present values and the locus of efficient combinations is constructed.[20] The appropriate discount rate is the *riskless* rate of interest.
>
> (b) After adjusting for the time value of money, the estimated "market price" of a unit of risk is used to find the optimal combination.[21]

---

[20] The actual computation can be facilitated using a variant of the computer program employed in Chapter XVI to calculate the efficiency curves for international portfolios.
[21] Alternatively the decision process can be set out in terms of *individual* proposals, rather than portfolios. Equation (13.20) of Chapter XIII, which sets out the risk–return relationship for *individual* securities, taking their contribution to the total risk of the optimal portfolio into account, determines the appropriate discount rate to be used when calculating the net present value of individual proposals. Note that the discount rate is composed of the riskless rate of interest plus a risk premium which reflects the variance of the individual project as well as its interaction with all other projects. Only projects whose NPV's are positive using this (variable) rate are accepted.

4. SUMMARY

In this chapter the portfolio theory of Part II was applied to two problems involving the business firm rather than the investor in securities: (a) conglomerate mergers, and (b) capital budgeting. In both cases appropriate analogues can be found, and the resulting analysis provides some new and thought-provoking insights into both problems.

QUESTIONS AND PROBLEMS

15.1 Explain briefly the difference between a horizontal, a vertical and a conglomerate merger.

15.2 Can an investor gain from a pure conglomerate merger in a *perfect* capital market?

15.3 Can an investor gain from a pure conglomerate merger in an *imperfect* capital market?

15.4 Assume a capital market which meets all of the conditions of a perfect market with the exception of the absence of taxation. Can an investor gain from a pure conglomerate merger in such a situation?

15.5 In what circumstances, may a firm rationally decide to accept an investment which has negative NPV?

15.6 Calculate the variance of the following investment project:

	First Year		Second Year	
Io	Xi	Pi	Xj	Pj
-100	60	1/3	100	1/3
	90	1/3	100	1/3
	120	1/3	160	1/3

Assume that the possible cash flows of the two years are related in the following manner: when 60 or 90 results in the first year, then 100 appears in the second, and when 120 is earned in the first year, then 160 is earned in the second. Assume that the firm's discount rate is $k = 10\%$.

15.7 Evaluate the variance of NPV as an appropriate measure of a capital investment project's risk.

SELECTED REFERENCES

Alberts, W. W., "The Profitability of Growth by Merger," in *The Corporate Merger*, W. W. Alberts and J. E. Segall, eds., Chicago and London: University of Chicago Press, 1966.

Hillier, F. S., "The Derivation of Probabilistic Information for the Evaluation of Risky Investments," *Management Science* (April 1963).

Judelson, D. N., "A Philosophy for a Conglomerate Company," *Business Horizons* (June 1968).

Levy, H., and Sarnat, M., "Diversification, Portfolio Analysis and the Uneasy Case for Conglomerate Mergers," *Journal of Finance* (September 1970).

———, "The Portfolio Analysis of Multiperiod Investments Under Conditions of Risk," *Engineering Economist* (September 1970).

Lewellen, W. G., "A Pure Financial Rationale for the Conglomerate Merger" *Journal of Finance, Papers and Proceedings* (May 1971).

Lintner, J., "Expectations, Mergers and Equilibrium in Purely Competitive Securities Markets" *American Economic Review, Papers and Proceedings* (May 1971).

———, "The Valuation of Risk Assets and the Selection of Risky Investments in Stock Portfolios and Capital Budgets," *Review of Economics and Statistics* (February 1965).

Mao, J. C. T., and Helliwell, J. F., "Investment Decisions Under Uncertainty: Theory and Practice," *Journal of Finance* (May 1969).

Molodovsky, N., "Corporate Mergers and Antitrust Policy," *Financial Analysts Journal*, (March–April 1968).

Mueller, Dennis C., "A Theory of Conglomerate Mergers," *Quarterly Journal of Economics* (November 1969).

Myers, S. C., "Procedures for Capital Budgeting Under Uncertainty," *Industrial Management Review* (Spring 1968).

Shapiro, D. L., "Conglomerate Mergers and Optimal Investment Policy," *Journal of Financial and Quantitative Analysis* (January 1970).

Smith, K. V., and Schreiner, J. C., "A Portfolio Analysis of Conglomerate Diversification," *Journal of Finance* (June 1969).

Turner, D. F., "Conglomerate Mergers and Section 7 of the Clayton Act," *Harvard Law Review* (May 1965).

Van Horne, J. C., "Capital-Budgeting Decisions Involving Combinations of Risky Investments," *Management Science* (October 1966).

———, *Financial Management and Policy*. Englewood Cliffs, N.J.: Prentice-Hall, 1968.

Weston, J. F., "Responses to Market Imperfection–Discussion," *American Economic Review* (May 1971).

APPENDIX XV-1
Proof of the Neutrality of Conglomerate Mergers in a Perfect Securities Market

The purpose of this appendix is to prove the "neutrality" of a pure conglomerate merger. For simplicity we assume a securities market in which the shares of only three companies are traded. Let p_1, p_2, and p_3 denote the proportions of investment in the shares of companies 1, 2, and 3 respectively and p_r the proportion invested in bonds,[22] subject to the constraint:

$$\sum_{i=1}^{3} p_i + p_r = 1 \qquad (15.1.1)$$

The variance of the investment portfolios is given by

$$V = \sum_{i=1}^{3} p_i^2 \sigma_i^2 + 2 \sum_{\substack{i=1 \\ j>i}}^{3} p_i p_j \, Cov(x_i x_j) \qquad (15.1.2)$$

The optimal proportion of investment in each of the three shares can be found by bringing the variance of the portfolio to a minimum for any given expected return, $\bar{\mu}$. This is accomplished by differentiating the following function with respect to each of the p_i and with respect to the Lagrange multiplier λ_1:[23]

$$C = \sum_{i=1}^{3} p_i^2 \sigma_i^2 + 2 \sum_{\substack{i=1 \\ j>i}}^{3} p_i p_j \, Cov(x_i x_j) + \lambda_1 \left[\bar{\mu} - \sum_{i=1}^{3} p_i \mu_i - \left(1 - \sum_{i=1}^{3} p_i\right) r \right]$$

$$(15.1.3)$$

---

[22] We assume that the bonds are riskless and that the individual investors, in building their portfolios, can borrow or lend at the riskless rate of interest r.
[23] See Chapter XIII.

PROOF OF THE NEUTRALITY OF CONGLOMERATE MERGERS

The differentiation yields the following set of four equations:

$$p_1\sigma_1^2 + p_2 \, Cov(x_1 x_2) + p_3 \, Cov(x_1 x_3) = \lambda_1(\mu_1 - r) \quad (15.1.4)$$

$$p_1 \, Cov(x_1 x_2) + p_2\sigma_2^2 + p_3 \, Cov(x_2 x_3) = \lambda_1(\mu_2 - r) \quad (15.1.5)$$

$$p_1 \, Cov(x_1 x_3) + p_2 \, Cov(x_2 x_3) + p_3\sigma_3^2 = \lambda_1(\mu_3 - r) \quad (15.1.6)$$

$$\bar{\mu} = p_1\mu_1 + p_2\mu_2 + p_3\mu_3 + \left(1 - \sum_{i=1}^{3} p_i\right) r \quad (15.1.7)$$

As we have shown in Chapter XIII this solution set gives the optimal proportions of investment in each security for *all* investors. Since the optimal ratio of investment proportions in any two shares is a constant for every investor in the market, it also follows that if the market is to be cleared, this ratio must be proportional to the relative size of the firms.[24] Thus in the case of companies 1 and 2, the following equilibrium relationship must hold:

$$p_1/p_2 = w/1 - w$$

Now let us assume that company 1 and company 2 are merged. Determining the *postmerger* optimum investment proportions (by the same method as above) yields the following set of three equations:

$$h_1\sigma_z + h_2 \, Cov(zy) = \lambda_2(\mu_z - r) \quad (15.1.8)$$

$$h_1 \, Cov(zy) + h_2\sigma_y^2 = \lambda_2(\mu_y - r) \quad (15.1.9)$$

$$\bar{\mu} = h_1\mu_z + h_2\mu_y + (1 - h_1 - h_2)r \quad (15.1.10)$$

where: h_1 = the optimal proportion of investment in the shares of the newly merged company
h_2 = the optimal proportion of investment in the third company
$y = x_3$ = a random variable denoting the return on the shares of the third company.

The problem is to prove that after the merger of companies 1 and 2, the following relationships must hold:

$$h_1 = p_1 + p_2$$
$$h_2 = p_3$$

and therefore no change in equilibrium share prices has been induced.

As a first step we substitute the following terms in the previous set of equations: x_3 for y; $wx_1 + (1 - w)x_2$ for z; and σ_3^2 for σ_y^2. This yields the

---

[24] It is this property of perfect capital markets which permits the aggregation implicit in the market equations of the text.

following equation in place of (15.1.8):

$$h_1 w^2 \sigma_1^2 + h_1(1-w)^2 \sigma_2^2 + 2h_1 w(1-w) \, Cov\,(x_1 x_2)$$
$$+ h_2(1-w)\,Cov\,(x_2 x_3) + h_2 w\,Cov\,(x_1 x_3)$$
$$= \lambda_2[w\mu_1 + (1-w)\mu_2 - r] \quad (15.1.11)$$

Rearranging terms, the equation can be written as follows:

$$w[h_1 w \sigma_1^2 + h_1(1-w)\,Cov\,(x_1 x_2) + h_2\,Cov\,(x_1 x_3)]$$
$$+ (1-w)[h_1 w\,Cov\,(x_1 x_2) + h_1(1-w)\sigma_2^2 + h_2\,Cov\,(x_2 x_3)]$$
$$= w\lambda_2(\mu_1 - r) + (1-w)\lambda_2(\mu_2 - r) \quad (15.1.12)$$

Carrying through the indicated substitutions, we can rewrite Equations (15.1.9) and (15.1.10) as follows:

$$h_1 w\,Cov\,(x_1 x_3) + h_1(1-w)\,Cov\,(x_2 x_3) + h_2 \sigma_3^2 = \lambda_2(\mu_3 - r) \quad (15.1.13)$$
$$\bar{\mu} = h_1 w \mu_1 + h_1(1-w)\mu_2 + h_2 \mu_3 + (1 - wh_1 - (1-w)h_1 - h_2)r$$
$$(15.1.14)$$

The optimal proportions of investment before the merger can be found by solving the set of Equations (15.1.4) to (15.1.7); the optimal proportion of investment after the merger can be found by solving the set of Equations (15.1.8) to (15.1.10), or equivalently, (15.1.12) to (15.1.14). After solving the premerger equations for p_1, p_2, p_3, and λ_1, we multiply Equation (15.1.4) by w and Equation (15.1.5) by $(1-w)$. If we then combine these two equations and substitute wh_1 for p_1; $(1-w)h_1$ for p_2; and λ_2 for λ_1 in this and the remaining two equations, the resulting set of three equations is identical to the set of Equations (15.1.12) to (15.1.14). Since the latter set comprises three equations with three unknowns, namely h_1, h_2, and λ_2, it follows that this solution is also the unique solution.

Since we found that $h_1 w = p_1$ and $h_1(1-w) = p_2$, it follows that $h_1 = p_1 + p_2$, that is, the optimal proportion of investment after the merger is simply the sum of the proportions which were invested in the individual companies prior to the merger. Thus the merger per se calls forth no market forces to alter the equilibrium share prices which existed prior to the change, and therefore we may conclude that the market value of the new company will not differ from the sum of the premerger market values of the two component companies.

Chapter XVI
International Diversification of Investments

1. INTRODUCTION

Risk diversification need not be confined to domestic assets. This chapter concludes the book by extending the portfolio model to problems of international investment.

2. CO-MOVEMENTS OF SECURITY PRICES

The degree to which diversification can reduce risk depends on the correlations among security returns. If the returns should display perfect negative correlation, diversification could completely eliminate risk and portfolio selection would become an analogue to the cancelling of risks in the insurance industry. On the other hand, if security returns were perfectly correlated, no amount of diversification could affect risk. The practical as well as theoretical importance of portfolio selection stems from the fact that while the observed security returns for any particular country are highly correlated, they are not perfectly correlated, which implies the reduction (but not the elimination) of risk through diversification.

This can be illustrated by considering the relationships among the prices of common stocks in the United States. Table XVI–1 sets out the correlation coefficients among the various stock price indices published by Moody's Investment Services during the period 1929–69. Within the economy, a strong tendency usually exists for economic phenomena to move more or less in unison, which gives rise to periods of relatively high or low general economic activity. This also holds true for individual securities and industries. For example, during the period 1929–69, Moody's price index of

530 INTERNATIONAL DIVERSIFICATION OF INVESTMENTS

TABLE XVI-1. Correlation matrix of U.S. common stock price indices, 1929–69

	Stock Price Indices					
	1	2	3	4	5	6
1. Composite	1.00000	0.99461	0.84277	0.81973	0.62362	0.98430
2. Industrials		1.00000	0.81697	0.79180	0.57332	0.97810
3. Railroads			1.00000	0.91661	0.88329	0.79983
4. Utilities				1.00000	0.89450	0.78741
5. N.Y.C. Banks					1.00000	0.58572
6. Fire Insurance						1.00000

SOURCE: Calculated from data appearing in *Moody's Industrial Manual, 1970*, pp. a24–a25.

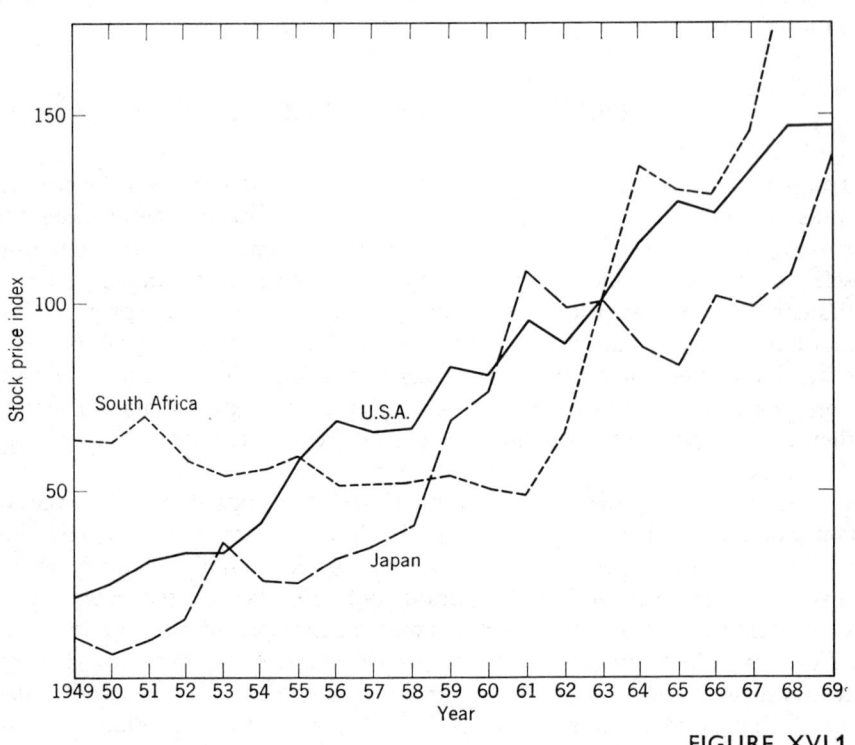

FIGURE XVI.1.

3. THE GAINS FROM INTERNATIONAL DIVERSIFICATION

industrial common stocks was positively correlated with the indices of railroad, public utilities, New York City banks, and fire insurance companies. The correlation coefficients were 0.82, 0.79, 0.57, and 0.98 respectively.[1]

The existence of a relatively high degree of positive correlation within an economy suggests the possibility that risk reduction might be facilitated by diversifying securities portfolios internationally. In Figure XVI.1 the common stock price indices of the United States, Japan, and South Africa are presented graphically for the period 1949-69.[2] A glance at Figure XVI.1 suffices to show that the correlation among the stock prices of these three countries is much lower than the correlation which we noted among the common stocks of the United States taken alone. For example, between 1949 and 1952, South African stock prices *fell* by 10%, while stock prices in the U.S.A. and Japan were *rising* by more than 50%. On the other hand, South African share prices rose dramatically between 1961 and 1965, a period in which the Japanese stock index fell by over 20%.

3. THE GAINS FROM INTERNATIONAL DIVERSIFICATION

To estimate the potential gains from international diversification a more refined analysis is required. Data on common stock prices must be adjusted for currency devaluations, that is, they must be expressed in some common currency unit such as U.S. dollars or Swiss francs, and the resulting data expressed as rates of return if meaningful comparisons are to be made. Finally, an operational method for applying the portfolio model must be found so that the optimal internationally diversified portfolios can be determined.

This sounds like a large order, and it is! The first step in the analysis, however, is straightforward and familiar. Taking as our sample 28 countries (see Table XVI-2) for which data were available, mean rates of return on the investment in common stocks were calculated for the period 1951 to 1969. The annual rate of return for each country was defined as the percentage change in the dollar value of its index of common stocks.[3]

$$r_{i(t)} = \frac{P_{i(t)} - P_{i(t-1)}}{P_{i(t-1)}}$$

---

[1] This phenomenon holds for other countries as well. For example, Israel's index of industrial stock prices is positively correlated with the indices of banking and insurance, real estate and investment companies.

[2] The data on the indices were obtained from various editions of International Monetary Fund, *International Financial Statistics*.

[3] The indices for the 28 countries were obtained from various editions of *Ibid*. Notice that we do not measure the maximum potential gain from diversification since we deal with indexes and not with individual stocks.

TABLE XVI-2. Mean rates of return and standard deviations of common stocks for 28 selected countries, 1951–69. (in percentage)

Country	Rate of Return	Standard Deviation	Country	Rate of Return	Standard Deviation
Australia	5.0	12.0	Mexico	1.3	17.4
Austria	14.5	26.6	Netherlands	9.7	19.0
Belgium	3.6	10.2	New Zealand	4.9	14.7
Canada	8.4	14.3	Norway	2.3	12.5
Ceylon	−0.2	19.7	Peru	−2.2	12.1
Chile	3.8	31.9	Philippines	9.2	39.4
Denmark	5.4	11.4	Portugal	7.2	17.7
Finland	9.5	22.4	South Africa	8.7	19.0
France	8.6	19.8	Spain	−2.7	17.2
Germany	17.1	27.0	Sweden	8.5	12.8
India	0.1	13.6	Switzerland	8.8	21.0
Israel	3.5	38.7	United Kingdom	6.2	15.9
Italy	10.6	21.1	United States	11.5	11.6
Japan	17.9	29.5	Venezuela	4.4	15.8

* Adjusted for changes in the dollar exchange rate.
SOURCE: Calculated from common stock indices and exchange rates appearing in various issues of the International Monetary Fund's *International Financial Statistics*.

where: $P_{i(t)}$ = the dollar value of the ith country's common stock index at the end of year t

$r_{i(t)}$ = the rate of return for the ith country in year t.[4]

Thus if the index for a particular country equaled 120 at the end of 1968 and rose to 132 at the close of 1969, the "rate of return" in 1969 is given by

$$\frac{132 - 120}{120} = 10\%$$

Since we defined the rate of return in terms of dollars, the indices must be adjusted to reflect any change in exchange rates during the year.[5] To clarify the calculation, let us consider a concrete example. Let us assume that an American invests $100 in the securities of a foreign country, for example,

---

[4] Owing to the lack of data for many of the countries dividends are not included; the rates of return, therefore, have a downward bias.
[5] Foreign currency values were converted into dollar values using the exchange rates which prevailed at the end of each year. Data on exchange rates were taken from various issues of *Ibid*.

3. THE GAINS FROM INTERNATIONAL DIVERSIFICATION

Israel; that he earns a 20% *nominal* rate of return on his investment; that the exchange rate was one dollar = one Israeli pound at the time of the investment; and that during the year the pound is devalued to 1.80 Israeli pounds to the dollar, that is, a dollar is now worth 1.8 pounds as compared with one pound at the beginning of the year. What is the "dollar adjusted" rate of return?

At the beginning of the year the U.S. investor acquires 100 Israeli pounds for $100 at the prevailing exchange rate and invests this sum in Israeli securities (represented by that country's index of common stock prices). At the end of the year he liquidates his Israeli investment and receives 120 pounds (that is, a rate of return of 20% in pounds); however, because of the devaluation he now can convert the 120 Israeli pounds into only 67 dollars ($120 ÷ 1.80 = $67), and his *dollar-adjusted* rate of return is negative—minus 33%! The investment process can be illustrated by the following simple diagram:

```
Beginning                  Exchange Rate
of Year      100 dollars  ───1 to 1───→   100 pounds
                                               │ 20% nominal
                                               │ rate of return
                                               ↓
End of       67 dollars  ←──────────────   120 pounds
Year                       Exchange Rate
                           1.80 pounds to the dollar
```

Table XVI–2 sets out the mean dollar-adjusted rate of return and the standard deviation of returns for each of the 28 countries included in our sample during the period 1951 to 1969. The mean rate of return for each country was calculated by taking the arithmetic average of the annual returns:

$$R_i = \frac{1}{N} \sum_{t=1}^{N} r_i(t)$$

where R_i = the mean rate of return for the ith country.

Since the annual rates of return have been adjusted for all changes in the dollar exchange rate during the period in question, Table XVI–2 sets out the relevant rates for investors in dollars or any other currency unit whose dollar rate of exchange remained constant during the period 1951–69. Thus, for example, the investment returns and the remaining analysis of this chapter are relevant for Switzerland as well as for the United States, but not for the United Kingdom, since the latter devalued its currency during the period under study.

The annual average dollar rate of return on common stocks for the period 1951–69 ranged from a high of 17.9% for Japan to a low of −2.7% for Spain. The intercountry differences in variability (standard deviations) were also very pronounced: three countries—Chile, Israel, and the Philippines—had standard deviations greater than 30%; while seven countries had standard deviations below 13%.

As might have been anticipated, the rate of return for the United States (11.5%) was relatively high while its risk level (standard deviation) was relatively low (the standard deviation was 11.6%); but, despite the relatively good performance of U.S. common stocks, portfolio theory suggests that American investors may still benefit from international diversification. For as we have already seen, so long as the correlation of returns among investment options is not perfect, a very strong case for portfolio diversification exists. Thus the addition of even relatively low-return foreign stocks might materially reduce the variance of the overall portfolio; moreover, three countries—Austria, Germany, and Japan—had rates of return which exceeded that of the United States during the relevant period.

4. THE EFFICIENCY FRONTIER

To make an empirical test of the benefits to the investor from international diversification, we must first calculate the set of efficient portfolios, an efficient international portfolio being defined as a combination of investments in various countries which either maximizes the rate of return, given the variance, or minimizes the variance, given the rate of return. The locus of all such points comprises the efficiency curve.

Clearly, the number of calculations necessary to isolate the efficient locus is extremely large, but fortunately standard computer programs are available which can be applied to the solution of our problem. As a first step a correlation matrix among the annual rates of return of the 28 countries making up our population was calculated and the variances and covariances were used in all subsequent computations. The variance for the ith country was defined as

$$\sigma_i^2 = \frac{1}{N} \sum_{t=1}^{N} [r_i(t) - R_i]^2$$

The locus of efficient points (portfolios) was found by deriving the investment proportions which minimize the variance of the portfolio, for given expected rates of return.[6] For this purpose the reduced gradient algorithm,

---

[6] A mathematical statement of this problem is given in H. Levy and M. Sarnat, "International Diversification of Investment Portfolios," *American Economic Review* LX, No. 4 (September 1970).

5. THE COMPOSITION OF THE OPTIMAL PORTFOLIOS

TABLE XVI-3. Mean portfolio returns and standard deviations for selected points on the efficiency locus (in percentage)

Mean Return	8.0	10.0	11.5	13.0	17.0
Standard Deviation	4.5	5.1	6.2	8.2	20.2

PHIMAQ, developed by Electricité de France, was used. Minimum variances for alternative levels of portfolio return were determined by raising the given portfolio return by half a percent and repeating the computation procedure.[7] Table XVI-3 gives some selected combinations of mean return and standard deviations for five points on the efficiency curve.

The entire efficiency frontier, that is, the locus of efficient portfolios, for the case in which investments potentially can be made in all of the 28 countries included in the study is given in Figure XVI.2. The curve, labeled A, summarizes the efficient risk–return combinations which were attainable to an investor who had the opportunity to build an internationally diversified portfolio of common stocks. Point F represents the risk–return combination for an investor who restricted his portfolio to a cross section of U.S. common stocks (mean return = 11.5% and standard deviation = 11.6%). It is clear from the diagram and from Table XVI-3 that point F represents a nonefficient point to the U.S. investor who could have achieved the same level of return (11.5%) at a much reduced level of risk (standard deviation of only 6.2%) by diversifying his portfolio to include investments in foreign countries as well as in the United States.

5. THE COMPOSITION OF THE OPTIMAL PORTFOLIOS

Each point on the efficiency frontier denotes a unique risk–return combination which results from a particular combination of investment proportions in various countries. However, to focus attention on the proportion of investment in each of the various countries a method must be found to reduce the efficiency locus to a single point (portfolio). Essentially this means that given a particular set of initial conditions we must find the optimum portfolio.

This can be accomplished by utilizing the market equilibrium model of Chapter XIII. The application of the model to the problem of international

---

[7] The computation procedure used restricts the range of proportions to the positive values between 0 and 1; that is, negative investment is not permitted. This is equivalent to assuming the absence of short sales.

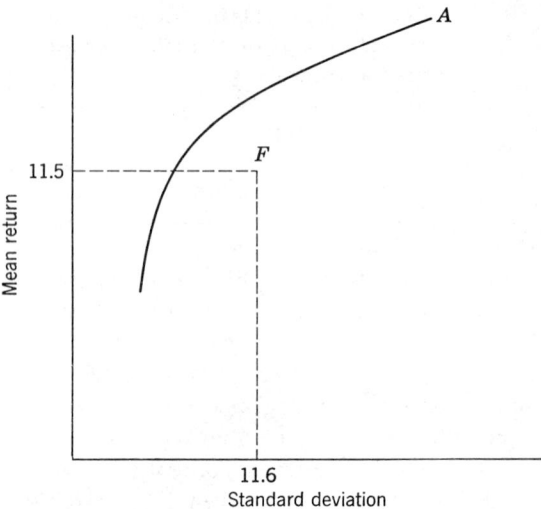

FIGURE XVI.2.

diversification is illustrated in Figure XVI.3, which reproduces the efficiency curve of Figure XVI.2. The market opportunity line r_1 rising from the 3% intercept on the Y axis reflects the assumption that riskless lending or borrowing, at 3%, can take place; similarly, the market opportunity line r_2 reflects the case where riskless borrowing or lending can take place at 6%.[8] The optimum unlevered portfolio for a particular interest rate is given by the point at which the appropriate market opportunity line is tangent to the locus of efficient portfolios, for example, points such as a and b in Figure XVI.3. In this context it should be recalled that the slope of the market opportunity line measures the trade-off between expected return and risk for all investors, independent of their tastes, and therefore uniquely determines the optimal unlevered share portfolio for all investors faced by the relevant interest rate.

One peculiarity of Figure XVI.3 calls for an explicit explanation. It is clear from the slope of the efficiency locus that the higher the interest rate (that is, the higher the intercept of the market opportunity line on the Y axis), the higher will be the point of tangency along the efficiency curve. We can conclude, therefore, that investors faced with a high interest rate will prefer an investment portfolio with both a higher risk and a higher average return than that chosen by an investor who is confronted by a relatively low interest rate.

[8] The two market opportunity lines can also be used to illustrate a case of an imperfect capital market in which the borrowing rate differs from the lending rate.

5. THE COMPOSITION OF THE OPTIMAL PORTFOLIOS   537

This preference for riskier unlevered portfolios where higher interest rates prevail may not be intuitively obvious, but it can be readily explained. A higher interest rate is equivalent to establishing a lower price for a unit of risk (that is, the slope of the 6% market opportunity line, r_2, is flatter (lower) than that of the 3% line, r_1 (see Figure XVI.3). In other words, given the higher interest rates the investor can more readily add risk to his unlevered portfolio, and he is therefore prepared to absorb more variance to acquire additional increments of return.

Figure XVI.3 sets out the market opportunity lines and tangency points for 3% and 6% interest rates. By constructing the appropriate market opportunity lines for alternative interest rates, a one-to-one correspondence can be established between the interest rate confronting investors and an optimal point on the efficiency locus.

Table XVI–4 sets out the investment proportions of four such optimal portfolios for 3, 4, 5, and 6% interest rates respectively. Although 28 countries are included in the study (see Table XVI–2), only eight countries are included in at least one of the optimal portfolios in the relevant range, and of these, two countries (Germany and Denmark) can be ignored since only a negligible proportion of two of the portfolios is invested in these countries. Investments in three countries, the United States, South Africa,

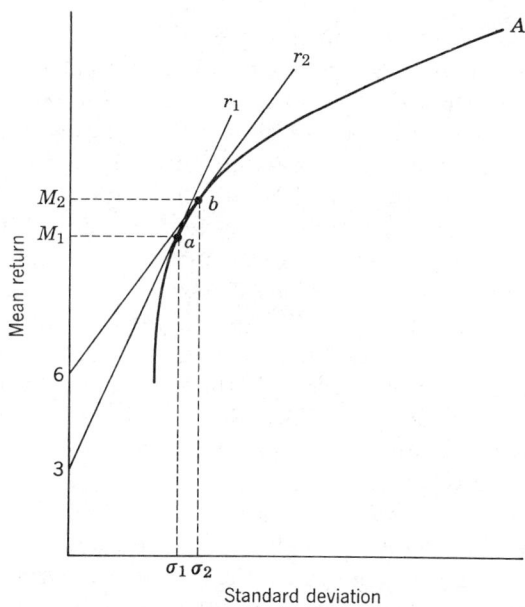

FIGURE XVI.3.

TABLE XVI-4. Composition of optimal portfolios for selected interest rates (in percentage)

| | Interest Rate | | | |
Country	3	4	5	6
Austria	7.6	8.4	9.0	10.5
Denmark	2.5	0.3	—	—
Germany	—	0.4	—	—
Japan	18.3	18.9	20.1	19.6
Portugal	5.1	5.8	5.6	5.0
South Africa	23.9	24.4	24.6	26.2
United States	28.4	29.3	29.8	31.6
Venezuela	14.4	12.6	11.0	7.1
Total*	100.0	100.0	100.0	100.0
Mean Portfolio Rate of Return	10.8	11.1	11.3	11.8
Portfolio Standard Deviation	5.6	5.9	6.2	6.5

* Detail does not always add to totals due to rounding.

and Japan, account for over 70% of the optimal portfolios, but with the exception of Austria the portfolios virtually exclude the developed countries of Western Europe. A noteworthy feature of the composition of the diversified international portfolios is the relatively high proportion of investments in developing or borderline income countries such as Venezuela, South Africa, Portugal, and Japan, the proportion of such investment accounting for about 60% of the aggregate portfolio. But perhaps the most surprising result is the fact that U.S. investments comprise only about 30% of the optimal portfolios, which strongly suggests that the U.S. investor can achieve very significant gains by diversifying his investments internationally.

An explanation for these results is not difficult to find. Table XVI-5 sets out the correlation matrix for the countries which were included in at least one optimal portfolio. The United States enters the optimal portfolios essentially on its own merits, the American investment returns having both a relatively high rate of return and only a moderate risk level. On the other hand Japan, which taken by itself is characterized by a high return but also by a high level of risk, has a relatively large share in the portfolio because of a very high degree of negative covariance with the other members of the set. The return on Japanese investments is negatively correlated with four countries: Portugal, South Africa, the United States, and Venezuela, while its correlation with the returns of Austria and Denmark is zero for all

5. THE COMPOSITION OF THE OPTIMAL PORTFOLIOS

TABLE XVI-5. Intercountry correlation coefficients for countries appearing in the optimal portfolios

Country	1	2	3	4	5	6	7	8
1. Austria	1.00	0.10	0.45	0.05	−0.21	−0.37	0.28	0.14
2. Denmark	——	1.00	0.22	0.06	0.39	−0.14	0.16	−0.13
3. Germany	——	——	1.00	0.24	−0.11	−0.17	0.41	−0.32
4. Japan	——	——	——	1.00	−0.05	−0.51	−0.26	−0.10
5. Portugal	——	——	——	——	1.00	0.12	−0.04	0.12
6. South Africa	——	——	——	——	——	1.00	0.18	−0.23
7. United States	——	——	——	——	——	——	1.00	−0.17
8. Venezuela	——	——	——	——	——	——	——	1.00

practical purposes. Thus, despite Japan's own relatively high standard deviation, because of covariance, its inclusion tends to reduce the risk of the overall portfolio. This is especially true since the investment returns of Japan are negatively correlated with those of the United States, and the latter accounts for a significant share of all the optimal portfolios. This can be seen very clearly by examining Figure XVI.4, which plots the annual rates of return on common stock for the United States and for Japan.

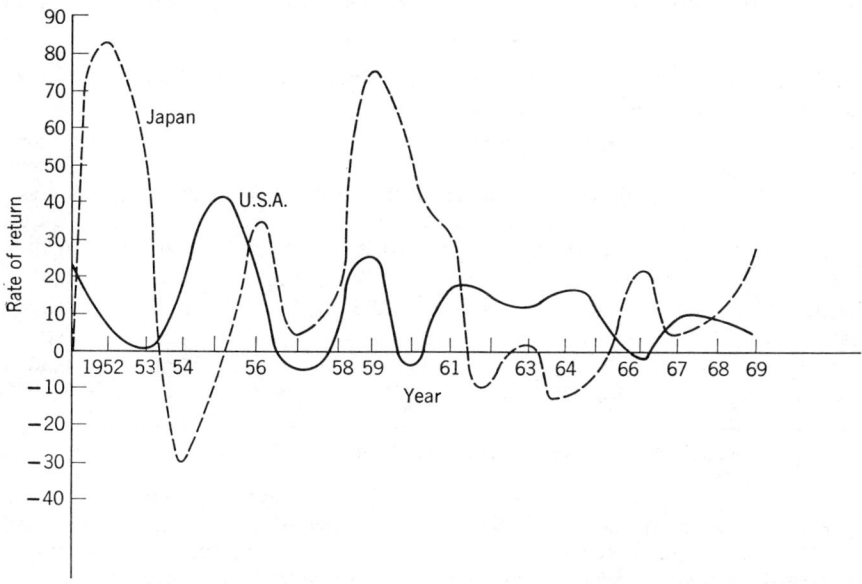

FIGURE XVI.4.

The case for the inclusion of South Africa and Venezuela in the optimal portfolios is somewhat different. Taken alone both of these countries represent inefficient alternatives to U.S. investments; their rates of return are lower while their standard deviations are higher than those of the United States. And in the case of Venezuela, the mean rate of return was very much lower (4.4%) than that of the United States (11.5%). Once again a glance at the intercountry correlation matrix of Table XVI–5 provides the explanation. The returns on Venezuelan common stocks were negatively correlated with those of the United States, Japan, and three other countries included in the optimal portfolios, while its correlation with the remaining two countries (Austria and Portugal) was very close to zero. South Africa, on the other hand, is included in the optimal portfolios largely on the strength of its unusually pronounced degree of negative correlation with the returns of Japan and Austria (−0.51 and −0.37, respectively).

The optimal investment portfolios are also notable for the countries which are excluded. The five highly developed common market countries do not appear in any of the portfolios.[9] Table XVI–6 helps clarify the reasons for this; the investment returns in the five common market countries included in Table XVI–6 are all highly correlated so that little gain can be realized from combining them in a portfolio of their own. But even the high degree of positive correlation among the common market countries[10] would not necessarily preclude the inclusion of at least one of the countries in the optimal portfolio. The last column of Table XVI–6, however, shows that

TABLE XVI–6. Intercountry correlation coefficients for five Common Market countries* and the United States

	Belgium	France	Germany	Italy	Netherlands	United States
Belgium	1.00	0.71	0.56	0.30	0.65	0.79
France	—	1.00	0.52	0.63	0.56	0.47
Germany	—	—	1.00	0.67	0.75	0.41
Italy	—	—	—	1.00	0.57	0.09
Netherlands	—	—	—	—	1.00	0.50
United States	—	—	—	—	—	1.00

* Comparable data for Luxembourg were unavailable.

[9] We can safely ignore Germany's negligible share in one of the optimal portfolios—less than 0.5% of the optimal portfolio when the riskless rate of interest is assumed to be 4%.
[10] The high degree of correlation constitutes impressive evidence of the economic integration among the capital markets of these countries.

5. THE COMPOSITION OF THE OPTIMAL PORTFOLIOS

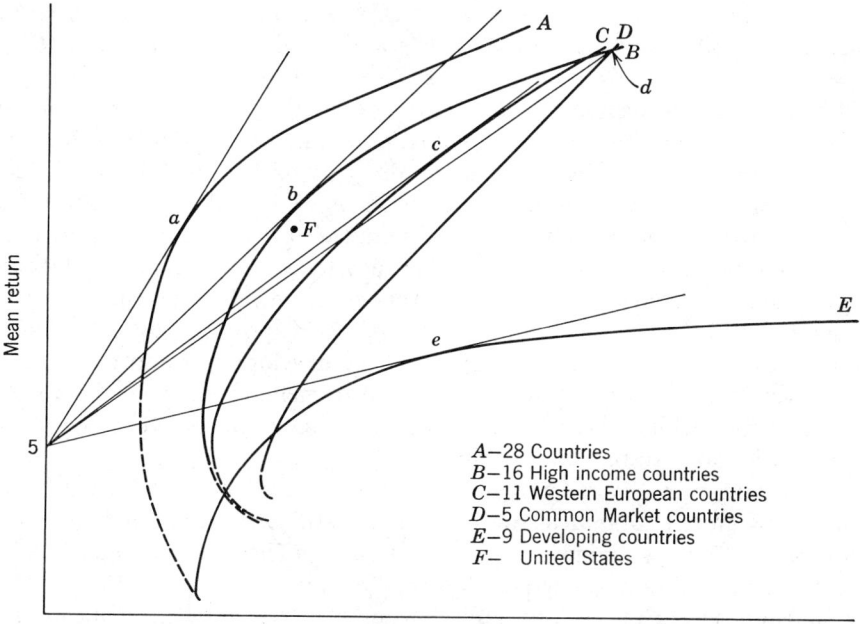

FIGURE XVI.5.

all of the common market countries have relatively high positive correlations with the United States. It is the high degree of positive correlation with the United States (and Japan as well) which excludes Germany from the optimal portfolio despite the fact that Germany's own rate of return was 17.1%, the second highest among the 28 countries included in our sample.

It is also interesting to note the absence of Canada from the optimal portfolios. Again the main reason stems from that country's very high positive correlation (0.77) with the United States, combined with the fact that the rate of return on Canadian investments was lower while the risk in Canada was greater than that for the United States (see Table XVI–2). As a result, the United States dominates Canada and the latter was eliminated from the efficiency curve in the relevant range.

The potential gains from international diversification can be seen more clearly by examining Figure XVI.5, which again sets out the efficiency frontier for the 28 countries included in our population as well as the curves for several subsets[11] of the population. The risk–return combination for a

---
[11] Three borderline countries—Israel, Japan, and South Africa—which are included in the total population are not included in any of the subsets of Figure XVI.5. For the classification of countries by the various subsets, see Appendix XVI–1.

portfolio invested in a cross section of U.S. common stocks is again represented by point F (11.5% rate of return and standard deviation of 11.6%). Clearly, an investor will suffer a loss if he must eschew investment in the United States and restrict his portfolio to developing countries, the common market, or Western Europe, all of whose curves lie below point F.[12] Perhaps even more striking is the fact that by diversifying his portfolio to include investments in other high-income countries as well as in the United States, the investor can make only a very marginal improvement in his portfolio, since point F lies very close to the efficiency locus B. Thus while diversification generally pays, it does not pay very much in this instance.

Only when the American investor diversifies his portfolio to include such countries as Japan and South Africa and the developing countries of South America and Asia does a significant improvement in his portfolio result; the efficiency locus for all the 28 countries included in the study (curve A) lies considerably to the left of point F.

The gains from diversification are quantified in Table XVI–7, which sets out the mean rates of return and standard deviations of the optimal portfolios for each subset assuming a 5% interest rate. (The data of Table XVI–7 correspond to the tangency points a, b, c, d, and e of Figure XVI.5.) The systematic nature of risk reduction through international diversification is reflected in the continuous reduction of the portfolios' variability (at all levels of return) as the opportunity set is broadened. Thus the best combination that can be created out of equities in the developing countries is a

TABLE XVI–7. Mean rates of return and standard deviations of optimal portfolios for a 5% interest rate (in percentage)

	Mean Rate of Return	Standard Deviation
Developing Countries	7.7	18.6
Common Market	16.9	26.7
Western Europe	16.1	23.0
High-Income Countries	12.6	12.2
All Countries	11.3	6.2

[12] This is not strictly true according to the Mean–Variance Criterion since some of the points on these curves represent efficient points relative to the United States. It is clear, however, that once borrowing and lending can take place, the investor can always reach a higher market opportunity line (and therefore a higher level of utility) by moving to point F, independent of the interest rate assumed. See Chapter XIII.

portfolio with a 7.7% return and an 18.6% standard deviation, as compared with a return of 11.3% and standard deviation of only 6.2% for the unconstrained optimum portfolio.

6. SOME FURTHER IMPLICATIONS OF THE ANALYSIS

Although the American investor should never restrict his portfolio to developing countries alone (the efficiency curve E lies far below point F), the inclusion of these and other borderline-income countries in the opportunity set materially improves his risk–return position. This has some interesting implications for the theory of international capital movements.[13] For example, the traditional approach to international investment, which compares returns in developing countries with those of the developed economies of the United States and Europe, understates the benefits of such investments. For as we have seen, low-yielding foreign investments in the developing countries may have a salutary effect on the overall portfolio variance of the investing country. Thus when stabilizing portfolio effects are taken into account, a much stronger case can be made for U.S. investment in countries whose economies are not highly correlated with that of the investing country.

Similarly, the portfolio analysis of international diversification provides some insight into the recent spate of international mutual funds. Independent of tax considerations, these funds, which typically include the securities of a dozen or more countries, reflect the fundamental fact that risk diversification can often be facilitated by including an international cross section of securities in the portfolio. Perhaps due to the nature of the operations of many of these funds, data are often difficult to obtain, but Table XVI–8 sets out the proportion of the portfolios of seven international funds accounted for by U.S. and Japanese securities.[14] As might have been anticipated from the analysis of the previous section, Japanese and U.S. securities tend to dominate the portfolio, comprising between 38 and 72% of the aggregate investments of the seven funds included in Table XVI–8.

---

[13] With regard to other countries, their efficiency curves must be defined in terms of each country's national currency unit. Thus the optimal investment proportions of England, France, or Germany will typically differ from that of the United States and from one another as well. In addition, the direction of the net capital movement depends not only on the proportion of investment in each country's securities but on the relative size of their capital markets as well.

[14] We purposely exclude funds with a stated policy of investing a large proportion of the portfolio in a given country, for example, the IOS Group's Fonditalia, more than half of whose investments are in Italy.

TABLE XVI-8. Share of Japanese and U.S. securities in the portfolios of selected international mutual funds, 1969. (in percentage)

Name of Fund	Japanese Securities	U.S. Securities	Total
Fonselex (Oct. 1969)	11	29	40
ITT (June 1969)	33	39	72
Robeco	8	32	40
Rolinco	14	24	38
Slater Walker	39	4	43
Tyndal International (April 1969)	30	17	47
Utilco	10	39	49

Finally, two warnings may be in order. First, we must remember that the above analysis has been carried out in terms of dollar-adjusted rates of return, that is, from the view point of a dollar investor or one whose currency is stable in terms of dollars.[15] Before generalizing our conclusions, the optimal portfolios of English, German, French, and other investors would have to be calculated since they will typically differ from the optimal dollar portfolio. Second, the analysis has been based on historical rates of return; no effort has been made to adjust the data to achieve a better prediction of future patterns since virtually no theory is available to assess the degree to which the *ex-post* results mirror *ex-ante* predictions.

[15] In an unpublished paper, A. A. Robichek, R. A. Cohn, and J. J. Pringle extend this type of analysis to cover other types of investment media such as bonds and real estate; see their "Returns on Alternative Investment Media and Implications for Portfolio Construction," Stanford, California: Graduate School of Business, Stanford University.

QUESTIONS AND PROBLEMS

16.1 In what way can a U.S. investor profit from international diversification?

16.2 Define the efficiency frontier for internationally diversified portfolios.

16.3 The efficiency curves of an American and a European investor are not necessarily the same even if they are confronted by the same investment opportunities. Appraise.

16.4 "Since U.S. stocks represent high return–low risk investments relative to the rest of the world, American investors should *not* include foreign stocks in their portfolios." Appraise.

16.5 How can you account for the fact that, other things being equal, a higher riskless interest rate implies "riskier" investment portfolios.

16.6 Draw the efficiency curves for the following cases:
(a) Investors are constrained to investments in two countries.
(b) Investors are constrained to investments in ten countries.

16.7 Draw the efficiency curve of investments in the Common Market countries. How do you account for its slope? (For this purpose, compare the Common Market curve with an unconstrained international efficiency curve.)

16.8 The table on page 546 shows the average annual nominal rates of return on investments in Israel and in the United States during the period 1951–1969. During this period, the Israel pound was devalued as follows:

(a) In 1952 the exchange rate was raised from 0.36 Israel pounds per dollar to one Israel pound per dollar.
(b) In 1953 the exchange rate was again changed from one pound per dollar to 1.80 Israel pounds per dollar.
(c) In 1962 the exchange rate was raised to 3 Israel pounds per dollar.
(d) In 1967 the exchange rate was again raised from 3 pounds per dollar to 3.50 pounds per dollar.

Rates of Return

(in percentages)

Year	Israel	United States
1951	23	23
1952	6	6
1953	12	0
1954	53	21
1955	17	42
1956	−15	17
1957	−13	−4
1958	−5	3
1959	37	25
1960	108	−4
1961	17	17
1962	8	15
1963	47	12
1964	−1	17
1965	−18	9
1966	−19	−2
1967	−9	9
1968	−12	8
1969	4	4

Assume that diversification can take place only between the U.S. and Israel, and past data will be used to estimate expected values.

(a) For an Israeli investor who wants to diversify his portfolio between Israel and the U.S., what are the *relevant rates of return* for calculating the efficiency curve? Calculate the appropriate rates of return.
(b) Answer part (a), assuming that the investor is an American.
(c) Are the efficiency curves of the two investors identical? Explain.
(d) Are the optimal investment proportions in Israel and the U.S. the same for two Israeli investors? Are the optimal proportions the same for two American investors? Explain.
(e) Assume that there had been no devaluations in Israel during the years 1951–69; how would this affect your answer to part (c).

SELECTED REFERENCES

Devlin, D. T., and Cutler, F., "The International Investment Position of the United States in 1968," *Survey of Current Business* (October 1969).
Grubel, Herbert G., "Internationally Diversified Portfolios: Welfare Gains and Capital Flows," *American Economic Review* (December 1968).
International Monetary Fund, *International Financial Statistics* Washington Annual Reports, 1951–1969.
Lee, C. H., "A Stock Adjustment Analysis of Capital Movements: The United States–Canadian Case," *Journal of Political Economy* (July–August 1969).
Levy, H., and Sarnat, M., "International Diversification of Investment Portfolios," *American Economic Review* (September 1970).
Miller, N. C., and Whitman, M. v. N., "A Mean–Variance Analysis of United States Long-Term Portfolio Foreign Investment," *Quarterly Journal of Economics* (May 1970).
Vasudevan, A., "The Portfolio Approach: Its Relevance to Under-Developed Economies," *Indian Economic Journal* (April–June 1969).

APPENDIX XVI-1. Classification of 28 countries by groups

Country	High-Income Countries	Western Europe	Common Market	Developing Countries	Intermediate-Income Countries
1. Australia	x				
2. Austria	x	x			
3. Belgium	x	x	x		
4. Canada	x				
5. Ceylon				x	
6. Chile				x	
7. Denmark	x	x			
8. Finland	x				
9. France	x	x	x		
10. Germany	x	x	x		
11. India				x	
12. Israel					x
13. Italy	x	x	x		
14. Japan					x
15. Mexico				x	
16. Netherlands	x	x	x		
17. New Zealand	x				
18. Norway	x	x			
19. Peru				x	
20. Philippines				x	
21. Portugal				x	
22. South Africa					x
23. Spain				x	
24. Sweden	x	x			
25. Switzerland	x	x			
26. United Kingdom	x	x			
27. U.S.A.	x				
28. Venezuela				x	

PART IV
TECHNICAL SUPPLEMENT

MATHEMATICAL SUPPLEMENT

This section is designed for the reader who is unfamiliar with higher mathematics but wants to go beyond the statement that the first derivative measures the rate of change of a function. The presentation is rather intuitive and makes no pretense at being rigorous. Despite this, the supplement should be adequate to familiarize the reader with some of the mathematical techniques mentioned in the text; for example, the concept of the *derivative* and the use of Lagrange multipliers as an optimization technique. Because of its extensive use special attention is given to the *integral*. We conclude the section with two brief comments concerning *geometric series* and *Taylor series*.

THE DERIVATIVE

DEFINITION

Given a single variable function $y = f(x)$ and looking at any point x_0, by changing the argument x by the amount of Δx, the value of the function can be expressed by

$$y + \Delta y = f(x_0 + \Delta x) \qquad (1)$$

and since $y = f(x)$, (1) is written as

$$\Delta y = f(x_0 + \Delta x) - f(x_0) \qquad (2)$$

which is the amount of change in y, caused by a change of Δx in the argument x. Furthermore, if we are interested in the relative change caused by Δx, we have

$$\frac{\Delta y}{\Delta x} = \frac{f(x_0 + \Delta x) - f(x_0)}{\Delta x} \qquad (3)$$

This quotient depends on Δx, because for different Δx we get different Δy. However, as we consider smaller and smaller changes in Δx, we assume that $\Delta y/\Delta x$ will tend toward a unique number, which we denote by $f'(x_0)$, or

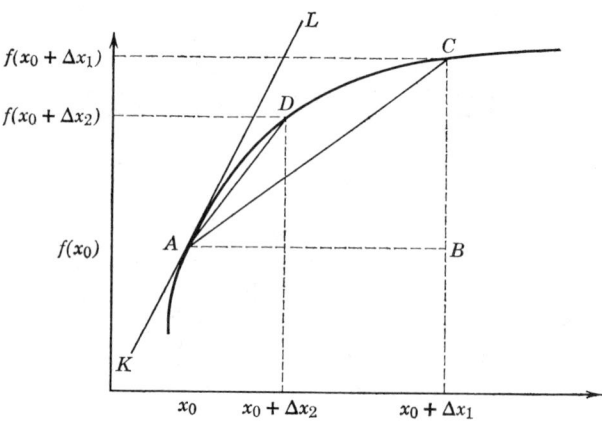

FIGURE 1.

$dy/(dx)_{x_0}$, or

$$f'(x_0) = \left[\frac{dy}{dx}\right]_{x_0} = \lim_{\Delta x \to 0} \frac{\Delta y}{\Delta x} = \lim_{\Delta x \to 0} \frac{f(x_0 + \Delta x) - f(x_0)}{\Delta x} \qquad (4)$$

GEOMETRICAL INTERPRETATION

Assume we have $y = f(x)$ as represented in Figure 1. It can easily be seen that $[f(x_0 + \Delta x_1) - f(x_0)]/\Delta x_1$ is the slope of the line AC. Taking a smaller increment Δx_2 gives $[f(x_0 + \Delta x_2) - f(x_0)]/\Delta x_2$ which is the slope of the line AD. By setting Δx smaller and smaller, the expression $[f(x_0 + \Delta x) - f(x_0)]/\Delta x$ will tend to coincide with the slope of the tangent KL to the function $y = f(x)$ at the point x_0. Therefore we can say that the derivative of a function $f(x)$ at x_0 is exactly the slope of the tangent to the function at this point.

THE DERIVED FUNCTION

Suppose we have a function $f(x)$ whose derivative can be found at each of its points. By finding the value of the derivative of $y = f(x)$ at these points, we define a new function: the *derived function*. This function is denoted by $f'(x)$ or dy/dx. Notice that $f'(x_0)$ or $(dy/dx)_{x_0}$ is the value of the derived function at one particular point: x_0. Bearing in mind the geometrical interpretation of the derivative, $f'(x)$ is nothing but a function which fits to any point x a value equal to the slope of the tangent to $f(x)$ at x as demonstrated in Figure 2. (Note that when $x = 1$ $f(x)$ reaches its peak and $f'(x) = 0$.)

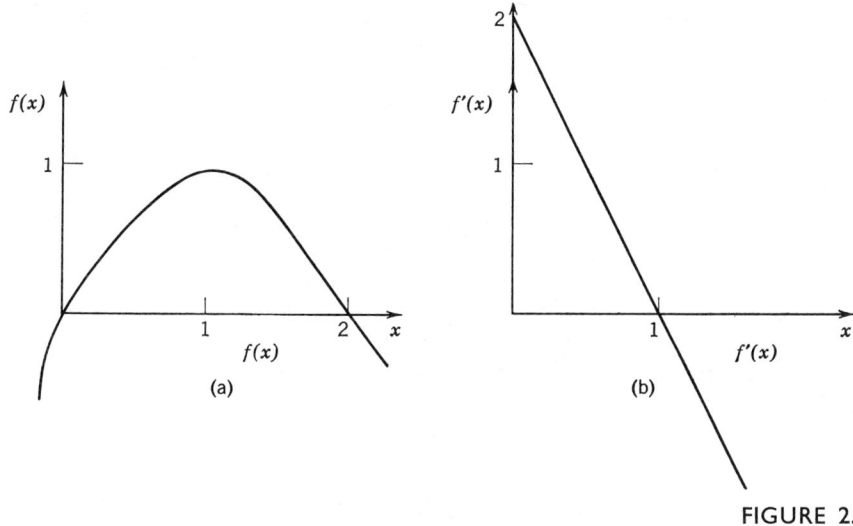

FIGURE 2.

INCREASING AND DECREASING FUNCTIONS

A function is said to be an *increasing function*, in some interval, if for each point in this interval higher values of x give higher values of $f(x)$. Adding a positive increment Δx results in

$$f(x + \Delta x) \geq f(x) \quad \text{for } \Delta x > 0$$

hence:

$$f(x + \Delta x) - f(x) \geq 0$$

and since $\Delta x > 0$

$$[f(x + \Delta x) - f(x)]/\Delta x \geq 0$$

This ratio holds for every $\Delta x > 0$, and therefore this inequality is also preserved when we set Δx equal to zero. Therefore, for an increasing function we have

$$f'(x) = \lim_{\Delta x \to 0} \frac{f(x + \Delta x) - f(x)}{\Delta x} \geq 0 \tag{5}$$

We leave it to the reader to prove that this result remains unchanged for $\Delta x < 0$.

A function $f(x)$ is defined as a *decreasing function*, over some interval, if higher values of x result in lower values of $f(x)$. For such functions we have

$$f(x + \Delta x) - f(x) \leq 0 \quad \text{for } \Delta x > 0$$

and in a similar way it can be shown that for a decreasing function and any increment Δx

$$f'(x) = \lim_{\Delta x \to 0} \frac{f(x + \Delta x) - f(x)}{\Delta x} \leq 0 \qquad (6)$$

RULES OF DIFFERENTIATION

The process by which we calculate the derived function is called *differentiation*. Formally this is done by finding the limit to which Equation (3) approaches, as Δx tends to zero. For example, take the function $f(x) = x^2$:

$$\frac{dy}{dx} = \lim_{\Delta x \to 0} \frac{(x + \Delta x)^2 - x^2}{\Delta x}$$

$$= \lim_{\Delta x \to 0} \frac{x^2 + \Delta x^2 + 2x \Delta x - x^2}{\Delta x} = \lim_{\Delta x \to 0} (\Delta x + 2x) = 2x$$

The derived function or derivative of $y = x^2$ is therefore $f'(x) = 2x$. The above procedure can be carried out for different types of functions. Following are the differentiation rules for some common classes of functions.[1]

$$f(x) = c, \qquad f'(x) = 0 \qquad (i)$$

where c is a constant

$$f(x) = x^n, \qquad f'(x) = nx^{n-1} \qquad (ii)$$

$$f(x) = u(x)v(x), \qquad f'(x) = u'(x)v(x) + v'(x)u(x) \qquad (iii)$$

$$f(x) = \frac{u(x)}{v(x)}, \qquad f'(x) = \frac{u'(x)v(x) - v'(x)u(x)}{[v(x)]^2} \qquad (iv)$$

$$f(x) = \log_a x, \qquad f'(x) = \frac{1}{x} \log_a e \qquad (v)$$

where $e = 2.718 \ldots$ is the base of the natural logarithm

$$f(x) = e^{ax}, \qquad f'(x) = ae^{ax} \qquad (vi)$$

$$f(x) = u[v(x)], \qquad f'(x) = u'[v(x)]v'(x) \qquad (vii)$$

[1] For a more formal discussion of differentiation see *Calculus* by Lipman Bers, Holt, Rinehart and Winston, 1969; or *Fundamental Methods of Mathematical Economics* by Alpha C. Chiang, McGraw-Hill, 1967.

RULES OF DIFFERENTIATION

SOME REMARKS

(a) From rule (v) it is apparent why mathematicians prefer to work with the natural logarithm rather than with the base 10, because with e as a base the differentiation rule becomes $f'(x) = 1/x$.

(b) Rule (vii) is known as the *chain rule;* it deals with the differentiation of a function of a function. For an example of such a function consider

$$v(x) = 2x - 1, \quad u[v(x)] = [v(x)]^2$$

then

$$f(x) = u[v(x)] = [v(x)]^2 = (2x - 1)^2$$

(c) From rule (iii) it follows immediately that for a constant a: $d[af(x)]/dx = af'(x)$. Thus the derivative of a function multiplied by a constant is the product of the derivative of the function multiplied by the constant.

Examples

$$f(x) = a + x^2 \cdot e^x + \frac{\log x}{x}$$

$$f'(x) = 0 + (2x \cdot e^x + e^x \cdot x^2) + \left[\frac{\frac{1}{x} \cdot x - 1 \cdot \log x}{x^2} \right]$$

$$= e^x(2x + x^2) + \left[\frac{1 - \log x}{x^2} \right]$$

We used rule (i) to differentiate each term. We then applied rule (iii) to differentiate the product and rules (ii) and (vi) to take care of the factors inside this term. Rule (iv) is applied to the quotient using differentiation rules (v) and (ii) for the numerator and denominator.

(2) As an example of the chain rule consider

$$f(x) = (2x - 1)^2$$

Then

$$f'(x) = 2(2x - 1) \cdot 2$$

where $2(2x - 1)$ is the derivative with respect to $2x - 1$ and 2 results from differentiating $2x - 1$ with respect to x.

HIGHER-ORDER DERIVATIVES

As we mentioned above the process of differentiation gives us the derived function. This derived function can also be differentiated, thereby yielding a *second order* derived function (whose value at a particular point is called the second derivative). In other words, if $f'(x)$ is the derived function then by differentiating this function we obtain

$$\frac{d[f'(x)]}{dx} = \lim_{\Delta x \to 0} \frac{f'(x_0 + \Delta x) - f'(x_0)}{\Delta x} \qquad (7)$$

The second derivative of $f(x)$ at x_0 is denoted by $f''(x_0)$ or $(d^2f/dx^2)_{x_0}$. Likewise we can define the nth-order derivative by

$$f^{(n)}(x_0) = \lim_{\Delta x \to 0} \frac{f^{(n-1)}(x_0 + \Delta x) - f^{(n-1)}(x_0)}{\Delta x}$$

Example: $f(x) = 2x^2 + 3x + 1$

$f'(x) = 4x + 3$ is the first derivative
$f''(x) = 4$ is the second derivative
$f^{(3)}(x) = 0$ is the third derivative

PARTIAL DERIVATIVES

Where we have a function of more than one variable: $Z = f(x, y)$, for example $Z = 2xy + x^2$, we can differentiate the function with respect to either one of the variables (x or y) while holding the other constant. To distinguish this type of differentiation from the regular one, it is usually denoted by $\partial f(x, y)/\partial x$ when differentiating with respect to x (y held constant) or $\partial f(x, y)/\partial y$ when differentiating with respect to y. The partial derivative with respect to x is defined as

$$\frac{\partial f(x_0, y_0)}{\partial x} = \lim_{\Delta x \to 0} \frac{f(x_0 + \Delta x, y_0) - f(x_0, y_0)}{\Delta x} \qquad (8)$$

We leave it to the reader to work out the definition for $\partial f(x, y)/\partial y$.

LOCAL MAXIMA AND MINIMA

Looking at the function $y = f(x)$ in Figure 3, we see that the function has a *local maximum* at points x_2 and x_4, and a *local minimum* at x_1 and x_3. A point which is either a local maximum or a local minimum is called an *extremum point*. Formally, what characterizes a local maximum (minimum) at any point x_0 is the fact that for any other x in the close neighborhood of x_0 the inequality $f(x_0) \geq f(x)$ (or $f(x_0) \leq f(x)$ for a local minimum) holds.

Figure 4 isolates the interval $x_1 x_3$ so as to facilitate an examination of the characteristics of the local maximum at x_2. As can readily be seen, in the interval (x_1, x_2), $f(x)$ is an increasing function; while in the interval (x_2, x_3) it is decreasing. Applying our previous discussion of increasing and decreasing functions we know that in the interval $(x_1, x_2) f'(x) \geq 0$. Furthermore, the closer we approach x_2, the smaller is $f'(x)$. Thus we can see that the slope of the tangent at B is smaller than that at A. With respect to the interval (x_2, x_3), $f'(x)$ is negative and the closer we come to x_2, the less negative the slope of the tangent. At the maximum point itself, x_2, the slope (derivative) is exactly zero. A similar type of argument can be used for the minimum point x_3, whose derivative at this point is also zero.

We can summarize by saying that in the neighborhood of a local maximum point, $f'(x)$ is a *decreasing* function with the value zero at the maximum point, and since $f'(x)$ is a decreasing function then $f''(x) < 0$, that is, the necessary and sufficient conditions for $f(x)$ to have a local maximum at a point x_0 are

$$\begin{aligned}&\text{(i) } f'(x_0) = 0\\&\text{(ii) } f''(x_0) < 0\end{aligned} \quad (9)$$

We leave it to the reader to show that the sufficient and necessary conditions

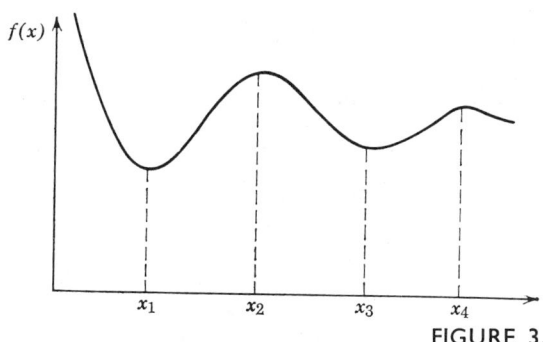

FIGURE 3.

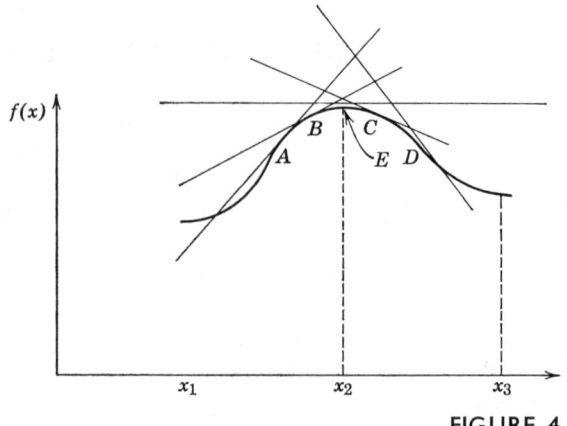

FIGURE 4.

for a function $f(x)$ to have a local minimum at a point x_0 are

$$\text{(i) } f'(x_0) = 0$$
$$\text{(ii) } f''(x_0) > 0 \tag{10}$$

It is worthwhile to mention that Equations (9) and (10) constitute the necessary and sufficient conditions only under the assumption that $f''(x_0) \neq 0$. Where $f''(x_0) = 0$ the conditions are somewhat more complicated: we require that the first derivative of order n, which is different from zero, will be negative for a local maximum and positive for a local minimum.

Examples

$$y = 2x^2 - 2x \tag{a}$$

Step 1: Differentiate and set the first derivative equal to zero

$$f'(x) = 4x - 2 = 0$$

$f(x)$ may have an extremum at

$$x_0 = \tfrac{1}{2}$$

Step 2: Check the second derivative at $x_0 = \tfrac{1}{2}$:

$$f''(x) = 4 > 0$$

Therefore $f(x)$ has a local *minimum* at $x_0 = \tfrac{1}{2}$.

$$y = x^3 + 2x^2 \tag{b}$$

Step 1: Differentiate and equate to zero

$$f'(x) = 3x^2 + 4x = 0$$

Therefore there are two possible points which can be extremum points:

$$x_1 = 0; \quad x_2 = -\tfrac{4}{3}$$

Step 2: Check the second derivative at these points:

$$f''(x) = 6x + 4$$

For $x_1 = 0$ $f''(x) = 0 + 4 = 4 > 0$ and the function has a *minimum* at $x_1 = 0$.
For $x_2 = -(\tfrac{4}{3})$ $f''(x) = 6(-\tfrac{4}{3}) + 4 = -8 + 4 = -4 < 0$ and the function has a *maximum* at $x_2 = -(\tfrac{4}{3})$

$$y = x^3 \tag{c}$$

Step 1: Differentiate and equate to zero

$$f'(x) = 3x^2 = 0$$

$f(x)$ may have an extremum at $x_0 = 0$.
Step 2, however, fails because there is no higher-order derivative which will be different from zero (that is, $f''(x) = 0$). Therefore $y = x^3$ has no extremum point. Looking at the graphical representation of this function in Figure 5, we see that at the point $x_0 = 0$ the function has an inflection point, but no maximum or minimum.

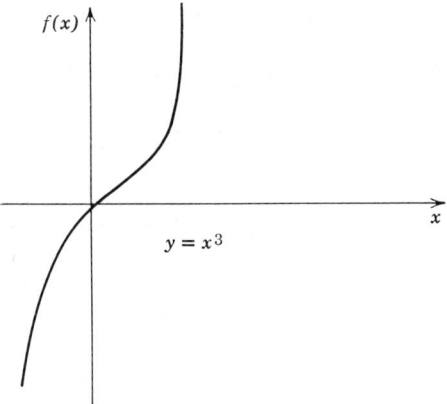

FIGURE 5.

CONSTRAINED MAXIMA AND MINIMA

The problem of scarcity of resources, with which every beginning economist has to deal, raises the problem of optimization under certain constraints. For instance: how much of a certain commodity should be consumed under a given budget limitation? How much should be invested in each of the available securities so as to maximize returns from the limited amount of money at our disposal? Let us take a concrete example:

Consider the following function:

$$\sigma^2 = P_1^2 \sigma_1^2 + P_2^2 \sigma_2^2$$

where: P_1, P_2 = the proportions invested in securities 1 and 2 respectively;
σ_1^2, σ_2^2 = the respective variances[2] of the returns on the two securities;
σ^2 = the variance of the return on the overall portfolio (assuming independence).

The problem is to minimize σ^2 given the constraint $P_1 + P_2 = 1$. Thus we must invest all of our money, but we cannot invest more than our initial resources. There are two ways to treat this problem.

THE ELIMINATION METHOD

Eliminate P_2 from the constraint:

$$P_2 = 1 - P_1$$

Substitute this expression in σ^2:

$$\sigma^2 = P_1^2 \sigma_1^2 + (1 - P_1)^2 \sigma_2^2$$

To find the investment proportions which minimize σ^2, we have to differentiate this function with respect to P_1 and set the derivative equal to zero:

$$\frac{d\sigma^2}{dP_1} = 2P_1 \sigma_1^2 - 2(1 - P_1)\sigma_2^2 = 0$$

$$P_1 \sigma_1^2 = (1 - P_1)\sigma_2^2$$

or

$$\frac{P_1}{1 - P_1} = \frac{\sigma_2^2}{\sigma_1^2} \tag{11}$$

---

[2] For the definition of the variance of a random variable see the Statistical Supplement.

CONSTRAINED MAXIMA AND MINIMA

which provides us with:

$$\frac{P_1}{P_2} = \frac{\sigma_2^2}{\sigma_1^2} \tag{12}$$

Thus the variance of the returns is at a minimum when the ratio of the proportions invested in the two stocks equals the *inverse* of the ratio of their variances.

LAGRANGE MULTIPLIER METHOD

Since $P_1 + P_2 = 1$ we have

$$P_1 + P_2 - 1 = 0$$

and can form the function

$$L = P_1^2 \sigma_1^2 + P_2^2 \sigma_2^2 - \lambda(P_1 + P_2 - 1) \tag{13}$$

which will be called the *Lagrangian function*. Note that as long as $P_1 + P_2 = 1$, the value of this function will be σ^2. λ is called a Lagrange multiplier, and L is a function of the three variables: P_1, P_2, λ. Looking for a minimum we differentiate with respect to each of these three variables, and set the derivatives equal to zero:

$$\frac{\partial L}{\partial P_1} = 2P_1 \sigma_1^2 - \lambda = 0$$

$$\frac{\partial L}{\partial P_2} = 2P_2 \sigma_2^2 - \lambda = 0 \tag{14}$$

$$\frac{\partial L}{\partial \lambda} = P_1 + P_2 - 1 = 0$$

By equating $\lambda = 2P_1 \sigma_1^2$ from the first equation and $\lambda = 2P_2 \sigma_2^2$ from the second equation we get $P_1 \sigma_1^2 = P_2 \sigma_2^2$ or

$$\frac{P_1}{P_2} = \frac{\sigma_2^2}{\sigma_1^2} \tag{15}$$

which provides the same result as the elimination method (Equation 12). The proportion P_1 can be found from the third equation:

$$\frac{P_1}{1 - P_1} = \frac{\sigma_2^2}{\sigma_1^2}$$

$$P_1 \sigma_1^2 = \sigma_2^2(1 - P_1) = \sigma_2^2 - P_1 \sigma_2^2$$

$$P_1(\sigma_1^2 + \sigma_2^2) = \sigma_2^2$$

so that

$$P_1 = \frac{\sigma_2^2}{\sigma_1^2 + \sigma_2^2} \qquad (16)$$

The same result can be reached without using the Lagrange multiplier method. However, technically this method is much more efficient when the number of the variables and/or the number of constraints are increased. For instance assuming independence:

$$\sigma^2 = \sum_{i=1}^{n} P_i^2 \sigma_i^2$$

In this case we form the function

$$L = \sum_{i=1}^{n} P_i^2 \sigma_i^2 - \lambda \left(\sum_{i=1}^{n} P_i - 1 \right) \qquad (17)$$

Differentiating with respect to $P_1, P_2, \ldots, P_n$ and λ we get $n+1$ equations with $n+1$ unknowns, whose solution gives the optimal proportion $(P_1, P_2, \ldots, P_n)$.

The Lagrange multiplier method is also very useful in cases where we have more than one constraint; for example, an investor who decides to invest half of his money in stocks 1 to 10 and half of his money in stocks 11 to 30. The first group of stocks might be utilities while the second is made up of industrials. Such a problem has the following form:[3]

$$\text{minimize} \quad \sigma^2 = \sum_{i=1}^{30} P_i^2 \sigma_i^2$$

$$\text{subject to the constraints} \quad \sum_{i=1}^{10} P_i = 0.5$$

$$\sum_{i=11}^{30} P_i = 0.5$$

The Lagrangian function will be of the form

$$L = \sum_{i=1}^{30} P_i^2 \sigma_i^2 - \lambda_1 \left(\sum_{i=1}^{10} P_i - 0.5 \right) - \lambda_2 \left(\sum_{i=11}^{30} P_i - 0.5 \right)$$

Differentiating L with respect to $P_1, P_2, \ldots, P_n, \lambda_1, \lambda_2$ yields $n+2$ equations with $n+2$ unknowns, and hence the system has a solution.

From the above discussion it would seem that the Lagrange multipliers have only technical significance; however, in Chapter XIII an economic interpretation is given to λ in terms of the price of a unit of risk reduction.

---

[3] We assume independence. See Statistical Supplement.

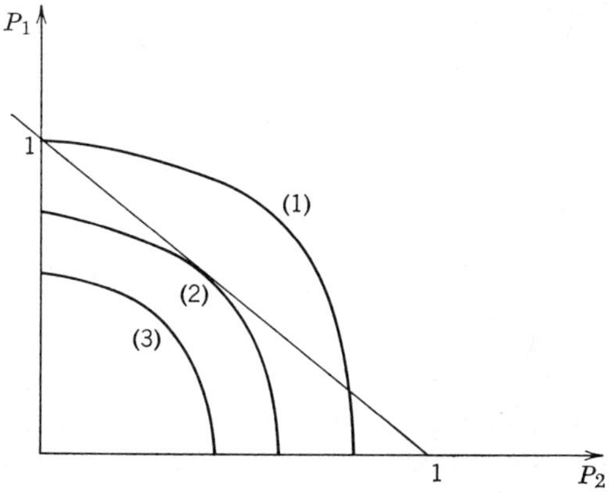

FIGURE 6.

GRAPHICAL INTERPRETATION OF THE CONSTRAINED MAXIMUM

The equation $\sigma^2 = P_1^2\sigma_1^2 + P_2^2\sigma_2^2$ can be drawn on the P_1P_2 plane. This equation provides us with a family of isovariance ellipses which can be written (by dividing by both sides of the above equation by σ^2) as follows:

$$\frac{P_1^2}{\left(\dfrac{\sigma}{\sigma_1}\right)^2} + \frac{P_2^2}{\left(\dfrac{\sigma}{\sigma_2}\right)^2} = 1 \qquad (18)$$

In the unconstrained case the problem of minimizing σ^2 is trivial: take $P_1 = P_2 = 0$ and get $\sigma^2 = 0$.[4] However, imposing the condition $P_1 + P_2 = 1$ means: Choose the lowest ellipse which intersects the line $P_1 + P_2 = 1$. This ellipse is the one which is tangent to this line, namely, ellipse 2 (see Figure 6).

INTEGRALS

Suppose we have a function $y = f(x)$. The *indefinite integral* of $f(x)$ is a function $F(x)$ which satisfies

$$F'(x) = f(x) \qquad (19)$$

---

[4] Notice that choosing $P_1 = P_2 = 0$ is tantamount to *not* investing at all.

Examples

(1) Let $f(x) = a$. Then $F(x) = ax + c$ because

$$F'(x) = \frac{d(ax + c)}{dx} = a = f(x)$$

(2) Let $f(x) = x^n$. Then

$$F(x) = \frac{x^{n+1}}{n + 1} + c \quad \text{(Verify by differentiation!)}$$

Notice that the indefinite integral is a function $F(x)$ whose derived function is our original function $y = f(x)$. This function is denoted by

$$\int f(x) \, dx = F(x) + c \tag{20}$$

Using this notation the above examples turn out to be

$$\int a \, dx = ax + c$$

$$\int x^n \, dx = \frac{x^{n+1}}{n + 1} + c$$

We now define the *definite integral* as

$$\int_a^b f(x) \, dx = F(b) - F(a) \tag{21}$$

Notice that the definite integral is a number which gives the value of the difference of the indefinite integral function $\int f(x) \, dx$ at two points: b and a. We call x the *integration variable*, while b is the *upper limit of integration* and a is the *lower limit of integration*. (a, b) is the *integration interval* and the function $f(x)$ is the *integrand*.

Examples

$$\int_a^b x^n \, dx = \left[\frac{x^{n+1}}{n + 1}\right]_a^b = \frac{b^{n+1}}{n + 1} - \frac{a^{n+1}}{n + 1} = \frac{b^{n+1} - a^{n+1}}{n + 1}$$

or numerically

$$\int_{-1}^3 x^2 \, dx = \left[\frac{x^3}{3}\right]_{-1}^3 = \frac{3^3}{3} - \frac{(-1)^3}{3} = \frac{27}{3} - \frac{-1}{3} = \frac{28}{3} = 9\tfrac{1}{3}$$

INTEGRALS

As an immediate result of the definition of the definite integral we can derive the following rules:

$$
\begin{aligned}
&\text{(i)} \quad \int_a^a f(x)\, dx = 0 \\
&\text{(ii)} \quad \int_a^b cf(x)\, dx = c \int_a^b f(x)\, dx \\
&\text{(iii)} \quad \int_a^b \{f(x) \pm g(x)\}\, dx = \int_a^b f(x)\, dx \pm \int_a^b g(x)\, dx \\
&\text{(iv)} \quad \int_a^b f(x)\, dx + \int_b^c f(x)\, dx = \int_a^c f(x)\, dx
\end{aligned}
\tag{22}
$$

THE INDEFINITE INTEGRAL AS AN AREA UNDER A CURVE

We shall demonstrate now how the definite integral can be used to measure x, the area under a curve: Suppose we have a function $y = f(x)$: and we want to find the area under $y = f(x)$ between the points a and b (see Figure 7). Our contention is that this area is given by

$$S(a, b) = \int_a^b f(x)\, dx \tag{23}$$

where $S(a, b)$ means the area between a and b. To show this, divide the interval (a, b) into n subintervals. The area under the curve in each of these intervals is given approximately by the area of the rectangle: $(f(x_i) \cdot \Delta x_i)$. It is clear that the smaller Δx_i (or the higher n), the better the approximation, since the deviation of the real area from that of the rectangle will be smaller.

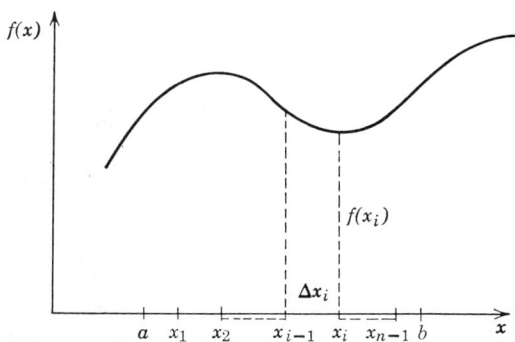

FIGURE 7.

Therefore the area from a to b is given by

$$S(a, b) = \lim_{n \to \infty} \sum_{i=1}^{n} f(x_i) \Delta x_i$$

or for any point x:

$$S(a, x) = \lim_{n \to \infty} \sum_{i=1}^{n} f(x_i) \Delta x_i$$

where the interval (a, x) is divided into n subintervals. Looking now at an interval Δx_i, its area can be expressed as the difference

$$S(x_{i-1}, x_i) = S(a, x_i) - S(a, x_{i-1})$$

But this is an approximation to

$$S(x_{i-1}, x_i) \approx f(x_i) \Delta x_i$$

or

$$S(a, x_i) - S(a, x_{i-1}) \approx f(x_i) \Delta x_i$$

Hence

$$f(x_i) \approx \frac{S(a, x_i) - S(a, x_{i-1})}{\Delta x_i}$$

or in the limit

$$f(x_i) = \lim_{\Delta x_i \to 0} \frac{S(a, x_i) - S(a, x_{i-1})}{\Delta x_i}$$

which by the definition of the derivative yields

$$f(x_i) = \frac{d[S(a, x_i)]}{dx_i}$$

or, since it holds for every x_i,

$$f(x) = \frac{d[S(a, x)]}{dx}$$

Applying now the definition of the definite integral we have

$$\int_a^b f(x)\, dx = S(a, b) - S(a, a)$$

but since $S(a, a) = 0$ (the area under the curve from point a to point a) we have

$$S(a, b) = \int_a^b f(x)\, dx \qquad (24)$$

which asserts our proposition that the definite integral gives us the area under $y = f(x)$ between the points a and b

INTEGRALS

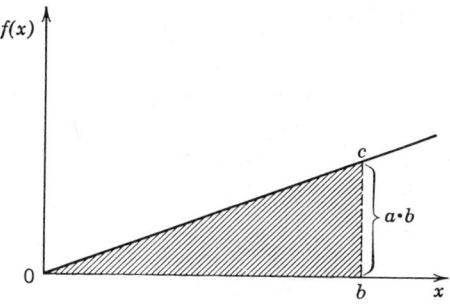

FIGURE 8.

Examples

(1) Let $y = ax$. The area under $y = ax$ between the points 0 and b is given by

$$S(0, b) = \int_0^b ax = \left(\frac{ax^2}{2}\right)_0^b = \frac{ab^2}{2}$$

which is the familiar result from high school geometry for the area of a triangle: $S = (ab \cdot b)/2$ (see Figure 8).

CHANGING THE INTEGRATION VARIABLE

Looking at the integral $\int_a^b f(x)\, dx$, how should this expression be changed if x itself is a function of another variable z? For example $x = u(z)$. The first step is to change the integrand $f(x)$ to $f[u(z)]$. Secondly, the integration limit should be chosen. Take that z which satisfies $a = u(z)$ as the lower limit of integration and that which satisfies $b = u(z)$ as the upper limit of integration. The last step is to find a substitute for dx. For this recall:

$$\frac{dx}{dz} = \frac{du}{dz}$$

Hence

$$dx = \frac{du}{dz}\, dz$$

so that the new integral will be

$$\int_{z_1}^{z_2} f[u(z)] \frac{du}{dz}\, dz = \int_a^b f(x)\, dx \tag{25}$$

Examples

Let $f(x) = x^2$ and look at $\int_{x=2}^{x=4} x^2 \, dx$. Suppose now that $x = 2z$. Then the integrand will be $x^2 = (2z)^2 = 4z^2$. As for the integration intervals, solve $2 = 2z_1$ to give $z_1 = 1$ as the lower limit and $4 = 2z_2$ or $z_2 = 2$ as the upper limit. As to the dx, since $dx/dz = d(2z)/dz = 2$ we have $dx = 2dz$, and finally we get

$$\int_2^4 x^2 \, dx = \int_1^2 4z^2 (2dz) = 8 \int_1^2 z^2 \, dz = 8 \left(\frac{z^3}{3} \right)_1^2 = 18\tfrac{2}{3}$$

We leave it up to the reader to show that the same numerical answer results when computing $\int_2^4 x^2 \, dx$ directly.

THE DOUBLE INTEGRAL

Given a function of two variables $z = f(x, y)$, this function spans a surface in the three-dimension space:

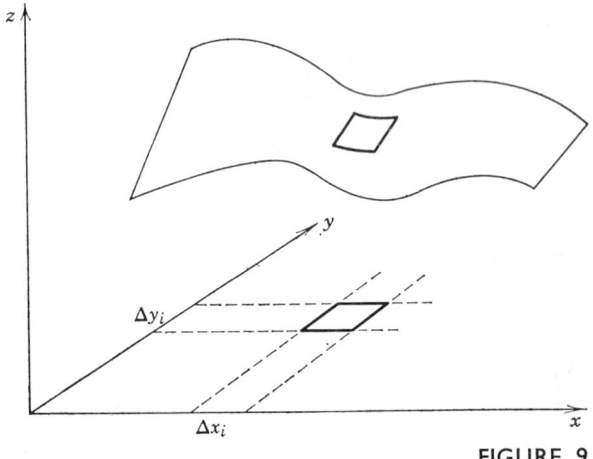

FIGURE 9.

The double integral procedure enables us to find the volume V under this surface (see Figure 9). The procedure is much the same as that for the single integral case. First we look at some rectangle which is the intersection of Δx_i and Δy_j. An approximate expression for the volume over it will be $f(x_i, y_j) \, \Delta x_i \, \Delta y_j$; continuing the same process, it can be shown that

$$f(x_i, y_j) = \frac{d}{dy} \left(\frac{d}{dx} V(x_i, y_j) \right)$$

or
$$V = \int_a^b \int_c^b f(x, y)\, dx\, dy \tag{26}$$

where the integration is made first with respect to x, keeping y constant and then with respect to y, keeping x constant.

Example

Suppose we have a joint distribution of the two random variables x and y given by

$$f(x, y) = \begin{cases} \dfrac{x \cdot y}{4} & \text{for } \begin{cases} 0 \leq x \leq 2 \\ 0 \leq y \leq 2 \end{cases} \\ 0 & \text{otherwise} \end{cases}$$

What is the probability that X will fall in the interval $(0, 1)$ and Y in $(1, 2)$? For this take:

$$p(0 \leq x \leq 1, 1 \leq y \leq 2) = \int_0^1 \int_1^2 \frac{xy}{4}\, dx\, dy$$

$$= \int_1^2 \left(\frac{x^2}{2} \cdot \frac{y}{4}\right)_0^1 dy = \int_1^2 \frac{1}{2} \cdot \frac{y}{4}\, dy = \int_1^2 \frac{y}{8}\, dy = \left(\frac{1}{8} \cdot \frac{y^2}{2}\right)_1^2$$

$$= \left(\frac{4}{16} - \frac{1}{16}\right) = \frac{3}{16}$$

THE SUM OF GEOMETRIC SERIES

A geometric series is of the form

$$A = a + aq + aq^2 + \cdots + aq^{n-1} + aq^n \tag{27}$$

where $0 < q < 1$.

In cases where n is not finite, the series is called an infinite geometric series. This kind of series is very useful in economics and finance (for the calculation of the net present value of investment, for the valuation of growth stocks, and so on).

Denoting the sum of the first m terms by Sm, then

$$Sm = a + aq + aq^2 + \cdots + aq^{m-1}$$
$$= a(1 + q + q^2 + \cdots + q^{m-1})$$

Hence
$$qSm = aq + aq^2 + \cdots + aq^m$$
$$= a(q + q^2 + \cdots + q^m)$$

Substructuring qS_m from S_m we get
$$Sm - qSm = a(1 - q + q - q^2 + q^2 - \cdots - q^{m-1} + q^{m-1} - q^m)$$
$$= a(1 - q^m)$$
or:
$$Sm(1 - q) = a(1 - q^m)$$
Hence
$$S_m = a \frac{1 - q^m}{1 - q} \qquad (28)$$

To find the sum of an infinite geometric series with $q < 1$ take
$$S = \lim_{m \to \infty} Sm = \lim_{m \to \infty} \frac{a(1 - q^m)}{1 - q} = \frac{a}{1 - q}$$
or
$$S = \frac{a}{1 - q} \qquad (29)$$

TAYLOR SERIES: POWER EXPANSION OF FUNCTIONS

The power expansion of a function is a common technique in economics and in other sciences as well. The main idea is to express a value of any function $f(x)$ in the neighborhood of a point x_0 by a polynomial in the powers of the difference: $x - x_0$:

$$f(x) = b_0 + b_1(x - x_0) + b_2(x - x_0)^2$$
$$+ b_3(x - x_0)^3 + \cdots + b_n(x - x_0)^n + \cdots \quad (30)$$

Our task is to find the coefficients of this polynomial. To do this, we first find the value of $f(x)$ at x_0 and get

$$f(x_0) = b_0 + b_1(x_0 - x_0) + b_2(x_0 - x_0)^2 + \cdots + b_n(x_0 - x_0)^2$$

or $f(x_0) = b_0$, which gives us the first coefficient. We then differentiate $f(x)$ at x_0 and find

$$f'(x_0) = 0 + b_1 + 2b_2(x_0 - x_0) + 3b_3(x_0 - x_0)^2 + \cdots + nb_n(x_0 - x_0)^{n-1}$$

TAYLOR SERIES: POWER EXPANSION OF FUNCTIONS

or $b_1 = f'(x_0)$, which gives us the second coefficient. To find the third coefficient we differentiate again and get

$$f''(x_0) = 0 + 0 + 2b_2 + 2 \cdot 3b_3(x - x_0) + \cdots + n(n-1)(x_0 - x_0)^{n-2}$$

or $b_2 = f''(x_0)/2$.

The fourth coefficient is determined as follows:

$$f'''(x_0) = 1 \cdot 2 \cdot 3 b_3 \quad \text{or} \quad b_3 = \frac{f'''(x_0)}{1 \cdot 2 \cdot 3}$$

and, in general,

$$b_n = \frac{f^{(n)}(x_0)}{1 \cdot 2 \cdot 3 \cdots n} = \frac{f^{(n)}(x_0)}{n!}$$

where $n! = 1 \cdot 2 \cdot 3 \cdots n$ is called n factorial. Putting all of these terms together we have

$$f(x) = f(x_0) + f'(x_0)(x - x_0) + \frac{f''(x_0)}{2!}(x - x_0)^2$$

$$+ \frac{f'''(x_0)}{3!}(x - x_0)^3 + \cdots + \frac{f^{(n)}(x_0)}{n!}(x - x_0)^n + \cdots \quad (31)$$

In Chapter VII this technique is used to show that expected utility, in general, is a function of *all* the distribution moments.

STATISTICAL SUPPLEMENT

The purpose of this supplement is to familiarize the reader with those statistical tools which are used in the text. We shall define and explain the concepts of a random variable and of a probability distribution and its characteristics. Since the normal and the uniform (rectangular) distributions are referred to extensively in the text, special attention is devoted to these two distributions.

By nature, portfolio selection deals with combinations of several random variables. The analysis of the relationship between the return and risk of the overall portfolio and the return and risk of the individual securities comprising the portfolio can be facilitated by introducing the statistical concepts of expected return, variance, covariance, and correlation.

A *random variable* is a numerical function defined over the sample space. This variable takes random values with a given probability assigned to each value.

Example 1: In tossing a fair coin we have two alternative outcomes: Heads (H) and tails (T) with equal probabilities 1/2 and 1/2. Hence the result of tossing such a coin constitutes a random variable. A random variable is not necessarily the actual result which occurs but might be defined as any function which assigns numerical values to these two outcomes. For instance, assume that if heads occurs you get a prize of $2 and if tails occurs you get $3. Then the prize that you get is a random variable, that is, $f(H) = 2$, $f(T) = 3$ is the random variable.

Example 2: In rolling a fair dice a random variable might be defined as a function which assigns to any outcome x the same value x: that is, $f(x) = x$. But $f(x) = x^2$ is also a random variable which gives to the player a prize equal to the square of the outcome of the throw.

A *probability function* is a function which assigns to any particular value of the random variable its probability of occurrence. Going back to the fair dice example, and defining the random variable $f(x) = x$, we obtain the following probability function:

$$P(X = x) = \begin{cases} 1/6 & x = 1, 2, 3, 4, 5, 6 \\ 0 & \text{for any other } x \end{cases}$$

Where $P(X = x)$ stands for the probability that the random variable X will get some particular value x.[1] Thus there is a probability of 1/6 that the random variable will get the values 1, 2, 3, 4, 5, 6 and a probability of zero to get any other value. Notice that $\sum_{x=1}^{6} P(X = x) = 1$ which means that there is a probability of 1 that at least one of the above values will occur.

Similarly, we can write other probability functions; for example, assume a common stock whose price at the end of the year is unknown. However, we do know that the probability that the final price will be \$110 is 1/2, the probability that this price will be \$100 is 1/4, and the same probability is assigned to a final price of \$90. Defining the stock's price as a random variable, we get the probability function

$$P(X = x) = \begin{cases} 1/2 & x = 110 \\ 1/4 & x = 90, 100 \\ 0 & \text{otherwise} \end{cases}$$

THE DISTRIBUTION FUNCTION

The probability function provides us with the probability that a random variable X will have a value x. We can use this function to define the cumulative distribution function, or in short the *distribution function*, which gives us the probability that a random variable will get any value smaller or equal to x, that is, $P(X \leq x)$. A common notation for this function is $F(x) = P(X \leq x)$.

Example: Assume that the following is a probability function of the price of some stock at the end of the year:

$$P(X = x) = \begin{cases} 1/4 & x = 80 \\ 1/4 & x = 90 \\ 1/4 & x = 110 \\ 1/4 & x = 120 \\ 0 & \text{otherwise} \end{cases}$$

If we want to know what is the probability that the final price will be smaller or equal to any value, we can derive the answer from the following

---

[1] As a general notation we denote the random variable by X while any particular value is denoted by x.

THE DISTRIBUTION FUNCTION

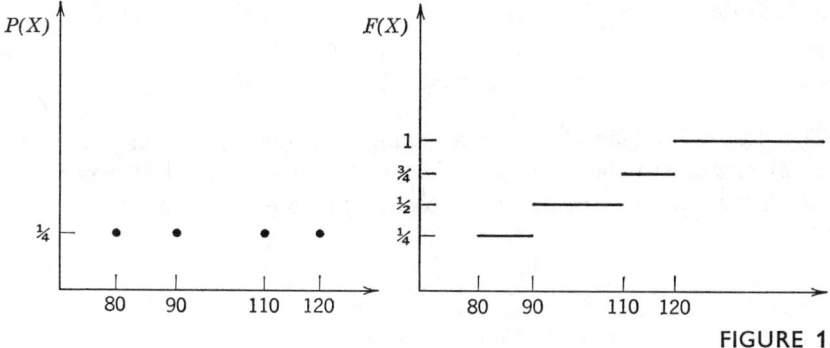

FIGURE 1.

function:

$$F(x) = P(X \leq x) = \begin{cases} 0 & x < 80 \\ 1/4 & 80 \leq x < 90 \\ 1/2 & 90 \leq x < 110 \\ 3/4 & 110 \leq x < 120 \\ 1 & x \geq 120 \end{cases}$$

If we want to know what is the probability that the price at the end of the year will be smaller than or equal to 112.5, we look at the appropriate interval ($110 \leq x < 120$), and find 3/4 as the answer. The graphical representation of this function is given in Figure 1.

To be exact, the probability distribution function is defined on the domain $(-\infty, +\infty)$. Thus, the function enables us to determine the probability of X having a value smaller than or equal to any number between $(-\infty, +\infty)$. However as by definition $P(X \leq -\infty) = 0$ and $P(X \leq +\infty) = 1$ for any random variable, it follows that the function $P(X \leq x)$ can take any value between 0 and 1. Furthermore, since this function is a cumulative function, the following relationship cannot hold: $P(X \leq x_1) > P(X \leq x_2)$ where $x_2 > x_1$. This means that the distribution function is nondecreasing.

A CONTINUOUS RANDOM VARIABLE

So far, we have considered discrete probability functions which are defined only on a finite number of events. What happens when we permit a stock to take on any value between $90 and $100? In this case our random variable is *continuous* rather than discrete. For the continuous case we define a probability *density* function which is the analogue to the probability function of the discrete case. The density function $f(x)$ is defined to satisfy

$$F(x_0) = P(X \le x_0) = \int_{-\infty}^{x_0} f(x)\,dx \tag{1}$$

That is, $f(x)$ is defined in such a manner that the area under $f(x)$ to some point x_0 is exactly the probability that the random variable will accept values which are smaller or equal to x_0. As immediate result we have

$$\int_{-\infty}^{+\infty} f(x)\,dx = 1 \quad \text{(why?)} \tag{2}$$

because all the probabilities must sum to one.

Example: Let X be a random variable with an equal probability $(1/20)$ of occurring between any two successive numbers in the interval $(90, 110)$. More specifically, the function is given by (see Figure 2),

$$f(x) = \begin{cases} 1/20 & 90 \le x \le 110 \\ 0 & \text{otherwise} \end{cases}$$

From the above probability density function we can calculate the cumulative distribution function in the interval $(90, 110)$ as

$$f(x) = \int_{-\infty}^{x} f(x)\,dx = \int_{-\infty}^{x} \frac{1}{20}\,dx = \left(\frac{x}{20}\right)_{90}^{x} = \frac{x}{20} - \frac{90}{20} = \frac{x-90}{20}$$

The cumulative distribution function helps us to find the probability that the random variable will occur in any interval (x_1, x_2) because

$$P(x_1 \le X \le x_2) = P(X \le x_2) - P(X \le x_1) = \int_{-\infty}^{x_2} f(x)\,dx - \int_{-\infty}^{x_1} f(x)\,dx$$

$$= \int_{-\infty}^{x_1} f(x)\,dx + \int_{x_1}^{x_2} f(x)\,dx - \int_{-\infty}^{x_1} f(x)\,dx = \int_{x_1}^{x_2} f(x)\,dx$$

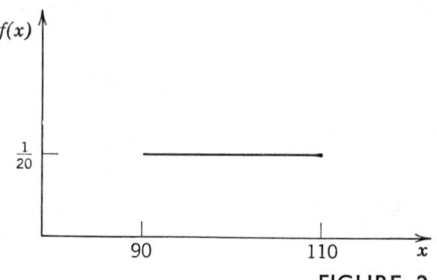

FIGURE 2.

MOMENTS

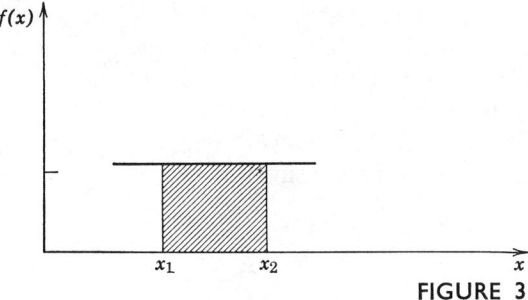

FIGURE 3.

Hence

$$P(x_1 \leq X \leq x_2) = \int_{x_1}^{x_2} f(x)\,dx \qquad (3)$$

Using the integral as a measure of area it means that the probability to find the random variable in this area is given by the area under the probability function in this interval (see Figure 3).

$$F(x) = P(X \leq x) = \begin{cases} 0 & x < 90 \\ \dfrac{x - 90}{20} & 90 \leq x \leq 110 \\ 1 & x \geq 110 \end{cases}$$

For example, from this cumulative distribution function we find that

$$F(105) = P(X \leq 105) = \frac{105 - 90}{20} = \frac{15}{20} = \frac{3}{4}$$

MOMENTS

The probability function can be characterized by a series of indices which are called "moments."

(1) *Expected Value.* The first moment is called the expected value and is defined by

$$\mu_1 = \sum_{i=-\infty}^{+\infty} x_i P_i(x) \quad \text{for the discrete case or}$$
$$\mu_1 = \int_{-\infty}^{+\infty} x f(x)\,dx \quad \text{for the continuous case} \qquad (4)$$

This moment is usually called the *expected value* or *mean* of X, and will be denoted by Ex or $\mu_1(x)$. Technically, this moment is the weighted average of all the values of the random variable, where the weight assigned to each value is the probability that this value will occur.

The expected value, or the mean, is a measure of the location of the distribution; the higher the expected value, the more to the right it is located. For example, the following two distributions are identical in every respect except for the first moment:

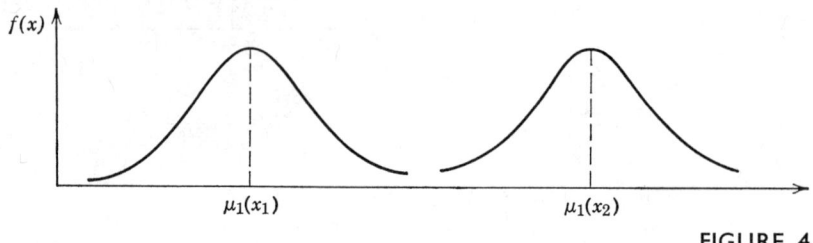

FIGURE 4.

In this case the features of $f(x_1)$ and $f(x_2)$ are identical; the only difference is that $f(x_1)$ is shifted to the left since $\mu_1(x_1) < \mu_1(x_2)$, see Figure 4.

(2) *The Variance.* The second moment, which is called the variance, is defined by

$$\mu_2 = E(x - Ex)^2 \qquad (5)$$

and is denoted by μ_2 or $Var\ x$ or $\sigma^2(x)$. More explicitly the variance can be written as

$$Var\ x = E(x - Ex)^2 = \sum_{i=-\infty}^{\infty} (x_i - Ex)^2 P(x_i) \qquad \text{for the discrete case}$$
$$Var\ x = E(x - Ex)^2 = \int_{-\infty}^{+\infty} (x - Ex)^2 f(x)\ dx \qquad \text{for the continuous case} \qquad (6)$$

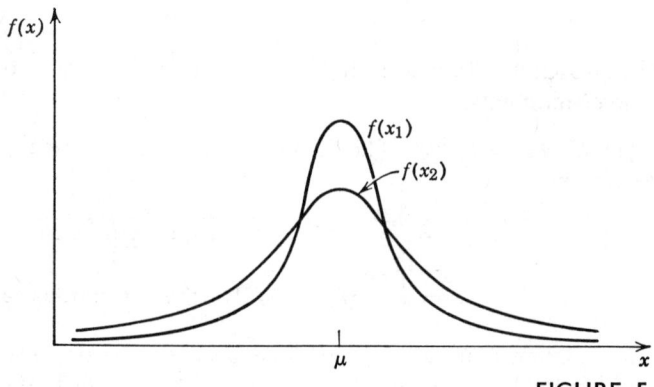

FIGURE 5.

MOMENTS

The variance is a measure of the dispersion of the random variable around the mean. The larger the variance, the more dispersed is the distribution. As can be seen in Figure 5, though $\mu_1(x_1) = \mu_2(x_2)$, $Var(x_1) < Var(x_2)$. Another measure associated with the second moment is the *standard deviation*, or square root of the variance:

$$\sigma(x) = \sqrt{Var(x)} = \sqrt{\sigma^2(x)} \tag{7}$$

where $\sigma(x)$ denotes the standard deviation.

(3) *The skewness*. The third moment, which is called the skewness of the distribution, is given by

$$\mu_3 = E(x - Ex)^3 \quad \text{or} \tag{8}$$

$$\mu_3 = \sum_{i=-\infty}^{+\infty} (x_i - Ex)^3 P(x_i) \quad \text{for the discrete case, and}$$

$$\mu_3 = \int_{-\infty}^{+\infty} (x - Ex)^3 f(x)\, dx \quad \text{for the continuous case} \tag{9}$$

Looking at Figure 6(a), the expression $(x - Ex)^3$ will be negative to the left of $E(x)$ and positive to the right. However, since there are relatively large numbers to the right, μ_3 will be positive. The reason is that we calculate the third power of the deviations from the mean, and even though we have only a small probability of getting such outcomes, these terms will determine the sign of μ_3. Therefore skewness to the right is characterized by a positive third moment of the distribution, and the distribution is said to have *positive skewness* ($\mu_3 > 0$). In a similar way we say that a distribution which is skewed to the left (Figure 6b) has a negative third moment or *negative skewness* ($\mu_3 < 0$). Notice that in case the distribution is symmetrical, the third moment around the mean is zero.

(4) *nth moment*. Similarly we can define any moment of order n as

$$\mu_n(x) = E(x - Ex)^n \quad \text{hence} \tag{10}$$

$$\mu_n(x) = \sum_{i=-\infty}^{+\infty} (x_i - Ex)^n P(x_i) \quad \text{for the discrete case or}$$

$$\mu_n(x) = \int_{-\infty}^{+\infty} (x = Ex)^n f(x)\, dx \quad \text{for the continuous case} \tag{11}$$

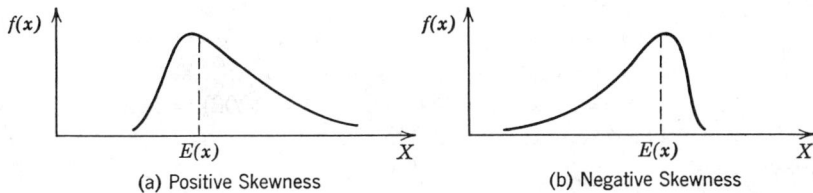

(a) Positive Skewness (b) Negative Skewness

FIGURE 6.

Examples and Further Developments

(1) Expected value in the discrete case:

Let
$$P(X = x) = \begin{cases} \frac{1}{2} & x = 80 \\ \frac{1}{4} & x = 100, 200 \\ 0 & \text{otherwise} \end{cases}$$

Then
$$Ex = \tfrac{1}{2} \times 80 + \tfrac{1}{4} \times 100 + \tfrac{1}{4} \times 200 = 40 + 25 + 50 = 115$$

(2) Expected value for the continuous case:

Let
$$f(x) = \begin{cases} 1/100 & 100 \leq x \leq 200 \\ 0 & \text{otherwise} \end{cases}$$

$$Ex = \int_{100}^{200} x \cdot \frac{1}{100} \, dx = \left(\frac{x^2}{200}\right)_{100}^{200} = \frac{40{,}000}{200} - \frac{10{,}000}{200} = \frac{30{,}000}{200} = 150$$

(3) We shall demonstrate now a simpler way to compute the variance of a random variable:

$$\operatorname{Var} x = E(x - Ex)^2 = E(x^2 + Ex^2 - 2xEx) = Ex^2 + (Ex)^2 - 2ExEx$$
$$= Ex^2 - (Ex)^2$$

$$\operatorname{Var} x = Ex^2 - (Ex)^2 \tag{12}$$

where $Ex^2 = \sum_{i=-\infty}^{\infty} x_i^2 P(x_i)$, which is nothing but the expected value of the random variable X^2.

$$\left[\text{Similarly for the continuous case: } Ex^2 = \int_{-\infty}^{+\infty} x^2 f(x) \, dx.\right]$$

(4) Variance of a discrete random variable:

Let
$$P(X = x) = \begin{cases} \frac{1}{2} & x = 80 \\ \frac{1}{4} & x = 100 \\ \frac{1}{4} & x = 200 \\ 0 & \text{otherwise} \end{cases}$$

Then
$$Ex^2 = \tfrac{1}{2} \times (80)^2 + \tfrac{1}{4} \times (100)^2 + \tfrac{1}{4} \times (200)^2$$
$$= 3{,}200 + 2{,}500 + 10{,}000 = 15{,}700$$
$$Ex = \tfrac{1}{2} \times (80) + \tfrac{1}{4}(100) + \tfrac{1}{4} \times (200) = 115$$
$$(Ex)^2 = (115)^2 = 13{,}225$$

Hence
$$\operatorname{Var} x = Ex^2 - (Ex)^2 = 15{,}700 - 13{,}225 = 2{,}475$$

MOMENTS

(5) Variance of continuous random variable:

Let
$$f(x) = \begin{cases} \frac{1}{100} & 100 \leq x \leq 200 \\ 0 & \text{otherwise} \end{cases}$$

Then
$$Ex^2 = \int_{100}^{200} x^2 \frac{1}{100} dx = \left(\frac{x^3}{300}\right)_{100}^{200} = \frac{8,000,000}{300} - \frac{1,000,000}{300} = 23,333\tfrac{1}{3}$$

$$E(x) = \int_{100}^{200} x \frac{1}{100} dx = \left(\frac{x^2}{200}\right)_{100}^{200} = \frac{40,000}{200} - \frac{10,000}{200} = 150$$

$$(Ex)^2 = (150)^2 = 22,500$$

Hence
$$Var\ x = Ex^2 - (Ex)^2 = 23,333\tfrac{1}{3} - 22,500 = 833\tfrac{1}{3}$$

(6) Third moment of a discrete random variable:

Let
$$P(X = x) = \begin{cases} \tfrac{1}{2} & x = 80 \\ \tfrac{1}{4} & x = 100 \\ \tfrac{1}{4} & x = 200 \\ 0 & \text{otherwise} \end{cases}$$

From (1) we know that $Ex = 115$. Then

$$\mu_3(x) = \sum_{i=1}^{3} (x_i - Ex)^3 P(x_i)$$

$$= \tfrac{1}{2}(80 - 115)^3 + \tfrac{1}{4}(100 - 115)^3 + \tfrac{1}{4}(200 - 115)^3$$

$$= \frac{-42,875}{2} - \frac{3,375}{4} + \frac{614,125}{4} = 131,750$$

(7) Third moment of continuous random variable:

Let
$$f(x) = \begin{cases} \frac{1}{100} & 100 \leq x \leq 200 \\ 0 & \text{otherwise} \end{cases}$$

From (2) we know that $Ex = 150$. Then

$$\mu_3(x) = \int_{100}^{200} (x - 150)^3 \frac{1}{100} dx = \left[\frac{(x-150)^4}{400}\right]_{100}^{200}$$

$$= \frac{(200-150)^4}{400} - \frac{(100-150)^4}{400} = 15,625 - 15,625 = 0$$

The fact that the third moment is zero reflects the fact that this distribution is unskewed, that is, it is a symmetrical distribution.

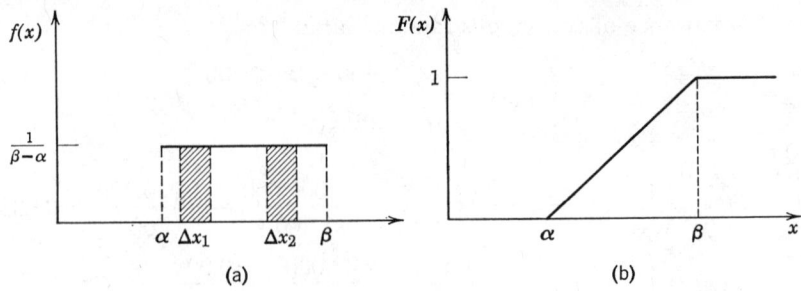

FIGURE 7.

THE UNIFORM (RECTANGULAR) DISTRIBUTION

In Example 2 above we introduced a distribution whose general analytic form is

$$f(x) = \begin{cases} \dfrac{1}{\beta - \alpha} & \alpha \leq x \leq \beta \\ 0 & \text{otherwise} \end{cases} \qquad (13)$$

This distribution is called the *uniform distribution* or the *rectangular distribution*. From the above expression we can derive the cumulative distribution function to be

$$F(x) = \int_{-\infty}^{x} f(x)\, dx = \begin{cases} 0 & x < \alpha \\ \dfrac{x - \alpha}{\beta - \alpha} & \alpha \leq x \leq \beta \\ 1 & x > \beta \end{cases} \qquad (14)$$

The diagrammatic representation of these two functions is given in Figure 7. The uniform distribution is characterized by the fact that the chances of the random variable occurring in two equal-length intervals Δx_1 and Δx_2 are the same.

$$\frac{\Delta x_1}{\beta - \alpha} = \frac{\Delta x_2}{\beta - \alpha}$$

THE EXPECTED VALUE AND THE VARIANCE OF THE UNIFORM DISTRIBUTION

Given a random variable X uniformly distributed over the interval (α, β) (denote: $X \sim U(\alpha, \beta)$)

$$f(x) = \begin{cases} \dfrac{1}{\beta - \alpha} & \alpha \leq x \leq \beta \\ 0 & \text{otherwise} \end{cases}$$

THE NORMAL DISTRIBUTION

or

$$Ex = \int_\alpha^\beta xf(x)\,dx = \int_\alpha^\beta x\,\frac{1}{\beta - \alpha}\,dx = \left(\frac{x^2}{2(\beta - \alpha)}\right)_\alpha^\beta = \frac{\beta^2 - \alpha^2}{2(\beta - \alpha)}$$

then

$$= \frac{(\beta - \alpha)(\beta + \alpha)}{2(\beta - \alpha)} = \frac{\alpha + \beta}{2}$$

or

$$Ex = \frac{\alpha + \beta}{2} \tag{15}$$

Hence the expected value of X is $(\alpha + \beta)/2$ or half the way between α and β. As to the variance, compute

$$Ex^2 = \int_\alpha^\beta x^2\,\frac{1}{\beta - \alpha}\,dx = \left(\frac{x^3}{3(\beta - \alpha)}\right)_\alpha^\beta = \frac{\beta^3 - \alpha^3}{3(\beta - \alpha)}$$

$$= \frac{(\beta^2 + \alpha\beta + \alpha^2)(\beta - \alpha)}{3(\beta - \alpha)} = \frac{\beta^2 + \alpha\beta + \alpha^2}{3}$$

$(Ex)^2$ is given above as

$$(Ex)^2 = \left(\frac{\alpha + \beta}{2}\right)^2$$

Hence

$$Var\,x = Ex^2 - (Ex)^2 = \frac{\beta^2 + \alpha\beta - \alpha^2}{3} - \frac{(\alpha + \beta)^2}{2} = \frac{(\beta - \alpha)^2}{12}$$

or

$$Var\,x = \frac{(\beta - \alpha)^2}{12}$$

THE NORMAL DISTRIBUTION

The density function of the normal distribution is given by

$$f(x) = \frac{1}{\sqrt{2\pi}\,\sigma}\,e^{-\frac{1}{2}(x-\mu/\sigma)^2} \quad \text{for} \quad -\infty < x < \infty \tag{16}$$

where μ is the mean of the distribution and σ its standard deviation. $\pi = 3.14\ldots$ is the familiar geometric constant, and $e = 2.71\ldots$ is also a constant, known as the base of natural logarithms. This distribution is very useful both in theory and practice since it represents many random phenomena. Graphically, the normal distribution has the form of a bell, hence

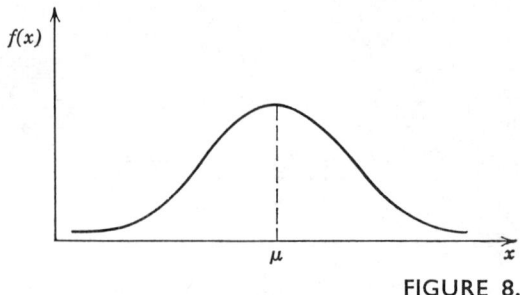

FIGURE 8.

the name "bell function" (see Figure 8). It can easily be seen that this distribution is symmetrical around the mean. The "width" of the curve depends on σ, the standard deviation; the greater the σ, the wider is the curve, which means that the distribution is more dispersed. Another characteristic of this distribution is that the probability of getting values of x is high in the neighborhood of μ and diminishes considerably as we move away from the mean. The normal *cumulative* distribution is given by

$$F(x) = \int_{-\infty}^{x} \frac{1}{\sqrt{2\pi}\,\sigma} e^{-\frac{1}{2}(x-\mu/\sigma)^2} dx \tag{17}$$

which is the area under the bell function to the point x. This area gives us the probability that the random variable X will have a value which is smaller or equal to x. To calculate this distribution there is no need to compute the integral, since special tables are available which give us the value $F(x)$ for every value x.

THE NORMAL DISTRIBUTION PARAMETERS

The normal distribution can be fully characterized by two parameters: the mean μ, and the standard deviation σ.

In Figure 9 we have a case of two distributions which differ only in their

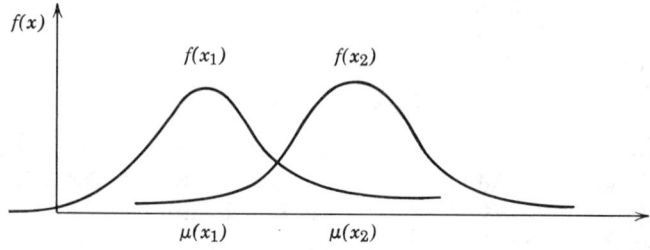

FIGURE 9.

THE NORMAL DISTRIBUTION

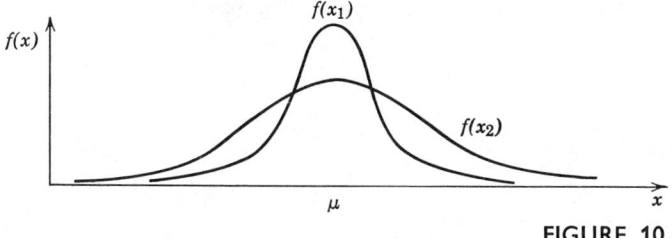

FIGURE 10.

means: $\mu(x_1) < \mu(x_2)$; the other parameter σ, which is a measure of the dispersion or variability, is the same, $\sigma_1 = \sigma_2$. Figure 10 gives us the opposite case: two normal distributions with the same mean, μ, but differing in their standard deviation ($\sigma_2 > \sigma_1$).

Normal distribution functions can differ both in their mean and the standard deviations (see Figure 11). However the area under a normal curve must, by definition, be equal to 1 regardless of μ or σ.

The cumulative distribution function of the normal distribution functions can be derived by summing up the area under the curve $f(x)$ (see Figure 12).

In Chapter VIII we use an important characteristic of the normal distribution. Given X_1 and X_2 such that $\sigma(x_1) \neq \sigma(x_2)$, the two cumulative functions intersect each other. We shall demonstrate this fact graphically: Assume first that $\mu(x_1) > \mu(x_2)$ but $\sigma(x_1) = \sigma(x_2)$. Then $F(x_1)$ is nothing but

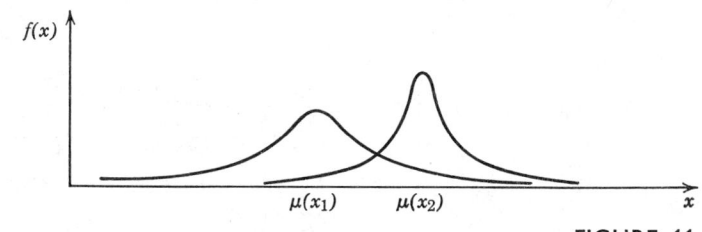

FIGURE 11.

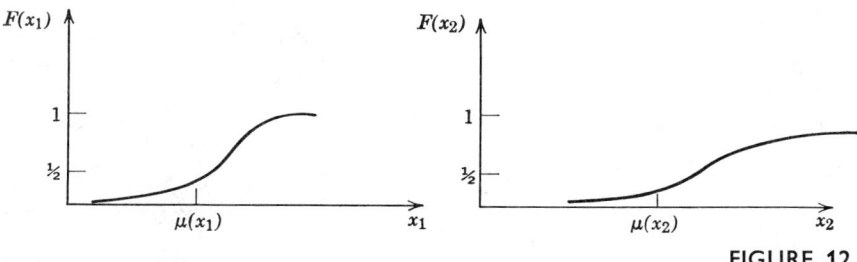

FIGURE 12.

a shift to the right of $F(x_2)$ (see Figure 13):

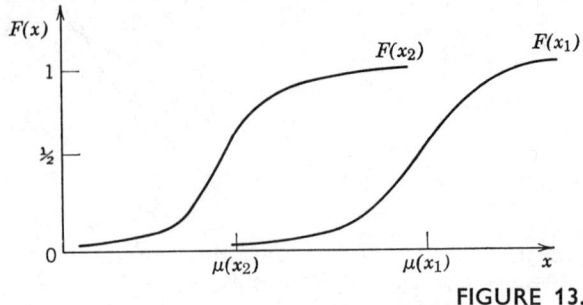

FIGURE 13.

In cases where $\sigma(x_2) > \sigma(x_1)$, even if both distributions have the same mean μ, the distribution $f(x_2)$ accumulates, up to any point a $(a < \mu)$, a larger area than $f(x_1)$ does. However, up to the point μ both of them accumulate the same area: 1/2 (see Figure 14):

$$\int_{-\infty}^{\mu} f(x_1)\,dx_1 = \int_{-\infty}^{\mu} f(x_2)\,dx_2 = \tfrac{1}{2}$$

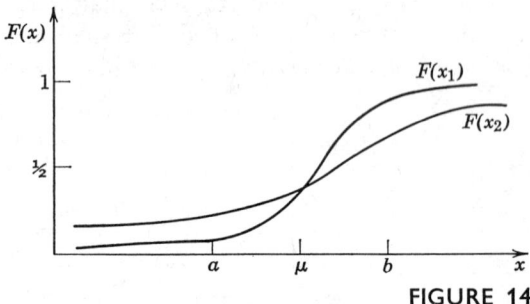

FIGURE 14.

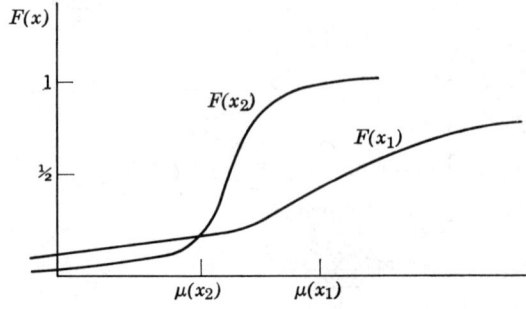

FIGURE 15.

LINEAR TRANSFORMATION OF RANDOM VARIABLES

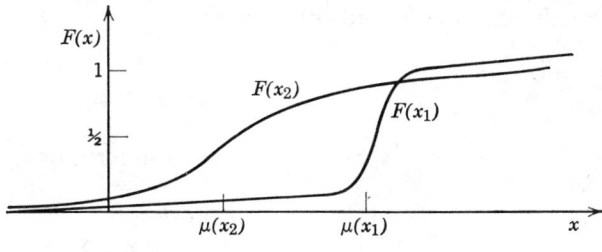

FIGURE 16.

The reader should note that the curves intersect at μ. The illustration of the case where $\mu(x_1) \neq \mu(x_2)$ and $\sigma(x_1) \neq \sigma(x_2)$ is given in Figure 15, in which $\mu(x_2) < \mu(x_1)$ but $\sigma(x_1) > \sigma(x_2)$. Another possible combination is when $\mu(x_2) < \mu(x_1)$ and $\sigma(x_2) > \sigma(x_1)$, which is shown in Figure 16.

LINEAR TRANSFORMATION OF RANDOM VARIABLES

We define a linear transformation of a random variable X as

$$Y = aX + b$$

Y itself is a new random variable whose statistical characteristics can be calculated.

Examples:

(i) $Y = 5 + 3X$
(ii) $Y = 3X$
(iii) $Y = 5$

are all linear combinations of X. We shall prove some rules concerning these transformations.

(i) The expected value of a constant number is the number itself, that is,

$$Ea = a \qquad (18)$$

This is a degenerated random variable which takes the value a with probability 1, and therefore

$$Ea = 1 \cdot a = a$$

(ii) Let X be a random variable and let b be a constant number. Then

$$E(bx) = bEx \qquad (19)$$

Since

$$E(bx) = \sum_{i=-\infty}^{+\infty} bx_i P(x_i) = b \sum_{i=-\infty}^{+\infty} x_i P(x_i) = bEx$$

combining rule (i) and (ii) we have

(iii)
$$E(a + bx) = a + bEx \tag{20}$$

(iv) The variance of a fixed number is zero, or
$$Var\ a = 0 \tag{21}$$

Since $Var\ x = Ex^2 - (Ex)^2$ and in this case $Ea^2 = a^2$ and $(Ea)^2 = a^2$, we obtain
$$Var\ a = a^2 - a^2 = 0$$

Intuitively this means that since a is a constant, it has no variance.

(v) Let X be a random variable and let b be a constant; then
$$Var\ (bx) = b^2\ Var\ x \tag{22}$$

By the definition of the variance we have

$$Var\ (bx) = E(bx - E(bx))^2 = E(b(x - Ex))^2 = b^2 E(x - Ex)^2 = b^2\ Var\ x$$

(vi) Rules (iv) and (v) can be summarized as follows:
$$Var\ (a + bx) = b^2\ Var\ x \tag{23}$$

COVARIANCE AND THE CORRELATION COEFFICIENT

So far we have been dealing with a single random variable. But in the more complicated cases we have to explore the relationships among several random variables. Consider an individual who invests part of his money in the construction industry. Since profits in this industry fluctuate strongly, he may be interested in investing part of his money in another industry to stabilize his income. This stabilization can be facilitated by investing part of his money in an industry whose profits fluctuate either independently or negatively with those of the construction industry. By so doing, the investor can achieve a fairly stable average return; when the return on one type of stock is relatively low, the return from the other stocks will be relatively high, and vice versa. The degree to which diversification stabilizes the return is a function of the relation between the two random variables. The two concepts which serve as quantitative measures of the relation between the fluctuations of two random variables are the *covariance* and the *correlation coefficient*.

COVARIANCE AND THE CORRELATION COEFFICIENT

THE COVARIANCE

We define the covariance of two random variables X and Y as

$$Cov\,(x, y) = E((x - Ex)(y - Ey)) \qquad (24)$$

In the discrete case we get

$$Cov\,(x, y) = \sum_{i=1}^{n} (x_i - Ex)(y_i - Ey)P_i \qquad (25)$$

where P_i stands for the probability of getting x_i and y_i simultaneously. The above definition of $Cov\,(x, y)$ can be found to be

$$Cov\,(x, y) = E[(x - Ex)(y - Ey)] = E[xy - yEx - xEy + ExEy]$$
$$= E(xy) - 2ExEy + ExEy = E(xy) - ExEy$$

or

$$Cov\,(x, y) = E(xy) - ExEy \qquad (26)$$

where $E(xy)$ is the expected value of the random variable XY. In the continuous case we have

$$Cov\,(x, y) = \iint_{x\,y} (x - Ex)(y - Ey) f(x, y)\,dx\,dy$$

or

$$Cov\,(x, y) = \iint_{x\,y} xy f(x, y)\,dx\,dy - \left(\int_x x f(x)\,dx \int_y y f(y)\,dy \right)$$

We can explain the intuitive meaning of the covariance as follows:
Look at the expression $(x - Ex)(y - Ey)$.

$$\text{Suppose } x - Ex > 0 \quad (x \text{ exceeds } Ex)$$
$$\text{and } y - Ey > 0 \quad (y \text{ exceeds } Ey)$$
$$\text{Then } (x - Ex)(y - Ey) > 0$$

We will get a positive value also when both x and y are below their average. However, if

$$(x - Ex) > 0 \quad \text{and} \quad (y - Ey) < 0$$

or

$$(x - Ex) < 0 \quad \text{and} \quad (y - Ey) > 0$$

which means that one of the variables is above its average and the other is below the average, then

$$(x - Ex)(y - Ey) < 0$$

Consequently if we get $Cov\,(x, y) = E(x - Ex)(y - Ey) > 0$, we have to conclude that x and y simultaneously tend either to exceed their respective average or to be below it. However, if $Cov(x, y) < 0$, we can say that they tend to disperse from their average in opposite directions. That is why our hypothetical investor will try to choose an industry whose returns have a *negative* covariance with the returns in the construction industry.[2]

CORRELATION COEFFICIENT

The covariance has been shown to be an indicator of the direction of the dependence between two variables. This indicator, however, changes with any change in the unit of measurement (cents, dimes, or dollars) of the random variables. We need, therefore, an indicator which will be independent of the units used in measuring the outcomes. Furthermore, we desire information concerning *both* the direction and the power of the relationship between the variables. The index which has the required characteristics is called the correlation coefficient and is given by

$$R(x, y) = \frac{Cov(x, y)}{\sigma(x)\sigma(y)} \qquad (27)$$

This coefficient always satisfies

$$-1 \leq R(x, y) \leq 1 \qquad (28)$$

and is independent of the units of measurement.

When $0 < R < +1$ the relation between the two variables is of a positive nature. The closer we approach to 1, the stronger is the relation. When $R = 1$ there is a perfect positive correlation. In other words, the relation is linear, which means there are b and a such that $y = a + bx$ where $b > 0$.[3] When $0 \geq R \geq -1$ the relation is negative and the smaller R, the stronger is the negative relation. In the extreme case where $R = -1$ we have

$$y = a + bx \quad \text{with} \quad b < 0$$

---

[2] It is worthwhile to mention that the relationship between X and Y can be written as

$$y_t = a + bx_t + e_t$$

where a, b are constants, t stands for year t, and e_t is the deviation of $y(t)$ from the straight line. The line which minimizes the $\sum e_t^2$ is called the regression line of Y on X. By using this "best" line we find that the slope of the line is:

$$b = \frac{Cov(x, y)}{\sigma^2(x)}$$

[3] See preceding footnote. This implies that if $R = +1$ then $e_t = 0$ and hence $\sum e_t^2 = 0$.

THE EXPECTED VALUE AND THE VARIANCE OF THE SUM OF RANDOM VARIABLES

Suppose X and Y are two random variables. What is the expected value and variance of the sum? Let us start with the expected value of the sum which we denote by $E(x + y)$. From the definition

$$E(x + y) = \sum_{\infty \leq i, j \leq +\infty} (x_i + y_j) P(x_i, y_j)$$

where $P(x_i, y_j)$ is the joint probability to get x_i and y_j, the expected value can be rewritten as

$$E(x + y) = \sum_i \sum_j x_i P(x_i, y_j) + \sum_j \sum_i y_j P(x_i, y_j)$$

$$= \sum_i x_i \sum_j P(x_i, y_j) + \sum_j y_j \sum_i P(x_i, y_j) \qquad (29)$$

But since $P(x_i, y_j)$ is the probability to get x_i when y_j occurs, we have

$$\sum_j P(x_i, y_j) = P(x_i)$$

$$\sum_i P(x_i, y_j) = P(y_j)$$

and (29) is

$$E(x + y) = \sum_i x_i P(x_i) + \sum_j y_j P(y_j) = Ex + Ey$$

hence

$$E(x + y) = Ex + Ey$$

and similarly

$$E(x - y) = Ex - Ey \qquad (30)$$

In the case of more than two random variables, we can derive

$$E(x_1 + x_2 + \cdots + x_n) = Ex_1 + Ex_2 + \cdots + Ex_n$$

or

$$E\left(\sum_{i=1}^n x_i\right) = \sum_{i=1}^n Ex_i \qquad (31)$$

What will be the variance of this sum?

$$\begin{aligned}
Var(x + y) &= E[(x + y) - E(x + y)]^2 = E[(x - Ex) + (y - Ey)]^2 \\
&= E[(x - Ex)^2 + (y - Ey)^2 + 2(x - Ex)(y - Ey)] \\
&= E(x - Ex)^2 + E(y - Ey)^2 + 2E(x - Ex)(y - Ey) \\
&= Var\, x + Var\, y + 2\, Cov\,(x, y)
\end{aligned}$$

or
$$Var(x+y) = Var\, x + Var\, y + 2\, Cov(x, y)$$
Similarly (32)
$$Var(x-y) = Var\, x + Var\, y - 2\, Cov(x, y)$$

Since $R(x, y) = Cov(x, y)/\sigma(x)\sigma(y)$ implies $Cov(x, y) = R(x, y)\sigma(x)\sigma(y)$,
$$Var(x+y) = Var\, x + Var\, y + 2R(x, y)\sigma(x)\sigma(y)$$

Substituting, $Var\, x = \sigma^2(x)$, $Var\, y = \sigma^2(y)$, $Var(x+y) = \sigma^2(x+y)$, we get
$$\sigma^2(x \pm y) = \sigma^2(x) + \sigma^2(y) \pm 2R(x, y)\sigma(x)\sigma(y) \tag{33}$$

Suppose the above random variables are multiplied by constant factors. What is $Var(ax + by)$ or generally $Var(\sum_{i=1}^{n} a_i x_i)$? From the definition

$$Var\left(\sum_{i=1}^{n} a_i x_i\right) = E\left(\sum_{i=1}^{n} a_i x_i - \sum a_i E x_i\right)^2 = E\left(\sum_{i=1}^{n} a_i(x_i - E x_i)\right)^2$$

$$= E\left[\sum_{i=1}^{n} a_i^2 (x_i - E x_i)^2 + 2 \sum_{i=1}^{n} \sum_{j>i} a_i a_j (x_i - E x_i)(x_j - E x_j)\right]$$

$$= \sum_{i=1}^{n} a_i^2\, Var\, x_i + 2 \sum_{i=1}^{n} \sum_{j>i} a_i a_j\, Cov(x_i, x_j)$$

$$Var\left(\sum_{i=1}^{n} a_i x_i\right) = \sum_{i=1}^{n} a_i^2\, Var\, x_i + 2 \sum_{i=1}^{n} \sum_{j>i} a_i a_j\, Cov(x_i, x_j) \tag{34}$$

and by equivalent substitution to that end we have

$$Var\left(\sum_{i=1}^{n} a_i x_i\right) = \sum_{i=1}^{n} a_i^2 \sigma^2(x_i) + 2 \sum_{i=1}^{n} \sum_{j>i} a_i a_j R(x_i, x_j)\sigma(x_i)\sigma(x_j) \tag{35}$$

and in the special case where $R(x_i, x_j) = 0$,

$$Var\left(\sum_{i=1}^{n} a_i x_i\right) = \sum_{i=1}^{n} a_i^2 \sigma^2(x_i) \tag{36}$$

CHEBYCHEV INEQUALITY

Suppose we have a random variable with an expected value μ and variance σ^2. We expect this random variable to have values around the expected values; and the further we move from the expected value the smaller is the probability that X will get these more remote values. The *Chebychev inequality* provides a tool which can be used to estimate the probability of this deviation from the expected value, even if we do not know the probability function of X. The contention is that the following inequality holds:[4]

$$Pr\{|x - \mu| \geq K\sigma\} \leq \frac{1}{K^2} \tag{37}$$

Thus the probability that X will differ from the expected value by more than $K\sigma$ is smaller than (or equal to) $1/K^2$. We shall prove this for the continuous case.

Define a new random variable $Y = X - \mu$, whose density function is $f(y)$. What we have to prove is

$$Pr\{|y| \geq K\sigma\} \leq \frac{1}{K^2}$$

To do this, examine the following inequality:

$$K^2\sigma^2 Pr\{|y| \geq K\sigma\} = K^2\sigma^2(Pr\{-K\sigma \geq y\} + Pr\{y \geq K\sigma\})$$
$$= K^2\sigma^2 \left\{ \int_{-\infty}^{-K\sigma} f(y)\, dy + \int_{+K\sigma}^{\infty} f(y)\, dy \right\}$$

Since in these intervals, $(-\infty, -K\sigma)$ and $(K\sigma, \infty)$, Y satisfies $|y| > K\sigma$ then $y^2 > K^2\sigma^2$, and by replacing $K^2\sigma^2$ for y^2 we get

$$K^2\sigma^2 Pr\{|y| \geq K\sigma\} \leq \int_{-\infty}^{-K\sigma} y^2 f(y)\, dy + \int_{K\sigma}^{+\infty} y^2 f(y)\, dy$$
$$\leq \int_{-\infty}^{+\infty} y^2 f(y)\, dy = Ey^2$$

But by definition $Ey = E(x - \mu) = Ex - \mu = \mu - \mu = 0$. Hence

$$\sigma^2(y) = Ey^2 + (Ey)^2 = Ey^2 - 0 = Ey^2$$

But since y differs from x by a constant μ we have

$$\sigma^2(y) = \sigma^2(x) = \sigma^2$$

Therefore $K^2\sigma^2 Pr\{|y| \geq K\sigma\} = K^2\sigma^2 Pr\{|X - \mu| \geq K\sigma\} \leq \sigma^2$. Dividing both sides by $K^2\sigma^2$ we get the required result:

$$Pr\{|X - \mu| \geq K\sigma\} \leq \frac{1}{K^2}$$

---

[4] Provided the first two moments exist.

Author Index

Italicized roman numerals refer to the preface while all other roman numerals refer to selected references at the end of each chapter.

Adler, M., ix
Alberts, W. W., xv
Alchian, A. A., iii, vi
Alexander, S. S., 29n, ii, xiv
Allen, R. G. D., 244n, 372n
Altman, E. I., xiv
Archer, S. H., xiv
Arditti, F. D., *vi*, vi, 248n, ix, 480n, xiv
Arlington, M. J., *vi*
Arrow, K. J., 201n, 215n, vi, ix, 382, 382n, 395

Bachelier, L., 493n
Bailey, M. J., 82n, iii
Barker, C. A., 138n, v
Bauman, W. S., iii
Baumol, W. J., 10n, 17n, i, 123n, 305, 305n, ix, 388, 388n, 389n, 391n, 392, 396, xiv
Baxter, N. D., iv
Baxter, W. T., ii
Bear, R. M., xiv
Bell, W. E., v
Ben-Horim, M., *vi*
Ben-Shahar, H., 80n, iii
Benishay, H., 173n, v
Bennington, G. A., xiv
Bernhard, H. B., iii
Bernoulli, D., 194n, 196, 197, 197n, 198, 200, 200n, 201, 217, 220, vi, 303
Bernoulli, N., 194, 194n, 200n
Bers, L., 554n
Biderman, R., ix
Bierman, H., iii, ix

Bierwag, G. O., vi, xiii
Blackwell, D., 299n
Block, F. E., ii
Blume, M. E., 480n, xiv
Bodenhorn, D., v
Borch, K., vi, ix
Boulding, K., 67n, iii, 431
Bower, D. H., 175n, v, xiii
Bower, R. S., 175n, v, xiii, xiv
Breen, W., xiv
Brigham, E. F., iii, 123n, v
Briscoe, G., vi
Brown, F. E., xiv
Brown, J. M., i
Bryan, G. L., vi
Buse, A., iv

Carleton, W. T., iii, iv
Carlson, R. S., xiv
Chen, A. H. Y., iv
Chiang, A. C., 554n
Chottiner, S., v
Clarkson, G. P., ix
Cohen, J. B., i, iv
Cohen, K. J., ix, xiv
Cohn, R. A., 544n
Cootner, P. H., 492n, 493n, xiv
Cottle, S., ii, iv, 131n, v
Cramer, G., 196, 200, 200n, 201, 201n, 217, 220, viii, 296n, 303
Cutler, F., xvi

Davidson, S., ii
Dean, ii, iii, 507n
Debreu, G., 215n, vi

595

Devlin, D. T., xvi
Diamond, P. A., xiii
Dice, C. A., i
Dietz, P. O., xiv
Dodd, D. C., ii, iv, 131n, v
Domar, E., 304, 304n, ix
Dryden, M. M., xiv
Durand, D., 116, 116n, 158n, 161n, 162, 169, 177, 183, v, vi

Edwards, W., vi
Eiteman, D. K., i
Eiteman, W. J., i
Ellsburg, D., vi
Elton, E. J., iii, v, ix
Evans, J. L., xiv

Fama, E. F., 330n, 430n, 451n, xiii, 492n, 493n, 495n, xiv
Farrar, D. E., ix
Farwell, L. C., i
Feldstein, M. S., ix
Feller, W., viii, 343n, 344n
Fellner, W. J., 194n, vi
Fischer, G. A., 122n
Fisher, I., 109n, 118
Fisher, L., 83n, iii, xiv
Fraser, D. A. S., 389n
Freimer, M., ix
Freund, W. C., iv
Fried, J., xiv
Friedman, M., 4n, vi, 235, 235n, 236n, 238, 239, 239n, 240, 240n, 243n, 250, 251, 252, 253, 254, 265, 416, 429, 429n, xiii
Friend, I., 480n, xiv
Furst, R. W., i

Gaumnitz, J. E., xiv
Gordon, M. J., 139n, 142n, v, ix
Goshay, R. C., ix
Graham, B., ii, iv, 131n, v
Graybill, F. A., 195n, 245n, 326n, ix
Greely, R. E., 476n
Grossman, H. I., iv
Grove, M. A., vi, xiii
Grubel, H. G., xvi
Gruber, M. J., v
Grunfeld, Y., 11n

Hadar, J., viii, 296n, 299n

Hakansson, N., vi, 243n, ix
Hald, A., 316n, ix
Hamada, R. S., 175n, v
Hamburg, M., 383n
Hanoch, G., *vi*, viii, 296n, 299n, 302n, ix, 339n, 388n
Hanssman, F., ix
Hanumanta, R. K. S., v
Hastie, K. L., ix
Heins, A. J., v
Helliwell, J. F., xv
Herman, E. S., xiv
Hester, D. D., ix, 383n
Hickman, W. B., 105n, 108n, iv
Hicks, J. R., ii, 118, 118n, 120n, iv, 304, 304n, ix
Higgins, C. A., xiv
Hillier, F. S., 512n, xv
Hirshleifer, J., iii, 215n, vi, 240n
Hoel, P. G., 303n
Holt, C. C., v
Horowitz, I., xiv
Hunt, P., v

Jacob, N., *vi*, 249n, 487n
Jensen, M. C., 407n, 480n, 487n, 490, xiv
Joyce, J. M., ix
Judelson, D. N., 507n, xv

Kahane, Y., *vi*
Kaplansky, I., vi, 248n
Kessel, R. A., 117n, 120n, iv
Keynes, J. M., 10, 10n, 11, 115, 115n, 118, iv, 201n, vi, 304, 304n, ix
Keynes, J. N., 4, 4n
King, B. F., 486, 486n, xiv
Knight, F. H., 189n, vi

Latané, H. A., ix, xiv
Lee, C. H., xvi
Leffler, G. L., i
Lerner, E. M., i, iv
Levy, R. A., ix, xiv
Lewellen, W. G., xv
Lintner, J., *vi*, 146n, v, ix, 422n, 425n, 447n, 451, 455, 455n, xiii, 479, xv
Litzenberger, R. H., xiii
Lorie, J. H., 83n, iii, xiii, xiv
Luce, R. D., 202n, vi
Luckett, D. G., 120n

AUTHOR INDEX

Lutz, F. A., iii, 118, 118n, 119n, 120n, iv
Lutz, V., iii

Malkiel, B. G., 118n, 123n, iv, v
Mandelbrot, B., xiii, 493n, xiv
Mao, J. C. T., iii, v, xiv, xv
Markowitz, H. M., *vi*, 3, 3n, 6, vi, viii, 303, 303n, 311, 331, ix, 383n, 430, 519
Marschak, J., 304, 304n, ix
Massé, P., viii
Matlock, W. F., 383n
May, C., v
Mazuy, K., 488n, 490, xiv
McEnally, R. W., v
McKenzie, R., 123n, iv
McWilliams, J. D., v
Meiselman, D., iv
Menger, K., 201, 201n, vi
Merrett, A. J., iii
Michaelsen, J. B., iv, ix
Miller, M. H., 144, 144n, 145n, 162, 163, 163n, 165, 165n, 167, 169, 170, 171, 173, 174n, 176, 177, 182, 183, v, vi, 247n
Miller, N., i
Miller, N. C., xvi
Miller, R. L., ix
Modigliani, F., 144, 144n, 145n, 162, 163, 163n, 165, 165n, 167, 169, 170, 171, 173, 174n, 176, 177, 182, 183, v
Molodovsky, N., i, v, xv
Montabano, M., iii
Mood, A. M., 195n, 245n, 326n, ix
Moore, B. J., xiii
Morgenstern, O., 201, 202n, 204, 205, 212, 218, 220, vi, 244, 258n, 334
Mossins, J., vi, 383n, xiii
Mosteller, F., vi
Mueller, D. C., xv
Musgrave, R. A., 304, 304n, ix
Myers, S. C., v, vi, xv

Naslund, B., ix
Nicholson, S. F., v
Niebuhr, W. D., 115n, iv
Niederhoffer, V., xiv
Nogee, P., vi
Nostrum, C., iii

Ophir, T., v

Pappas, J. L., iii, v
Patinkin, D., 109n
Pease, F., iv
Peles, Y., 216n
Pilcher, J. C., iv
Pogue, J. A., xiii, xiv
Porterfield, J. T. S., iii
Pratt, J. W., vi, ix, 382, 382n, 395
Priest, W. W. Jr., xiv
Pringle, J. J., 544n
Pye, G., 122n, iv, xiii
Pyle, D. H., ix

Quandt, R. E., 123n
Quirin, G. D., iii
Quirk, J. P., viii, 296n

Raiffa, H., 202n, vi
Ramsey, F. P., 201, 201n, 202, vi
Rappaport, A., iii
Renshaw, E. F., i, ix, xiv, 506n
Renwick, F. B., xiii, xiv
Richter, M. K., vi, viii, 383n
Roberts, H. V., xiv
Robichek, A. A., *vi*, i, 115n, iv, v, 215n, vi, 544n
Robinson, R., iii
Rosett, R. N., vi
Rothschild, M., 299n
Roy, A. D., ix, 390n
Russel, W. R., viii, 296n, 299n

Samuels, J. M., vi
Samuelson, P. A., 66n, iii, iv, ix, 493n, xiv
Saposnik, R., viii, 296n
Sarma, L. V. L. N., v
Sauvain, H., iv
Savage, J., xiv
Savage, L. J., iii, vi, 235, 235n, 236n, 238, 239, 239n, 240, 240n, 243n, 250, 251, 252, 253, 254, 265, 416, xiv
Schreiner, J. C., xv
Schrock, N. W., ix
Schwartz, E., v
Schwartz, R. A., xiv
Seligman, D., 494n
Shapiro, E., 139n, v
Shapiro, D. L., xv

Sharpe, W. F., *vi*, vi, ix, 407n, 430, 430n, 451n, 455, xiii, 479, 480, 480n, 482, 486, 487, 490, xv
Shelly, M. W., iv
Shelton, J. P., iv
Smidt, S., iii
Smith, A., 492n, 506
Smith, K. V., xv
Smith, W. F., xiv, 507n
Smyth, D. J., vi
Soldofsky, R. M., iv, v, ix
Solomon, E., iii, v
Solomons, D., 29n
Sprenkle, C. M., v
Stevenson, R. A., iv, xiv
Stiglitz, J. E., 163n, 165n, v, 299n
Sykes, A., iii

Tatham, C., ii, iv, 131n, v
Tito, D. A., xiv
Tobin, J., *vi*, 3, 3n, 303, 303n, 311, 331, ix, 342, 348n, 420n, 430, 446, 446n, xiii, 519
Treichrow, D., iii
Treynor, J. L., *vi*, 480n, 482, 483, 486, 487n, 488n, 490, xiv
Turner, D. F., 512n, xv
Turnovsky, S. J., ix

Tuttle, D. C., ix
Tversky, A., vi

Van Horne, J. C., 14n, i, iv, 519n, xv
Vasudevan, A., xvi
Vickers, D., 139n, v, xiv
Vogel, R. C., ix
von Neumann, J., 201, 202n, 204, 205, 212, 218, 220, vi, 244, 258n, 334

Wallingford, B. A., ix, xiv
Weingartner, H. M., iii
Wendt, P. F., v
West, S., i
Weston, F. T., ii
Weston, J. F., iii, 507n, xv
Whinston, A., ix
Whitman, M. N., xvi
Williams, J. B., 139n, v
Williams, W. D., ii
Wilt, G. A. Jr., 122n
Wippern, R. F., xiv
Wu, H. K., 494n

Yaari, M. E., vi, 240, 240n
Young, W. E., xiv

Zakon, A. J., 494n
Zinbarg, E. D., i, iv

Subject Index

Numbers in bold refer to sections.

Absolute return, 76, 76n
Absolute risk aversion, 382
  definition of, 382n
Accounting analysis, 29-32
  vs economic analysis, 29
Allocation ratio, 39
Bankruptcy (*see* risk of bonds)
Baumol's criterion (*see* expected
    gain–confidence limit criterion)
Bernoulli's solution, 196-200
  (*see* maximum return criterion; utility)
Blue chip average, 21
Bonds,
  convertibility of, 123-24
  coverage ratio of, 107
  indenture, 106
  prices of, 111-13
  rate of return on, 99-100
  risk of, 111-114
    (*see* risk of bonds)
  short-term bonds and certainty, 109n
  yield to maturity, 101
  yields on, 100-104
Borrowing,
  and lending in a perfect capital
    market, 431-33
Call provision, 122
Capital budgeting,
  variance as a measure of risk in, **512-18**
Capital costs,
  of conglomerate mergers, 511-12
Capital investments, **512-21**
  diversification of, **512-18**
  portfolio analysis of, **518-21**
  (*see* capital budgeting; diversification)
Capital market,
  definition of, 7

Capital market (*continued*)
  vs money market, 7n
Capital structure,
  and valuation, **163-67**
Cash dividends, 83, 84, 139
Cash flows, 29, 67n, 80, 133, 513
Central limit theorem, 326n
Certainty,
  definition of, 189-90
  short-term bonds and, 190n
Characteristic line,
  definition of, 483
Chebychev inequality, 305, 389n, 592
Coefficient of variation, 248, 305
Concave utility function, 207, 207n, 208,
    209, 311, 390
  (*see* risk, attitudes to; utility functions)
Conglomerate mergers (*see* mergers)
Continuity axiom, 203
Convertibility,
  of bonds and preferred stocks, 123-25
Convex utility curve, 207, 209, 209n, 210
  (*see* risk, attitudes to; utility functions)
Covariance,
  and correlation coefficient, **588-90**
Coverage ratio,
  of bonds, 107
Cramer's solution, 200-201
  (*see* maximum return criterion; utility)
Credit risk (*see* risk of bonds)
Cubic utility function, 249n, 250n
  (*see* utility functions)
Current ratio of firm,
  definition of, 109

Debt, 161-68, 170
Debt equity ratio, 170
Depreciation, 30
Derivative, 233, **551-63**
Devaluation, 531
Discount rate (*see* rate of return)

599

Dispersion of returns (see distribution of returns)
Distribution,
  asymmetry of, 248
  function, 574-77
  moments of, 577-582
    (see moments of distribution)
  normal distribution function, 584-87
  of returns, 248, 304-305
  probability, 190, 245, 265, 289
  range of, 303n
  risk attitude in the stock market and, 244
  symmetrical, 314
  two-parameters, 325-30
  uniform (rectangular), 582-83
  variance of, 248, 290, 303
Diversification,
  capital investments and, 512-21
  conglomerate mergers and, 505-12
  efficiency criteria and, 285-90
  gains from, 363-70, 531-34
  international, 529-43
  multiple-stock portfolios and, 443-50
  synergism, 507
Dividend policy,
  and valuation, 143-47
Dividends,
  cash, 83, 84, 139
  current, 83
  present value of, 139-43
  stock, 37, 39, 41
Dow-Jones averages (see index of prices)

Earnings,
  adjustment of (see earnings per share)
  per share (see earnings per share)
  present value of, 60-61, 133-36, 164
  price-earnings ratio, 136-39, 170-75
  retained, 140, 142, 147
Earnings per share,
  adjustment of, 35-49
  definition of, 33
  financial leverage and, 154
  present value of, 133-36
  price-earnings ratio, 136-39, 170-75
Economic analysis, 29-30, 30n
Economic risk,
  and financial leverage, 153
Efficiency criteria,
  comparison of alternative, 393-95

Efficiency criteria (continued)
  diversification and, 285-90
  relative effectiveness of, 410-14
  (see efficiency criterion)
Efficiency criterion,
  concept of, 261-64
  definition of, 261
  optimal, 264, 269n
    (see optimal efficiency criterion)
  (see Baumol's criterion, general efficiency criterion, mean-variance criterion, risk-aversion criterion, two-stage criterion)
Efficiency Frontier, 319n, 370-73, 391-93, 519n, 534-35
Efficient sets, 261, 267, 309-10, 402
End of period value, 208, 210, 213
Equilibrium prices, 439-41, 452-55
Exchange community, 12-13
  role of specialist in, 16-17
Expected Gain–Confidence limit criterion, 388-95
  concave utility function and, 390
  mean-variance criterion and, 390
  quadratic utility function and, 391
Expected return (see expected value)
Expected utility, 201, 201n, 202-204, 241n, 305
  vs expected return, 198
Expected value, 9, 289, 351, 513, 577-78, 582-83
  definition of, 193n
  maximum-return criterion and, 193-94
  mean-variance criterion and, 308
  profitability of, 303, 305
  random variable and, 591-92
  vs expected utility, 198

Financial leverage, 153-57
Fixed-income securities, 99, 121-25
Friedman-Savage hypothesis, 310-11, 235-40, 265

General efficiency criterion, 264-78
  Friedman-Savage hypothesis and, 265
  risk-aversion criterion and, 279
Geometric mean rate of return, 80-83, 100
Geometric series, sum of, 569-70
Growth stocks, 147-53, 477

IBM paradox, 150-53

SUBJECT INDEX 601

Index of prices,
  Dow-Jones, 19-23, 478, 487, 489
  Moody's, 21n, 38n, 105, 136n, 529
  Standard & Poor, 21, 21n, 105, 136n, 478, 479, 487, 489, 490n, 491
Integrals, 563-69
Interest rate,
  multiple, 441-43
  unique, 439-41
Interest rate risk (*see* risk of bonds)
Internal rate of return, 67-79, 80, 135,
  definition of, 67
  Net Present Value and, 69-73
  ranking investment proposals and, 73-79
Investment,
  liquid assets, **341-49**
  performance, **479-84**
    (*see* Sharpe-Lintner model, Treynor's performance indicator)
  retained earnings, 140-42, 147
  returns, discounting of, 67n, **406-10**
  risk, 304-307
Iso—profit line, 351
Iso—return line, 351
Iso—variance curve, 354
Iso—variance ellipse, 356

Kolmogorov-Smirnov test, 327n
Kurtosis, 248
  (*see* moments of distribution)

Lagrange multiplier method, 372, 372n, 448, 449, 526, **561-63**
Lending (*see* borrowing)
Leverage,
  Modigliani-Miller analysis of, **162-70**
  valuation and, **157-62**
  (*see* financial leverage)
Limit order, 15
Linear utility function, 212-15, 277
Liquid assets,
  definition of, 113
  investment in, **341-49**
Liquidity, 113
  preference, 115
Local maxima, 372n, **557-65**
  constrained, **560-65**
Local minima, 372n, **557-65**
  constrained, **560-65**
Margin trading, 17-18

Marginal efficiency of money, 67n
Marginal utility of money, 196-200, 207, 209, 210-11
Market line, 436
Market order, 15
Market price, 10, 39-43, 244
Market value,
  firm, 11n
  investment, 84
Marketable assets, 31
Markowitz-Tobin mean-variance model
  (*see* mean-variance criterion)
Mathematical expectation, 305
  (*see* moments of distribution)
Maximum expected return (*see* maximum return criterion)
Maximum-Return criterion, **192-201**
  Bernoulli's solution, 196-200
  Cramer's solution, 200-201
  expected return and, 193-94
  St. Petersburg paradox and, 194-96
  uncertainty and, 204
Mean-variance criterion, **307-23**, 344, 404, 435
  concave utility curve and, 311
  diversification of investments and, 519-20
  quadratic utility and, 310-11, 383-85, 388
  utility foundations of, 310-15
Mergers, **505-12**
  conglomerate, 506
  diversification and, 505-12
  horizontal type, 505
  vertical type, 506
Modern Theory of utility, **201-206**
Modigliani-Miller analysis, **162-73**
  debt and, 161-62
  price-earnings ratio and, 171-73
  valuation of capital structure and, 163-67
Moments of distribution, 246, 276-78, 305, 310, **577-82**
  (*see* expected value, skewness, variance)
Money market,
  vs capital market, 7n
Monotonicity axiom, 203
Monotonically nondecreasing function, 277
Moody's price index (*see* index of prices)
Multiple interest rates, 441-43
Multiple-Stock portfolios, **443-52**
Mutual funds,
  investment performance of, **476-99**

Mutual funds (*continued*)
 investor's behavior and mutual funds
  returns, 244-48
 (*see* investment performance)

Net Asset Value approach, 131-33
Net assets,
 definition of, 132
 per share, 132
Net income, 157-62
Net operating income, 155, 157-62
Net present value, **62-66**, 66n, 69-79
 (*see* present value)
New issues market, 8
New York Stock Exchange, 11-17
Nonstochastic variable, 403-404
Normal distribution parameters, 584-87
 (*see* distribution function)

Objective utility approach (*see* subjective utility approach)
Odd lots shareholders, 15
Open-end investment company (*see* mutual funds)
Opportunity costs, 30, 66, 66n, 77
Optimal efficiency criterion, **268-78**
 definition of, 268
 vs optimal investment option, 269n
Optimal investment option, 446-51
 definition of, 264
 vs optimal efficiency criterion, 264
Optimal portfolios,
 composition of, **535-43**

Payout ratio, 147
Perfect capital market, 146, 431, 508-10
Pledge of assets, 106
Preferred stocks, 99, 100
 yields on, 99-104
Present value, 60-61
 dividends, 139-43
 earnings, 133-36, 164
Price-earnings ratio, **136-39**
 adjustment of, 137-39
 financial risk and, 170-75
 stock splits, 138.
Price determination in the stock market
 (*see* equilibrium in the stock market, multiple-stock portfolios, Sharpe-Lintner model, single-stock portfolios)
Primary securities, market,
 definition of, 8

Probability distribution, 245, 249, 289
 cumulative, 265
 objective vs subjective, 190
Probability function,
 definition of, 573
Profitability,
 expected returns, 303, 305
 financial investments, 79-84
 net earnings, 32-33
 present value, 135
 risk aversion criterion, 283
Profits,
 accounting vs economic, **29-32**
 corporate, 34
Purchasing power risk (*see* risks of bonds)

Quadratic utility, 91, 249, 404
 absolute risk aversion in, 282
 criterion, **385-88**
 function, definition of, 379
 meaning of, **379-83**
 mean-variance criterion and, 310-11, 383-85, 388

Random variable, 245, 265
 continuous, 575-77
 definition of, 573
 expected value, 591-92
 linear transformation of, 587-88
 variance of, 591-92
 wealth as a, 403-406
Random Walk hypothesis, **492-96**
Range of distribution,
 definition of, 303n
Ranking, 71-73, 76
Rate of interest, 104, 109, 110
Rate of return,
 absolute, 76, 76n
 adjusted, 10, 83-88, 521
 bonds, 99-100
 common stocks, 22, 80-82
 discount, 67n, 406-410, 521
 dispersion of, 304-305
 expected, 451-52
 financial leverage, 154
 geometric mean, 80
 internal, 67-79, 80, 135
 net present value, 62
 preferred stocks, 99-100
 risk-adjusted, 10, 215, 521
 time value of money, 60

SUBJECT INDEX

Rate of return (*continued*)
variance, 245, 304, 351, 582-83
Regression analysis, 246-47
Reinvestment,
cash dividends, 84
rates, 76-78
vs compounding, 81
Retained earnings (*see* earnings)
Retirement provisions, 121-22
Returns (*see* rate of return)
Reward-to-variability ratio, **480-82**
Rights issues, 39-43, 83, 138
Rights offering (*see* rights issues)
Risk averter,
definition of, 207
(*see* risk, attitudes toward)
Risk,
attitudes toward, 189-90, 207-12, **244-50**
aversion, 243, 382, 382n
definition of, 190
financial, 170-75
index, 303-305
investment, 304-307
liquid assets, 346
optimal investment proportion, 450
premium, 104, 109, 120, 306, 434
rate of return, 10, 215, 514-521
reduction, 249-50, 478
systematic vs unsystematic, 483-86
(*see* concave utility function, convex utility curve, risk aversion criterion, risk of bonds)
Risk aversion criterion, 201, **278-85**
Risk lover,
definition of, 209
(*see* convex utility curve; risk, attitudes toward)
Risk of bonds,
bankruptcy, 106
credit risk, 104-109
interest rate risk, 111-14
purchasing power risk, 109-11
sinking funds provision, 121-22
Round lot, 13, 15n, 37n
definition of, 13

Secondary securities market, 8-11
definition of, 8
Securities Exchange Act, 12, 17
Sharpe-Lintner performance model, 430, 479-82

Short selling, **19-24**
Single-stock portfolios, **431-43**
lending and borrowing, 431-36
multiple interest rates, 441-43
unique interest rate, 439-41
Sinking funds provisions (*see* risk of bonds)
Skewness, 248, 314, 579
(*see* moments of distribution)
Specialist,
role in Stock Exchange, 16-17
Standard deviation (*see* variability, variance)
Standard & Poor (*see* index of prices)
State-preference theory, **215-17**
Stieltjes-Lebesgues integrals, 296n
Stochastic variable,
wealth as a, 404-406
Stock,
allocation ratio of, 39
dividend component, 39, 41
dividends (*see* stock splits)
exchange, 9-11
market, 11, 11n
price index, 19-24
(*see* index of prices)
relative price of, 136
splits, 37, 37n, 83, 123, 138
St. Petersburg Paradox, **194-96**, 200-202
Subjective utility approach, **240-44**
vs objective approach, 240n
Symmetrical distribution, 314
Synergism, 507
definition of, 507n
Systematic risk, 483-86
definition of, 485

Tax,
credit risk, 107-108
earnings per share, 34
leverage, 154
Modigliani-Miller analysis, 163-70
perfect capital market, 431
preferential tax treatment, 34
price-earnings ratio, 171-75
Taylor series, 244, 249n, **570-71**
Three-security portfolios, **359-63**
Time-adjusted rate of return, 80
(*see* rate of return)
Time-adjusted risk, 514
(*see* risk)
Time-discounted measure of investment worth (*see* internal rate of return, net present value)

Time-interest earned ratio, 107
  (see credit risk)
Time value of money, 59-62
  (see present value, end of period value, value of money)
Tobin's separation theorem, 446
Total coverage ratio (see coverage ratio)
Treynor's performance indicator, 482-83, 486-87
Two-parameter distribution, **325-30**
  (see distribution)
Two securities portfolios, **349-59**
Two-stage criterion, **315-18**

Uncertainty, 189, 191, 204
  (see risk)
Uniform distribution, **582-83**
  definition of, 582
  (see distribution)
Unique interest rate, 439-41
Unsystematic risk, 483-86
  definition of, 485
Utility,
  absolute return, 76n
  Bernoulli's solution, 196-200
  Cramer's solution, 200-201
  expected, 198, 201-204, 201n, 241n, 305
  Friedman-Savage hypothesis, 235
  general efficiency criterion, 265
  loss, 209
  marginal utility of money, 196-200, 207, 209, 210-11, 215
  maximum expected, 204
  meaning of, 204-206
  mean-variance criterion, 310-15
  modern theory of, 201-206
  objective approach to, 240n
  quadratic utility, **379-83**
  quadratic utility criterion, **385-88**
  subjective, 210-11, **240-44**
    (see utility functions)
Utility functions,
  concave, 207-209
  convex, 207-209

Utility functions (continued)
  cubic, 249n, 250n
  linear, 212-15, 277
  von Neumann-Morgenstern, 204-206, 244
  quadratic, 249

Valuation,
  capital structure and, 163-67
  dividend policy and, 143-47
  leverage and, 157-62
Value of money,
  future value, 60
  present value, 61
  (see end of period value, net present value, present value, time value)
Variability (see variance)
Variance, 578-79
  as measure of risk, 512-18
  Baumol's criterion and, 390
  coefficient of variation, 248, 305
  covariance, 588-90
  distribution, 248, 290, 303
  random variable, 591-92
  reduction in, 290, 366
  returns, 245, 304, 351, 582-83
  risk index, 303
  Taylor's series, 245
  undiscounted, 514
  uniform distribution, 582-83
  (see mean-variance criterion, moments of distribution)
Volatility, 482-83
  (see Treynor's performance indicator)
von Neumann-Morgenstern axioms, 204-206, 244

Warrants, 124
Wealth, 402-406

Yield curve, **114-21**
Yields,
  bonds, 99-104
  capital structure, 167-70
  preferred stock, 99-104
Yield to maturity, 101

DATE DUE